Cooking With
Mrs. Appleyard

Cooking With Mrs. Appleyard

LOUISE ANDREWS KENT
AND
ELIZABETH KENT GAY

CONTAINING

MRS. APPLEYARD'S KITCHEN
MRS. APPLEYARD'S SUMMER KITCHEN
MRS. APPLEYARD'S WINTER KITCHEN

Keats Publishing, Inc. New Canaan, Connecticut

COOKING WITH MRS. APPLEYARD

LIBRARY OF CONGRESS CATALOGING-IN-PUBLICATION DATA

Kent, Louise Andrews.
Cooking with Mrs. Appleyard / Louise Andrews Kent and
Elizabeth Kent Gay.
p.   cm.
Includes indexes.
Contents: Mrs. Appleyard's kitchen — Mrs. Appleyard's
summer kitchen — Mrs. Appleyard's winter kitchen.
ISBN 0-87983-597-4 $19.95
1. Cookery, American.   I. Gay, Elizabeth Kent.   II. Title.
TX715.K357   1993
641.5973—dc20   92-30293
                                                            CIP

Printed in the United States of America

Published by Keats Publishing, Inc.
27 Pine Street (Box 876)
New Canaan, Connecticut 06840-0876

Mrs. Appleyard's Kitchen

BOOKS BY LOUISE ANDREWS KENT

Novels

THE TERRACE

PAUL REVERE SQUARE

MRS. APPLEYARD'S YEAR

———————

MRS. APPLEYARD'S KITCHEN

Stories for Young People

DOUGLAS OF PORCUPINE

THE RED RAJAH

TWO CHILDREN OF TYRE

HE WENT WITH MARCO POLO

HE WENT WITH VASCO DA GAMA

HE WENT WITH CHRISTOPHER COLUMBUS

JO ANN, TOMBOY (with Ellis Parker Butler)

IN GOOD OLD COLONY TIMES (with Elizabeth Kent Tarshis)

Mrs. Appleyard's

Kitchen

LOUISE ANDREWS KENT

Keats Publishing, Inc. New Canaan, Connecticut

TO

M. W.

with whom some of the
best meals were eaten

Preface

A SLIGHT BATTLE took place between Mrs. Appleyard and her Editor as to whether there should be a Preface to this book. Mrs. Appleyard, who had become interested in a chicken curry, felt that her duty was at the stove. The Editor maintained that a book without a Preface was like a dinner without hors d'oeuvres. Luckily for the Editor, this well-directed simile coincided with the moment when Mrs. Appleyard dropped the last grain of rice into the violently boiling water, and she was at leisure for a moment.

'Just a few words about what sort of book it is,' said the Editor, in the sweetly persuasive editorial tones of one who conceals a whip behind his back.

'I thought you were writing the Preface,' said Mrs. Appleyard vaguely, beginning to peel an onion.

The Editor, with praiseworthy firmness, took the knife away.

Thus badgered, Mrs. Appleyard made the following statement:

'This book will never displace real cookbooks — books like the Hesseltine and Dow *Good Cooking*, for instance. I don't know how brides got along without that, because it has everything in it that anyone ever heard of cooking, and it's practical. If I'd had it when I was a bride everything might have been different. I might never have made those choke-dogs, for instance. . . .'

'Brooding never did anyone any good,' said the Editor tersely, 'and please talk about your own book.'

'Oh, yes — well, I still think there's room for the smaller, more personal book, for the kind that is based on one person's experience, rather than the encyclopaedia of cooking that has all the wisdom of the ages in it. The smaller ones are fun to read, too, even if you never cook out of them.'

'Is your book for wartime?' asked the Editor.

'Not specifically,' said Mrs. Appleyard, 'but I think it might be helpful. Its point of view is that you eat things when they are at their best rather than dragging them over the country when they are out of season. And that you have a few things and take pains in making them, rather than many and give them only part of your attention.

'I hope it makes cooking seem like something that's fun for a family to do together. I have no patience with the martyred mother who loves her martyrdom more than she does her family — the kind that monopolizes all the unselfishness and comes to the table too tired to eat, or faints just before the meal because she has been standing over the hot stove on the hottest day in summer, making three different kinds of pie when the family would much rather have her look cool and comfortable while they eat some plain raspberries. We're all going to have some cooking as part of our war work and we might as well enjoy it and let our families enjoy it with us. It's a challenge to our ingenuity to get the most out of what we have.

'I didn't leave out the things that took sugar, because I don't think the war is going to last forever, and I think we're going to win it and there will come a time when someone says, "How was it we used to make that foamy sauce?" Imagine if everyone had forgotten! I learned how to make that sauce from my husband's mother, and she'll always be remembered while it's made — just as no one eats fish chowder in our house without thinking of my grandmother. Don't you think a chowder is a lot nicer than a bronze tablet?'

The Editor agreed to that and asked if the recipes were mostly family ones.

'In our family we say "receipts,"' said Mrs. Appleyard, 'and I'll tell you why. It's a question of Latin. "Recipe" is the imperative form of the verb — what I'd say to you if I wanted to tell you how to make cornstarch pudding, for instance, or cough syrup, or any other unlikely substance. "Take — *recipe*," I'd say, "two tablespoonfuls of cornstarch and throw it into the sink." Those directions would be the *receipt* — the instructions that you received from me, because the word is derived from the past participle — is that clear?'

'As clear as imitation Hollandaise sauce,' murmured the Editor.

'I'm glad,' said Mrs. Appleyard, 'because I just made it up. Of course when we don't want to embarrass anyone we just call them "rules,"' she continued. 'Yes, a good many of them are family receipts and others came from friends, and some are things we worked out ourselves. There isn't anything in the book that we haven't made at some time or other, and when we get something so that we think it's right, we have always written down just what we did at the time, including warnings about the difficulties. I think it's almost as important to know what not to do in certain things you cook as it is to have the positive instructions you need. Having made a good many peculiar mistakes in my time I can at least serve as a horrible warning if not as an example. I've tried to tell you about the various dishes so that you can cook them even if you haven't done much cooking before.'

'Do you call these recipes — I mean receipts — economical as well as practical?'

'In the larger sense of the word — yes. If you mean that I suggest lots of perfectly delicious ways of making things without eggs, butter, flour, or sugar — no. I'd always rather save up until I could make the thing properly, and in the meantime eat bread and cheese. There's nothing so wasteful as an "economical" dish that the family won't eat. It wastes time and temper as well as materials. Cut down on the number of things you serve but use the best materials for those you make. Remember that if you serve dried beef instead of porterhouse steak, you can afford cream for it and still be away ahead; that if you will bake your potatoes perfectly to go with it, making the family wait for the potatoes instead of the other way, and take pains with the other vegetables you serve, you will have a good meal instead of a poor one.

'Don't serve the family's favorite kind of meat, vegetable, and dessert all at the same meal. Stagger them (not the family, the favorites!). Have strawberry shortcake the day you have meat loaf instead of the day you have broiled chicken. Of course it's a poor heart that never rejoices, and there will be times when you produce all the treasures for one meal; but for everyday menu planning it's good management — which is economy, as I seem to remember being told — to have some favorite food at every meal rather than all the dull ones at once and all the more interesting ones at another time. And don't forget that a good hot bowl of soup with people you like tastes a lot better than chicken croquettes with béchamel sauce and warm ice cream, with after-dinner speeches ahead of you; and that cooking for your family is Family Fun, if you will make it so, and that we're all lucky if we have families to cook for.'

'You mean that your book won't be much help unless you do your own cooking?'

'I think the people who do their own cooking will use it most, but, you know, even if we have people to help us, there are likely to be gaps. There are Thursday and Sunday evenings when you can have your kitchen to yourself, and there are those periods when the children say, "When Hilda is on her vacation will you make cream puffs with chocolate sauce?" And there are picnics. Besides, I hope it's going to be partly for my convenience. People keep saying to me, "Mrs. Appleyard, I do wish you would give me your rule for oatmeal cookies." And then, poor idiot that I am, I do, knowing well that they will lose the paper before they get home and then try to do it out of their heads, and then blame me because the cookies didn't come out right. Now I shall just say, "Look on page 69 of my book," and that will end the discussion.'

'Your point is well taken,' said the Editor. 'Perhaps they'll stop writing to me about green peas and things too. I hope that in your book you have told about all the things to eat that were in *Mrs. Appleyard's Year.*'

'I think we have. May I go back to my curry now?'

'Yes, indeed,' said the Editor, who was beginning to be hungry. 'Will you give me the recipe — excuse me, receipt?'

'Look on page 162,' said Mrs. Appleyard firmly, and went on cutting up onions.

Contents

1

A Cook in spite of Herself. Some of the best
reading in the world, Mrs. Appleyard says, is found in cookbooks. She ought to know because she began to read them
as literature long before she took to wielding the egg beater.
There have been frequent periods in Mrs. Appleyard's life
when she was on short rations. Her doctor has told her to
lose three hundred pounds and she has. No, she has not
vanished in the process. She is still moderately substantial.
She has merely lost ten pounds thirty times. During those
periods when her too, too solid flesh was melting, she has
learned to sublimate her yearnings for chocolate cake and
lobster Newburg by reading cookbooks. She has fortunately discovered that she can get a pleasantly stuffed feeling simply by moving her eyes rapidly from left to right
over menus that begin with twenty assorted appetizers and
end with Baked Alaska.

Mrs. Appleyard is the reader all writers have been looking
for. If the hero of a book climbs a peak only slightly lower

than Mount Everest — some cone as hard to negotiate as lemon sherbet with stars like spun sugar fizzing around it against a sky as dark as a Concord grape (the similes are Mrs. Appleyard's) — there she is panting and puffing behind him. Probably he is saved only by her hot breath blowing down his neck. When the heroine takes to the tropics and acts like a langorous panther, Mrs. Appleyard lies limply — though lumpily — on a couch draped with hibiscus blooms and mosquito netting. Her laugh becomes low, thrilling, and just slightly sinister as it hisses from between lips that are a scarlet gash in her gardenia-white face. Her eyes lengthen and narrow. She wears a sarong. . . .

What she can do with a cape when the hero is a bull-fighter would delight Mr. Hemingway. How crisply witty she was during her Jane Austen period only Mrs. Appleyard knows. It was perhaps her happiest phase, although she also enjoyed her life in Barchester when she was the Archdeacon and Mrs. Proudie both at once. Sometimes, too, she thinks back wistfully to the days when she was Becky Sharp, decked with diamonds, and waltzed wickedly at Waterloo — with Rhett Butler or somebody.

When Mrs. Appleyard reads a cookbook she eats.

Having now eaten her way through cookbooks where everything is smothered in whipped cream, through the kind that lets no innocent piece of meat escape without an overcoat of sauce, through helpful advice about garnishing pheasants with artichoke bottoms, through the spirally bound collection of the Appleyard Centre Woman's Club (twenty rules for doughnuts, four for green tomato mincemeat, six versions of sour-cream cookies, for any one of which the owner will pull hair!), through books dainty and delectable, books hearty and homely, Mrs. Appleyard has naturally decided to give the book of her own kitchen to the world.

There are good reasons for this step.

Mrs. Appleyard had not read more than twenty or thirty cookbooks when she began to have an uneasy feeling about this form of literature. Cookbooks, she thought, ought to tell someone who does not know how to cook something how to cook it. Yet frequently the writer approaches the subject assuming airily that the reader knows all about it anyway. In that case, Mrs. Appleyard thinks it would be better for the writer to tell about her trip to the Gaspé or how to crochet an openwork afghan. There are also writers about cooking who, from pure malice, Mrs. Appleyard thinks, deceive the trusting reader about some simple process — cooking string beans, for instance.

In book after book the reader is told to break string beans into inch pieces and cook them for various lengths of time ranging from twenty to sixty minutes. Beans broken in this way and cooked an hour look and taste like pieces of somebody's ski boots, Mrs. Appleyard says. If you cook them twenty minutes, they may look and taste better, but as you can't chew them the improvement in appearance and flavor is of somewhat academic interest. Mrs. Appleyard here states, and is willing to have her book judged at this point by what she says, that the cooking of string beans depends greatly on how they are cut. If you do not care to take the trouble to cut them on a long diagonal so that a large amount of cut surface is exposed to rapidly boiling water, why don't you have squash or open a nice can of corn? Furthermore, all the water that you use ought to cook into the beans so that all their flavor and minerals and vitamines are in them and not thrown down the sink or on the petunias. They should cook in this way in about half an hour. They will be tender, a delicate shade of natural olive green, and all they need on them is a little butter and salt. If you like them with cream, be sure they stand in it long enough so that they absorb some of it.

Now, it seems that the writers of cookbooks must know this simple fact about cutting string beans, yet they blithely advise you to break them into inch pieces, and then they begin to chatter about sultana roll. Yet string beans have to be eaten frequently and if you really want sultana roll, you can get it from the caterer. He is a lot more deft about imitation green coloring, and combining glue with raspberry and claret extract than — for instance — Mrs. Appleyard.

'The trouble with most cookbooks,' she says, 'is that they assume that people live the way they don't live. They talk as if you still made soup by cooking a knuckle of veal for three days when as a matter of fact you open a red-and-white can in three seconds. Cookbooks are often very good about telling you what to do — generally something you don't want to do — but they don't tell you what not to do, which is sometimes just as important. I don't know that I have much to contribute,' she added, in one of her rare moments of modesty, 'but at least when I think I know anything I am going to Tell All.'

Mrs. Appleyard began by speaking of her qualifications as a cook. They seemed to consist chiefly of the fact that when she was married, her mind was a blank page upon which any receipt could be written. She had never even made fudge. Because as a child she had always had her nose in a book, her family had decided to make a librarian of her. They did not know that reading books is no more a

virtue in a librarian than drinking cocktails is in a bar-
tender. Mrs. Appleyard found it out the first week, but
was too lethargic to say so. She decided that if she were
supposed to be leading an intellectual life she would not
have to be domestic. She thought, poor moron, that she
didn't like domesticity. She just didn't like it without Mr.
Appleyard. In his society, she discovered, opening a can
of corned-beef hash became a romantic gesture. So was
mending his socks.

'Unless,' Mrs. Appleyard has been heard to remark
(Record 4567 B), 'you think it would be fun to mend his
socks, don't marry him.'

Mr. Appleyard adapted himself to his wife's cooking with
extraordinary amiability. He did, it is true, murmur at
times about the sour-cream johnnycake that his grandmother used to make, and he would occasionally speak in
a homesick fashion of the salt pork with sour-cream gravy
that his mother made. Still, as Overbrook Hill was far
outside the sour-cream zone, Mrs. Appleyard never had
to do much but listen sympathetically while she planned
whether Cicely's spring coat had better be pink or blue.
Of course Mr. Appleyard was one of those men who 'had
that for lunch,' but what man hasn't?

Besides, Mrs. Appleyard soon checkmated that dinner-
table gambit. She got a job testing receipts for a magazine.
That phase of her career has always needed some explaining. Why, it has been asked, would a magazine pay
for the materials and also pay, for testing things, someone
who had never cooked anything more complicated than
tomato soup — the condensed kind — and canned peaches?

'That was why,' Mrs. Appleyard explains. 'If I could
cook it, so could anyone. Those rules just had to be good.'

It must have been nervous work for Mr. Appleyard. Rare indeed were those times when he was able to anticipate and duplicate at noon what he was going to have for dinner. Those pungent curries, those weird and wonderful desserts full of marshmallows and maraschino cherries, those thirty-nine ways of disguising eggs so that their own mother would never know them, those soufflés that rose only to fall again, those casseroles with pretty nearly anything in them — no man ever had those for lunch! Then there was the seasonal rhythm. Much has been written about how editors read Christmas stories in June, and in December have to writhe in their chairs while poets make the exciting discovery that June rhymes with moon — approximately. It remained, however, for the Appleyards to discover how strange life can be when you eat suet pudding on the Fourth of July and revel in cooling drinks and ice cream at Christmas.

Mr. Appleyard bore it all nobly. It is true that he did say once with a patient expression — it was while Mrs. Appleyard was trying out 'twenty new thoughts about spinach,' a good many of the thoughts containing garlic — that perhaps it would be better if Mrs. Appleyard would try it on the dog instead of on the visiting economist who was coming to dinner. He said there was no such thing as a little garlic. . . . Still, for the most part he ate what was set before him in the silence that — in a man — implies praise.

Mrs. Appleyard still has an interesting little collection of scrawls on paper that she 'hasn't got around to trying yet.' She will not include any of them in her book. Neither is she going to put in any rules for economical cakes. When she feels economical she does not make cake. She prefers a raw carrot stick to any cake that has been constructed from motives of economy. She also states that, while this is not an advertising pamphlet, she will call things by their trade names if she feels like it. This is her book and it is going to tell the way she cooks — and inspires cooking in others. Luckily there have always been adventurous souls who seemed to like to help in the Appleyard kitchen. This book should really belong to them. Perhaps also to Hugh.

He was standing beside his mother looking over her shoulder while she was copying some rules into her private cookbook. He was ten years old, perhaps. After a while he said, 'Mother, when I am married, will you give my wife that book?'

Mrs. Appleyard considered the question, realized with gratitude how unassertive her mother-in-law had been in the matter of that salt pork with cream gravy, and answered: 'Well, I don't know if I would, Hugh. I could show it to her, of course, and tell her she could copy anything she liked out of it, but I don't believe I'd give her the book.'

'That's all right, mother,' Hugh said kindly. 'I expect the kind of girl I'm planning to marry will have a cookbook of her own.'

This is Mrs. Appleyard's own book, and anyone is welcome to copy anything out of it.

2

Weights and Measures. Mrs. Appleyard believes in weighing and measuring. She has deep admiration for the cook who operates on inspiration, but she herself is not gifted that way and she clings to the measuring cup. Unfortunately, all cookbooks do not use the same system. Some chat in terms of ounces and others in cups. In unravelling these directions — including her own — Mrs. Appleyard has found the following facts helpful.

3 teaspoonfuls (t.)	equals	1 tablespoonful (T.)
16 T.	equals	1 cup (c.)
½ c. butter	equals	¼ pound (lb.)
2 T. butter	equals	1 ounce (oz.)
2 c. butter	equals	1 lb.
2 c. granulated sugar	equals	1 lb.

It takes almost three cups of powdered or light·brown

sugar to make a pound, so always measure them by cups instead of dumping in a package at a time.

4 c. pastry flour	equals	1 lb.
2 T. flour	equals	1 oz.
4⅓ c. coffee	equals	1 lb.
1 sq. Baker's chocolate	equals	1 oz.
9 large eggs	equals	1 lb.
2 c. Hamburg steak	equals	1 lb.
Pinch of salt	equals	⅛ t.

3

'*Beverages.*' Why are things to drink always called beverages in cookbooks? Mrs. Appleyard says she has no idea. Perhaps it's refined or something. Anyway, far be it from her to flout tradition. A glass of water is a beverage; so is a glass of champagne. Mrs. Appleyard is fond of both, though her experience has been chiefly with water.

She sometimes feels that not enough attention is paid to water. There seems to be an idea that all water is alike. Nonsense! Water varies just as much as wine. It doesn't cost enough so that it pays to advertise it, that's all.

Fond of water though she is, she never appreciated it so much anywhere as in England. English waiters do not approve of the nervous American habit of water-drinking. Probably they know the water is needed to season the potatoes or else they think that if you drink it, you will have no room for cabbage. At any rate when you sit down at the table you are invited to slake your thirst on some good sturdy bread. Mrs. Appleyard soon discovered that if she wanted water at all, she must be firm.

She learned to brave the pitying look with which the waiters said to themselves, 'Ah, an American!' and also that it was not enough to say, 'May we have some water?' but that, in order to save the whole family from desiccation, she must add: 'Six glasses, please. One for each of us.'

A further complication was that the Appleyards, although they like water cold, do not like ice in it. They want it the way it comes out of the springhouse at Appleyard Centre — as when Mrs. Appleyard says: 'Dinner's almost ready. Get the water from the spring. Don't dip it. Hold the pitcher under the pipe.'

Realizing, because they are an adaptable family, that Simpson's-in-the-Strand probably did not have a springhouse with thimbleberries growing around it, they were willing to drink London water in its native lukewarmness. Mr. Appleyard was even detected fishing out lumps of ice with a spoon. The most elegant-looking of the waiters had just put it in. He had heard Mrs. Appleyard's American accent and went to work at once. Mrs. Appleyard felt sorry for his honest perplexity at the capriciousness of Americans. 'All Americans drink ice water' was an article of faith with him, and here were six who didn't.

Mrs. Appleyard also felt drawn to the waiter because he was wearing a frock coat like the one Mr. Appleyard was wearing the first time she ever saw him. This reminded her so pleasantly of her courtship that she actually ate most of her broad beans. She did not wish to hurt the feelings of anyone in a coat like that. She also prevented Mr. Appleyard from asking maliciously if the beef were really English, thus averting a split of no mean proportions in Anglo-American relations.

Ah, that beef! Was there ever anything better? or half so good? Except possibly the saddle of mutton. Is there a better dessert than English strawberries in a punnet — which is a small round basket, lined and covered with fresh strawberry leaves — and Devonshire cream? Except perhaps the raspberries. Appleyard Centre raspberries are no better even when you pick them off the bush yourself. What is so good to eat with cheese as English biscuits? What fish is better than English sole eaten at a restaurant that has been looking out over Piccadilly for a couple of centuries?

There is plenty of poor cooking in England — just as there is in America — but some of the best food in the world is English, if you know where to look for it. English writers have a genius for describing terrible meals, Mrs. Appleyard says, and she thinks they don't spend enough of their time telling about the good ones that you may have: the wonderful teas, the breakfast with bacon that makes you realize you never ate bacon before, the Yorkshire hams, the salmon that was swimming up the river that morning —— But she was supposed to be talking about things to drink, wasn't she? All right, all right!

WATER

Water should be cold, but it should not be cold enough to paralyze the palate. If you are not lucky enough to have a cold spring piped into your front yard, you can help to make the outside of the pitcher agreeably frosty by putting in a few ice cubes and after a few minutes, fishing them out. Or you can leave them in if Mr. Appleyard is not one of the guests. Or, as far as Mrs. Appleyard is concerned, you can serve the water lukewarm. She really doesn't care so long as it's wet.

TEA

By exerting immense self-control, Mrs. Appleyard will not say what she thinks of tea made with tea bags. Why should she blast a great industry, the product of American ingenuity? She simply declines to mention how to manipulate those little mechanisms known to some as the mouse in the teacup. Merely saying that she would as soon think of making lobster soup by boiling a lobster buoy, she passes on to the making of tea.

For four people:

A quart teapot — earthenware	2 qts. boiling water
Another quart teapot	5 t. of the best tea
A tea-strainer	you can afford

Into a quart earthenware teapot that is *hot* and *dry* put the tea. Set the teapot on the stove near the kettle. Never bring the kettle to the teapot: always the teapot to the kettle. Run two quarts of fresh cold water into the kettle and bring it rapidly to a real bubbling boil. As soon as it is boiling hard, pour enough water over the tea to fill the teapot nearly full. Cover the teapot. An English tea cozy is the best thing, but anything that will keep it warm will do — a towel folded several times, for instance. Let it stand at least five minutes, never more than seven. If you want it stronger, use more tea, not longer steeping. Now strain it into another warm teapot, which may be silver if you like. Put the rest of the hot water into another teapot or into a silver teakettle, or into anything you have handy, according to the degree of elegance that you are maintaining at the moment. This is for the feeble souls who like hot water flavored with tea. There are always some of these around — Mrs. Appleyard is ashamed to admit being one of them — and it's just as well to face the fact. Of course the pleasantest thing is to have a silver teakettle with an alcohol lamp under it that really works, but this is a rare sight in these times, and you can have good tea without it.

The point of these manoeuvres, Mrs. Appleyard says, is this: The fragrance of tea is best extracted by steeping it as near the boiling point as you can get it without its actually boiling. If you leave it on the grounds too long, you get bitterness instead of fragrance.

Making tea is so simple that it is amazing how much bad tea there is available. Even a moderately priced tea is good to drink if it is carefully made, and the most expensive kinds can be ruined by water that is not freshly boiled, or not really boiling when it hits the tea, or by being steeped too long, or not long enough.

Mrs. Appleyard likes several kinds of tea: Lapsang Souchong, Ming Cha, Earl Grey's Mixture, Flowery Tip Orange Pekoe are all good — and so is your favorite brand, whatever it is. And as we are lucky to have any tea at all, it's worth taking pains to make it right.

COFFEE

Mrs. Appleyard approaches the subject of coffee with a certain amount of nervousness. Theoretically she knows how to produce a good cup of coffee. In practice she is always sure that it might have been better. She has tried various methods, and as she has probably had her worst results with percolators, she will leave that subject to those who know how to dominate them.

On one or two points she is fairly sure. Coffee should be freshly roasted, freshly ground, and served as soon as it is ready. Why is coffee always so good on a picnic? Partly because you are on a beach or a hilltop, and because the air is fresh and you are hungry — yes; but also because everyone is gathered around the fire, breathing in the smell of coffee and wood smoke, and as soon as the coffee is cleared and the grounds have settled, it is poured out and you drink it. It has no chance to stand around and get bitter.

Also on a picnic there is generally someone who is particular about his coffee and he is asked to make it and gives his whole soul to it. Give him a cooking space to himself — a fire between four stones will do — a new enamel coffee-pot, a vacuum tin of coffee that he opens on the spot, water from the spring, an egg right out of the henhouse, and he will produce something that makes everyone say, 'That's the *best* coffee!'

One of these picnic coffee chefs told Mrs. Appleyard how he did it and it sounds simple. (If it were, hers would probably taste more like it.)

Use plenty of coffee, he says, at least two tablespoonfuls to a cup of water. You can weaken it with cream or milk, you know, but you can't make it stronger after you've once started. Crush the egg, shell and all, with the grounds and put in no more than five *grains* of salt to a cup of water. Stand right over it so that you know when it comes to the boil, and time it with your watch. Let it boil exactly one minute, dash a little cold water into it, and let it stand just five minutes for the grounds to settle. Be sure that it keeps hot but that it doesn't boil again. Under his supervision coffee never boils over and wastes all its goodness on stones, ants, and grasshoppers, but keeps it where it belongs — in the pot.

Probably in these days when coffee is not ground or roasted at home, the best coffee comes out of a freshly opened vacuum tin. People sometimes forget that once a vacuum is broken, there is no more magic to that can than there is to any other open can of coffee. Buy coffee in small quantities and from a shop that sells a large amount so that you know the stock is frequently replaced. Wash and scald and sun everything that you use in coffee-making. Always use enough coffee.

Even with these precautions the picnic coffee is still perhaps better than the coffee made in the kitchen, because it is served out of the pot in which it was made instead of being decanted into that handsome Georgian silver coffee-pot. Coffee made in a glass coffee maker in sight of the guests also has the virtue of being served as soon as it is ready. However, it is possible to produce with one of these appliances something that tastes as if the grapes of wrath had been squeezed into it. Mrs. Appleyard has done so and knows of what she speaks.

Perhaps drip coffee is safest for the amateur. An earthenware pot is better than a metal one. Neither coffee nor tea is really at home in metal. Like any other sort of coffee-pot, all parts of the drip pot should be scalded and dried in the sunshine. Always use plenty of coffee and be sure it is ground right for drip coffee. The water must be freshly boiled and boiling hard when it is poured over the coffee.

Have the pot warmed before you put in the coffee and plug the spout with tissue paper so that the fragrance stays in the coffee instead of rising to the attic. Pour over a few tablespoonfuls of water at first and then let it stand a minute before you add the rest. Keep the water boiling and do not pour it on too fast. The water should be in contact with the grounds for about seven minutes. Put the pot where it will keep hot while the water is dripping through the grounds, but never let it boil. If your sense of beauty or vanity requires you to serve it in another pot, be sure that the second pot is freshly scalded and hot enough to take the shellac off your table. (It won't hurt Mrs. Appleyard's, because hers is finished with linseed oil — a substance she really knows how to use. Perhaps it would be better if she stuck to it and let Mr. Appleyard make the coffee. . . .)

ICED COFFEE

Never use left-over coffee for iced coffee. If your hand and arm become paralyzed when you think of pouring coffee away, make coffee jelly with it; or learn to make the right amount.

For iced coffee use at least two tablespoons of coffee to each cup of water. Make it your favorite way — boiled, dripped, or percolated — and pour it over cracked ice in tall glasses just before you are ready to serve it. People vary so much in their ideas about sugar and cream that it is better to serve them separately. Cream may be whipped, but Mr. Appleyard has views on whipped cream of such a firm nature that in Appleyard Centre the substance is pretty nearly illegal. Rich yellow cream that has the taste of June grass in it is what he prefers — and why not? Leave enough room in the glasses for the cream to be poured in. Those who like it generally like plenty. Long spoons for stirring in cream and sugar are almost an essential for iced coffee. There are few drearier sensations than being confronted with a glass of iced coffee with the cream and sugar all at the top and a limp cellophane straw.

COFFEE FOR TWENTY

There comes a time in most lives when a lot of coffee has to be made and no ordinary pot is big enough. You can produce something that most of your guests will accept as coffee by putting a gallon of water on to boil in a large enamelware saucepan and three quarters of a pound of coffee into a cheesecloth bag. The bag must be big enough so that there is room in it for nearly twice as much coffee as you put in. Be sure it is tied tightly at the top. Crush a whole egg, shell and all, with the ground coffee — if you like it made with egg — and add a few grains of salt.

Just as the water comes to a full bubbling boil, put in the bag and let it boil one minute. Then cover the kettle tightly and let it stand where it will keep very hot but not boil for six minutes longer. Remove the bag and pour the coffee into a freshly scalded coffee-urn.

If you are serving forty people do not try to double the quantity in the bag, but make a second batch while the first one is being served. If you have the water ready in the teakettle, you will have time before the first lot is used up. Use a new bag, because you will not have time to wash and scald the first one properly and if you do not, your second lot of coffee will be bitter. Be sure your kettle is thoroughly scalded in between times, too.

CHOCOLATE

Chocolate, Mrs. Appleyard says, is usually cocoa, and weak at that. This is a slander on a noble drink. Cocoa is a nice drink for children, and you will be quite safe in making it if you follow the directions on the package. You may use powdered chocolate, if you like, or you may even brew a drink out of cocoa shells — and Mrs. Appleyard will say nothing against it; at least she won't if she does not have to drink any of these concoctions under the name of chocolate. She means *chocolate*.

It's a nuisance to make real chocolate. It uses more dishes than tea or coffee. It's fattening. It keeps you awake at night — if it happens to. Nevertheless there's something about a well-made cup of hot chocolate that is very cheering on a cold January afternoon. It is associated in Mrs. Appleyard's mind with frosty moonlight nights, sleighbells, straw around your feet, a chinchilla muff — you could blow holes in the fur — the creak of runners on the crisp snow, the steam from the horses' breath, the driver humped in bearskin with big mittened hands and earlaps on his peaked cap, bare elms against a green-and-silver sky. You sang — whether you could sing or not. Everyone can sing on a sleigh ride. 'Jingle bells' ... 'Nelly Gray' ... 'Over the River' ... 'She's got rings on her fingers' ... 'Old Black Joe' ... 'The Merry Widow' ... 'Up the Street' ...

And afterward you stamped your numb feet and laughed a good deal at nothing special and the hot chocolate made you warm again down to the tips of your fingers and toes.

And here's how it was made.

For twelve people:

6 sqs. Baker's cooking chocolate	6 T. sugar
1 c. water	8 c. rich milk
¼ t. salt	½ pt. cream, whipped

1 T. brandy (or 2 t. vanilla)

Grate the chocolate and put it into the top of a large double boiler with the water, salt, and brandy. Stir until the chocolate is melted and when the mixture is smooth, add the sugar and keep stirring. Stir in the milk and when it is scalding hot, beat the chocolate with an egg-beater until it froths. It must be served at once or there will be skin on the top. It will not taste of the brandy, which simply makes it extra smooth and rich. Serve the whipped cream separately for those who have no regard at all for their silhouettes. Some deceive the eye though not the palate by floating marshmallows — or compounds thereof — on top of chocolate. Of this subterfuge Mrs. Appleyard says little, but that is not because she has no opinions about it.

Coffee Chocolate is good if you don't mind staying awake at night. Even if chocolate does not keep you awake, you can be pretty nearly sure of a clear-minded night by substituting a cup of strong coffee for the water in this rule. Either of these drinks is good iced. Put cracked ice in tall glasses, make the chocolate or coffee chocolate fresh, pour it over the ice. Put a tablespoon of thick cream — or of whipped cream if you prefer it — on top, stick in a sprig of mint, and relax. For iced chocolate you may need to add extra sugar, as cold drinks taste less sweet than hot ones.

For Mint Chocolate add six drops of peppermint extract for each glass of iced chocolate to be served. Plenty of mint in the top, of course — enough to make a real bouquet to smell.

Iced Chocolate may also be made by shaking cold milk and chocolate syrup together in a glass shaker with some ice cubes. Chocolate syrup may be bought readymade, but it is easy to make it at home and it is convenient to have it on hand in the refrigerator.

CHOCOLATE SYRUP

4 sqs. Baker's unsweetened ⅛ t. salt
    chocolate   6 T. sugar
2 c. water

Grate the chocolate and put it into the top of the double boiler with the water. Stir it over the direct flame until the chocolate is melted, then add the salt and sugar and cook it over hot water three minutes longer. Cool it, put it into a jar with a tight cover, and keep it in the refrigerator until you need it.

To make a Chocolate Milk Shake put two tablespoonfuls of this syrup and eight ounces of rich milk into a glass shaker with an ice cube. Add whatever flavor your customer likes — two drops of peppermint extract, two drops of almond, or one quarter teaspoon of vanilla. Let him shake it himself and give him a tall glass for it. This is a good way to make some of the skinny members of the family take extra milk.

CIDER

Cider with preservative in it is often a beautiful clear dark amber color and comes in a jug of exotic shape with a handsome label printed in seven different tints. It looks fine on a fruit stand and, according to Mr. Appleyard, should be left right there.

Cider should be bought the day it is made from the mill where it is made. The right kind of mill can generally be identified by its unprofessional appearance. The roof slants at various interesting angles. There is a smell of apples with overtones of vinegar. (Mills where they use preservative never let any cider turn to vinegar.) The jugs in the right kind of mill are clean, but there are no seductive labels on them picturing an apple the size of a large turnip and colored like a peach and probably, Mr. Appleyard says, tasting like a turnip and having the same amount of juice. It is the sort of apple that Adam would have immediately handed over to Eve, he says.

He seems to imply that it would serve her right, but Mrs. Appleyard, who is sampling the day's run of cider from a paper cup, fails to snatch up the insult. Fresh cider must have a soothing effect on her. . . . She also likes it as it mellows to the happy stage where the cork comes out of the jug with a resounding pop and the cider fizzes a little as it is poured into the glasses.

She always puts most of it into the refrigerator, where it will slowly reach the fizzy state, but also leaves out a gallon or two in a warm place where it will turn to vinegar. It is much better in watermelon pickle or mincemeat or raspberry shrub than vinegar that is made in vinegar works.

She can, however, in recommendation of commercial vinegar, honestly say that when poured over some rusty nails and left standing for a few days, it makes a very fine wart-remover. There are various charms that you are supposed to say as you apply the black and sticky result, and it is a good idea to get someone — a grandmother is a likely philanthropist — to buy your warts. They will vanish in about two weeks. . . . Used straight, bottled vinegar can be applied to your table top to bleach it — if you were ever silly enough to darken it with ammonia. Combined with salt it helps in cleaning an old brass kettle. Probably Mrs. Appleyard could think of other uses for it, but she would rather talk about cider.

There is nothing especially technical about serving cider if you bought it at the right place and kept it cold long enough for it to harden a little. A sixteen-pound turkey from Craftsbury, Vermont, makes a very nice background for a few glasses of cider. So do mince and pumpkin pie.

There are also occasions when *Hot Spiced Cider* is a pleasant drink. Either sweet cider or some that is beginning to harden may be used for this.

For twelve people:

12 c. cider	2 T. stick cinnamon, broken fine
12 whole cloves	¼ t. nutmeg

Put the cider into a saucepan with the spices. Bring it slowly to the boiling point. Strain it. Serve it hot with toasted cheese and chutney appetizers (see page 145).

RUM PUNCH

Anyone who comes into the kitchen and finds Mrs. Appleyard removing the peel from several dozen lemons is correct in guessing that something exciting is going on in the family. It takes at least an engagement to stir her to this particular activity.

For sixty people she takes:

24 lemons	4 oz. yellow Chartreuse
4 lbs. lump sugar	2 T. Orange Pekoe tea
2 gal. water	4 oz. apricot brandy
2 c. New England rum	2 oz. orange curaçao

Take the thin peel off the lemons. She says you ought to cut it so thin that you can see through it. Put it into a large bowl with the sugar. If possible get the old-fashioned roughly cut kind of lump sugar instead of the too civilized package variety. Put the water into a large kettle and bring it to a boil as quickly as possible. While it is heating, squeeze the lemons and pour the juice over the peel and sugar. Just as the water reaches a full bubbling boil, toss the tea into it and let it boil *exactly* one minute — no more and no less. Use your watch to time it. Too long boiling makes it bitter; too short cooking fails to bring out the flavor. Remove it at once from the fire and strain it over the lemons and sugar. Stir it hard until the sugar is melted. Add the rum, apricot brandy, Chartreuse, and orange curaçao. Keep on stirring.

Now put it away in a cool place — not the refrigerator — for at least a day to blend and ripen. It may then be strained into scalded jugs until you are ready to use it. If it is not to be used within a day or two add a little more rum to the top of each jug.

When serving the punch put ice cubes — a block of ice is better, if you can get it — into a large punch bowl. Add diced fresh pineapple and maraschino cherries. Strawberries or raspberries may be added if they are in season or a few stoned black cherries, or some slices of banana or of fresh peach. Freshly sliced lemon and orange may be used.

too. But not too much fruit, please. You aren't making fruit compote! Decorate the bowl with some sprays of fresh mint.

CIDER AND RUM PUNCH — HOT

Half spiced cider (see page 23) and half this rum punch heated together makes a good drink after skiing. Mrs. Appleyard sometimes adds a little raspberry vinegar to it. Not bad a bit, is the verdict.

TEA PUNCH (NO ALCOHOL) NO. 1

1 gal. boiling water	2 qts. pale dry ginger ale
16 lemons	1 qt. purple grape juice
1 T. tea	Cut-up fruit
4 oranges	Fresh mint
	2 c. sugar

Put the water on to boil. Slice the oranges and lemons very thin. Add the sugar and pound it into the fruit with a pestle until it makes a thick syrup with the fruit juice. Do not pound it too long or you will bring out the bitterness in the rind. When the water is boiling, throw in the tea. (Mrs. Appleyard likes Earl Grey's mixture for this, but Orange Pekoe will do.) Let it boil exactly one minute. Strain it over the fruit juice and sugar mixture. Put it away to cool and ripen. When it is cool, add the grape juice. When serving, strain it over a chunk of ice in a punch bowl and add some fruit — sliced orange, strawberries, peaches, and bananas — and a few very thin slices of cucumber. Last of all add the chilled ginger ale and the mint.

TEA PUNCH (NO ALCOHOL) NO. 2

1 gal. boiling water	2 qts. pale dry ginger ale
16 lemons	1 qt. white grape juice
1 T. tea	or pineapple juice
4 oranges	2 c. sugar

Make this just as you do Tea Punch No. 1. A good combination of fruit to put into the punch bowl for this version is freshly sliced lemon, strawberries, and diced pineapple. Decorate it with mint.

Either of these rules serves thirty people, only you have to keep the small boys from coming back for seconds before their less enterprising elders are served. Mrs. Appleyard would be glad to hear from anyone who has a real solution for this problem. She doesn't consider muzzling them is hospitable.

LEMONADE

Mrs. Appleyard and her friend Mrs. Teasdale are rivals in the construction of lemonade. Each dallies appreciatively with a long cool glass of the other lady's beverage, and they frequently say to each other, 'Now do tell me just once more how you do it.' Each is completely sincere but when confronted with lemons and sugar she always reverts to type. It is difficult to get precise instructions from either of the rivals, but Mrs. Teasdale is especially abstruse. Can it be that she does not really wish to give away her secret? She has a good deal to say about how it is impossible to be sure, now that the green glass pitcher is broken and she thinks the sugar scoop she has in Overbrook Hill isn't the same as the Appleyard Centre one. However, spies sent

into her kitchen disguised as thirsty tennis players have reported that the formula is about like this:

3 lemons	4 c. cold spring water
1 orange	Ice
1 lime	1 c. sugar

This makes enough for three tall glasses of lemonade
and enough to fill them again before they are empty.
'What's the use of a small glass of lemonade?' Mrs. Teasdale
says — a very sound remark, according to Mrs. Appleyard.

Put the sugar in the pink glass pitcher (the green one,
alas, being broken). Pour the strained fruit juices over it
and stir until they are thoroughly dissolved. Add part of
the water and stir some more, then the ice and the rest of
the water. If you have any doubt about its being well
mixed, pour it into something else and then back into the
pitcher. (This may be how pitchers get broken.)

Some people, Mrs. Teasdale says, might like this sweeter,
but this combination has always been perfectly acceptable
to Mrs. Appleyard while the two friends are sitting in a
shaded room with a breeze blowing through it on a hot day,
and saying how remarkable each other's children are.

LEMONADE WITH SUGAR SYRUP

There are people so prudent that they have sugar syrup
on hand in the refrigerator for making lemonade. Mrs.
Appleyard is not one of these. The presence of sugar syrup
merely inspires her to make a lot more lemonade than
usual and have the neighbors in. When an emergency
arises she is just where she would have been anyway. However, for those who have the strength of character to make
the syrup and put it away in case Uncle Roswell, Aunt

Cynthia, and three thirsty little Haliburtons drive into the front yard it is a good thing, and this is how you make it.

4 c. granulated sugar   4 c. water

Boil the sugar and the water together for ten minutes. Pour it into jars that have been boiled and are still hot, and seal them. Keep it on hand if you can and remember to make some more when you use it up.

The juice of six lemons, three cups of water, and one and a half cups of sugar syrup make a good smooth lemonade that will not be sour on top and with unmelted sugar at the bottom of the glass. If the syrup is kept in the refrigerator, one or two ice cubes will be enough to chill it. If you are making a fruit drink to be used later the same day, shave off the thin yellow peel of the lemons and drop it into the boiling syrup for a few minutes. The syrup should then be cooled and the lemons can be squeezed when you are ready to serve the lemonade. If you have used the peel when you cooked the syrup, you can use slightly more water when you mix the drink. This is very good with a cup of strawberries, crushed and carefully strained, added to it when you add the lemon juice.

For her final word on the subject of lemonade, Mrs. Appleyard now reveals to a waiting world the secret of

GRANDMOTHER APPLEYARD'S LEMONADE

Grandmother Appleyard left behind her many happy memories. She was an unequalled teller of the tales of the countryside. She could always think of some ingenious way to use something for a purpose for which the maker of it was a lot too unenterprising to intend it. She was generous. The expression 'She would take her dress off her back and give it to you, if she thought you needed it' will always describe Grandmother Appleyard to her daughter-in-law, who once actually saw her mother-in-law do just that. She had clever fingers. Two bedspreads with quilted patterns of shells and feathers among the pink and green roses and tulips show how skillful she was with her needle. But even if the quilts were not there, even if she had not once broken up an old stove with a grindstone, she would still be remembered for her lemonade.

The big yellow mixing bowl that she used is still there. Into it she used to put:

12 lemons	4 c. granulated sugar
4 oranges	16 c. water

Slice the lemons and the oranges — the thinner the better, she said. Have the sugar beside you as you work and sprinkle it over the slices from time to time. When all the fruit and all the sugar are used, take a wooden pestle and crush them. 'Scrunch' is a better word for the process, perhaps. It consists of grinding the juice out of the fruit with the sharp sugar crystals and the dissolving of the sugar in the juice. Do not work over this too long. The idea is to get the juice out of the slices and the flavor out of the rind. Pounding it too long or too hard will only bring out the bitterness of the white skin under the rind. The result should be a thick lemony syrup that has the flavor of rind and juice but no bitter taste. Three or four minutes of crushing is about enough if you have cut the lemons really thin. If you don't mind an occasional seed in your lemonade, all you need to do now is to put in some ice, pour in the spring water, stir it well, and skim off any seeds that come at once to the top.

If there are city folks around who might be made nervous by seeds, you have Mrs. Appleyard's permission to strain it over a chunk of ice into your best punch bowl.

This scrunched-up lemon and sugar is used in Appleyard Centre as the basis for several kinds of fruit punch.

Around Fourth of July a box of ripe strawberries is always crushed along with the lemons and pale dry ginger ale takes the place of part of the water. Sometimes the added liquid is a third water, a third pineapple juice, and a third ginger ale; or white grape juice may be used in place of the pineapple juice. In raspberry season there are always raspberries floating around in it. Once in a while there are a few mint leaves crushed with the fruit, and there are almost always sprigs of mint stuck into the bowl.

It is hard to specify how many people can be served with this lemonade because there has never yet been any left. All Mrs. Appleyard generally gets is a somewhat feeble decoction made by adding some more water to what is left in the bottom of the bowl. A gallon is supposed to serve twenty people (caterers allow thirty), but as small sticky hands always appear under Mrs. Appleyard's elbow before she finishes serving the first round she is pretty vague about the numbers. She swears every year to make more next time.

For hot August evenings a good thirst-quencher is:

MRS. APPLEYARD'S RASPBERRY SHRUB

2 qts. raspberries	2 c. cider vinegar
4 c. sugar	2 c. boiling water

The vinegar you make yourself by leaving some cider around in a warm place is the best kind to use.

Crush the fruit with the sugar, pour the vinegar over it, and heat it until the sugar and the vinegar are well blended. Do not boil it. Set it aside to cool. Cover it and let it stand in a cool place for two days. Cook it again gently for twenty minutes, adding a little water if it seems too thick. Strain it through a very fine sieve, pouring the two cups of boiling water slowly through it to get all the color and flavor out of the pulp.

Water and ice cubes may be added to this amount of shrub — there should be about two quarts — enough to make a gallon of liquid. The Appleyards, however, like to use it in the kind of lemonade made by crushing lemons and sugar together (see page 28) — about a cupful of shrub to a gallon of lemonade.

Or if the raspberry flavor is to predominate, Mrs. Appleyard crushes three thinly sliced lemons with one cup of sugar and adds two quarts of the raspberry shrub, two quarts of water, and a few fresh raspberries. Ginger ale may be substituted for part of the water. It is a good idea to taste this frequently, Mrs. Appleyard says, as the shrub has a good deal of tang to it and you may like it a little sweeter or diluted further. After all, the person who constructs the drinks ought to be allowed to sample them, as that may be all she'll ever get anyway. To any and all rules that contain lemon, Mrs. Appleyard is apt to add a lime or two if they are handy.

Mr. Appleyard is fond of *Vermouth Cassis*, and he makes it by putting into a highball glass two ice cubes, an ounce of dry vermouth, and half an ounce of crème de Cassis, and filling the glass with club soda. (Mrs. Appleyard wonders if when the Cassis is gone — and it won't be long now — she can't do a little good in the world with some of the red currants by the carriagehouse and the black raspberries by the springhouse. There may just possibly be something in it.)

Fortunately there are still likely to be cranberries, so that Mr. Appleyard can still make

THE MAGIC COCKTAIL (J. H. C.)

This is called the Magic Cocktail, because the formula came from a famous magician to a distinguished surgeon, who revealed the secret to his friend Mr. Appleyard, and gave him permission to tell Mrs. Appleyard, and thus bestow it on a thirsty and appreciative world.

First catch your cranberry cider. This project presents certain difficulties as there is apparently only one place in Massachusetts where it is made. If you happen to take any other route than 128 to the Cape, you are not in the least likely to find it. However, you may be able to get pretty good results with a bottle of cranberry juice from the grocery store. Whichever you use, begin by pouring out a quarter of it. This need not be thrown away; your wife can drink it. Substitute for it an equal amount of pure grain alcohol, shake it up and let it stand for a few days to blend.

For each cocktail Mr. Appleyard uses three ounces of the fortified cranberry cider, one ounce of Jamaica rum, and a dash of lime juice. He shakes it well with ice and when he pours it out, it is a handsome pale pink. There is enough for a 'dividend.'

4

Brides Must Bake. Most cooks like to bake, and Mrs. Appleyard is no exception. There is probably no more thrilling moment than the one when the broom straw (sterilized, of course, in these aseptic times) is thrust into the cake and comes out clean and shining without the least hint of stickiness. Then that wonderful smell just as the biscuits are done and before they begin to scorch — why has Chanel never bottled it? What a boon it would be to a young bride if she could sprinkle a little on her flowered Austrian skiing-folk-dancing-and-cooking apron so that at least she would be a pleasant advertisement for her baking — no matter what the facts in the case might be.

Mrs. Appleyard, like all other cooks who studied in the school of experience, has turned out her quota of biscuits that were better for throwing than for eating. She offers her rule for them with some hesitation because making biscuits, like riding a bicycle, is one of those things that come all at once. No amount of telling how it is done seems to have much effect. However, there has to be a first time and you might as well try it this way, and don't blame Mrs. Appleyard if your husband implies that any members of his family tree constructed them differently. Even brides' husbands' ancestors had to learn.

BAKING–POWDER BISCUIT

2 c. flour	1 t. salt
4 t. baking powder	2 T. butter
¾ c. milk (more if needed)	

Mix the dry ingredients. Mrs. Appleyard always sifts them four times and measures the flour after the first sifting. Work in the butter with your fingertips — or cut it in with a pastry blender if you'd rather — until it is all through the flour in lumps that are almost too small to see. Use an extra tablespoon of butter if you like them very short. Cut the milk in with a table knife. Toss the dough on a floured board, pat it into the shape of a fat pincushion, roll it out lightly not too thin, three quarters of an inch is about right. Shape the biscuits with a cutter and put them into a tin pan or on a baking-sheet. Bake them in a hot oven (450° F.) about twelve minutes.

If they are baked in too slow an oven, the gas from the baking powder will escape without having raised the biscuits. The less biscuits are handled the better, and the emergency kind is often the lightest. These are made with the above mixture, only more milk is added and they are not rolled out, but pushed from the end of a large spoon onto the baking-sheet one and a half inches apart, brushed lightly with thick cream, and baked in a hot oven from eight to ten minutes.

MRS. APPLEYARD'S DATE-NUT BREAD

This is a very adhesive kind of bread. It sticks to the
fingers, to the ribs, and to the sides of the pan unless precautions are taken. It is generally eaten slightly warm with
plenty of butter. The addition of some cottage cheese and
some fruit is considered a satisfactory dessert by the simple
dwellers in Appleyard Centre.

1 c. dark molasses	½ c. nuts, chopped
2 c. graham flour	1 c. sour cream
2 large eggs	1 c. white flour
1 t. baking powder	1 t. baking soda
1 c. dates, cut in	½ t. salt
pieces and floured	

Sift the dry ingredients. This does not mean that the
bran is discarded from the graham. It will stay in the sifter,
but it must be stirred back into the flour. Mrs. Appleyard
mentions this because once one of her pupils carefully
removed the bran. She also repeats that she always sifts
the flour once before she measures it, then adds the salt and
baking soda and baking powder and sifts everything together three times more. Some people add soda to the
cream or molasses — probably because it's fun to see it
fizz. Mrs. Appleyard believes that the fizzing ought to go
on during the baking and not be wasted beforehand. The
careful sifting distributes the soda through the bread, and
it is all ready to combine with the acid in the cream and
help to raise the bread during the baking. Soda and baking
powder are two different substances. You'd better take
Mrs. Appleyard's word for this or you will get some only
too interesting results. (She knows a young lady who
thought they were interchangeable. She is the same one

who cut out an opera cape with a pair of nail scissors.) There is no use going into the chemistry of the matter any further, because Mrs. Appleyard's ignorance on the subject would probably embarrass you.

Stir the molasses and the cream together and add the eggs, well beaten. Next add the dry ingredients, beating them in well. Then stir in quickly the floured dates and nuts. These may be walnuts, pecans, or — if you are lucky — butternuts. Put the mixture into a bread tin that has been buttered, lightly floured, and lined with heavy waxed paper. Bake the bread in a moderate oven (375° F.) one hour. This makes one large loaf.

SOUR-CREAM GRAHAM BREAD

2 eggs, well beaten	1½ c. sour milk
1⅓ c. maple syrup	2 c. graham flour
½ c. thick sour cream	1½ t. salt
2 c. white flour	2 t. soda
2 t. baking powder	

Sift the dry ingredients together. Beat the eggs well and stir them into the cream, milk, and syrup. Beat in the dry ingredients. The batter should be quite stiff. Add a little more of the graham flour if necessary. Butter bread tins and line them with heavy waxed paper. Fill them two-thirds full with the mixture. Bake in a moderate oven (375° F.) for one hour, reducing the heat the last part of the time. Test with a broom straw. When it comes out clean, the bread is done.

Mr. Appleyard likes this for dessert with butter, powdered maple sugar (see page 82), and thick cream.

Why wouldn't he?

PUFFED MONTPELIER CRACKERS

These are a nuisance but the customers say it's worth it. 'Worth it to whom?' Mrs. Appleyard has been heard to inquire, when in one of her less melting moods, for even she can sometimes resist flattery.

Boston Common crackers may be used in those benighted regions where Montpelier crackers have not yet penetrated. What is so wonderful, cynical outlanders have been known to ask, about an ordinary soda cracker?

To be sure they have no exotic flavor. No one pretends they are Camembert, caviar, or Bar-le-Duc. Yet for all three — and for many other things — they are the perfect background. They are larger than an ordinary soda cracker and at once crisper, fluffier, and flakier. There is a story told in Montpelier that a big baking company in the West once hired away the baker from the Montpelier firm that made the crackers, offered him a large salary, and provided him with everything that he asked for: the specially ground flour, the soapstone ovens — everything that was part of his secret.

But the first batch of crackers was a failure, and so was the second — and so on. They had everything — the money, the secret rule, the baker, the ovens — everything but the Vermont water. Water for Montpelier crackers, it seems, has to run out of those special hills. Out of special clouds, too, perhaps. Snow and hail and sleet and thunder all have their part in it. Maple trees, too, that are powdery gilt in the spring and hot gold in the fall hold it around their roots, and it trickles under the roots of pasture apple trees loaded with pink drifts of blossom, and under pointed firs like church steeples when the snow is on them. It filters through limestone and around granite boulders and slate. It chuckles in brooks where there are trout, and quietly washes a bank where there are freshwater clams with pearls in them, and tells no one about them. It reflects gentian and jewel weed and the pointed wings of swallows. The sun draws it up in straight gold bands behind Hunger Mountain and lets it fall again — and they make crackers with it. Like all other good Vermonters in the region of the Winooski (or Onion) River, the Appleyards always have a box on hand.

The crackers are good broken into a bowl of rich Guernsey milk and eaten with Vermont cheese. They are good split, buttered, and put into the oven for a few minutes. They take kindly to having almost anything spread on them. Mixed with French bread crumbs they make the best cracker crumbs in the world for stuffing, for scalloped oysters, for anything au gratin. In fact the only way that Mrs. Appleyard cannot conscientiously recommend them is the way one fifteen-year-old six-footer ate them. He was the type of boy with hollow legs, and always went off to bed with a large sandwich or two to help him through the night. One night he was heard rummaging in the pantry, but others had been before him. For once everything was scraped clean — no forgotten hunk of Washington pie, no peanut butter, no sardines, no marshmallows — in fact none of those substances that would produce a restful night, either in combination or singly. However, he emerged with his sandwich just the same. It consisted of a Montpelier cracker, split, with another Montpelier cracker in between.

This type of sandwich would be best consumed, if at all, under water, Mrs. Appleyard says. It makes her thirsty just to think about it.

It may seem like painting the lily to soufflé them, but here's how you do it. The materials are simple:

Montpelier crackers   Butter
Ice water

Be sure to split enough crackers. Allow at least two whole crackers apiece.

Put ice cubes into a large bowl of cold spring water. When the water is very cold, put in the split halves of crackers. Have ready some clean damask napkins — the kind that are getting a few thin places in them. At the end of three minutes — or sooner, if they seem to be getting too soft — remove the crackers from the ice water. A pancake-turner with holes in it is best for this gesture. If the crackers stay in too long, they will fall to pieces; if not long enough, they will not puff.

When they have drained for a few minutes — five, perhaps — put them into iron dripping-pans and dot them over thickly with soft butter. Dust them with paprika, if you like it. Have the oven hot (450°–500° F.) and bake them until they are puffed, crisp, and golden brown. They should be done in from twenty-five to thirty-five minutes. It is hard to get on too much butter. Always allow at least an hour for the whole process, as nothing is less attractive than a puffed cracker that has changed its mind and decided to be a wet blotter. It should show no symptoms of ever having been near the water. If you didn't put on enough butter the first time, add some more halfway through the baking. There is no use making them if you are not going to be reckless with butter. If you are feeling cautious, why not have a few prunes? They might be just as good for you.

BOSTON BROWN BREAD

1 c. rye flour	1 c. graham flour
¾ t. soda	¾ c. molasses
1 c. corn meal	¾ t. salt
1¾ c. sweet milk	

Sift the dry ingredients together thoroughly. Mix the milk and molasses together, make a hollow in the flour mixture, and pour in the other mixture, beating it in well as you do so. Put the batter into greased tins that can be covered tightly. The tins should be taller than they are wide. A half-pound coffee tin of some brands is a good size and proportion. Do not fill the tins more than two-thirds full. Steam the bread for three hours. Be sure that the tins do not rest on the bottom of the kettle; there must be a chance for the water to circulate freely underneath them. Cover the kettle tightly so that as little steam as possible escapes. A lot of water can vanish in three hours and it is important for the kettle not to cook dry. The bread will steam more evenly if you do not have to uncover the kettle and add water during the steaming process. At the end of three hours, uncover the tins and set them in the oven for from five to ten minutes to dry out.

Add raisins if you like them: the Appleyards don't. Half a cup would be about right, Mrs. Appleyard thinks, but her opinion on this point is not worth much. Of course the usual place for this bread is alongside baked beans, but don't forget that when it is cold sandwiches of it, cut thin and either buttered or spread with a combination of butter and horse-radish, are good with any kind of shellfish. If you are going to use it for this purpose, a baking-powder tin is a nice size to steam the brown bread in.

BLUEBERRY MUFFINS

Bakery blueberry muffins are generally trying to make up their minds whether to be muffins or cake. Mrs. Appleyard's are frankly and honestly muffins, and if you prefer the cake variety, ask someone else how to make them. Hers have lots of berries in them and are never likely to be mistaken for currant cakes that have been in a fight.

¼ c. butter	2⅔ c. flour
½ t. salt	1 c. milk
⅓ c. sugar	4 t. baking powder
1 egg	1 heaping c. blueberries

Heated iron gem pans with plenty of melted butter in them are the secret of baking these muffins so that they are beautifully browned all over.

Cream the butter, work in the sugar, and add the egg, well beaten. Put in two eggs if they are small, and leave out a little of the milk. Save out about a quarter of a cup of the flour. The rest you have, of course, sifted with the baking powder and the salt. Did you measure the flour after the first sifting? Mrs. Appleyard hates to keep nagging about this, but feels that it is her duty.

Put the berries into a bowl with the flour you saved out and roll the berries around in the flour until each one looks like Couching Lion seen through heat haze in August. Beat the rest of the dry ingredients into the butter-and-sugar mixture, alternating with the milk. Last of all add the berries, stirring and folding them in. A spoon with holes in it is good for this process.

Fill the hot buttered gem pans two-thirds full. Have the oven hot — 475° F. Bake until the muffins have risen above the tops of the pans and are a handsome tan, punctured here and there with spots of Tyrian purple.

SOUR–CREAM BISCUIT

It is sad to think that there are a great many people in the world who never see sour cream rolled off a pan of milk that has just turned to clabber. Mrs. Appleyard enjoys taking the skimmer that was her husband's grandmother's from the nail where it has hung for a hundred years, and with it removing the thick old-ivory cream and revealing the quivering alabaster below. Biscuits made with cream and clabber are tender and light. Be sure not to get in too much soda. Biscuits that taste of it are, perhaps, appreciated by the family pig, but no other eater for them has yet been discovered. Mrs. Appleyard learned from Mr. Appleyard's mother to use only enough soda to neutralize the acidity of the milk and to add baking powder to help with the rising process. For freshly soured milk and cream the proportions are about like this:

1 c. thick sour milk	1 t. baking powder
½ c. sour cream	½ t. salt
¾ t. soda	2 c. flour

You may need a little more flour than this. The dough should be rather stiff, as it is not to be rolled out and there is no butter to melt in the baking. Mix the soda and baking powder with the milk and cream. Taste it to be sure you have not put in too much soda. If there is the least taste of soda, add a little more milk or cream until you are sure that there is no taste of soda and also that the sour taste of the milk is neutralized. This takes courage but it is the only way you can learn. It is difficult to judge the exact amount of acid in sour milk, and even women who have used it all their lives will, if they depend on luck, turn out an occasional batch of biscuits that taste of soda. The only sure way to tell what you are doing is to taste the milk after you have mixed the soda with it. Or — if you sifted the dry ingredients together and then worked in the milk and cream — to taste the dough. In either case, correct it, if necessary by working in a bit more milk and cream. This of course will make more flour necessary — and you can keep this up far into the night. When the dough is just right, push it off the end of a large spoon onto a baking-sheet. Bake the biscuits in a hot oven (475°–500° F.) for ten minutes.

You may have a failure, but suppose you do? The whole process only takes about fifteen minutes: you can start all over again and next time it will come right. When you once get the hang of it, you will wish you always had sour milk for your biscuits.

POPOVERS

What makes popovers pop is one of those crucial questions that is often asked by the young and never answered by the old — probably because their mouths are too hot to speak.

Mrs. Appleyard thinks this desirable chemical change is produced by starting the popovers in hissing hot iron gem pans in a hot oven, but there is another school of thought that advises starting them in cold pans in a cold oven and letting everything heat up together. Frankly Mrs. Appleyard believes that this is just folklore, but of course she can't stop any adventurous spirit from trying it; in fact she means to try it herself some day. Anyway, the batter is the same. The lightness is given by the eggs and lots of beating.

1 c. milk	¼ t. salt
1 c. flour	2 eggs, well beaten

Sift the flour with the salt four times. Add the milk slowly and then the beaten eggs. Beat the batter for two minutes. Pour the mixture into hot buttered iron gem pans and bake in a hot oven (450° F.) for twenty minutes. Then reduce the heat to 350° F. and bake fifteen to twenty minutes longer. Serve at once with plenty of butter. With maple syrup or with hot chocolate sauce, they make a good cold-weather dessert.

YORKSHIRE PUDDING

Yorkshire pudding is really only a popover batter treated a little differently. What is better with roast beef? No one needs to turn up his nose at English cooking until he has tasted English roast beef with Yorkshire pudding — and then he certainly won't. All right — suppose they do have four vegetables, three of which are cabbage. A lot worse things can happen to you than some well-cooked cabbage (gooseberry tart with custard made of imitation eggs, for instance, or, nearer home, doughnuts that have soaked fat, or pale, tough piecrust).

Batter for Yorkshire pudding is made of

1 c. milk	3 eggs, well beaten
1 c. flour	½ t. salt

Sift the flour and salt four times. Add the milk slowly, then beat in the eggs. Beat the batter two minutes with an egg-beater. Into an iron dripping-pan pour fat from the roasting beef half an inch deep. Pour in the batter and bake it for twenty minutes at 400° F. Cut it into squares and put it around the beef. Baste it with the drippings from the roast and let it cook ten to fifteen minutes longer. It should be light and crisp and a dark golden brown.

CORN MEAL IN BAKING

Mrs. Appleyard remembers several things about the war once innocently called the Great War with some disfavor. She had an experience with whale meat that she has been known to mention to her family — probably not more than twenty or thirty times (see the Appleyard children's under-the-table notebook for accurate statistics on this point). Whale meat, she says, is all very well as described by Herman Melville in *Moby Dick*. As cooked by Mrs. Appleyard it resembled tough round steak that had been in swimming with a mackerel — all her fault, no doubt.

It was, however, no pang to the Appleyards to eat their ration of corn meal instead of white flour. They liked it already. When the young Appleyards learn to cook, they always begin with:

CORN-MEAL MUFFINS

1 c. corn meal	¼ c. sugar
½ t. salt	2 T. melted butter
2 eggs	1 c. milk
1 c. white flour	4 t. baking powder

Mix and sift the dry ingredients. Add the milk, the well-beaten eggs, and the melted butter. When you start to mix the batter, light the oven and put into it your iron gem pans with a dab of butter in each compartment. Fill them half full of the batter and bake the muffins twenty to twenty-five minutes at 400°–425° F. If the pans are large this makes a dozen muffins. They should be crusty at top and bottom, soft inside, golden brown all over. Honey and butter disappear rapidly in their presence, also marmalade.

SCALDED JOHNNYCAKE

One charm of scalded johnnycake is that it is an entirely different thing according to the pan in which it is baked and the thickness to which it is spread. The first version is a rugged one for hearty appetites.

1 c. corn meal, yellow or white	1 c. boiling water
1 t. salt	¼ c. milk
1 T. butter	2 T. fat — for browning

Put the fat — it may be sausage fat, bacon fat, or butter if you prefer — into a medium-sized iron frying-pan, and put the pan where the fat will melt slowly while you are scalding the meal. Boil your water in a saucepan and when it is boiling hard, pour it over the corn meal, to which you have added the salt and the butter. Always bring the bowl of meal to the stove, never the water to the meal. The water should be as near boiling as possible when it strikes the meal. Stir thoroughly until you are sure that the meal has absorbed all the water that it will take. Then add the milk. You may find that you have to add more water. It is hard to give the amount of water accurately as different kinds of meal absorb different amounts of liquid. The batter may seem too wet at first, but it will swell and take up water as it stands. It should not be thin and sloppy, but do not worry if you have made it a little too wet: it will simply take a bit longer to bake. Do not make the mistake of adding more corn meal after you start the scalding process unless you scald it separately and add more butter.

Now pour the batter into the pan containing the melted fat. Let it get hot for a few minutes on the top of the stove. When the batter begins to bubble up around the edges put the pan into the oven — 475° F. — and bake the johnnycake for half an hour. After the top has crusted over, which it should do in about ten minutes, put some more dabs of butter on top.

It should be a glazed golden brown underneath, rough and brown on top, rather soft inside. Like the cocoon, it makes the butterfly (an ancient joke sometimes served with this johnnycake in the Appleyard family). Cut it in wedge-shaped pieces. There is no harm in putting maple syrup on it.

THIN SCALDED JOHNNYCAKE

Use the same mixture given above. When it has absorbed all the liquid it will take, spread it very thin on a greased cooky-sheet. Use a spatula or a round-bladed knife and wet it from time to time as you spread. Either spread the johnnycake in a whole sheet and mark if off in squares, or drop it in dabs and spread them out in circles. Bake it in a hot oven (475° F.) for ten minutes. At the end of five minutes, put a small dab of butter in the middle of each square or round. The result to be desired is something like cassava cakes. The cakes should crumble in your fingers. They are good either hot or cold.

There are variations. One substitutes a teaspoonful of celery salt for the salt. This gives an interesting flavor that arouses curiosity in the consumer. There is also the trick of sprinkling grated cheese over the cakes during the last five minutes of their career in the oven. Mrs. Appleyard advises starting with them plain. Getting the plain ones right is enough of a trick without introducing foreign substances. If you add too much water, they will be leathery; if not enough, they will not stay together. Don't, Mrs. Appleyard says, be discouraged if the first batch is not just right. It does not take long to make them, and even Mrs. Appleyard herself has been known to throw away a whole panful and start over. In both kinds of scalded johnnycake, rather coarsely ground corn meal gives the best results. It's not much use trying to make it of the very finely ground kind, she says. She adds that the directions seem more dismaying than is really necessary. When you get the hang of it, you can make it in your sleep.

RHODE ISLAND JOHNNYCAKE (S. W. E.)

Mrs. Appleyard writes the name rather hesitantly. She means it as a compliment to one of her favorite states, but she realizes that some of its inhabitants may have some other formula for this most delicious of corn-meal dishes. All she can be perfectly sure of is that a good Rhode Island neighbor gave the rule to Mrs. Appleyard's grandmother and that the resulting johnnycakes have tempered many a cold morning when she was about to start for her morning trudge to school. This is how they were made.

2 c. white Rhode Island meal	2 T. butter
1 t. salt	2 c. boiling water (about)
½ c. milk	Extra butter for frying

Put the meal, mixed with the salt and butter, into a bowl and set it on the stove. When the water is boiling hard pour it over the meal. Be sure it is really boiling as it strikes the meal. Two cups of water should be enough, but it must absorb all it will take. Add the milk and let the mixture stand for two or three minutes so that you are sure it is wet enough. If you have to add more boiling water do so in very small quantities.

The batter should be soft but not wet. Drop it by large tablespoonfuls on a well-buttered griddle. When the cakes look brown around the edges, add a little more butter, turn the cakes, and brown them on the other side. Have the oven warm and have a dripping-pan ready in it. As the cakes brown put them into the pan. A little baking improves them but do not have the oven so hot that it dries them up. They should be a crisp brown outside, white and soft inside. Serve them with anything you like.

Mr. Appleyard, feeling that Vermont and Rhode Island ought to combine their talents, demands maple syrup — and gets it, of course. Mrs. Appleyard, a natural purist, thinks plain butter is sufficient dissipation.

SPOON BREAD

Wandering still farther afield Mrs. Appleyard thinks about spoon bread. This rule was given to her under the name of Southern Spoon Bread. Not having collected it on the spot she merely asserts that this is the way they make it in the southern part of Appleyard Centre — south of the millpond, the elm tree, and the old stage road to Canada. She generally makes double the amount given below in a four-quart milk pan and finds that recent mountain-climbers will not leave a scraping. Probably the quantity given would be enough for six ordinary appetites.

1 c. corn meal (white is best but yellow will do)	1 c. milk
	3 eggs
2 c. boiling water	2 t. baking powder
6 T. melted butter	½ t. salt

Scald the meal mixed with the salt and baking powder. Add four tablespoons of the melted butter, the milk, and the eggs, well beaten. Put the rest of the butter into a hot baking-dish, pour in the batter. Bake until the spoon bread is brown — about thirty-five minutes in a moderate oven (375° F.).

It's good instead of potatoes with either chicken or fish. Serve it in the dish in which it was cooked. You will want plenty of butter with it. If there is no maple syrup on the table Mr. Appleyard will ask plaintively if the sap didn't run last spring. However, it is not necessary to pattern your conduct after that of a man who can eat maple syrup with a spoon from a saucer.

SPIDER CORN CAKE

This is halfway between johnnycake and spoon bread. Like all things made with sour milk, it takes judgment, but if you get it right, your husband will rise up and call you blessed

1½ c. sour milk — part cream	½ c. white flour
1⅛ c. corn meal	1 t. salt
3 t. baking powder	1 egg
¼ c. sweet cream	1¼ c. sweet milk
1½ t. soda	2 T. melted butter

Sift the dry ingredients together. Pour in the sour milk

and half the sweet milk. Beat well. Stir in the egg, well beaten. Melt the butter in a large iron frying-pan, pour in the mixture, add the rest of the milk and the cream. Do not stir. Bake thirty minutes at 350° F., or until it is well browned.

This corn cake will have a soft layer in the middle. Serve it with butter and tart jelly — raspberry and currant, for instance — or maple syrup.

CORN PUDDING

Mrs. Appleyard is slightly confused as to whether this is a kind of bread or a vegetable. She ought to know because she invented it one day when there was not enough corn to go around for some unexpected visitors. Perhaps they had some theory about it, but all she knows is that they ate it. In times of stress she has also made it with canned whole-grain corn or with frozen corn instead of corn on the cob.

1 c. yellow corn meal	3 eggs
2 c. boiling water	2 t. baking powder
6 T. melted butter	½ t. salt
1 c. milk	1 c. corn, cut from the cob

Melt two tablespoons of the butter in a baking-dish. Mix the baking powder and the salt with the meal, add the rest of the butter. Scald the meal with the boiling water. Add the milk and the beaten eggs. Beat. Add the cut corn.

Bake thirty-five minutes in a moderately hot oven — about 400° F. Especially good with ham or sausage.

Even the scrapings are, among the Appleyards, a subject of keen competition. They like it baked long enough so that there is plenty of brown crust on the bottom.

CORN AND CHEESE SOUFFLÉ

3 T. butter	½ t. salt
3 T. flour	¼ t. paprika
1 c. milk	3 eggs, separated
1 c. corn, cut from the cob	½ c. grated cheese

Make a white sauce (see page 251) of the butter, flour, milk, and seasonings. Add the corn and the grated cheese. Then add the three egg yolks, beaten light. Last, fold in the stiffly beaten egg whites. Put the mixture into a greased baking-dish. Set the dish on a rack in a pan of hot water. Bake slowly at 375° F. for half an hour, or until puffed and brown. Serve at once. Guests must wait for the soufflé because the soufflé won't wait for them.

Supper is a good time to serve it — with a green salad and tomato marmalade.

Perhaps this soufflé ought not to have wandered into this section. Somehow one thing led to another. Mrs. Appleyard hastily wrenches the conversation back to

CREAM OF WHEAT SPOON BREAD

2½ c. boiling water	1½ c. milk
⅔ c. Cream of Wheat	1 t. salt
4 T. butter	3 t. baking powder
3 eggs, separated	2 T. flour

Add the Cream of Wheat to the boiling water so slowly that it never stops boiling. Cook over hot water for five minutes. Add butter. Let cool slightly and add milk, flour mixed with the salt, and the well-beaten egg yolks. Last of all fold in the stiffly beaten egg whites. Put the mixture into a well-buttered baking-dish. Dot more butter on top. Bake it in a moderate oven (375°–400° F.) for from thirty-five to forty-five minutes. Serve it from the dish in which you baked it as a vegetable instead of potatoes.

This is also delicious made with hominy but is a little more trouble, as the hominy needs longer cooking. Use about three cups of cooked hominy grits in place of the Cream of Wheat and boiling water.

5

Cakes — and Cookies, too. After baking a successful batch of muffins, it was generally only a matter of days before the thoughts of the young Appleyard novices turned toward cake. No blame attaches to them for this impulse: it is as natural as the thrusting green of the skunk cabbage in the spring woods, as inevitable as the auction purchase by young Appleyard boys of pairs of polished buffalo horns, as spontaneous as the combination of Mrs. Appleyard, a crescent of broken glass, and a tavern table with red paint on it.

However, the impulse, although powerful, can be guided, and it had better be guided toward sponge cake. Before beginning to sift the flour, the impatient cook has to hear Mrs. Appleyard's thoughts on cake.

'Don't make cake at all, if you feel economical. Toast yourself a Montpelier cracker or make some hot biscuits to have with maple syrup, or eat some raisins. There is nothing especially noble about having your cake cover the largest possible area with the smallest number of eggs. It is all right for a dachshund to be low slung, because that is his nature, but sponge cake should rise. If you want your cake to rise, it's got to have eggs in it. Most economizing on eggs is done in the country — where eggs are plentiful. That is because they are taken to the store and exchanged for some instantaneous cereal that tastes like last year's mullein stalks and a pineapple cherry cake wrapped in cellophane and made with baking powder and chicken fat. This keeps the wheels of business turning.'

Mrs. Appleyard had plenty more to say on this subject, but seeing a yawn, she simply added in a solemn tone, 'Never put baking powder in a sponge cake.'

Being assured by her pupils that they would avoid any such social error, she proceeded to give forth her knowledge on this vital topic.

SPONGE CAKE

6 eggs, separated	1 T. lemon juice
1 c. sugar	¼ t. salt
1 c. flour, measured	Grated rind of
after sifting	1 lemon

Sift the flour and measure it. Add the salt, sift three times more. Separate the eggs and beat the yolks until they are thick and lemon colored. Sift the sugar twice and add it gradually to the egg yolks, beating it in well. Add the lemon juice and the grated rind. Beat the egg whites until they are stiff but not dry. Fold them into the yolks and sugar, alternating with the flour. Do not beat at this stage. Put the batter into a large ungreased angel-cake tin and bake one hour at 325° F. After ten minutes sprinkle the top of the cake with a little granulated sugar. This will melt and combine with the batter to form a sugary crust. The cake is done when it springs back when lightly pressed with the fingertip. Turn it out onto a cake-cooler and let it stand until cold. Loosen it with a spatula, and it will slide from the pan with its own lightness.

ANGEL CAKE

The great problem with angel cake is what you do with the egg yolks. There is Hollandaise sauce, to be sure, but even Mrs. Appleyard, who likes it on everything but ice cream, feels that the lake of Hollandaise resulting from ten egg yolks would be a little difficult to dispose of. Still, it is not necessary to use them all at once, and there is foamy sauce to go with blueberry pudding, and velvet sauce to go with lemon soufflé, and perhaps you can work one or two into custard for chocolate ice cream. After all, it isn't Mrs. Appleyard's business what you do with them. You may buy from the bakery a cake made of powdered chalk for all she cares.

10 egg whites	1 c. sugar
⅛ t. salt	1 t. cream of tartar
⅞ c. flour	1 t. vanilla

Sift the flour and measure it. Add the salt and sift four times more. Sift the sugar twice. Beat the egg whites until they are stiff but not dry. Remember that even a very small bit of the yolk in them will keep them from beating stiff. Never beat them until everything else is ready, because the air bubbles go out of them quickly and it is the imprisoned air bubbles that are going to hold up the cake. Add the sugar, gradually beating it in. Add the vanilla. Fold in the sifted flour. Put the mixture into a large, well-greased angel-cake tin and bake it fifty minutes at 325° F. Do not slam the oven door or let the younger set play leapfrog around the stove while the cake is baking. This might be a good time for them to go in swimming.

When the cake is done, turn the pan upside down on a wire cake-cooler. After a while the cake will fall out. You can put some ice cubes wrapped in wax paper on top of the tin if you want to hurry things, but it is better to allow enough time for the cake to drop out of its own weight.

APPLEYARD CENTRE GINGERBREAD

Gingerbread is a good transition between sponge cake and the more difficult butter cakes. Mrs. Appleyard generally bakes it in two large layer-cake tins. When the first cake is done, it is removed from the pan and placed on the dish on which it is to be served. A large earthenware platter with crinkled blue edges is much esteemed for this purpose. The gingerbread is spread lightly with butter. Marshmallows torn in pieces — a dozen or so — are scattered over it, the second layer of gingerbread is laid over the first, and the dish is set into the oven with the door open. The gingerbread keeps hot and the marshmallows melt while the family are eating their fish chowder. This is a filling dessert and goes well with a meal that is not too heavy. Sometimes whipped cream and shredded crystallized ginger are served with the gingerbread, and there are some epicures who like thick sour cream with it.

1 c. sugar	½ t. ginger
1 c. dark molasses	½ t. nutmeg
⅔ c. melted butter	½ t. salt
1 c. thick sour milk, part cream	2½ c. flour
1 t. soda	2 eggs, well beaten
1 t. cinnamon	

Sift the flour and measure. Add the salt and spices and sift three times more. Mix together the sugar, molasses, butter, and milk. Beat the dry ingredients into the wet mixture, and add the well-beaten eggs. Fill buttered layer-cake tins half full. Bake twenty minutes at 400° F.

It may also be baked in heated, buttered iron gem pans for twenty minutes at 425° F.

CAKES WITH BUTTER IN THEM

Mrs. Appleyard thoroughly agrees with a piece of advice that she read in a French cookbook. If you must use two grades of butter, it said, use the better one in cooking and put the inferior one on the table where people can avoid it. Mrs. Appleyard solves the problem by using only one grade. If you feel you cannot use the best butter in cake, better express yourself in junket, or boiled rice, or go without something else — monogrammed playing-cards or peculiar hats.

In mixing butter cakes be sure that your eggs are fresh and cold. If they are to be separated, keep the whites in the refrigerator until you are ready to beat them. Have your butter soft but not melted, your sugar sifted and free of lumps; your flour dry and sifted four times. Be sure your pans are well buttered. If the rule calls for waxed paper, use plenty. Use a strong wooden spoon for creaming the butter, and a deep bowl. Never mix or bake a cake in a hurry. Cake mixtures are very sensitive to temper and haste.

Baking is as important as mixing. Well-mixed cakes — even of the best materials — can be spoiled by being shoved into the oven and neglected. Never try to bake a cake while you are baking something else in the oven. It would be a pleasant coincidence if both things needed the same temperature at the same moment, but it is as unlikely as a Jersey cow with a wreath of gardenias around her neck. It could happen, but it doesn't.

Divide the baking into four periods. In the first quarter the cake is rising. In the second quarter it keeps rising and starts browning. In the third it goes on browning. In the fourth it is getting baked inside, it browns more, it shrinks away from the sides of the pan. Reduce the heat during the second half of the time if the cake seems to be browning too quickly. It is all right to look at the cake frequently during baking so long as you do not move the pan until the cake has finished rising, and you handle the oven door gently. If the oven is too cold at first, the cake may rise too fast and run over the sides of the pan. If it is too hot, the cake may brown too quickly and split on top. This will also happen if you have used too much flour. If you use bread flour for making cake, take a little less than if you use cake flour.

Turn the cake upside down on a wire cake-cooler as soon as you take it from the oven. If it seems as if it were going to stick to the pan — and that happens to everyone sooner or later — keep calm, loosen it around the edges with a spatula, put ice cubes wrapped in wax paper on top of the pan, and hope for the best. If the misfortune occurs of the cake's coming out and leaving a piece behind, look upon it as a picture puzzle. Remove the broken piece gently with a spatula, tailor it neatly into the yawning gap, and give the cake a good thick coat of frosting.

If your frosting is the uncooked kind, put it on while the cake is still slightly warm. If you use cooked frosting, the cake may just as well be cool.

Cupcakes are easier to bake than loaf cakes, and take **a**

slightly hotter oven and a shorter time to bake than larger cakes. With these thoughts in mind, Mrs. Appleyard remarks to her panting listeners, you had better begin with:

MADELEINES

4 eggs	½ c. butter, melted
1 c. sugar, sifted	1 t. vanilla
1 c. cake flour	1 t. baking powder

These are small light cakes that are easy to make because the baking powder makes them pretty sure to rise well. Also because the butter is melted and the eggs are put in whole. They are not rich cakes and their charm is partly in their appearance — the way they are frosted and decorated.

Sift the flour and measure it. Add the baking powder and sift three times more. Beat the eggs well. Add the sugar and keep beating. Add the melted butter and the flavoring. Have the cake tins buttered — always use your smallest ones — and lightly sprinkled with flour. Fill them half full. Bake in a fairly hot oven (375°–400° F.) for fifteen minutes.

Frost with Seven-Minute Frosting (page 78) or with Almond-Butter Frosting (page 76). Decorate with candied cherries, almonds, or pecans.

When you have conquered these try:

LEMON QUEENS

1 c. sugar	1 T. lemon juice
½ c. butter	1¼ c. flour
¼ t. soda	4 eggs, separated
Grated rind of 1 lemon	

Sift the flour and measure it. Add the soda and sift three times more. Cream the butter, add the sugar, beat it in well, and add the lemon rind and juice. Keep beating. Add the yolks of the eggs, beaten until thick and lemon-colored, and beat in the sifted flour. Beat the egg whites until they are stiff but not dry. Fold them into the mixture. Fill small cake tins two-thirds full with the batter. Bake twenty to twenty-five minutes in a moderate oven — 375° F.

Frost with two tablespoonfuls of thick cream in which confectioner's sugar is stirred until it is thick enough to spread. Flavor it with vanilla or with a very little lemon extract.

Or frost them with Almond-Butter Frosting (page 76) or Boiled Frosting (page 78). They may also have a small piece removed from the centre and be filled with Lemon Filling (page 75). Cover the filling with the crusty top of the piece that you cut out and dust the whole top with powdered sugar. Properly baked Lemon Queens are level on top. Their consistency is that of a very delicate pound cake. A careless hand with the flour is fatal to them.

CHOCOLATE–PEPPERMINT CUPCAKES

This happy surprise in small cakes occurred because someone once gave Mrs. Appleyard a box of peppermints — the kind that are about the size of a half-dollar, and are sometimes white and flavored with peppermint, and sometimes other pastel shades and flavored with whatever the ingenious makers had in the house. Being — as usual — on a diet, Mrs. Appleyard could not very well eat the peppermints; the children were away, so they were no help.

She amused herself against their return by inventing these cakes. They are simply small chocolate cakes with a peppermint neatly inlaid in the top and rich chocolate frosting concealing it from the public.

Henry James has remarked that there are two different types of intellectual pleasure — the pleasure of recognition and the pleasure of discovery. Of course he took five pages to say it, but that was the idea. Chocolate-peppermint cakes embody both pleasures: the surprise of finding that something lurks in the chocolate ambush and the pleasure of recognizing that it is actually a peppermint, or a pink disk flavored with checkerberry — as the case may be.

The drawback of these cakes was soon apparent. There were favorite colors, and in the lottery of Fate the right customers did not always receive them. This problem became a family crisis. ('Is it fair for Sally to poke the cakes before she chooses?' — 'Go on — change with me Hugh. You know you like green and I've eaten hardly any of it.' — 'Oh gosh, pink again,' etc., etc.)

Of late years the peppermints have all been white.

CHOCOLATE CUPCAKES

2 sqs. Baker's chocolate	1 t. soda
¼ c. butter	2 eggs
1 c. milk	2 t. vanilla
¾ c. sugar	Pinch of salt
1¼ c. flour	

Sift the flour and measure it. Sift it three times more with the salt and soda. Grate the chocolate and melt it over hot water. Add the sugar and the beaten eggs and beat them well together. Add the sifted flour and the milk alternately in small amounts, beating them in thoroughly. Last of all, add the vanilla. If the batter seems too stiff, a little more milk may be added. Fill small, greased cupcake tins half full. Bake for twenty minutes at 375° F. These cakes should be quite level if they are baked carefully. If they rise too high in the middle, cut off small pieces before you put on the peppermints. Cover them with Chocolate Cream-Cheese Frosting (page 79).

Fortunately the tide of family receipts can flow up as well as down. This fudge cake is something that Cicely taught her mother how to make.

FUDGE CAKE

2 c. sifted flour	½ t. soda
3 t. baking powder	2 eggs, separated
½ c. butter	1¼ c. milk
1 c. sugar	1 t. vanilla
3 sqs. chocolate (melted)	Pinch of salt

Sift the flour once and measure it. Add the soda, baking powder, and salt and sift three times more. Cream the butter, add the sugar, beat till light. Add the egg yolks, well beaten, and the melted chocolate. Add the flour and milk alternately in small amounts. Beat smooth after each addition. Add the vanilla. Fold in the egg whites. Bake in three layers at 350° F. for from twenty to twenty-five minutes. Fill and frost with:

FUDGE FROSTING

2 c. sugar	2 T. butter
⅔ c. milk	2 sqs. Baker's chocolate
2 T. maple syrup	6 marshmallows
1 t. vanilla	

Grate the chocolate and cook it with the sugar and milk, stirring until the sugar is dissolved. Let it boil, watching it as a cat does a mousehole unless — Cicely says — you would like to let it boil over and gum up the burner of the oil stove for the rest of the summer. It also has a very adhesive effect on gas and electric stoves.

Cook until the syrup forms a soft ball (238° F.). Remove from the fire. Add the butter. Cool until lukewarm. Add vanilla, and beat until the frosting is ready to spread. Put part of it between the layers of the fudge cake. Cut the marshmallows into small pieces and cover the top layer with them and then with the frosting. Sprinkle a few chopped nuts over the top if you like.

As this cake will all be eaten before you know it, perhaps you had better toss off a little dark fruit cake the next day. Mrs. Appleyard bakes fruit cake in the afternoon when the oven is not needed for anything else. If the spasm strikes her late in the day, there may still be spicy and fruity smells seeping in from the kitchen during the evening.

'Go along to bed!' she has been heard to remark. 'I have to sit up with a fruit cake.'

Sitting up with a fruit cake and a thrice-read volume of John Buchan — *Mr. Standfast*, perhaps, or *The Courts of the Morning* — is Mrs. Appleyard's idea of a nice quiet evening.

A favorite fruit cake in Mrs. Appleyard's family was affectionately known as huckleberry gingerbread. Mrs. Appleyard's grandmother, Mrs. Elmore, used to keep a supply of this cake on hand in case of company. It was so spicy and rich that it was considered good enough for visiting clergymen when they came to supper — along, of course with pound cake, scalloped oysters, Parker House rolls, mince turnovers, chicken salad, six kinds of preserves, three kinds of cheese, and other delicacies of a spiritual sort. One lean and lank young minister who had eaten his way through one of Mrs. Elmore's suppers as if food were a novelty that he had only recently discovered, was asked if he wouldn't take a little something.

'Nothing at all,' replied the guest, raising a thin, ascetic hand, and then — moving it toward the place where the fruit cake rested, dark and spicy under its mantle of white frosting — 'except possibly another slice of your huckleberry gingerbread....'

This is how it was made:

HUCKLEBERRY GINGERBREAD

1½ c. butter	1 t. nutmeg
1 c. milk (or ½ c. strong coffee and ½ c. brandy)	1 t. clove
	½ t. soda
6 eggs, separated	½ t. salt
3 c. sugar	1 lb. seeded raisins
½ c. dark molasses	1 lb. currants
4 c. sifted flour	¼ c. citron, thinly sliced
2 t. cinnamon	½ c. nuts (optional)

Sift the flour and measure it. Flour the fruit with half a cup of it and sift the rest three times with the dry ingredients. Add the sugar, sifted, to the creamed butter. Beat till light. Add the egg yolks, beaten thick. Add the milk or other liquids (Mrs. Appleyard uses brandy) alternately with the flour. The molasses goes in with whatever liquid you use. Add the floured fruit and fold in the egg whites, beaten stiffly.

Bake in a large round graniteware pan, lined with buttered brown paper and waxed paper, for three hours at

275° F. the first hour and 250° the rest of the time. Have a pan of water on the bottom of the oven. This keeps the bottom of the cake from cooking too quickly.

WEDDING CAKE (MRS. APPLEYARD)

When there is a wedding of one of the Appleyard daughters — either real or adopted — the family works for days slicing citron and candied peel and chopping nuts and beating eggs. The cake is baked in a five-quart milk pan and watched over for hours. Mrs. Teasdale lends her electric mixer. Patience Barlow from up the road brings down her cake-froster and begins to think up designs for initials and scrolls and flowers. In short, it becomes a community project.

The cake is eaten between rounds of 'Hull's Victory' and 'Money Musk,' accompanied by pants and puffs on the accordion, and pretty soon there is nothing left of the wedding punch but lemon peel and nothing of the cake but crumbs. *Sic transit gloria mundi.*

This, however, is not Mrs. Appleyard's philosophy. She is all ready to start in on another cake even before the confetti and the paper rose leaves are out of the lilacs. Here's the method:

1 lb. butter	1 c. orange marmalade
2 t. cinnamon	1 lb. currants
1 t. baking soda	½ lb. candied lemon peel
1 c. brandy	¼ lb. candied ginger
4 T. lemon juice	12 eggs
4 T. orange juice	4 c. flour
2 lbs. seedless raisins	½ t. each of mace, clove,
½ lb. candied orange peel	allspice

½ lb. candied cherries
1 lb. sugar
1 t. nutmeg
1 t. salt
1 T. apricot brandy
Grated rind of 4 lemons

1 t. vanilla
1 T. orange curaçao
1 t. lemon extract
1 lb. seeded raisins
1 lb. citron
½ lb. nuts

Get the fruit ready the day before the cake is to be baked. Slice the citron, the lemon peel, and the orange peel very thin and cut them into small pieces. Cut the cherries into four pieces and the ginger into small cubes. Chop the nuts — they may be butternuts, pecans, or walnuts — not too fine. Mix all these together in a large bowl and add the raisins and the currants, the grated lemon rind, the marmalade, and the vanilla and lemon extract. Pour over them the brandy, liqueurs, and fruit juices and mix them well with the fruit. Cover the bowl and let it stand in a warm place overnight. By morning the fruit should have absorbed most of the liquid.

Cream the butter and beat in the sugar. Mrs. Appleyard sometimes uses some of Mr. Appleyard's granulated maple sugar (page 82) for this, but white or light-brown sugar will do. Now beat in the eggs, one at a time. While one member of the family is doing this, another is attending to the flour. Sift it before measuring it, put it into a shallow pan for a few minutes, and set it into the oven with the door open. Stir it occasionally. When it is warm and dry, sift three cups of it with the spices, salt, and soda, and beat it slowly into the egg mixture. Dredge the rest of it — which should be quite hot — over the fruit. If the fruit has not absorbed all the liquid, drain it before dredging it with the flour. Save this liquid and add it to the batter. Now mix the fruit in well. If the batter is too stiff to stir easily, add a little more brandy or cordial.

Line the pan — or pans — with one thickness of buttered brown paper and four thicknesses of heavy waxed paper. Set the pan into another one containing hot water. Have a wire cake-cooler in the outside pan so that the water can circulate freely under the cake. During the first part of the baking, cover the cake with a double thickness of buttered brown paper. The oven should be at 250° F. The cake should rise during the first half-hour. Keep the outer pan filled with hot water until the last half-hour. The top paper may be removed then, too. A large cake — this whole mixture in one pan — will take at least five hours to bake. It may take more. Test it with a clean broom straw. When the straw comes out clean, the cake is done.

Have a cake-cooler big enough to cover the whole top of the pan. Place it over the pan and over it place a pastry board. Turn the whole thing upside down. This takes two people and enough cooperation for the whole Russian ballet. Cover the pan with cloths wrung out of cold water and some ice. It is hard to leave it alone at this stage, and it is hardly human nature not to fiddle with the pan to see if the cake has actually emerged. Don't. It won't help a bit more than it does to dig plants up by the roots to see how they are growing. After a while — and you really might as well take a rest, and goodness knows you will need it — the cake will leave the pan of its own weight, and then comes the fascinating occupation of peeling off the paper and tasting an occasional stray crumb. Better do this alone or the cake will begin to look moth-eaten.

Frost it the next day with boiled frosting (page 78). Make three times the amount given.

Keep this cake at least a week before you cut it.

Cake-baking is an undertaking needing a certain amount

of quiet and concentration. Cookies can be made in the middle of any hurly-burly that is going on. There is a game played on the lawn outside the kitchen at Appleyard Centre that is like deck tennis except that it is played with the lid of a tin biscuit can. This pastime, with its accompanying shrieks from the gentler sex and the occasional crash of broken glass, has often been the background for cooky-baking. So have the voices of croquet battlers and of those turning cartwheels, the crack of rifles aimed at tin cans, and the grunts that go with a form of wrestling known as pig-piling. Or, if the weather is rainy those who look forward to dividends of broken cookies crowd into the kitchen, joggle the elbow of the cook and keep her mind active with a peculiarly searching form of Twenty Questions. It is under these circumstances that Mrs. Appleyard turns out a batch of:

OATMEAL LACE COOKIES

½ lb. butter, melted	½ t. salt
2¼ c. Mother's Oats	1 egg, slightly beaten
2¼ c. light-brown sugar	1 t. vanilla, or almond
3 T. flour	if you like it

If Mrs. Appleyard is remembered by posterity, it will be for these cookies. Here — for the first time, by special arrangement — she tells all.

'What you are trying to achieve,' says Mrs. Appleyard, 'is an irregular circle of lacy crispness brown at the edges, golden in the middle, glazed underneath. It is no use trying to skimp on butter or to use the quick-cooking kind of oatmeal or the dark, moist sugar that looks like snow in Boston after three days. The right kind of sugar is light beige in color, dry and powdery in consistency. It does not lurk in packages but lives in a hinged bin, is removed with a generous scoop, and comes to you in an honest brown-paper bag tied up with string. You can still get it if you make enough fuss about it, and you can still get the kind of rolled oats that has not had all the taste steamed out of it and then been run through a vacuum cleaner. The best brand is Mother's Oats and if you are lucky, you get a china cup and saucer with rosebuds in it on the package; though sometimes — to be sure — it's only a cereal dish.

'Never make the mistake of adding more flour because the mixture looks too wet. Never try to bake anything else in the oven at the same time. Don't try to get along with less than three pans. They should be large iron dripping-pans. The best ones have been used for years, washed but never scoured, and have a patina like ebony. These can sometimes be bought at auction.

'Begin by looking at the weather. It is no use trying to bake these cookies on a hot sticky day. Make brownies or sponge cake. The day should be cool and crisp with a few white clouds high up in the blue. The wind should be in the northwest. The smell of newly cut hay, the sound of a downy woodpecker tapping on the apple tree, cowbells in the distance, and the silky rustle of maple leaves are desirable but not absolutely essential. It is only honest to admit that, given the right materials and the zeal, oatmeal cookies may be made against a background of carbon monoxide, English sparrows, squealing brakes, and the scuffing of feet on cement sidewalks.

'Get out the big yellow bowl — or that old Bennington one with the crack in it — and begin.

'Put the rolled oats, flour, salt, and sugar into the bowl

and stir them thoroughly together. Melt the butter. Let it get quite hot but not bubble. Stir it well into the mixture until the sugar is melted. Add the slightly beaten egg and the vanilla, and stir all together.

'Your oven should now be ready at 375° F. Each batch of cookies — there will be about six — will take about seven minutes to bake. Watch them carefully. If they are not cooked enough, they will be sticky in the middle. If they cook too long, they will be scorched around the edge. Never leave the stove. Let the telephone ring.' (Mrs. Appleyard admits that it is largely for purposes of making cookies in peace that she uses the neighborhood telephone up the road.)

'Push the batter off the end of a large spoon with a spatula. Make small lumps two inches apart. Do not smooth them down: they will attend to that themselves. Set your first pan on the top shelf of the oven. Fill the second. Move the first pan to the lower shelf and put the second pan on the top shelf. Fill the third pan. The first pan will soon be done. Take it out. Put it on the table to cool for a minute or two. Move the second pan to the lower shelf. Put the third pan on the top shelf.

'With your spatula test the edge of one of the cookies in the first pan. If it is cool enough — and not too cool — you can slide a pancake-turner under the cooky, holding the spatula in the other hand in case of need. Transfer the cookies to a large earthenware platter. Have enough platters or plates ready so that you do not have to put the cookies on top of each other.

'When you have removed all the cookies from the first pan, fill it again. Keep up this whole cycle until all the batter is baked. If you have good luck and no one comes in to ask you how to play Mah Jongg, or to ask whether any socks came home in the wash, you should have just about enough time to get one batch of cookies off the pan and the pan filled again while the next batch is baking. At the end of the time you should have about fifty cookies — minus any that were wheedled out of you and the ones you ate yourself to be sure you were doing all right.

'Be sure they are cold before you put them away. A large box with a tight cover is the Appleyard repository for them, and they are put in between layers of waxed paper. They will keep crisp as long as there are any left.' Mrs. Appleyard says she kept some once for almost two days.

BROWNIES

¼ c. butter, creamed	½ c. nut meats (chopped)
2 sqs. melted chocolate	1 c. sugar (white or brown)
½ c. flour	2 eggs, broken into the mixture
	½ t. vanilla

Mix in the order given. Spread in a shallow cake pan and bake at 350° F. for 15 minutes. If you shake a little sugar on them just before you put them into the oven, it gives them a glossy appearance that is rather handsome. If your favorite brownies are the thick kind like cake, this is not the right rule. These are more on the chewy side.

DELMONICO WAFERS

These are to the winter season what oatmeal lace cookies are to the summer. They should be made on a day when snow has just fallen and trees throw blue shadows across it;

when blue jays call across it from one frosted pine to the next, and chickadees hang upside down from elm twigs.

1 c. butter	½ c. flour
2 c. molasses	⅔ c. coconut
	1 t. soda

Boil the butter and molasses together for half an hour. Add the flour, sifted with the soda, and the coconut. Boil ten minutes, stirring constantly. Drop in small lumps into a buttered dripping-pan. Bake the wafers in a moderate oven (375° F.) until they bubble. Let them stand a minute or two. Then slip a spatula under them and lay them flat on a cold tin or platter. Or, choosing a proper stage of pliability — this can only be learned by experiment — curl them around the handle of a wooden spoon or over the thick edge of a mixing bowl. Keep the three pans going as described so lyrically in the case of oatmeal cookies (see page 69).

6

Candy, Frostings, and Cake Fillings.
A small sponge cake or a Madeleine responds happily to
being made into a surprise package. Cut out a small cyl-
inder-shaped piece. Use the top for a lid. Someone can
usually be found to eat the bottom. (Swabbing the bowl
you made the filling in is rather a popular way of disposing
of these pieces.) Fill the cavity with whatever filling you
prefer and put back the lid. Frost the top or dust it over
with powdered sugar. Almond, lemon, and orange filling
are all good.

ALMOND–CUSTARD FILLING

1 c. milk	½ t. almond extract
Yolks of 2 eggs	1 t. cornstarch
½ c. sugar	⅛ t. salt
1 c. chopped blanched almonds	

Bring milk to a boil. Add the cornstarch dissolved in **a**

little cold water. Beat egg yolks light with sugar. Pour hot milk over them, put the mixture into the top of the double boiler and cook till it thickens. Fill cakes or use it between the layers of cake for Washington Pie. Cover with Boiled Frosting (page 78) or Almond-Butter Frosting (page 76).

ORANGE FILLING

½ c. sugar	½ T. lemon juice
2½ T. flour	Yolks of 2 eggs
Grated rind of one orange	1 t. butter
¼ c. orange juice	A little grated lemon rind

Mrs. Appleyard prefers fillings of this kind made with flour rather than cornstarch, but it's a question of taste.

Mix sugar and flour together. Add the yolks of the eggs, well beaten, the fruit juices and rind, and the butter. Cook in the top of the double boiler, stirring occasionally until the mixture coats the back of the spoon.

LEMON FILLING

This may be made like the orange filling above, only substituting lemon for orange juice. Perhaps it is even better when it is made without any thickening except what is supplied by the happy harmony that exists between eggs and lemon juice.

2 oz. butter	¼ c. lemon juice
⅔ c. sugar	3 egg yolks, well beaten
Grated rind of ½ lemon	

Put the butter in the top of the double boiler. When it has melted, stir in the sugar, then the lemon juice and rind.

and, last, the beaten egg yolks. Keep stirring until the mixture thickens. Do not leave it over the fire too long or it will separate. Take it off when it coats the back of the spoon thickly.

ALMOND–BUTTER FROSTING

½ c. butter	½ c. blanched, toasted,
1½ c. confectioner's	chopped almonds
sugar	2 egg yolks

Cream the butter, add the sugar and egg yolks. Add the almonds finely chopped. Have a few extra to chop coarsely and sprinkle on top of the frosting.

SOUR–CREAM ALMOND FROSTING

This is the country cousin of almond-butter frosting. Some consider the latter fit only for city slickers. Mrs. Appleyard remains neutral and simply says that if you want to make it, you use half a cup of sour cream instead of the butter, and half a teaspoon of almond extract. It is easier to make than the other kind because you don't have to cream the butter.

You may use professionally-made salted almonds, of course, for either of these, but they are likely to be too salty. Mrs. Appleyard likes to fix them herself. She began to do it when she was eight years old, and it remained one of the few household tasks that were considered suited to her mentality.

There is something pleasantly languid about blanching almonds. You can't hurry it. The skins simply won't come off until they are ready. You keep stirring the almonds around in a bowl of water with a spoon with holes in it, fishing up an occasional one and seeing whether it is ready to slip out of its corduroy overcoat. As the water cools, you put your hands in bravely. Perhaps someone is telling you a story about a leprechaun. The Boston terrier lies under the stove where the kettle will not boil over on him. Once was enough. The hairs came in white. The mark is like an arrow.

Pretty soon it is hard to tell which are your shrivelled fingertips and which are the almonds. Both are neatly ribbed. Now comes the drying of the almonds between layers of old clean damask, after which you are ready to toss them in butter. (Mrs. Appleyard has always loved that expression — there's something light-hearted about it.)

Put the nuts in a dripping-pan and give them the merest sprinkling of salt. Add a little more butter if you have any doubts about the thoroughness of the tossing process. Bake them until they are a delicate brown, stirring them occasionally in a fairly hot oven.

Naturally the child was not allowed to bake them. That took brains. Mrs. Appleyard thinks that the wonderful range that looked like a combination pipe organ and Early American settle probably produced a temperature of around 400° F. Ah — the mince turnovers that came out of one of its four ovens — the lower right hand one!

But perhaps it would be better not to start Mrs. Appleyard crying into her cup of weak tea with lemon and over her bristly health biscuit. This seems a good point at which to take up a frosting which, being of the mushy kind, is no special temptation to her. It is the young who like to bury their faces in it. They could learn to make it, too, if they would put their minds on it for seven minutes.

SEVEN–MINUTE FROSTING

¾ c. granulated sugar   White of 1 egg, unbeaten
3 T. cold water   1 t. vanilla or other flavoring

Put all the ingredients except the flavoring into the top of a double boiler and beat over boiling water for exactly seven minutes. Remove from the fire, add the vanilla. Beat until the frosting is ready to spread.

For chocolate frosting melt one and a half squares of cooking chocolate and beat it in during the last two minutes.

If the white frosting is used, decorate it with candied cherries, thinly sliced citron, nuts, or a small pool of melted semisweet chocolate. Ginger is all right too, or candied lemon peel. In fact the only substances that do not seem to have occurred to Mrs. Appleyard in this connection at some point are raw oysters and French fried onions.

BOILED FROSTING

1 c. sugar   1, 2, or 3 egg whites
½ c. cold water   ½ t. vanilla or almond extract

Put the sugar and water together into a saucepan. Stir until the sugar is dissolved to keep crystals from forming on the sides of the pan. Then boil without stirring. Use a candy thermometer. If you are going to use one egg white, cook the syrup until it will spin a thread that will turn up at the end — 238° F. For two egg whites the syrup must be hotter — soft-ball stage, 244° F. Still hotter for three egg whites — hard-ball stage, 254° F. Remove the syrup from the fire and let it cool a little while you are beating the egg whites stiff. Then pour it over the egg whites in a thin stream, beating steadily. It takes two people to do this unless you have either four hands or an electric mixer. Perhaps this is why many people prefer to make uncooked frosting.

UNCOOKED FROSTING

1 egg white	½ c. confectioner's sugar
	½ t. vanilla

Beat the egg white stiff, add the sugar gradually. Keep beating till the mixture is smooth and ready to spread. Beat in the flavoring.

MRS. APPLEYARD'S FUDGE FROSTING

2 c. sugar	2 sqs. Baker's cooking chocolate
⅔ c. milk	1 t. vanilla
2 T. butter	6 marshmallows
2 T. maple syrup	¼ c. chopped nuts

Grate the chocolate and put it into a saucepan with the milk, syrup, and sugar, stirring until the sugar is dissolved. Cook until a drop holds its shape in water — 238° F. Remove from the fire. Add butter. Cool by setting the pan into a pan of cold water. Add ice cubes to the water if you are in a hurry. Add the vanilla. Beat until the frosting is ready to spread. Put bits of marshmallow before you frost it. Sprinkle the top with chopped nuts.

CHOCOLATE CREAM–CHEESE FROSTING

2 c. confectioner's sugar	3 sqs. Baker's chocolate,
1 small cream cheese	melted
2 T. cream	1 t. vanilla

Mash the cream cheese and beat the cream into it, add gradually the confectioner's sugar and the melted chocolate. Beat well and stir in the vanilla. Mrs. Appleyard uses this

on Chocolate-Peppermint Cupcakes (page 61). Sometimes she flavors it with three drops of peppermint extract
instead of vanilla.

SALLY APPLEYARD'S FUDGE

When Mrs. Appleyard contemplates a pan of Sally's
freshly made fudge, she sometimes thinks that it will be
Sally's name that will be long known as that of the *cordon
bleu* of Appleyard Centre. The place where the pan is hidden is the oven of a disused stove. This stove, a bandy-
legged item with many arabesques in iron upon its ample
surface, is not used for cooking because no one living now
understands its temperament, but it stands where it has
always stood because it has always stood there. Besides, like
Lewis Carroll's snark, it is handy for striking a light — especially when there is cellophane to burn up. Also it has a
warming oven that conceals shoe polish, rat poison, and
ancient tin candlesticks. The warming oven is Chippendale
in outline. The real oven is different — Duncan Phyfe, perhaps. A versatile man — its designer.

This oven door opens with a peculiar clank. Fudge, to
the young Appleyards, speaks with this voice, just as to
their mother it spoke with the lid of a certain box of enam-
elled Venetian glass. No doubt the clank of the oven is as
musical to their ears as the clink of the glass box cover,
stealthily lifted by her small brother's hand, was to Mrs.
Appleyard's half a century ago.

Whether it clinks or clanks, this is good fudge.

⅔ c. milk, part cream	¼ lb. butter
3 sqs. Baker's chocolate	1½ c. light-brown sugar
1⅓ c. white sugar	⅛ t. salt
1 t. vanilla	

Grate the chocolate. Save out about a tablespoonful of it and the same of the butter. Boil everything else — except the vanilla — together in a large saucepan. Scrape it away from the edges so that crystals will not form until the sugar has dissolved. Then boil without stirring until it will form a soft ball when dropped in cold water — 238° F. Take the pan from the fire. Drop in the extra butter and the chocolate. Let the fudge cool a few minutes. Add the vanilla and beat until it will hold its shape when it is dropped from the spoon. Pour it out quickly on a buttered pan that you may have decorated with pieces of marshmallow, candied cherries, and nuts. Crease in squares, give any small boys the pan and spoon to scrape, put the fudge furtively into its hiding-place, shut the door softly, and hope for the best.

HOREHOUND CANDY (MISS J. L. R.)

It was at least forty years ago that Mrs. Appleyard first tasted this candy. The same kind neighbor who made it then sent some over the other day. Time seems to have made her, if anything, a little more skillful at making it.

3 c. granulated sugar	½ t. cream of tartar
¼ oz. horehound	1 pt. boiling water

Cut about a quarter-inch from a package of pressed horehound herb. You buy it at the drugstore. Pour the boiling water over it and let it steep for three minutes. Strain it through fine cheesecloth over the sugar mixed with the cream of tartar. Let it come to the boil, scraping the crystals away from the sides until the sugar is dissolved. Then boil without stirring until it is brittle when tested on

a cold plate (290° F.).   Boil it in a saucepan that has a large
evaporating surface.   Crease the candy into half-inch
squares before it is cool.   Make deep creases.   Make this
candy on a bright, crisp day.   It looks like clear amber and
is excellent when you have a cough or a dry throat — or if
you haven't.

MR. APPLEYARD'S DRY MAPLE SUGAR

When the sap begins to stir in the trees Mr. Appleyard
naturally feels homesick for Vermont, and he brings up a
can of vintage syrup from the cellar. He takes a kettle that
will hold two gallons or more and pours a half-gallon of
syrup into it. Soon the house is full of maple fragrance.
When the children were at home this used to be a signal for
them to rush out and fill saucepans with newly fallen snow
— there always seemed to be some in those far-off times — so
that the first dipping from the kettle would be caught on the
snow and run over it in patterns of gold lace. After they had
reached the stage where they began to think with interest
only of pickles, Mr. Appleyard would pour the rest of the
syrup into a big yellow bowl and began to stir it steadily.
It would change from dark to light amber, then to light
brown, and at last to a pale beige shade. Mr. Appleyard
keeps working over it until it is in coarse grains. He likes it
best with small lumps left in it, but occasionally he sifts it
through a coarse sieve and gets to work on the lumps that
are left. This is for his wife when she is going to use it in
cooking. The result looks something like a coarse light-
brown sugar, but it tastes of bare maple trees and crusty
snow, and sap running into the buckets, and the sun hot on
your cheek. In fact, strangely enough, it's maple sugar.

Mr. Appleyard lists the following temperatures for the different stages of the boiling syrup.

Sugar on snow:

Waxy	230° F.
Lacy	232° F.

Sugar stirred and poured over

butternut meats on plate	232° F.
Sugar stirred and granulated	238° F.

7

Cheese: How to Cook It, also How to Make It. Mrs. Appleyard likes the story about the two French peasants who, before the Revolution, were sitting under a pear tree eating pears and cheese.

One said, 'After all, my friend, there is nothing in this world to eat that is so good as fruit and cheese.'

'Hush!' said the other. 'Speak more softly — the aristocrats might hear you.'

Mrs. Appleyard is quite willing the aristocrats should have pheasant and venison if she can have cheese and fruit. Only it's got to be the right cheese. It should be made, she says, of June milk — milk that has young, juicy grass in it — grass that grows when the clouds are high up in the air, when there are fireflies lighting the mist at night under the apple trees, and the bobolinks are chasing each other through the air all day in patterns of black and white. There are wild roses in bloom and Mrs. Appleyard is making potpourri.

This cheese is not ready until October — a month that has many other good things about it. People know the others better than they do about the cheese. Buy a whole cheese. Cut out a wedge. Coat one side of the cut cheese with Parawax and cut off the other side until it is all gone — which will be a lot sooner than you think. Any pieces that are dry may be grated and used with onion soup, or in baked bread-and-cheese. This cheese with a green salad is good enough for anyone — even Mr. Appleyard, who deserves the best.

This does not mean that the Appleyards do not think wistfully sometimes of a perfect bit of real Camembert or Roquefort, that they do not appreciate Stilton or cheeses from Switzerland or Holland. They simply know they are lucky to have a sound dairy cheese where they can cut off a hunk any time. These are some of the things Mrs. Appleyard does with it:

BAKED BREAD–AND–CHEESE

6 slices of bread	½ t. salt
1 c. grated cheese	⅛ t. red pepper
1 c. milk	⅛ t. nutmeg
2 T. butter	Slice of onion

Slice home-made bread, not too thin. Cut off the crusts. Butter each slice and cover it thickly with cheese. Cut the slices into inch strips and build them up in a buttered baking-dish. Heat the milk with the onion and seasonings. Remove the onion and pour the hot milk over the bread and cheese. Sprinkle a little more cheese over the top. Bake it in a moderate oven (375° F.) for about twenty minutes, or longer if you like it very brown. Baste the bread with the milk occasionally. Serve it in the dish in which you baked it. A French casserole is a good kind of dish for it.

CHEESE CUBES

12 cubes bread, ¾ in. square	1 egg
6 drops Worcestershire sauce	½ c. grated cheese
¼ c. butter	½ t. paprika

Cream the butter, add the seasonings and the egg, lightly beaten; dip the cubes into the mixture and then roll them in the grated cheese. Put the cubes on a baking sheet and bake them at 375° F. until the cheese is melted and the cubes begin to brown. These are good served either hot or cold.

CHEESE RUSKS (to serve with salad)

1½ c. grated cheese	1 t. Worcestershire
1 t. salad oil	sauce
1 t. butter	½ t. salt
1 t. dry mustard	1 t. paprika
2 t. red wine garlic vinegar	⅛ t. soda

Mix the cheese with the oil, vinegar, and seasonings. Add the soda and beat until it is light and creamy. Spread it on rusks, or on French bread sliced thin, or on Montpelier crackers. Toast them in the oven until they begin to brown. Good with soup too.

CHEESE CLUB SANDWICHES: OPEN-FACED STYLE

Slice of bread	A little chopped green
Slice of tomato	pepper
Thin slice of Spanish onion	2 slices of bacon
Slice of cheese	

Make as many of these as you have people. Put them to.

gether in the order given. Bake twenty minutes at 375° F.
— or until the bacon is the way you like it. Beer goes well
with them.

PIMENTO CHEESE

1 lb. dairy cheese	1 small onion, sliced
6-oz. can of pimentos	1 t. salt
¾ c. cream	½ t. paprika

Put the onion into a wooden chopping-bowl and chop it
fine. Add the cheese and pimentos and keep on chopping.
Put the cream into a double boiler, stir in the seasonings,
add the cheese mixture, and stir until it is melted and well
blended. Put it into scalded jelly glasses and keep it in the
ice chest till you need it. This is a good filling for toasted
sandwiches. Spread one slice with butter and the other
thickly with the cheese, put them together and toast them.

CHEESE BISCUITS

These look like innocent and uninteresting cookies. The
plate will sometimes stay well filled until some conscientious guest who has been investigating the table says,
'These are cheese — try one.' The rest is history, and there
is no hope that the family will get any for a quiet midnight
snack while they are talking over the party.

½ lb. dairy cheese, grated	1 T. paprika
6 oz. butter	½ t. salt
1¼ c. flour	¾ t. baking powder

Sift the flour and measure it. Sift it with the baking
powder and seasonings three times. Put the butter in a

warm bowl and soften it with your hand. Work in the
cheese with your hand until it and the butter are well
blended. Stir in the flour with a spoon until the mixture is
stiff enough to handle. Toss the dough on a floured board
and knead in the rest of the flour lightly. Roll it out gently,
not too thin — about twice as thick as for sugar cookies.
Cut with a crimped cooky-cutter. Keep the cutter well
floured. Bake the biscuits about ten minutes at 400° F. The
length of time you must bake them depends upon how thin
you rolled them. They should bake thoroughly but not
brown.

Mrs. Appleyard generally bakes a sample to test the oven
and the thickness of the biscuit and the amount of flour in
the dough before she puts in a whole batch.

CHEESE PUFFS

1 c. water	½ t. paprika
½ c. butter	1 t. salt
1 c. pastry flour	¾ c. dairy cheese,
3 eggs	finely grated

Put the water and salt in a saucepan. When the water
boils, dump in the flour. Stir till the mixture leaves the
sides of the pan. Remove from the fire. Cool a little. Add
the unbeaten eggs one at a time, beating hard after adding
each one. Beat in one half-cup of the grated cheese. Line a
dripping-pan with waxed paper. Put the mixture into a
Swedish cooky press and squeeze it out into flower or star
shapes. Sprinkle with the rest of the grated cheese. Bake in
a moderate oven (375° F.) until they are thoroughly done.
It will take at least thirty-five minutes. If you take them
out too soon, they will fall the way cream puffs do. Be sure

there are no bubbles of moisture on the outside before you take them out.

These are good with salad, either plain or filled with

CHEESE CUSTARD FILLING

3 T. butter	¾ c. grated cheese
2 egg yolks	½ t. salt
3 T. flour	½ t. paprika
½ c. thick cream	

Melt the butter, rub in the flour sifted with the seasonings. Take from the fire and add the cheese and the beaten egg yolks. Cool. Beat the cream until it starts to whip and beat it into the mixture. Keep the filling in the ice chest and fill the puffs only as they are needed. This is only for those whose digestions are those of an ostrich.

CHEESE SOUFFLÉ

½ c. butter	2 c. grated cheese
6 T. flour	1 t. salt
6 eggs, separated	1 t. paprika
2 c. milk	

Make a white sauce (page 251) of the butter, flour, milk, and seasonings. Cook until the sauce thickens. Add the cheese. Stir till the cheese melts. Cool. Add the beaten egg yolks. Fold in the stiffly beaten egg whites. Put the mixture into a buttered baking-dish. Bake in a moderate oven — 375° F. — until it is firm on top. Either set it in a pan of water or put a pan of water on the shelf below it. Baking will take about forty-five minutes. This receipt serves six. The guests must wait for the soufflé because if they don't, all they will get is either a half-cooked layer at the bottom, or some shoe leather enclosing a few weary air bubbles.... Yes, in her youth these things happened even to Mrs. Appleyard. Now the soufflé never approaches the oven until the visitors have driven through the lower gate. That means that soufflé is for those who live within the walls, not for people who come for a single meal. It is hardly worth spoiling a beautiful friendship because someone is late to lunch. Better have something that can wait — like curry — or something you must put together at the last minute anyway — like Eggs Benedict.

Less strain on the nerves because it stays up a little better is

TAPIOCA CHEESE SOUFFLÉ

1 c. milk	1 c. grated cheese
3 T. tapioca	1 t. salt
3 eggs, separated	

Scald the milk in a double boiler and cook the tapioca — which, by the way, you had better soak first for a couple of hours, unless you really prefer it like bullets — until it is clear. This will take about fifteen minutes. Add the cheese and salt. Cook until the cheese melts. Cool. Beat the egg yolks well and add them to the mixture. Beat the whites stiff and fold them in. Turn the mixture into a buttered baking-dish. Bake at 375° F. with water either under or around it for forty-five minutes or till it is firm to the touch on top. Serve at once.

WELSH RABBIT

This is quite generally and correctly regarded as the king of cheese dishes, but it must be made right. Among those who make it best is Mr. Appleyard. His usually benevolent countenance is darkened as by thunderclouds when he hears this dish described as containing flour, milk, tomato soup, or chopped olives. Yet there are handsomely bound books with luscious-looking pictures that recommend all these atrocities. Almost as annoying to Mr. Appleyard is to hear it called a 'rarebit.' It is, he says, a rabbit in the same sense that codfish is Cape Cod turkey, that a Scotch woodcook has hard-boiled eggs in it, that an English monkey is a cheese mixture, and a Bombay duck is a very dead fish that has been dried a long time.

This is how Mr. Appleyard makes a Welsh *rabbit:*

2 T. butter	2 t. Worcestershire sauce
2 lbs. mild, soft dairy cheese	2 t. dry mustard
cut in small pieces	½ t. salt
1 c. beer	¼ t. Cayenne
2 egg yolks, lightly beaten	

There is in the Appleyard treasure house a chafing-dish of antique design. Long before the Appleyards were married, the silver had begun to disappear from the bottom, rubbed off by the stirring of many spoons. It is now all gone and a fine brave blush of copper has taken its place. Mrs. Appleyard sometimes wonders when the next layer of silver will appear, and how soon after that there will be a hole that will send an entire rabbit down into the flickering blue flame of the lamp beneath. It might be any time now.

Mr. Appleyard will not use a hot-water pan underneath the top pan for two reasons. In the first place he feels that it isn't sporting. He says it's like shooting a duck sitting. In the second place, the chafing-dish was once lent, hot-water pan and all, to a church supper, and the pan that Mrs. Appleyard brought home in the redistribution of wealth has always made the chafing-dish appear like a large man in a small hat.

So Mr. Appleyard begins by melting the butter directly over the flame. This helps to keep the rabbit from sticking to the bottom of the pan. If you have ever washed one that rabbit has been cooked in, you will appreciate the value of this suggestion. Next he pours in the beer. When it is good and hot he puts in the seasonings and stirs them until they are well blended with the hot beer and butter. Now he adds the cheese. It was Mrs. Appleyard who cut it into those small, easily melted cubes. That is not chef's work, and she is proud to be the kitchenmaid on these happy occasions. Now the cheese is melting and Mr. Appleyard is working over it gently but firmly with that strong wrist of his — the same with which he used to deliver that reverse-twist service that burned up the grass on the Overbrook tennis courts, and made many an opponent wonder if he had not better see his oculist.

During the last few minutes of the melting process — it doesn't take long because cheese doesn't take much cooking — he graciously allows the lady on his left to beat the egg yolks in a small bowl with a silver fork. Mrs. Appleyard, in the meantime, is toasting and buttering English muffins, one to a customer and a few over.

Mr. Appleyard accepts the bowl of beaten egg yolks, spoons into it an ample dollop of the rabbit, beats the mixture lightly, pours it back into the chafing-dish, and blends it in with a few powerful swirls. Now he stirs it rather quickly — the great moment approaches.

'Now! Now!' says Mrs. Appleyard, coming in with the hot, buttery muffins. (It is too much to expect her to do no back-seat driving at all.)

Mr. Appleyard takes half a muffin. He dunks it into the rabbit. It emerges veiled in ambrosia and gold, dripping, succulent, ready to go on a hot plate and receive a final spoonful of rabbit. Beer foams in the tall glasses. Major Grey's Chutney circulates around the table. There is a moment of solemn hush. Then — 'This,' says Mrs. Appleyard, 'is one of your best.'

There is enough for six and everyone is happy.

GRANDMOTHER APPLEYARD'S DUTCH CHEESE

People are divided sharply into two groups, both vocal, those who like Dutch (or cottage) cheese — and those who don't. Few are indifferent. If you are one of those who enjoy it, you will like the way Mr. Appleyard's mother always made it. If you do not, you will sympathize with the small boy at Appleyard Centre who took a large mouthful of it under the impression that it was popcorn. Being a child of character, he swallowed it, and having done so remarked quietly, 'It has a dampish sour taste.'

He never joined the Appleyard Centre Dutch Cheese Club.

Grandmother Appleyard always began by scalding a five-quart milk pan and pouring into it three quarts of milk that had never been cooled or pasteurized. She let it stand in a warm — not hot — place two or three days, at the end of which it would be thick clabber, just starting to whey.

Do not try, Mrs. Appleyard says, to hurry this process. If you do, you will produce a rubber substitute as resilient as a ping-pong ball, but not nearly so edible. Probably much of the cream has been skimmed off for cooking, but if it is milk from a Guernsey cow in a Vermont pasture, more has risen. There should be several tablespoonfuls on the top of the pan.

Set the pan in the sink; fill the pan up with boiling water. Let it stand until it is cool. The whey will separate and the curd will sink to the bottom of the pan. Test the curd once in a while. When it feels just slightly rough between your thumb and finger, it is ready. If when it is cool it still feels slippery, add a little more hot water. Pour the curd into a colander. Let it drain for half an hour. If it still feels slippery, pour a little more hot water through it. Add about two tablespoonfuls of salt. This will take out the rest of the whey. If it tastes too salty, pour cold water through it and let it drain. Mrs. Appleyard likes it best when it has that deceptive popcorn look and has ivory shadows in it. The question of how dry it is to be is one of individual taste. The more hot water you put on it the drier it will be. If it seems too dry, add a little sweet cream — or some sour cream, whichever you prefer.

Good with salad, good with fruit, good with crackers, good with apple pan dowdy. Good with about anything. Oh, well — not with banana ice cream, if you are going to be fussily accurate. But *good* (if you like it).

Even those effete souls who do not care for cottage cheese sometimes respond to treatment with

MRS. APPLEYARD'S APPLE-TREE CHEESE

Perhaps another tree would do, but an apple tree with its stout curved twigs sticking out so handily, its low-hung branches, its dapple of sun and shade, is the Cream Cheese Tree, *par excellence*.

This cheese is made of cream that has thickened well and

is only just slightly sour. To make it Mrs. Appleyard brings new milk, fresh, frothing, ivory-colored, slowly to a temperature of 150° F., keeps it there for half an hour, and then pours it into a scalded milk pan. She likes to have at least four quarts. She sets the pan in a warm place for twenty-four hours. By then the cream should have risen so that most of it can be easily skimmed off without getting much milk. She then puts four thicknesses of cheesecloth over a bowl and pours the cream, which she has beaten a little with a fork, on the cheesecloth. Now she ties the cloth together at the top with a strong piece of string. Being a string-saver she has no difficulty in finding an appropriate piece. There is some that once belonged to Hugh's kite that has been helpful for many years. It was Mr. Appleyard's string first.

The cream should be thick enough so that not much will drip through the cheesecloth, but she carries the bowl along through the winter kitchen, the summer kitchen, and the woodshed. Then out into the warm July afternoon and to the Dutchess apple tree, which is reaching out a curved twig just right for a cheese-hanger. If she has chosen the right day — and usually, with the same instinct that makes goldfinches wait for thistledown to build their nests, she has — the cheese will be ready by the afternoon of the next day.

There will have been no blazing heat by day, no thunderstorms, no dank chill at night, but under the apple tree a warm green-and-gold twilight all day, a breeze just strong enough to rustle the leaves and dry the gently swinging bag, only the thinnest clouds across the stars at night. If there is a moon it shines with warmth and softness. At dawn there is silver mist down the valley, and when the sun comes out there will be cobwebs on the grass.

By late afternoon of the second day, the whey will all have drained out of the bag and the cheese will be ready. Leave it another night if it seems too soft and if there is whey still dripping from the bag. Otherwise brush the ants off the bag, take the cheese out, salt it a little, eat it with strawberries and cream, with raspberries, with raspberries and currant jelly, with apple sauce made from the apples that, in August, hang around it. You can make it in August if you choose the right day. September is too cold at night.

This cheese has a delicate sub-acid flavor and is, so Mrs. Appleyard's father used to say, the nearest thing to Devonshire cream that grows on this side of the Atlantic.

There was one interesting variant of this cheese that is not likely to be repeated. Mrs. Appleyard read somewhere that Roquefort cheese occurred because a French workman left his lunch, consisting of bread, butter, and cheese, in a cave and forgot about it. When he went back and happened on it sometime later, the cheese had become Roquefort. At the time that she learned this engaging fact — if it is one — Mrs. Appleyard had some of her cream cheese on hand. Naturally she experimented. She took about half of it and put it between two slices of buttered bread, wrapped it in waxed paper, put it in a dark corner in the cellarway, and forgot about it. She did not in fact remember it until one of her children remarked, 'I wonder what has died in the cellarway!'

Mrs. Appleyard is now in a position to state that Roquefort cannot be entered into so lightly and unadvisedly. However, the cheese was interesting and unique — something like Camembert that had met some Limburger in a bad temper. Since then Mrs. Appleyard has done her cheese-making in the wide-open spaces.

8

Desserts — if You Must Have Them.

Mrs. Appleyard's idea of a good dessert, as has been mentioned before, is some fruit and crackers and cheese. A Royal Riviera pear, for instance, and a perfect piece of Camembert will tempt her jaded appetite. Mr. Appleyard is quite happy with nuts and raisins and a glass of Madeira. Why not?

There are, however, other types of appetites; Mrs. Appleyard knows one or two things that seem to dull their sharpest edges, and feels like talking about them at this point. Ice cream, pastry, and pudding are taken up in their alphabetical place. This arrangement is just a symptom of Mrs. Appleyard's escape from being a librarian. Two of her classmates were once heard wondering why she had involved herself in such a career.

'Probably so she can classify her hats,' they finally decided.

The reference was to a little masterpiece that consisted of a bed of roses with two swallows perched among them. There was also a diamond buckle. Animal, vegetable, or mineral: it was anybody's guess. It was too hard for Mrs. Appleyard and she gave up the whole idea. However, she has never completely recovered from a tendency to file things.

Under desserts she first puts:

CREAM PUFFS

½ c. butter	1 c. boiling water
4 eggs	1 c. flour

Put the water and the butter into a saucepan. When they come to a boil, dump in the flour all at once and stir hard until it leaves the sides of the pan. Remove from the stove, and add the unbeaten eggs, one at a time, beating hard each time you add one. Like women, dogs, and walnut trees, the more they are beaten, the better. Indeed, the best ones Mrs. Appleyard ever made were some that she beat for fifteen minutes. This display of energy occurred because she asked one of her interesting children to watch the clock for her and tell her when five minutes had gone. The clock-watcher focussed on the hour hand. In the Appleyard family the rest is history.

Drop the batter by spoonfuls on a buttered baking-sheet one and a half inches apart. Shape them with the handle of the spoon — the curved metal kind — into circular or éclair shapes. Heap them up slightly in the middle. This makes eighteen small puffs or twelve large ones.

Bake them for thirty minutes at 400° F. and then reduce the heat to 350° F. They are done when there are no longer any iridescent bubbles on them. Watch them the way an eagle watches an osprey that has caught a fish. The puffs will fall if they are taken out too soon. When you think they are done, take one out. If [it stays up, take out the rest; cool them, cut a slit along one side, fill them, frost them.

The Appleyards like them filled with vanilla ice cream and served with hot chocolate sauce, or crushed strawberry sauce, or with custard filling and peach sauce. They are also thought well of when filled with Lemon Filling (page 75) and frosted with Boiled Frosting (page 78).

Mrs. Teasdale has been known to fill them with creamed chicken. Mrs. Appleyard sometimes makes them mouthful size and fills them with caviar and sour cream, or with lobster or chicken salad. They are in fact a versatile form of food, well worth the danger of a little neuritis in the arm that whirrs the egg-beater.

APPLE SAUCE MARIE

The inventor of this dish saw the Dutchess apple tree with its full quota of pink-striped yellow apples. She had in her hand a package of Zo — a dry cereal popular with the Appleyards. Zo is rather like toasted crumbs of graham bread. There is a habit at Appleyard Centre of eating this cereal involved with a banana split. Mrs. Appleyard has nothing to do with this bedtime snack, except to watch in horrified fascination while the young intelligentsia split bananas, add marshmallows, peanut butter, three kinds of jam, and anything else within reach and pour cream over the whole thing. It is simply not true that she ever ate one of those collections. She did, however, sample Marie's apple sauce and found it very sustaining on a cold summer evening.

2 qts. Dutchess apple sauce	½ c. seedless raisins
2 T. butter	½ c. light-brown sugar
½ c. Zo	⅛ t. cinnamon
12 marshmallows	

Put the apple sauce into a buttered baking-dish. Stir in the raisins. Sprinkle Zo and brown sugar and cinnamon, mixed together, over the top. Dot with butter. Cover with marshmallows. Put in the oven and bake till the marshmallows brown. Serve with cream or Hard Sauce (page 222). This is a good emergency dessert if you have apple sauce on hand. It can be made with canned apple sauce.

MRS. APPLEYARD'S PANDOWDY

3 lbs. Dutchess apples, pared and quartered	3 c. light brown sugar
½ lb. butter	⅛ t. cinnamon
1 clove	Piece of thin lemon peel, 1 in. square

Melt half the butter in a large granite dish: Mrs. Appleyard uses a milk pan. Add two cups of the sugar and mix well. Add the seasonings. Put in the apples and the rest of the butter in small pieces between them. Put the dish in the oven. When the butter begins to bubble up and the apples start to cook, cover them with biscuit dough, mixed soft and dropped from the spoon in small lumps. When the biscuits have risen, sprinkle the rest of the sugar over them and dot them with a little more butter. Use either the rule for Baking-Powder Biscuit (page 34) or Sour-Cream Biscuit (page 42). Bake until the biscuits are well browned at 475° F. It will take about half an hour.

Serve with thick cream, either sweet or sour, or hard
sauce.

PEACH PANDOWDY

This can be made with canned Elberta peaches, though
fresh peaches from North Carolina are even better. Mrs.
Appleyard has pleasant memories of the bushel baskets of
peaches that used to come from there to Vermont. It was a
treat just to put your head into the cellarway while they
were ripening. A bushel of peaches gives you some scope,
especially if they were like those miracles of sweetness. For
ice cream, short cake, upside-down cake, cut up in a Sandwich-glass dish, eaten in the hand over the kitchen sink —
there was nothing better.

For a pandowdy for ten people use about eighteen
peaches. Peel and quarter them. Do not put in any spices
but use instead three drops of almond extract. You won't
taste it — it just brings out the peach flavor. Make the
dough as above, using either Baking-Powder Biscuit (page
34) or Sour-Cream Biscuit (page 42).

When there are no apples yet and no peaches, in the leafy
month of June when strawberries are still sulking under
their leaves, when — in Vermont — leaves are about the
only thing that has ripened, Mrs. Appleyard sometimes
makes

PINEAPPLE PANDOWDY

She uses the same amount of butter as for the apple or
peach kind, the rind and juice of one lemon, but no spices.
She uses two cans of pineapple, cut into small wedges, and

dots a little orange marmalade over the top and stirs about a tablespoonful of marmalade into the dough. She uses either Baking-Powder Biscuit dough (page 34) or Sour-Cream Biscuit dough (page 42).

This dish has some very faithful adherents and so, of course, has

PINEAPPLE UPSIDE-DOWN CAKE

1 can of sliced pineapple	2 c. light-brown sugar
¾ c. butter	Small jar of maraschino cherries

Melt the butter and sugar in a large iron frying-pan. Arrange the slices of pineapple in the pan. Put a cherry in the centre of each slice. Add a little of the liquid from the cherries. Set the pan into the oven and when the butter and sugar begins to bubble, pour on the following batter:

2½ c. cake flour	½ t. salt
2½ t. baking powder	3 eggs
1½ c. sugar	1 c. milk
6. T. Melted butter	

Sift the flour with the baking powder and salt three times. (You sifted the flour before you measured it, didn't you? Good.) Mix the milk, sugar, butter, eggs, and vanilla together with the egg-beater and beat them into the flour until the batter is smooth. Pour it over the hot fruit and bake until a clean broom straw shows that it is done (about thirty-five minutes at 375° F.).

Turn it upside down on a hot platter that is big enough for it. This takes courage, speed, a strong wrist, and a pancake-turner. Serve it with cream, vanilla ice cream, or Foamy Sauce (page 227).

PEACH UPSIDE–DOWN CAKE

This is made just the same except that the batter is flavored with one quarter-teaspoonful of almond extract instead of vanilla. Halve the peaches; fourteen is the number prescribed by Mrs. Appleyard for that large frying-pan. Put a cherry in the middle of each half, and place it cut side down in the hot butter and sugar mixture. You do this with a pancake-turner. Serve the cake with thick cream, or a sauce made by crushing raspberries and sugar, or vanilla ice cream, or Foamy Sauce. It serves ten and they will probably be languid about supper. You can safely plan for soup and a green salad — with perhaps a few after-dinner mints — soda mints, for instance. . . .

Mrs. Appleyard loves to make these indigestible concoctions, but she really prefers something like

GRAPEFRUIT AND SHERBET

For this she allows half a large grapefruit for each person. She removes the seeds, takes out the fruit neatly and puts it into a bowl with the juice, and adds to it some sugar, a little white wine, some peeled sections of Temple oranges — those best of Florida oranges that are a little like a tangerine, only twice as large and six times as juicy. She allows one orange to two grapefruit. She puts the fruit back into the grapefruit shells, which have been carefully scraped out, filling them a little more than half full. She puts in only a little of the juice. Sometimes she makes sherbet of the rest of the juice herself, adding lemon juice to it, but if she feels both lethargic and thirsty — which is a lot more likely — she drinks the juice and buys the sherbet. Either way, at serving time she fills up the grapefruit halves with sherbet — orange and grapefruit or plain orange, lemon, or pineapple — decorates the tops with candied cherries and sprigs of mint. These are pleasantly cooling, especially if there was curry first.

CANDIED APPLE SAUCE

Again the Dutchess apple is the heroine of the occasion, though Yellow Transparents are delicious, too, and Gravensteins are all right if you have to pick your apples off a fruit stand instead of finding them under the tree in the thick grass or gently pulling down a loaded branch and taking only those that drop into your hand as you touch them.

1 c. sugar	A few grains of nutmeg
1 clove	2 c. water
⅛ t. cinnamon	
12 pared and cored and quartered Dutchess apples	
Thin yellow peel of ½ lemon	

Pare the apples while the syrup is heating. Add the seasonings and the lemon peel to it. When it begins to boil, begin dropping in the apple quarters and cook them until they are transparent. Stand by the stove all the time and keep paring the apples. As you take out one piece and put it into your Thousand-Eye glass dish, drop in another. Make more syrup if necessary. When all the apples are done, there should be about a cup of syrup left. If there is more — there may be if the fruit is very juicy — cook it down to a cupful and pour it over the fruit. Do this long enough ahead so that the fruit will be cold and the syrup a candy-like jelly. Serve it with Oatmeal Lace Cookies and some

Apple-Tree Cheese. Fate will not harm you — you will have dined that day.

STRAWBERRY SHORTCAKE

2 c. flour	1 c. cream, plain
¾ c. milk	or whipped
1 c. sugar	⅓ c. butter
4 t. baking powder	1 qt. strawberries
Extra butter	whole strawberries

Crush the strawberries with the sugar and set them where they will be slightly warm. Never let them get hot, as it spoils the delicate flavor. Mix and sift the flour, salt, and baking powder four times. Work in the butter with the fingertips. Mix in the milk with a knife. Toss the dough on a floured board and roll it out half an inch thick. Cut it with a good-sized biscuit-cutter. Mrs. Appleyard's antique model is square, but there is no rule about this. Excellent shortcakes have been discovered in the circular form. Bake the biscuits twelve to fifteen minutes in a hot oven — 450° F. When they are done, split them, butter them with the extra butter, which should be soft, but not melted. Put crushed fruit on the bottom half. Turn the top half upside down and place it on the bottom half. Cover it with the crushed fruit, then with the whipped cream, topping it with one of the whole berries. Since Mr. Appleyard has strong feelings about whipped cream, there are always two shortcakes on the platter from which this feminine substance has been omitted. (*Note* by Mr. Appleyard: 'We hold this truth to be self-evident: that making a dessert out of cake and strawberries and calling it *shortcake* is a felony. The injured party automatically takes custody of the children, removing them to some place — preferably in Vermont — where their innocent minds will not be corrupted. This travesty on a noble dish is an *agrarian outrage*. It is said that one of our ambassadors to the Court of St. James's taught the English that *cake* stuck together with a few berries and whipped cream was shortcake. If so, this was a fraud upon a gallant and friendly people who have the best strawberries in the world.' — S. D. A.)

PEACH SHORTCAKE

Never make peach shortcake, Mrs. Appleyard says, unless the peaches drip when you cut them. Some other use must be found for those handsome deceivers that are fuzzy inside and out. Perhaps they might be all right for pillows for hay-fever sufferers.

Pare the peaches and slice them rather thin. Cover them with sugar. Squeeze lemon juice over them. Let them stand long enough for the sugar to dissolve. Proceed as for Strawberry Shortcake (page 105).

RASPBERRY SHORTCAKE

Mash the berries with sugar. A few red currants may be added to supply a little extra juice if it is needed. Proceed as for Strawberry Shortcake.

SHORTCAKE GUILFORD

This is named in honor of the young gentleman who, on being asked by Mrs. Appleyard whether he would have peach or raspberry on his shortcake, replied, 'I would like both.'

So he got thinly sliced peaches with a squeeze of lemon juice and a little sugar between the layers, and crushed raspberries, currants, and sugar on top. Also a cloud of whipped cream and a raspberry like a rare jewel on top of that. This started what amounted to a mutiny in Appleyard Centre — they all threatened to down forks unless they got peaches and raspberries too. It's a sort of country-style Peach Melba. Mrs. Appleyard, who remembers Madame Melba, thinks she would have liked it.

MRS. TEASDALE'S POPCORN

There comes a chilly evening, and the mind turns lovingly toward popcorn. It is good any time, including dessert time. Bear-paw popcorn is good. It comes off an ear that is shaped like a bear's paw. Perhaps it is no better than what comes in cellophane, but it seems to taste better when you shuck it off yourself. Mr. Appleyard is skillful at getting the corn off the cob without getting the corn on the floor or the skin off his fingers. He rubs two ears of corn together and the kernels rain into the tin pan like hail on the porch roof. Mrs. Appleyard has never learned the knack, but she can look on and admire. The Appleyards usually pop corn over the open fire, but they admit that Mrs. Teasdale's method produces fewer unpopped and scorched grains. When they pop it for sociability, they use the popper. When they are going to use it for dessert, they imitate Mrs. Teasdale.

She puts the corn into a big saucepan with a cover that can be clamped down tight. She puts in only enough corn to cover the bottom of the pan and a generous lump of butter — about one and a half tablespoonfuls for a three-quart pan. Then she begins to shake it over a hot fire — the top of a coal stove, a gas burner, or an oil stove — anything that produces plenty of heat. Popcorn has to be surprised into exploding. Soon comes the first faint pop and a grain hits the top of the kettle. She keeps on shaking until no noise of popping is heard. She lets it stand a minute or two before she takes off the cover, because she claims that makes it more crisp and tender than if it cools too quickly.

The Appleyards have been known to eat it for dessert with maple syrup, chocolate sauce, molasses, or cream. It's good with soup, too, instead of crackers — which is Mrs. Appleyard's favorite use for it.

9

Eggs: the Good Mixers. No one has yet really decided that controversy about whether the hen or the egg came first. If it was the hen, there must surely have been a bleak period before the first eggs were laid. Mrs. Appleyard has often wondered who it was that first discovered that you could separate the yolk and the white and that when beaten, the white would turn to snow. Her opinion is that it was a woman, and she rates the invention considerably higher than bombs on wings and poison gas.

An egg is like those people who are not witty themselves but the cause of wit in others. Alone, there is nothing very exciting about it — except perhaps when it is boiled and you chip the shell, not knowing just how soft-boiled it is. But how it combines with other things...

> With hot buttered toast, with ham!
> With mushrooms, with cream, with jam!
> With chives and cheese — and to cram
> With all except cold roast lamb!

Excuse it, please... Mrs. Appleyard merely means to say that among the infinite variety of egg dishes that she could think up between now and supper, she will mention only a few, because the topic is well covered by almost everyone that ever wrote about cooking.

EGG RING WITH MUSHROOMS

4 eggs	¼ t. salt
2 c. rich milk	⅛ t. paprika

Beat the eggs well, add the milk, salt, and paprika. Butter a ring mould. Cover it, set it in a pan full of hot water. Bake it in a slow oven — 300° F. — till it is firm. It should be done in about thirty minutes, or when a knife blade stuck into the middle of the custard comes out clean.

Serve with Mushroom Sauce (page 257) in the centre.

EGGS IN RAMEKINS

A beautiful set of porcelain ramekins is one of Mrs. Appleyard's proudest possessions. She treasures them so tenderly that for six months she served devilled ham at practically every meal so that she could get enough of the vermilion jars in which her favorite brand comes. She needed them to bake eggs in, she said, when questioned about a certain monotony in her menus.

This is simple and pleasant to do as soon as you have acquired the red jars. All you need is eggs, butter, chives, cheese, cream, and salt.

Butter each jar, leaving a half-teaspoonful of butter in the bottom. Mix the chives, finely cut, the cream, grated cheese, and seasonings. Put a little of the mixture in each jar, break in the eggs, cover them with the rest of the mixture. Set the jars in a pan of hot water and bake them at 300° F. until the whites of the eggs are set. Serve thin slices of freshly made buttered toast with them. The guests may eat the toast in their fingers and try to get the egg out of the jar with the implements provided. (No one ever supplies a vacuum cleaner, unfortunately.) Or, if they are practical, they will spoon the whole thing onto the toast and go on from there.

A few tips of fresh asparagus, cooked, are good worked into this mixture.

SPAGHETTI, EGGS, AND CHEESE

Boil the spaghetti ten minutes. Hard-boil the eggs and slice them. Place slices of large ripe tomatoes, dotted with butter, under the broiler for a few minutes. Chop a large onion very fine, add it to two cups of Cheese Sauce (page 254).

Drain the spaghetti, put it on a fireproof platter. Lay the tomatoes on the spaghetti. Spread the egg slices with devilled ham and put them between the tomatoes. Cover the whole thing with the cheese sauce. Sprinkle with paprika. Put it under the broiler for a minute. Serve it right away. It was in her devilled-ham period that Mrs. Appleyard invented this — obviously: it takes two jars.

EGGS BENEDICT

It takes three people to make these, but that is no reason for not having them at home — rather the reverse.

> 6 eggs
> 3 English muffins, split, toasted, buttered
> 6 slices of baked ham, cut to fit the muffins
> Hollandaise sauce (page 255)
> A sliced truffle, or 6 mushroom caps, grilled

One of the team toasts the muffins. Another poaches the

eggs in rings the size of the muffins. The third — that large lady in the smock made out of a certain number of red bandanas; why, yes, it *is* Mrs. Appleyard — makes the Hollandaise. She has the ham ready and also the mushrooms or truffles.

Put the ham on the muffins, the eggs on the ham, the Hollandaise over the eggs, the mushrooms on top. All right — everyone may sit down now.

CURRIED EGGS

That last was pretty exhausting. Mrs. Appleyard will take up the subject of curry intensively when she feels equal to dealing with a whole chicken and a flock of relish dishes. At present all she cares to say is that when chickens are scarce, eggs are a great help. You hard-boil them and make Curry Sauce (page 163), using canned chicken soup if you have no chicken stock on hand. If your rice is well cooked (page 163) and you have plenty of relishes — especially chutney — this is a very good substitute for chicken curry.

EGGS AND SPINACH

1 box of frosted spinach, cooked	1 t. grated onion
6 eggs	½ t. salt
A few grains of nutmeg	2 T. butter
¼ t. paprika	Grated cheese

Divide the cooked spinach into six portions and put each one into a small buttered baking-dish. The Mexican kind is good for this purpose. Season the spinach with the nutmeg, salt, pepper, and onion. Make a depression in the spinach, put a lump of butter in it, and put the egg in on top of the butter. Cover the egg thickly with grated cheese and dot it with butter and sprinkle with paprika. Set the dishes into a pan of hot water and bake them in a slow oven (300° F.) until the whites of the eggs are set — about twenty minutes.

STUFFED EGGS IN ASPIC

Here's another use for that devilled ham.

Aspic is, in the professional cookbooks, a word that they use to frighten young housewives with, so that they run and hide in the delicatessen. This terror is unnecessary if they supply themselves with the kind of consommé that jellies in the can, and the more amiable sort of can-opener. These eggs are good either in a ring mould or in individual moulds. Whichever you use, begin by rinsing the moulds with cold water.

2 cans of consommé	2 oz. devilled ham
6 hard-boiled eggs	12 stuffed olives
Finely cut chives	2 T. cream
2 pimentos	

While the eggs are cooking, heat the consommé slightly and pour a little of it into the bottom of the moulds and set them in the refrigerator. Shell the eggs. Cut them in halves. Take out the yolks and mash them with the ham and the chives. Moisten them with the cream — or mayonnaise if you prefer. Fill the egg whites with this mixture. Keep what is left over in the ice chest for sandwich filling. Put the halves of the eggs together again and wrap a thin strip of pimento around them to conceal the cut place. By the time you have performed this bit of first aid, the consommé in the moulds ought to have stiffened a little. Put a slice of stuffed olive at the bottom of the mould, the egg on it and the rest of the sliced olives around it, and pour the rest of the consommé over the eggs so that they are covered and the mould is full.

If you use a ring mould, when you unmould it fill the middle with a green salad that has watercress in it, and decorate it with radish roses. If the eggs are in individual moulds, turn them out on plates and put some green salad beside them. Russian Dressing (page 243) is good with this kind of salad. It is a good deal easier to unmould six small aspics than to get a large one out of a ring without any catastrophe. Don't say Mrs. Appleyard didn't tell you.

EGGS AND BACON AND CHEESE

After all, one of the happiest affinities in the world was not between Antony and Cleopatra but between bacon and eggs.

'Butter a shirred-egg dish,' Mrs. Appleyard says, 'slide an egg into it — preferably a large brown egg, unless you are a New Yorker. It seems hard enough to be a Yorker without having to eat white eggs besides, but then everyone has his burden. There are Yorkers no doubt' — Mrs. Appleyard omits the customary adjective — 'who are not a bit interested in brown eggs, or about Vermont's being a republic in the eighteenth century, and declaring war on Germany in September, 1941.' It must be a little dull, Mrs. Appleyard thinks, to live in a place where you don't get into an argument with a total stranger on the other side of a hotel dining-room just by quoting something Ethan Allen said at Ticonderoga — but doubtless there are compensations. Mrs. Appleyard had some very good broiled kidneys in New York about twenty years ago and some excellent chicken soup some fifteen years later. Perhaps not so good as Hartwell Farm's chicken soup, but a praiseworthy effort. . . .

Let's see — wasn't she cooking some eggs?

'Having put the egg into the buttered dish,' she continues, 'lay four thin strips of bacon across it in a square, sprinkle it thickly with grated cheese, dust it with paprika and a little salt. Put the dishes into a fairly hot oven — 375° F. — and bake until the whites of the eggs are set. If you have the type of personality that demands very crisp bacon, better cook it a little beforehand.'

10

Fish: Shell and Otherwise. For people who never live somewhere near the sea, Mrs. Appleyard has a profound pity. Fortunately most of the inland dwellers do not need the pity because they do not know what they are missing. Fish that has to travel on ice for days is satisfactory to them, and that is quite all right with Mrs. Appleyard so long as she doesn't have to have any of it.

'Eastern' lobster pursues the traveller across the continent and is even offered as a great delicacy on the Pacific coast, Mrs. Appleyard discovered recently. She had to use considerable ingenuity to avoid it and to get chili con carne instead. She believes in eating the food of the country where she happens to be. The food of Kansas, for instance, is definitely not lobster, but Mrs. Appleyard had a steak in Kansas once that was a pattern by which all steaks, past and future, will be judged. Lobster she does not care to eat much farther west than Durgin-Park's.

She clings to this prejudice in spite of the malicious story about any cargo of lobsters that comes to Boston. The real fighters, so runs this myth, are sent to Los Angeles. Fairly active ones go to Denver. If they can still crawl, they are sent to Chicago, and if they are so limp that their tails barely snap when pulled, they are kept in Boston.

Mrs. Appleyard, who was brought up in the summer on an island in Frenchman's Bay, a happy paradise where a lobster car in the cove was as essential a piece of furniture as the table for twelve around which the lobster was eaten, here firmly asserts that next best to lobster out of your own lobster car is lobster out of any other Maine lobster car, and that next best to that is lobster from the Boston market.

One of the best ways to eat lobster is a way almost no one ever does eat it outside its own haunts; and that is plain boiled, just as it comes out of the kettle, with plenty of butter to dip the pink-and-white chunks into as you pry them out. No buttery crumbs, no chopped-up mushrooms, distract your attention. Oh, possibly a few hot Parker House rolls, and afterward perhaps some wild strawberries and cream and a hunk of chocolate layer cake — nothing elaborate. Mr. and Mrs. Appleyard went to a Maine island on their wedding trip and that was what they had to eat for supper every evening. With such a beginning it is no wonder that Mrs. Appleyard has enjoyed married life.

Cold boiled lobster with melted butter is good too, if you don't happen to be around when it's hot, Mrs. Appleyard says. Only you must see the lobster brought up from the shore in a basket, squirming and fighting and snapping with its green-bronze claws. Otherwise it's all right to eat it à la Newburg or even in cutlets, with Mrs. Appleyard's kind approval.

No one who has ever lived by the sea feels quite at home when fish comes out of a can. The first thing these exiles ask for on coming home is fish. When Hugh came in from the West the other day, Mr. and Mrs. Appleyard did not even wait until they got him out of the South Station, but rushed him into the oyster bar and revived him with a dozen freshly opened raw oysters. It was pleasant to see the color flow back into the boy's pale cheeks and the sparkle return to his lustreless eyes.

Oyster stew can sometimes be used in such cases with a fortunate effect. Here is how Mrs. Appleyard makes it.

OYSTER STEW

Allow at least eight oysters to a person. The more recently they are opened, the better the stew is.

1 qt. oysters	2 c. cream
4 c. milk	½ T. salt
½ c. butter	¼ t. pepper

Clean the oysters by putting them into a colander that is standing in a saucepan and pouring three-fourths of a cup of cold water through them. Strain the liquid in the pan through cheesecloth into another pan large enough to hold the stew when it is finished. Add the butter and seasonings and bring it to the boiling point. In the meantime in another saucepan, scald the milk and the cream.

As soon as the oyster liquor is boiling add the oysters and cook them gently until they begin to curl around the edges. Get the milk and cream as hot as you can without scorching it. If your nerves are of the tense sort, you can heat it in the double boiler. Many a good batch of oysters has been ruined by a suggestion of scorched hay in the milk department.

As soon as the oysters are ready, pour the hot milk over them. Have your tureen and its cover hot, pour the stew into it. Serve with it oyster crackers or — popular with the

Appleyards — pilot biscuit that have been buttered and put into the oven until the butter froths and the crackers just start to brown.

This is enough stew for four people who like stew. You could serve more people with this amount, if some of them were indifferent to its charms, but why waste it on them? The rest of the meal is not important, though perhaps by dessert time they will be ready for some pumpkin pie.

MRS. APPLEYARD'S OYSTER, MUSHROOM, AND CELERY SOUP

1 qt. of oysters	⅓ c. flour
1 bunch Pascal celery	½ t. paprika
⅛ t. nutmeg	2 c. cream
1 t. chopped parsley	1 small onion
⅛ t. pepper	½ c. butter
4 c. milk	1 t. salt
1 lb. mushrooms	2 T. white wine
Bit of bay leaf	

There is some doubt in Mrs. Appleyard's mind as to whether this prescription had better go with soup or with fish, but as it has leaped into her mind with oysters, and as it is one of those hearty soups that can be the main dish for supper or luncheon, she has decided to speak of it here.

Cook the celery until it is soft enough to put through a fine sieve. Save the juice. Chop the onion fine. Peel the mushrooms. Use only the caps, which should be cut rather fine. Save the stems and skins for soup stock for another day. Wash the oysters as for Oyster Stew (see page 118) and save the liquor.

Fry the onion slowly in the butter until it begins to soften. Add the mushrooms and cook until they are tender

— about five minutes. Remove them from the pan and rub in the flour: add a little more butter if necessary but be sure it froths before you put in any flour. When the butter and flour have cooked together gently for three minutes, work in the cream and milk slowly, and add the seasonings. When the sauce thickens, add the mushrooms, the celery purée and juice. Set the pan where it will keep warm until you are ready to finish the soup. This first part may be done some time beforehand. When you are ready to serve the meal, heat up the oyster liquor and cook the oysters in it until their edges curl. Do this in a saucepan big enough to hold all the soup. As soon as the oysters are ready pour in the first mixture. Stir thoroughly, add the white wine, and put the soup into your hot tureen. Sprinkle the chopped parsley over the top. Croutons are nice with this — or oyster crackers.

Oysters and lobsters are happy together in the same dish and are good with other fish in

MRS. APPLEYARD'S SEA FOOD

1 lb. fresh crab meat	2 c. oyster liquor
1 qt. oysters	2 c. scallop liquor
1 qt. Cape scallops	1 qt. heavy cream
Meat from a 2-lb. lobster	2 c. rich milk
1 lb. mushroom caps, quartered	½ c. white wine
	2 egg yolks, beaten
1 green pepper, cut fine	Bit of bay leaf
	¼ t. nutmeg
1 small onion, finely minced	1 T. salt
	½ t. paprika
½ c. butter	⅛ t. cayenne
½ c. flour	¼ t. pepper

Fry the minced onion in the butter, add the mushrooms

and cook until they are tender. Remove them while you blend in the flour, sifted with the seasonings, and work in the milk and the cream. Put them back and add the lobster, crab meat, and the green pepper. Now set the pan where it will keep warm until serving time. Clean the oysters and scallops by pouring two cups of cold water through them and strain the liquor.

Just as you are ready to serve the sea food, bring the strained liquor to a boil and cook the scallops and oysters in it until the edges of the oysters begin to curl. Do this in a kettle large enough to hold all the sea food. The scallops, like oysters, should not be overcooked, and by a wise arrangement of Providence they both take about three minutes. As soon as they are ready, stir in the first mixture, stirring it well. Add the wine and the egg yolks. Beat them with a fork, stir in a little of the sauce, and then stir them back into the sauce in the kettle. This distributes the eggs more evenly through the sauce than you can do in any other way.

Be sure that no real cooking goes on after the addition of the wine and the eggs, or your sauce will separate. If you have chafing-dishes with hot-water pans, they are ideal for serving sea food, but it may also be served from a large, hot soup tureen, or from covered casseroles. It does not matter so long as the dish is hot, and will keep hot for a reasonable length of time.

While you are cooking sea food, have some extra cream and rich milk on hand so that you can add it if the sauce seems too thick. There ought to be plenty of sauce. If you have to add more cream, you had better put in a little more wine, too, and some extra seasonings. Be sure to taste the sauce as you go along, Mrs. Appleyard says: that's part of the fun. She also warns you not to forget to take out the bay leaf before you serve any sauce or soup that you put it into. Her face turned slightly pink when it was called to her attention that she had never said when it went into the sea food.

'The bay leaf always goes in with the milk,' said Mrs. Appleyard, 'and I don't intend to keep harping on it. Cooks mustn't be pampered all the time or they won't learn anything.'

This seems a little late for Mrs. Appleyard to take such an attitude, but it is probably only a phase.

French bread, cut about three-fourths of an inch thick, toasted and buttered, goes well with sea food, she says. Neat triangles of bread with the crusts cut off and toasted look more ladylike, and on that ground alone are generally rejected by Mrs. Appleyard. She never feels very refined after she has made a kettle of sea food, and has an appetite like a snapping turtle's.

BAKED OYSTERS

Allow six oysters apiece for these. Buy them in their shells. Your fish man will open them for you and fasten them together again.

Shallow Pyrex dishes are good for this if you have some large enough to hold six oyster shells. They take up more room than you think. You must have a dish for each person. Fill the dishes with coarse rock salt and set them in the oven to heat. For four people take

24 oysters on the deep shell	¼ lb. butter
	½ c. French bread crumbs
2 T. onion	1 T. minced parsley

1 bean garlic	2 T. white wine
2 slices bacon	½ t. salt
Juice of 1 lemon	¼ t. black pepper
6 drops Worcester-	⅛ t. red pepper
shire sauce	

Dry several thin slices of French bread in a slow oven, crumble and pound it into fine crumbs. Use crust and all. In a saucepan melt part of the butter and cook the onion, finely minced with the garlic, in it slowly until the onion is a pale straw color. Put in the lemon juice and the seasonings, and stir well. Add the wine and the bread crumbs. Add a little more wine if the mixture seems too dry, but do not get it wet and mushy. Now sink the oysters on their deep shells into the salt that you have heated in the pans. Be careful not to spill the oyster juice. Cover each oyster with the buttered crumbs. Sprinkle with parsley or with minced chives if you prefer, and put small squares of the bacon on top. Bake them ten minutes at 500° F.

Layer-cake tins will do if you have no glass dishes. When serving them, set them on dishes that are fireproof. Those dishes of salt are *hot*.

These are something like Oysters Rockefeller, but without the absinthe. Even if Mrs. Appleyard knew how to make a sauce out of absinthe and spinach she would think it only right to let concealment prey upon her damask cheek, like a termite in a beam. She really likes scalloped oysters better anyway. Why, she wonders, do cookbooks say 'escalloped'? Probably for the same reason that some people stick out their little fingers when holding a water glass. . . .

SCALLOPED OYSTERS

1 qt. oysters	1 c. Montpelier cracker
½ c. oyster liquor,	crumbs
strained	1 c. French bread crumbs
2 T. cream	½ t. salt
2 T. sherry	¼ t. pepper
½ c. melted butter	⅛ t. nutmeg

Roll the Montpelier crackers fine. (Oh, all right — common crackers if that's all you have.) Dry some slices of French bread in a slow oven. Pound the crust and all into crumbs. Mix with the cracker crumbs. Add the seasonings and mix well. Stir in the butter, cream, sherry, and oyster liquor. Do not get the mixture too wet. The oysters themselves supply some moisture. Butter a shallow Pyrex glass baking-dish, put a thin layer of the crumb mixture into the bottom of the dish, then half the oysters. Cover them with more of the crumb mixture, put in the rest of the oysters, cover them with the rest of the crumbs. Dot with a little more butter. Bake for thirty minutes at 400° F.

Scalloped oysters should never consist of more than two layers of oysters. If you use more layers the middle layers will still be half-raw when the top and bottom layers are properly cooked, or else the middle layers will be right and the outer ones tough. There are two sad results that wrong timing can produce: undercooking — and also too many bread crumbs and too much liquid — all tend to make a singularly unattractive form of poultice; overcooking — especially when combined with too little liquid, too little butter, and too large a proportion of cracker crumbs — may enliven the meal with a dish of sawdust containing some frizzled-up gray objects that may be either oysters or the children's old mittens.

OYSTERS AND MUSHROOMS

Scalloped oysters may be varied by making them with half oysters and half mushrooms. Use a little extra butter and fry the peeled and sliced mushroom caps in it, and also a little grated onion, until the mushrooms are tender. Prepare the crumbs as for scalloped oysters, put in half the oysters and half the mushrooms in each of the two layers, cover them with a layer of crumbs, and bake until the crumbs are brown.

HADDOCK

Life, however, cannot be all lobster and oysters. Consider the humble haddock an uninteresting fish when fried in large chunks, but one that responds cheerfully to kind treatment. It used to appear, on that island of which Mrs. Appleyard has already spoken, under the name of Turbot à la crême. During her innocent youth Mrs. Appleyard thought it was all one word and the name of a separate fish. Pronounced rapidly it is certainly a very stylish name, but the dish is still all right if you call it

SCALLOPED HADDOCK

A 5-lb. haddock, cut for chowder	½ t. white pepper
	1 t. thyme
3 c. milk	¾ c. butter
1 c. cream	1 t. salt
½ c. flour	½ c. cracker crumbs
½ t. minced parsley	½ c. French bread crumbs
1 onion, finely minced	¼ c. grated cheese
2 egg yolks	

Boil the haddock. There is more flavor to the haddock if

you boil the head with it and throw it away later instead of
beforehand. You need not, so far as Mrs. Appleyard is concerned, make the eyes into waistcoat buttons in the silent
night. Leave that to some aged man sitting on a gate.

Remove the bones. Flake the fish into small pieces.
Melt a half-cup of the butter in a large saucepan and fry
the onion in it until the onion is a pale straw color. Shove
the onion to one side of the saucepan and rub into the butter
the flour, sifted with the pepper and salt. Work in the milk,
add the cream, the parsley, and the thyme. Fresh thyme,
finely minced, is best, but dried will do. Beat the egg yolks
with a fork, dilute them with a large spoonful of the sauce,
and stir them into the sauce in the pan. Now butter a
large casserole, put in a layer of the sauce, a layer of the
fish, and so on. Finish with the sauce and add the crumbs,
into which you have stirred the rest of the butter melted.
Add a few more dots of butter if the crumbs seem at all
dry. Sprinkle over the grated cheese and bake at 375° F.
for from fifteen to twenty minutes or until the crumbs are
well browned.

BAKED HADDOCK

A 5-lb. haddock, cut	½ t. salt
to bake	2 t. melted butter
¼ lb. fat salt pork	1 t. minced parsley
6 slices of bacon	1 lemon, sliced

Stuffing

¾ c. cracker crumbs	¼ t. pepper
¾ c. French bread crumbs	1 onion, finely minced
⅓ c. butter	½ t. Bell's poultry seasoning
½ t. salt	1 egg, beaten

Make the stuffing first. Roll the crackers fine. Dry some

slices of French bread, and roll crust and all into fine crumbs. Stir the dry seasonings into the crumbs, then the butter, melted, the minced onion, and the beaten egg.

Brush the fish inside and out with melted butter and sprinkle it with a little salt and pepper. Put in the stuffing. If you pack it in neatly, there is no real reason for sewing. There will be a crust on the outside and by using two pancake-turners you can get the fish out of the pan whole. Perhaps you like to sew fish — in which case, go right ahead. Mrs. Appleyard prefers smocking or Italian cutwork, or even mending stockings. However, the fish is not in the pan yet. . . .

Butter an iron dripping-pan, lay the stuffed fish in it, put over it the salt pork cut in thin strips. Add a very little water — just enough to keep it from drying out during the first few minutes. Fish has more flavor if it is baked without water. Bake the fish for forty to fifty minutes — at 425° F. for ten minutes, and the rest of the time at 350° F. Baste it with the fat that runs into the pan. During the last fifteen minutes put the slices of bacon over it. Transfer it to a hot platter, pour the liquid in the pan over it, surround it with slices of lemon, and sprinkle it with the chopped parsley.

FISH CHOWDER

This rule was inherited by Mrs. Appleyard and the chowder is always eaten with gratitude to the hands that used to make it. The best kettleful that Mrs. Appleyard ever ate was cooked over an open fire built on the rounded pebbles of a beach on Frenchman's Bay. The haddock had not been out of the water more than half an hour. The salt air, the scent of the pointed firs, the smell of the burning driftwood, all seemed to be added to the chowder. Still, it is pretty good cooked on a prosaic gas stove. You can have good chowder without smoke in your eyes, but not without plenty of salt pork and onions. Without them it is just a fishy dish of potatoes and milk. Do not try to make it with cooked potatoes or without the head and the bones of the fish. Much of the flavor of the fish is in them.

CHOWDER (FOR SIX)

A 4-lb. haddock, cut for chowder, head and all	3 large onions, finely sliced
3 c. milk	6 medium potatoes
1 c. cream	1 t. salt
8 pilot crackers	1/4 t. black pepper
1/2 lb. salt pork, diced	1/2 t. paprika

Slice the potatoes 'as thin as fourpence.' Mrs. Appleyard has never seen a fourpence, but she estimates the thickness as about that of a nickel. In other words, you slice them so thin that there is no danger of there being half-raw lumps of potato in your chowder. Furthermore, pork dice means dice — not hunks. Fry the dice till they are a delicate cracker brown. Dip them out with a skimmer and put them on a saucer. Fry the onion in the pork fat until it is a light straw color. Take out the onion with your skimmer and put it on the saucer with the pork. Now rinse out the frying-pan with a little hot water and pour the water into a large kettle. In this way you don't lose the onion flavor. Lay in your pieces of fish. Add the potatoes, the onions, and the pork. Rinse the saucer on which the pork was with a little more hot water and pour it into the kettle. Add the seasonings and enough more hot water to cover the fish and potatoes. Cover the kettle and let the fish cook slowly for forty minutes, or until the fish is falling from the bones and the potatoes are done.

You are now ready to serve the chowder, so add the milk and cream. Let it come to the boil but not boil. Taste it and be sure it is seasoned to suit you. If the pork was not very salty, you may need to add more — gently, though: it's a lot easier to put in than to take out. Put two of the pilot crackers, broken in quarters, into a large hot soup tureen. It does not look right to Mrs. Appleyard in anything but blue Canton, but please yourself.

Now take the large pieces of bone out of the chowder and discard them. Drop in the rest of the broken pilot crackers. Take a large ladle and transfer the chowder to the tureen, dipping it up from the bottom. Throw away the head if you have not already done so. Unless the fish slips easily from the bones the chowder is not done. You will not be able to get all the bones out. 'Look out for bones!' is a motto that ought to be cross-stitched on a silver cardboard, and served with each plateful. Mrs. Appleyard will attend to that later. At the moment she simply urges you again to taste the chowder once more for seasoning before you send it to the table. Having been brought up in a family where one of the favorite expressions was 'This dish is poisoned with salt!' she is likely to put in too little for some tastes.

The Appleyards like a few extra pilot crackers, buttered generously and put in the oven until the butter froths and the crackers begin to brown around the edges. A little paprika sprinkled over them looks rather cheering. The Appleyards take their chowder seriously and eat enough of it so that the next course is likely to be dessert. Something about lemon meringue pie makes it seem a fitting conclusion to this meal.

BROILED SHAD ROE

When the Appleyards leave for Vermont they cannot forget that they spend most of the year near the sea. They are lucky in having some fishermen in the family, but the trout do not always bite. Most canned fish does not appeal to them, but an exception is shad roe. Shad is a fish that is not at its best even as near home as Boston. Lucky cities like Baltimore and Philadelphia deserve the best and get it. The next best, in Mrs. Appleyard's opinion, is the canned roe, done when the fish have just leaped out of the water, and plenty good enough for the Appleyards when they reach the point that even the goldfish in the pool look tempting.

Mrs. Appleyard brushes the roe with melted butter, sprinkles a very little salt and pepper on it, broils it, about three minutes on each side, basting it while it broils with the juice of a lemon mixed with two tablespoonfuls of melted butter. With it she serves plenty of bacon and garnishes the dish with quartered lemons and sprigs of parsley. Asparagus, Country Style (page 284) and Creamed Potatoes (page 305) are likely to turn up in company with shad roe.

Someone seems to have distracted Mrs. Appleyard's attention from chowder. Fish chowder, she says, turning away from a tantalizing can of shad roe in scarlet and gold, and deciding to keep it for just one more emergency, may be slammed through light-heartedly; clam chowder is a serious project. Mrs. Appleyard is still seeing red from an article that she read about chowder.

'A good chowder,' wrote the well-meaning author, 'is made by substituting milk for the ordinary tomato juice.'

Mrs. Appleyard began by punctuating this quotation with an exclamation point. Then she put another one and, as her temper rose, strung them out to the edge of the page. Finding that even that number did not express her feelings, she decided on the following understatement:

'A * * * * * [fill in adjectives at pleasure] concoction is sometimes made by substituting tomato juice for the usual milk and cream. Steps will be taken to see that no one making it is allowed to cross the Massachusetts border, the Connecticut, or Lake Champlain.'

Mrs. Appleyard would gladly have talked till next day, but she felt that the lesson must end. Here is how some very intelligent people have been making clam chowder since the days when you paid for the clams in wampum.

NEW ENGLAND CLAM CHOWDER

1 qt. Duxbury or Ipswich clams	¼ t. pepper
1 c. cold water	4 T. butter
4 c. potatoes	2 c. milk
¼ lb. fat salt pork	2 c. cream
1 t. salt	4 T. flour
½ t. paprika	8 pilot crackers
	1 lemon, sliced very thin

Put the clams into a strainer, set into a bowl. Pour a cup of cold water over them. Save the liquor. Separate the soft parts of the clams from the rest and set them aside. Put the tough parts through the meat-grinder.

Cut the pork into very small dice and cook them until they are a delicate cracker brown. Take them out with a skimmer. Fry the onion in the pork fat until it is a pale straw color. Cut the potatoes into small neat cubes and parboil them five minutes in just enough water to cover them. Drain the water off, using it to rinse out the dish in which you cooked the onions and pork. Save it. Melt a little of the butter in a kettle. Put a layer of potatoes into it, add some of the ground clams, dredge with a little of the flour, sifted with the seasonings, and put in part of the pork and the onions. Repeat this until you have used all the ground clams, potatoes, pork, onions, and two tablespoons of the flour. Add the water you drained off the potatoes and enough more hot water to cover the mixture. Cook fifteen minutes. Add the soft parts of the clams. Cook three minutes. Then add the milk and cream. Let it come to a boil, but not boil. Into the same frying-pan you used before, put the remaining butter. Rub in the rest of the flour as soon as the butter froths, and cook gently for three minutes. Blend into it the strained clam juice. Cook a few minutes longer. Add this to the chowder just before serving. It will tend to make the milk separate if it is added too soon.

Have a hot tureen ready. Put into it some of the pilot crackers, broken. Pour the chowder over them. Put the rest of the crackers on top. Add the sliced lemon. This may be left out of the chowder and passed separately if you feel there is likely to be sales resistance to it among your public. Serve a few extra pilot crackers well buttered and sprinkled with paprika and toasted in the oven for a few minutes.

BOUILLABAISSE

Bouillabaisse is just a chowder that has had the advantages of foreign travel. In Mrs. Appleyard's rag-bag mind there turn up every now and then Thackeray's lines about this famous dish.

> Green herbs, red peppers, mussels, saffron;
> Soles, onions, garlic, roach, and dace —
> All these you eat at Terré's Tavern
> In that one dish of Bouillabaisse.

Even if you can't follow the whole prescription, you can at least get the saffron from the drugstore, use a mixture ot fish and shellfish, and produce something that is distinctly good to eat. Perhaps it ought to be called fish stew, but why take the romance out of life?

NEW ENGLAND BOUILLABAISSE, MRS. APPLEYARD

A 3-lb. haddock, cut for chowder	1 T. celery, chopped
A 1-lb. halibut	3 tomatoes, chopped
1 lb. flounder fillets	1 t. parsley, minced
1 lb. fresh crab meat	1 t. thyme
A 2-lb lobster.	½ t. saffron
1 qt. oysters	2 bay leaves
1 pt. Cape scallops	1 t. salt
1 T. lemon juice	½ t. pepper
1 c. salad oil	½ t. paprika
2 large onions, chopped	Small can of pimentos
1 bunch of leeks	1 c. white wine
1 t. garlic, minced	Half a long loaf of French bread

Mrs. Appleyard assembled these things partly from the ballad, partly from an old French cookbook, partly from observation, having once eaten bouillabaisse in a French restaurant. Of course you are supposed to have mussels in it, shells and all, and if you really like the shells, you could put in some small clams to steam and open while the rest of the fish is cooking. She really likes it better without, but perhaps that's just ignorance. Anyway, this is her version and she sticks to it.

Cut up the fish into neat pieces, not too small. Save all the bones and trimmings, including the lobster shells (be sure the lobster is well cleaned), cover them with water, and cook them gently for at least half an hour. Be sure the head of the haddock and the flounder bones are in this. There should be about a quart of fish stock.

Put the oil into a large frying-pan. Fry the onions, leeks, and garlic in it until the onion is light straw color. Use the green tops of the leeks as well as the white and cut them into half-inch pieces. Add the cut-up fish and the crab meat and lobster meat. Pound up the lobster coral fine and put it in. Of course you may use some other combination of fish, but have lobster if possible.

Cook the fish five minutes, add the tomatoes, celery, lemon juice, and seasonings except the saffron and parsley. Add the fish stock and the pimentos, cut in strips, and simmer twenty-five minutes with the pan covered. Then add the oysters and scallops and cook them until the edges of the oysters curl. Add last of all the saffron, parsley, and wine.

Put the French bread, cut one and a half inches thick and toasted, into a large hot tureen or covered casserole. Pour the bouillabaisse over it. Serve the rest of the loaf of bread, some unsalted butter, radishes, olives, and raw celery with the bouillabaisse. Have some white wine to drink with it. This serves eight people. All you will want for dessert will be some fruit and cheese.

FISH MOUSSE

A 1-lb. halibut or salmon	¾ c. cream, beaten
2 eggs, beaten	¼ t. salt
¼ c. milk	¼ t. white pepper

A few grains of Cayenne

This is for a small ring mould.

Put the fish through the food-chopper. Mousse is better made with raw fish. Be sure to remove all bones and skin before you begin to chop it. Add the milk with the seasonings in it, the beaten eggs, and the cream, beaten until it begins to thicken. Butter the ring mould — or one shaped like a fish if you happened to inherit it. Put in the mixture, cover the mould with heavy wax paper, set it in a pan of hot water, and bake it until the mousse is firm. In the middle of the mould, if it is a ring, or around it, put either Mushroom Sauce (page 257), Hollandaise Sauce (page 255), or Lobster Sauce — made by simmering diced lobster in cream sauce (page 254) and, just before serving, adding one tablespoonful of white wine for each cup of sauce — Egg Sauce (page 254) or Fish Sauce made as follows:

Bones and trimmings of the fish	¼ t. salt
1 small carrot, sliced	2 c. cold water
1 onion, sliced	2 T. butter
Sprig of parsley	3 T. flour
Bit of bay leaf	1½ c. heavy cream
¼ t. pepper	Yolks of 2 eggs
	2 T. white wine

Cover the fish bones and trimmings with the water. Add the seasonings, carrot, and parsley. Cook the stock down so that there is only one cup. Melt the butter; when it bubbles, rub in the flour, cook gently for three minutes, add the fish stock and the cream. Beat the egg yolks, dilute them with an equal amount of the sauce, and pour the mixture back into the sauce, stirring it in well. Add the wine and pour it over the mousse.

SALMON AND FLOUNDER

This is a way of making your salmon go further.

Take some small chunks of salmon, wrap small fillets of flounder around them. Fasten the fillets with toothpicks, put the fish into a cheesecloth that you keep for fishy manoeuvres. Have some boiling water ready in a kettle, put in the cloth containing the fish, and poach it for from thirty-five to forty-five minutes. Never let it boil hard. Season the water with some salt and pepper.

Serve the fillets with the Fish Sauce described on page 135 or with Hollandaise Sauce (page 255) or with Lobster Sauce made as described on page 135.

Cucumbers sliced very thin, soaked in salted water, drained, and marinated in a good French dressing are nice with this. How about an old-fashioned strawberry short-cake afterward? Perhaps you prefer bread pudding — suit yourself. Mrs. Appleyard is perfectly satisfied: all the more strawberries for her.

CODFISH IN CREAM

Although there is probably good creamed codfish in Gloucester, it is in Vermont that Mrs. Appleyard first found out that it was an edible substance. That is because when Vermonters say 'cream' they mean it. So codfish in cream was considered such an exotic delicacy during the last century that it was reserved for company. A cousin of Mr. Appleyard's, who had left the state for the West, once returned and made a round of visits to various relatives who were still in the Green Mountains. He dined with Cousin Sarah — codfish in cream; with Uncle Abdiel — codfish in cream. The codfish was also in excellent form at Great Aunt Susan's, and at Cousin James's, and as he drove into the yard at Cousin Horatio's he heard a voice from the kitchen say: 'Horatio, that looks like George's boy that just drove in. Go over to the store and get me a cod-fish. I've got cream.'

There is no mystery to this dish — if you have cream. Freshen your codfish by soaking it in cold water. Change the water several times. When you cook it start it in cold water, bring it to the boiling point and then put it where it will be hot but not boil while you are making the sauce. Make a cream sauce (page 254) and boil some eggs hard. Flake up the fish, discarding any tough pieces, and put it into the sauce in the top of the double boiler to keep hot and mellow until you need it. Have plenty of sauce in pro-portion to the amount of fish — three cups of sauce to a pound of fish is about the way Mr. Appleyard likes it. Slice the hard-boiled eggs and strew them over the sauce and fish. With it have either baked or boiled new potatoes, according to which is best at the moment. A pound of fish serves from four to six people, depending on where they were born.

SALT–FISH DINNER

This is an easy way to a man's heart. It seems to take care of the same instinct that makes mud pies a favorite occupation.

For six people:

1½ lbs. salt codfish	6 carrots
3 cups egg sauce (page 254)	6 small white turnips
½ lb. salt pork	6 beets
6 onions	6 boiled potatoes

Soak the fish in cold water overnight. Change the water three times. Before you start to cook the vegetables, put the fish in a large frying-pan, cover it with fresh water, bring it to a boil but do not boil it. Set it where it will cook gently below the boiling point until you are ready to use it. Cook each of the vegetables separately. If they are very young and small, allow several of each kind instead of the one apiece called for above. There is of course no harm in cooking some extra anyway, but this is a filling dish and second helpings are not generally needed. While the fish and the vegetables are cooking, make the egg sauce and dice the salt pork fine and try it out until the pork scraps are brown and crisp. When everything is ready put the fish in the middle of a large hot platter and arrange the vegetables around it. Serve the egg sauce in a large bowl and the pork scraps with the pork fat in a sauce boat.

It is a pretty sight to see Mr. Appleyard attack a salt-fish dinner. He takes a potato on his plate and cuts it up rather fine, and then cuts into it the fish and the various vegetables. He keeps on cutting, and works into it some pork scraps and some of the tried-out pork fat, and last of all he takes a generous amount of the egg sauce and cuts that in. The result is a superb mound that fills the plate, in which the different flavors and textures are blended into something that is different from anything that went into it, and yet has the virtues of all its parts. Be sure that the vegetables are cooked freshly and all the water cooked out of them, that the fish is tender and well drained, the pork scraps crisp, that the sauce is made with plenty of cream, that the plates are stinging hot — and everyone will be happy.

Watermelon pickle is not part of the essential ritual but it is good with this dinner, and Mr. Appleyard thinks the dessert ought to be Indian Pudding (page 235), so you'd better have johnnycake for breakfast.

11

Hors d' Oeuvres. Appetizers, Mrs. Appleyard says, are generally eaten most by those who need them least. This paradox, however, does not prevent their being frequently the best part of the meal. She advises anyone who sees something really hot and tempting among the hors d'oeuvres to eat it as rapidly as he can without scorching his tongue, and so continue, for after all, he may be going to encounter frozen peas with soda in them and a feminine dessert. This strategy originated with Mr. Appleyard, who believes that a hot sausage in the hand is worth more than a fruit salad in the bush — especially if the bush is garnished with marshmallows.

The most popular appetizer is caviar. Shakespeare is responsible for the idea that it is something liked only by the sophisticated. It may be an acquired taste, but unfortunately it is acquired only too easily. Put out a lot of appetizers on a large silver platter and see which ones vanish first. Either everyone likes caviar or those who do like it have no self-control at all.

Mrs. Appleyard sighs for the days of imperial gray beluga, but the imitations — either red or black — are better than nothing. Perhaps the most comfortable way to eat caviar is to have a good-sized bowl of it on the table around which you are sitting. Caviar should be cold but not frozen. With it serve crusty French bread, sweet butter, sour cream, finely chopped onion, quartered lemons. Fingerbowls are a pretty good idea, and don't hurry with the next course. People sitting around eating caviar are having a good time. Take advantage of this fact if you are serving the meal yourself.

There are, however, moments when caviar served wholesale is not the thing. For these less expansive occasions Mrs. Appleyard makes

CAVIAR CANAPÉS

Thinly cut sandwich bread, not too fresh, is essential to making good canapés. In ordering a sandwich loaf, always order it the day before you are going to use it. It is possible in some shops, operated by benefactors of humanity, to get sandwich bread sliced wafer thin. This is not so thin as the most skillful cook can do with a very sharp knife, but it is a lot thinner than most of us can do in a hurry with the knife our little ones borrowed for cutting the string that tied their new skis together, Mrs. Appleyard says.

Quantities needed for twelve canapés:

4-oz. jar of caviar	¼ lb. unsalted butter, softened
Juice of ½ lemon	1 hard-boiled egg
4 large stuffed olives	1 t. grated onion

Cut out rounds of the thinly sliced bread with a cooky-cutter. Toast them lightly on one side. Spread them with softened sweet butter, then with caviar that has been mixed with a little chopped onion and a squeeze of lemon juice. Spread it thickly. Caviar spread thin is just an annoyance. Decorate it around the edge with finely chopped white of hard-boiled egg and sprinkle a little of the grated yolk over the top. A slice of a large stuffed olive in the middle looks rather cheerful and does no special harm.

CREAM PUFFS WITH CAVIAR

Make 24 very small cream puffs (see page 98).

FILLING

1 4-oz jar of caviar	4 T. sour cream
2 t. grated onion	1 t. paprika
Juice of 1 lemon	

Mix caviar with the seasonings. Split the puffs halfway through and fill them with caviar. Top them with a dash of sour cream dusted with paprika.

Either red or black caviar may be used; neither of them ever met a sturgeon, but they do their best in a hard world. In those unhappy districts where cream comes in a bottle and lives in a refrigerator, a passable substitute for sour cream may be made by mashing a small cream cheese and beating a tablespoonful or two of thick cream into it. Mrs. Appleyard does not really approve of this stratagem, but admits she has used it when hard pressed.

PLATE OF APPETIZERS NO. 1

If the rest of the meal is to be light, a plate of appetizers may be served at the table as the first course. It might include:

Half a hard-boiled egg stuffed with a paste made by mashing the yolk with one teaspoonful of devilled ham and a little mayonnaise.

A small tomato stuffed with cream cheese mixed with olive butter, and chopped chives, and moistened with a little cream. To a small cream cheese use:

1 T. olive butter	2 t. cream
1 t. chopped chives	½ t. salt

A sardine on a small oblong of toast made from wafer-thin sandwich bread, lightly toasted and spread with softened butter to which a few drops of Worcestershire sauce have been added. Sprinkle the sardine with finely minced chives.

A crisp stalk of celery stuffed with cheese. Use part Roquefort, or Argentine Blue, and part cream cheese mashed together with a little thick cream. Dust it with paprika.

A small cream puff stuffed with caviar (see page 142) or with pâté de foie gras, or with crab meat and mayonnaise, or lobster. In any case a small lettuce leaf sticking out advertises the fact that there is something good inside.

PLATE OF APPETIZERS NO. 2 (FOR SIX PEOPLE)

6 lettuce hearts	6 large stuffed ripe
6 celery hearts	olives
6 slices of tomato	3 radishes, thinly sliced
12 anchovy fillets	12 green olives stuffed,
6 sardines	sliced
6 thin slices of tongue	6 thin slices of dried beef

Arrange these on individual plates and pour over them a dressing made of:

½ t. dry mustard	1 T. oil from sardines
½ t. salt	5 T. olive oil
¼ t. pepper	1½ T. lemon juice
½ t. paprika	1 T. red-wine vinegar
2 T. chopped chives	½ t. anchovy essence
1 t. finely minced onion	

TOMATO AND CAVIAR CANAPÉS

Toast wafer-thin rounds of bread on one side. Spread the other side with soft butter. Place on it a thin slice of peeled tomato lightly spread with mayonnaise. Spread it with black caviar (née cod roe, but don't look at the label), squeeze lemon juice over it, sprinkle it with grated egg yolk.

Made with a rather generous round of bread and tomato and caviar in proportion, this is enough for a first course.

TOMATO AND ANCHOVY CANAPÉS

1 hard-boiled egg	1 small peeled tomato
2 T. tuna fish	½ green pepper, finely
6 anchovy fillets	minced

Chop all these together. Moisten with one teaspoon of mayonnaise, one teaspoon of chili sauce, and a few drops of Worcestershire sauce. Spread this mixture on six rounds of thin sandwich bread that have been buttered and put into the oven for a few minutes. Decorate the canapés with stuffed olives. Put a slice of olive cut across in the middle, and four slices cut lengthwise radiating from it. A spray of watercress wreathed around these looks rather attractive. Mrs. Appleyard considers these good but a waste of time.

TRAYS OF APPETIZERS

These are some of the things that Mrs. Appleyard likes to put on the small sticks used for spearing hot hors d'oeuvres: innocent young sausages an inch long that have been baked awhile in the oven and finished off under the broiler; large stuffed olives wrapped in bacon and broiled; oysters treated the same way; mushroom caps dotted with butter and a little salt and broiled.

It is a ticklish business to get the mushrooms broiled just right. If you cook them too much they get flabby and if you get on too much butter, your guests may avoid them. Hostesses might as well remember that if it is a choice between a man's shirt front and the rug, he will choose the rug. Perhaps you had better play safe and make

MUSHROOM AND BACON APPETIZERS

1 lb. mushrooms	½ t. salt
1 slice of onion	4 t. thick cream
4 T. butter	1 t. sherry
2 T. flour	6 slices of bacon

Chop the mushrooms and the onion fine and fry them slowly in the butter. When they are tender sprinkle the flour over them and the salt and cook a little longer. Add the cream and last of all the sherry. Spread the mixture on rounds of sandwich bread. Put a small square of bacon on top of each canapé. Cook them under the broiler until the bacon is done.

CHEESE AND CHUTNEY APPETIZERS (MRS. APPLEYARD)

¼ lb. butter	1 t. finely minced onion
½ lb. dairy cheese	6 drops Worcestershire sauce
1 cup Major Grey's chutney	

Cream the butter, add the cheese, finely grated. Chop

the onion and then in the same bowl the chutney and stir this mixture into the cheese and butter. Add the Worcestershire sauce and enough juice from the chutney so that the mixture will spread easily. Spread it on rounds of sandwich bread and put them on a baking-sheet into a very hot oven (500° F.) for about three minutes.

This amount will make about three dozen appetizers.

SARDINE AND OLIVE APPETIZERS

1 small can of sardines	3 drops Worcestershire sauce
2 T. butter	1 t. cream
1 t. lemon juice	

Mash the sardines with their own oil. Add the butter, lemon juice, Worcestershire sauce, and cream. Toast rounds of bread and spread them with the mixture and decorate them with slices of stuffed olives and hard-boiled egg if you have it.

Mrs. Appleyard feels that it is really safer to pass your appetizers than to make an arbitrary selection for the guests and serve it on a plate. Imagine, for instance, the chagrin of the hostess at finding that some of the guests toy lightly with those sacred caviar puffs and leave them half-eaten. Certainly pass them if you have one of those Chinese trays into which dishes of celadon or turquoise-colored porcelain are fitted. However, even if you haven't, it is possible to improvise an attractive tray. Mrs. Appleyard has encountered one with dishes from Woolworth's where the dishes and their contents were both full of charm.

The dishes may contain any of the things mentioned above — better keep all the hot things on one tray — and besides, shredded carrot and cabbage salad, potato salad, anchovies, stuffed olives, green and ripe, smoked sausage, artichoke bottoms, pickled mushrooms, sardines. One of them may even contain pickled beets.

Mrs. Appleyard is very unlikely to live down the fact that, when being helped from a table of such delicacies in a New York restaurant, it was noticed by her loving friends that the only thing out of the dozen presented to her notice that she did not take was the beets.

In a good many restaurants west of Chicago they bring you salad as soon as you sit down. This is a surprise to Eastern visitors who expect to begin with either soup, fruit cup, grapefruit, or oysters. There is a good deal to be said for this practice of setting salad before the hungry guest — especially from the point of view of the restaurant: it keeps the guest busy while he is waiting for the rest of his order, and perhaps makes him satisfied with a smaller portion of the main course than he would otherwise expect. There is a tendency in the East now to follow the same strategy, only they bring you relishes and Melba toast and butter. It is a pretty sight, Mrs. Appleyard thinks, to see ladies on a reducing diet virtuously choose a piece of Melba toast and cover it with butter.

If salad is going to be served first, try salad à la Max. Max was a genius who had a small restaurant in Boston — a hundred years ago, more or less, it seems to Mrs. Appleyard. This is the salad he always set before his guests, as she remembers it across the years.

He put four or five crisp leaves of native lettuce on a plate — in those innocent times iceberg lettuce was still in its native icebergs, right where it belongs — and over them he put four fillets of anchovy. In and around the anchovies he put thin slices of radishes and stuffed olives, some green and some ripe. He put a shrimp in the middle of each plate and sprinkled the whole thing with grated egg yolk. Just before he sent it to the table he poured over it a dressing made with red-wine vinegar. Mrs. Appleyard does not know exactly how it was made, but Mr. Appleyard's French dressing is a good deal like it. She says that you may add a teaspoonful of anchovy essence to it if you like. The rule for Mr. Appleyard's salad dressing is on page 239.

Of course this dressing should really be made with olive oil, but we can eat cottonseed and like it. Mr. Appleyard says you had better season it a little more heavily than you would if you were using olive oil.

Mrs. Appleyard was once turned loose at a smorgasbord where the following hors d'oeuvres were spread out. Even her excellent appetite did not allow her to sample them all, and she lists them simply as pleasant recollection of the past and a rainbow promise of the future, which she trusts will not be too distant.

1. Hot anchovy and chutney rolls. These seemed to consist of fresh bread spread with butter and chopped chutney and rolled around an anchovy fillet. The useful hors d'oeuvres sticks fastened them and they were toasted brown.

2. Small sausages on sticks.

3. Toasted cheese sandwiches.

4. Toasted mushroom sandwiches.

5. Grilled shad roe. It was cut in chunks and wrapped with bacon, skewered on toothpicks and broiled.

6. Sardines on toast with hot mustard sauce.

7. Thin slices of salami.

8. Liver paté.

9. Potato salad.

10. Dried-beef cornucopias filled with cream cheese and horse radish.

11. Thin slices of ham rolled around cream cheese mixed with chutney.

12. Caviar with chopped onion, lemon, grated egg yolk, Melba toast.

13. Celery stuffed with Roquefort cheese.

14. Rolled asparagus sandwiches.

15. Rolled watercress sandwiches.

16. Salad of raw carrot, shredded white and purple cabbage, purple onions, and watercress with French dressing.

17. Conserve of spiced fruits.

18. Tomato marmalade.

19. Watermelon pickle.

20. Chutney.

This collection seemed to be supplying something for every taste. Yet after all, Mrs. Appleyard says, is there anything better than some cold crisp celery, some jumbo-sized green olives, some very young radishes, a few sticks of raw carrot, with French bread and unsalted butter?

12

Ice Cream and Sherbet. The electric refrigerator is a great blessing to humanity, but it has something chalked up against it because of what it has done to ice cream. The whole theory of ice cream is that it is *beaten and frozen at the same time.* Nothing made in the drawer of a refrigerator is ever so good as what is cranked by hand in a White Mountain freezer, no matter how often you may take it out of the drawer and stir it. Of course it is better if you stir it than if you leave it alone to sulk, but it never has quite the cool smoothness produced by a hand freezer. Besides, there is no dash to lick. Think of the arid childhood of one who has never been handed the dash (or dasher, but never called so in this connection), a bowl, and a spoon, and who actually, in the melting sweetness, never finds a shred of peach or strawberry. . . . Let's not think of it — too sad.

Mr. Appleyard in his youth froze so much ice cream that he invented a board seat that fitted over the freezer, so that he could sit down on it and keep the freezer steady while he cranked with his right hand, and in his left held a copy of *King Solomon's Mines* by H. Rider Haggard. Mrs. Appleyard, too, has put her inventive genius to work. She thought up a cylinder with a beater inside that would fit into her refrigerator freezing compartment. This good idea occurred to her in her bath. Probably she is distantly related to Archimedes. She planned to have a small motor attached to the cylinder and a flat rubber cord that would go through the refrigerator door and not stop it from shutting. She was going to plug it into a socket near by.

No sooner said than done. All Mrs. Appleyard has to do is to think about an invention and someone else, someone who has wrestled with aluminum and motors and patent lawyers, and rubber, promptly puts it on the market. She exercises this strange power rather infrequently, because she feels that it is a serious responsibility. Within two weeks — which was certainly quick for an invention — one of the cylinders was whirring away busily in Mrs. Appleyard's refrigerator, beating up some strawberry ice cream that even Mr. Appleyard admits was just as good as any he ever made with Rider Haggard's help — or Conan Doyle's either, for that matter.

In case anyone else gets one of these Hamilton Beach Freezers, Mrs. Appleyard has a word of caution. Be sure your refrigerator freezing compartment has a space big enough to hold the cylinder. Always set your control at its coldest point. Follow the directions for using the freezer *exactly*. They were not written in any frivolous spirit. At one time Mrs. Appleyard thought she knew better. This was pure conceit: her Archimedes complex. She was wrong. She admits it. She feels sure lots of people will like to hear about this.

STRAWBERRY ICE CREAM

There should be nothing in strawberry ice cream but perfect strawberries, cream, and sugar. This does not seem like a very revolutionary statement, but as most strawberry ice cream is constructed of cornstarch, gelatine, milk, artificial coloring and flavoring, and powdered eggs, perhaps it is worth mentioning.

2 c. thick cream
1 qt. strawberries, picked that morning
1 c. sugar

Mash the berries with the sugar. Put them through a fine strainer or through the potato-ricer. Don't worry if there are a few seeds and an occasional bit of strawberry pulp. What kind of ice cream is this, anyway? The amounts of cream and fruit stated above give a fine pink ice cream, but one of the charms of home-made ice cream is that it is not always exactly the same. If you have not quite two cups of cream on hand, don't worry — it will just be a slightly pinker pink.

In those happy days before the Hurricane blew down Mr. Appleyard's sugar place, Mrs. Appleyard actually used to think up ways to use up maple syrup. This was one of her inventions that turned out pretty well:

MAPLE MARRON MOUSSE

1¼ c. maple syrup
Yolks of 4 eggs
2 c. heavy cream
1 c. light cream

12 marrons (the kind
in vanilla syrup)
A few grains of salt

Beat the egg yolks till they are thick and lemon colored.

Heat the syrup and pour it over them, beating it in gradually. Cook the mixture over hot water until it coats the back of the spoon. Cool — you can hasten the cooling by setting the pan in cold water with ice cubes in it. Add the marrons, cut up into small pieces, the salt, and the cream. Freeze in a hand freezer, or in the electric freezer.

This is not too bad, frozen in the refrigerator tray, if you can burden your mind with stirring it occasionally, so that the syrup will not settle at the bottom, and so that the crystals are broken up. Of course in that case you whip the cream before you add it. Pounded-up nut brittle may be substituted for the marrons. Be sure that the refrigerator is at its coldest point when you put in the mixture.

What is sadder than chocolate ice cream without enough chocolate in it? Nothing leaps to Mrs. Appleyard's mind at the moment. It ought to be dark brown and velvety, not pallid with an occasional freckle of undissolved chocolate. It may be made simply with cream (Rule I) but it is very smooth and good made with a custard (Rule II). Mrs. Appleyard lives in a dairy country where when the cream is gone that's just all there is about it, so she makes it either way according to the state of the cream supply.

CHOCOLATE ICE CREAM NO. 1

4 c. thin cream	1 t. vanilla
1 c. sugar	A few grains of salt
3 sqs. Baker's chocolate, grated	2 T. hot water

Put the grated chocolate into the top of the double boiler, add the hot water, and when the chocolate is melted add the sugar and the salt and mix well. Scald the cream — do not let it boil — and add it to the chocolate a little at a time.

If you do this carefully with the chocolate and the cream at about the same temperature, you will not find specks of chocolate in the frozen cream. Cool, add the vanilla. Freeze.

CHOCOLATE ICE CREAM NO. 2

2 c. milk	2 t. vanilla
3 T. flour sifted with a	2 c. thick cream
few grains of salt	3 sqs. Baker's chocolate,
1 c. sugar	grated
4 egg yolks	

Put the cold milk and the grated chocolate in the top of the double boiler. When the chocolate is melted, beat with a rotary beater until smooth. Mix sugar and flour and salt and stir into them enough of the milk-and-chocolate mixture to dissolve the sugar. It must be thin enough to pour, and you next pour it back into the double boiler with the rest of the milk, cover it, and cook it ten minutes, stirring occasionally.

In between times beat the egg yolks slightly, add them to the chocolate mixture, and cook one minute. Scald the cream — be sure not to boil it — and add it to the chocolate mixture, which by now should coat the back of the spoon. Add the vanilla. If by any oversight the chocolate has lumped at all, strain the mixture, but this should not be necessary if you have followed directions. If you are going to freeze it with ice and salt, cool it first. In the electric cylinder the heat will simply help to make the good freezing contact that is essential for freezing. Did any kind friend ever tell you to touch the tip of your tongue to metal on a zero day? If so, you will understand why your cylinder freezes better if it starts hot.

POUNDED NUT GLACÉ

1 c. sugar	1 c. nuts, broken in pieces

The nuts may be pecans, almonds, walnuts, cashews, or any mixed nuts you like. Do not include peanuts in the mixture, as it will taste only of peanuts. Use them separately if you like.

Put the broken nuts into a buttered pan. Melt the sugar in a frying-pan. When it is golden brown, pour it over the nuts. This is one of the things you make on a clear, crisp day. When the glacé is cool, pound it up. It's good either frozen into a mixture — such as maple mousse — or sprinkled over plain ice cream from the drugstore. So as a matter of fact is peanut brittle that you buy in a package.

Another good dodge for turning drugstore ice cream into something rich and strange is to get it ahead of time, and pack it into your refrigerator tray with the indicator set at its coldest point for an hour. Just before you serve the ice cream, cut it into rather thick slices and roll them either in nut glacé or in powdered macaroon crumbs. Put the slices on a cold platter. Sprinkle some more crumbs over the whole thing and get it to the table with what speed you can muster at that point.

Or perhaps it would be better to make

LEMON MILK SHERBET

4 c. milk	Juice of 3 large lemons
1½ c. sugar	½ t. grated lemon rind

This is for the freezer only and occurs in regions where you look in the ice chest and say: 'Goodness, how that milk is piling up! What had I better do with it? No, definitely *not* rice pudding....'

Mix the lemon juice, rind, and the sugar. Don't let the fact that the milk may separate slightly dismay you. It will smooth out as it freezes. Freeze it either in the electric cylinder or in ice and salt in the hand freezer. This is about the simplest of the frozen desserts, but it is always popular at Appleyard Centre, where it is associated with hot days when scythes are ringing and swallows are flying over the place where the green oats are falling.

If you have no milk to absorb, try

LEMON WATER ICE

4 c. water	¾ c. lemon juice
2 c. sugar	½ t. grated rind

Make a syrup of the sugar and water. Cook it for fifteen minutes. Cool it. Add the lemon juice and rind. Freeze. Three parts of ice to one of salt is a good mixture for water ice or sherbet.

RASPBERRY ICE

4 c. water	2 T. lemon juice
2 c. sugar	2 c. raspberry juice

Make a syrup of the sugar and water and boil it fifteen minutes. Cool it and add the raspberry juice. It will probably take about a quart of berries to make the two cups of juice. They should be mashed and strained through a very fine sieve. Add the lemon juice. If the raspberries are not juicy a few currants may be added. Freeze this either in three parts of ice and one of salt in the hand freezer or in the electric cylinder.

FROZEN RASPBERRIES OR STRAWBERRIES

1 qt. fruit	2 egg whites or
1 c. sugar	½ c. thick cream
1 t. lemon juice	

Mash the fruit and the sugar together. Strain the fruit through a fine sieve and add the lemon juice and freeze. Taste it and sweeten it more if necessary. Ice-cream mixtures always taste sweeter before they are frozen than they do afterward. Freeze — by hand or in the electric cylinder. When the fruit is partly frozen fold in some partly whipped cream or the whites of two eggs beaten stiff, and continue the freezing.

ORANGE ICE

2 c. water	Grated rind of 2 oranges
2 c. sugar	1 t. grated lemon rind
2 c. orange juice	¼ c. lemon juice

Make a syrup of the water and sugar. Cool the syrup, add the fruit juices and grated rind, and let it stand a few minutes so that the syrup will absorb the flavor of the rind. Strain and freeze, either by hand or in the electric cylinder.

Never grate the rind of any oranges that are marked 'Color Added' — if you like candle wax in your sherbet, add it separately. Mrs. Appleyard likes Temple oranges for sherbet. They are the natural color without benefit of colored wax, and the rind has a particularly pleasant tang.

In Mrs. Appleyard's family it is felt that there is a special

harmony between orange ice and macaroon ice cream —
with macaroons in it!

MACAROON ICE CREAM

2 c. thin cream	¾ c. sugar
2 c. thick cream	2 t. vanilla or a
2 c. macaroon crumbs	little brandy

Take fresh macaroons and dry them in a very slow oven
(250° F.). Pound them, mix the crumbs — after measuring
them — with the sugar, and stir them into the cream. If you
like vanilla, use it, but Mrs. Appleyard thinks a very little
brandy brings out the flavor of the macaroons better. It
ought not to taste of the brandy. For her a teaspoonful is
plenty.

If you are actually going to embark on the project of making macaroon ice cream and orange sherbet on the same
day, make the ice cream first and pack it when frozen into
the bottom of your deepest refrigerator tray. Then get to
work on the sherbet, which freezes more quickly and needs
less ripening. Pack it in on top of the ice cream as soon as it
is frozen and let it stand awhile. Take a day off and do this
sometime. Mrs. Appleyard made some one morning while
four men were putting up a portable garage in her back
yard. They got through before she did. The garage is still
there and the ice cream vanished twenty years ago, but she
still thinks it was worth while.

PEACH ICE CREAM

Like strawberry ice cream, Mrs. Appleyard says, peach
ice cream should never be made with a custard. Neither
peaches nor strawberries are the same fruit if they have ever

been cooked, or even if there are cooked eggs and milk with them. The fresh flavor of the fruit is so delicate that it takes very little to change it. Never use any fruit that you would not like to eat plain. This does not necessarily mean the largest and handsomest fruit, but the juiciest and sweetest. Ice cream is no better than what you put into it.

Really good sliced peaches with some thick cream to pour over them are, in Mrs. Appleyard's opinion, a much better dessert than any peach ice cream that you can buy; or than anything you can make yourself out of peaches that happened to turn out either woolly or rubbery. Alas, both these substances can lurk under a skin of perfect beauty.

Mrs. Appleyard saw some peaches once in England. They were wrapped in cotton wool and cost three shillings apiece — but perhaps she had better not bring that up now. She will sing instead of Georgia, of North Carolina, of Delaware, and mention, diffidently of course, the peaches that sometimes ripen in an inconspicuous state with an unsingable name for which she has a sneaking affection. Massachusetts is its name, and she loves it in spite of its roadside fungus of hot-dog stands and signs. Yes, in spite of its politicians and its dowagers, its poison ivy and brownstone buildings, its traffic lights and those who honk their horns thereat; in spite of the fact that its baked beans are small and slippery and its winter winds as cold as raw smoked salmon, she cherishes Massachusetts.

Has it not cranberries, the pinkest apple blossoms, the loveliest lilac plumes, Chestnut Street in Salem and Salem Gibraltars, a Sacred Cod under a golden dome, and codfish balls? Listening to the best symphony orchestra in the world are there not more women with beautiful white hair than in any other space of its size in the Western Hemisphere?

Where but in Boston and Worcester are there museums with so little pompous trash among so much that is exciting and charming? In what other city than Boston can you ride in a swan boat and chuckle over Dahl's cartoon and see sunlight through tulip petals all at the same time? For the elms on its village streets, for the Charles River winding wherever you go, for the Lynn Marshes at sunset and the Custom House Tower at sunrise, for the Berkshires folding into each other in purple haze, for small girls in riding clothes and with bands on their teeth, for skinny, lumpy boys in football helmets, for Marshfield strawberries, for Bailey's candy, for the smell of S. S. Pierce's on Christmas Eve, for snowplows with storms of silver spraying over them, for cock pheasants in the autumn woods, and for — every two or three years — a good crop of *peaches*, let us all praise Massachusetts!

Mrs. Appleyard here breathed hard and returned to the subject of . . .

PEACH ICE CREAM

2 c. light cream	2 c. peach pulp and juice
2 c. heavy cream	Peach kernels
1 c. sugar	

Peel ripe, juicy peaches and crush them through a potato-ricer. Mix with the sugar and put the bowl in the ice chest for a while. In the meantime crack two of the peach stones, blanch the kernels, and let them stand in the cream. It is a question in Mrs. Appleyard's mind as to whether this has any real effect. Probably it's only a ritual. Anyway you soon remove them; very likely a drop of almond extract would do as well. Some people add a little lemon juice, but Mrs. Appleyard sticks to her story: if the peaches are good enough, they need no other flavoring.

Now freeze the mixture, either by hand or in the electric cylinder. Slice some more peaches and serve them with it. Sprinkle a little sugar over them, but they won't need much.

Mrs. Appleyard has always wished she could make spun sugar. She loves the idea of laying white wrapping paper on the floor, putting new broomsticks between two chairs — she thinks they ought to be Hepplewhite for such an elegant process, only perhaps a Sheraton back would be a better shape — and spinning sugar over the broomsticks. However, as she realizes only too well that the result would be sugar on stove, sink, table, on her favorite painting of a white mare and a black colt — which she keeps in her kitchen because she likes art where she can see it — and of course the ceiling, she has so far denied herself this pleasure. Still, the day may come, and when it does she can be counted upon to tell about it. Up to that time she thinks you had better buy spun sugar from the caterer.

13

Meat: from Roast Through Hash. Just because Mrs. Appleyard says nothing about roasting beef, lamb, or veal is no sign that she is the only one of Les Amies de Françoise Fermière that cannot put a piece of meat into the oven, and take it out again later in a fair state of preservation. Others, notably the patron saint of the order, have covered the topic so thoroughly that to read the average cookbook you would think that people had a tip of the sirloin every day or so. Mrs. Appleyard, with a humble bow, leaves them the field, and the problem of what to do with the cold lamb, and turns her attention to the other days. You might, for instance, be thinking wistfully about the time you had

CURRIED CHICKEN (S. E. D.)

A 6-lb. fowl (or two 3½-lb. roasting chickens)	2 onions
	Sprig of parsley
1 stalk celery	½ t. pepper
1 carrot	1 t. salt

Have the fowl cut up at the market and simmer it for

two and a half hours with the vegetables. Add the salt and pepper the last half-hour. Take the meat out, separate it from the skin and bones, return the bones to the broth and cook them for another hour. Strain the broth and set it aside to cool. Skim off the fat.

For the sauce:

> 4 t. butter
> 4 t. flour
> 2 T. curry powder

Melt the butter (you may use some of the chicken fat if you prefer), and when it bubbles, rub in the flour and the curry powder. (If you like it very hot, add more of the powder.) Stir the chicken broth into it. The broth should be cooked down so that there are four cups of it. Let it simmer awhile until the flour is thoroughly cooked and the curry powder well blended in. Then add the chicken and set the pan where it will barely simmer while you are cooking the rice. Just before you serve the sauce, add a cup of thick cream. Mrs. Appleyard generally begins this sauce by frying minced onion, but that is not necessary unless you like, as there was onion cooked in the broth anyway. Optional also is about half a cup of strained apple sauce made from tart apples. If you use it, add it when you add the chicken.

The rice for curry is as important as the curry itself, Mrs. Appleyard says. You can spoil a good curry by serving soggy rice with it. The rice should be fluffy, and each kernel should stand apart from the others and yet it should not be really dry. Each grain should have a chance to take up all the water it really needs. To do that, it must be well washed. That, to Mrs. Appleyard, means changing the water twelve times. Probably this is more than is strictly necessary, but she would rather wash it too much than not enough.

For one cup of rice she has three quarts of water boiling violently with one tablespoonful of salt in it. She drops the washed and drained rice in so slowly that the water never stops boiling. She cooks it uncovered, until the kernels are soft, not mushy, when felt between the thumb and forefinger — about twenty minutes. Then she puts it into a colander and pours hot water over it. This removes any starch that has not been washed away and makes the grains separate. After letting the rice drain a few minutes, she sets the colander into a warm oven with the door open so that the rice can warm and dry out.

When she is ready to serve the curry she has a large, hot platter ready. She takes a teacup, fills it with the rice, and turns the rice out in small mounds around the platter. Then she pours the curried chicken into the middle of the platter and serves it.

In the meantime her daughters have set nine Sandwich-glass dishes — eight small ones and one large one — on a big tray and have been busy filling them with the following things: chopped white of hard-boiled eggs, grated yolks of hard-boiled eggs, finely minced raw onion, finely chopped parsley, red tomato relish, piccalilli, shredded coconut — fresh, if possible — chopped peanuts, Major Grey's or Colonel Skinner's chutney. The large dish is for the chutney.

Each guest takes a mound of rice, covers it with curry, then helps himself to any combination of relishes that he likes — generally, Mrs. Appleyard notices, he takes some of each — and mixes everything together. Fried bananas are also served with this, and the dessert is something cooling — lemon sherbet, for instance.

CURRY OF LAMB

Curry of lamb is very much like chicken curry. The great point about a meat curry is that it should be made from meat cooked for the purpose and not from dry chips of roast meat that you can't think what else to do with. You need stock for the sauce, and the way to get it is out of the meat you are going to have in the curry. A less expensive curry than the chicken kind described above is made from a shoulder of lamb, cut up at the market and treated just like the chicken. The only difference is that instead of the cream that you put in the sauce you add a cup of tomato purée. Mrs. Appleyard, being languid about the purée process, uses a can of thick tomato soup for this. Be sure to get your lamb broth cool enough so that you can get all the fat off before you start to make your sauce. Almost no one really loves mutton fat.

Serve the relishes just as you would with the chicken curry, or substitute any you may prefer. A little green-apple sauce is rather good for one. Some people put tart apples into the sauce. They should be so tender that they cook down and disappear. Four apples, peeled and quartered, is about right for two cups of sauce. Mint jelly goes well with lamb curry. Have whatever you like, only it's fun to have a lot of kinds to choose from.

BEEF CURRY

This is a short cut for times when you feel both economical and hurried. Cook your rice as above. Make your stock from canned consommé or bouillon. Add a can of tomato soup, a cup of cream, two tablespoonfuls of curry powder, more if you like it very hot. Have a pound and a half of the bottom of the round ground twice. Make it into cakes and broil it. Put it on the platter with the mounds of rice around it, pour the curry sauce over it. Serve it with a lot of relishes, one of which had better be mustard pickle.

MRS. APPLEYARD'S VEAL LOAF

2 lbs. of veal and 1 lb. of lean pork
Put twice through the grinder together

½ lb. calves' liver	1 t. white pepper
½ lb. baked ham	1½ t. salt
2 truffles	1 t. Bell's poultry seasoning
6 Montpelier or Boston	⅛ t. thyme
Common crackers	4 slices of bacon
2 eggs, well beaten	1 T. flour
2 large onions	1 T. butter

The marketman will grind the veal and pork together for you. Cook the liver the day before, blanching it and simmering it till tender, and chop it very fine. Mrs. Appleyard generally uses ham cut from a ham that she has baked herself because she is likely to serve ham sliced thin along with the veal loaf, but a slice of boiled ham half an inch thick cut into dice will do.

She begins by chopping the onions very fine and then chopping the liver into them and then the veal and the pork until everything is well mixed. She rolls the crackers into fine crumbs, mixes the seasonings with them, and mixes them in. Next go in the beaten eggs, and last of all the ham cubes and the sliced truffles if you can get them. Their nutty fragrance is delicious with the veal and pork.

Now she butters a bread tin and puts in the mixture, pressing it well into the corners. She dredges the top with flour and a few very fine crumbs and covers it with the bacon cut into small strips. She sets the pan on a rack in a covered roaster, surrounds it with water, and bakes it for two and a half hours at 375° F., reducing the heat if it seems to be getting too brown, and adding more water until the last half-hour. Be sure to chill it thoroughly before serving. This slices beautifully. Mrs. Appleyard generally serves with it Mushroom Sauce (page 257), sliced baked ham, and Vegetable Salad (page 244).

VEAL–AND–HAM PIE (MRS. APPLEYARD)

Mr. Appleyard once caused a waiter in an English restaurant great pain by sending back the veal-and-ham pie with the indestructible crust, saying — to Mrs. Appleyard — that he preferred what he had at home. She was both pleased and embarrassed by this tribute. Since hers can actually be bitten into, she does think that perhaps Mr. Appleyard was right. Veal-and-ham pie, like other things in England, is wonderful if you get it at the right place — even better than Mrs. Appleyard's. (This is just an attack of false modesty on his wife's part, Mr. Appleyard says loyally. If you get a pie that has been made since George the Fourth was king you are lucky, and even then Mrs. Appleyard's is just as good.) Well, leaving history out of it this is how she makes a small one.

2 lbs. veal cutlet	1 sprig parsley
2 lbs. veal bones	Bit of bay leaf
1 lb. baked ham (page 183)	1 t. pepper
1 carrot	1 t. salt
2 onions	4 hard-boiled eggs
1 T. poultry seasoning	

Cover the veal and the bones with cold water, add the

seasonings and the onions, let it come to the boiling point slowly, and simmer for two hours. Remove the meat from the broth and cut the veal into small pieces. Cook the broth down until there is only a pint of it. Butter a baking-dish, put in the veal mixed with the ham, which may be either cut in small cubes or sliced very thin. Use only the lean part of the ham. Put in a layer of the meat, then thick slices of the hard-boiled eggs around the sides, then the rest of the meat. Add half the broth. Cover the pie with pastry; you know — *pastry* (page 212), not a tough overcoat of flour and water. Leave a hole in the crust. Bake the pie one hour at 375° F. When the crust is a good brown, take out the pie and pour the rest of the broth through the hole in the pastry, using a small funnel.

Serve it cold. The broth jellies among the pieces of meat. This is very good served with a green salad — also filling.

LAMB CHOPS DE LUXE (FOR SIX)

6 kidney chops, cut thick	¼ lb. sausage meat
6 mushroom caps	Salt
1 t. minced onion	Pepper

Have the chops cut from a large loin, double thick, and have them boned. Mix the sausage meat with the onion, fill the mushroom caps with the mixture, wrap the tails of the chops around the mushrooms and fasten them with skewers or sew them into place.

Have the broiler very hot. Sear the chops on both sides for a minute on each side — time it carefully — turning them with two pancake-turners. Lower the heat and cook the chops five minutes on each side if you like them rare, or seven minutes on each side if you like them well done.

Serve with potato balls rolled in chopped parsley and buttered and Mint Butter or Mint and Currant Sauce.

MINT BUTTER

Mint leaves
Butter
Paprika

Chop enough mint leaves to make three tablespoonfuls. Cream two tablespoonfuls butter and work in the mint leaves. Spread it on the chops just as they come out of the oven and dust them with the paprika.

MINT AND CURRANT JELLY SAUCE

2 T. mint leaves, finely minced   1 t. grated lemon rind
6-oz. glass of currant jelly   ¼ c. hot water

Heat the water, put in the jelly, lemon rind, and the mint leaves. When the jelly is melted and starts to bubble, the sauce is ready to serve. Serve it in a silver bowl with a silver ladle. Some other kind will do, but the color is nice with silver.

CLUB SANDWICHES

The Appleyards prefer their club sandwiches made with two pieces of toast to the ordinary three-decker style, which always seems to consist, somehow, chiefly of toast. The best ones, they think, are those made on the Consumers' Cooperative plan: one person makes the toast, another cooks the bacon, a third slices olives, tomatoes, and onions. A fourth gets the chicken and lettuce ready. Each person puts his own sandwich together and is soon back for another. After the first round it is a question of making your own toast and assembling the filling from what you find on various platters. After a while you get down to dark meat and cooking some more bacon, but by then it is generally too dark to see. You have beer to drink with these, if you like, and you eat them in front of an open fire. Mrs. Appleyard feels she could do with a round pretty soon.

MUSHROOM CLUB SANDWICH

For each sandwich:

2 slices of buttered toast	1 t. cream
2 strips of cooked bacon	¼ t. salt
4 large mushroom caps	1 t. butter
1 slice of broiled tomato	1 stuffed olive
Grated onion	

Peel the mushrooms. Chop the stems fine and fry them in butter with the grated onion. Add the cream. Spread the toasted side of the bread lightly with the mixture. Broil the mushroom caps, the sliced tomato, and the bacon, dotting the mushrooms and the tomatoes with butter and sprinkling them with salt and a very little pepper. Cover the mushroom toast with lettuce leaf, mayonnaise, tomato and bacon, and the mushroom caps. Decorate the top slice with lettuce, bacon, and half a stuffed olive. These can be put together on the assembly-line system too.

CHICKEN

Beef coming chiefly off cows, lamb generally leaping straight from field to frying-pan, fish, on the other hand, swimming in all too leisurely from the sea, the Appleyards, when in Appleyard Centre, eat a great deal of chicken.

Rhode Island Reds doubtless thrive splendidly in their native state, but they cannot well be better than when they have been brought up among the Green Mountains.

PAN-BROILED CHICKENS (WHITE MEAT ONLY)

Breasts of young chickens that weigh at least 3½ lbs.
Allow one wing and breast piece for each person

Large tomatoes, thickly sliced	Parsley
Sliced bacon	Salt
Wild mushrooms (*Agaricus campestris*)	Paprika
Sweet potatoes	Butter

Put some butter in a large frying-pan and brown the chicken breasts in it lightly. Transfer them to a large dripping-pan and set it into the oven. Cover the pan and cook the chicken for forty minutes at 400° F. Then take off the top pan, put the bacon over the chickens, and cook ten minutes longer.

In the meantime you have parboiled the sweet potatoes and cut them into thick slices. Spread them with butter and sprinkle them lightly with salt and pepper. Broil them till they are a good brown and arrange them around a large hot platter. The mushroom caps are to be broiled too. They take less time than the potatoes and had better be done separately unless you are sure you can manage them with the potatoes. Either broil the tomatoes with the potatoes or dip them in milk and then in seasoned flour and fry them in the same pan in which you browned the chicken. Put them on the hot platter. The chicken is almost done now, so you had better make the gravy.

GRAVY FOR PAN-BROILED CHICKENS

You are saving the livers for a purpose to be disclosed later, so you will use only the gizzards and hearts, which you have been simmering all the morning with salt, pepper, and some slices of onion. Before you began to broil the potatoes you minced the gizzard and the onion very fine. From the pan in which the chickens are cooking take three tablespoonfuls of fat. Put this into the frying-pan that has been your best friend all the morning and when it is hot, rub in three tablespoons of flour sifted with one half-teaspoonful of salt and a little pepper. Then add the minced giblets and onions and cook gently for three minutes. Stir in the juice in which they were cooked and add one tablespoon of thick sour cream, a cup of sweet cream, and a teaspoonful of finely minced parsley. If your cream supply is running low, use a little milk. This makes enough gravy for four people and some left over for the next day, on which Mrs. Appleyard fixes her eagle eye, because she has plans about it. Perhaps she had better tabulate the directions for the gravy, although making it is one of those affairs where you may have to vary it from day to day.

CREAM GIBLET GRAVY (FOR SIX)

Gizzards and hearts of 3 chickens	$\frac{1}{4}$ t. pepper
1 onion	1 c. juice from giblets
3 T. fat from the pan	1 T. thick sour cream
3 T. flour	1 c. sweet cream
$\frac{1}{2}$ t. salt	1 t. minced parsley

Put the gravy in the tureen — the one with the tiny sprigs of flowers that was Mr. Appleyard's grandmother's and that has the ladle to match. Put the chicken breasts and bacon in the middle of the big hot platter with the fluted green edge — the platter that Mrs. Appleyard found in the back buttery. The tomatoes and sweet potatoes and mushrooms are already on it. Pour any juice that is left in the pan over the chickens. Garnish with parsley.

'I suppose that is all you had,' the Editor said to Mrs. Appleyard.

'Well, we did have some raspberry and currant jelly, and I happened to have pretty good luck with my mint chutney, so I just put on a little for them to taste, and Stan brought in a few peas he'd picked about half an hour before dinner, so we had those, and I put on a few new potatoes in their jackets in case anyone didn't like sweet ——'

'And dessert?'

'Oh — I hardly remember. Probably just some wild raspberries and cream and cottage cheese and some oatmeal cookies.'

'Stop! Stop!' said the Editor. 'You're making me cry. . . .'

'Perhaps,' said Mrs. Appleyard, kindly, at this juncture, 'you would like to hear what became of the second joints and drumsticks of the chicken. Of course it was company that got the white pieces. The family had to put up with the rest.

'You had better,' she said, sandpapering a cradle about two inches long that she was making for some sinister purpose of her own, 'start this some morning when you ought to be doing something else you don't want to do, because this dish will take you all the morning. I call it

CHICKEN POCKETBOOKS

6 second joints and drum- sticks of 3½-lb. chickens	½ t. Bell's seasoning
	2 mushroom caps, chopped
⅓ loaf of French bread	3 chicken livers
6 T. cream	1 small onion
⅔ c. giblet gravy	½ c. sausage meat,
(left over)	preferably Montpelier
1 t. salt	4 T. butter, melted

'You take the bones out of the second joints and drumsticks.' (This sounds easy, but Mrs. Appleyard admits that she often uses three knives, the kitchen shears, and the poultry clippers. However, it must be possible for the least athletic, since she does it.)   Dry the bread, cut into slices, and pound it into fine crumbs. Mix it with the cream, gravy, seasonings, and mushrooms. Mince the livers fine with the onion and the piece of sausage meat and combine the mixtures. If it seems too moist, add a few more bread crumbs. It should hold its shape.

'Stuff it into the places where the bones were, folding back the drumstick part. Either tie the whole thing up or sew it with heavy linen thread. Toothpicks come in handy in this project. Manage it without sewing if possible, be-cause you won't enjoy unsewing it at the last minute.

'Put the pockets in a buttered pan in the oven, brush them over with melted butter, and cook them for forty min-utes at 450° F. The pan should be covered. Uncover them after the forty minutes, put strips of bacon over them, and cook them until the bacon is the way you like it — ten to fifteen minutes.

'You had all the peas that were ready from the garden yesterday. Today you will have innocent young beets — and save a few and their juice to make bortsch tomorrow. There will be no gravy, so the potatoes will be creamed (page 305). There are still some oatmeal cookies left, a hiding-place having been found in one of Great-Grand-mother Appleyard's covered dishes. It is still raspberry time, so the dessert is Raspberry Ice (page 156). Any com-plaints?'

When the chickens get big enough, Mrs. Appleyard says, they will be roasted. It would be hard indeed to roast one of Leonard Bealls's Rhode Island Reds so that it wasn't good. You'd have to make a real business of spoiling it. However, part of the goodness is in the stuffing. In Mrs. Appleyard's theory of life, stuffing should not be a highly seasoned mass of wet dough but a delicately flavored trap for the juice of the roasting birds. This is how she goes about it.

STUFFING — FOR THREE SMALL CHICKENS OR TWO
LARGE ONES

5 c. French bread crumbs	½ c. milk (part cream)
2 Montpelier crackers, or common crackers	2 large onions, finely minced
½ c. butter	2 t. Bell's seasoning
2 T. sausage meat	1½ t. salt
2 eggs	½ t. pepper

The chickens have been brushed inside with soft butter and are covered outside with a blanket of butter and seasoned flour. This is in addition to the butter in the stuffing.

Slice the French bread and dry it in the oven. Make it into fine crumbs, using crust and all. Roll the crackers fine and mix them with the bread crumbs and dry seasonings. Add the minced onion and chop in the sausage meat. Add the melted butter, the eggs lightly beaten, and the milk. This stuffing may seem rather dry when you put it in, but it will moisten during cooking. It will also swell a little, so do not pack it in too tightly. You may add a little chopped celery if you have it, but it is not necessary.

Make the gravy for these chickens like the gravy for Pan-Broiled Chickens (page 171), only use the livers as well as the gizzards.

Mrs. Appleyard's father always liked bread sauce with roast chicken and she sometimes makes it still, to go either with chicken, turkey, or Guinea chickens.

BREAD SAUCE

2 c. milk	½ t. salt
1 c. dried French bread crumbs	¼ t. white pepper
(inside of loaf only)	⅛ t. nutmeg
½ small onion	1 bay leaf
3 T. butter	1 sprig of parsley

Tear out the inside of the loaf, dry it in the oven, and roll it into crumbs. Be sure that it does not brown. Sift it, saving the coarser crumbs — about half a cup. Put the fine ones into the top of the double boiler with the milk, onion, and seasonings. Cook fifteen minutes. Skim out the bay leaf, onion, and parsley. Add a tablespoon of the butter.

Now fry the coarse crumbs in the rest of the butter. It should froth before you add the crumbs. Cook them until they are a light golden brown — about two minutes. Stir them all the time so that they will not burn. Put the sauce into a hot tureen, and sprinkle the bread crumbs over it.

This sauce is not like a poultice.

It is fun to cook things *sous cloche*, but if you do not have the cloches you can get nearly the same effect, Mrs. Appleyard has discovered, with covered Pyrex dishes: — that is, the same effect so far as the taste is concerned. You don't of course get quite the illusion that you are lunching at the Ritz.

When the chickens still weigh about two pounds apiece, this is a good way to use the breasts.

BREASTS OF CHICKEN UNDER GLASS (FOR SIX PEOPLE)

Breasts of 3 broilers	6 slices of very dry toast
1 qt. chicken stock	2 T. butter

6 thin slices of baked ham	½ t. salt
24 mushroom caps	¼ t. pepper
2 c. cream	½ t. paprika
1 onion, finely minced	

Cook the chicken breasts in a covered pan in the stock to which you have added the salt, pepper, and onion — for ten minutes. Use canned chicken soup if you have no stock on hand. Have ready the toast lightly buttered, cut to fit the bottoms of the baking-dishes. Butter the baking-dishes. Put in the toast and cover it with the slices of ham, cut the same size. (In emergencies Mrs. Appleyard sometimes spreads the toast with devilled ham.) Cook the broth down so that there is two cups of it. In another pan melt two table-spoons of butter. When it froths blend the flour with it and let it cook slowly for three minutes. Pour the broth on slowly, stirring it well. As it thickens, add the cream. Set the pan where it will just simmer. Put the chicken breasts on the toast and ham, surround the chicken with the peeled mush-rooms. Pour some of the sauce over each of the chicken breasts. Cover the dishes tightly and set them into a mod-erately hot oven (475° F.) for half an hour. Serve them while the sauce is still bubbling hot.

It is easier for the guest, Mrs. Appleyard thinks, if the dishes are set on separate plates in front of the dinner plate, not on it. That is because on his own plate, before the meal has progressed very far, he will find Spoon Bread (page 49), young peas and carrots cooked together, and some of Mrs. Appleyard's currant jelly. The dessert is as likely as not to be a wreath of dark red strawberries with their hulls on and a mound of powdered sugar in the middle and a big lemon sponge cake, torn to pieces with two forks — not cut with a knife.

The next day the family will get the second joints, broiled with bacon, string beans cut very thin and left to mellow in cream and butter for half an hour before they are served, Watermelon Pickle (page 209) and, as the oven is not being used for anything else, Strawberry Shortcake (page 105).

CHICKEN PIE

Mrs. Appleyard sometimes uses chickens for this, but she thinks that young fowls really have more flavor. They should weigh at least five pounds.

For ten people:

2 5-lb. fowls	1 T. salt
3 onions, sliced	⅛ t. pepper

Begin the day before you are going to make your pies. Have the fowls cleaned and cut up, each into eight pieces. Put the meat and the onions into a large kettle. Cover the meat with cold water, bring it slowly to the boil, and cook slowly for three hours. During the last hour add the seasonings. When the meat falls from the bones, set a large colander into another kettle and pour the meat into it. Strain the broth and set it away to cool. Now pick over the meat, removing the skin and the bones. Save them, put them back into the first kettle, cover them with water, add a teaspoon of salt, and cook them for at least two hours. Strain this broth and set it away to cool. In the morning skim the fat off the two bowls of broth. If the broth has not jellied, put both lots into one kettle and cook a little longer. There should be about two quarts of the jellied chicken stock.

Now put the chicken into a large shallow baking-dish. There are some Bennington ones like old tortoiseshell that

have always been in the pantry for the last century that
Mrs. Appleyard likes, but if they are busy in some other
good work she uses a four-quart milk pan. Whichever it is,
she butters it lightly and puts in the meat.

Next she makes a sauce with the chicken stock, using

> 4 T. chicken fat
> skimmed from the stock
> 4 T. flour
> 2 qts. stock

She melts the chicken fat; when it is hot she works the
flour into it and lets it cook very gently for three minutes.
Then she stirs in the chicken stock slowly, tastes it, adds
more salt if necessary, lets it simmer for a few minutes, and
pours enough of it over the meat to cover it well. Then she
sets the pan into the oven (475° F.), and while the pie is
heating she stirs up some Sour-Milk Biscuits.

SOUR-MILK BISCUITS (FOR TEN PEOPLE)

2⅔ c. flour	¾ t. salt
½ t. soda	6 T. butter
2 t. baking powder	1 c. thick sour milk

Sift the flour with the baking powder and salt and soda
three times. Work in the butter with the fingertips, cut in
the sour milk with a knife. The mixture should be rather
stiff. Taste it to be sure you have not put in too much soda.
Add a little more milk and flour if you have. As soon as the
chicken broth is bubbling hard around the meat, drop the
dough in small lumps on top of it. Bake the pie until the
biscuits are brown — about thirty-five minutes in a hot
oven — 475°-500° F. If you have no sour milk, use the rule
for Baking-Powder Biscuits (page 34), but add extra butter
and do not roll out the dough but drop it on in lumps.

Serve Giblet Gravy with this, made as on page 172. You made it some time earlier when there was a free moment. If you were able to save any of the chicken stock for it, put it in, but it is good made with the water the giblets were cooked in. At the chicken-pie dinners in the church in Gospel Hollow they always serve with the pie white cabbage, finely shredded, mixed with salad dressing, pickled beets, mashed potato, pickles, and six kinds of pie for dessert.

Mrs. Appleyard, not requiring potato on top of pie for building up her silhouette, serves thick slices of tomatoes with French dressing. She says you don't know what a tomato is unless you have eaten them in Vermont fresh from your neighbor's garden. On the same principle — care for the hostess and her figure problem (as it is so elegantly called in the specialty shops) — you will not get six kinds of pie for dessert — or even one — but just some Dutchess apple sauce and cottage cheese with perhaps a few Brownies in case the chicken pie did not take the edge off your appetite.

Chicken is good, but life would be monotonous if you ate nothing else. In fact after two or three days of chicken Mrs. Appleyard notices that the family turns kindly eyes upon the humble dried beef. In Vermont dried beef does not mean something you get in a four-ounce jar with a fancy label. It comes off a large hunk of something that looks like petrified wood from somewhere near the Painted Desert. You buy it where you buy the Montpelier sausage and stand there while a machine of more than human skill shaves it into dark red translucent sheets that curl as they fall.

Mr. Appleyard once came home reporting that he did not approve of the new clerk who cut the beef for him.

'He saw the scales go down and took off two slices,' Mr. Appleyard reported. 'They can't have weighed more than half a picture postcard.'

Mrs. Appleyard made suitable sounds of disapproval over such ill-timed parsimony, and said, a little nervously, 'Did you say anything?'

'No,' replied her husband and favorite marketer. 'I just picked them up and ate them. . . .'

This is how Mrs. Appleyard cooked that accurately weighed half-pound of dried beef.

DRIED BEEF IN CREAM

½ lb. dried beef	1 c. sweet cream
2 T. sour cream	4 hard-boiled eggs, sliced
2 T. butter	½ t. paprika
1 c. milk	3 T. flour

Freshen the beef by pouring hot water on it, letting it stand ten minutes and draining it. Make the sauce by putting the butter into a pan, heating it till it froths, rubbing in the flour, cooking it slowly for three minutes, then adding the sour cream (lower the heat while you are doing this), the sweet cream, and the milk. Put it where it will just simmer, add the dried beef and the sliced hard-boiled eggs. There should be lots of sauce. If it gets too thick add a little more milk and cream.

Serve it with the first new potatoes that are big enough to bake, or with mashed potato. Once at a friend's house Mrs. Appleyard had it poured over French toast made by dipping stale bread in a batter of milk, eggs, and salt and browning it on both sides in a well-buttered frying-pan. That was quite an experience — she's hoping for another invitation.

If you serve the beef with baked potatoes, give the customers a chance to get their potatoes ready, mashing butter and pepper and salt into them, before you pass the dried beef.

FRIED SALT PORK WITH SOUR-CREAM GRAVY

This is a favorite Vermont dish and is made in about as many ways as there are cooks. Naturally Mr. Appleyard thinks that his mother's way was the best, and this is how she used to do it.

Boil a chunk of salt pork for an hour. Drain it, cool it a little, cut it into slices a quarter-inch thick. Dip them in milk, then in flour. Fry them rather slowly until they are a light cracker brown on both sides. Remove them from the pan and put them on a platter that is covered with brown paper to absorb any surplus fat. Cook the fat in the pan down so that there is only two tablespoonfuls or pour off some of it. Work in two tablespoonfuls of flour. Add half a cup of thick sour cream and half a cup of sweet cream. Cook very gently until the gravy has thickened. Serve the pork on a hot platter and the gravy in a hot tureen.

Baked potatoes with this, please, Mr. Appleyard says, a green vegetable — beet greens, spinach, Swiss chard — and something tart and sour for a relish — piccalilli, perhaps. Lemon Milk Sherbet (page 155) for dessert.

One of the great steps in the march of progress, Mrs. Appleyard says, was when hams began to appear already boiled and wrapped in silver paper, preferably with holly and mistletoe printed on it. Oh, well, there's no special objection to Easter lilies, but the notion that hams are especially appropriate to Easter is, in her opinion, just something thought up by the same people who have decided that Mothers' Day is a lovely opportunity to give your mother everything from a polo mallet to a knitted shawl. Mrs. Appleyard has laid down the principle that she expects her children to treat her nicely three hundred and sixty-five days in the year and one extra on Leap Year. She looks with no favor on the idea of being forgotten on three hundred and sixty-four of them and remembered on the odd one with a sense of guilt, carnations, and a hot-water bottle.

Ham, she says, is good on Easter, Mothers' Day, or Labor Day, but on the whole she likes it best in cold weather when she has fresh cider to pour around it.

BAKED HAM

A ham — weight after boiling 10 lbs.	3 c. cider
1 c. French bread crumbs	Whole cloves
½ c. light brown sugar (or maple sugar)	½ t. cinnamon

Skin the ham, if it has not been skinned already. If you have boiled it yourself for the last twelve hours, let it cool a little. Then take a knife and score the fat across diagonally with the lines about three-fourths of an inch apart, so that it is marked off diagonally into fine diamonds. Dry the French bread and roll it into very fine crumbs. Mix the crumbs with the sugar and cinnamon and rub about half of the mixture into the fat of the ham. Then press the cloves into the points at which the scored lines cross. Sprinkle the rest of the crumb mixture over the ham, put it on a rack in the dripping-pan, pour the cider around it, and bake it slowly at 375° F. until it is brown, basting it from time to time with the cider. It should be baked for at least forty-five minutes. Reduce the heat if it seems to be browning too quickly.

The cider should have been kept long enough in a cold place so that it has just started to fizz a little.

Pineapple juice or ginger ale may be used when cider is not available. If you are going to serve it hot, put pineapple slices around it. Baste them as the ham cooks and serve them on the platter with it. Add a little red wine if you like it.

A small shoulder is good, done the same way and served hot with pineapple, spinach, and Corn Pudding (page 51).

There is a lot of solid comfort in having a ham in the house, but ultimately it gets to the point where it seems that grinding it up would have to be its reward from a grateful public. This reminds Mrs. Appleyard that she had better make

HAM MOUSSE

2 c. cold baked ham, ground fine	1 t. dry mustard
1 T. Minute gelatine	⅛ t. cayenne
½ c. hot water	½ c. thick cream

This is for a small mould for about six people.

Dissolve the gelatine in the hot water, add the ham pounded in a mortar after you have ground it. Be sure to use only lean meat. Beat the cream stiff and add the seasonings (add a teaspoonful of horse-radish if you like it) and mix well with the meat. Dip a mould in ice water, put in the mixture. Chill thoroughly in the refrigerator for at least three hours. Remove it from the mould. Serve it with Mushroom Sauce (page 257).

HASH

A certain relative of Mrs. Appleyard's gives the following rule for hash.

'Look longingly,' he says, 'at the roast of beef while it goes through the stages of hot with Yorkshire pudding and cold with salad. When you have cut yourself off enough for a bedtime sandwich from the last chunk that is in the ice chest, put on an appealing expression and ask your hostess if she is considering *hash*. A few blandishments about how you haven't forgotten that day, etc. . . . and how hers is really etc. etc., *ad lib.* . . . come in well here. You might also remind her that you noticed a bone from a porterhouse steak, too.'

She will then proceed as follows.

She hews the meat into gobbets. (Hash is a manly dish and calls for strong measures — and expressions.) She hurls them into a saucepan with a big onion hacked into chunks.

'Do not,' she says firmly, waving a large knife in a way calculated to produce respect for her advice, 'try to make hash by putting meat through the grinder and using odds and ends of potato, boiled, mashed, or baked. Take the long view; give such trifles to the hens or the pig and get them back later in edible form.

'Cover the meat — accompanied, of course, by its bosom friend the onion — with water and let it cook slowly till it is tender and most of the water has cooked away. Salt it during the last half-hour of cooking. When the meat is done, put on the potatoes and parboil them twenty minutes. They *must* be freshly cooked (furious wave with the knife). Cook enough so that you will have rather more potato than meat — three cups of potato to two of meat is about right. While the potatoes are cooking take out the meat and the onion from the pan. Let the broth go on cooking until there is only half a cup of it to two cups of meat. Pick over the meat carefully, removing any gristle and any large pieces of fat, and the bones. Very small pieces of fat may stay in. The meat should be so tender that it falls apart.

'Now try out the large pieces of fat in an iron frying-pan. Perhaps you saved the fat that ran down from the roast while you were cooking it, and perhaps if you were prudent you may have a cup that will have some of the dish gravy in it. It will consist of some garnet-colored juice or jelly and some creamy fat on top. Put the juice in the broth and use the fat for frying the hash. However, the tried-out kind will do very well, and failing either you may use butter. You are not, though, quite ready for the frying-pan yet.

'Chop the meat,' Mrs. Appleyard says, 'in a wooden chopping-bowl — a big one. As soon as the potatoes are ready, chop them in with the meat, not too fine. If you have two cups of meat with three cups of potatoes it will be just about the right amount for your large frying-pan — that big black one. Now add the broth that you have been cooking down.

'Heat the fat in the frying-pan. There must be plenty. It should cover the bottom of the pan and be at least a quarter of an inch deep. If there is not enough beef fat, add some butter. Put in the hash, mix it well for a minute or two over a hot fire. Then reduce the heat and let it cook slowly for about twenty minutes. You may like to do this on the bottom shelf of the oven if you do not interfere with anything else you are cooking. You may also set it on a flat gas toaster over one of the burners with the flame turned low. Whichever you do, watch it as a cat watches a robin's nest and when it is well browned around the edges, take it out.'

'That sounds easy,' Mrs. Appleyard's relative says, 'and apparently it is, if you have the muscles of Joe Louis and the dexterity of Houdini. Mrs. Appleyard begins by making a cut across the middle of the pan at right angles to the handle. She rests the pan on a platter hot enough to scorch the finish off any table not finished with linseed oil and elbow grease (Advt.), and with the pancake-turner she folds the half of the hash toward the handle over the lower half, as you would an omelet, and then teases the whole thing out onto the platter. It was a glazed, beautiful brown, like an old cherry table (one without shellac, of course), and it tasted like...' Finding no suitable comparison the speaker added weakly, '... like hash. How singularly fortunate I was to have allied myself with such a family!' he concluded with feeling, for affection for a good pan of hash is one of the keenest emotions known to man....

Mr. Appleyard sometimes likes poached eggs with hash. Mrs. Appleyard accordingly serves them, generally muttering something about painting lilies. She thinks her own brand of chutney (page 202) and some scalloped tomatoes go pretty well with it.

DUCKS WITH ORANGES IN CASSEROLE

2 young ducks	4 Temple oranges, rind
6 small carrots, sliced	and juice
2 c. peas, shelled	1 glass currant jelly
3 onions, sliced	¼ c. red wine
1 c. lima beans	1 t. salt
6 slices bacon	½ t. paprika

Have the ducklings cut in serving pieces at the market. Put a rack in your roaster. Put a cupful of water in the bottom of it, put in the vegetables. Some other combination will do, but have a variety. This is a good way to use frozen vegetables when fresh ones are hard to get.

Brown the pieces of duck in a frying-pan for a few minutes and lay them over the vegetables. Cover the roaster and cook for one hour at 375° F. Now have your individual casserole dishes ready — Mexican, French, Pyrex glass are all good. Make a brown gravy from the juice in your roaster, using two tablespoons of flour, well browned, the juice of the oranges and their grated rind, the currant jelly, and the red wine. Add the salt and pepper and paprika. Taste it and season it more highly if you wish. Put some of the vegetables into each casserole, put the pieces of duck on top. Add some of the sauce. Put on top a rosette of mashed potato sprinkled with a little more of the orange peel and some chopped parsley. Put a slice of bacon that has been partly cooked (there is enough fat from the ducks already in the dish) on top of the potato. Set the casseroles into the oven for a few minutes at 475° F., just long enough to finish cooking the bacon and to be sure that everything has blended and that the gravy is sizzling hot.

As this is the whole meal, meat and vegetables, in one dish, serve with it only some crusty rolls and some red wine. For dessert some plain lettuce salad made at the table with French dressing, toasted crackers, and cheese.

ROAST PORK

7-lb. loin of pork	*Mixed Vegetables*
1 t. poultry dressing	Peas
½ t. paprika	Carrots
4 T. flour	Wax and string beans
1 t. salt	Celery, finely cut
¼ t. cinnamon	Onions
1¾ t. cloves	

Have the loin cut so that it is easy to carve it into chops.

Sift the flour and seasonings together and rub the mixture well into the surface of the meat.

Have the oven hot — 500° F. — put the pork on a rack in the roaster and cook it for ten minutes uncovered. Then reduce the heat to 300° F. and add a little water and cook the pork for two and a half hours. Then put the vegetables around the pork and cook covered for an hour longer. If it has not browned enough, cook it uncovered for a few minutes longer while you are preparing the gravy, which you make by thickening the gravy in the pan with some well-browned flour. Put the meat and the vegetables on a hot platter and pour the gravy over them. Serve with mashed potato and green apple sauce made from early summer apples — Dutchess or yellow transparents.

For dessert: blackberries, lemon queens.

Sometimes Mrs. Appleyard varies this by cooking whatever vegetables she is going to cook separately, and the last half-hour putting around the pork a dressing made like the chicken stuffing on page 175, only moistening it with an extra egg and a little more cream. When this is brown she cuts it into squares and puts it around the pork. She makes a brown gravy with the juice and serves it separately. It is necessary to cook pork thoroughly and it is hard to cook it too long, provided you do not let it dry up. Never try to get it ready unless you have plenty of time.

POT ROAST OF BEEF

7 lbs. beef chuck	1 c. shelled new peas
6 small carrots, sliced	½ lb. beef suet
4 large onions, sliced	3 T. flour
1 c. celery, cut fine	½ t. cinnamon
½ c. young white turnips, diced	3 cloves
6 small radishes	½ t. Bell's seasoning

Pot roast, Mrs. Appleyard says, is always better the second day, so she always starts it the day before, if you understand what she means.

Have the meat tied in a neat round. Try out some of the beef suet in a large frying-pan and brown the meat on all sides in it. Now put it into a deep roaster large enough to hold the meat and the vegetables, cover it tightly, add a little water and the seasonings and cook it slowly at 250° F. for at least three hours. That's all for that day. The next day heat it up again slowly and cook it two hours longer. Add more water if necessary and turn the meat (it should have been turned at the end of the first two hours the day before, by the way). At the end of the second hour the second day, put the vegetables in. It will take another hour to cook them. Baste them and the meat well with the juice in the pan, add a little more water, but don't overdo it as there is a considerable amount of moisture in the vegetables. Do not put in the peas at first with the other vegetables but cook them separately the shortest possible time and add them and their juice — there should be very little — to the others just before you are ready to make the gravy.

This dish is of such a noble nature when it has been given a mother's care for two days that Mrs. Appleyard considers it well worth one of your best platters. She thinks it looks well on Sheffield with the grape pattern around the edge. She makes the gravy by thickening the juice in the pan with some well-browned flour, and after this has simmered she pours it over the meat and vegetables.

The radishes, she says, will never be recognized as such. They taste like very delicate young turnips, only slightly more spicy.

With the pot roast she serves mashed potato and perhaps

some asparagus, Country Style (page 284) or String Beans and Mushrooms in Cream (page 299). The dessert is sliced peaches with port-wine jelly and angel cake.

Port-wine jelly comes in a glass jar from a grocery store that she and her husband refer to simply as 'The Grocery Store' because they disagree about the pronunciation of its short and simple name. Whichever version is correct, they certainly know how to stir up a good port-wine jelly.

14

Menus: for Everyday or Holiday

LADIES' LUNCHEONS

Ladies are generally on a diet. They would faint at the sight of a baked potato but they can always eat cream.

1   Mushroom Soup (*page* 281)
Baked Eggs in Ramekins (*page* 110)
Lettuce with French Dressing (*page* 239)
Montpelier Crackers, Puffed (*page* 37)
Raspberries and Cream   Oatmeal Lace Cookies (*page* 69)

2   Mushroom Broth (Canned) with Sherry Added
Melba Toast
Eggs Benedict (*page* 111)   Green Salad (*page* 243)
Cottage Cheese (*page* 93)
Strawberries to dip in sugar   Brownies

3   Cold Consommé Cardinal
Broiled Chicken   Vegetable Salad (*page* 244)
Cantaloupe Filled with Lemon Sherbet

At Appleyard Centre the main meal is generally in the middle of the day. If, however, there are hungry mountain-climbers coming home late, it is in the evening. Those who are left at home get for lunch what they would otherwise have had for supper.

MAIN MEALS — FOR HUNGRY PEOPLE

These assume that the people who eat them swim, mow lawns, build log cabins, cook, build dams in the brook, fish, run tractors, ride hay carts, do sword dancing, and rest by wrestling, scraping furniture, and picking vegetables. They are more interested in plenty of one or two things that they like than they are in elaborate menus. Mrs. Appleyard likes to cater to these appetites. As she and some of the other members of the family are often cooking the meal, she seldom serves soup at this time because you can't serve soup, make Hollandaise, and be at the table with your friends all at once. Soup is usually served at the lighter meal — lunch or supper, whichever it is.

These are some combinations that have found favor with log cabin and fireplace builders:

1   Mrs. Appleyard's Oven-Cooked Broilers
with Pineapple and Bacon
Creamed Potatoes (*page* 305)   Green Peas (*page* 291)
Raspberry Shortcake *page* 106)

2   Lamb Chops (*page* 168)   Asparagus
Hashed Brown Potatoes
Strawberries and Cream   Oatmeal Lace Cookies (*page* 69)

3 Peas and Potatoes and Salt Pork Cooked in Cream (*page* 293)
Mrs. Appleyard's Graham Bread and Butter (*page* 36)
Pineapple Upside-Down Cake, Foamy Sauce
(*pages* 102 and 227)

4   Montpelier Sausage Cakes   Apple Sauce
New Potatoes in Their Jackets with Butter
and Cream to Mash into Them
Young Carrots and Peas, Cooked Together (*page* 287)
Strawberry Shortcake (*page* 105)

5   Chicken Curry and Rice with Relishes (*page* 162)
Lemon Milk Sherbet   Chocolate Cakes (*page* 62)

6   Baked Ham (*page* 183)   Green Salad (*page* 243)
Mrs. Appleyard's Chutney (*page* 202)
Raspberries and Cream   Filled Lemon Queens

7 Broiled Shad Roe (*page* 130)   String Beans in Cream
Baked Potatoes
Peach Pandowdy (*page* 101)   Hard Sauce (*page* 222)

8   Montpelier Dried Beef in Cream (*page* 181)
Green Peas   Young Beets
New Potatoes with Chopped Chives, Butter, and Parsley
Blueberry Pudding (*page* 226)   Foamy Sauce (*page* 227)

9   Pot Roast of Beef (*page* 189) with Vegetables
Rhubarb and Strawberry Conserve
Raspberry Sherbet   Madeleines

10   Codfish in Cream *page* (136)
Baked Potato
Strawberries to Dip in Sugar

11   Veal Loaf (*page* 166)   Mashed Potato
Corn on the Cob (*page* 287)   Green Salad
Dutchess Apple Sauce (*page* 104)

12   Broiled Schrod.   Corn Pudding (*page* 51)
Sliced Tomatoes, French Dressing   String Beans, Buttered
          Blueberry Pie   Cheese

13 Pan-Broiled Chickens, Sour-Cream Giblet Gravy (*page* 171)
        Spoon Bread (*page* 49)   Young Beets
      Apple Pandowdy   Hard Sauce (*page* 222)

14 Roast Lamb Currant, Mint, and Orange Sauce (*page* 258)
     Potatoes Browned Around the Meat   Peas in Cream
      Chocolate Ice Cream   Angel Cake (*page* 56)

Mrs. Appleyard can think of plenty more, but she declined to go on any further on the ground that she was hungry. She was, however, persuaded to speak of the Last Day dinner.

Mr. Appleyard enjoys a table full of serious eaters. He says it makes him feel like a patriarch. If carving serenely, superbly, and generously is the mark of a patriarch, then Mr. Appleyard is one. Mrs. Appleyard likes to supply him with an audience of suitable proportions, and during this particular summer, by judicious borrowing, the family consisted at times of twenty people. There was a good deal of coming and going and it became a habit to remark to Mrs. Appleyard: 'Won't you have swordfish and blueberry pudding — or chickens and peach shortcake — or whatever the favorite objects were — tomorrow? You know it's my Last Day.'

Probably no woman is more easily susceptible to flattery than Mrs. Appleyard, and for a while she continued Last Days as requested. However, even on her this occupation began to pall and she finally — as the end of the season drew near and departures loomed — announced that there would be one official Last Day for everyone. They could write down on slips provided for the purpose their choices of hors d'oeuvres, soup, meat, or fish, three vegetables — one of which might be a salad — a dessert, either cake or cookies, something to drink. They could even mention things on the Emergency Shelf: nothing was sacred. And she would be alone, she said firmly, with this project.

The menu-makers left the house by ten o'clock with strict instructions to climb something high. From then on until seven-thirty Mrs. Appleyard seems to remember having been in constant motion. After comparing the various requests, she evolved, acquired the food for, and cooked the following

LAST-DAY DINNER

Caviar Canapés (Red and Black)
Cottage Cheese and Chives   Sardines on Toast
Bortsch with Sour Cream   Puffed Montpelier Crackers
Baked Broilers with Pineapple and Bacon
Raspberry and Currant Jelly
Sour-Cream Giblet Gravy (*page* 172)   Candied Sweet Potatoes
Corn on the Cob   Broccoli: Hollandaise
Sliced Tomatoes: French Dressing
Dutchess Apple Sauce with Vanilla Ice Cream
Oatmeal Lace Cookies (*page* 69)
Grandmother Appleyard's Lemonade (*page* 28)

The human system is a very remarkable invention. After consuming this meal in heroic quantities and then washing the dishes while singing choruses from Gilbert and Sullivan, the young anacondas turned to and acted a few charades. Somehow Mrs. Appleyard does not remember a great deal about them.

SUPPERS

Suppers are of several types. Mrs. Appleyard's favorite kind is the one that she improvises on a cold summer evening. Mrs. Appleyard is apt to say bitterly about six times a summer, 'I have suffered more from cold than I ever did from heat in this summer resort.' When asked by someone with a logical mind why she continues to patronize it, Mrs. Appleyard replies, 'Well, I've got to get myself toughened up for winter in Boston, haven't I?'

Still, with plenty of hot soup she manages to get through the summer. She always makes enough for two helpings all around — which means that some get three.

SUPPERS FOR COLD EVENINGS

1 Onion Soup with Custard   Toast and Cheese (*page* 268)
Chocolate Pudding (*page* 234)

2 Bortsch with Sour Cream   Montpelier Crackers Toasted
Apple Pandowdy: Hard Sauce

3 Black Bean Soup with Hard-Boiled Egg and Lemon
Toasted Cheese and Bacon Sandwiches
Vegetable Salad   Chutney

4 Toasted Club Sandwiches (*page* 169)
Hot Chocolate (*page* 19)
Blackberries and Cream   Lemon Queens (*page* 60)

5 Mr. Appleyard's Welsh Rabbit (*page* 90)
Green Salad   Coffee   Fruit

On hot evenings the Appleyards drag their suppers out to a table on the lawn or to some hilltop where the sunset is easy to look at if they are not too busy eating. The menus are constructed so as to make these migrations as easy as possible for Mrs. Appleyard. Materials for making sandwiches rather than made-up sandwiches are transported. Sometimes each has his own supper strapped to him — known as Supper at the Belt. One of the various versions of Appleyard Centre lemonade goes along in a thermos pail. The most important thing is plenty of knives for spreading.

In this connection the problem arises as to whether each person has a knife or whether each thing to be spread has a knife. Mrs. Appleyard has never really solved this, but she generally brings enough extra knives so that it is not really necessary to spread sandwiches of sardines and of strawberry jam with the same knife. No set menu is suggested — as the whole point is that you make it up as you go along — but these are some of the things that seem to be easily consumed on Vermont lawns and hilltops.

Home-made graham bread.

Boston brown bread (at least a day old so it will slice well).

Sliced white bread — whatever loathsome form is being foisted upon a supine public at the moment. The bread is all the same, but it has some new seductive title each summer, such as Butter Crunch Bread or Grandmother's Sunshine Cream Loaf. Aside from the fact that neither grandmother, sunshine, nor cream enters into its composition and that you cannot crunch it, these names are accurate. It does come in the form of a loaf and the waxed paper is handy around the kitchen. Mrs. Appleyard would just as soon eat the paper as the bread. However, the younger generation finds it useful as a basis for heaping things on, so sliced bread is likely to stray into the baskets.

Mrs. Appleyard sometimes wonders what will happen to us when we have to face the facts of life and slice our own bread. She herself takes a loaf of Pepperidge Farm Bread and slices it as thin as blotting paper and rejoices that this is the only resemblance between the two substances.

One basket contains:

Cottage Cheese (*page* 93) or Apple-Tree Cheese (*page* 94)
Strawberry Jam   Peanut Butter   Devilled Ham
Pâté de Foie Gras   Sardines   Orange Marmalade
Snappy Vermont Cheese

If supper is to be on the lawn, the salad is mixed beforehand in a big wooden bowl. If the eating is going to be done away from the house, the salad goes in various glass containers. In them there are likely to be:

A jar of mixed vegetables, marinated with a little French dressing.

Mayonnaise.

Sliced tomatoes — or whole ones. (There are always some earnest admirers of Appleyard Centre tomatoes who prefer to eat them from the hand. This means plenty of paper napkins. Tomatoes and peaches, Mrs. Appleyard says, are no good unless they have to be eaten bending over.)

Lettuce — curly and bronze around the edges.

Sliced onion.

Cold meat wrapped in waxed paper: ham, tongue, chicken, or veal loaf.

Dried beef.

The dessert consists of the cold drink out of the thermos jar and whatever cake or cookies were found in the pantry with five-quart milk pans turned over them. There may be chocolate fudge cake, oatmeal cookies, Toll House cookies, brownies — it's all a matter of luck.

After these trifles have been consumed there are no scraps of waxed paper, no bread crusts, no squashed paper cups to show that anyone ever ate supper on that particular spot.

The Appleyards' friends the Teasdales often invite the whole Appleyard horde for a meal out-of-doors. Mr. Teasdale can build a stone fireplace in less time than it takes Mrs. Appleyard to make a batch of blueberry muffins. When you meet the Teasdales at their picnic place, you find that they have three or four fires going, a throne of slate stones for the grandmother of the party, hemlock logs for the children to roost upon, seats in shade or sunshine, and even a bed of hemlock boughs for anyone suffering from sacroiliac trouble. The table may be a rock or a grassy bank or some boards supported by sap buckets that have seen better days. Mr. Teasdale is roasting corn in the husks over one fire and Mrs. Teasdale is cooking Hamburgers over another. One of the Teasdale boys is doing bacon over a third and another is carefully turning sausage cakes, or inquiring whether you would like your egg sunny side up. Frankfurters have already been steamed and Bob Teasdale will grill one for you if you like. There are Frankfurter and Hamburger rolls warming in a reflecting oven near one of the fires. On the table are sliced tomatoes, sliced onions, pickles, pepper hash, butter, lettuce, mayonnaise.

There is a large lake of Mrs. Teasdale's lemonade and an angel cake a foot high, for which she apologizes on the ground that the oven wasn't just right or she only had sixteen eggs.

Anyone who cannot fix himself a succulent meal at the Teasdales' must certainly be lacking in initiative. Of what is left over campers have been known to equip themselves for a three-day trip.

15

Preserves. Mrs. Appleyard is never happier than when she is putting up something. She has an idea — of course this applies only to people like herself and not to any really virtuous housewife — that preserving is used chiefly as a defense. No woman who is making quince jelly or cucumber pickle can possibly be asked to sew on buttons or be urged to talk to the Ladies' Aid on 'The Arrangement of Flowers' or 'The Lighter Side of Chemistry.' She is so obviously busy and she has so much to show for it. There are the steaming kettles; there are all the magnificent jars and glasses with the sunshine glowing through them. Such a tangible achievement is a valid excuse for skulking at home even after everything is sealed with Parawax. There is something pleasant about having a duty to a large watermelon or a crate of strawberries. And when you come back to the country next year and find that the ravening hordes actually missed a few jars of this and that, it is like finding a pearl in an oyster. At least Mrs. Appleyard supposes that finding pearls is at times a rewarding occupation: the only ones she ever found were boiled.

Among the treasures that she sometimes finds on hand when June comes rolling round again there may be a jar of chutney that she made when the apples were ripe last year. This is what went into it:

APPLE–MINT CHUTNEY

12 Dutchess apples, cored, pared, and quartered	½ c. seedless raisins
	⅓ c. chopped mint leaves
4 ripe tomatoes — big ones	3 cloves
3 large green peppers	3 c. cider vinegar
2 lemons, sliced very thin	2 t. dry mustard
1 orange, sliced	2 t. salt
3 onions, chopped	½ t. cinnamon
½ lb. preserved ginger	1 t. ginger
1½ c. seeded raisins	4 lbs. brown sugar

Begin by chopping the mint very fine; add the onions and chop fine; then add the peppers, split and cleaned of seeds, and chopped medium fine, next the apples, and last of all the tomatoes, leaving them chopped fairly coarse. Add the sliced lemon and orange cut into quarters. Scald the vinegar with the sugar, syrup, and spices, pour over the fruit. Add the raisins and the preserved ginger very finely shaved into slices. Stir well. Cook half an hour the first day and let it stand overnight. The next morning reheat the chutney and cook it fifteen minutes. The third day cook it till the syrup is thick. It will probably take about twenty minutes after it begins to cook.

Watch it carefully, stirring to make sure it does not stick to the bottom of the kettle. Pour it into scalded jars. Parawax them and try to keep the chutney if you can. This amount makes about twelve pint jars.

Earlier in the summer Mrs. Appleyard makes a combination of rhubarb and strawberries that is all gone by the time the chutney is ready.

RHUBARB AND STRAWBERRY CONSERVE

12 c. rhubarb cut fine	1 c. red currants
12 c. small strawberries	Thin yellow rind of 1 lemon
1 can sliced pineapple	Juice of 1 lemon
(no juice)	16 c. sugar

Put everything together in large granite pans — those milk pans Mrs. Appleyard keeps talking about. Bake the fruit in a moderate oven — 375° F. — for one hour. Then put the fruit into a large kettle and cook it until the juice jellies on a cold saucer. This amount fills twelve pint jars.

An accident, such as might happen in any home — if Mrs. Appleyard happened to be in it — produced an interesting variant on this conserve and also a word for the Appleyard family dictionary. There were not quite enough strawberries for the full twelve cups, it was discovered after Mrs. Appleyard had been out and pulled up the rhubarb from behind the springhouse and had cut it into juicy green and pink cubes. Remembering that she had seen a bowl of crushed strawberries in the ice chest, she got it out and with a sweeping dramatic gesture poured it over the rhubarb and strawberries. Now, the flavor of onion is a delicious one, but not usually associated with strawberries. The bowl, in point of fact, contained about a quart of bortsch with plenty of onions in it.

No one needs to think that our heroine was dismayed by

this happening. She simply added a half-teaspoon of cloves, a teaspoon of cinnamon, a little nutmeg, two more lemons thinly sliced and quartered, and proceeded as above. The conserve was a peculiarly handsome color and of a flavor that — luckily, perchance — defied immediate analysis. Some brave spirits preferred it to the established variety even after they knew what was in it.

It was natural, after this episode, for the verb 'to bortsch' to establish itself in the family dictionary. It is defined as 'to add some unexpected ingredient to a mixture, as "to bortsch the conserve." ' (You can bortsch a dinner party, too, Mrs. Appleyard says — but not always with such happy effect.)

So far she has never put any onion into her brandied fruit and she is not planning to do so. Brandy is not generally considered a sedative, but Brandied Fruit is a peaceful sort of preserving that Mrs. Appleyard finds a restful change after some of her activities. It goes on all summer and lasts all winter — if you make enough.

BRANDIED FRUIT

Take as many quart jars as you think you will need. You will use about half a pint of brandy for each one, so let your supply of brandy be your guide. Mrs. Appleyard uses California brandy. She puts into each jar the different kinds of fruit as they come along and adds, each time, about half as much sugar as fruit. She begins with strawberries, both wild and cultivated, adds fresh ripe pineapple, finely diced (canned will do), red raspberries, red and white currants, black raspberries, sliced peaches, and blackberries. She covers the first lot of fruit and sugar with the brandy and from time to time adds a little more brandy as she puts in fruit and sugar. The result is a fine dark reddish-purple syrup with fruit floating in it. She uses it to put on ice cream or for pudding sauce.

Some cooks insist on making cottage pudding. Mrs. Appleyard has never had much sympathy for this habit, but she thinks you might take part of the curse off it by using this sauce.

BRANDIED HARD SAUCE

½ c. butter
1 c. powdered sugar

½ c. brandied fruit
1 egg, well beaten

Cream the butter, add the sugar gradually, stir in the brandied fruit and the egg well beaten. Beat all together with a wire whisk. You can control the consistency by the amount of the fruit juice that you add, according to whether you prefer a thick or a thin sauce. This makes a rather thin one.

POTPOURRI

You can't eat it, even on cottage pudding, but if you have roses, it is fun to make it. Rugosa roses have very fragrant petals and their petals keep their bright color in the potpourri for a long time.

Gather the roses in the middle of a clear morning when the dew is off them. If you have rose geranium, lemon verbena, or syringa blossoms, add those too, but be sure there are three or four times as many rose leaves as of the other sorts. Put the petals to dry in the shed chamber, spread out on newspapers. What — no shed chamber? Well, that's hardly Mrs. Appleyard's fault, is it? Anyway choose a dry place where they will be out of your way.

To two quarts of dried petals use:

2 oz. allspice	8 drops oil of rose
2 oz. stick cinnamon	¼ pint brandy
½ oz. whole cloves	Thin peel of 1 orange
1 oz. orris root	Salt
2 oz. dried lavender flowers	

Put the dried rose petals into a large bowl. Sprinkle them lightly with salt. Do this for several days until you have enough petals. Stir it up every time you add a fresh lot. At the end of about a week, mix the spices with the petals and let them stand covered for a day. Then add the orris and put the potpourri into your jars, placing a little of the orange peel and the brandy in each. What Mrs. Appleyard made in 1937 is still fragrant. It is nice to scatter in the drawers where you keep your sheets.

Also easy to make and more appealing to the practical members of the family is Tomato Conserve. This can be made with either fresh or canned tomatoes. Three large cans of tomatoes about equal four quarts of whole tomatoes. Mrs. Appleyard thinks that unless you have tomatoes that come from your own or your neighbor's garden the canned tomatoes are about as good for this purpose. Their color is often better than that of ordinary tomatoes that you buy in the city. The bright color is one of the attractive things about this conserve. Cook it in a shallow pan so that the liquid will evaporate rapidly and it will keep its color.

MRS. APPLEYARD'S TOMATO CONSERVE

4 qts. ripe tomatoes	½ oz. stick cinnamon
(measured whole)	1 c. seedless raisins
3 oranges	sugar
3 lemons	2 t. salt

Peel the tomatoes by holding them by a fork over the gas flame until the skins pop and sizzle. Peel off the skin, slice the tomatoes. Cut them up and pour off about a quart of their juice and keep it to drink chilled or to use in soup.

Measure the tomatoes and add an equal amount of sugar or maple syrup. Slice the lemons and oranges paper thin. A sandwich-slicer is a great help for this, but you can do it by hand if you have patience and a sharp knife. Cut the slices into quarters — a kitchen shears comes in handy at this point. If you heat the sugar in the oven, it will dissolve more readily than if you have it cold. If you use syrup heat it a little first before pouring it over the tomatoes. Tie the spices in bags and put them into the kettles — you had better use two so that the conserve will cook quickly — with the tomatoes, lemons, oranges, and raisins. When the juice of the tomatoes begins to bubble add the heated sugar or syrup. Cook, stirring often from the bottom, until the juice begins to crinkle when tested on a cold saucer. Put the conserve into sterilized jars. Serve it with cold meat, meat loaf, fish, or curry.

RED–PEPPER RELISH (TO SERVE WITH CURRY)

12 red peppers	1 lemon, sliced thin
6 green peppers	1 qt. cider vinegar
6 tomatoes	2 c. sugar (or maple syrup)
3 large onions	1½ T. salt

Split the peppers and take out the seeds. Mrs. Appleyard left some in once, with surprising results. She also once cut a large batch of them by hand very fine. It took most of the skin off her hands. She is glad someone else is a bride now.

Chop the peppers in a large wooden bowl. Cover them

with boiling water, let them stand ten minutes, drain, pour over some more water, let them stand five minutes, and drain again. Add the onion chopped fine, peel the tomatoes, by holding them over the gas flame until they pop and taking off their rubber overcoats. Chop them in with the peppers, not too fine. Add the lemon sliced thin and quartered.

Heat the vinegar, sugar or syrup, and salt and let them boil five minutes. Then add the chopped pepper mixture. Bring it to the boil again and cook ten minutes. Let it stand overnight. In the morning cook ten minutes longer, stirring carefully. Put it into sterilized glass jars. Good with meat or fish as well as with curry.

PICCALILLI (TO SERVE WITH CURRY)

Frost comes early in Vermont and always leaves some green tomatoes that were hastily picked off the vines some evening when the sun went down in a windless sky behind Mount Hunger, and the moon came up over Spruce as sharp-edged as a new axe, and the crickets chirped so slowly you thought they had stopped for the winter.

The next day is the day to make Piccalilli.

½ peck green tomatoes	2 t. stick cinnamon, broken
3 green peppers	1½ t. allspice
3 large onions	½ t. mustard
1 sweet red pepper	1 c. sugar
1 bunch celery	3 t. salt
1 t. whole cloves	Vinegar

Chop the onions fine. Split the peppers and take out the seeds and chop the peppers with the onion. Add the celery and keep chopping, not too fine, and last of all the tomatoes and chop all together. Put the mixture into a kettle, add the salt, and let it stand overnight. In the morning pour off the juice. Add the spices in a bag and cover the chopped vegetables with cider vinegar. Cook slowly until the peppers are tender. Taste it and add more salt if you like. Good with hamburg or hot dogs.

Watermelon, Mrs. Appleyard says, is good for two purposes — to look at and to make into watermelon pickle. Anyone who does not mind eating water flavored with water is welcome to the pink part, she says. It is to her the most deceptive of all foods. Nothing is so delectable-looking, and nothing but a green pear — in her opinion — is so tasteless. Let her have the cool green rind and everyone will be happy.

WATERMELON PICKLE

4 lbs watermelon rind	3 lemons, juice and thin yellow peel
4 lbs. sugar	1 t. whole cloves
1 qt. vinegar	¼ c. salt
1 qt. water	4 t. stick cinnamon, broken

Cut the pale green part of the watermelon rind away from the hard green outside rind. If it is inconvenient for you to weigh it (it almost never *is* convenient for Mrs. Appleyard to weigh anything but herself, and the whole idea depresses her), it is fairly safe to figure that four quarts — cut up — amounts to about the same thing. A pint's a pound the world around, isn't it? It's true of water and logically should be true of watermelon. Anyway Mrs. Appleyard proceeds on that theory.

Make a brine of the water and salt and cover the rind with it and let it stand overnight. If there is not enough brine to cover all the rind, make some more of the same strength. The rind must be all covered: it is the brine that makes the pickle crisp instead of flabby and mushy.

The next morning drain off the brine, pour some more cold water over the melon, drain it again, add enough more clear water to cover it, and cook it till its tender. Sometimes it seems as if this were going on all summer, but cheer up, the end is in sight. Let it stand once more overnight, drain it again in the morning, and cut it into small cubes. Peel the lemons so thin that you get none of the white part of the rind. Squeeze their juice over the lemon rind, spices tied in a bag, vinegar, and sugar. Heat this up and when it is just starting to boil, add the melon cubes. Cook over a hot fire until the melon cubes are transparent. Take out the spices, put the rind into sterilized glass jars, pour the syrup over it.

If there is not enough syrup, make some more out of vinegar and sugar or heat some maple syrup. Whichever you do, put back the spice bags into it again. Be sure you divide the rind and syrup that it was cooked in so that no jar contains only the second lot of syrup. If you have to add a second batch, be sure to cook it down enough. Better put some more lemon peel in it too.

Probably — although it is hard to judge just how much syrup you need — being obliged to make a second lot is just something that happens to Mrs. Appleyard.

16

Pastry: Mostly Pies. Almost everyone who likes pie at all has strong opinions about piecrust. Mrs. Appleyard supposes it is all in how you were brought up. Probably there are perfectly worthy, honorable people to whom a pallid, white pie looks attractive. Mrs. Appleyard was educated in a circle of pie-eaters that liked the crust brown, and flaky, and crisp at the edges. There was in fact at one time a demand for pies baked in an oblong tin, because there arose in it a peculiarly fine opportunity for crusty pieces at the corners. This fad died out because if you cut the pie in six pieces, two of them were not corner pieces. There were enough opportunities for family competition without this situation, so the circular tin came back into style. It was fortunate for our language that the original form of tin was preserved. Otherwise the word "pie-shaped," meaning, of course, shaped like a wedge, would have lost its true significance.

Mrs. Appleyard's family cherished pie in various forms,

but not for breakfast. There must always have been some slight radical tendency in the family, some flaunting of tradition. Even in Emerson's day Mrs. Appleyard's ancestors contented themselves with a breakfast consisting of fruit, cereal, coffee, chops or steak, omelet and bacon if you preferred it, toast, honey, and three kinds of hot bread.

Mr. Emerson, so tradition runs, when asked if he ate pie for breakfast, replied with grave sweetness: 'Why, what is pie for?' It was also this well-loved sage who — on being offered some cherries in between meals — replied: 'What — set the whole fearful and wonderful machinery of my digestion at work upon a single cherry! No, I thank you.'

What kind of pie he had had for breakfast that morning is not recorded.

Not for breakfast, but for dinner and supper and an occasional setting of the digestive machinery to work in between meals were the pies and turnovers that Mrs. Appleyard's grandmother made. This is how she made her pastry. (Don't read this if you belong to the school of thought that admires blondes among pies.)

4 c. flour	½ t. salt
1 c. butter	Extra flour for rolling
1 c. lard	out
1 c. ice water	Extra butter for enrich-
⅛ t. soda	ing crust later

Sift the flour, measure it. Sift it three times with the baking soda and salt. Have the lard and butter very cold. Put them into a wooden chopping-bowl with the flour and chop them with a cold chopping-knife until they are in small lumps the size of your little finger tip. Put an ice-cube in a cup, fill the cup up with water and when your ice is melted, add the water, half a cupful at a time, blending it in with your chopper. Chop a little more, mixing the whole thing together.

Flour your pastry board and roll out the paste with a floured rolling-pin. Be gentle: pastry hates to be thumped. Roll it out about three-fourths of an inch thick. Cut it in thirds with a cold spatula. Do not touch it with your hands. With the spatula and a chilled pancake-turner pile the outside pieces over the one in the middle. Turn your board ninety degrees and repeat the process, cutting the pastry in thirds each time, rolling it out gently to the original thickness and putting the outside pieces over the middle one. Keep turning the board ninety degrees and do this four times, always as gently as if you were handling a week-old baby.

Have a cold platter ready with a cold, damp napkin on it, wrung out of ice water. Put the pastry on it and wrap the ends around it. Always make the pastry long enough before you want to use it so that you can chill it for several hours. It is even better to make it the day before you plan to use it.

When you roll it out for your pies, put a few extra dots of cold butter on it, because with the flour you have used on your board and rolling-pin you will find that it will stand some enrichment.

Bake in a hot oven — 450°–500° F. at first so that the chilled spaces that you made by your turning and cutting will suddenly expand, and so that your shortening will blend with your flour before the fat melts and gets oily. If it does melt, your pastry will be tough. When the crust begins to brown, you can reduce the heat a little. Pies with a double crust and a fruit filling need longer cooking than pies with a single crust and custard filling. They all need careful watching.

MINCE-PIE MEAT

3 lbs. round of beef
Tart apples, twice as much as meat, measured after they
   are pared and quartered and after the meat is cooked
   and chopped

1½ lbs. suet	¼ t. clove
1 gal. sweet cider	1 T. cinnamon
1 lb. citron	2 t. allspice
½ lb. candied orange peel	4 grated nutmegs
2 lbs. seedless raisins	2 T. lemon extract
1 lb. seeded raisins	4 lemons — rind and juice
3 lbs. currants	3 c. brandy
2 T. salt	Stock from meat

Begin the day before you plan to make your pies. Put the
beef on in cold water, let it come to the boil, and keep it
simmering until it is tender. It will take five hours probably. Be sure not to let the water cook away. Cool the
meat, remove any gristle, and chop the meat fine by hand in
a wooden chopping-bowl. Measure it.

Now pare, core, and quarter tart apples, and chop them
fine. Fix enough so that you have twice as much apple as
meat (the apple will cook down so there will not be too
much). Chop the suet fine and mix it with the meat and
apples. In the meantime you have put your sweet cider on
to boil with the citron and the candied peel cut in pieces.
When it has cooked down to two quarts, moisten the meat
mixture with one quart of it and let the other go on cooking
with the citron and peel until they are tender. Take them
out, chop them fine, and add them to the meat. Add also
at this time the raisins, currants, and spices, the lemon
extract, juice of the lemons and their grated rind.

Then add the liquor that the meat was cooked in and

simmer the whole thing for two hours over a slow fire. During the last hour add gradually the rest of the cider and the brandy. Cook a little longer if the mixture seems too moist.

Mrs. Appleyard's grandmother used to make turnovers with this mincemeat and keep them in a certain crock in the china closet. There was a spicy smell about the place that lasted winter and summer. Huckleberry gingerbread probably kept the good work going during the summer months. The turnovers were intended for children on their way home from school. They had a healing effect on scholars who had been wrestling with the more spiteful forms of mathematics and coming off second best. Even the division of fractions, the Theory of Limits, and circles with dotted lines skew-angling about them seemed better after a mince turnover or two.

The turnovers were also all right filled with dried-apple sauce. Mrs. Appleyard does not know, she says, just how the apple sauce was made, but she does know that the apples were not bleached with sulphur. They hung on strings from the kitchen ceiling and turned a nice pigskin brown. Anyone who wanted sulphur in those days took it where it belonged — in a large spoon with molasses in the springtime.

One of Mrs. Appleyard's saddest memories is connected with these dried-apple turnovers. There was a picnic on an island in Frenchman's Bay about a mile from Great Porcupine, where Mrs. Appleyard's grandmother, Mrs. Elmore, had a summer place. Mrs. Elmore was in many ways wiser than her granddaughter is ever likely to become, and one way was that when the rest of the family went on picnics she stayed at home. Thus she preserved the serenity that was one of her great charms. Her only defect — if she had one — was that she was likely to provide the picnickers with more food than they really needed. And she did not want any of it brought home. It must all be consumed on some other island, or on some pointed-fir-covered point on the mainland, in a becalmed catboat, on a sandy beach part way to Grand Manan, or on their own Shag Ledge with the tide coming in. It was a matter of indifference to her under just what conditions of sun, fog, wind, or tide they ate it — so long as they ate it all.

On this particular picnic when the bacon, broiled by setting up a salty driftwood board in front of a driftwood fire and pinning the bacon to the board, was all gone and they had eaten all the buttered toast with the marks of forked alder twigs through it and many more things that Mrs. Appleyard preferred not to mention, she said, because she was hungry enough anyway, the apple turnovers were produced.

Try as the picnickers might they could not eat them all. To be sure, Mrs. Appleyard would willingly have immolated herself, but for reasons of a statistical nature, accurately recited to her, she was denied the opportunity of making the supreme sacrifice. Some were even coarse enough to refer to her age — it was eight — and mention that they had to go home in the boat with her.

So the turnovers — there were two of them — were placed a little way below high-water mark; neatly they were placed on a shingle, sadly the shingle was laid on the smooth pebbles of gray and white and dull orange and porphyry color. Below the seaweed wreath at the tide mark with the driftwood like a deer's antlers sticking out of it lay the shingle with its precious freight.

The tide was coming in fast, and as the boat shoved off with that still hungry, skinny eight-year-old, Susan Markham, in the bow, the waves began to lap gently around the edges of the brown crinkly crust, and pretty soon one wave larger than the rest lifted the shingle. . . .

'Oh, well, I too have lived in Arcadia,' says Mrs. Appleyard. 'Perhaps I'd better talk about pumpkin pie now.'

The best pumpkins for pie, she says, are the small ones. They have less string and more sweetness than the jack-o'-lantern style. Cut them in halves, take out the seeds and string, cut them into large pieces and steam them until they are tender. Separate the pulp from the shell and put the pulp through a fine strainer.

Mrs. Appleyard has often gone all through this process, and she has on other occasions opened a can of pumpkin. Mr. Appleyard disapproved of anything but the home-grown product — never having tried anything else. He is, however, a man of reason, so when his mother and his wife conspired against him and made two pies — one of canned pumpkin and one of fresh — and he, poor innocent, voted for the canned one as being a trifle the more utterly delicate of the two, he simply beamed upon the plotters when they confessed, and had another piece of each pie. He has never since been so crude as to inquire which kind Mrs. Appleyard was devoting to his nourishment this time, and if he can't tell, no one can.

However you acquired your cooked pumpkin, either by steaming and straining it yourself or by opening a can, you have really only just begun. You take a large iron frying-pan, butter it lightly, put in the pumpkin, and cook it down until it is dry and brown. This cooking, plenty of cream, a delicate accuracy in seasoning, rich flaky crust, are the essential things in turning out a good pumpkin pie. The cooking in the frying-pan is well worth the trouble of standing over it and stirring it constantly. It will scorch if it is not stirred often, and what you are trying to do is to dry the moisture out of it and just slightly caramelize the natural sugar that is in the pumpkin. If this is done right, turning the whole mass over so that it all comes in contact with the hot pan from time to time, it brings out the flavor and sweetness of the pumpkin. Drying out the pumpkin in the oven is *not* a substitute for cooking it in the pan on top of the stove. In the oven it is likely that the pumpkin will simply dry on the outside and still be moist inside. Keep turning it over as the steam puffs out of it. It will take about twenty minutes and at the end of that time it should be a rich golden brown all through instead of orange, and thick and smooth instead of watery. There should be about one and a half cups if you are planning to make two large pies.

PUMPKIN PIE (B. H. K.)

1½ c. cooked and browned pumpkin	1 t. cinnamon
	½ t. ginger
2 T. flour	⅛ t. mace
2 eggs	3 c. rich milk
1 t. salt 1 c. sugar	1 c. cream

Put the pumpkin in a bowl, sprinkle it with the flour, and stir in the flour thoroughly. Butter the bottom of a saucepan and scald the milk in it. Add the cream and the seasonings. Pour it over the pumpkin mixture and add the eggs — well beaten. Get pie shells ready, built up around the edge, and nicely fluted or crimped (for pastry see page 212). Do not have the pie shells too full of the mixture; three quarters of an inch deep is about right. If your tins are only of medium size this will be enough for another small pie tomorrow. Bake only what you are going to eat within twenty-four hours. Both pastry and filling will keep in the ice chest until you need them. Cut cheesecloth into inch strips or use one-inch strips of gauze, moisten it a little and put it around the edge of your pies. This will keep them from browning too fast at first.

Bake the pies in a fairly hot oven — 450° F. for forty-five minutes, reducing the heat to 325° F. if they seem to be cooking too fast. They are done when they will just shake in the middle when moved.

To leave out some Vermont cheese when you serve the pie is a serious offense in the Appleyard family.

If you want to make squash pie, go right ahead, but don't expect any help from Mrs. Appleyard, who would rather speak about Lemon Meringue.

It is not true that Mrs. Appleyard has the digestion of an anaconda. Her constitution is really an organism of peculiar delicacy; for instance, she is allergic to cornstarch. Anyone who wishes to make lemon pie — or anything else, such as that pudding that tastes like slate pencils — had better carry on his researches somewhere else.

LEMON PIE WITHOUT CORNSTARCH (B. H. K.)

5 eggs	3 T. water
1 heaping c. sugar	Grated rind of 1 lemon
½ c. lemon juice	

Separate the eggs. Beat the yolks slightly, add the sugar, lemon juice, finely grated rind, and water. Beat all together. Have a large pie shell ready with one crust, built up and fluted around the edge, pricked all over, baked ten minutes. Fill it, put a strip of gauze around the edge so that it will not brown too quickly. Bake it for ten minutes at 450° F., then reduce the heat and bake for twenty minutes longer at 325° F. Remove it from the oven, cool it, and cover it with a meringue made, while the filling is baking, as follows:

MERINGUE NO. 1

Whites of 5 eggs
1 heaping c. powdered sugar
2½ T. lemon juice

Put the whites of eggs in a bowl and beat till the mixture will hold its shape. Add the lemon juice, a drop at a time, and keep beating. This will take about half an hour.

If you have a feeling of lethargy or have not an electric mixer, both of which drawbacks are generally keeping Mrs. Appleyard in a relaxed state, better do it this way:

MERINGUE NO. 2

Whites of 5 eggs
1 t. lemon extract
1 c. powdered sugar

Beat the egg whites stiff. Add a quarter of the sugar gradually, and beat hard; then another quarter, keep on beating. Fold in all the rest at once and add the flavoring — vanilla, if you prefer. Heap it on the pie and return pie to the oven for a few minutes until the meringue starts to brown.

These directions are for a large pie and a lot of meringue. The Appleyards consider a small pie something made simply to annoy.

Apple pie depends, strangely enough, on the apples of which it is made. They should be tart and juicy. Dutchess, Yellow Transparents, Gravensteins, Mackintosh Reds all make good pie and all slightly different. There are so many possible faults in apple pie that it is depressing to mention them all, but perhaps the two worst, assuming that your crust is good, are apples still partly raw because they were hard and dry to start with, and too much spice. An apple pie should taste of *Apple*. A very little lemon juice or rind, the merest hint of cinnamon or nutmeg do bring out the flavor of the apples, but they are dangerous substances, to be used, like arsenic, in small medicinal doses.

APPLE PIE

6 apples with a tang	1 c. sugar
¼ t. lemon juice or ⅛ t.	1¼ t. cinnamon
lemon rind	⅛ t. nutmeg
1 t. butter	

Better not put the spices in at all if you cannot trust yourself not to scatter them about. If you use them, mix them thoroughly with the sugar so that they will be evenly distributed through the fruit. Line your pie plate with well-chilled pastry (page 212). Work a little more butter into the top crust than into the bottom crust. Never grease a pie plate: good pastry does its own greasing. Set the plate and the top crust back into the refrigerator while you are getting the apples ready. Pare the apples, core them, slice them very thin. Be sure to fix plenty. Put them into the pie plate on the lower crust, shaking the spiced sugar over each layer. Dot the top layer with the butter and sprinkle it with the lemon juice. Cover the apples with the top crust. Gash it in three places to let the steam escape. Bake the pie for forty minutes. Have the oven at 450° F. for the first ten minutes and then reduce the heat to 425° F. for the remaining half-hour.

Apple-tree Cheese (page 94) is good with this, and so is vanilla ice cream, if you like your pie à la mode. The Appleyard children do. One of them ordered beef à la mode at a restaurant once and asked when it came, 'But where's the ice cream that goes with it?' Mr. Appleyard, however, says there is nothing better with apple pie than a piece of a well-ripened Vermont June cheese, and his wife is inclined to agree with him.

Double the amount of apples baked in a large earthenware dish with one crust is a good way to make your first apple pie, and you can graduate to the two-crust style later. This is a fine way to use the later apples when the early ones have gone. Be sure to slice them thin. Baldwins are good in a deep-dish pie. This may be spiced a little more than a pie made of early apples, but don't overdo it. It will probably take fifty minutes to bake a large pie. Begin with the oven at 450° F., and after the first ten minutes reduce the heat to 400° F.

Because of her youngest child's tastes Mrs. Appleyard generally serves vanilla ice cream with this, but some of the others like Hard Sauce and get it when their turn to be pampered comes.

HARD SAUCE

½ c. butter	¼ t. nutmeg
1 c. powdered sugar	1 T. powdered maple sugar
½ t. vanilla	

Cream the butter. Work the sugar in gradually. Add

the vanilla. Do not get the sauce too stiff — you may like to leave out part of the sugar. Sprinkle it with the nutmeg and powdered maple sugar (page 82). You are not really likely to have any unless you know Mr. Appleyard intimately. It's not a bad idea to learn to make it, though. Of course you can take a cake of maple sugar and grate it if you would rather.

The annual expedition to the top of Catamountain to get blueberries results in a certain monotony in the Appleyard menus. Blueberry pudding, blueberry pie, blueberry muffins all have their adherents among the pickers. Mrs. Appleyard makes them all: pie for dinner, muffins for supper, and pudding the next day.

Pie is the most sensitive of the three, so it is made with the freshest and best berries. In blueberry pie there should be *nothing but blueberries and sugar*. The suggestion that there should be flour dredged over the berries is one that is so shocking to Mrs. Appleyard that she can hardly think that it can be meant to be taken seriously. She has also heard of the macabre notion of adding a few green grapes 'to improve the flavor.' Where could blueberries have been picked that need improving in any such way? Not in Vermont, nor yet in New Hampshire, Mrs. Appleyard is sure; and Maine, too, is innocent of any such crop. If grapes, Mrs. Appleyard inquires, why not a few spoonfuls of cornstarch, some gooseberries, and a little almond extract?

At this point the Editor, realizing that talk of this sort was not doing Mrs. Appleyard's blood pressure a bit of good, tactfully led her back to her Queen Anne chair and the subject of pie.

'Blueberries,' she continued more calmly, 'should have on them a bloom that is like the sky above Catamountain, over a skin as dark as the mountain itself when seen just before a thunderstorm, some August afternoon. Pick the stems and leaves out of the berries. Take out any that are mashed. Handle them as little as possible. If there are a few that are still a reddish purple or even slightly green, leave them in. They'll do instead of those green grapes to add a little tartness. Line the biggest Bennington pie dish with pastry (page 212). To fill this particular dish you will need two and one-half cups of berries and one cup of sugar.

'Mix them well together, being careful not to crush the berries. Perhaps it is not necessary to mention that the berries should not be washed, but stranger things have happened — there were those grapes.

'Have the top crust a little more enriched with butter than the lower one. Put in the berries and sugar and cover them with the top crust. Make three gashes in it and be sure that the edges of the under and upper crusts meet neatly everywhere. Brush the lower crust with water very lightly before putting on the upper one and press the two crusts gently together with the back of a fork. Bind the edge of the pie with a strip of gauze. This will help to keep the juice in and stop the edge from browning too quickly. The only possible excuse for putting in flour is to keep the pies from leaking. It is not necessary if you bind the edges. Have the oven at 450° F. for ten minutes and then reduce the heat to 425° F. and bake the pie for thirty to thirty-five minutes longer.

Be sure your pie is well browned. There are few lovelier color combinations for interior decoration, Mrs. Appleyard says, than the golden brown of piecrust and the rich purple of blueberry juice.

'Green grapes indeed!'

Mrs. Appleyard goes off muttering, but turns back to say over her shoulder: 'And now, children, you had better all brush your teeth. I can't have you looking like chow dogs. . . .'

17

Puddings, and Sauces for Them

STEAMED BLUEBERRY PUDDING

This is Mr. Appleyard's favorite dessert, as it was his father's, and we hope that the Appleyard boys will choose wives who will take this hereditary task seriously. Few words have ever pleased Mrs. Appleyard more than some from her husband in praise of her blueberry pudding. This is how he likes it:

2 c. flour	1¼ c. blueberries
1 c. milk	½ t. salt
4 t. baking powder	2 T. butter

Sift the flour and measure it. Sift it three times more with the baking powder and salt. Work in the butter with the fingertips. Add milk and berries — which you have jounced up and down with a little of the flour — alternately. Put the batter into a buttered tin that has a tight cover. A quart coffee can, the kind that is higher than it is wide, is a good shape and size. Vacuum-packed cans are no good. An old Chase & Sanborn can is a great treasure. Mrs. Appleyard's whole career as a wife and mother was almost wrecked once because the tin she used got thrown away by some non-New Englander. However, she found another one at an auction, and cherishes it with the fond devotion of a motorist for his spare tire.

Steam the pudding one and a half hours. Steaming is easy if you have the mould (née coffee can), a kettle with a tight cover, a rack to set the mould on, and something heavy — Mrs. Appleyard uses an antique stovelid retired from active service for this — to put on top of the can containing the pudding so that it will not tip over. If the pudding stands upright and if the water never stops boiling, there is no reason why your pudding should not fill the mould and be fluffy inside and a delicate biscuit tan outside with rich purple spots through it.

Do not fill your mould more than two thirds full. Be sure that the water comes halfway up around the can and that it does not cook away. You will have noticed that the pudding is made with a biscuit dough — not a cake batter. The richness is in the sauce.

FOAMY SAUCE

½ c. butter	1 c. powdered sugar
2 eggs	1 t. vanilla

Cream the butter. Add gradually the sugar, the eggs well beaten, and the vanilla. Cook in the top of the double boiler, beating with a wire whisk or an egg-beater, until the mixture thickens. It takes only a few minutes. Mrs. Appleyard has the butter and sugar ready in the top of the boiler and finishes the sauce while the table is being cleared.

This is supposed to be enough to go with one can of pudding. It does indeed supply enough for a liberal coating of six thick slices (try saying that fast) into which the pudding is cut. (Not over three quarters of an inch thick, says Mr. Appleyard.) However, on glancing through Mrs. Appleyard's book of rules — that battle-scarred volume — the Editor noticed a remark, deeply underscored, which was deciphered to read 'Never enough.'

ALMOND RING (E. M.)

Whites of 4 eggs	½ t. almond extract
1⅔ c. ground, blanched almonds	4 macaroons
1 c. sugar	

Make the macaroons into fine crumbs. Butter a ring mould and dust the crumbs over it. Beat the eggs to a stiff froth, fold in the sugar and the almonds alternately. Put the mixture into the mould. Bake in a moderate oven — 375°–400° F. — for half an hour. Serve the ring either hot or cold. Strawberries, slightly crushed with sugar, and some vanilla ice cream are good with it if it is served cold. Chocolate sauce is nice with it if it is served hot.

CHOCOLATE SAUCE

2 sqs. Baker's chocolate	½ c. light brown or maple sugar
1½ t. butter	½ c. boiling water
1 c. white sugar	½ t. vanilla

Melt the chocolate, add the butter. Pour on gradually, stirring well, the boiling water. Bring to the boiling point add the sugar, and cook fifteen minutes. Cool slightly and add the vanilla.

This sauce is good on cream puffs, pudding, or ice cream.

Mrs. Appleyard's rule for plum pudding was given to her by a friend from South Carolina at whose house everything to eat ought to have been recorded in shorthand on the spot. Unfortunately being then young and frivolous, Mrs. Appleyard missed her opportunity. She regrets that she never learned how to cook those soft-shell crabs, that hominy in her hands never has quite its full charm, that her stewed tomatoes just miss some subtle flavor, that she never could have greeted with quite the same aplomb the episode of the turkey.

Mrs. Rodman was one of those who can always inspire good cooking in others, even when the material seems unpromising. The material at hand when the turkey was roasted was a willing but inexperienced little Swedish girl named Sigrid. She was round and slow, with earnest blue eyes. It was a mistake to think that she was stupid and Mrs. Rodman did not think so, but it was also a mistake for her to try to move faster than her own rhythm dictated. It was unfortunate that, filled with zeal and pride over its splendid appearance, she tried to hurry the Christmas turkey into the dining-room.

It was an enormous turkey. It had, Mrs. Appleyard seems to remember, oyster stuffing inside it. Chains of brown sausages were draped over its noble breast. Parsley and celery wreathed it artistically. It was on a silver platter so large that Sigrid's plump arms could hardly go around it, and her platinum head with its neat braids came just high enough above the crackly brown turkey for you to see the pride in her blue eyes and the pink flush that baking the sizzling bird had given her.

Sigrid's pride lasted only just through the swinging door and around the Chinese screen. She herself had waxed the floor to the polish of an old mirror. Turning the corner by the screen at unusual speed was too much for her. Her feet went out. The platter rolled one way, the turkey another. Parsley, celery, sausages flew through the air.

Mrs. Appleyard remembers that Mrs. Rodman always looked the way a French marquise ought to look — only probably one never did. She may have recently taken off her cooking-apron, but she never brought the kitchen into the dining-room. This neutrality toward a meal after it was ready she carried out in the case of the skidding turkey.

Into the silence that fell upon the eleven people around the mahogany came her voice, saying kindly but crisply, 'Pick up the turkey, Sigrid, and bring the other one.'

Of course there was no other turkey, but when the first one emerged from the kitchen once more, it looked as handsome as ever. Its roll on the immaculate waxed floor had done it no harm. Sigrid's face was saved. The guests, according to their own discretion, had either the satisfaction of thinking that there really were two turkeys or of enjoying the joke.

When Mrs. Rodman was asked later why she knew that Sigrid would respond in the emergency, she replied, 'I've cooked with her.'

It is still, Mrs. Appleyard thinks, a good way to know another person.

After the turkey came the plum pudding. It arrived safely in blue flames with a spray of holly stuck in the top, and this was the way it was made.

PLUM PUDDING (A. C. R.)

1 lb. beef suet, ground fine	1 t. each of cloves, cin-
½ lb. citron, diced	namon, and allspice
½ lb. raisins	Juice of 1 lemon
¼ lb. candied cherries	2 T. rose water
½ lb. currants	2 T. rum
½ lb. almonds, blanched and ground	1 c. sherry
2 c. French bread crumbs	10 eggs
½ nutmeg grated	2 c. sugar
½ t. salt	1 c. flour

Dry the French bread — inside of the loaf only — and make it into very fine crumbs. Mix it with the chopped suet, almonds, citron, raisins, currants, and cherries. Sprinkle the spices and salt over the fruit and mix well. Pour the rose water, lemon juice, sherry, and rum over them. Stir. Cover the bowl and let it stand overnight. The next day beat the yolks of the eggs well and add them to the sugar. Beat the whites stiff but not dry and fold them into the yolks. Add this mixture to the fruit mixture. Scatter the flour over the whole thing and fold it in.

This will make about eight pounds. Use coffee cans, large baking-powder cans, anything with a tight cover to steam the pudding in. Butter them well. Fill them not more than two thirds full. Set them on a rack in a large kettle with a tight cover. Steam them for five or six hours.

Mrs. Rodman used to make these puddings and send them to her friends for Christmas — a pleasant custom. In serving hers Mrs. Appleyard used to steam it long enough to heat it through, stick holly into it, pour brandy around it, and bring it in lighted. She never did so without thinking of her friend saying, 'Sigrid, pick up the turkey. . . .'

In fact she has told the story often enough so that it is entered in her children's under-the-dinner-table notebook under Food and Wine Anecdotes, No. 87.

There are various kinds of sauce that are good with plum pudding. Hard Sauce (page 222) is good. So is Foamy Sauce (page 227). Mrs. Appleyard sometimes makes hard sauce and puts a little of her Brandied Fruit (page 204) with it, but as there is perhaps already enough brandy in the pudding for some tastes, she sometimes makes

VELVET–PUDDING SAUCE

½ c. butter creamed	1 egg, well beaten
1 c. powdered sugar	½ t. vanilla

This is very easy to make as it is not cooked.

Cream the butter, add the sugar gradually and then the beaten egg. Add the vanilla. This can be fixed, except for the egg and the flavoring beforehand. It takes only a minute to beat in the egg.

If you like rice pudding — Mrs. Appleyard can't see why anyone does — this kind has at least the advantage of being creamy and delicately flavored.

RICE PUDDING (S. W. E.)

2½ T. rice (level measurement)	1 qt. milk
3 T. sugar	¼ c. seedless raisins
¼ t. lemon extract or	½ t. salt
¼ t. vanilla	

Wash the rice in several changes of water. Butter a thick pottery baking-dish. Put in the milk and stir into it the rice, sugar, raisins, and flavoring. Bake it for at least two hours in a slow oven — 300° F. During the first hour, stir it three times. There will be skin over the top and you must slide your spoon carefully under it at the side and stir the contents without breaking the skin. Reduce the heat if the skin is browning too fast.

Purists, those who like rice pudding, often prefer it without the raisins. Mrs. Appleyard sees no point in taking sides in this argument. There is a tradition in her family that she always wept at the sight of rice pudding — large silent tears trickled down her upturned nose and made her look somehow more than ever like the King Charles spaniel that she was said to resemble.

She has learned since not to shed tears, but that is as far as she plans to get. Still, she has acquired a taste for horehound candy, cottage cheese, and spinach — all substances to which the average child is hostile. Perhaps she will graduate to gruel, rice pudding, and rennet. Nothing is impossible. She may even learn to cherish tripe — that dishonest dish that looks like a waffle, feels like a raw eel, and tastes like an umbrella.

Mrs. Appleyard shudders, and turns to her own chocolate pudding. It happened one day at Appleyard Centre that, owing to world conditions or something, there was discovered in the pantry a third of a chocolate cake and half a stale coconut frosted cake. This circumstance is something like the likelihood of Mars, Jupiter, and Venus all hanging in the west in a straight line in a primrose-and-blue sky with rose-colored clouds above them — yet both things have happened in Mrs. Appleyard's lifetime, and may again. Anyway, sponge cake would do and you would just add more chocolate and some coconut. You have to be a little daring in this world every now and then.

CHOCOLATE PUDDING (MRS. APPLEYARD)

One-third of an 8-inch chocolate cake with chocolate frosting
Half an 8-inch coconut cake
2 c. milk
1 t. vanilla
½ c. sugar

2 sqs. chocolate
¼ t. salt
2 T. Zo or Grapenuts
2 eggs
2 T. light-brown or maple sugar

There should be about three cups of cake crumbs when you have rolled them fine. Heat the milk, add the sugar and the chocolate, grated. Stir till well mixed, add the vanilla and the salt, and pour the mixture over the cake crumbs. Beat two eggs light and beat them well into the mixture. Butter a baking-dish, put in the mixture, sprinkle the top with the Zo and brown sugar mixed together. Bake for half an hour at 400° F. The top should be crisp and crusty. Serve it hot with Hard Sauce or Foamy Sauce, or cold with thick cream.

The best Indian pudding that either Mr. or Mrs. Appleyard ever ate was in a little Vermont inn not far from the Connecticut. Mr. Appleyard would not rest until he found out how it was made. He turned on his full charm and the waitress guaranteed to wheedle the rule from the cook.

When she came back, she said, with blushes and giggles, that the cook did not want to tell. She was of the opinion — as Vermonters usually are when asked for a receipt — that it was not fit to eat anyway, that she didn't think she'd had extra good luck with it, and that if Mr. Appleyard knew how it was made, he'd never eat her cooking again.

These preliminaries being disposed of, the secret was then revealed: there happened to be some cold johnnycake left

from breakfast and the pudding was made from that. Mr.
Appleyard thinks that the fact that the corn meal in the
jonnnycake had already been cooked and that the johnnycake had plenty of eggs and sour cream in it helped to make
the pudding especially good. This was how it was done:

INDIAN PUDDING (CONNECTICUT RIVER VALLEY)

Square of cold johnny cake 6 by 8 inches.
Spider Corn Cake (see page 50) may be used

1 qt. of milk	½ t. salt
½ c. molasses	½ t. nutmeg
2 eggs	½ t. cinnamon

Crumble the johnnycake very fine. Pour the milk over
it and soak it well. Add the molasses and seasonings, mix
well, and let it stand on the back of the stove for a while.
Beat two eggs and add them. Taste it and add more
molasses if you like. Put it into a buttered baking-dish,
earthenware, and bake it for one and a half hours at 350° F.
Stir it three times the first hour, slipping the spoon in at
the side and taking care not to break the skin.

Serve with thick cream and powdered maple sugar
(page 82) or vanilla ice cream. What a surprise it would
be to an Iroquois to find vanilla ice cream on his pudding!...

18

Salad, and Salad Dressings. Assuming
that whatever vegetables go into a salad are in good con-
dition — and why make salad at all if they are not? — Mrs.
Appleyard thinks that the dressing is more important than
the precise combination in the salad bowl. Therefore she
begins with some different dressings. What you put them
on is really your own affair, she says. Coming from her this
is unusually liberal treatment.

Ideally all salad dressing made with oil should be made
with olive oil, but probably for the next few years we are not
going to see much of it. Mrs. Appleyard, who has cooked
and eaten through one war, thinks that there are worse fates
than cottonseed oil in your salad dressing. We all eat a
good deal of it in commercial salad dressing without notic-
ing it much, she says. If you have olive oil on hand, treasure
it for your French dressing and begin by using part olive oil
and part Wesson oil. Gradually increase the proportion of
the Wesson oil and you will hardly know when the olive oil
is gone. Some people even get so that they prefer cotton-

seed oil. In using it, season the dressing a little more highly than you would for olive oil, use the very best vinegar, always have some chives on hand, and you'll get by somehow.

A good many of us are going to have to practice forgotten economies and ingenuities. We have also got to stay at home more because we are not going to have cars at our disposal when it occurs to us that it would be fun to drive out to Ye Olde Blacksmythe and Plumbinge Shoppe for lunch. As long as we have got to give up this pastime — the tantalizing, sticky rolls, the agonizing choice between lobster and chicken, the ball of ice cream set like a rare jewel in its small paper frill, the brightly colored vegetables that all taste alike — and stay in that half-familiar house quaintly known as home, perhaps we might as well spend some time making our own mayonnaise. That isn't a bad place to start our new life. By all means do it if you are lucky enough to have an electric mixer.

If you make it by hand, use a bowl with a rounded bottom. Use a French whip or a rotary beater. Have the bowl, beater, and eggs, well chilled.

MAYONNAISE DRESSING

2 raw egg yolks	1 t. salt
3 T. vinegar or lemon juice	¼ t. pepper
2 c. salad oil	½ t. paprika
1 t. powdered sugar	1 t. dry mustard

Mix the dry ingredients together, add them to the egg yolks, beat well, and add the vinegar or lemon juice (use some of each if you prefer) and beat some more. Then add the oil gradually, drop by drop at first, later in larger quantities, beating all the time. If the dressing begins to curdle, start over again with a third egg yolk, beat a little of the remaining oil into it and then work in the curdled dressing. Remember that mayonnaise should be kept in a cool place but not in the very cold part of the refrigerator. It separates if it gets too cold. A good cool cellarway like the one at Appleyard Centre is an ideal place to keep mayonnaise. As this is not yet standard equipment for city apartments, perhaps it is better to make mayonnaise in quantities that will be quickly consumed.

Remember too that mayonnaise separates if you mix it with the salad too long ahead of time, and that mayonnaise to which cream is added will be thinner than plain mayonnaise.

When you get the trick of it there is a quick way of making mayonnaise that is much easier than the version given above. The difficulty about this way is that you have to exercise judgment about the amount of oil used, and that is something you have to learn by trying.

QUICK MAYONNAISE (M. W.)

1 whole egg, unbeaten	1 t. powdered sugar
1 T. vinegar	¼ t. pepper
1 T. salad oil	½ t. paprika
1 t. salt	Extra salad oil — at
1 t. dry mustard	least a cup

Mix the seasonings together and put them into a chilled bowl with the egg, vinegar, and one tablespoonful of salad oil. Beat them together thoroughly with the egg-beater. When the mixture is thick and well blended, splash in the rest of the oil, beating all the time, and put in all the mixture will hold. If it separates, start over again with another egg, beat in a little of the oil, and add the rest of the dressing. If you like tarragon vinegar, use it in this. You can make it yourself by pouring some mild cider vinegar over a few fresh tarragon leaves. One plant in your garden will produce enough tarragon leaves for a whole year's supply of vinegar and some to give away. Mrs. Appleyard buys sweet cider in the fall — the kind without any preservative — and leaves some of it in a warm place.

It obligingly turns to vinegar, and Mr. Appleyard is very handy about straining it through cheesecloth. This gives you a supply of vinegar for no trouble and fifty cents a gallon. Mrs. Appleyard makes some into tarragon vinegar, uses some plain in mayonnaise or anything that calls for it, and uses the rest in pickles of different kinds. The time soon arrives when she wishes she had made more.

For French dressing, however, she buys red-wine vinegar and puts one or two beans of garlic in the bottle. That is one reason why people ask Mr. Appleyard how he makes his French dressing.

It has been often wisely said that there is no such thing as a little garlic. Either you have garlic or you don't have garlic. Mr. Appleyard says that a bean of garlic in a quart of vinegar really produces something that may be honestly described as a little garlic. It's there but you don't know it: all you know is that the dressing has some zip to it.

This is how Mr. Appleyard makes French dressing for a bowl of native lettuce:

FRENCH DRESSING (MR. APPLEYARD)

1 T. garlic red-wine vinegar	½ t. salt
½ t. dry mustard	A few grains of cayenne
¼ t. black pepper	3 T. salad oil
½ t. paprika	

Mr. Appleyard begins by putting all the dry seasonings into a large wooden spoon (blessings be upon the head of the giver of that salad spoon and fork a quarter of a century ago) and mixing them together with the fork over the blue Canton soup plate in which he is going to mix the dressing. He really likes to have this plate set into a larger one with ice in it, but he doesn't make too much fuss about it. Next he pours into the spoon over the mixed seasonings a tablespoonful of garlic red-wine vinegar and goes on mixing with the fork. This may begin to splash out into the plate a little, and it does not matter because he needs room for the oil in the spoon, and pretty soon he fills up the spoon with the oil, still mixing all the time, of course. By now the seasonings are well blended and he dumps the whole spoonful into the plate and fills up the spoon again with oil until he has used three tablespoonfuls, adds it to the vinegar mixture, and stirs hard. After a little while he takes a small piece of bread crust, dips it into the dressing and tastes it, looking wise.

Mrs. Appleyard accuses him of doing this because he likes the taste, but it is true that he does sometimes make some minute addition to the seasoning — his private preference being for more mustard than he has found others like — and he has been known to add a drop or two of Worcestershire sauce.

The salad — plain lettuce with some chopped chives sprinkled over it or some combination of greens — is now ready in a bowl that is big enough to mix it in. He pours in the dressing with a handsome flourish, and turns over the greens with the fork and spoon gently so that each leaf is coated with the dressing. It is a waste of good dressing, he says, to pour it into the bowl without this thorough mixing.

If you hurry it, the dressing goes to the bottom of the bowl and the salad is still just a collection of rabbit food and the dressing is ultimately poured into the sink, where its only effect is that the sink is hard to clean.

If there is more than the usual amount of lettuce, Mr. Appleyard starts all over again on a second batch of dressing. He says you can't mix it thoroughly enough with large quantities and get the seasonings really blended with the oil and vinegar.

VARIATIONS OF FRENCH DRESSING

Roquefort Dressing. Add 1 T. crumbled Roquefort cheese after you add the oil. Argentine or Wisconsin blue cheese may be used instead of Roquefort, and Gold N' Rich cheese, crumbled, is also good.

Anchovy Dressing. Omit ¼ t. of the salt and add 1 T. anchovy paste before you add the oil. This is good for a salad of lettuce hearts garnished with strips of anchovy fillets. If there is oil with the anchovies, use it in the dressing.

Olive Dressing. 1 T. ripe olives chopped, 1 T. green stuffed olives, chopped, half a green pepper — minced, 1 hard-boiled egg — white chopped, yolk grated), 1 T. chopped chives. Make a double quantity of the French dressing. Put all the other ingredients into a jar, pour the dressing over them, cover the jar tightly and shake it hard. Good with a salad of lettuce and tomatoes. Give the jar another good shaking before you pour the dressing over the salad.

Chutney Dressing. 2 T. of Major Grey's chutney, minced fine. Mix well with the dressing and serve it with plain lettuce, mixing it in well. Serve toasted cheese sandwiches with this.

SOUR-CREAM DRESSING (FOR POTATO SALAD)

½ c. thick sour cream	½ t. paprika
½ t. salt	¼ T. pepper
½ t. powdered sugar	1 T. chopped chives
1 T. lemon juice	1 T. minced parsley

Mix all together and beat well. Use tarragon vinegar in place of the lemon juice if you prefer. The sugar may be omitted from any of these rules: it merely serves to bring out the flavor a little and is not strictly necessary if you are on short rations of it. These amounts are so small, however, that it seems as if the saving might better be done on a larger scale.

LEMON MAYONNAISE (FOR FRUIT SALAD)

Make regular mayonnaise (page 237) with lemon juice. Take off the thin yellow peel of one lemon, let it stand in a half-cup of thick cream for half an hour. Remove the lemon, whip the cream, and add it to the mayonnaise.

CREAM DRESSING (FOR SHREDDED CABBAGE)

¼ c. thick sour cream	1 t. powdered sugar
1 whole egg, beaten	½ t. salt
¼ c. mild vinegar	¼ t. pepper
1 t. mustard	½ t. paprika

Mix the vinegar and the dry seasonings. Beat the egg and beat the cream into it. Just before serving beat the two mixtures together and mix them thoroughly with the shredded cabbage. Some grated carrot and a little grated onion combine well with the cabbage.

RUSSIAN DRESSING

1 c. mayonnaise (page 237)	1 T. chopped chives
2 T. chili sauce	1 t. chopped green pepper
1 t. Worcestershire sauce	½ t. paprika

Probably this dressing is no more Russian than Mrs. Appleyard, but anyway it's good on a salad of raw cauliflower and tomato, and also good to serve in a bowl with raw cauliflower broken up to dunk in it.

Mix everything up together and stir it into the Mayonnaise.

SALAD MATERIALS

Combination 1. Lettuce, chicory, asparagus tips, tomatoes. Serve with French dressing into which you have mixed 1 t. pickled beets, finely chopped, 1 t. minced parsley, 1 t. chopped onion.

Combination 2. Lettuce and watercress with finely chopped herbs — fresh tarragon, chives, parsley, chervil, thyme, a very little sage. French dressing.

Combination 3. Curly bronze lettuce, romaine, plain lettuce, sliced cucumbers, radishes. Olive Dressing (page 241). With this serve toasted Montpelier crackers and Frozen Cheese made by blending ½ lb. cottage cheese, ¼ lb. Roquefort or Argentine blue cheese, 2 t. minced chives, ½ t. Worcestershire sauce, ½ t. salt, ½ t. paprika, and ¼ c. cream. Chill the mixture in the refrigerator tray for an hour. Cut it in cubes and toss it in with the salad.

Combination 4. Shredded iceberg lettuce, shredded white cabbage, romaine, chicory, sliced tomatoes, small cubes of tongue or chicken, and ham, crisp chopped bacon, sliced stuffed olives. French dressing.

All these are good and so are many others. So is the Vegetable Salad that is served on the lawn at Appleyard Centre on warm evenings.

APPLEYARD CENTRE VEGETABLE SALAD

Mrs. Appleyard brings out the big oblong wooden salad bowl — it was once used for working butter. It has seen hard times, but lately it has enjoyed life. Mrs. Appleyard, with sandpaper, broken glass, and steel wool — none of which ingredients appear in the salad — has brought it back to something fairly close to its old smoothness. Not caring for the flavor of linseed and turpentine in her salad, Mrs. Appleyard uses French dressing to finish her salad bowls. This makes a better furniture polish than those without an analytical mind might think. The vinegar bleaches the wood, the dry seasonings act as a slight abrasive, the oil protects it from absorbing liquids that might stain it. A bowl finished this way should never be scoured. Just rinse it out, rub it hard, and put it in the sun to dry.

Mrs. Appleyard has told elsewhere [1] how she finishes table-tops with linseed oil and powdered pumice. She did not however at that time tell the Editor that, after starting a table with linseed oil and getting the grain well filled up with the hardened oil, you can keep it shining simply by rubbing in anything that comes handy — a dash of salad dressing, a little Hollandaise, and especially cream. You can generally identify anyone who has ever spent a summer at Appleyard Centre by an absent-minded habit of rubbing cream into any table at which he is sitting. This is one of those local customs — like that practiced automatically by

[1] *Mrs. Appleyard's Year.* Houghton Mifflin Company, 1941.

Harvard students who have eaten at their native tables, of wiping the silver on the napkin before use — that sometimes draws a raised eyebrow from the hostess. It is distinctly not politic to try to rub cream into a damask or lace tablecloth. ...

There is also, Mrs. Appleyard has read somewhere, the possibility of finishing a table with orange juice. There is something attractive about this idea, but Mrs. Appleyard's first attempt can hardly be rated as a success. You were supposed to rub the juice in with the peel. She did, but it seems that there is more in it than meets the nose. The only point on which she has no doubts is that grapefruit or orange juice spattered on a table makes little lacquered spots that have to be washed off with warm water. Perhaps, therefore, if you had enough orange juice, you could really lacquer a table with it. Mrs. Appleyard, however, prefers to drink it and, for a heat-, water-, and alcohol-proof finish, to depend on that old reliable bottle of two parts boiled linseed and one part turpentine, the finest powdered pumice, plenty of rags, and shoulder power. In spite of old saws about elbow grease, it is with your shoulders and back that you do most of the rubbing.

This isn't the way to get the salad bowl filled, is it?

The ingredients are usually: cauliflower, carrots, beets, tomatoes, celery, green peas, green and wax beans, onions, curly lettuce, sliced hard-boiled eggs.

In the middle of the bowl Mrs. Appleyard puts a small but perfect head of cauliflower, cooked. Next a ring of tiny new beets, cooked. Then a ring of very small carrots, cooked and diced. The next row is getting pretty big, so it will probably consist of small heaps of different kinds of vegetables: crisp raw celery, bright green peas, the yellow and the green beans, cut fine and cooked, some cubes of cooked potato mixed with chopped chives and parsley. Next come slices of ripe tomatoes, peeled and cut thick, and last of all is a border of green and bronze lettuce.

All these vegetables are first marinated in some French dressing that has in it several teaspoonfuls of onion, minced so fine that you hardly know it is there. This supplies most of the flavor, but to please the eye there is Quick Mayonnaise (page 238) to which some sour cream has been added dotted here and there among the vegetables. Mrs. Appleyard obligingly answered the following questionnaire on vegetable salad.

'How much does this bowl you mention — I believe you referred to it as a butter boat — hold, Mrs. Appleyard?'

'Oh, I don't know. A couple of gallons, I suppose.'

'How long does it take to fill it?'

'Well, including picking the vegetables, about a day, I think.'

'You consider that a good way to spend your time?'

'I do.'

'What did you do with what was left over?'

'I don't know.'

'You don't know? Now really, Mrs. Appleyard, our radio audience isn't going to believe that — just try to think. No coaching, please....'

'There never was any.'

'Do you know any other kinds of vegetable salad?'

'What am I — a Quiz Kid? Of course I do....'

VEGETABLE SALAD 2

This time Mrs. Appleyard takes another wooden bowl, a big round one, and sets into the middle of it a glass dish of mayonnaise. She surrounds it with the following vegetables that have been marinated in a French dressing with plenty of minced onion in it: cooked beets, asparagus tips, peas, raw carrot and cucumber cut into matchstick pieces, finely cut celery, purple onions — sliced, red tomatoes — sliced, yellow tomatoes — peeled and left whole. Chicory and watercress go around the edge.

VEGETABLE SALAD 3

This kind is all mixed together. It has raw cauliflower separated into flowerets, raw carrot, cooked beets, cooked potato, string beans, peas, chopped onion, white cabbage — finely shredded, green pepper — minced, cubes of baked ham and tongue.

It is first marinated in French dressing, then has mayonnaise mixed with it. It goes into a big yellow pottery bowl with curly lettuce around it. There is of course no end to the different combinations of vegetables that you may use. One charm about these salads is that they are never twice exactly alike. They are distinctly country salads, meant for hearty appetites and depending for their goodness on the vegetables' being perfect of their kind.

POTATO SALAD

6 potatoes, baked or boiled in their jackets	1 T. finely minced onion
½ t. salt	¼ t. pepper
2 T. cider vinegar	1 T. finely minced parsley

As soon as the potatoes are cooked — Mrs. Appleyard thinks the baked ones have the best flavor — dice or slice them into a mixing-bowl. Sprinkle over them the vinegar mixed with the seasonings and the onion. Cover the bowl. When the potato is cool, set the bowl into the refrigerator. When you are ready to serve the salad, stir into it some Sour-Cream Dressing (page 242) and the minced parsley, mixing it all gently together. This has much more flavor than salad made out of any left-over potatoes that you happen to stumble over when you are looking for those egg whites you know you had left from the Hollandaise yesterday.

CABBAGE AND RAW CARROT SALAD

White cabbage	Onion
Raw carrots	Mayonnaise

Grate white cabbage and raw carrot until your elbow gives out. Grate a little raw onion and mix the whole thing together with mayonnaise or part mayonnaise and part sour-cream dressing.

This is especially good with sausage, roast pork, or pork chops.

VEGETABLE SALAD DE LUXE

1 c. cubes of cooked carrot	1 onion, minced
1 c. cubed potato	2 hard-boiled eggs
1 c. cooked peas	2 T. red caviar
1 c. cooked lima beans	Smoked salmon
1 c. beets, cooked and cubed	Anchovy fillets
1 c. raw celery, cut fine	Watercress
2 T. minced parsley	Lettuce

Put the vegetables in separate bowls and marinate them with French dressing and add a little of the chopped onion to each bowl. In the middle of a large deep platter put a silver bowl or a glass dish of Russian Dressing (page 243). Arrange the lettuce and watercress around the edge of the platter and then make wedge-shaped sections of the vegetables around the bowl of dressing, alternating the bright colored ones with the green and white ones. Divide the sections with lines of minced parsley. Garnish two of the sections with smoked salmon, two with anchovy fillets (or sardines, if you like them better), one with chopped egg white, one with grated egg yolk. Dot a little of the red caviar here and there. This is a good salad to serve with Baked Ham (page 183).

SPRING SALAD WITH CHOPPED BACON

Watercress	Cucumber, thinly sliced
Chicory	Tomatoes (little hothouse ones,
Lettuce	sliced)
Radishes, sliced	Bacon, fried crisp and
Purple onion	crumbled

Put all the salad materials into a large bowl. Scatter the bacon through them. Make the French dressing at the table, pour it over the salad, mixing it gently and thoroughly so that every bit of it is coated with the dressing.

Boston Brown Bread (page 40) sliced thin and buttered and made into sandwiches is good with this.

19

Sauces. If you are going to make sauces for meat, fish, or vegetables, there are certain things that are convenient to have on hand. Among them are:

Worcestershire sauce (always pronounced Worcester)
Dried onion flakes (when you want only a suggestion of onion or run out of onions)
Bay leaves (ten cents' worth will last for years)
Dried parsley (in case fresh is not available)
Tarragon vinegar
Cloves of garlic
Garlic red-wine vinegar
Pepper, ground: white, black, cayenne
Whole black peppercorns
Paprika
Spices, ground: cloves, nutmeg, allspice, mace
Whole cloves, stick cinnamon, whole nutmegs
Curry powder
Celery salt
Dry mustard

Canned tomato soup or tomato paste
Canned consommé
Canned chicken broth
Currant jelly
Lemons
Fresh or dried sage, thyme, marjoram
Bell's poultry seasoning

This magnificent list makes it seem as if Mrs. Appleyard bathed everything in sauce. As a matter of fact, she is generally eating plain cold lamb and wishing there were some mint-sauce left from yesterday. Still, when she is in a mood to make sauce she likes to have the seasonings needed, and they last a long time after you have once bought them. Whole books have been written about sauces — and a lot of nonsense incidentally. There is supposed to be some dark mystery about them that keeps ordinary people from dealing with anything more exciting than brown gravy. Yet a lot of people who are not exactly Doctors of Philosophy manage to make them, and you certainly can make the ones that Mrs. Appleyard mentions if you will remember the simple principle that unless you use the best materials it is a lot better not to have any sauce at all.

WHITE SAUCE

Mrs. Appleyard sometimes thinks there ought to be a law against white sauce.

'Go out into our fair land,' she says, 'so beautiful for fields of amber grain, and eat your lunch where you happen to stop. You will get the impression that a lot of the amber grain has gone into the making of paperhanger's paste and then, by some strange industrial accident, been transferred to dishes prankishly listed as creamed potatoes, creamed carrots, creamed fish, and so on.

'I have even,' she says, 'in a city that I hesitate to name, having received much kind hospitality there, encountered the same substance, only colored a bilious yellow and travelling under the name of Hollandaise. . . .'

Here Mrs. Appleyard began to pace the floor, uttering low imprecations, but was calmed down by the application of a few puff-paste cheese straws, and went on to say with only a moderate amount of bitterness that Hollandaise sauce should contain eggs and butter, and that cream sauce should be made with cream. (This woman is certainly a fearless, original thinker.)

Cream sauce, she said, should not be a mixture of skim milk and half-cooked flour. If you feel cream is too expensive, put on a little butter and let it go at that. Never try to make a white sauce with less butter than flour: always use at least equal amounts, and use rich milk with the cream left in it and add a little more cream.

So many dishes — soups, sauces, soufflés, scalloped dishes — depend on white sauce as their basis that you should know how to make it well and quickly, even if you do not use it often on vegetables. Your rule may call for thin, medium, or thick white sauce. Use these proportions:

THIN WHITE SAUCE

1 T. flour	1 T. butter
½ c. cream	½ c. milk
¼ t. salt	⅛ t. pepper

MEDIUM WHITE SAUCE

2 T. flour	2 T. butter
½ c. cream	½ c. milk
¼ t. salt	⅛ t. pepper

THICK WHITE SAUCE

3–4 T. flour	3–4 T. butter
½ c. cream	½ c. milk
¼ t. salt	⅛ t. pepper

Melt the butter. When it bubbles and froths, rub in the flour sifted with the seasonings. Reduce the heat and cook this roux of butter and flour very slowly for three minutes — this is how to get the taste of raw flour out of your sauce. Stir it carefully and be sure it does not get darker than a deep rich ivory color. Now stir in the cold milk, a little at first, and rub it to a smooth paste with the back of the spoon. Be sure you get out all the lumps at this stage unless you like to meet them later. When this paste is perfectly smooth, add the rest of the milk and then the cream. Cook it slowly for another ten minutes below boiling point — a double boiler is a good place for this. Taste it and add more seasoning if you like.

Into each life some rain must fall, and it happens to almost everyone sooner or later that the white sauce has lumps in it. Perhaps the telephone rings or that delightful gentleman with the brushes-of-more-than-human-intelligence comes to the door. You relax your grip on the sauce just at the crucial moment and chaos results. Don't worry too much. Strain it through a fine sieve, rubbing all you can of the flour through, and no one will ever know — especially if you remember to wash the strainer.

Mrs. Appleyard generally makes white sauce in an iron frying-pan. She likes the sauce to cover a large area as it cooks. She thinks it is easier to cook raw flour thoroughly and slowly this way.

CREAM SAUCE

Use all cream instead of milk and make like thin white sauce. Add whatever you are creaming — chicken, eggs, a vegetable — add the seasoning you like — a little onion, some paprika for Mrs. Appleyard — and let the sauce and whatever you have added to it mellow and blend for twenty minutes in the double boiler while you are doing something else.

CHEESE SAUCE

Add ½ c. grated cheese, ½ t. grated onion, ⅛ t. mustard, and ½ t. paprika to medium white sauce.

EGG SAUCE

Add 1 hard-boiled egg and ¼ t. grated onion to medium white sauce. Remove the onion when you serve the sauce.

OYSTER SAUCE

Heat ½ pint of oysters in their own juice for each cup of thick white sauce. Cook them until their edges curl. Cook a slice of onion with them. Add them to the sauce. When you serve it, sprinkle some paprika over it and remove the onion. Good to serve with boiled fowl.

ONION SAUCE

Mince three large onions fine for each cup of medium white sauce. Cook them with butter until they are tender. Add enough more butter to make two tablespoons and work in the butter, milk, and cream. Add about a teaspoon of minced parsley. Good with fish.

CHICKEN CREAM SAUCE

To 1 c. cream sauce add 1 c. chicken stock. Canned chicken broth will do. Add some slices of onion. Beat two egg yolks. Spoon some of the sauce over them, mix well, and put the mixture back into the sauce. Cook in the top of the double boiler. Add a pinch of nutmeg. When serving, remove the onion and add some minced parsley.

HOLLANDAISE SAUCE

This is generally considered hard to make, but Mrs. Appleyard says that if you follow the directions it is really less trouble than almost any other sauce.

½ c. butter	1 T. lemon juice
¼ t. salt	Slight grating of lemon rind
Yolks of 2 eggs	Pinch of cayenne

Use only the very best butter. Divide it into three pieces. Put the egg yolks, unbeaten, the salt, pepper, lemon juice, and rind into the top of the double boiler over hot, not boiling, water. Begin beating with a wire whisk and add the first piece of butter. Keep beating and as the butter melts, add the second piece. The sauce will start to thicken and you keep on beating and as the second piece of butter disappears, you add the third piece. Here's your danger point. Just as this last piece of butter melts — keep on beating all the time — remove the sauce from over the hot water. If you leave it even a second too long it will separate Don't have hysterics if it does, because it can be brought back by beating in about a teaspoonful of cream. Be sure the cream is well chilled. Put the sauce into a warm — not hot — bowl.

There is no such thing as keeping Hollandaise sauce hot. It must be served *at once*. This is the only difficulty about it. Making it simply means that you must plan an extra five minutes just before you are going to send the asparagus — or what ever you serve it with — to the table.

This rule makes a thick sauce. It may be thinned by adding two teaspoonfuls of cream and one of hot water mixed together so that they are not too hot.

Always make plenty of Hollandaise and never spurn any that is left over. You can work it into salad dressing, or sandwiches, or into some other sauce. Just use your ingenuity.

BÉARNAISE SAUCE

This is very much like Hollandaise. Use white-wine vinegar instead of lemon juice. Cook a tablespoonful of chopped shallots or young onions and a teaspoon of tarragon leaves first in the vinegar. Start with enough vinegar to cover the leaves and cook it down to a tablespoonful. Strain it and go on from there as you did with the Hollandaise and at the end add a teaspoonful of minced parsley. Mrs. Appleyard remembers pleasantly some thick lamb chops with this sauce on them. Good with steak, too — but then, what isn't?

HOLLANDAISE TOMATO SAUCE

You can make a rather handsomely colored sauce, good with white fish, by adding two tablespoonfuls of thick tomato soup to Hollandaise. Have the soup warm — not hot — and beat it in just before the last of the butter melts. (Mrs. Appleyard thinks Hollandaise is better plain.)

MUSHROOM SAUCE (MRS. APPLEYARD)

1 lb. mushrooms, peeled, caps only	1 c. light cream
4 T. butter	1 T. sherry
2 t. flour	Bit of bay leaf
½ small onion minced	½ t. salt
1 c. heavy cream	¼ t. pepper
	⅛ t. nutmeg

Save the mushroom skins and stems for soup (page 281). Cut the peeled caps into quarters. Fry them gently in the butter with the onion till they are tender — about five minutes. Take them out and put them into the top of the double boiler. Now rub in the flour as you would for white sauce, adding more butter if necessary. There should be at least two tablespoonfuls in the pan. Be sure the roux is thoroughly blended and let it cook very slowly for three minutes. Now add the thin cream, slowly at first to make a thin smooth paste free from lumps, and then more rapidly. Add the seasonings — or sift them in first with the flour — and add the heavy cream and the bay leaf. Let the sauce cook gently — but do not let it boil — for five minutes and then pour it over the mushrooms in the double boiler. This sauce will be all the better if you make it ahead of time and leave it to blend in the double boiler. Add the sherry just before you serve it. Good with fish, ham, or chicken mousse.

CURRANT-JELLY SAUCE (MRS. APPLEYARD)

1 8-oz. glass of red-currant jelly	Thin peel of 1 orange
½ c. consommé	Juice of 1 orange
Thin yellow peel of 1 lemon	1 t. lemon juice

Mix the consommé, the peel, and the lemon and orange juice. When it starts to boil, add the currant jelly and let it melt. Set it aside where it will keep hot. Remove the peel and have it very hot when you serve it.

Mrs. Appleyard sometimes solves her cold-lamb problem by heating it up — cut in thick slices — in this sauce. It is supposed to taste like venison and does taste at least as much like venison as it does like cold lamb, and that's something anyway.

Variations of this are:

Currant Bitter-Orange Sauce. Instead of the orange and lemon juice and peel add two tablespoonfuls of orange marmalade. Good with duck.

Currant Mint Sauce. Add two tablespoonfuls of finely minced fresh mint leaves. Good with roast lamb.

Currant Raisin Sauce.

1 8-oz. glass of currant jelly	1 c. seedless raisins
1 c. consommé	3 cloves
1 lemon, sliced thin	⅛ t. cinnamon
2 T. orange marmalade	

Cook the raisins in the consommé until they are tender. Add the rest of the ingredients and serve when the jelly is melted and the sauce is very hot. A smoked shoulder is much cheered up when served hot with this — good with pork or tongue, too.

SPANISH SAUCE FOR OMELET

1 tomato	6 mushrooms
1 green pepper, seeded	4 T. butter
1 small onion	½ t. salt
2 sprigs parsley	½ t. paprika
1 stalk celery	⅛ t. cayenne

Chop everything together. Add the seasonings. Simmer

in the butter until the pepper is tender. Put half the sauce inside the omelet and the rest on top with grated cheese sprinkled over it.

TOMATO-CHEESE SAUCE

2 T. butter	½ t. mustard
2 T. flour	½ c. grated cheese
1 c. cream	½ t. salt
1 t. minced onion	¼ t. pepper
2 c. thick tomato soup	6 drops Worcestershire sauce

Fry the onion in the butter, make a roux of the butter and the flour, sifted with the pepper and salt. When it is thoroughly cooked add the cream slowly. Add the cheese. Stir until it melts and add the tomato, mustard, and Worcestershire sauce. Beat thoroughly. Serve it with spaghetti or rice.

BROWN GRAVY

The success of brown gravy depends on the thorough browning of the flour — which does not mean burning. The fat that you use generally comes from a roast and is brown enough anyway. Use two tablespoons of flour to two of fat. Cook the roux well before you add either a cup of consommé or a cup of boiling water in which you have dissolved a soup cube. Taste it and add more seasoning if you like. A few drops of Worcestershire sauce or a little kitchen bouquet help it.

Strain it, if there are any lumps, and then — as far as Mrs. Appleyard is concerned — throw it away, and eat the gravy that runs out of the roast into the well of the platter when Mr. Appleyard has sharpened his knife and made the first cut. It is a pleasant sight, Mrs. Appleyard always thinks, to see his skillful and benevolent carving. Perhaps that is why the dish gravy tastes so good.

20

Soup. Let's be honest about soup, Mrs. Appleyard says.

Most cookbooks are written as if the readers spent their time dallying with large shins of beef, cooking them three days with herbs, and spices, and vegetables, straining, skimming, clearing with egg, throwing away the vegetables — and then being just ready to start making soup. Yet among the facts of life is the homely truth that the chief gesture now used in soup-making is the circular motion by which you guide a cutting edge around a can.

The reason why there are twice as many soup cans as any other kind of can in people's ash barrels is that there are certain kinds of canned soup that are better than anything the average cook can turn out, even after one of those epic struggles with a shin of beef. Canned consommé is stronger, clearer, and better than home-made consommé. Canned black-bean soup is smoother and better flavored than most amateur attempts. Consommé cardinal is more beautifully colored and clearer than anything you can do with white of egg and cheesecloth. Canned tomato soup tastes better than tomato soup made out of anything except the very best tomatoes from your own garden. There are plenty of other good kinds of soup, too, and if your time and patience are worth anything to you, it may be actually more economical to use canned soup than to make your own. By the time you have paid for the materials and the fuel, you may even be out of pocket when your work is over.

However, Mrs. Appleyard does not recommend that one kind of canned soup should follow another just as they come from the can. She regards them rather as a basis for experiment. She frequently combines them, almost always changes the seasoning somewhat, and very often adds to them other stock that she saves, or juice drained from vegetables, or small quantities of vegetables themselves. She seldom serves canned cream soups without adding real cream to them, because somehow when it comes time to add the cream the manufacturers get absent-minded.

There are certain soups that have not yet been canned so that they equal the home-made variety.

Canned chicken broth is useful in cooking where you need a small amount of chicken stock in a hurry, but don't expect it to be quite the same as the chicken soup from Hartwell Farm in Lincoln, Massachusetts, where they use seven or eight chickens to a gallon of soup. This soup is so good that people drive for miles to get it and refuse to believe that there is not some great mystery about the way it is made. Yet there is nothing more to it than this — according to the proprietors of the old weathered farmhouse that has been standing under the huge elm since before the Revolution.

HARTWELL FARM CHICKEN SOUP

To make a gallon of soup they cut up seven or eight plump young fowls, put them into a big aluminum kettle, and cover them with two gallons of water. They think perhaps the water from Sandy Pond in Lincoln may have something to do with the goodness of the soup and also of their coffee. There is certainly, they say, a difference in any cooking you have to do with water that is heavily chlorinated. Sandy Pond water is without the pungent flavor of chlorine.

The chickens go on cooking slowly until they are tender — two or three hours — and until the liquid has cooked down to about five quarts. They take the chickens out and lay them on platters to cool. The meat is to be used in salad or one of their other special dishes. When the stock has jellied around the chickens, the cooks scrape off all the jellied stock that is on the platter and put it back into the soup kettle with the stock. They season the liquid, allowing half a teaspoonful of salt and one quarter of a teaspoonful of pepper to each quart. Next they make a paste of some flour with some of the soup — it takes one cup of flour for a gallon of soup. They strain this back into the soup so that there will be no lumps in it and simmer the soup for seven or eight minutes.

Now the soup is strained into a big aluminum container that has a spigot at the bottom, to keep it hot until it is needed. It is allowed to stand a little while before any of it is drawn off so that any fat that has not blended with the flour can rise to the top. They think one reason why the soup is so good is that it is drawn off from under this floating seal of fat. There is about two inches of it in their big cylindrical container on a gallon of soup. The fat is drawn off and discarded before another lot of soup is put into the container.

The soup is served in earthenware tureens, so hot that you can hardly eat it, and when you have had three plates of it, the waitress comes around and asks you if you would like some more!

Now, the equipment and the number of chickens are not exactly the usual thing for home soup-making, but Mrs. Appleyard has made soup at home by a method quite similar and almost as good. She cooks the young fowls — two usually — cut up and covered with water until the meat falls from the bones. It takes about three quarts of water to cover them and the soup cooks down to about two. The meat she uses for salad or creamed chicken. She puts the jelly on the platter on which the chicken is placed to cool back into the kettle. She also puts back the bones and the skin of the chickens after she has removed the meat from them, and lets them cook a little longer. At this point — there is now about a quart and a half of stock — her practice has been to depart from the Hartwell Farm method because she has no shining kettle with a spigot at the bottom.

Mrs. Appleyard strains the soup into a bowl and sets it away to cool overnight. The next morning she carefully skims off the fat. The soup will be so stiffly jellied that it is easy to separate the fat from it. She takes four tablespoonfuls of the fat and makes a roux of it with an equal amount of flour. When the flour and fat have cooked together for three minutes, she adds a little of the chicken stock warmed enough to melt it, but not hot, works it in, and then adds the rest. She lets it cook gently for a few minutes, tastes it, and adds a little salt, just enough to bring out the chicken flavor. Half a teaspoonful is enough for her, but you may like more — that's your problem. The soup is improved by slow cooking after you add the flour: the top of the double boiler is a good place.

This is a good soup, though not quite so good as the Hartwell Farm version. Perhaps it's that Sandy Pond water (Appleyard Centre water is pretty good too). Or it may be those big tureens like bean pots, or the enormous fireplaces with the big logs blazing in them, or that aluminum tank, or the generous way everything is served, or the whole way in which you are made welcome. Anyway the lesson is: if you want chicken soup, put some chicken in it. It's all right to cook the bones of roast chicken, turkey, or duck for stock, but remember that the poor exhausted creatures have already given you their juice in the meat and in the gravy you made with the juice in the pan. It is unreasonable to expect them to provide a strong soup besides. By all means get what stock you can out of them — it will be useful in many ways, but don't expect miracles.

Returning to those brilliantly labelled cans that certainly should be on your emergency shelf, Mrs. Appleyard is far from spurning them, but she likes to improve on Nature. These are some of the things she does:

Black-Bean Soup is always served with its traditional accompaniment of sliced hard-boiled eggs and lemon. She allows one lemon and two eggs to each can. She also adds a tablespoonful of sherry just before she serves it. If the situation arises where an extra guest drops in at the last moment and it is necessary to spread out the soup a bit, she dilutes it, not with water but with consommé and more sherry.

Mock Turtle is improved, she thinks, by the addition of sherry and sliced lemon.

Consommé is helped by sherry, lemon, and a little very finely minced parsley. Consommé is also changed into something new and different by adding a tablespoonful of chili sauce for each cup. Let it simmer a few minutes and then strain it into cups with slices of lemon in them.

Chicken Soup is a good deal more exciting if you add some heavy cream and a little curry powder to it and shake a little paprika over the top of each cup.

Pea Soup is mixed with tomato soup to make *Purée Mongole*. Add a very little curry powder, and if you are feeling energetic, some carrots, leeks, and white turnip, finely diced and cooked gently in butter until tender. Half a cup of the vegetables is plenty for a quart of soup.

Pea soup responds gratefully to a little finely chopped mint sprinkled over it. It's always tactful to find out if anyone is allergic to mint in soup before you do it. Almost everyone likes fresh mint in drinks, but those who don't like it with soup or meat are very firm in their prejudice.

Tomato Soup is good thinned with consommé instead of with water or milk. It is also good with cream added to it — half a cup of cream and half a cup of milk to one can of condensed soup — and served with croutons and a few roasted peanuts scattered over each cup.

Mushroom Broth — the best canned mushroom soup — is much helped by the addition of sherry.

Concentrated Celery Soup and Asparagus Soup are both better if you dilute them with chicken broth than with water or milk, and if you add some cream or a little white wine. Almost any canned cream soup is helped by a little white wine, a teaspoonful to the cup. You hardly taste the wine, but the soup is more interesting than without it.

These are all familiar ideas about soup — Mrs. Appleyard just mentions them in case they have slipped your
mind.

There are some other things that she does that take
slightly more thought. There is, for instance, a soup that
she invented one cold evening when there wasn't enough of
anything for some unexpected and hungry company. She
calls it Mexican Tomato Bisque. The only reason for
dragging Mexico into it was that some of her children had
just visited it and had had such a wonderful time that the
word Mexican became a handy word of praise. Also Mexi-
cans do put whole beans in soup sometimes; also the returned travellers liked the soup.

MEXICAN TOMATO BISQUE

2 cans Campbell's tomato soup	2 c. hot baked beans
1 c. rich milk	½ t. red pepper
1 c. cream	Pinch of soda

Dissolve the soda in the milk, add the cream and stir it
slowly into the soup. Heat it to the boiling point but do not
boil it. Put a tablespoonful of the baked beans into each
plate or soup bowl — brown Mexican pottery is nice for
this — and pour the soup over the beans. Serve the soup
with Thin Scalded Johnnycake (page 47). This is enough
like tortillas for Mrs. Appleyard, who does not see herself
getting up at dawn to grind the corn, even if when she sees
herself in a shop window she does sometimes wonder if she
is a fresco by Diego de Rivera. Brown Bread (page 40),
cold-sliced and buttered and made into sandwiches or buttered and put into the oven until the butter melts, is good
with this too.

ONION SOUP (MRS. APPLEYARD)

Allow for each person:

1 large onion	1 T. butter
1 can Campbell's consommé	1 bouillon cube
2 T. grated cheese	A few drops of Kitchen
2 slices French bread,	Bouquet
½ inch thick	1 T. red wine

Slice the onions and fry them gently in the butter. They should not be cooked too soft at this stage — a delicate straw color is the right tint for them. Stir them well so that they do not brown. Now add the soup and a can of water for each can of soup. Don't worry about its being too weak — the water is going to cook out again. Add the soup cube and the Kitchen Bouquet and let the soup simmer for a while. Toast the bread lightly on both sides. Put the soup into a large earthenware casserole, add the wine, put the slices of toast on top of the soup. Cover them thickly with the grated cheese. Set the casserole in the oven and cook for half an hour or until the cheese is well browned.

Serve it from the casserole at the table into pottery bowls. With a substantial dessert this is a good supper.

ONION SOUP DE LUXE (MRS. APPLEYARD)

Mr. and Mrs. Appleyard had this once in a French restaurant, and as Mr. Appleyard expressed great approval of it his wife went rapidly home and invented how to make it. The soup is made just like that described above up to the point where it goes into the casserole. When it has sim-mered long enough so that the onions are tender and the

soup has cooked down to its original strength, add the
wine

Earlier in the day you made the following:

CONSOMMÉ CUSTARD (FOR FOUR PEOPLE)

1 egg	4 T. cream
Yolk of another egg	1 t. salt
2 T. consommé	¼ t. pepper

Beat all the ingredients together. Have a small buttered
mould ready — a baking-powder tin makes a good one.
Fill it two-thirds full with the custard, put it on a rack in a
baking-pan and surround it with boiling water. Bake it ten
minutes in a moderate oven — 350° F. — or until it is set.

When serving the soup (use your best soup plates for this,
as it is for company) put a slice of toasted French bread in
the plate. Cover the bread with a slice of the custard. Pour
the soup over it, being sure that everyone gets some onions,
and sprinkle grated cheese over the custard. Pass some more
cheese and some more of the toasted bread with the soup.

BORTSCH

The chief difficulty about this soup is spelling it. Mrs.
Appleyard chose this version because it seemed the hardest.
She loves to see five consonants together: it makes her feel
intelligent. This is a soup that is pleasant to have because
you can vary it according to what you have on hand. The
only absolutely essential thing is the beet juice. In fact,
Mrs. Appleyard makes it because she can't bear to throw
the beet juice away. She uses either fresh or canned beets.
Beets are an accommodating vegetable: they do not resent
canning as peas and beans and spinach do. Try to get Mrs.

Appleyard to serve canned string beans and see what happens to you. . . . Fresh beets are superior, but there is not that wide gulf between the best brand of canned miniature beets that there is in the case of beans.

For ten people she uses

1 pt. beet juice	2 cans thick vegetable soup
2 cans consommé or strong soup stock	1 c. tomato juice
	2 c. water
6 small beets, finely chopped	3 large onions, sliced
	3 T. butter
½ c. shredded cabbage	1 c. sour cream

She begins by frying the onion and the cabbage in the butter, using a large iron frying-pan and adding more butter if necessary. She cooks them, stirring constantly until the onions are a light straw color. Then she adds the consommé, water, tomato juice, the chopped beets, and the vegetable soup. If she has small quantities of other vegetables on hand such as cooked carrots, peas, string beans, or celery, she adds them, and also any water drained off them while they were cooking. If she has a little jellied chicken stock, she adds that too. She lets the whole thing simmer for forty minutes. When she serves it she passes the sour cream and those who like it take some and stir it into the soup. The soup itself is a fine dark red. The cream changes it into an equally enticing shade of pink.

Sandwiches of Boston Brown Bread (page 40), either buttered or filled with a mixture of cream cheese and horse radish, go well with this. With Bortsch and a hearty dessert — Apple Pandowdy (page 100), for instance — even sixteen-year-old boys with hollow legs seem to think they have had enough for supper.

OYSTER AND CELERY SOUP (FOR FOUR)

This is another short cut that is made possible by canned soup.

1 can celery soup (condensed)	1 T. white wine
	Bit of bay leaf
1 c. cream	Slice of onion
1 c. oysters	⅛ t. nutmeg
½ c. oyster liquor	1 T. butter
½ t. celery salt	4 large mushroom caps

Scald the cream with the bay leaf and onion and strain it over the celery soup, to which you have added a half-cup of hot water. Set this where it will simmer. Heat the oyster liquor and cook the oysters in it till their edges curl while you are also cooking the mushroom caps in butter. This is a good plan because it keeps you mentally active. Add the oysters to the soup. Add the wine to it also and the nutmeg. Put the mushroom caps into heated soup plates and pour the soup over them.

VICHYSSOISE

Canned chicken broth comes in handy when you make this, although Mrs. Appleyard prefers home-made chicken stock.

4 leeks (white stalks only)	1 sprig of parsley, chopped fine
½ c. butter	1 T. chives, chopped
1 stalk celery	1 c. cream
4 raw potatoes, sliced very thin	1 t. salt
2 c. chicken broth	¼ t. pepper
2 c. water	⅛ t. nutmeg

Mince the leeks and the celery fine and cook them slowly

in the butter for ten minutes. Do not let them brown. Stir them all the time. Add the sliced potatoes, the chicken stock, and the water and seasonings. Cook slowly for half an hour. Now either add the cream and the chopped chives and serve it hot with croutons, or strain it through a fine sieve, stir in the cream, pour the soup into cups, chill it, and serve it very cold with the chopped chives scattered over the top just before serving. Mrs. Appleyard thinks it looks especially beguiling in those scarlet jars that the devilled ham came in of which she has spoken before. Better have some extra ones, because someone will want two.

If you have no thick cream on hand you can make the soup richer by adding two egg yolks when you are ready to serve it, if it is to be eaten hot, and after you have strained it if you are going to chill it. Beat the egg yolks slightly, spoon two tablespoonfuls of the hot soup into them, beat it into them, and stir the mixture back into the soup. Never cook the soup after you have done this or it will separate.

You may use sorrel instead of parsley in the soup. Almost anyone who neglects a garden conscientiously is rewarded by having sorrel spring up in it. Half a cupful of the leaves are chopped and added to the leeks with the stock and strained out again before you chill the soup and add the cream and eggs.

When amateurs plant vegetable gardens lots of seeds and vegetables are wasted. It's astounding what one small package of lettuce or spinach seed will do. Mrs. Appleyard has been confronted by a wilderness of green leaves for years, and although she can hardly say that she has really subdued the lettuce jungle, she does manage to use a good

deal of it. Here is a way that you might not think of —
something to do when you are tired of salad, but still have
an active conscience toward your garden and the crops you
raised up in it.

Suppose you have also a roast chicken that still has a
little meat on it, a problem child among chickens. There
isn't enough to cream but there is too much just to abandon
it to those who raid the refrigerator for sandwich materials.
Perhaps there is also a chunk of ham too small to do anyone
much good, the day is too chilly to make cold cuts and salad
attractive, your garden has no corn or peas in it, but more
spinach, lettuce, and Swiss chard than you know what to
do with; no one has caught any trout or perch; the meat
cart won't be around till tomorrow. In short it is one of
those days!

Confronted with this combination of circumstances Mrs.
Appleyard makes

GREEN SOUP

She begins the day by putting on the chicken carcass to
boil. A little stuffing clings to it. She cuts the meat off,
puts the remnants of stuffing with it, breaks up the bones,
covers them with cold water in a large kettle, sets them
to simmer over a low flame, puts on a broad-brimmed
hat and a pair of dingy gloves, and goes out into the
garden. There she inspects the green-leaf situation and
begins to pick things into a basket that will hold about a
peck. Curly lettuce she puts into it and the plain green
kind. She picks Swiss chard and spinach, a few sorrel
leaves, some beet tops and turnip tops. There will be young
beets and turnips on the end that are still almost too small

to see, but they will all go into the soup. If she can find half a dozen young onions she will pull them up, and a few leeks too. Next she will visit her daughter's herb garden and help herself to a sprig of thyme, one of lemon thyme, a few sage leaves, a sprig of summer savory, parsley, chives, a leaf or two of chervil, the same of tarragon. She wishes she had some watercress and vows to get someone to plant some next year down by the brook.

When she gets home with her basket and her bouquet of herbs, the soup has begun to boil and she turns the heat down so that it will simmer, and begins to pick over the vegetables. The beets and turnips have to be cleaned carefully, and any dirt washed out of the whole collection, but naturally they were carefully picked so it is not much trouble. She probably has a white cabbage on hand and she takes a few of the outside leaves of that. If there is celery, she cuts off some of the tops, and if she has a stalk of broccoli, she uses that. If she found no young onions, she slices up some old ones.

By the time she has made her collection and talked to the neighbors about this and that, and picked over the greens, it is time to start chopping. She takes the biggest wooden chopping-bowl, strips the leaves from the tough stems such as the thyme, puts all the washed greens and the herbs together in the bowl, and starts chopping. She puts in the young onions or leeks if she has them, but if not she begins by chopping up three sliced onions and then chops the greens in with them. She chops the greens for about five minutes and then adds them to the chicken broth — from which she has removed the bones — and lets it cook hard while she is cutting the chicken meat and the ham into neat cubes. She adds these to the soup and lets it go on cooking. If she has no ham she may add some bacon, cut in cubes and tried out a little, or some salt pork. She sometimes adds them anyway even if she has the ham.

At this point she is quite likely to decide that there is not enough broth, and if so she adds a couple of cans of chicken soup to the kettle. She tastes it and adds salt and pepper. Dinner time is now approaching — don't think for a moment that she has not made two blueberry pies and a batch of Dutch cheese and some Corn Muffins (page 45) in the pauses — and it is time to thicken the soup. She does this by making a roux of four tablespoonfuls of butter and the same of flour, cooking them three minutes slowly together, blending some of the broth with the roux, cooking it a few minutes longer and then returning it to the kettle. She cooks it very slowly now, watching it carefully to be sure it does not scorch. If the family are standing around looking hungry — and as they have been smelling the soup all the morning it's rather likely that they are — she adds a few sliced pimentos out of a can, stirs everything well together and puts it into a big hot brown bowl. If she thinks there is anyone around whose native refinement would suffer, she may put the soup through a fine strainer before adding the meat and the pimento, but she herself prefers it with all its native ruggedness.

Veal and pork bones may be added with the chicken bones, and small pieces of veal may be added with the meat. Duck and turkey may be used too. In fact this is a very versatile soup and Mrs. Appleyard feels as if she could hardly wait till summer. She has already found in the seed catalogue some watercress that sounds as if, given favorable conditions, it might grow about the size of a lilac bush. She is certainly going to have some around her lily pool. She thinks it would provide a nice shelter for the frogs — unless of course it cut off too much sunlight from the lilies. She thinks she could keep it down fairly well by making plenty of soup.

ASPARAGUS SOUP (FOR FOUR)

If you cook your asparagus country style (page 284), you will have some very good strong asparagus liquor left over. Here is a chance for a good soup.

1 c. asparagus liquor	½ t. salt
1 c. milk	¼ t. pepper
1 c. cream	⅛ t. nutmeg
1 c. chicken soup	1 egg yolk
4 T. butter	2 T. asparagus tips
4 T. flour	1 t. white wine
1 small onion, sliced	

Make a white sauce of the butter, flour, seasonings, milk, and cream (method on page 251). Put the sauce into the top of the double boiler. Cook the onion in the asparagus liquor and strain it into the sauce. Just before you are ready to serve the soup, beat the egg yolk slightly, add a tablespoonful of the soup to it, mix well, and return it to the soup. Put a few asparagus tips into each cup and fill them with soup.

CREAM OF SPINACH SOUP

2 c. spinach purée	1 egg
1 qt. chicken stock	Slice of onion
2 T. butter	½ t. salt
2 T. flour	⅛ t. nutmeg
1 c. cream	

Wash the spinach thoroughly, cook it as quickly as possible with only the water that clings to it. Put it through a fine sieve. Melt the butter; when it froths, rub in the flour sifted with the seasonings and cook slowly for three minutes. Add the soup stock and put it into the top of the double boiler. Add the spinach and let it cook uncovered for twenty minutes. It should be quite thick. Add the cream. Just before you serve it add the beaten egg yolk, first beating into it some of the soup. The soup when done should be of the consistency of thick cream. Serve it in cups with Cheese Biscuits (page 87).

CREAM OF SQUASH SOUP

Make this just like Cream of Spinach Soup, above, substituting squash for the spinach. This is a beautiful color as well as good to eat. You may use part milk in either of these if you have not enough chicken stock.

CONSOMMÉ CARDINAL WITH PEARLS

Among the best of the canned soups and one of the hardest to make well at home is the beautifully clear red consommé that is known as consommé cardinal. It jellies by itself in the refrigerator and is delicious on a hot evening simply served with a slice of lemon. It is also good hot, and Mrs. Appleyard likes this way of serving it.

For six people:

4 cans consommé cardinal	6 slices of lemon
6 T. pearl tapioca	1 c. cold water
4 T. sherry	2 c. boiling water

Soak the tapioca in cold water for at least two hours.

It must be the old-fashioned kind like small bullets. Drain, add it to the boiling water, cook in a double boiler until the tapioca is transparent. This will take about half an hour. Be sure the tapioca is really clear. Nothing is worse than half-cooked tapioca. Add the soup and the sherry and let it cook a few minutes longer. Add more consommé if it seems too thick. Serve it hot in your very best soup plates with a slice of lemon in each one.

LOBSTER SOUP

3 small lobsters	3 c. cream
A 3-lb. haddock	⅛ t. nutmeg
3 c. milk	2 egg yolks
1 small onion, sliced	½ T. butter, extra
6 T. butter	6 toasted and buttered
6 T. flour	rusks
2 t. salt	2 T. sherry
½ t. paprika	2 T. cream, extra

Have the haddock cut for chowder and cook it all, including the head, until the fish slips from the bones. Remove the fish from the bones and save it for scalloped fish the next day. Return the bones to the broth, add the onion and seasonings, the lobster shells and claws, and the pounded-up lobster coral. Let this cook for at least an hour. It should cook down so you have about two cups of strong fish stock The haddock simply serves to enrich it and bring out the lobster flavor.

Cut the lobster meat up neatly but not too fine. Now make a white sauce (page 251) with the butter, flour, milk, and cream. Put it into the top of the double boiler to keep hot and add the lobster. When you are ready to serve the soup, put a toasted rusk into each soup plate, stir the strained fish bouillon into the white sauce, add the sherry and the extra cream. Then add the beaten egg yolks, first diluting them with some of the soup and then stirring them into the soup. Slip in the extra bit of butter — it should be cold and hard. Stir the sauce until the butter melts. Put some of the lobster meat on each rusk, pour the soup over the rusk boats with their cargo of lobster, and serve.

Serve with Soufflé Crackers (page 37) which have been thickly sprinkled with soft crumbled cheese and paprika the last few minutes of their cooking time.

Canned soups, as Mrs. Appleyard has been admitting cheerfully and perhaps too often, are a great help. We may however have to cut down on their use, or even get along without them. Luckily there are good soups that you can make without them and without much trouble. Some of the best soup Mrs. Appleyard ever remembers eating was served in a Southern family where they kept a soup kettle going. Into it they put bones and trimmings of meat, juice from cooked vegetables, and the vegetables themselves if there were any left over. There was always onion in it and generally tomato, but its virtue was largely in its never being twice the same.

It is simple to make soup this way if you have a range where it can simmer gently without attention, but it is possible to manage with other types of heat. With modern refrigerators vegetables and their juices can be saved until there are bones with which to cook them, or vice versa. If you have plenty of onions you can make good soup, can or no can, so let no lamb or beef bone escape you until it has given its all.

Don't forget either the soups without stock such as

POTATO AND ONION SOUP

6 potatoes	2 T. flour
3 large onions	1 T. salt
3 c. milk	¼ t. pepper
1 c. cream	Chopped peanuts
4 T. butter	

Pare the potatoes and slice them thin. Slice the onions thin. Cook them in water, covered, until they are tender and the water has nearly all cooked away. Make a white sauce of the butter, flour, seasonings, and milk. Put the onions and potatoes into the top of the double boiler, pour the white sauce over them, mix well, add the cream. If you do not like the pieces of onion and potato in the soup, rub it through a fine strainer. In either case sprinkle the chopped peanuts over each plateful before you send it to the table.

CREAM OF LEEK SOUP

1 bunch of leeks	1 t. salt
3 c. milk	¼ t. pepper
1 c. cream	½ t. paprika
6 t. butter	Yolk of 1 egg
6 T. flour	Grated cheese
1 t. minced parsley	

Slice the leeks thin, using the green and white parts both. Fry them slowly in the butter. Remove the leeks to the top of the double boiler and make a white sauce of the butter in the pan and the flour, seasonings, and milk. Pour it over the leeks, stir in the cream, and cook forty minutes in the double boiler. Just before serving time add the egg yolk, first beating it slightly and diluting it with some of the soup, and then stirring the mixture into the soup. Serve the soup with the parsley and paprika sprinkled over each plateful and pass the grated cheese with it. Sandwiches made by buttering bread and spreading it with devilled ham and then toasting the sandwiches lightly are good with this.

MUSHROOM SOUP

Skin and stems of 2 lbs. mushrooms	2 T. flour
	½ small onion, sliced
Caps of 6 mushrooms	1 bay leaf
2 c. milk	⅛ t. nutmeg
1 c. cream	1 t. salt
4 T. butter	1 T. sherry

This must be started the day before you serve it. Chop the stems of the mushrooms fine, add the skins, the salt, bay leaf, and onion, cover with cold water, and simmer for at least an hour — two is better. This should give you a cup of strong mushroom broth. Add a bouillon cube and a little Worcestershire sauce if it is not strong enough.

Make a white sauce of the butter, flour, and milk, add the cream and the mushroom stock. Put the soup in the double boiler and cook it forty minutes. If it seems too thick, dilute it with a little cream or rich milk. If it is thinner than you like, thicken it with an egg yolk, first blending the beaten yolk with a tablespoonful of the soup, and stirring it in well. Add the sherry and serve at once. Into each plate or cup put one of the mushroom caps, either broiled or fried in a little butter.

21

Vegetables: Including Spaghetti. Mrs. Appleyard's proudest moment was when her friend Mrs. Teasdale said to her, 'I learned a great deal about cooking vegetables from you.'

Mrs. Teasdale and Mrs. Appleyard once spent a summer cooking co-operatively. They ate their breakfasts and suppers alone — if you call alone eating supper with your husband, four children, three kittens, two turtles, and any visitors of strong nerves — but took turns cooking dinner for the combined families.

There was a great deal of merit in this plan. Each of the *cordons bleus* had a day off every other day, and when there was anything left from a meal, which happened seldom, it was the other cook that had to exercise her ingenuity upon it. There was excitement for everyone in this plan, especially for the families, because of course the cooks naturally tried violently to outdo each other all summer, with interesting results. It certainly speaks very well for everyone that with this threat to digestion the competitors still remain friends. Their families must have been tough.

Mrs. Teasdale may have learned about vegetables, but it was Mrs. Appleyard who learned about chicken salad in cream puffs, and how to roast corn and pop it, and some valuable facts about walnut wafers.

Mrs. Appleyard's vegetable cookery has nothing very mysterious about it. She is simply firm in the notion that the juice of vegetables with its minerals and vitamines ought to be in the vegetables, or in soup or stew the next day, and not down any sink. She cooks vegetables in the smallest possible amount of water and as quickly as they can be cooked. She watches them carefully to be sure that the water does not cook away before they are cooked and to be sure that it does cook into them just before they are sent to the table. If by chance there is any water left, she saves it and dilutes canned soup with it instead of using plain water, or adds it to the meat she is using for stew.

She does not put soda into vegetables because she has had it well beaten into her head that soda kills the vitamines and she knows it takes all the taste away, except of course the taste of soda, to which anyone is welcome who wants it. She considers it a poor business deal to swap delicate flavor and vitamines for a shade of green that never was very becoming to her anyway. And besides, she says, if you pick vegetables just before you cook them and cook them quickly without much water, you keep most of the color.

In following the policy of cooking water into vegetables she has scorched her quota of beets, it is true, and there has been an occasional batch of carrots that had rather more caramelized carrot-sugar at the bottom of the pan than was really necessary. However, her average is fairly good — as witness Mrs. Teasdale's tribute. (Of course what she learned may just have been not to try to paint a blue jay on your living-room walls while you were cooking beets, but Mrs. Appleyard prefers to swallow compliments like oysters — whole and with trust.)

She says she thinks it isn't necessary for her to go through the entire list of vegetables in the cookbook, from asparagus to zucchini. There was a certain sadness in her voice as she remarked: 'People who have always thrown the water from vegetables down the sink and seasoned them with soda when they weren't poisoning them with salt are going to do it just the same even if I tell them not to thirty-nine times. If they are going to learn, they'll learn without my screaming and flying up the lace curtains. If I had any.

ASPARAGUS, COUNTRY STYLE

Those handsome stalks of asparagus that always remind Mrs. Appleyard of a tenor playing Faust in green tights, the ones that come from the West and are so expensive — not the tenor, stupid, the asparagus — in the spring are naturally cooked whole and placed handsomely on a Minton platter. Mrs. Appleyard is not talking about these, but about the kind that come in your own garden or from a roadside stand in the apple-blossom country, which is also asparagus country. Some places seem to have all the luck! The stalks will not be all the same size and they twist around at strange angles. Trying to tie them into a neat bunch is hard as well as silly, so this is how you cook them:

Start your water to heat and go out and cut the asparagus. Break off the tough ends. Any part of it that won't break easily is too tough to cook, so throw it away. Now with the kitchen shears cut the stems into pieces about three quarters of an inch long. Leave the tips an inch long and put them into a separate pile. Salt the water, which by now should be boiling hard, drop in the cut stems and cook them fifteen minutes. Then put in the tips and cook them ten minutes longer. By that time the tips should be tender and the water almost cooked away. If the tips are done and there is still water not cooked away, either:

(1) Drain the asparagus into a hot dish and put some soft butter on it, saving the juice for soup (page 276), or

(2) Drain the asparagus into a hot dish containing some buttered toast, cook the rest of the juice down rapidly until there is only two tablespoonfuls, take it from the fire, add butter to it, and pour it over the asparagus, or

(3) Instead of the butter in either of these methods, pour Hollandaise over it and send it to the table — quick like a mouse, or

(4) Keep the asparagus cooking until you are sure there is only a spoonful of water (this means standing over it and shaking the pan), then add thick cream, put it into the top of the double boiler and let it stand long enough to soak up some of the cream. Pour it over hot buttered toast.

Any of these ways will make you utter kind words in memory of the man who planted the asparagus bed ten years ago. Asparagus once started is as hard to kill as a dandelion. For all Mrs. Appleyard knows, the same bed from which Samuel Pepys used to get his may still be growing. An asparagus bed is a much better monument than a granite tomb and not half so expensive. Really, she has almost talked herself into planting one.

There are two pitfalls to be avoided in this way of cooking asparagus: you may forget to put the tips in soon enough;

you may let the water cook out. If you do the latter, open all the doors and windows and wish you had decided on raw celery. If you do the first, go on and cook it some more. Mrs. Appleyard has committed both these crimes. The first is not really serious unless it leads to the second — which unluckily it is likely to do — just as one murder leads to another in the mystery stories. Fortunately the consequences are not necessarily fatal: you open a can of beets and like them.

CARROTS

There was a time when carrots used to be considered as something you gave a horse to make his coat shine. The horse very sensibly ate his carrots and never told anyone that a young carrot is better raw than any other way — wanted to keep them all himself, probably. Human beings at last learned to cut carrots into sticks and serve them with radishes, celery, olives, and young onions with French bread and unsalted butter, either as an appetizer or instead of a salad.

There is almost as much difference between young carrots that you yourself pull out of the warm earth while the water is boiling and the carrots you buy, as there is between asparagus you pick and asparagus you buy. The sugar in them hasn't had time to change into whatever it is it changes into. They are still sweet and they need very little cooking.

Cut them into rather thin slices. Cook them in the smallest possible amount of water and cook every drop of water out of them. Either add thick cream and let them stand in it awhile in the top of the double boiler or add soft butter and serve at once. If the carrots are getting large you may add a very little light-brown sugar and some butter to them just as the last of the water cooks away.

CARROTS AND PEAS

There are a few days in the summer when the carrots are very young and innocent and the supply of peas is getting rather low, when Mrs. Appleyard cooks carrots and peas together. She starts the carrots first. When they are nearly done, she drops in the peas. She stands right over them as they cook. In five minutes' time the water should be all cooked out and the peas tender and a lovely emerald green among the orange and gold of the carrots. Add either butter or thick cream, whichever you prefer. Mrs. Appleyard likes butter. Vegetables cooked this way need very little salt. Add it after they are about half cooked.

CORN

No corn is better than what Mr. Teasdale cooks over a fire in his outdoor fireplace. The corn is Golden Bantam and it is cooked in the husks. Mr. Teasdale keeps turning it over on the grate over the fire with a forked stick. He knows by instinct when it is done so that the milk is still in the kernels and the skin has just begun to brown. A pretty good guide is if the silk tassel has scorched away and the husk at the tassel end is getting black. It depends on the fire. If there is a good bed of coals, it takes about fifteen minutes.

Plenty of butter, plenty of salt, corn just off the stalks, a crisp September evening, and there you are.

However, even lacking Mr. Teasdale's practiced hand

and smoke-proof eyes, you can still have some good corn if you cook it soon enough after you pick it. Mrs. Appleyard sometimes roasts it in the oven in the husks, turning it often. The oven must be as hot as you can get it. Unless you can give it your whole attention — which you can't if you are broiling swordfish, making Hollandaise, and baking blueberry muffins at the same time — she thinks it is better to boil it.

She starts the water in a big kettle and a tight lid while she is picking and husking the corn. She puts in only about a third of the water that the kettle will hold and she makes everyone she can lay hands on husk corn for her. When the corn is ready and the water is boiling hard, she packs the kettle full of corn and clamps down the lid. She watches it carefully to check the time when the water begins to boil again. This will vary with the amount of corn. After the kettle is steaming hard again, five minutes is long enough to cook the corn. For a big kettle of corn, picked on a cool evening the whole thing may take fifteen minutes. Have ready a hot platter with a clean damask napkin on it and don't let anyone be late to supper.

CELERY

Cut celery into small pieces. Don't be afraid to use the green part: it has more vitamines than the white part and just as much flavor. Cook in salted boiling water to cover it and either cook out all the water or save it for soup. Add either some soft butter or some thick cream. If you use the cream put celery, cream, and some paprika into the top of the double boiler and let them get well blended. Just as a personal favor to Mrs. Appleyard don't half-cook celery and cover it with paperhanger's paste. If you're saving up for a mink coat, better eat your celery raw.

BRAISED CELERY

This doesn't happen often. When it does, it's an event.

2 bunches Pascal celery	1 sprig of parsley, minced
2 cans consommé	1 leek, sliced fine
2 c. water	1 bean of garlic, minced
1 t. salt	1 t. whole peppercorns
½ t. paprika	1 sprig fresh thyme
⅛ lb. salt pork, diced	(or ⅛ t. dried thyme)
1 carrot, sliced	1 T. butter
1 onion, sliced	

Put the diced pork into a large dripping-pan and try it out a little. Add the butter, carrot, onion, leek, parsley, and seasonings except the salt and paprika. Cook this mixture (it is Mrs. Appleyard's version of what the French call a *mirepoix*) until the onion is just beginning to brown. Lay over the *mirepoix* the celery, washed, with the leaves cut off. Leave on just enough root to hold the branches together. Season it with the salt and paprika. Pour over it the water and consommé and let it boil hard for five minutes. Then set the pan into the oven — 400° F. — for forty minutes. Cover the celery with a sheet of buttered brown paper. When you serve it, take out the celery and put it in a hot dish, strain some of the juice over it, and save the rest and the *mirepoix* to use in soup the next day.

This is good to serve with meat loaf and may be cooked in the same oven. Better have creamed potatoes — which you can also cook mostly in the oven (page 305) — and Tomato Sauce (page 259) with the loaf.

When you serve the humbler vegetables, it helps if you make them look attractive. This way of serving spinach happens because your own garden always seems to grow enough spinach but never enough peas. Serve it sometime with ham or tongue.

SPINACH: COUNTRY STYLE

½ peck young spinach	2 hard-boiled eggs
16 very small beets	4 T. butter
16 young carrots	1 T. light-brown sugar
Slice of onion	1 T. chopped parsley
2 t. salt	

Begin by cooking the beets with a half-teaspoonful of the salt until they are tender. While they are cooking start the carrots with the onion, and another half-teaspoonful of the salt. When they are almost done, start the spinach, well washed, and cook it with only the water that clings to it with the rest of the salt. Chop it fine as it cooks. It will take only a few minutes and you stand right over it all the time, because you are not trying to produce something that looks like weary old seaweed, but something green and cheerful as a background to the other vegetables.

You are also — Mrs. Appleyard thinks she'd better break the news to you now — serving Inside-Out Potatoes (page 306) at this meal, so you have already baked them, starting them when you did the beets, and they have already been mashed and put back into their shells and are at present browning in the oven.

All right! By the time the spinach is nearly done the water should be cooked out of the carrots. Add to them two tablespoonfuls of the butter and the sugar, and set them where they will just simmer gently. Your eggs are cooked and cooled (if you were Mrs. Appleyard you probably put them in with the beets and fished them out some time ago, but you may use your own judgment on this point).

Everything is getting done at once now and Mrs. Appleyard is going to 'dish up.' The ham is already sliced and it is on the table. So is the chutney. Now the potatoes are a delicate brown on their swirled-up tops and the spinach is green and tender. Mrs. Appleyard has a hot dish ready — probably it will be better if no one speaks to her just now (anyone who does is likely to get a dusty answer) — and she puts the spinach into the middle of it, with the rest of the butter. She makes a depression in the middle and into it puts half the beets. She puts the rings of sliced hard-boiled egg around on the spinach and surrounds it with the rest of the beets and the carrots, alternating them and sprinkling them with the chopped parsley.

Out of the way, everyone!

PEAS

You are lucky in Appleyard Centre if you get peas by the Fourth of July. Mrs. Appleyard has been known to transport most of a Penobscot salmon into the hills if it seems as if it were likely that there will be peas to go with it. She sees the noble fish packed into a thermos jar with cracked ice and it is never really out of her thoughts on the long trip. It is one of the few sadnesses of her life that salmon is not at its peak of perfection in the Green Mountains and that peas are never really peas in Boston. It is at times like these that she remembers that island off the coast of Maine where salmon and peas met together in a happy harmony never, she believes, duplicated anywhere else. However, she does her best.

The peas are picked just before she is ready to cook them and are shelled by everyone within range. Croquet-players must drop their mallets — though not on each other's toes. There must be no covers from cracker tins hurled from hand to hand. Sally must stop playing her flute and Tom must lay down his recorder. Mr. Appleyard must emerge from his book, for he has had a nice rest, it being fully twelve minutes since he stopped cleaning robins' nests out of the gutters. Hugh had better get off his hands the pitch from those logs he is hauling for his cabin — what else did his mother make that very powerful soap for? Put down your knitting, Cicely; wriggle out of those accordion straps, Stan. Leave the lawnmower where it is, Guilford, and, Paul, never mind pruning that apple tree. Dicky — this is no time for Southern languor. Nancy, stop squinting into that microscope. There are peas to shell!

'Always,' says Mrs. Appleyard, 'have the water boiling hard and have less than you think you need. You must cook it all out again and the peas are full of juice themselves. An inch at the bottom of the kettle is plenty. Eight minutes from the time you put the peas in is long enough to cook them. Stay right with them. Stir them so the same ones won't be on top all the time. If they are young — and why else are you cooking them, for goodness' sake? — five minutes, perhaps even less, after they start boiling again is long enough to cook them. Eat one every now and then and as soon as they are soft, put in what salt you like, stir them well, and begin ladling them out into a very hot dish with some butter in it. By all that you hold sacred — not too much salt. No sugar either. Peas cooked within three hours of the time they are picked have their own sugar in them, and when they have been off the vines only twenty minutes they are melting with it. When you have transferred the last of them to their mauve-and-ivory dish — you do this with a ladle with holes in it — there will still be a little juice at the bottom of the kettle. Cook this out rapidly over your hottest fire and just as it is down to the last teaspoonful pour it over the peas, which are waiting with big lumps of soft butter beginning to melt among the tender green globes.'

> *Now*
> Sound flutes and recorders,
> Thump the bass drum.
> PEAS ARE READY.
> Everyone come!

PEAS COUNTRY STYLE WITH NEW POTATOES

This assumes that the peas are not picked out of your garden. They will be good even if they came from a garden a little farther up the road, but they may perhaps lack just that last shade of delicate subtlety of your own.

The potatoes must be tiny new ones, the first digging of the season. Scrub them well but do not peel them. Have some boiling water ready and put into it two quarts of potatoes. Cut half a pound of salt pork into half-inch cubes and try them out until they are a delicate straw color. With them cook a small onion chopped fine. Do not let it brown. Add pork and onions to the potatoes and cook until the potatoes are done. Twenty minutes is all the cooking they need after the water starts boiling again. Do not use more water than will just cover them — you want it to cook away.

While the potatoes are cooking, shell the peas — there

should be at least a quart after they are shelled. Cook them in a very little rapidly boiling water for three minutes after they begin to boil. Add them, with any of their juice that has not cooked away, to the potatoes and pork, which you have just transferred to a big fireproof brown bowl. Now add a cup of thick cream. Put the bowl over a very low flame, where it will keep hot for a few minutes so that everything will blend. When the cream just begins to bubble around the edges, send the bowl to the table.

This is Mr. Appleyard's pet dish. For all anyone knows, this pampered creature, who has probably done nothing whatever all the morning except clean up the woodshed, get shingles for the church roof, inspire his sons to take the trash to the dump, and chase three Jersey heifers out of the corn, will get blueberry pudding for dessert. Even the peas, though, will make him smile with particular kindliness upon his little kingdom.

BROCCOLI

Broccoli is one of the few good things that have happened to the world in the last fifteen years, Mrs. Appleyard says. Before that it was just a luxury, and a joke about its being only spinach with a college education. Now it is available most of the year. Unlike most vegetables, broccoli is actually better in winter than in summer, and what travels over the continent from California is better than what grows nearer home. Broccoli has usually been sprayed, so be sure to stand it upside down for a while in plenty of water and rinse it well. Always cut off the tough part of the stems and if they are large, split them for most of their length. Always cook broccoli in plenty of boiling, salted water in a saucepan in which you can stand it with the flowers up. Have the water come well up around the stems and let the flowers cook in the steam. If they cook in the water with the stems they will be mushy. The water will stop boiling when you put them in. Time them when it starts boiling again. The broccoli should be tender in about twenty minutes. Serve it with Hollandaise Sauce (page 255) or with this Tomato Sauce.

Mrs. Appleyard learned this sauce from her fruit man. It was the way he used to have it at home — his mother made it. He told about it with such gusto that Mrs. Appleyard went right home and made it. She wishes she knew what army camp he is in now. She is afraid they haven't the rule.

JOHN'S TOMATO SAUCE

6 T. olive oil	½ t. red pepper
2 carrots, sliced	2 cloves
1 stalk of celery, chopped	1 t. salt
2 t. parsley, minced	1 green pepper, chopped
1 bean of garlic, minced	4 T. butter
2 onions, sliced	4 T. flour
⅛ t. cinnamon	2 t. light-brown sugar
½ t. white pepper	2 qts. fine red tomatoes
¼ t. powdered thyme	

If the tomatoes are not really red and juicy, use two cans of tomatoes instead. They are better than the pallid, woody things that sometimes travel — and travel a lot too far — under the name of tomatoes.

Put the olive oil (or Wesson oil) into a large iron frying-pan and put into it everything else except the tomatoes, flour, and sugar. Stir carefully while the mixture cooks over a slow fire until the onions are soft. Shove the vegetables to one side and rub the flour into the hot fat. When it is well blended add a quart of cold water, slowly, and the tomatoes. Mix well and cover the frying-pan and set it where it will cook slowly for an hour and a half. The lower rack in the oven with the oven at 300° F. is a good place. Stir it from time to time and uncover it during the last half-hour.

Strain it through a fine sieve. This makes a lot of sauce It keeps well in the refrigerator and is good to use with spaghetti or to season soups or to pour over meat loaf.

Speaking of spaghetti, which Mrs. Appleyard supposes is a vegetable — anyway it's neither an animal nor a fruit and ought not to be cooked so that it seems like a mineral, although it sometimes does — this is the Appleyard Centre way of dealing with it; or rather two ways.

SPAGHETTI, APPLEYARD CENTRE NO. 1

1 package of spaghetti	1 lb. mild cheese
4 T. flour	1 t. finely scraped onion
4 T. butter	Crumbs from 2 Montpelier
3 c. milk	crackers
1 c. cream	Crumbs from 2 slices
1 t. salt	of French bread
½ t. pepper	

Mrs. Appleyard's project is to make enough spaghetti for ten people. She has her eye on a certain Bennington baking-dish, which she butters. First she cooks the spaghetti for ten minutes in rapidly boiling water. While she is cooking it she makes a white sauce of the butter, flour, seasonings, and milk (method page 252) and adds the onion to it and the cream. When the sauce is well blended she adds to it the cheese, cut into small pieces. She saves some of the cheese for the top of the dish. As soon as the cheese melts, she stirs the cooked spaghetti into the sauce, lets it cook slowly a minute or two, and then pours it into the baking-dish. She scatters the crumbs over the top, adding the rest of the cheese and a few dots of butter. Then she sets the dish into the oven — 400° F. — and bakes the spaghetti until the top is well browned — about fifteen or twenty minutes.

Don't try to scrimp on the cheese, she pleads. This is your main dish for supper with a green salad and it had better be good.

SPAGHETTI, APPLEYARD CENTRE NO. 2

This generally happens because Mrs. Appleyard is trying to use up a jar of devilled ham to get the jar so she can serve Vichyssoise in it. Make the spaghetti just as in the rule above, only add two tablespoonfuls of devilled ham to the sauce. Add also a can of thick vegetable soup, a can of tomato soup, and some extra milk. Put the crumbs over it and bake it until they are well browned. This will take the edge off twelve hungry appetites. If Mrs. Appleyard has any of her pet tomato sauce around she uses it instead of the soup.

Speaking of tomatoes, don't forget to broil some or fry some on one of those cool September evenings.

FRIED TOMATOES

Choose tomatoes for this that are not too ripe. Slice them rather thick, dip them in seasoned flour, fry them in some fat from the Montpelier — or similar — sausage that you are cooking to go with them — Mrs. Appleyard hopes. There will be enough flour in the pan so that you can probably make your gravy with it, but be sure you rub it all smoothly into the fat — add some butter if you haven't enough fat. When your roux is ready, there should be about two tablespoonfuls of it, reduce the heat and add two tablespoonfuls of thick sour cream and a cup of rich milk, part sweet cream. Be sure your sauce is smooth — strain it if necessary — and add a tablespoonful of minced parsley. Serve it in a gravy tureen. New potatoes cooked in their jackets will be very good with this gravy mashed into them.

How about a little watermelon pickle (page 209) with this combination?

STEWED TOMATOES

Most stewed tomatoes, Mrs. Appleyard thinks, are not stewed nearly enough. They generally seem as if they had been in a can within fifteen minutes. This is, of course, all right if you like it, but she thinks it is better to put them, either fresh and cut up, or canned, into a shallow pan with a little onion, a little brown sugar and the same amount of butter, some salt and pepper, and either simmer them over a slow fire or put them into the oven. Use the oven if you have something else in it that takes long, slow cooking — a fruit cake, for instance. Stir the tomatoes occasionally. They should cook down to a rich dark red savory sauce. Serve them with rice or spaghetti. Baked pork chops with pineapple and rice are made even better if this kind of stewed tomato is present on the same plate.

STRING BEANS AND MUSHROOMS

1 qt. string beans	1 T. minced onion
1 lb. mushrooms — caps only	½ t. salt
1 c. cream	2 T. flour
4 T. butter	

Cut the string beans in long narrow diagonals, drop them into rapidly boiling water, and cook them until they are tender — about twenty-five minutes. Do not salt them until they are nearly done. By that time the water should be almost all cooked out. In the meantime you have peeled the mushroom caps (make stock out of the stems and skins for soup the next day — page 281) and cut them into medium-sized pieces. Fry them now with the onion in the butter until they are tender — about five minutes. Take them out and put them into the double boiler, rub the flour into the butter, and let it cook slowly for three minutes. Add the cream and the pepper, let the cream get hot, but not boil, and pour it over the mushrooms mixed with the beans in the top of the double boiler. Keep them hot until you are ready to serve them. Taste the sauce, add more salt if you like and a sprinkle of paprika. The beans should stand in the double boiler for at least twenty minutes before they are served, and standing longer does them no harm, so this is something that is good to have with broiled meat or fish that must be cooked at the last minute.

Frozen French-cut beans may be used if good fresh ones are not available.

RICE

For the way of boiling rice so that it is fluffy and the grains stand apart, see page 163.

A sauce to serve with rice that makes a little of several things go a long way is made as follows:

1 c. rice, boiled	2 T. butter
¼ lb. baked ham, cut	1 c. cream
in small cubes	2. T. paprika
1 c. meat from a roasted	½ t. salt
chicken, cut in squares	6 cakes of Montpelier sausage
½ lb. mushrooms	6 slices of bacon

Cook the onions in the butter. When they are tender add the mushrooms — caps sliced and stems chopped fine. Cook five minutes. Add the cream, seasonings, ham, and chicken. Put this all in the double boiler to blend. Cook the rice and while it is drying out cook the bacon and sausage cakes. When you are ready to serve the rice, stir about half the sauce into it and the rest on top. Add the sausages and the bacon.

A raw vegetable salad with a French dressing goes well with this. Shredded white cabbage, shredded purple cabbage, a little raw purple onion, carrot sticks, and watercress make a good combination.

BAKED BEANS

Even Mrs. Appleyard is a little hesitant about telling anyone else how to cook baked beans. Feelings run high on this point. Still, she was reminded by the Editor, suppose one of your great-grandchildren should say: 'I don't believe my Great-Grandmother Appleyard knew how to bake beans. There wasn't a word about them in her book.'

Thus challenged, and with an amount of humility that raised suspicions that perhaps she wasn't feeling quite well,

Mrs. Appleyard revealed her method for this controversial dish.

4 c. yellow-eye beans, soaked overnight	1 t. mustard
	2 onions
4 T. maple syrup	1 lb. salt pork
½ t. salt	

In the morning drain the beans. Cover them with fresh water and heat them slowly. Keep the water below the boiling point and cook the beans till the skins crack when you take some out on a spoon and blow on them. Drain them. You will like the flavor of your kitchen better if you don't pour the water down the sink. Perhaps you have a few plants outside that are yearning for a little bean water. Don't scald them, though. Few plants really enjoy being boiled.

Cut a thin slice off the pork and put it in the bottom of your bean pot. On it put the onions whole. You don't need to eat them and probably you will never know they are there — that is, not as onions; they just bring out the flavor of the beans. Now put the salt, mustard, and maple syrup into a cup of boiling water. Put some of the beans into the bean pot. Put in the pork, rind side up. There should be cuts in the rind about an inch deep. Surround it with the beans, letting the rind show at the top. Pour over the beans the water with the syrup and seasonings dissolved in it, and add enough water to cover the beans. Cover the bean pot and set it into a slow oven — 300° F. for eight hours. Add more water from time to time. The last hour uncover the beans and let the rind of the pork get brown and crisp.

Mrs. Appleyard, still in that gentle mood, says that you may use molasses instead of maple syrup if you like. Mr. Appleyard is not in favor of telling anyone about using maple syrup. There isn't enough to go around now, he points out. He likes chutney with his beans and he doesn't like his brown bread toasted. Mrs. Appleyard supplies some toasted — that is, spread with butter and heated in the oven for a few minutes — and some plain.

'Did you ever,' she inquired wistfully, 'have for breakfast the next morning brown bread that had been quickly fried in the fat from the sausages you had just cooked? Of course not, and probably no one ever will again,' she added, looking with disfavor upon her glass of spinach juice, and turned hastily to the more cheerful subject of Lima beans.

Dried Lima beans are very good baked, she says. Soak them overnight just as you would yellow-eye beans, drain and parboil them in the same way. Put some butter and a few slices of onion in a small bean pot; a small casserole will do. To a cup of beans add a cup of cream and half a teaspoonful of salt. Cover them and cook them in a slow oven until they are tender. Add more cream if necessary. Two hours should be enough.

LIMA BEANS AND MUSHROOMS

Fresh Lima beans, or frozen ones for that matter, are very good cooked with mushrooms in the same way as string beans (page 299) and in the same proportions.

MUSHROOMS IN CREAM

For this Mrs. Appleyard gets out her small covered glass casseroles. You may of course, she says, use a large casserole, but the mushrooms are really better in small ones. She allows a pound of mushrooms for three dishes — caps only

— and saves the skins and stems for soup.   For six dishes:

2 lbs. mushrooms	¼ t. white pepper
3 c. heavy cream	¼ t. nutmeg
3 T. butter	2 t. minced onion
2 t. salt	1 bay leaf, cut into bits
½ t. paprika	3 T. sherry

Into each dish put the mushroom caps skin side down. The dishes are buttered and butter is dotted between the layers of mushrooms and over them.   Put the seasonings, except the sherry, into a saucepan with the cream and heat it until it starts to bubble around the edges.   Pour it over the mushrooms and put the dishes into a fairly hot oven — 425° F. — cover them tightly and cook until the mushrooms are tender.   It will take about half an hour.   The sherry is to be added just before the mushrooms are served.   If the mushrooms are to be eaten from the dish in which they are cooked, have rounds of thin dry toast cut to fit the bottom of the dishes and when you put in the sherry, slip the toast under the mushrooms.   If the mushrooms are to be taken out of the dishes, bring the dishes in on separate plates and have a pile of hot buttered toast to serve with them.   Each person takes a piece of toast and spoons the mushrooms and the hot juice out onto it.

Don't, Mrs. Appleyard says, try to cook the toast in with the mushrooms all the time, because it soaks up all the liquid and gets mushy.   The sherry has to be added last because it tends to make the cream separate.

GRILLED MUSHROOMS

Peel large mushroom caps.   Into each one put a small lump of butter, 2 drops of Worcestershire sauce, ¼ t. of sherry, and ⅛ t. of salt.   Place them in a buttered pan and broil them under a hot flame. If the broiler is well heated, two minutes is enough. This is a good way to make a meat loaf more interesting. Allow two large or three medium mushrooms for each person to be served. Pour the juice in the pan over the loaf and put the mushroom caps around it.

POTATOES (MRS. APPLEYARD)

Butter a large dripping-pan or a large iron frying-pan. Use at least two tablespoonfuls of butter, melt it and get it evenly distributed. Peel potatoes — allow one large one for each person to be served and one or two extra — and slice them very thin. Put a layer into the pan, dot it over thickly with butter, sprinkle it with crumbled soft cheese, finely minced onion, salt, pepper, and paprika. Do this until you have four layers. Put an extra amount of butter on the top layer. Now pour in a mixture of milk and cream — half and half into the pan. It should come up to the top layer but not cover it. Bake the potatoes for forty minutes at 450° F. When they are done they should be brown on top and a glazed brown underneath. They will absorb all the liquid. Serve them cut into serving portions on a hot platter. If you greased your pan well to begin with, you should be able to get them out neatly by using two pancake-turners or a turner and a spatula.

Even those who 'never eat potatoes' eat these.

POTATOES HASHED IN CREAM

6 baking-size potatoes, not too large	½ t. pepper
	3 T. butter
1½ c. cream	2 t. finely minced onion
2 t. salt	2 T. butter (extra)

Bake the potatoes for about half an hour at 450° F. Peel

them and chop them medium fine. Warm the cream, add the three tablespoonfuls of butter, the salt, pepper, and onion. Stir in the chopped potatoes. Melt the rest of the butter in the frying-pan. Put in the potato-and-cream mixture and cook over a slow fire until the cream is absorbed and you can see brown around the edges. Treat it as if it were an omelet: cut across at right angles to the handle of the pan, turn the top half over the other, and slide the whole thing out on a very hot platter.

CREAMED POTATOES

Never, NEVER, says Mrs. Appleyard, try to make creamed potatoes with cold potatoes. If she had any supply of larger letters she would print 'NEVER' bigger and blacker. If you do use cooked potatoes, you lose both the mineral salts and the taste. Besides, the way she approves is less trouble, though that's a detail.

Peel the potatoes, taking off the thinnest peel that you can manage. Cut them fine or chop them if you like. For each six potatoes use one large onion. Mince it fine and fry it in two tablespoonfuls of butter until it is a light straw color. Add another two tablespoonfuls of butter, stir in the chopped potatoes. Sprinkle over them two teaspoonfuls of salt and some paprika and stir some more. Pour in two cups of rich milk and 1 cup of cream. If you have a little sour cream that is unemployed at the moment, this is an excellent situation for it. Stir everything together, cover the pan, set it into a medium oven — 375° F. — and bake for forty–fifty minutes. If your oven is not going, you may do it on the top of the stove over a very low flame. The potatoes are not supposed to be brown on top. If you think they are drying up, add some more cream or rich milk. The dish will be a little like hashed brown potato except that it will be distinctly creamy. There will be a light golden crust on the bottom. Make plenty.

CANDIED SWEET POTATOES WITH PEANUTS

Parboil sweet potatoes twenty minutes. Let them cool. When they are cool enough to slice easily without breaking, cut them lengthwise into rather thick slices. Put them into a well-buttered baking-pan, dot each slice thickly with butter and light-brown sugar, put the pan into a moderate oven — 375° F. — and bake about fifteen minutes, by which time the sugar and butter should have melted and the potatoes have become tender. Allow a tablespoonful of chopped peanuts to each whole potato. Sprinkle them over the slices and cook a few minutes longer.

There is something about the young of the human species that makes it like marshmallows. Mrs. Appleyard outgrew this taste some years ago, but she sometimes caters to it by putting marshmallows on top of a dish of candied sweet potato. She parboils the potatoes, and slices them into a buttered baking-dish with lots of butter and sugar and just enough water to keep them from scorching before the butter melts. These get baked until they are sticky — about forty minutes. Then the marshmallows are put on and the dish returned to the oven until the marshmallows are a delicate brown.

INSIDE-OUT POTATOES

That's what they are called in the Appleyard family, although there is doubtless some more de luxe name for them.

Bake fine large potatoes until they are nearly done — about forty minutes at 475° F. Cut a piece off the side and scoop out the potato. Don't break the skin — you're saving it for a cold winter. Be sure to have the dish into which you scoop them hot and have in it for each potato ½ T. of butter, ¼ t. of salt, ¼ t. of paprika, and 1 T. of thick cream. Mash the potatoes thoroughly with the back of a fork into this mixture and beat them up light. Don't let the potato get cold. Pile it lightly back into the shells, sprinkle a little more paprika on it. Don't mash it down but make wavy lines on it with the tines of your fork if you like. Set the potatoes on a baking-sheet and put them back into the oven. If in ten minutes the tops are not a nice brown, slip them under the broiler flame for a minute. Watch it — no scorching allowed. Have some small sprigs of parsley ready to stick into the tops.

Mr. Appleyard considers this all nonsense. All he wants is a good baked potato — it doesn't have to come wrapped in pink tissue paper (we won't quote him directly on this point). Give him butter, salt, his pepper-grinder, fresh paprika, and a pitcher of cream, and he'll fix his own.

CAULIFLOWER BAKED IN TOMATO (E. K. T.)

1 cauliflower, parboiled	½ t. mustard
2 c. thick tomato soup	1 T. light-brown sugar
2 T. butter	½ c. grated cheese
2 T. flour	⅛ t. Worcestershire sauce
½ t. salt	1 t. grated onion
⅛ t. pepper	

Melt the butter. When it bubbles, work in the flour, cook three minutes slowly, add the canned soup, the seasonings, onion, and the grated cheese. Cook until the cheese melts — about two minutes. Grease a French earthenware casserole. Put the cauliflower into it, pour the sauce over the cauliflower, and on top put some buttered crumbs — half Montpelier or Common crackers and half dry French bread — and some more grated cheese. Bake it for half an hour at 400° F. or until the top is well browned.

22

The Most Important Ingredient. It will
be apparent to the thoughtful reader that there are strange
gaps in Mrs. Appleyard's cooking. What! An adopted
Vermonter and she never tells how to make doughnuts!
Where is her rule for griddle cakes? Can a woman who
doesn't mention French-fried potatoes really hold a good
man's affection?

These are all pretty sharp, pointed questions, and Mrs.
Appleyard's face — if not red — was at least a becoming
pink as she answered them. She had just taken a batch of
oatmeal cookies out of the oven, so it may have been only
her baking flush. Her hair net was broken because she had
just been chasing a Siamese kitten into a rosebush before the
urge to make cookies came upon her. She had on that
scarlet bandanna smock that makes her look like a fire
engine — on a small scale, of course. She had managed to
get a little flour on her nose. Mrs. Appleyard's nose is the
style that used to be called tip-tilted in the more sentimental

books of her youth. There's not room for much flour on it. Some was on her right cheek, too.

Still, in spite of these minor difficulties, Mrs. Appleyard preserved her poise. So does the Statue of Liberty, for that matter — in spite of this and that.

'I have seventeen wonderful rules for doughnuts and I never made one in my life,' she announced, apparently without shame. 'Why should I make them when my neighbors do it a lot better and send me in the results? Did you ever hear about the Covered-Dish Party in Gospel Hollow? You know everyone takes a covered dish and then at a moment of tense excitement, the covers are removed and the dishes are passed around. Usually one person has salad and another cake and another macaroni and cheese or baked beans. This time at Gospel Hollow when they opened the dishes everyone had brought doughnuts. Except the one who had marble cake. They have committees now. If I'd been there I'd probably have brought popcorn. As to griddle cakes,' Mrs. Appleyard went on, 'I am the sort of cook that sometimes has good luck with my griddle cakes — need I say more? Mr. Appleyard doesn't like French-fried potatoes. If he did I'd cut myself up into small pieces and fry the potatoes in it.'

Mrs. Appleyard made this somewhat obscure statement at a critical moment of taking cookies swiftly off a pan and did not seem to have time to explain it.

This was a favorable time to interview Mrs. Appleyard — for the interviewer — to whose share fell certain fragments of a quite exceptional character.

'Now, just one more question, Mrs. Appleyard,' the Editoi said, hoping she would break another cooky. 'I've heard it said that a well-known painter when asked what he mixed his paints with, said, "With brains." Now do you feel that — to sum up what you've told me — people should cook with brains? May I quote you?'

Mrs. Appleyard put another batch of cookies into the oven.

'Brains aren't enough,' she said. 'You have to like things: the dishes you cook with, the people you buy the butter from, the field where the crows fly over the corn and the wind that blows through their wings. You have to like the table you put the food on, and the people who sit around it. Yes, even when they tip back in your Hitchcock chairs, you have to like them. You don't just like how food tastes — you like how it looks and smells and how the egg-beater sounds. You like the rhythm of chopping and the throb of the teakettle lid. You like to test the frying-pan with water and see it run around like quicksilver. You like the shadows in pewter and the soft gleam of silver and the sharp flash of glass. You like the feel of damask napkins and the shadows of flowers on a white cloth. You like people eating in their best clothes in candlelight, and in their dungarees on a beach in the broiling sun, or under a pine tree in the rain.

'You like that last moment before a meal is served when the Hollandaise thickens, the steak comes sputtering out of the broiler, the cream is cooked into the potatoes and the last drop of water is cooked out of the peas.' Here she was silent long enough to take the correctly lacy and golden cookies off the pan. 'Not with brains,' she repeated, putting down the spatula. 'With love.'

Index

The
Summer Kitchen

Mrs. Appleyard's Summer Kitchen

LOUISE ANDREWS KENT
AND
ELIZABETH KENT GAY

DECORATIONS BY JOHN O'HARA COSGRAVE II

Keats Publishing, Inc. New Canaan, Connecticut

For
JOHN TREVILLE LATOUCHE
one of whose many kindnesses to the authors
was reading the manuscript of this book

Contents

Contents

NOTE

* *Indicates recipes printed in this book.*

† *Those found in* Mrs. Appleyard's Kitchen.

‡ *In* ". . . with Kitchen Privileges."

The
Summer Kitchen

The Summer Kitchen

I_T'S ABOUT TIME," Cicely Bradshaw said to her mother, "that you wrote another cookbook."

Mrs. Appleyard — for it was she — briskly swept her new car around one of those reverse curves so dear to the hearts of Vermont road builders, reached into her pocketbook and handed her eldest daughter a rather weary-looking pencil. Also an envelope kindly contributed by a grower of Dutch bulbs.

"You write it," she said firmly.

From these few words there developed a contest of wits and wills to see which of these strong but amiable characters would do the writing and which would read over the manuscript and say: "That's fine, splendid, just what I had in mind — but did it ever occur to you . . ."

On the first day, however, everything went serenely. This was partly because Mrs. Appleyard was driving and had therefore automatically won the first round. Also, the first hint of a new book is like the scent of boiling coffee or the smell of a new car — a fragrance all the more exciting because you know it will never be quite realized. What coffee ever tasted the way it smells? What car ever quite became the magic carpet implied by the aroma wafted out as you opened the door for your first drive? What book — ?

Still, as Cicely pointed out, September is a good time for new enterprises.

"Think of all the parties we've been to and the different menus and the remarkable people we know. We'll put them all in," she said.

"Perhaps we had better not," her mother said cautiously.

Cicely had been reading Harriet Wilson's memoirs. She suggested that they might imitate that lady and ask people how much they would pay to have their names left out.

"An excellent idea," Mrs. Appleyard said. "I leave the negotiations entirely to you. Somehow I don't feel that blackmail is one of my talents . . . Which of these roads would you advise me to take? They both seem to have a good deal of grass growing down the middle."

They chose the left fork, which ended in the dooryard of a farm. Hillcrest View Farm it was called. It had a fine collection of barns carefully placed so as to shut out a Grade A Vermont view from the house. They tried the right fork. It led up to a camp covered with imitation brick siding. A sign said "Reduce Speed. Men Drinking."

The view in this case was obscured by another camp, also covered with an imitation of one of the uglier styles of brick and cowering under a collection of paper clips and old hairpins which suggested that the cultural advantages of television were available to the inhabitants. The name of the camp was "Duneatin."

"Very appropriate," said Cicely looking sternly at her mother. "After today's menu I wonder we dare write a cookbook."

Mrs. Appleyard was seen to blush. It was she who had provided the materials for the picnic lunch from her freezer. She had, she confessed, forgotten that it took longer to thaw things out in October than it did in June. The Pepperidge Farm bread came in chilled slices more suitable for shingling a roof than for making sandwiches. The stick of unsalted butter resisted the knife to the last. A small jar of pâté would have made a good billiard ball.

Choosing a picnic spot is always difficult when more than one person is involved. The compromise on this particular day was in a dark and chilly "gulf" — Vermont for wooded glen — through which the wind beat steadily. The picnic table stood beside a rocky stream; its benches creaked perilously. To finish off this arctic meal a small can of frozen orange juice had been provided; luckily the can opener was missing.

"It is possible," said Mrs. Appleyard calmly, "that the season for picnics is over.

"Vermonters certainly have a great natural talent for ugliness," she added. "I suppose it's a reaction from living in the most beautiful place in the world."

"No doubt it's annoying to have to see all those colors," Cicely agreed.

Indeed there was a wide variety of colors to dislike. The

leaves turned early that September, turned without a touch of frost. No leaves had yet been burned brown, but had ripened in sunshine to their full brilliance. Wind and rain had carried none away. The maples shone under the blue and silver sky in shades of crimson and maroon, in scarlet, apricot and rose, in orange, yellow and dull gold, in pale green tipped with coral. Steeple firs were dark accents among them. Larches were changing from green to bronze. Ash leaves were yellow stained with purple, beech leaves yellow and russet. Discs of gold and silver quivered on birches and poplars.

The lakes were dark steel-gray mirrors that day. Hardly a ripple broke the reflections of the hills. Clouds drifted slowly across the sun, making deep purple shadows on the lion-colored mountaintops. Fields were still as green as Vermont fields in May. It was, in short, just an average autumn day, a suitable day for the 251 Club to inspect the country.

This Vermont club consists of people who have visited or intended to visit all the two hundred and fifty-one towns in the state. Mrs. Appleyard and her daughter have already colored in more than half the towns on their map. Cicely's daughter Camilla is also a member. Luckily she is a child who resembles her mother and grandmother in that she "likes to go." This is one of the most damaging things one Vermont woman can say about another. If you want to be equally scathing about a man you say he is "moderate." Well, at least no one in the Appleyard family is moderate. Cicely and her mother have attacked the 251 Club project with their usual spirit.

"We are writing our book," they now say every day as they start down the road in a cloud of dust. "Back at six." Even Tommy Bradshaw, an earnest advocate of the theory that mothers and grandmothers ought to stay at home while boys and men are out in the woods with guns, accepts this excuse. He realizes that interesting meals result from such a project.

However, it was in a tone with a slight edge of suspicion that he inquired, "What is the name of this book?"

"*The Summer Kitchen*," his mother replied glibly.

Tommy stirred the pound of sausage he was cooking for a light lunch for himself and asked, "Why?"

Because — his mother told him — we are writing about the things people like to eat in the summer, especially at parties. You know how in all the houses around here people have two kitchens, a cool airy one for summer and a warm crowded one for winter. You can't have a hundred people to supper so easily in the winter but you can in the summertime.

"I like both Grandma's kitchens," Tommy said. "The summer one is nice and cool, all green and white. I like Beatrice Duncan's picture of the old dance hall. But I like the winter kitchen best, with a fire in the wood stove, cake in the oven, steak in the broiler, oatmeal cookies in the red tin box. Gosh, I'm hungry. So why won't you write about winter?"

"This book," his mother said firmly, "is about summer. Your grandmother planned it that way."

"Cicely," Mrs. Appleyard was saying at about the same time, "feels that this ought to be a summer cookbook — full of useful hints about what you serve when a poet and two composers and a subsistence farmer drop in for a game of croquet. Or what to do when a playwright lays the beet greens he is cutting up on your great-grandmother's needlepoint chair. It ought to be a practical book, she says."

So, happily supplying alibis for each other, these writers began work on *The Summer Kitchen*.

May

Ordeal by Birthday

CICELY BRADSHAW was up attic, sorting out old snapshots. Having decided that morning to give a large party the following Saturday, she naturally began her housecleaning and general preparations at the point farthest removed from the part of the house normally seen by guests. Whether she would get the kitchen floor mopped, the table set and her dress on in time for the arrival of the guests was another matter; at least she would be clothed in a virtuous glow and the knowledge that the garage was in perfect order.

A birthday was a fine excuse for a party, thought Cicely,

but this year she would not announce the reason for her celebration. The debris of her own life and that of many other people lay about her in the dusty sunlight of the shed chamber, and she emphatically did not wish for more things to look after, to keep in good repair, to make decisions about and to shove up attic when their usefulness was past. She had not the character to take these cast-offs to the dump, and she clung to the New England principle that each discarded treasure would one day come in handy again. This happened just often enough to confirm her in her squirreling ways.

Camilla, her youngest child, and the only one not at school, had draped herself in a bedraggled boa of lavender feathers and was trying on a green glass lampshade for a hat.

"Give me that," said her mother briskly. "It's just the thing for Geoffrey Toussaint's housewarming present. I hate it and he will adore it and we shall both be happy."

She stopped her trancelike absorption in the box of snapshots and set to repairing the lampshade with that characteristic rapidity of motion which often terrified those who usually saw her in a state of amiable lethargy. People did not realize, Cicely had to explain, that this was the way most Vermonters did their work, and that the leaning against farm buildings and the propping up by shovels and rakes was simply the gathering of energy for the most economical use of muscle and sinew.

As she worked, the menu for the party began to arrange itself in her mind, for she was blessed with the capacity of visualizing in full color and three dimensions.

It would undoubtedly be a cold evening, she decided, just right for hot spiced tomato juice, with a dash of rose hips for Geoffrey's sake. Mrs. Appleyard's cheese biscuits to go with it, cut in small fancy shapes. Then veal cut in small squares, pounded flat, lined with prosciutto and filled with parsley, garlic and lemon, finely chopped, the whole thing pinned together and braised in a white wine sauce; with the veal, green peppers Wellfleet, lightly cooked and marinated, and a salad of avocado, grapefruit and orange sections with watercress; for dessert her specialty, a many-layered meringue torte, chocolate filled and whipped-cream decorated.

Cicely found her imagination so compelling that even though it was only eleven-thirty she couldn't wait for lunch. She and Camilla abandoned their housecleaning in favor of scrambled eggs unusually ambrosial.

By the end of the week the cleaning-up process had wound its way through the upstairs and the less prominent portion of the downstairs. Cicely was calm in the knowledge that her closets were tidy, her desk drawers in order and that she had found a number of items missing since Christmas, including the belt to her best dress. The green peppers were marinating in their garlic-laden dressing, the veal had been pounded and stuffed and the mocha torte mellowed in the refrigerator; by Saturday afternoon Cicely had got round to laying out silver and napkins, in between sliding pans of cheese biscuits in and out of the oven.

Having sent the children off in all directions to spend the night with patient friends, Cicely settled down to the final marshaling of forces. From childhood she had been one of those who likes to eat a little bit of everything on her plate so that the last forkful contains nicely balanced portions of meat, vegetable and gravy. So she now enjoyed bringing the various elements of the party to a climax. The meal was almost ready now, timed to give leeway for the almost certain late arrival of at least one third of the guests. The fire was

laid with white birch logs and the first footstep on the porch
would be the signal for lighting it. Cicely had been able to
change her clothes and do her hair. What could go wrong?

That something would go wrong was the lesson that Cicely
had learned through long experience. The departure of the
children had eliminated four possible disaster areas — they
could neither make demands on her nor attack each other at
a critical moment. She would not be called away to serve
drinks of water, admire a new hairdo, observe the charm of
a repeating cap pistol, find a lost arithmetic book. As she set
the plates to warm and the water pitcher to chill, she reviewed
all the possible catastrophes, feeling that this gave her some
power over them. Short of a tornado the electricity should
stay on through the evening. The gas tank was a fresh one
and couldn't give out during the final cooking; the furnace
would hardly be needed, but if it were there was plenty of oil.

Striving for perfection was doubtless a fault, Cicely supposed,
arranging the forks in chevron pattern on the faded red tablecloth. She was well aware that the kinds of disasters that
commonly beset her were more endearing than otherwise.
Who but she would be sprayed by a skunk in her own yard
while wearing a brand-new skirt? Who but she would quietly
tip her station wagon over a five-foot bank while calling good
night to the teacher whom she had sedately driven home from
P.T.A.? In such situations there was nothing to do but laugh.
She had even been able to laugh when her house burned down
in Arizona, for how else could you greet the brisk consumption
of all your belongings, including a new wing just completed
for the children that same week? Also it had sent her to
Vermont to live.

Still, she could always hope, and perhaps the only flaw in

the evening would be the almost inevitable clash between Geoffrey Toussaint and Clifton Carroll, both powerful personalities and accustomed to getting and holding the floor at any gathering. Cicely had to admit that she rather looked forward to the fireworks. She was betting on Geoffrey, who was rather more ruthless than Clifton, though no more entertaining.

One merit in being always slightly behind schedule, Cicely found, was that you never had to endure for long that fateful pause when you know everyone has forgotten the date, the time, the place, the whole occasion. The only time she had been utterly deserted by her guests was on Christmas Eve last year, when an icestorm had so glazed the roads that not even the Hiltons, always valiant, had dared to venture out. In defiance of fate and the elements Cicely had packed punch, fruit cake, cookies in a basket, and with the children shrieking and sliding with excitement had walked to the Teasdales' for one of the happiest parties of any Christmas.

Whatever pitfall was being digged for her this gentle May evening, lack of guests was not one of them. As she heard the purr of the Hiltons' station wagon she forgot her star-crossed past and, running first to light the fire, she opened the door to find that not only the Hiltons were coming up the steps, but behind them the Davenports and the Holts, always prompt.

Cicely always enjoyed her own parties as much, or possibly even more, than anyone present, especially this unacknowledged celebration of her birthday. For the guests, too, this first party of the season had a special interest, for the summer people coming up for weekend inspection of cottages and houses, and the all-year-round people putting on spring clothes for the first time, all had winter's tales to tell each other, plans to outline and absent characters to blacken or brighten according to their humor.

The last of the veal had been polished from the platter, the salad bowl was empty save for a little pool of dressing in the bottom, the mocha torte had vanished to the last crumb of meringue — Cicely as usual refusing to impart its secret — before Geoffrey Toussaint and Clifton Carroll entered the conversational lists. The long living room held small groups of Cicely's friends — Fair and Eleanor Davenport's flashing kingfisher gaze caught her eye in one corner; Wallace and Prue Holt's bright brown glance in another. Molly Hilton was asking Morris Houston about the theatrical season just past. All round the room there was the steady hum of a successful party.

Little by little, however, small groups formed larger ones until at one end of the room half the gathering listened to Clifton's stories of the modern robber baron for whom he was chief counsel, while at the other Geoffrey was spinning tales of his South Carolina youth, of fallen grandeur, seedy plantations, patronesses of the arts who did all their own work. Somehow keeping an ear on each half of the party, Cicely hoped that bringing Geoffrey and Clifton together would not result in either being vanquished on his chosen field. However, the party remained exactly divided and equally rapt, and diversion came while the battle was still equally joined.

Myrtle, the ancestral black cat of the household, just then stalked through the living room with a small limp object in her mouth, making for Cicely's downstairs bedroom. She went in and immediately came out again, returned to the kitchen and soon was back with another kitten, damp and obviously newborn. At first, in the shadowy, firelit room, her goings and comings were not much noticed, but after the third trip Eleanor Davenport, who like Cicely was partial to matriarchal cats, caught her eye and began to count softly.

Cicely sat still, trying to think where Myrtle could be taking the kittens — which spot in the clothescloset, which bureau drawer — and, more important, where she was getting them. *Four, five, six* — Myrtle seldom had more than four kittens, occasionally five — *seven, eight;* by now all conversation had lapsed and all tension vanished. As Myrtle appeared with the ninth kitten, Cicely pulled herself together and went to the kitchen. How could she have forgotten that the evening might well include diversion by the animal kingdom?

The comfortable carton she had suggested to Myrtle only yesterday sat untenanted and tidy behind the stove. Had she had them among the pots and pans again? No, all the cupboard doors were shut, for a wonder. There was the washer — but that was silly; heavens, of course, the drier! What could be more suitable — warm, dark, quiet, except, of course, when it was whirling rapidly with its light on! She peered in the open door and saw — not Myrtle's black sleekness but the arrogant green eyes and leonine ruff of Myrtle's daughter Penny. Lying with her on the pile of freshly dried, still-warm clothes were the last kittens of the two batches that had been born during and after dinner, eleven in all. Perhaps Myrtle had realized that the drier was only a temporary shelter. In any case, she had got the kittens so thoroughly mixed up that no one could ever decide which were hers and which Penny's, especially as both mothers nursed the whole lot of them in relays, one of them always on the job.

Cicely did not mind in the least sharing her bed with two cats and eleven kittens that night. After all, she owed them something for saving her party from breaking up into two armed camps. What a popular birthday mine is, she thought as she sank into contented sleep.

MENU FOR A BIRTHDAY DINNER

Hot Spiced Tomato Juice with Rose Hips *
Mrs. Appleyard's Cheese Biscuits †
Veal with Prosciutto *
Green Peppers Wellfleet *
Avocado, Grapefruit, Orange and Watercress Salad
Mocha Torte *
Coffee

Hot Spiced Tomato Juice with Rose Hips

Any good brand of tomato juice can be used for this. Cicely likes the Co-op brand particularly. She adds a slice or two of lemon stuck with a few cloves and a stick of cinnamon. Salt, pepper and a dash of soy sauce and garlic salt can also be used if Mrs. Appleyard is not coming. Cicely made a purée of rose hips from her ordinary garden roses when the fruits were plump and bright orange. They are said to have fifty times the vitamin C of oranges. She simmered the pulp with half a lemon for each cup of cut-up rose hips, put it through the Foley food mill and into hot sterile jars. She has to confess that it added nothing perceptible to the tomato juice except the virtuous glow of knowing so much health was there. The tomato and rose hip mixture should not be allowed to boil. Serve hot in cups, with cheese biscuits, small size, on the side.

Veal with Prosciutto

Buy enough veal, cut thin for cutlets, so that there will be one third of a pound per person. Dredge with flour, seasoned to taste, and pound with a wooden mallet till very thin. Cut in squares about four inches each way. Cut prosciutto squares the same shape. With a big French knife chop fine some thin lemon peel, garlic and parsley, also a little fresh basil if you can get it, otherwise a pinch of the dried will do. Blend the whole into a paste and smear on the squares. Add salt, pepper and a dash of cayenne and sprinkle with grated Parmigiano cheese. Put the prosciutto on top of the veal like a sandwich, roll and fasten with toothpicks. Brown the rolls in butter and set on one side. In the same frying pan — Cicely hopes you have a heavy cast-iron one — sauté some chopped green onion, a couple of capers and a cup of chopped mushrooms. Add a cup of stock and simmer for a few minutes. Stir in a teaspoonful of flour. Return the rolls to the sauce and add half a cup of white wine. Cover and cook slowly till the sauce is well blended and the rolls heated through.

Green Peppers Wellfleet

Take firm green peppers and remove the skins. Cicely puts them in a very hot oven for about ten minutes, after which it is possible to peel them. Others plunge them into boiling water or hold them over a hot flame. Either way it is a messy job and the whole process should be done at least twenty-four hours before you plan to serve your dinner. Once having got the skins off, slice the peppers lengthwise, about one half inch wide. Prepare a simple French dressing with olive oil, wine vinegar and two or three cloves of garlic. Cover the peppers with this and set them aside to absorb the flavor and the dressing. The slices will be limp and delicious.

Mocha Torte

First you must make the meringue layers for the Torte. Separate 3 eggs and beat the whites very stiff, slowly adding 1 cup sugar and 1 teaspoon almond extract. Line buttered layer cake pans with brown paper. This will make three 8-inch layers. Bake in a slow (250°) oven till done; that is, firm and a pale light brown. Cool before removing the paper.

For the filling, melt 1 package chocolate bits over hot water. Add 6 egg yolks, ¼ cup water, 2 tablespoons instant coffee, ¼ cup sugar. Blend well and cool. Beat in ⅓ pound very soft butter. To put the Torte together, spread each meringue layer with the filling and then with whipped cream. Pile them on each other and finish with whipped cream. Garnish with shavings of bitter chocolate.

Pie Plant

Spring in Vermont brings new and sometimes curious items to local menus. Long before greens of the domesticated sort are up in the gardens, wild greens are sought out, cooked and eaten. Some swear by dandelions, for salads and for cooked greens; the bitter taste must mean they are good for you, and besides, the fewer the dandelions in the lawns and fields the better. Everyone knows this except the dandelions, which continue to multiply, golden and serene, until whole fields are orange-yellow, carpeted with sunshine.

Marsh marigolds — called cowslips — outline old watercourses with their lacquered golden shine. Some cook the stems and young leaves, or toss a few of the petals in an early salad. Fiddleheads — the unfolded leaves of certain ferns — are much fancied by connoisseurs. They are said to taste like asparagus. Cicely and Mrs. Appleyard incline to prefer the real thing. On the same grounds they would rather have lobster than rattlesnake meat.

The Appleyard ladies make dandelion and cowslip wine, in an attempt to bottle the first spring sunshine for winter consumption. But for true eating pleasure they watch for the first upthrust of rhubarb through last year's tangled grass. A rhubarb plant, like horseradish, is almost eternal, and no matter how much you cut it, it still greets the spring with unimpaired zeal.

True to their principle of eating everything in season, Cicely and her mother, the latter in town briefly to see that her house is still standing after the winter, keep large bowls of stewed rhubarb on hand in the refrigerator. Patience Barlow constructs latticed rhubarb pie. Rhubarb baked with sliced oranges adorns the luncheon table. Vanilla ice cream displays a rhubarb sauce. The wry astringent flavor of pie plant can be met during every course of the meal on certain over-enthusiastic days. It deters Mrs. Appleyard and her daughter not at all that the rest of the members of their family do not share their passion for rhubarb. All the more for them.

The ancestral Appleyard rhubarb plants are of a medium red strain that produces a beautiful pink sauce. As long as they pick only the fresh young stalks the sauce will be neither bitter nor stringy. Part of the pleasure in the rhubarb season is in the picking. Cicely's plants are down beside the brook, so that as she fills her basket she can inspect the water level, check on the wild flowers in the ravine where she planted them last year and see whether the bluebird has taken advantage of the hollow in the apple tree for this year's nest.

As Mrs. Appleyard pulls her stalks of rhubarb beside her back steps, the barn swallows swoop over her head and across her man-made pond in the pasture, now blending into the landscape. She sees that the frost has as usual pulled the carriage house about and that the barn floor lists still further to the south than it did. Somehow all Vermont buildings are trying to get to Florida. One more limb has gone from her bird tree. Soon it will be fit for nothing but a pecking post for pileated woodpeckers.

As the rhubarb season blends into the strawberry season, Mrs. Appleyard and Cicely make preserves combining both these favorites of theirs. This too is a good sauce for ice cream or on a plain cake. They halfheartedly freeze a little rhubarb, but their passion for it is waning. They toy with the idea of rhubarb ice cream and postpone it till next year. As the tones of the new leaves lose their distinction and blend more and more into a uniform green, as the orchard grass grows long and hides the rhubarb plants, these ladies occupy themselves more and more with their gardens. Rhubarb is part of the wild open look of early spring, not sedate enough for summer when the greens march in neat rows across the tamed earth.

Supper Menu in Rhubarb Time

Smothered Chicken *
Cream of Wheat Spoon Bread
Spinach Ring * with Mushroom Sauce (p. 116)
Rhubarb and Strawberry Conserve *
Hot Mocha Chocolate
Rhubarb Ice Cream
    or
Latticed Rhubarb Pie with Vanilla Ice Cream
    or
Baked Rhubarb and Orange Slices *

Smothered Chicken (V. H.)

Have a broiling chicken weighing at least 2½ pounds cut into four pieces. Use the wing tips, neck and carefully scrubbed and manicured (or is it pedicured?) feet to make a broth with onion, celery, carrot and whatever seasonings you like. While this is simmering you may do whatever you wish for a couple of hours. Mrs. Appleyard enjoys a good game of chess but does not consider it necessary to impose this preference upon the general public. About an hour and a half before serving time put some seasoned flour into a paper bag and toss the pieces of chicken around in it until they are thoroughly coated. Then brown them carefully in a mixture of half butter and half lard over a rather low flame, turning them from time to time. Use a heavy iron frying pan. They should be an even golden brown. Now strain in about two cups of the broth. Turn the heat down as low as it will go and simmer the chicken until it is tender, about an hour and a quarter. Add a little broth occasionally. There will be a delicious light brown gravy in the pan when the chicken is done. The small pieces of meat, the vegetables and the rest of the broth can be used in a risotto another day.

Variation (Mrs. Appleyard): Make your broth with tomato juice instead of water. Add to the chicken green pepper, sliced onions, mushrooms sautéed in butter just before you pour the broth over it. Add chopped parsley when you serve it.

Variation No. 2: Make your broth with water. Add sautéed mushrooms and onions when you pour the broth over the chicken. Just before serving time, remove the chicken from the pan. Blend in a little white wine, about two tablespoons, and half a cup of sour cream. Let it heat but not boil or it will curdle. Sprinkle a few minced chives or some minced parsley over it.

Spinach Ring

One of the few things that is better out of a cellophane bag than it is from your own garden, Mrs. Appleyard says, is spinach. Somehow no amateur ever gets the sand out of spinach so well as the people who wash it professionally. Perhaps they have a kind of super-Bendix that whirls it clean. Prue Holt tried it in her washing machine, and the problem was not so much how to get sand out of the spinach as how to get spinach out of Wallace's shirts for the next few weeks. Anyway, there it is, clean, curled and green. Your only problem is to get rid of the bag.

"I saw in the paper that you can use cellophane for mulch in the vegetable garden," Mrs. Appleyard remarked to Venetia Hopkins.

Venetia is the kind of gardener who will herself distribute a ton of straw between her rows of lettuce and peas. She grows delphinium eight feet high and lilies the size of Gabriel's trumpet. There is a story, circulated by some rival lover of compost, no doubt, that a weed was once seen in her asparagus bed.

Mrs. Appleyard doesn't believe a word of it.

"You save the cellophane and use it from year to year," she added.

Venetia made the noise usually written "Humph," and Mrs. Appleyard put the cellophane in the stove, touched a match to it and went to work as follows:

For a ring mold that would serve six people she took:

2 bags of washed spinach	¼ cup water
1 tablespoon finely minced onion	4 eggs, not separated
	3 tablespoons flour
1 cup milk, part cream	¼ teaspoon nutmeg
3 tablespoons butter	¼ teaspoon pepper
4 slices Pepperidge Farm bread	salt to taste

Make croutons from 4 slices of Pepperidge Farm bread and brown them slowly and lightly in 2 extra tablespoons of butter. Toss them frequently. Use garlic butter if you like it and are sure your guests will.

Cook the spinach and onion in the water until the spinach is thoroughly wet and limp, turning it over frequently. This takes about 4 minutes. Put ⅓ cup of the milk and water from the spinach in the electric blender. Add half the spinach and purée it thoroughly, then the rest in two more lots. Or use your own purée method. A food mill is a good tool for this. Or chop it and run it through the finest blade of the meat chopper. Anyway, get it fine and it should be cooked so little that it is still bright green. Light the oven at 325° and put a pan of hot water on the lower shelf.

Melt the butter, add flour and seasonings slowly and rub the mixture smooth. Remove from heat and slowly stir in the remaining ¾ cup of milk. Cook over a low flame till it thickens. Stir in the spinach purée. Mix in the eggs, one at a time, beating after each addition. Give it a final beating, pour it into a well-buttered ring mold, set it in the oven and bake until a knife blade dipped into it comes out clean — about 35 minutes. Run a spatula around the outer edge, a small knife around the inner one. Invert the mold on a circular dish.

Fill with Mushroom Sauce (p. 116). Surround with the croutons.

Baked Rhubarb and Orange Slices

To 4 cups rhubarb washed and cut in inch-long pieces add 4 oranges, peeled and cut in slices, 2 cups of sugar and a twist of lemon rind. Fill an earthenware baking dish with alternate layers of rhubarb and oranges, sprinkling with sugar in between. Bury the lemon peel in the middle. Bake in a fairly hot oven — 375° — till it bubbles around the edges. Serve with hard sauce. This also makes a good filling for a deep dish rhubarb pie.

Rhubarb and Strawberry Conserve

In any standard recipe for jam, take equal parts rhubarb and strawberries and follow the usual procedure. This makes a good ice-cream sauce.

Birthday Picnic

THE APPLEYARD FAMILY has many picnic sites. There is Jump-on-Appletree Pasture, where the stunted trees have been nibbled down by generations of cows till their twigs are like iron, capable of supporting a middle-sized child. There is Where-Grandma-Spilled-the-Lemonade-and-Was-Cross — a cow pasture halfway up Spruce Mountain referred to in awed terms by Mrs. Appleyard's children; their mother has often mislaid things, but seldom her temper.

Over toward Catamount is the pasture where the Bradshaws and the Hiltons were dining *al fresco* together when they found the first wild mushrooms. In the other direction is an overgrown cellar hole on a hillcrest overlooking Millbrook Pond. A birch tree and a maple have grown up in the cellar hole and the Appleyards sit on the wide granite doorstep and watch the wind send catspaws over the pond.

However, for the picnic with which Mrs. Appleyard and Camilla, the youngest Bradshaw, celebrate their joint birthday, the family almost always decides on Stone Houses for their picnic spot. Just at the edge of the spruce woods that border the Appleyard sugarbush is a series of ledges. The slates have been used to make a fireplace and two thronelike chairs for the guests of honor. One of them was always haunted for Cicely by the shade of her Grandmother Appleyard, energetic, salty of tongue, earthy of wit. Cicely remembered her playing billiards in her petticoat during a thunderstorm, going out to the garden at midnight to peel and eat a cucumber, sending her a check for a thousand dollars as a graduation present, to do with as she pleased.

The view from the picnic seats spread the whole of Appleyard Center before them like a toy village. They could see Henry Gould drive the last of his sleek brown Jerseys into the barn for milking and Marcia shutting up the hens for the night. Frank Flint drove his yellow mail car down the hill, pausing at each box to slide the papers and letters in with the deftness of long practice. They watched in turn the Goulds, the Marshes, the Balches come out to get their mail. In the still clear air of late afternoon every sound rose to them undiluted, and they could hear Sandra Marsh call to her husband and see him come out on the porch.

"There must be a letter from Jim," said Mrs. Appleyard. "I do hope it's good news." She knew from her own long years of waiting for letters from Stan and Hugh while they were in the service how hard it was to be calm when any series of letters was interrupted.

Tommy Bradshaw was building a fire and fitting the grate over it for Hamburg Specials. Cicely laid out brown bowls of fixings — sliced tomatoes, green pepper rings, mild onion slices, lengths of sharp cheese from the creamery over the ridge, last year's chutney and red pepper relish. Cynthia Bradshaw, formerly nicknamed Moppet, toasted the hamburger rolls to order. Joan handed out wooden plates and paper napkins. Camilla prepared to circulate with the salt grinder and pepper grater. She was too giddy with birthday excitement to sit still on her throne.

Mrs. Appleyard, however, was content to look about her and be waited upon. What did it matter if the hamburgers were a little charred on the outside, a little raw within, the rolls unevenly toasted, more pepper on her skirt than on her meat? Lately her birthdays had drifted by her with increasing frequency, but she could still share the intensity of Camilla's anticipation of the joys of being five.

Hamburgers having been devoured, Cicely retired into the spruce trees and came out with the birthday cake lit with six candles.

"I knew you wouldn't object to having Camilla dictate the number of candles," she said to her mother.

"Certainly not," said Mrs. Appleyard. "I don't care to have my cake bristling like a porcupine."

"You came to see me in the hospital, Grandma," said Camilla suddenly. "I was as big as a cat and I had black eyes."

"So you did, and black hair too," said her grandmother. "I liked you right away. Here, blow out the candles and I'll cut the cake."

With a great puff Camilla blew out all the candles. Cicely removed the daffodils from the center of the cake, her mother cut it in generous pieces and in no time at all there was nothing left but a smear of yellow frosting and a few crumbs. Angel cakes were a tradition for Appleyard birthdays, trimmed with flowers of the appropriate season, frosted and colored according to individual taste. Hugh always used to have pussy willows on his, Cicely pansies, Sally lilacs and Stan roses. But that was in Massachusetts, and Vermont birthdays for the same

people had different flowers. Thus Mrs. Appleyard who in
Brookline shared lilacs with Sally, in Appleyard Center was
put back to daffodils.

By the time the picnic odds and ends had been burned,
the sun was heading for the gap between Catamount and
Hunger Mountain and the shadows were creeping up the
fields toward Stone Houses. Joan and Camilla were called
away from a building project on the lower ledge where generations of Appleyards had made Druid circles, villages of
cones and twigs, quartz pebbles, twisted roots. Tommy had
collected enough spruce gum to last about a week.

Cynthia's sharp eyes saw the car turn in to her grandmother's
yard before the rest had noticed anything. It was a long, low-
slung black convertible with the top down. Since the passengers
had alighted and were standing on the porch, the scarlet leather
upholstery was brilliantly visible.

"Ah," said Mrs. Appleyard, "I expect I am wanted below."
She meant, of course, that she hoped she was wanted.

Who doesn't?

"We're just going anyway," said Cicely. "Give your grandmother a hand, Tommy — no, not the one with the spruce
gum in it. Is it the Emperor Geoffrey Toussaint the First?"

"None other," replied her mother joyfully. "Probably he
wishes to consult me about some satin-backed wallpaper or
a marble dressing table. I heard that he was to be in residence
today."

Now, she thought, things would begin to hum around
Appleyard Center. One composer would start to play Bach
on that piano that sounds like a banjo when you put down
the middle pedal while another was trying over his new twelve-
tone piece on the Steinway. Painters would begin painting

their friends with four eyes, all crossed. Writers would hide their tape recorders in their hosts' living rooms and transcribe the tapes with pens dipped in a nice blend of maple syrup and vitriol.

"Come on, children," she said aloud. "Summer's begun!"

MENU FOR A BIRTHDAY PICNIC

Hamburg Specials *
Red Pepper Relish †
Apple Chutney (p. 103)
Angel Cake with Flowers of the Season *

Mrs. Appleyard lived so long before the invention of electric grinders that it was many years before she knew there was such a thing as Hamburg steak. In her innocent youth tough steak was pounded, and usually not enough. On the whole, in case any archaeologist of the future would like to know, she considers the Ground Meat era superior to the Pounded Meat period. She would like, however, to record the fact that, like a freezer, you can't really get better meat out of a grinder than you put into it. Tenderer, yes, but not better flavored or with a better proportion of lean to fat meat. She thinks it is worthwhile to pay more and have chuck or bottom of the round ground — twice — for you. She also asserts that hamburgers ought to be big enough, at least a third of a pound apiece, and that one large one is better than two small ones.

The length of time they are cooked will be a matter of taste. She likes them brown on the outside, pink — not raw —

inside and achieves this effect by doing them two minutes on each side in a heated iron frying pan. In getting them ready she mixes about a tablespoonful of cold water with a pound of ground lean meat, shapes and pats each cake firmly, and conceals a small lump of butter, half a teaspoonful, in the center of each.

With sliced young onions from the garden, rich red tomato slices still warm from the vines, her own piccalilli and chutney, mustard pickle and horseradish with sour cream, she considers the eating of hamburgers no penance. She just wishes the rolls were not made out of cotton. She knows that the production of cotton is one of our major industries but she thinks it ought to be used for the lining of comforters. Perhaps, she says generously, it would be better with caraway seeds in it. At least it would be a good place to put them. Mrs. Appleyard was charmed, on a brief visit to Mexico, to learn that the importation of caraway seeds into that country is prohibited.

She ate one of the best meals she ever had in her life in a cave dug out of a brown hill in Mexico. Inside, the cave was painted a sinister neon blue. No caraway seeds in anything. No hamburgers either. Juicy steak, two inches thick. *Viva Mexico!*

Returning to everyday life, Mrs. Appleyard recalls with pleasure a way Venetia Hopkins has of treating Hamburg steak.

Hamburg Pie

For four people use an 8-inch frying pan and 1¾ pounds of ground meat. Butter the pan lightly, put the meat in, all in one thick cake pressed down evenly. Cook it for 5 minutes on top of the stove over a hot flame, then for 4 minutes under a preheated gas broiler or radiant electric broiler. This produces a medium-rare effect. Increase both times slightly if you like it better done.

To go with it, in a separate frying pan, she makes either a tomato sauce with garlic and green pepper (p. 53) or a mushroom sauce (p. 116), pouring it, bubbling hot, over the Hamburg Pie just before she brings it to the table.

Variation: Hamburg Pie Pretty Nearly Stroganov

Who was Stroganov? No one has been able to answer this question for Mrs. Appleyard. All anyone replies is "Well, you take some sour cream . . . " Mrs. Appleyard took a cupful, but first she began by slicing three onions thin and cooking them in butter until they began to brown. Then she poured 2 cups of hot water over them and turned the heat down. When she next looked at them all the water was cooked out and the onions were a deep amber color. She then proceeded to cook the Hamburg Pie as above (1¾ pounds of ground steak in an 8-inch buttered frying pan, 5 minutes on top of the stove, 4 minutes under the electric broiler). In the meantime she stirred the sour cream into the onions and let it stand, unheated. Just before the Hamburg was ready she heated the mixture to the boiling point, then poured it around the edge where the "pie" had shrunk from the pan, sprinkled it with parsley on top, and served it in the pan. The Hamburg cooked this way was juicy enough so that juice ran into the onion and sour cream mixture.

"Very good," pronounced Hugh Appleyard who was greeted with this invention at the end of a thousand-mile drive. "Well worth coming for."

He also enjoyed kasha, and peas twenty minutes from the vines. They drank Stroganov's health, whoever he was, in a glass of Burgundy.

Angel Cake

Mrs. Appleyard has made a good many angel cakes in her career in which she actually dealt with 13 egg whites and later with 13 yolks. She tells how she used to do this in *Mrs. Appleyard's Kitchen* (p. 56). That, however, was not a summer kitchen. It was quite a while before Cicely and her mother admitted to each other that their fine old New England moral fiber had relaxed so that they were using packaged angel cake mix. In fact they probably never would have admitted it to each other if they had not happened to meet at the counter in the Co-op, Cicely with a package of Swansdown, and her mother with one of Pillsbury's. Each maintains staunchly that her own brand is the best. The public — and this is definitely embarrassing — doesn't seem to be able to tell the difference either between one package and another or between a package and the 13-egg masterpieces of Auld Lang Syne. Mrs. Appleyard's advice is to choose whatever kind attracts you and to follow the directions *exactly*.

MENU FOR A SUPPER IN MAY

Fried Chicken
Wild Rice with Sautéed Mushrooms
Asparagus with Horse-radish and Sour Cream (p. 62)

Tossed Fruit and Scallion Salad *
Orange Cake *
Coffee

When Mrs. Appleyard was opening her house for what in
Vermont is quaintly called the summer — a season consisting
of a warm weekend in late July — it was May. Hills were
freshly frosted with snow. She had lunched on a lettuce sandwich. Of course the day was beautiful. Spring peepers were
tinkling. Meadows looked up at the blue sky out of bluer pools
of melted ice. Gray poplars were hung with silver catkins.
Brooks ran fast and green, foaming white over hidden rocks.
Under the golden willows rivers brimmed their banks.

Still, Mrs. Appleyard cannot live entirely on the landscape
and she was delighted when Laura Parkes asked her to supper.
Laura claims she is not a bit interested in food, hates to cook
and the meal would be terrible. Mrs. Appleyard knew that
Laura, though originally from Massachusetts, had lived in her
big white house in Montpelier long enough to have picked up
some Vermont attitudes. She did not worry about supper.
Mrs. Parkes might not be interested in what she ate herself
but she was far from indifferent to the appetites of her guests.

It was no surprise, therefore, when Laura bade her guest sit
down and listen to E. Power Biggs playing a Bach fugue on
an ancient Dutch organ and then, apparently without lifting
a finger, produced the above menu. Her generosity did not
stop there. After the meal was over she read to Mrs. Appleyard out of her own hand-written cookbook, read slowly
enough so Mrs. Appleyard could write it all down and pass
it along.

Tossed Fruit and Scallion Salad

sections from 1 grapefruit and 1 orange
1 avocado, diced

1 green pepper, sliced thin
1 bunch scallions, finely cut
lettuce

Toss all together with your favorite French dressing.

Orange Cake

Grind together:

1 cup raisins
1 cup walnuts

rind of 1 orange

In the mixer cream ½ cup butter with 1 cup sugar.
Beat in 2 eggs.

2 cups flour sifted with 1 teaspoon soda

1 cup sour milk or ¾ cup sweet milk and ¼ cup malt vinegar

Combine mixtures. Bake at 325° until the top springs back when pressed with the finger and the cake shrinks from the side of the pan — about 40 minutes. Remove from the pan and while the cake is still hot pour over it the juice of a large orange in which has been thoroughly dissolved ¾ cup sugar. This cake keeps well and is the kind of thing to give you courage to face the spring. Mrs. Appleyard was given a large chunk of it and found it extremely nutritious.

June

The Garden is Green

W<small>HEN</small> M<small>RS</small>. A<small>PPLEYARD</small> drives into her yard in June the first thing she notices is the way it smells. The spice pinks are out in a scented pink ruff around the bed of hardy perennials. These are well-named plants as only the hardiest can survive Mrs. Appleyard's patronage, which somehow produces more grass than flowers. Syringas, however, continue to send out perfume in response to her affectionate neglect. White rugosa roses positively revel in it. Pekin lilac demands no care to produce a fountain of creamy white, sweet-smelling spray.

Roger Willard has cut the grass, and in the fields across the brook tall timothy with clover in it is freshly mown. To shut off your engine and put your head out the car window is like opening the lid of an enormous jar of pot-pourri.

It is not possible to live entirely on pot-pourri, as Mrs. Appleyard soon remembers. It takes only a little longer to realize that in Appleyard Center she must drop back into a sort of neolithic age in which the procuring of each item of food is a personal triumph for the hunter. The weapons are different it is true. Little can be accomplished with bow and arrow; much with a wide-ranging car, a keen eye and a persuasive tongue.

Perhaps it is only because she drives forty miles to get it, but Vermont asparagus seems to have a distinctive flavor. She learned long ago from Mr. Appleyard to eat whatever is in season every day while it is at its best; that when the season is over something else comes along. So she eats asparagus: country style, with Hollandaise, as soup, as shortcake with cream sauce, cold with French dressing, hot with garlic croutons. By the time asparagus is getting stringy there are radishes and lettuce, five kinds of it, in her own garden, and the purple flowers of chives are coming up among the spice pinks.

It is obviously time to make spring garden salad and invite some guests who like garlic. She will serve Mr. Appleyard's Welsh Rabbit too. She will not buy any English muffins constructed with a view to using as much air and as little flour as possible. She states that she will make crumpets herself for the Welsh Rabbit to cascade over.

There is plenty of the 1955 chutney in the cellarway and it was a fairly good vintage, she remembers, and likely to have mellowed with age. Strawberries will be in season so soon that those left in the freezer from last year had better be used, she tells Patience Barlow. Perhaps for sauce on some angel cake. Patience gets out her egg beater and suggests that some guests with good digestions had better be chosen.

"And what," she asks with a slight touch of severity, "are you going to do with thirteen egg yolks?"

She should not have challenged Mrs. Appleyard's ingenuity. That lady stops mixing her crumpets long enough to assert that fish mousse with plenty of Hollandaise sauce, and crème brûlée will take care of most of them. Cicely suggests a gold cake that will cope with the rest.

"I'll invite some people who are on a bland diet for that menu," Mrs. Appleyard adds, and names over a few of her friends who have ulcers, or, as she has heard them called, dental difficulties. "I'll ask the ones with gallstones another day," she adds considerately.

"Well, don't serve spoon bread the same time you do fish mousse," Patience Barlow advises.

She is referring to one of Mrs. Appleyard's less well-planned luncheons during which a nearsighted guest put maple syrup on the fish mousse and Hollandaise on the spoon bread.

"I always knew Vermonters served a great deal of maple syrup but not with fish," the lady is reported to have said with an air of bewilderment.

Mrs. Appleyard simply remarked cheerfully that it was fortunate that no one had put hard sauce on the green beans or horseradish with sour cream on the chocolate soufflé. (Both were available.) She then set her crumpet batter to rise and did a little work on her velvet painting. June — that charming chilly month — usually brings out her latent handcraftiness. This year it is taking the form of trying to paint on velvet as well as her great-grandmother did a hundred and thirty years ago. So far her great-grandmother is still ahead. As she combines grapes and peaches and plums in a blue bowl, Mrs. Appleyard admires her ancestress more and more.

"Of course hers has had time to mellow," she says. "But I'll soon fix that."

As a gentle beauty hint one of Mrs. Appleyard's descendants once presented her with some pancake make-up. Mrs. Appleyard tried it but soon concluded that she looked too much like a beech leaf left over from last autumn and stopped using it. Naturally, being a Vermonter if only by association, she did not throw it away. It proved to be just the thing for mellowing velvet paintings. Mrs. Appleyard has plenty on hand in case a similar problem arises.

LUNCHEON MENUS

Mr. Appleyard's Welsh Rabbit † with English muffins
　　　　or
Cheese Fondue with Toasted French Bread
Asparagus, Country Style
Absent-Minded Meringue,* Crushed Strawberries
Tea

Fish Mousse with Hollandaise †
Asparagus with Garlic Croutons
Inside out Potatoes *
Tossed Salad
Crème Brûlée *
Coffee

Iced Vichyssoise

Rock Cornish Chickens *
Corn Pudding †
Asparagus Vinaigrette *
No Dessert except Soufflé Crackers † and Cheese

Absent-Minded Meringue

5 egg whites	1½ cups sugar
1 teaspoon cream of tartar	1 teaspoon vanilla

Beat the egg whites till they begin to thicken. Sprinkle in the cream of tartar and beat them until they are thick. Beat in half the sugar, a little at a time; fold in the rest and the vanilla. Put the mixture into an 8-inch aluminum pan lined with brown paper and bake it at 350° for half an hour. Turn off the oven. Forget the meringue and leave it in the oven all night.

You will have to arrange your own system for overlooking this delicacy. Mrs. Appleyard did it by being called to the telephone for a long distance talk with one of her favorite characters (note: Long distance in this case refers to the time consumed in conversation, not to the physical distance which is 1¼ miles) and prudently turning off the oven, planning to turn it on again later. Luckily she forgot and began to read *Wuthering Heights* for the seventeenth time. In the morning the meringue was a delicately tinted square of crispness which she split, filled with ice cream, and served with fresh raspberries.

Meringues

5 egg whites	1 cup granulated sugar, sifted
	1 teaspoon vanilla

In case you are in a mood to pay attention to the baking of meringues, Mrs. Appleyard, who has produced her share of flabby and sticky ones in her time, gives the following baking suggestions.

Beat egg whites in a cold bowl until they are thick but not stiff. Light the oven: 275°. Add sugar a tablespoon at a time, beating well, until you have used ¾ of a cup. Fold in the remaining ¼ cup of sugar and the vanilla. Cover a cooky sheet with a double thickness of white typewriter paper. (This is Mrs. Appleyard's favorite use for this substance. She always uses the best grade. The ordinary kind is plenty good enough for writing per cent signs when she means — well, what? Better not be too precise.) Spoon on the mixture in circular heaps. This amount makes ten large ones. Bake them until there are no shiny bubbles on them. *None. Not any.* It will take at least an hour. If your oven does not bake evenly, turn the pan. Be careful to do it gently and as quickly as possible so that the cold air does not strike them for any length of time. Mrs. Appleyard speaks, if at all, while shifting the pan in much the same low voice that she uses when she is shown her newest grandchild. She says meringues, like her descendants, behave best when the barometer is rising. Remove them immediately from the paper. Store them until you use them in a tin box with a tight-fitting lid.

Inside out Potatoes

Scrub large symmetrical potatoes, allowing one to a person and one or two extra. They need not be Idahos but they should be oval in shape and without bumps. Allow an hour and five minutes from sink to plate. Have the oven preheated at 450°.

Bake the potatoes at this temperature for twenty minutes, turning them often the first 10 minutes. Reduce the heat to 350°, turn them again and bake thirty minutes longer. Take them out of the oven, split them carefully lengthwise, remove the contents to a warm bowl containing softened butter, salt and freshly ground pepper to taste, and a little thick cream stirred together. Mash the potatoes briskly into the butter and cream. A large fork with twisted blades or a sturdy spoon with holes in it will help you at this point. Heap the mixture into the shells, set them in a pan and run it under the broiler briefly until a golden brown color appears.

Variations: Chopped chives or parsley may be stirred into the mixture.

It may be topped with thinly sliced Cheddar cheese.

Bacon cooked on one side, drained, and cut into small pieces may be put on top, cooked side down.

Crème Brûlée

8 egg yolks	1 quart light cream
2 tablespoons sugar	2 teaspoons vanilla
1 cup (about) light brown sugar	

You must have dry light brown sugar. The package will be labeled yellow brown or golden brown. Dark brown *will not do.*

You will need a cup, possibly more. The amount will vary with the size of the dish you use. Mrs. Appleyard likes a 9 x 13 Pyrex one. This gives plenty of top in proportion to the depth.

Heat the cream but do not scald it. Add sugar and vanilla

and pour the mixture over the well-beaten egg yolks and then into the Pyrex dish. Set the dish into a pan of warm water and bake it at 350° until a silver knife slipped into the middle comes out clean (about 20 minutes). Chill the custard — that's what it is, we may as well face it — for several hours or overnight. When it is very cold, cover it ¼ inch deep with the light brown sugar which is well sifted and free from lumps.

Now the broiling: an electric infra-red broiler is fine but it can be done in a gas broiler. Light either one ahead of time: gas, 5 minutes, electric infra-red 1 minute. The idea is brief exposure to intense heat. You must watch the Brûlée every second or it will scorch. All you are trying to do is to melt the sugar as fast as possible. When it begins to brown, remove it at once from the flame.

The center usually melts first so it is a good idea to slide first one end of the pan and then the other under the flame. The whole melting process takes three minutes, perhaps less. Now chill the Brûlée again. The top should be like golden ice and when tapped with the spoon should give forth a pleasant resonance.

Rock Cornish Chickens

These come frozen, beautifully trussed, encased in plastic bags and stuffed with wild rice. There are cooking directions printed on the plastic and they are helpful, but Mrs. Appleyard naturally has a suggestion or two.

Put the birds — one apiece — into a covered roaster right in their plastic bags. Have the oven 325°–350°. After an hour remove the bags. This is not so easy as it sounds, something

like juggling a hot greased pig. After you have won the battle
— and good luck to you! — pour melted butter over the
chickens, then dredge them with flour seasoned as you like
it. You were saving, Mrs. Appleyard hopes, some chicken
fat and some broth for just such an emergency. Put the fat
into the pan. There will soon be enough liquid to baste the
birds. Do this every fifteen minutes until they are brown and
tender. This should be in about another hour. Now remove
them to a hot platter and make gravy in the roaster.

Mrs. Appleyard uses for four birds:

2 tablespoons flour	2 tablespoons onion relish (p.
2 tablespoons chopped parsley	217) or finely minced onion
1½ cups milk	1½ cups chicken broth, hot
salt to taste	

Cook the onion till it softens. Rub flour into the fat. Cook
till it thickens and starts to brown. Turn off the heat, blend
in the stock and the milk. Add any seasoning you like, or
leave it to lead its own life. Reheat, sprinkle the parsley over
it and serve birds and gravy.

Asparagus Vinaigrette

When you have served Asparagus with Hollandaise, with
lemon butter, country style, made shortcake and used the tips
moistened with heavy cream for filling, or put piles of it with
green mayonnaise around cold boiled salmon, you might like
to change and try it vinaigrette, like this:

Break off the stalks of two and a half pounds of asparagus
where they snap easily, boil them until tender in your aspara-

gus cooker if you have one. Otherwise tie them in a neat
bunch, trim off the stems so the bunch will stand up. They
should cook standing for ten minutes and then covered by
the boiling water for another seven to ten minutes. Do not
overcook or the tips will break off.

Drain, and while the asparagus is still warm, pour over it
the following sauce.

6 tablespoons olive oil	1 tablespoon tarragon vinegar
2 tablespoons Wesson oil	2 tablespoons cider vinegar
1 tablespoon minced piccalilli	1 tablespoon green pepper
1 teaspoon minced parsley	minced

1 tablespoon minced chives
Seasonings to taste: salt, 1 teaspoon paprika, pepper from the
grinder, ½ teaspoon mustard.

Put these all in a jar and shake well. Put the asparagus into a
serving dish lightly rubbed with garlic. Set the dish into the
refrigerator. Serve it very cold. If the evening is hot, set the
dish into another containing cracked ice. Garnish with grated
egg yolk and strips of pimento.

Mrs. Appleyard always feels slightly abused when the subject of asparagus comes up, as it does every spring. For a long
time her wistfully hungry expression expressed regret that she
hadn't planted a bed of it the season before. Years passed; in
fact, decades passed. At last the time, the place and the loved
one all synchronized. Mary Washington was her name. Her
appearance was something that only Shakespeare, George Mere-
dith and the man who wrote the catalogue, probably assisted
by Robert Browning, could properly describe. A thousand
roots cost only $20.

"Was this the face that launched a thousand roots?" murmured Mrs. Appleyard, writing out the check lightly though with emotion.

So they came and were planted and the rest had better be silence. We did just happen to hear Mrs. Appleyard announce, one crisp May evening when everyone else within ten miles of Appleyard Center was saying: "I wonder when the peas will be ripe. I get kind of tired of asparagus this time of year . . . " that at least she was the only gardener she knew whose asparagus had cost her ten dollars a stalk.

"One of them," she added proudly, "was as large as my fourth finger."

Luckily the neighbors are generous.

Eating up the Freezer

ONE of the interesting features of Mrs. Appleyard's return to Vermont is seeing what she left in her drawer in the Locker Plant the year before. There are said to be individuals who keep accurate records of the frozen food they have on hand, who can tell with a quick glance at a filing card how many green beans are left and when they ate the last of that uninteresting batch of chicken soup. Not so Mrs. Appleyard. To her everything is a glad surprise — well, a surprise anyway.

The Locker Plant is a sort of gastronomic grab bag. Some of the grabs are more popular than others. As she examines the pearls of her dietetic rosary and counts them over one by one before putting them back into her own freezer, Mrs. Appleyard makes certain resolutions.

She will not, she promises herself, freeze any more succotash. There's a two years' supply on hand now. It must have been pure nervousness in 1953 that caused her to construct all that spaghetti sauce. Why, there's still enough to take a bath in. Also she will use everything up before she puts anything more in. And she will pack everything systematically, the oldest on top.

These virtuous resolves have something hauntingly familiar about them. They last several days. Within a week she has returned to her old habits — using the creamed mushrooms and letting the succotash sink to the bottom, cooking fresh rhubarb when she ought to be eating 1952 blackberries, bringing out her own peach ice cream and letting the sherbet of the professionals keep its own granite hardness and flavor. Still, she does find a delicious pot roast she had forgotten. She discovers that some of her guests — the ones who went with her on a picnic to visit a clairvoyant, for instance — are hungry enough in the open air to eat a casserole containing *both* the spaghetti sauce and the succotash.

Everyone knows that there is something special about Vermont turkeys and maple syrup, but few realize that Vermont clairvoyants also have their peculiar excellence. There is something charmingly cosy about prophecy combined with understatement. No crystal ball, no cobwebs are needed, no mystic symbols, no dingy shawls. A Vermont clairvoyant can operate in a sunshiny room with crisp ruffled curtains at the windows.

You may find her washing dishes at her spotless sink, wearing an apron flowered like a June meadow. She helps you state your problem by offering you coffee and freshly made doughnuts.

Even Mrs. Appleyard, a natural skeptic, likes a clairvoyant who says "I guess." Certainly the episode of the Bradshaws' silver takes some explaining. Somehow it vanished at the time their house in Arizona burned down. Cicely was quite sure she had not taken it to Arizona, and yet when she came back to Vermont to live there was no trace of it. Her mother knew nothing about it. She remembered buying it at the time of Cicely's wedding, remembered the maroon bags it came in and the plain pattern like her own, her mother's and her grandmother's, but she had not seen it for years. A common characteristic of the younger generation, Mrs. Appleyard has noticed, is that, for sensible reasons to do with the vanishing of servants, they are not metal polishers. The Bradshaws eat happily with stainless steel. However, there are occasions when a dozen teaspoons and salad forks come in handy, and when one of these arose Cicely missed her silver. Always efficient, she decided, rather than to ransack the house any further, to go to Berylla Casilani's.

Berylla lives on the other side of a substantial range of hills (mountains to southerners from Massachusetts). Mrs. Appleyard decided to take anyone in the neighborhood who had a problem in the lost-and-found department and a picnic lunch. She got out her various containers for hot and cold dishes, constructed her casserole and extracted other items from the freezer, reducing its contents to a satisfactory extent.

The travelers ate their lunch on a picnic table in a mountain glen beside a noisy foaming brook. The blackflies had been planning apparently to lunch on the picnickers. How did they know lunch was coming?

"Consulted Berylla, perhaps," Mrs. Appleyard said, and produced a bottle of 612 from the basket, for like Mrs. Swiss Family Robinson she comes prepared for pretty nearly everything. Thus garnished, the party consumed the casserole in peace and ate the 1953 cinnamon buns. They drank the punch, left over from Labor Day last year. They ate the Brown Betty made from last year's applesauce. The hard sauce was contemporary, but the cheese had been aged, though not by Mrs. Appleyard.

Thus refreshed they drove on through lanes of elms hung with fresh green, along the river bottom with its serpentine steep-banked stream, past a tiny sway-backed covered bridge and so to Berylla's tidy farmhouse.

Found after conference this day were one Stillson wrench, one platinum and diamond wrist watch, one Jersey heifer and a certain amount of flat silver. Perhaps the circumstances of the finding of the watch were the most unusual. Its owner had visited Berylla to inquire about a diamond ring (it was right where she left it, on the kitchen table with a Sandwich glass salt cellar turned over it). Not long afterward she missed the watch. Berylla handed it to her as soon as she spoke about it.

"The children found it in the road," she said. "I kinda guessed the owner would turn up. You musta dropped it last time you were here. No, I won't take a cent, no charge for storage."

A clairvoyant who would not make capital of such a heaven-sent occurrence must be of a really devastating honesty, Mrs. Appleyard decided. Apparently it never occurred to her to put the watch in a hollow tree and send the owner there blindfolded at midnight, telling her to put her hand in the hole when the owl hooted thrice. But then Berylla does not write mystery stories.

She was now thinking about Cicely's silver. She rocked a little in her old Boston rocker. She was knitting a pink baby blanket and her needles stopped clicking for a minute as though she were drowsy.

"Well," she said gently, "I guess your silver didn't burn up in any fire. I don't know as it's in Vermont, though. Seems 'sif I see it in some other state south of here. It's in a kind of a big house, a white house up a ways from the street, quite a few steps. It's not a country place, but there's a lot of grass and trees. The silver's quite high up in the house, about as high as you can get. I guess ther's something near it that's dark red . . . I'm afraid it's not much help," she added apologetically, "but you're entitled to another reading in case you don't find it."

No other reading was necessary. The next time Cicely visited the Green she climbed the steps to her mother's house, making her way over the tricycles, stuffed animals, bald-headed dolls and collapsed balloons assembled by the children who have kitchen and other privileges in that mansion. As she went up two flights of stairs the banister rails were being polished by descending small boys as she passed. She climbed the attic stairs, but she was not yet as high as she could get. Luckily there was a stepladder near the tall cabinet. On top of the cabinet was a pillow covered in dark red satin, and beneath it the silver in its maroon bags.

Berylla had, as usual, helped her neighbors.

MENU FOR A CLAIRVOYANT PICNIC

Casserole of Succotash *
Cinnamon Buns *
Labor Day Punch *
Brown Betty with Hard Sauce
Crowley Cheese

Succotash Casserole

In New England succotash means corn and shell beans, not limas. Corn and limas are good together when both are freshly picked, but the true succotash bean is the kind called Horticultural or Cranberry, with cranberry-sauce colored splashes on the pods. In 1954 both cranberry beans and golden bantam corn ripened before the frost and Mrs. Appleyard froze a good many packages. The beans were shelled and cooked until almost done and most of the water had cooked away. The corn was cut from the cob. Butter was melted in the frying pan and the corn was simmered in it with a finely scraped onion, a teaspoonful to a pint, for a few minutes. Very small beef cubes, tried out and crisply browned, were mixed with the beans, which were added, water and all, to the frying pan of corn.

Somehow there was more of this delicacy than Mrs. Appleyard remembered, and as spring made its grudging and gingerly advance she needed a little ingenuity to put it into circulation. Perhaps the best of these experiments was a large casserole that needed not only two packages of the succotash but two pints of tomato sauce to fill it; 1954 was a good tomato year too. The casserole was made by merely thawing out both the succotash and the tomato sauce in a large double boiler, transferring them to a casserole and topping the mixture with buttered Pepperidge Farm bread crumbs and thin slices of Cheddar cheese. By a tremendous effort Mrs. Appleyard here restrained herself from saying what she thinks about processed cheese. Instead she simply stated gently that she wants her cheese cut while she is looking at it from a large cheese she has tasted. She likes Crowley cheese, a zippy Vermont cheese, or mild Cheddar from Cabot in the same state, but she also has kind words to say about Cheddar from New York State and Wisconsin. No honest cheese need fear harsh words from this lady, but — well, perhaps we had better take up the tomato sauce.

Tomato Sauce

6 tablespoons olive oil	2 teaspoons light brown sugar
2 carrots, chopped	⅛ teaspoon cinnamon
1 stalk of celery, chopped	½ teaspoon pepper from
2 tablespoons parsley, minced	grinder
cloves from one whole head of	¼ teaspoon powdered thyme
garlic, crushed	½ teaspoon hot red pepper
2 large onions, sliced thin	2 cloves
1 green pepper, chopped	salt to taste
2 quarts fine red tomatoes	1 quart chicken or beef stock
skinned and quartered	4 tablespoons butter

4 tablespoons flour

Put the olive oil into a large iron frying pan. Put everything into it except the tomatoes, flour and sugar. Stir over low heat till the onions are soft. Shove the vegetables aside, blend flour and fat. Add tomatoes, flour and sugar. Mix well, cover frying pan, set it into a slow oven, 300°, and let it simmer for an hour and a half. Stir it occasionally. Uncover it the last half hour. Strain it through a fine sieve, or use it as it comes. This will keep in the refrigerator, for years in the freezer. It is good with meat loaf, Hamburg Pie (p. 31) or Spaghetti Loaf (p. 115).

Cinnamon Buns (I.G.O.)

2 cups boiling water	8 cups sifted all-purpose flour
½ cup sugar	2 yeast cakes
1 teaspoon salt	¼ cup lukewarm water
¼ cup shortening	1 tablespoon sugar

2 eggs, well beaten

Dissolve the sugar, salt and shortening in the boiling water. Cool to lukewarm. Dissolve the yeast cakes and 1 tablespoon sugar in the ¼ cup lukewarm water. Add to the first mixture. Add 4 cups of the flour. Add the eggs and the remainder of the flour. Stir thoroughly. Let rise in greased bowl in warm place till twice the bulk. Use at once or store for refrigerator rolls. For cinnamon buns roll out the dough, spread with brown sugar, cinnamon and butter, currants if desired. Roll up and cut in slices. Lay cut side down in greased pan. Let rise to double the bulk. Bake at 400° for 10–15 minutes depending on the size. Also good baked in individual cupcake pans.

Labor Day Punch

1 quart strong tea infusion made by boiling 2 tablespoons tea for 1 minute in 1 quart briskly boiling water and straining it.

6 lemons, thinly sliced, crushed with 2 cups sugar.

Add 1 quart cold water and let this stand in a cool place to mellow.

Use frozen fruit juice concentrates and make:

2 quarts orange juice	1 quart pineapple juice
2 quarts lemon juice	1 quart frozen strawberries

½ teaspoon mint extract

When you are ready to serve it put ice cubes in a large bowl, mix the tea and the fruit juices and pour them over the ice. Add the frozen strawberries and mint extract. Decorate the bowl with sprays of fresh mint.

This serves forty. It can be successfully refrozen for use another season.

Tea with the Fates

Summer could not really begin for Mrs. Appleyard without a visit to the Duncans. She has known them since they all had hair of reddish gold. It is white now, that shining white that has once been really golden. No one has yet invented a rinse that will produce this effect. Mrs. Appleyard once thought of making her fortune this way but has discarded the idea, along with woodcarving, plans for hunting for uranium and the imbedding of wildflowers in plastic.

There have to be a few things she doesn't do, she says reasonably. Using a Geiger counter among the Vermont hills would not be good for her blood pressure; the arrangement of violets and trilliums that she selected for her first experiment in plastic-as-an-art-form turned out so wry, withered and miserable that she threw it away at once. Twenty years ago she bought a set of woodcarving tools. This summer she tried them out and after half an hour put them back in the box, announcing that her instinct in never taking them out had been a sound one.

She has given up the project on which she meant to use them. It involved an old fanlight, a paneled door from Remember Appleyard's old house, discarded by Cicely in favor of three windows across the south front of this earliest house in Appleyard Center, and a good deal of co-operation from Roger Willard. As Roger is at present painting Mrs. Teasdale's addition, building a grape arbor for Geoffrey Toussaint and adjusting the plumbing here and there, this seemed like a pretty good time for Mrs. Appleyard not to be a woodcarver. Some mild surprise has been expressed by her friends at her having been defeated by anything. They wonder if she is feeling all right. Of course, an attack of common sense is likely to be painful, at whatever season it occurs. Otherwise she is in excellent health.

It was a fine cold bleak June day when she and Cicely started across country to see the Duncans. Wild apple trees were pink snowdrifts on pasture ledges. Pointed firs still cut black silhouettes against the thin new leaves on the hills. Brooks were full and foaming, ferns uncurling. Frost might still scorch tomato vines, kill the bees before they fertilized the apple blossoms, stunt the corn. Camilla rode with her mother and grandmother as she had ridden each year since she was a charcoal-eyed infant in the ancestral, pink-quilt-lined baby basket in which all Cicely's babies had accompanied their mother on social errands.

Frost or no frost, the Duncans had moved from their warm apartment in Montpelier to the old yellow tavern in Sprucebury where Fiona has her antique shop in the high-ceilinged, spring-floored dance hall in the ell. They had a good fire going in the wood stove and they were making the biggest and handsomest braided rug Mrs. Appleyard had ever seen. They reminded her, she told them, a little of the Three Fates, a little of an assembly line.

Fiona was choosing the materials from what she described as "a lot of calamity" — a refined term for culch — and cutting them into narrow strips with her sharp, flashing shears. Beatrice braided whatever was handed to her — maroon, green, gray, black. Daisy sewed the braids, her needle moving with butterfly swiftness. Unlike the Fates, who deal in prophecy, they spoke of the past as they worked — of who wore the gray striped trousers and tore them on a barbed-wire fence, of how the maroon tablecloth was scorched by a flatiron left too long in one spot, of a smudge of paint on Beatrice's green dress.

"There wasn't a thing wrong with my navy suit, except the girls said I should have a new one to go to legislature," said Daisy, attaching a dark blue braid neatly to a gray one.

Daisy dresses in the utmost simplicity, yet suggests lavender and old lace. She is small, daintily precise, brave and sensible about the larger perils, terrified of mice, spiders and thunderstorms. Unless you read about her in *Life* you would never guess that she is the oldest woman legislator in the country. If there were about a hundred more like her, equitably apportioned, the affairs of the nation, so Mrs. Appleyard thinks, would be carried on with far more efficiency and economy, although bounties on wildcats would jump several dollars, that being Daisy's special legislative interest.

The rug was getting so large that it was a long journey round it.

"Time to stop for the day, girls," Fiona said with a final click of her shears, and the assembly line went out of action as though a switch had been pulled.

Mrs. Appleyard went up with Fiona into the antique shop and inspected the newest treasures and some that she has been coveting for some time. Possibly her resistance was lowered by the winter cold that still seemed to linger in the old ballroom with its coved ceiling and its rows of small-paned windows. She resisted purple glass and pink luster teacups and ivory chessmen, but came downstairs looking guilty and clutching a large pastel of four warmly shawled and crinolined ladies said to be the Four Seasons. From the ten-cent table Camilla had chosen a walnut shell lined with thin blue silk and concealing a pair of china dolls half an inch long under a blanket of pinked flannel.

By the time they got downstairs again Daisy was setting the table with the thin silver teaspoons and the white gold-banded teacups. Beatrice had retired to her painting room and was at work on a ghostly white horse pulling an empty sleigh through whirling snow. Pictures finished and unfinished leaned against the walls. There is nothing of wild artistic disorder in Beatrice's studio. She paints as tidily in her hotel bedroom as in this big room with its sleigh bed and brightly papered walls. Beatrice's pictures are full of lively figures. In the old dance hall, now the antique shop, girls in fluffy dresses kick up their heels while a tall fiddler saws on his violin and his dumpy wife thrums her harp. Outside the red schoolhouse you can almost hear the children squealing as sleds whizz down the hill and skaters trip each other up. Here is an eerie pond by moonlight. Branches of a great black tree writhe across the moon and a fire blazes on the ice. The figures round it have the air of being ghosts of skaters.

There is a blind man in many of the pictures. He stands still with his stick poised and listens to the laughter. Here he has left the skating party and moved to the tropics. There is a tree of life heavy with bright birds on the hill above him. Father Time is moving along briskly with his scythe like any last-century farmer behind in his haying. Has he just cut the ground from under the feet of the young lady in the brown and yellow redingote? She seems to be floating up toward the tree, but perhaps it is only that her parasol is acting like a parachute in reverse.

The blind man is outside the white church too, listening to the guests at the June wedding as the bridal party drive away in the fringed carryall drawn by the ghostly white horse, the ringing of the bell in the crooked steeple and the cows cropping the grass among the tombstones. He is at the barn-raising where he can hear the hammers and smell the boiled dinner.

Mrs. Appleyard smells something delicious too and she, Cicely and Camilla are asked to share it, although Daisy, who is folding over a perfect omelet, assures her that it isn't a meal at all, just a snack.

"I'm afraid to cook for you," she says, and looks so much

as if she meant it that Mrs. Appleyard hastens to tell her that all this talk about her being an epicure is a lot of nonsense.

"I'm just as likely as anyone else to have a cold lamb sandwich for lunch and eat it walking around the kitchen," she says. "I am merely the most appreciative eater that is likely to drop in. Do I really smell asparagus? And popovers? And don't tell me Fiona has whipped up a deep dish rhubarb pie! What is this — the Garden of Eden?"

After the snack they set to work at the rug again.

"Fiona planned it," said Daisy. "She's really a genius at planning."

"It's lucky I'm a genius at something." Fiona laughs goodnaturedly. "It gets kind of monotonous hearing how remarkable Daisy and Beatrice are."

"We'd never get anywhere without you," Beatrice says.

They are in one of their mutual-admiration moods, Mrs. Appleyard notices, and waits for the tart comment that often varies it. It's a sound principle, she thinks, rather like serving pickles with maple sugar on snow.

"I'd have been up to see you," Beatrice says, "but the girls keep me right at my painting. They used to love to have me help in the kitchen. It would be 'Beatrice, you do make such lovely sponge cake,' or 'nobody can do bacon as well as you can.' Now it's 'don't think of washing a dish, Bee. Just go right in and paint. You know you have to get Geoffrey Toussaint's picture finished.' Sometimes I'm sorry I ever took to painting, they're such slavedrivers."

She braided deftly as she spoke.

"I wish you'd tell Bee to finish her pictures better," Fiona says. "You have a lot of influence with her."

"I'd as soon tell Picasso how to paint," said Mrs. Appleyard hastily.

"We'd have gone round by your place before," Fiona says, "but Daisy thinks the road is too rough."

"Too rough for the way Fiona drives at night," Daisy asserts.

"Daisy's afraid of every ditch between here and Montpelier," Fiona says, clicking her shears rapidly.

"I'd rather be a coward on the road than brave in a ditch." Daisy flashes a twinkle from behind her glasses at Mrs. Appleyard. Her diamond rings and her needle flash too.

"Mr. Toussaint admired our rug, too," said Beatrice. "He wants one just like it, only twice as big. When he was here to breakfast Tuesday afternoon he as good as ordered it along with four paintings, one for each season."

"Do you usually serve breakfast in the afternoon?" Mrs. Appleyard raised one eyebrow slightly.

"Well," said Daisy, her needle poised like a dragonfly over her work, "he wanted to come to breakfast with us, so we said, yes, any time, and it turned out to be about four o'clock, wasn't it, Fiona?"

"Four twenty-seven we sat down," said Fiona. "Of course, we knew he usually gets up around noon, so we began to expect him about two. I figure his hours are about three times as long as ordinary people's. Still, we had a good time when he came. We always do."

"So do we," said Mrs. Appleyard. "It must be nearly four twenty-seven now, Cicely. Your children will be wondering where you are. How pleasant to be a grandmother and escape so much domination by the young."

"I wouldn't mind so much," sighed Cicely, "if only they wouldn't go out the minute I get home. Still, I suppose it's better than not being noticed at all."

The Appleyard ladies had said their goodbyes and expressed

their thanks before they thought of inquiring what the menu had been at the belated breakfast.

"Never mind," said Cicely on the way home. "I shall make one up." So she did.

MENU FOR A HIGH TEA

Omelet with Minced Chives and Parsley
Asparagus with Horse-radish and Sour Cream *
Popovers
Mousse au Chocolat *

Asparagus with Horse-radish and Sour Cream

Cook the asparagus either in full length stalks or broken into short pieces. Pour a little melted butter over it or pass with it the following sauce:

Mix a tablespoon of powdered horse-radish with a little sweet cream. Heat a cup of sour cream over hot, not boiling water. Add salt and freshly ground pepper to taste and stir in the horse-radish. Have ready some coarse bread crumbs browned in butter. Put the sauce in a bowl and sprinkle the crumbs over the top of the sauce.

Mousse au Chocolat

1 package semi-sweet chocolate   6 egg yolks
       bits   ¼ cup water
                         6 egg whites

Melt the chocolate bits over hot water, with the water and egg yolks, stirring all the time. Don't let the water touch the top part of the double boiler. Remove as soon as the chocolate melts. Now fold in the stiffly beaten egg whites until the mixture is thoroughly blended. Pile in small glass serving dishes. This will resemble closely the French dessert of the same name. A variation is to add a heaping tablespoonful of powdered coffee to the mixture over the hot water. Whipped cream can be added but rather paints the lily.

HIGH BREAKFAST WITH A GENIUS

Orange-Banana Whip *
Grilled Bones *
Guacamole *
Tutti-frutti in Cream *

Orange-Banana Whip

The menu that Cicely imagined for Geoffrey Toussaint's entertainment was probably not at all like the one that the Duncan sisters provided for him, but she felt that hers would have catered to some of his more Oriental tastes.

Orange-Banana Whip is made by combining one can of frozen concentrated orange juice, one can of water, ¼ cup dried non-fat milk and 1 ripe banana in the electric blender and running the blender for about 1 minute. Full of nourishment and vitamins.

Grilled Bones

"I always hoped I'd have a grilled bone some day," Geoffrey Toussaint had said wistfully.

Mrs. Appleyard was delighted to know of this yearning. She felt great happiness at the idea of being able to fulfill a wish for Geoffrey, that scatterer of gifts, who travels in a haze of electric frying pans, chiffon stoles, circus tickets for entire families, sets of china, books on psychic phenomena, albums of long-playing records — all wittily inscribed, all flying away from him by centrifugal force.

"I will use the short ribs from the roast of beef we had yesterday," she said, and fell to making the sauce, thus:

For four people:

8 short ribs of beef from a 14-pound roast
2 tablespoons flour
2 tablespoons butter
1 onion minced
1 tablespoon parsley, minced
¼ teaspoon fresh ground pepper
¼ teaspoon cayenne
¼ teaspoon nutmeg
2 cups hot beef or chicken stock

2 tablespoons beef fat and cracklings from it
2 tablespoons tomato ketchup
4 teaspoons Gulden's mustard
2 tablespoons Worcestershire sauce
1 teaspoon curry powder
½ teaspoon chili powder
4 tablespoons flour
salt to taste

1 cup beef jelly from the roast

Put the 4 tablespoons flour into a paper bag. Put in the bones and shake them until they are thoroughly coated. Lay them on a plate. You will need your largest frying pan for the bones and a smaller one for the sauce. Into the smaller pan melt the butter and cook the onion till it is soft. Lower the heat and rub the 2 tablespoons flour mixed with the dry seasonings with the butter. When it is well browned pour on the hot stock slowly and blend it in well. Add the ketchup, Worcestershire sauce and mustard and the beef jelly saved from the roast.

In the meantime, in the larger pan, cracklings cut from the roast have been trying out over a low flame. Put in the floured beef bones and brown them on all sides. This takes about 8 minutes. When you are ready to serve them, pour the sauce over them, adding a little more hot stock if the sauce seems too thick. Sprinkle the parsley over them.

There is very little meat on the bones but what there is of it is good with the sauce. Rice, mashed potato, or Yorkshire Pudding (p. 221) are all good to soak up the sauce.

Guacamole

This can also be made in the blender although it is not necessary to do so. Mash together 1 well-ripened avocado, 1 finely chopped green pepper, 1 finely chopped tomato, 1 small grated onion. Season with salt, pepper and cayenne. Stir in 1 tablespoon olive oil and ½ tablespoon lemon juice.

Tutti-Frutti

Cut in small pieces with scissors:

½ pound pitted dates ½ pound figs
½ pound apricots ¼ pound pitted prunes
¼ pound golden raisins
1 pint heavy cream

Soak for several hours in 1½ cups honey and ½ cup lemon juice. Just before serving, whip 1 pint heavy cream, flavor with ½ teaspoon almond extract and 3 tablespoons brandy; add to fruit mixture. Add 1 cup broken walnut meats or almonds. Chill and serve.

All these three dishes are *terribly healthy*. They also taste good.

July

Fan Mail

IN RESPONSE to those well-bred mystery stories she writes, Mrs. Appleyard has always received a certain amount of fan mail. She is not like Geoffrey Toussaint who has to employ a secretary to answer admiring letters about his books and to keep his accounts. Mrs. Appleyard never has any great difficulty in keeping her accounts except the usual ones about subtraction and a certain unjustified optimism about her finances when the Director of Internal Revenue forgets to cash her last check. She wonders if he is keeping her autograph on the June one for a souvenir.

Mrs. Appleyard takes this way of letting him know that she will be delighted to autograph anything she receives, that is, if the return postage is prepaid, by an early mail. She makes no charge for this service and wants him to understand that the item in her tax return — "Answering Fan Mail, $1.64" — is just for those replies where postage was not enclosed. As a matter of fact she had several other letters where it was.

It was one hot evening in July that she received her first letter from Horace. It was written in a most scholarly hand, postmarked Appleyard Center and dated Cranberry Hill. Now Cranberry Hill is where Geoffrey Toussaint lives. Cranberries are scarce there but poets, composers and painters are as thick as devil's paintbrush.

Which was Horace? Mrs. Appleyard wondered.

It was a somewhat petulant letter, differing from her on the proper method of cooking Hearts of Artichoke à la Princesse Lointaine. Now the truth of the matter is that when Mrs. Appleyard is writing a murder mystery she gives her imagination free rein about the food. If there ever were any artichokes cooked in the manner of a faraway princess with asparagus and pâté de Périgord and a sauce of sweetbreads and champagne it is one of the most purely coincidental coincidences that ever attended a murder in good society. Still, Horace, that was how he signed himself, seemed to have strong opinions on this dish. She had left out the cardamom seeds, he said. It was not thus, he added, that things were done in Provence.

He seemed to be taking a course in the works of Appleyard, because next day he spoke, more in sorrow than in anger, on the topic of Frangipani Cream. Why, he asked, inject New England rum into that delicate harmony of macaroons and orange flowers? Didn't she know that it originated in seven-

teenth century Italy? No wonder there was a murder. And
he was sincerely hers, Horace.

That was Tuesday. On Wednesday he took up Bouillabaisse. If she had eaten it in Marseilles she would know that
the saffron should be added only during the last five minutes,
he wrote. Mrs. Appleyard, who by this time was wishing she
had never given her characters anything more exotic than a
peanut butter sandwich to eat, decided that steps must be
taken to penetrate Horace's disguise.

"What," she asked Mary Angell, the postmistress, "are the
names of the professors who are staying up on Cranberry Hill?"

She had hit the mark the first time. Their names were
Douglas Wright and Horace Carter.

Mrs. Appleyard then produced a letter, directed with unusual legibility to "Horace, Appleyard Center, Vermont," and
asked Mary to put it in the appropriate box. The letter was
a challenge to Horace to settle his differences with her with,
so to speak, egg beaters at twenty paces. The menus were to
be constructed by each submitting dishes of certain categories.
Slips bearing the names would be drawn by some neutral eater,
if any such pusillanimous individual could be found in Appleyard Center. Each could enlist the services of not more than
two assistants, and two or more guests could be invited. The
different rounds in the tournament would be held at the houses
of the contestants and would continue until one of them cried
"Hold! Enough!"

Horace agreed to the terms, and succulent aromas of simmering and baking were soon blended with the scent of newmown
hay. Mrs. Appleyard began hostilities one warm evening with
salmon in tomato aspic with watercress and green mayonnaise.
Brown bread sandwiches with cream cheese and garlic, new

potatoes and peas in cream with beef cracklings were served with this. Patience Barlow, summoned to her neighbor's aid, constructed a Lady Baltimore cake as light as milkweed fluff. Venetia Hopkins contributed some of her own raspberries to go with it.

Horace, who turned out to be less severe in person than on paper, had no word of condemnation for this menu. He even admitted that it might be possible to cook sweetbreads without cardamom seeds. It was rather generally admitted that Mrs. Appleyard had won the first round. However, when the tournament was moved to Cranberry Hill, Horace Carter triumphed. He made Mrs. Appleyard eat tripe and like it!

The meal began with a French pâté de foie gras, generously truffled in a way Mrs. Appleyard has not seen since the first World War. When asked how such a treasure was acquired in the neighborhood of Cranberry Hill, Mr. Carter said that he had brought it with him from France on his last visit and had been carrying it around with him in case he met anyone who would appreciate it. Proud of having been found worthy of such a talisman, Mrs. Appleyard enthusiastically ate the main course: perfectly cooked polenta containing a number of delicious flavors and textures. She did not discover until she was eating Zuppa Inglese for dessert that one of the ingredients of the sauce for the polenta had been tripe. She hereby withdraws any earlier harsh remarks she has made about this substance, though she still thinks it should be cooked with discretion, preferably by Horace Carter.

Supper Menus for Hot Evenings on the Lawn

Iced Vichyssoise
Salmon in Tomato Aspic * with Watercress and Green
   Mayonnaise *
Brown Bread Sandwiches with Cream Cheese and Garlic
New Potatoes and Peas in Cream *
Lady Baltimore Cake *
Fruit Cup *

      Pâté de Foie Gras with Truffles
      Green Garden Soup
      Polenta with Tripe in Tomato Sauce
      Tossed Salad
      Zuppa Inglese

Salmon in Tomato Aspic

The inspiration for this adventure with salmon in aspic was
a copper mold in the shape of a fish. It was hanging on the
wall in Venetia Hopkins' kitchen where it presented a handsome appearance. Mrs. Appleyard was in one of her "let's
make something we never made before" moods when her eye
encountered the fish. Up to that time its owner had probably thought of it as a decorative piece of still life. Soon
everything was in motion and Mrs. Appleyard was murmuring
incantations over a kettle of court bouillon. If you are going
to make this dish, she suggests that you start the day before if
you are going to serve it for lunch, or early in the morning
if supper is your goal. You will need for a large mold:

3 pounds of Penobscot or Gaspé
   salmon
salmon bones
1 carrot
1 onion
a small piece of bay leaf, a sprig
   of thyme, parsley, pepper, salt
   to taste
fresh tarragon leaves, peppercorns

1 lemon
1 quart tomato juice
2 envelopes plain gelatin
2 eggs, hard-boiled
oak leaf lettuce
egg shells for clearing soup. (If
   you didn't make sponge cake
   or soufflé that day, use two
   egg whites.)

Make the court bouillon, using the carrot, onion, thyme, bay leaf and parsley, salmon bones and two quarts of water. Cook them all together for half an hour. Strain through cheese-cloth over the fish. A Dutch oven of heavy aluminum or iron or an electric frying pan is a good container; something in which the fish can be simmered gently for about 40 minutes. Now remove the fish and put it aside to cool. Add the tomato juice to the bouillon and cook it down until there is about a quart. Add the peppercorns the last few minutes of cooking: they turn bitter if cooked too long. Add the egg shells. If you do not have plenty with some white clinging to them, add one or two extra whites. When the whites are cooked hard, strain the bouillon again through cheesecloth.

Soak the gelatin in the juice of the lemon and a little cold water for a few minutes. Pour the hot bouillon over the mixture and stir until the gelatin is dissolved. Wet the fish mold with cold water. Pour in a little of the jellied bouillon, lay six tarragon leaves crossed on top of it and set the mold into the refrigerator. While it is getting stiff, remove the skin and bones from the fish and peel and slice the hard-boiled eggs.

When the jelly has stiffened, lay the egg slices around the

sides of the mold and put in the fish. Mrs. Appleyard tries
to have the fish look as if it came in one piece and was really
curved in the sportive fashion indicated by the outlines of
the mold. Now pour in the rest of the jellied bouillon and
set the mold in the refrigerator. Your only problem now is
to get it out of the mold intact the next day.

Have your best silver platter ready and plenty of fresh
parsley and sliced lemon at hand. Set the fish mold in a pan of
warm, *not hot* water. Watch it. In a minute you will see the
first softening of the jelly around the edge. Remove the mold
immediately from the water. Wipe it dry. Put the platter over
it and turn the whole thing upside down. (This is the only
kind of exercise Mrs. Appleyard really enjoys.) If the jellied
fish does not leave the mold immediately, wring a cloth dry out
of hot water and apply it to the top of the mold. Just when
you think it is never coming out, it will. Lift off the mold.
Surround the fish with the oak leaf lettuce, parsley and sliced
lemon, and the green mayonnaise. Put it where it will keep cold
and take a deep breath.

Green Mayonnaise

The easy way to make this is in the electric blender. However, you have Mrs. Appleyard's permission to chop and purée
the greens in the way you find most convenient. You need
only a fourth of a cupful, so it is not a very exhausting task.
She puts into the blender:

2 tablespoons of lemon juice
¼ cup chopped greens — a
little watercress, parsley, a
leaf or two of spinach, a slice
or two of a scallion or a slice
of onion

Run the blender until you have some bright green pulp. Add:

1 whole egg
¼ cup oil (olive oil or part olive, part salad oil)
dry seasonings: mustard, pep-per, salt to your taste, which she is willing to bet is not hers, sugar

Run the blender about five seconds or until everything is well blended.

Now add, a small amount at a time, ¾ cup oil.

Run five seconds after each addition. Run a few seconds after the last oil is added.

Use the same method, only with longer beating, with the electric mixer. If you do it by hand, it is very convenient if someone will beat while you pour the oil. This is called executive ability. Non-executives get someone else to pour the oil while they beat. It took Mrs. Appleyard about forty years to find this out. Sometimes it seems as if she were not awfully bright.

New Potatoes and Peas in Cream

This dish is something like a transit of the sun and Jupiter. The ingredients for it — if it is to be perfect — do not come together every fine summer day by any means. The potatoes should be so young and innocent that they are not much bigger than golf balls. The peas should be no larger than good-sized pearls and they should be picked no longer than twenty minutes before they are cooked. The cream — but perhaps we had better not listen to Mrs. Appleyard on the subject of cream. Incidentally, we have known that lady to construct a fair approximation of this delicacy out of some potatoes from a neighboring state, peas she found in her freezer with a date in her own handwriting two years earlier and cream from a cow born and raised outside Vermont. She used to make it with salt pork but has now changed to beef cracklings and thinks the flavor is more subtle.

For six people you will need:

18 potatoes the size of golf balls (about 2 quarts)	1 onion finely minced
1 quart of shelled peas	¼ pound beef cracklings made from the fat of roast beef or
1 cup thick cream	steak

Begin by cutting the beef fat into half-inch cubes and set them over a very low flame to try out. Stir them occasionally and pour off some of the fat. Save this in a marked jar. Nothing is so good for browning hashed brown potatoes. The cubes should shrink to half their size and be a delicate tan in color. Mrs. Appleyard, who used to cook new potatoes and peas in cream in several separate pans and serve them in a Bennington bowl, has now become so dashingly modern that she recommends doing the whole thing in a frying pan or a Dutch enamel dish that comes right to the table. She likes the dish — a pale green one — best but says they taste all right out of a scarlet and ivory frying pan too.

When the cracklings are almost ready, put in the onion and cook till it is pale yellow. Don't let it brown. Turn off the heat while you are scrubbing the potatoes. You don't peel them. Add them to the contents of the dish, pour in some boiling water, not too much: you want most of it to cook away. Let them cook partly covered so that the steam will escape while you are shelling the peas — about 20 minutes.

When they are almost done and the water has mostly disappeared, add the peas. They should cook in 5 minutes. Stir them well into the potatoes. When they are tender but not mushy, add the cream. Let it just come to the boil. Turn off the heat, cover the dish and leave it to mellow a few minutes.

This is a good thing to serve when you are wondering if there is enough cold beef to go around, or even if you are not considering anything of the sort.

Lady Baltimore Cake

Mrs. Appleyard, not being strong on arithmetic, hesitates to say just how long ago it was that she ate her first piece of Lady Baltimore cake. Even though her culinary triumphs up to that time had consisted entirely of one rather scorched pan of fudge, she sat down immediately with her hostess's manuscript cookbook and copied down the receipt in an innocent and strangely legible hand. Something must have warned her that half a century or so later Horace Carter would be coming to supper.

Naturally such an emergency led to a good deal of discussion between Mrs. Appleyard and Patience Barlow. It was felt by both ladies that the occasion demanded something really stupendous, historic, monumental — served, of course, as nonchalantly as if they launched such delicacies upon the world every day. They turned over instructions for various types of guided missiles until at last Mrs. Appleyard announced, in a tone familiar to her family, a tone prophetic yet wistful, rather like that of a tiger about to spring upon a water buffalo: "I have never made this before."

Patience, recognizing that destiny had spoken, promptly got out three 10-inch layer cake tins and the fun began.

There are three stages involved in making a Lady Baltimore and unless you feel like devoting most of a day to it, Mrs. Appleyard advises you to get a package of somebody's cake mix and relax.

First you make the cake batter, then you make a syrup, last you make the frosting and filling.

Batter

1¼ cups butter	2½ cups sugar
5 large eggs	1¼ cups milk
4⅓ cups sifted flour	5 teaspoons baking powder
2¼ teaspoons almond extract	2½ teaspoons vanilla

Grease 3 large layer cake pans with Spry. Sift the flour four times with the baking powder. Light the oven at 350°. Even if the electric mixer was invented long after Lady Baltimore it is all right to use it, Mrs. Appleyard says. Cream butter and sugar. Break in the eggs one at a time and beat well. Beat in the flour alternately with the milk, using the rubber scraper to keep the batter away from the sides. Add the flavoring. Put the batter in the greased pans. Bake 30 minutes, reducing the heat to 325° after the first ten minutes if the layers are browning too quickly.

Now make the syrup.

1¼ cups sugar	¾ cup water
½ teaspoon almond extract	½ teaspoon vanilla

This should cook until it is rather thick. Don't let it discolor. Take your layers out of the pans and spread them with the warm syrup while they are still warm. This keeps the frosting, which you will now make, from making the layers soggy.

Lady Baltimore Frosting

The night before you are going to make the cake, mix:

3 cups seeded raisins, cut fine   1 cup sliced blanched almonds
2 cups chopped pecans   15 figs cut in small pieces
                    ½ cup candied cherries

and cover with ½ cup brandy, 1 teaspoon vanilla, 1 teaspoon almond, 1 tablespoon lemon juice. Stir occasionally so that all the fruit will absorb a little liquid.

Beat three egg whites until they make firm peaks.

Mix 1 cup water, 3 teaspoons corn syrup and 3 cups sugar. Boil together until it makes a firm soft ball — 234°.

Pour the syrup slowly on the beaten egg whites and get someone else to keep beating them all the time. Add the fruit and nuts. Spread between the layers, on top of the cake and around the sides. Do this on the cake plate on which you serve it, covering the plate first with four triangles of wax paper, points toward the center, which you will pull out when the frosting has had time to set.

Fruit Cup
DESSERT FOR A HOT EVENING

Mrs. Appleyard thinks that the fresh fruit that comes all cut up in glass jars is a great alleviation to anyone who has bursitis or is even, like herself, just plain lazy.

(One of her relatives who was looking over her shoulder as she was writing these remarks murmured: "And so I suppose was Napoleon. Also Susan B. Anthony, Thomas Alva Edison and Theodore Roosevelt!")

Take a quart jar of fruit, Mrs. Appleyard continued imperturbably, and a package of frozen melon balls. Anyone who is energetic enough to cut melon balls is welcome to do so, she added. Now mix

½ cup white wine
2 tablespoons lemon juice
strained juice from 1 cup fresh
    raspberries crushed with 2
    tablespoons sugar

3 drops peppermint extract
sprigs of fresh mint

Combine the fruit and melon balls. Mix the other ingredients except the sprigs of mint, pour over the fruit and set the bowl into the refrigerator for the flavors to blend. When you serve it, put a sprig of mint into each cup.

Mallets and Balls

I T was in July that the croquet tournament broke out. Every summer since the lawn was leveled and graded in 1925 the croquet set has been put out on the side porch. Every autumn what is left of it has been carried back into the woodshed. At present it consists of portions of two sets, one perhaps five years younger than the other, but both so weathered by rain and sun that it is hard to tell the green ball from the brown one.

Some colors are missing entirely, the balls having been cloven in twain, the shafts of the mallets split, by players who confused croquet and golf. However, there is enough equipment left so that Mrs. Appleyard's grandchildren can still, in moments of irritation, threaten each other with the same mallets used for that purpose by their parents. Balls can still bounce off the well-rusted wickets or miss by a hair's breadth the broken-topped stakes. They can still disappear into the raspberry bushes and turn up next spring, their stripes fainter than ever. The old arguments can still arise.

It is a long time since Mrs. Appleyard has had a mallet in her hand, and it was a happy surprise to her to find, one hot evening while she was serving supper on the lawn, that she could still occasionally send a ball through a wicket. She also made several brilliant hits, as unexpected to her opponents as to herself, and missed the easiest shots by wide margins. She was, in short, in her usual form.

Oddly enough, she and her partner, Colin Dalzell, the composer, did not win. They did, however, give the champions, Venetia Hopkins and Kendall Royce, a battle of a spirited sort. This began soon after the hummingbirds had left the larkspur, continued while the hermit thrushes were singing in the woods across the pond and lasted until the fireflies were doing their best to illuminate the croquet ground. Unfortunately there were not enough of them on duty, and before the match was over the players were using cigarette lighters to find their balls. Mrs. Appleyard had the interesting idea of marking the wickets with luminous tape, the kind used on the rear bumper of her car. She thought it would shine in reflected firefly and starlight. She was mistaken.

A better illuminated match was held at Kendall Royce's the next week. When the guests arrived they drove under an arch made by a yellow banner stretched between two pine trees. There were bright blue letters on the banner, saying "Welcome, Cranberry Hill Croquet Meet, 1955."

The Royce croquet set was new and shining. Balls, mallets and stakes displayed the proper colors. The course, however, had some unusual features. One was a small hill near the second stake. The player who hit his ball too gently saw it reach the top and roll back to his feet. Hit too hard, the ball traveled along the ridge and downhill into the goldenrod. Even Cicely had trouble with a hollow near the center wicket, and her partner, who was trying in vain to hit a ball that was resting in the hollow, could be heard chanting in a tone of resentful disgust: "It hopped right over it! It hopped right over it!"

Naturally, with the emotional and physical strains produced by croquet under these conditions, sustaining food is needed. Kendall Royce had filled a big ironstone tureen with a seafood bisque, rich with cream, chopped clams, shrimp and lobster, garnished with parsley, chives and slivered almonds. With it he served French bread spread with garlic butter, dusted with sharp cheese and paprika. The salad in its huge wooden chopping tray held all the young vegetables and lettuces that his garden could provide — radish roses, tiny raw peas, carrots and green beans, loose-leaf lettuces soft as butter, head lettuce dark and crisp, bitter chicory, bland watercress from his brook.

By dessert time the players were back at the course, bite-size mince and apple turnovers in their hands and the red wine punch floating its cucumber circles in the big brown mixing bowl within easy reach. Cicely and Carleton Welch were playing a final challenge round with Venetia Hopkins and Kendall Royce. Cicely had, by bitter experiment, learned the nasty intricacies of Kendall's course and was displaying the same sort of terrifying virtuosity which had made her undisputed champion of Appleyard Center at fifteen.

"You are too nice," she said to Kendall as she drove his ball into the dusk of the pine grove. "In this game it is the least pleasant person who wins." She took her ball and Carleton's the length of the course in a single turn and banged them both against the stake as the first stars pricked through deepening sky.

It was thought later that it was this display by Cicely of ruthless skill that caused her paying guest, a pink-cheeked, stiff-gestured young Englishman, much taken, by his own account, with the vitality of American civilization, to pack his bags and leave suddenly by the noon train the following day. The note he left on the bureau said that, frankly, he was bored. The other croquet players, however, subscribe to the theory that he was shocked by an excess of American vitality.

More Menus for Supper on the Lawn

Seafood Bisque *
Garlic Bread
Tossed Salad,   French Dressing *   Cheese Cubes *
Red Wine Punch
Mince or Apple Turnovers
Coffee

> Cold Borschtch
> Caged Lobster *
> Green Garden Salad *
> Corn Dodgers *
> Fresh Peaches in Brandy *
> Coffee

Tomachicko *
Veal and Ham Pie *
  with Two-Thousand-Layer Pastry *
Lettuce Salad *   (Five Kinds), French Dressing
Scalded Johnnycake
Coffee Angel Cake *
Lemon and White Wine Punch (Croquet Cooler) *

Seafood Bisque

For six servings take:

1 can minced clams	1 diced onion
1 pound lobster meat	1 stalk of celery, cut up
1 pound shrimp	½ cup blanched almonds
	parsley, chives

Cook them slowly and lightly in butter for about 5 minutes. Make a white sauce with 3 tablespoons butter, 2 tablespoons flour, 2 cups milk, 1 cup cream. Season with a little cayenne pepper, add a little diced pimento, salt to taste. Reheat the shellfish in the bisque — do not boil. Just before serving add ½ cup blanched almonds cut in slivers. Sprinkle with chopped chives and parsley. Serve in a big tureen.

French Dressing for Tossed Salad

¾ cup olive oil	salt to taste
¼ cup red vinegar in which you have soaked a clove of garlic	½ teaspoon dry mustard
	¼ teaspoon curry powder
	ground pepper
1 teaspoon paprika	1 teaspoon Worcestershire sauce
1 teaspoon sugar	1 medium onion, diced

Put everything in a screw-top jar and shake well. Chill. Just before you serve it, strain it and add 1 teaspoon each of parsley, tarragon and chives, finely chopped.

Cheese Cubes to go with Tossed Salads

You will need unsliced bread, homemade or Pepperidge Farm, for these.

3 slices of bread ¾ inch thick	4 teaspoons melted butter
1 egg, beaten	1 cup dry dairy cheese, grated

Cut the crust off the bread and cut it into ¾-inch cubes. Mix the egg and melted butter. Dip the cubes into the mixture and then roll them in grated cheese. Put them on a buttered baking sheet and bake them at 375° until they start to brown — 6 or 7 minutes.

It will be better for all concerned if you double the rule.

Caged Lobster — Vermont

To get to Vermont, lobsters need wings. Luckily this is no trick at all to the hardy Green Mountain airmen. They always seem ready to dash over to the Maine coast, snatch a load of lobsters and zoom back while their freight is still aggressive enough to snap each other's claws off. An episode over which Vermonters have done a little boasting, in a quiet refined way, of course, occurred when chefs from all over New England got together and cooked lobster for a jury of old experienced lobster eaters. The Vermont version was pronounced the best. Encouraged by this victory, Mrs. Appleyard tells how she fixes lobster in the only New England state without a sea coast.

Winged lobsters, she says, naturally need cages. You begin

by making them out of homemade unsliced bread. They should be four inches long, three inches wide and two inches high. You will have a by-product of a good many bread crumbs. Mrs. Appleyard at such times is not in a mood to care what you do with them.

Hollow out the bread, leaving a thickness of half an inch at sides and bottom. Butter the cages thinly all over, inside and out, with softened butter. Set them in the oven for a few minutes until they are slightly brown. Don't brown them too much — they are going back later.

Now make whichever you prefer: lobster Newburg, creamed lobster, lobster salad by your favorite rule. The sauce should not be too thin. In any event, fill the cases with the mixture, put mayonnaise on top of the lobster, set them on a baking sheet until the mayonnaise browns and puffs. You will not need anything else to eat for quite a while.

Variations: The boxes may be filled with creamed crabmeat and mushrooms, with chicken salad, or creamed chicken and mushrooms — in fact whatever you like. An easier method is to use hard dinner rolls, hollowed out, brushed with butter, filled and heated through.

Green Garden Salad

This is a local version of Caesar Salad and it occurs as soon as there are several kinds of lettuce ready in the garden. Mrs. Appleyard always plants several varieties because the descriptions in the catalogue are so ingeniously tempting. It is a literary feat she greatly admires, she says, to make you think one kind of lettuce is really going to taste different from another.

Fortunately they do actually look different, and an enormous old wooden bowl, one of the oblong kind once used for working butter, is a handsome sight when it is filled with a variety of shapes and colors.

Mrs. Appleyard likes to combine the long greenish-white leaves of romaine, the soft clusters of oak leaf with their deeply indented edges, crip bunches of iceberg that bear little resemblance to the tasteless tennis balls wrapped in cellophane of the winter season. There are darker greens too — Big Boston, Black-seeded Simpson, rosettes of bronze-tinged Mignonette, Matchless with leaves like a deer's tongue. At least the catalogue says so. Mrs. Appleyard has never seen a deer's tongue and bases her impressions solely on the slender pointed leaves of Matchless.

Another kind of lettuce said to be especially sweet and succulent is Bibb, which is also said to be a gourmet's favorite. The inner leaves are creamy yellow. Gourmet Appleyard cannot really detect anything very subtle about its flavor but admits that it is decorative in the salad bowl. She does not wish to enforce any of these varieties on those who have their own favorites but simply says mildly that one charm of this salad lies in its being made of several kinds of lettuce, well washed, well dried, and that one of them should be romaine. Also she states that she knows that it is the custom to tear the leaves for this salad into convenient pieces. However, with lettuce picked early in your own garden, leaf by leaf, this is not necessary. She chooses small leaves, cutting them off with scissors. This method leaves roots and dirt in the garden and brings only the lettuce into the kitchen. So, for six people:

1 large bowl of various kinds of lettuce including romaine
1 cup olive oil (part salad oil if you prefer)
1 whole raw egg
juice of 1 lemon (2 tablespoons)
peppercorns in a grinder
salt to taste
1 teaspoon dry mustard, ¼ teaspoon cayenne, ¼ teaspoon sugar

1 teaspoon paprika
½ cup dry cheese grated
4 slices Pepperidge Farm bread ¾ inch thick, crusts cut off
chopped chives and minced parsley if you have them growing
garlic — at least 4 good "ears," "cloves," "beans" or whatever you call them. More if you like

Begin several hours before you are going to mix the salad by making some garlic oil. This is simply pouring a cup of oil over the peeled and sliced cloves of garlic and leaving it in a cool place. Now pick the lettuce, wash it, drain and dry it well, and put it into the lowest part of the refrigerator to chill and crisp. Slice the bread into ¾-inch cubes, chop the chives, mince the parsley. Now take the cheese, and mix it with the mustard and other dry seasonings except the pepper. If you have real Parmesan, use it. Mrs. Appleyard says any honest dry chunk of dairy cheese is better than imitation Parmesan flavored with monosodium glutamate. Better not uphold the virtues of this substance in that lady's hearing. Those are fighting words. She could say more but will get on with the salad.

Anyway it is now time to relax, smell the newly cut grass, clover, syringas, spice pinks. After all, this is summer. The salad is to be mixed when the guests are sitting down and ready for it. Just before they come, you gently fry the croutons in the garlic oil, using about a half of it, and then put them in a slow oven for a little while to dry out and crisp up.

First you begin by giving a slight nervous shock to those who have not been exposed to this salad before by breaking the raw egg over the greens. The purpose of this is to help the dressing to coat every leaf. Toss the leaves carefully, gently, till the egg disappears. Sprinkle in the chives and parsley. Keep tossing. Grind in plenty of pepper. Toss some more. Now add the oil and lemon juice, mixed together. If there are not 6 tablespoons of oil to 2 of lemon juice add some more oil. Keep lettuce moving. Every leaf should be coated and there should be no excess dressing in the bottom of the bowl. Mix in the cheese and other seasonings, still tossing. Last of all add the garlic croutons. By this time the guests are so hungry that they could eat two-weeks-old iceberg lettuce flavored with m-n-s-d-m gl-t-m-t-, but never mind. The hostess is happy anyway.

Corn Dodgers (F.G.B.)

3 cups boiling water	1 tablespoon butter
1 scant teaspoon salt	1 cup Indian meal

Add meal slowly to the boiling water, stirring carefully so it doesn't lump. Add butter and beat well. Drop by spoonfuls on buttered baking sheets. Bake 25 minutes or until puffed and lightly browned in a hot oven, 450°–475°.

They should be crisp outside and hot enough so that the soft part inside burns your tongue and melts butter. Incidentally, Mrs. Appleyard uses an extra tablespoonful of butter and dots some more on the top but — as a co-worker of hers was once heard to remark — "It's just as well to look the other way when she gets out the butter." She says honey is good on these johnnycakes — that's what they are; also maple syrup.

Fresh Peaches in Brandy

Peel the peaches, dipping them briefly in boiling water and, as soon as you have removed the skins, halve them and put them into a bowl containing a can of frozen lemonade concentrate diluted with one can of water. (This supplies both sugar and lemon juice to keep them from turning brown.) For six people allow nine large peaches. Add to the bowl ½ cup of brandy and 1 teaspoon of almond extract. Chill until you are ready to serve them.

Tomachicko
FOR A HOT EVENING

The last time you cooked a fowl you saved some of the stock, Mrs. Appleyard hopes. And cooked it down until it jellied when you chilled it? And you carefully skimmed off the fat? Good, you will be glad you did.

Slice up an onion. Pour 3 cups of tomato juice over it. Juice from your own tomatoes is best but canned will do. If you like other seasonings, add them, but don't overdo it: this is delicately flavored. Mrs. Appleyard thinks that one leaf of fresh basil, one of rosemary, one of tarragon are enough. Let it stand a couple of hours in the refrigerator. Then combine it with three cups of chicken stock, straining out the herbs and onions. This is good hot too.

Veal and Ham Pie

Mrs. Appleyard has recently worked out an improved technique for making this delicacy and hereby tells all. She began by putting into a large kettle the veal, chicken feet, bones and seasoning, carefully manicuring the chicken feet first, of course. They were a present from her butcher and no doubt yours would be equally generous. They add flavor to the broth and make it jelly easily. As the great feature of the pie is that the meat is surrounded by a sort of savory aspic, this is important. Perhaps some laggards in cookery might use gelatin. Mrs. Appleyard shuts her eyes to this suggestion and does not even attempt to estimate how much would be needed. Colburn's ham, a Montpelier product, is her favorite kind but your own favorite will do.

Take:

2 pounds veal cut from the leg	4 eggs, hard-boiled
1½-pound slice of Colburn's Vermont ham	½ teaspoon nutmeg
	½ teaspoon cinnamon
6 chicken feet	6 whole cloves
veal bones	½ teaspoon pepper
celery tops	3 onions, sliced
3 sprays of parsley	1 carrot, sliced

pastry (p. 93)

Put the ham on to simmer, removing all the fat you can, in a frying pan with plenty of water, which should be changed occasionally. The water is a good basis for split-pea soup and may be saved for those in a mood for such a dish. At the same time put on the veal, bones, chicken feet, seasonings, onion and carrot to simmer. While they are cooking she has plenty of time to make some Two-Thousand-Layer pastry (p. 93) and to be beaten at a couple of games of chess. At one time she used to bake the pastry on top of the pie. She now advocates baking a lid, neatly tailored to fit the top of the dish, and putting it on when the pie is served. This was a suggestion of Venetia's over the chess board — she said it was a pity to let the pastry lose any of its lightness and fragility by being baked with liquid under it and served cold. Mrs. Appleyard was so struck with this idea that she was checkmated soon afterwards and was able to give her complete attention to cooking.

After both veal and ham are tender, strain off the veal broth. Set it to cool, then put it into the freezer. Cut veal and ham into neat cubes. In a Pyrex dish, loaf size, arrange a layer of meat, hard-boiled egg slices against the side of the dish so they can be seen through the glass, then more meat and more eggs. Fill the dish with the rest of the meat. Now the broth should be cold enough so the fat can be easily removed. There should be about 4 cups. Pour it over the meat until the dish is well filled. Save out a cup of it and reduce it to half a cup. In the meantime set the dish, covered but not too tightly, into a 350° oven and cook until the meat and broth are well amalgamated — about forty minutes. Add the broth you have cooked down, set the dish in a cold place. When it is well chilled the spaces between the meat should be filled with sparkling savory aspic. Put the pastry lid on and serve it with a tossed salad.

Two-Thousand-Layer Pastry

4 cups flour (measured after sifting. Save what is left over to flour
  the board)
extra flour for rolling out, as little as possible
1 cup butter, very cold
1 cup lard, very cold
1 cup ice water

Put flour, butter and lard into a large wooden chopping
bowl. Have the chopping knife cold. Chop until butter and
lard are in cubes the size of your little finger tip. Add the
water half a cup at a time, blending it in with your chopper.
Now flour your pastry board and rolling pin. Get the paste
out of the bowl with the chopper and a spatula. Never touch
it with your hands.

Roll it out about ¾ inch thick. Cut it in thirds, using the
spatula and a chilled pancake turner. Pile the outside pieces
over the ones in the middle. Be gentle. Pastry hates rough
handling. Repeat the process seven times, turning the board
90 degrees each time. Your pastry will now have 2187 layers.
If you do not believe Mrs. Appleyard's arithmetic, you may
do the calculation yourself, but really you had better not take
your mind off the pastry. Have a chilled plate ready with
wax paper on it. Wrap the pastry up and chill it several hours
before using it. When you roll it out, add a few little dots of
butter to it to enrich the extra flour you used on your board
and rolling pin.

Bake it in a hot oven — 450°. This is so the air spaces between your layers will expand suddenly. When it begins to
brown, reduce the heat slightly. It takes about 45 minutes to

cook a pie with two crusts thoroughly, less for single crust pies or tarts. Good luck to you!

Coffee Angel Cake

Here is a good way, Mrs. Appleyard says, to disguise the fact that you did not make your angel cake yourself, some hot July morning, but sensibly bought it.

1 tablespoon plain gelatin, soaked in ¼ cup cold water	1 teaspoon almond extract
1 cup powdered sugar	2 tablespoons hot strong coffee
8 egg yolks	2 cups heavy cream
1 teaspoon vanilla	½ cup blanched and toasted almonds

Put the soaked gelatin in the top of a double boiler, add the coffee and when the gelatin is dissolved, the sugar. Cool. Beat the egg yolks until light and lemon colored. Add flavorings. Fold in gelatin mixture. Whip the cream and add it. Chill. Cut the angel cake in halves horizontally. Spread the coffee mixture between the layers and on the top and sides. Sprinkle the toasted almonds on top.

Croquet Cooler
(LEMON AND WHITE WINE PUNCH)

6 lemons, thinly sliced	1 quart cold water
2 cups sugar	1 quart white wine
1 tablespoon tea	1 quart ginger ale
1 quart boiling water	¼ cup mint leaves

sprigs of mint

Cover the sliced lemons with the sugar and crush them with a potato masher till the sugar dissolves. Add the mint leaves and crush gently. When the water boils, throw in the tea and boil exactly one minute. Strain over the lemon and sugar. Stir. Add the cold water. Set aside to cool and blend. An hour before serving time add the white wine, chilled. At serving time add the ginger ale and the sprigs of mint. No harm is done to anyone by floating a few strawberries in it.

The Hotter the Better

IT WAS during the visit of the Princess to Cranberry Hill that everyone started to serve curry so feverishly.

"Is there any other way to serve it?" inquired Geoffrey Toussaint, who happened to walk into the summer kitchen one afternoon, finding Mrs. Appleyard mixing cayenne pepper and curry powder with a lavish hand.

"I could easily make you some Cream of Wheat," Mrs. Appleyard replied hospitably. "I think you will find," she added, "that this tastes like curry."

"Now why don't you be more like your mother?" Geoffrey asked Cicely, who was valiantly chopping onions. "When I make a statement to you or ask you a question, you always come up with a contradiction or a brash answer that cuts the ground from under me. But your mother — I remember the first time I met her I said: 'The Albigensians were named after a bishop called Albi.' She went right on beating eggs for a Crème Brûlée and said, oh so gently: '*I think you will find* that they were named for a *place* called Albi.' And of course the Encyclopedia agreed with her."

"Most people ask me — 'and are you as clever as your mother?' " Cicely replied, wiping away her onion-inspired tears. "It's refreshing to meet someone who recognizes at once that I am not. The other question is so extremely difficult to answer without insulting somebody. How are you making curry this time, Mother?"

"The way the Princess taught me," Mrs. Appleyard said. "You'd have learned too if you hadn't gone to Cape Cod."

"Is the Princess the lady with the raven tresses I met sunning herself on your terrace, Geoffrey?" asked Cicely.

"She washed her hair every morning and then oiled it thoroughly after lunch. She's a better than average blues singer, but she's sadly deficient in yoga and Hindu philosophy," replied Geoffrey.

"Deficiencies which you could no doubt correct handily between lunch and dinner," Mrs. Appleyard said. "Are you finished with the onions, Cicely?"

"Did the Princess cook right here in this very kitchen?" asked Joan Bradshaw, Cicely's third child. "When I went to New York with her on the plane she wore a kind of brown sheet with pink showing through and gold all round the edge."

"That was her traveling costume," said her grandmother. "The evening she came here to make curry her sari — what you called a sheet — was white and gold. I thought of having

the kitchen done over with mother-of-pearl tiles studded with
an occasional ruby. Perhaps a few gold frying pans with turquoise handles. Too late now, though. Still, it was a pretty
sight, just as it was. As though a Bird of Paradise had lighted
on my white phlox.

"The curry was excellent," she added. "We didn't have
anything with it except some of my 1954 chutney and some
brown rice. She said I cooked the rice very nicely. That
was my proudest moment."

"I went to a curry party where there were fresh frozen
mangoes," Cicely said, "and fresh coconut. I believe some
was combined with cucumbers and sour cream."

"That's fresh coconut in that bowl," her mother said.

"Where did you get it?" asked Cicely.

"I bought a coconut for fifteen cents and spent five dollars
worth of time getting it open and grating it," Mrs. Appleyard
replied. "Not to mention those gouges I made on the table
while I was pounding it with a croquet mallet. It will take
three hours to get them out with oil and pumice. I'm glad
now," she added, stirring sour cream and coconut milk into
the curry sauce, "that I never took my five favorite books
and went to live on a desert island. I would have starved rather
than deal with coconuts."

She tasted the sauce, added a trifle more curry powder and
said, "There, I think that is almost good enough for the Princess."

It is generally agreed that if Mrs. Appleyard only had a
suitable sari — something matronly in purple and gold — she
would be able to turn out a highly acceptable curry. She
has given up buying any gold frying pans but has brightened
the summer kitchen with a set enameled with scarlet outside

and ivory within. These are so handsome that she serves food right in them, placing them on wrought iron trivets on her well-polished table. By arranging these judiciously and setting out twelve dishes of condiments she is able to cover up most of the scars of the Battle of the Coconut.

"Your table," said Geoffrey Toussaint, who had moved a trivet, "has certainly received cruel and abrasive treatment."

Mrs. Appleyard mentioned her plan for eradicating the scars with linseed oil.

"Better add some of the curry sauce," suggested Mr. Toussaint, gasping for air. "That'll burn them off."

Weak spirits, Mrs. Appleyard says, may use half as much curry and cayenne as the Princess suggests.

No one died of internal combustion after Mrs. Appleyard's curry dinner, but those who vied with her in Oriental cookery did indeed modify the amount of spice in the sauce. Cicely produced a creditable minced beef and green pea curry which she claimed resembled one called "kofta" that she had eaten in an East Indian restaurant in England. (It was here that she encountered the menu which had two parts — hot and more hot — not to mention a lemon containing liquid fire.)

Colin Dalzell and Bolton Smith concocted a chicken curry served with toasted coconut slivers and tempered with a huge salad, green and cooling. The range of side dishes became ever more varied — some served baked bananas laced with honey and lemon juice, others cut theirs in chunks and rolled them in toasted coconut. Great was the chopping of parsley, the crisping of bacon, the peeling of onions, the grating of hard-boiled eggs, the pulverizing of peanuts, the selection of sweet and sour relishes, the diagnosis of chutnies. And then, as quickly as it had come, the vogue for curry passed, and the

Appleyard Center cooks turned their talents to that challenging item, the Covered Dish.

MENUS FOR CURRY SUPPERS

Twelve-Boy Curry of Lamb Mrs. Appleyard *
Broiled Bananas *
Lemon Sherbet
Oatmeal Cookies ‡
Coffee

The Princess's Curry of Chicken *
Chutney *
Lettuce Salad, French Dressing
Macaroon Trifle *
Tea (Smoky Souchong)

Twelve-Boy Curry of Lamb Mrs. Appleyard

Curry is like tribal lays, concerning which, the poet states, there are a large number of ways of reciting them "and every single one of them is right." Everything about one curry may be a little different from the next, yet both may be excellent. Mrs. Appleyard thinks that on the whole the best curry is made when you meant to all the time and when you are generous with the curry powder. No very distinguished result can be achieved, she says, by suddenly deciding that some uninteresting scraps of meat and some tired gravy would be improved by a dash of curry powder.

This is how she made one that, in the curry cycle, received several kind words.

For six people she took:

A 6-pound shoulder of lamb cut up into slices ¾ inch thick	2 onions sliced
the lamb bones and trimmings	2 tart apples sliced
4 tablespoons butter	1 cup light cream
4 cups stock (the bones simmered with a carrot, onion, branch of celery)	½ teaspoon cayenne pepper
	½ teaspoon pepper from the grinder
	salt to taste
4 tablespoons flour	extra butter, about 2 tablespoons
4 tablespoons curry powder	

She began by simmering the bones and vegetables for 2 hours. This was done the day before she served the curry so that there was time for the fat to rise and be skimmed off.

The next morning she cut the lean meat into cubes, put them into a paper bag with the flour, curry powder and seasonings and tossed them until they were thoroughly coated. Leaving them in a bag for a few minutes she put the butter into her biggest frying pan with the onions and apples, tossed them until they began to soften, then removed them and set them aside. Adding extra butter to the pan, she next gave the pieces of meat a final shaking, put them into the pan and browned them on both sides. She then returned the onion and apple mixture to the pan, scattered in the flour left in the bag, stirring it well into the butter, and added the stock, strained, skimmed and heated.

Mrs. Appleyard then covered the pan, turned the gas low and left the mixture to simmer until the meat was tender, about 2 hours. She looked at it occasionally and added a little hot water. When she was ready to serve it she added the cream. She tasted the sauce at intervals by dipping a piece of bread crust into it. She admits that no useful purpose was served by this gesture because all she did was to say: "Hm, not bad!" but she asserts that if she had felt that it needed more curry she would have added it. No doubt this is so.

She was not idle while the meat was simmering. She was getting the "boys" ready. She has been told — and likes to think that it is so — that in the Orient a different boy carries in each separate relish that accompanies the curry. As this parade is not practical in Vermont, Mrs. Appleyard merely sets out Chinese bowls on trays and lets her guests help themselves.

This lamb curry was a Twelve-Boy Curry and the bowls contained:

Chutney	Peanuts, chopped
Parsley, minced	Yolk of Egg, grated
Spiced Apple Sauce	Green Pepper Relish
White of Egg, chopped	Ginger Marmalade
Tomato Conserve	Fresh Coconut
Onion, chopped fine	Kumquat Preserve

Also served with the curry were broiled bananas and, of course, rice.

When interviewed on the subject of rice Mrs. Appleyard said that she felt too tired to enter into controversy about it at the moment. She merely murmured that when she said "wash it in twelve changes of water" she meant it. Anyone who didn't believe her, she added, was advised to use the quick-cooking kind and do what it said on the package. "Make *plenty!*" she concluded and turned her attention to:

Broiled Bananas

Allow one banana for each person. Slice them lengthwise and cut the slices in halves. Put them cut side up on the tray of the electric grill or in a pan that will fit under your gas broiler. Squeeze lemon juice over the slices, dot them with butter. The broiling takes only a short time — 2 or 3 minutes. Watch them carefully. Bananas should not be green but do not need to be completely ripe.

The Princess's Curry (M.R.)

It was a handsome sight to see the Princess in her white and gold sari bending over the stove in the summer kitchen. If a Baltimore oriole had flown in and started to whip up a chocolate soufflé, Mrs. Appleyard would hardly have been more surprised. However, she preserved her equanimity enough to see how the Princess made the curry.

For eight people she used two broilers, each cut into four pieces and began by browning them carefully in plenty of butter. In the meantime Mrs. Appleyard had chopped three onions and washed brown rice in twelve changes of water. When the chicken had browned, the Princess began to sprinkle curry powder over it, a tablespoon, then another . . . then another . . . then the rest of the bottle. She turned the pieces of chicken carefully, using a spoon and fork, with her sari draped over one arm. Mrs. Appleyard, when she can get some suitable material, changeable red and purple brocaded with silver, perhaps, intends to run up a sari and try this gesture, but hasn't got round to it yet. At present she is still using a pale blue smock, a present from Patience Barlow. It's fine for making cream puffs and oatmeal cookies but she thinks she ought to have something more sophisticated for curry.

While Mrs. Appleyard was brooding on this subject and boiling the water for the rice, the Princess began to sprinkle the chicken with cayenne pepper. She said you should put in plenty and suited the action to the word. Then she added the chopped onions and a quart of tomato juice. Mrs. Appleyard made it herself in the blender. The Princess endorsed this brew and spoke kindly, too, of Mrs. Appleyard's 1955 chutney, so they served some and some crystallized ginger with the curry.

"Is she," Mrs. Appleyard's youngest granddaughter was heard to ask Geoffrey Toussaint, "a real princess?"

"Get me half a split pea and we'll put it under her mattress and find out," answered that gentleman.

Whether the Princess tossed uneasily because of the presence of the slight lump under the mattress or not, Mrs. Appleyard is sure she is a real princess.

Chutney

Mrs. Appleyard's ambition has always been to make her chutney taste like Major Grey's or Colonel Skinner's. She thinks her 1955 version comes as near as anything to the product endorsed by those revered gentlemen. This is how she made it. Into her largest preserving kettle she put:

24 tart early apples (Dutchess, Peach, Yellow Transparent, Gravenstein), quartered
8 small onions, chopped
3 large cucumbers, cubed, soaked in brine two hours, drained
4 quarts tomatoes, measured whole, skinned and quartered
1 green pepper, sliced thin
1 4-ounce can pimentos, sliced
3 whole heads of garlic, peeled, sliced
1 pound seeded raisins
1 pound seedless raisins
½ pound currants
3 slices of pineapple, cut fine
3 tablespoons candied ginger, diced
1 cup red wine vinegar
1 cup cider vinegar
2 teaspoons cayenne
3 tablespoons curry powder
2 teaspoons cinnamon
2 pounds brown sugar
2 tablespoons dry mustard
2 teaspoons allspice
6 cups white sugar

Scald the vinegar with the spices and sugar and add it to the mixture of fruits. Bring the contents of the kettle to a boil and cook it for an hour, stirring occasionally. Let it stand overnight. The next morning bring it to a boil again. Better put an asbestos mat under it. It sticks easily at this stage. Cook ½ hour, stirring carefully. Sterilize your jars and rubbers. Remove fruit with a spoon with holes and distribute it in the jars, filling them ⅞ full. Cook the syrup left in the kettle until it is good and thick and fill up the jars with it. About this time it will be safe to invite the neighbors in for curry.

Macaroon Trifle

Mrs. Appleyard, who reads chiefly for the exercise, it is her favorite kind, started in on Thomas Mann's *Buddenbrooks* in German recently. She had read very little German for a number of years. Don't ask us what she was doing instead:

we might tell you and that would be fatiguing for everyone.
At first the language flowed over her without bringing a
great deal of meaning with it. Suddenly however there was
a succulent description of what the Buddenbrookses had to
eat on Christmas Eve. Soon Mrs. Appleyard laid down her
book and uttered words with which her family have long been
familiar. Like other phrases that have produced a great deal
of activity such as "Don't fire till you see the whites of their
eyes," "Carthago delenda est," "My kingdom for a horse," the
remark was simple and direct.

"I think," said Mrs. Appleyard, "that I could make that."

She did indeed, only why, as a guest who was having his
third helping remarked, does she call it a trifle?

You will need, she says, a sponge cake and two dozen macaroons. She does not actually say that you have to make them
yourself, so perhaps it would be just as well to start in before
she begins to indulge in such fantasies.

1 9-inch sponge cake   1 cup candied fruit (orange
24 macaroons, small   peel, lemon peel, cherries)
1 cup sherry   ½ cup blanched almonds
          ½ cup currant jelly

Custard:

4 cups scalded milk   ½ cup sugar
yolks of 6 eggs   ½ teaspoon almond extract
          1 teaspoon vanilla

Make the custard and let it cool while you are arranging the
trifle. Beat the eggs slightly with a wire whisk or fork. Add
the sugar and beat it in. Pour on the scalded milk, stirring all
the time. Cook in a double boiler until the mixture thickens

and coats the back of a spoon. This takes about twenty minutes and it cannot be left alone for any length of time but must be stirred pretty constantly. It will curdle if it is left too long, so look out. Add the flavoring. Chill.

Now your handsomest bowl, please. Mrs. Appleyard favors a large one of thousand-eye Sandwich glass which rings when struck like a bell buoy on a foggy day in the Bay of Fundy.

Cut the sponge cake in rather thin slices, spreading each one with the currant jelly, irrigating them slightly with sherry, and sticking the almonds into them as you go along. Arrange a layer of macaroons, sprinkle over some candied fruit and repeat the two layers, first of cake, then of macaroons, till the bowl is full. Macaroons should be on top and will loom up above the custard, which you now pour on, like rocks at low tide. You don't have to do another thing except to chill it for three or four hours and eat it.

Covered-Dish Supper

MOST PEOPLE think of the Fourth of July as the crucial day of that energetic month. Not so Mrs. Appleyard and the Refreshment Committee of the Community Club. In Appleyard Center the Fourth passes almost unnoticed, now that fireworks are forbidden, but as the end of the month approaches, tension mounts. By the last Friday in July barometers are nervously tapped. Thermometers are inspected. Every cloud is assessed to see if it has rain in it. Radios are listened to for rumors of hurricanes, and sufferers from sacroiliac trouble are asked with unusual solicitude whether their backs feel all right. Is it, in short, going to be a good day for the Covered-Dish Supper?

If it is a fine evening — not rainy, not too hot, too windy or too cold — there may be two hundred people to supper on Mrs. Appleyard's lawn. Every casserole will be scraped clean. Cicely Bradshaw and Eleanor Davenport will dash home and make others. Mrs. Appleyard herself may be detected in the twilight snatching materials from her vegetable garden to make extra salads.

Maria Flint's Parker House rolls vanish — all four hundred of them. She hastily bakes a batch of biscuits and sends them over. There isn't a crumb of Marcia Gould's chocolate chiffon cake left, but Cicely finds two angel cakes in her mother's freezer. They were there for an emergency. This is it. When the evening is over and the profits counted, everyone is happily exhausted and there will soon be new shingles on the roof of the Community Club.

If the weather is bad — well, at least, Mrs. Appleyard thinks, everyone who comes has a good time, and you can quite possibly get your casserole back intact and freeze it. For an emergency. People buy the rolls and cakes that are left over. There is plenty of supper left for the workers. They may even get some of Alice Richards' fish casserole.

Organizing this project takes only about the same amount of executive ability as it does to run the General Motors Corporation, so of course everything goes smoothly. Guests and workers take it for granted that coffee will be hot and salads cold. The only person who is surprised by this phenomenon is Mrs. Appleyard. Her burdensome tasks — such as asking Patience Barlow to make corn pudding, and peas and potatoes in cream, getting out the big red tablecloths, arranging flowers in big brown jugs — are over early.

If she tried to do anything else someone is sure to remind her that she has heart trouble. This is a convenient disease, since it can be switched on and off like electricity. Deciding to switch it on, this favorite of fortune relaxes, enjoys the party and marvels at the quiet efficiency of the committee.

Perhaps what she enjoys most is to see the residents of Cranberry Hill — composers, novelists, poets, painters, stage directors — marching in bearing their casseroles. They are all distinguished cooks and it is a dizzy experience to choose among their various masterpieces. It was rumored one summer that they had all chanced on the same cookbook, and another year Martha Carroll was said to have been called on at the last moment to make a substitute casserole for a composer who had let his burn while jotting down a new sonata. But whatever the source the contents are delicious.

The long table is soon loaded with covered dishes: copper, pottery, glass, Swedish iron. There are jellied salads on glass platters and tossed salads in wooden bowls. The best baked beans for miles around — Beth Flint's, Irene Olcott's — are steaming in big enameled pans. Alice Richards' fish casserole has arrived. It's the red one with the blue lining. Mrs. Appleyard just mentions this because someone took the dish home by mistake and Alice wants it back, and no wonder.

There is one table thickly paved with cakes of a toothsome

appearance, being cut into generous squares and triangles by the committee members' judicial knives. These cakes are as good as they look. Another table has an enormous coffee percolator on it, a silver tower guarding a flock of white cups, flanked by large white cream pitchers and glass sugar bowls.

All three tables are in the Carriage House, a building that has been used for many purposes since the carriages were moved out of it forty years ago. It was a workshop at one time. Later it was a dormitory for the Appleyard boys and their friends. When they grew up and went to the wars, Mrs. Appleyard, tired of seeing the empty beds, turned it into a dance hall for the next generation. When they in turn grew up and went away, she installed there the books that she lends: children's books and her unrivaled collection of mystery stories. Later she added the materials for whatever handicraft she was learning by main strength. Highboys six inches tall have been made here. Pictures have been framed, chairs stenciled, fabrics painted.

At the moment it is simply a peaceful place to sit and listen to music, but there are still traces of earlier periods. It has never been possible to get all the sawdust out of the cracks in the floor. A sign reading "No Loitering around the Station" is still nailed to a beam above where Hugh's bed used to stand. One of his guns, a long rifle a century old, leans up against a cupboard Stan made. The blue coverlet from his bed is still lying on the sofa.

Her sons' collection of tall beaver hats still hangs from pegs on the wall, ready to be snatched off and arrogantly worn by small boys. There is a great pile of Sally's favorite records. Stuffed birds, bought at auction by Cicely, who caters to her mother's weakness for them, look glassily down from the tops of cabinets. Paint has been worn from the floor by dancing feet. Shoes for a small pony still rest on a wooden bar where they have been for twenty-five years.

Outside on the grass are the Windsor benches borrowed from the church in Gospel Hollow. Seated on these, taking their pleasure with silent solemnity as Vermonters like to do, are people with well-loaded plates. Of course the menu never gives complete satisfaction. There are always some guests who expected "that spoon bread we had last year," or who report that "the man in front of me got the last chunk of pork out of the beans, a real big one. It ought to have been cut smaller."

The complainers are usually men, Mrs. Appleyard notes with interest. There are, of course, a few tigress mothers who feel that their little ones have been slighted.

"Cyril will never *touch* sponge cake," one says with melancholy pride. "Take a piece of the maple butternut, darling, and sit down right over here where we can watch in case anything chocolate is brought in."

"Lilly doesn't have much appetite today," another announces as her child languidly fills her plate for the third time.

Children come for half price and make up for it by eating twice as much as their parents.

Still, on the whole, the customers seem reasonably well pleased. Indeed, one of them, a spry youth of eighty, approaches Mrs. Appleyard and tells her that he spends his time attending church and community suppers throughout the state. He gives this one a good mark, well up toward the top of the list, he says.

"There are good cooks around Sharon, too," he adds; "I'll be down there for a turkey dinner with the Elks next week," and departs with a ghoulish smile.

Tommy Bradshaw has organized his friends into a clean-up squad. They get their supper free in return for their services. Partly out of pride in their work, partly out of interest in what is going to be left when their turn comes, they hover over the guests, ready to snatch plates and cups before they are empty. Mrs. Appleyard prevents, she hopes, several cases of nervous indigestion by feeding the clean-up squad a preliminary sample, about enough for a pride of young lions, and promising them more later.

She wanders into the summer kitchen and succeeds in drying a few coffee cups before she is detected and chased out again.

"Have you had supper? Go out and mingle with your guests," she is told with stern kindness by Cicely.

The guests Mrs. Appleyard really likes best are right here in the kitchen, making coffee, heating rolls, stirring up spaghetti sauce. However, she goes meekly out, joins the queue at the Carriage House, pays her dollar, succeeds in getting some of her own peas and potatoes, Cicely's chef's salad, a piece of her own angel cake.

She thinks it is a pretty sight to see the contributors to the supper helping themselves out of their own covered dishes. There is something rather touching about this preference for the homely familiar over the exotic. It reminds her of the time that Cicely, then four years old, was taken to the bird house at the Zoo. She quietly listened to the screams of macaws and cockatoos; she stared seriously at the toucans and pelicans, then wandered off to look at the parakeets. Suddenly she came running back flushed with excitement.

"Come quick, Mother! Look, in this cage right over here! I've found a *robin!*"

Yet Marion Morris, Cicely's friend from Scotland, had just

jumped as something flew past her showing a breast of orange russet, a back of brownish gray and two white tail feathers and asked: "What is that exotic bird?"

"It's a — a sort of thrush," Mrs. Appleyard said. "We call it a robin."

Marion was a delightful visitor. She liked all sorts of exotic things: robins, baked beans, drive-in movies, supermarkets. She also liked dark green lakes, rocky hilltops and tumbling brooks. They reminded her of Scotland, she said, and added, "You must forgive me for saying that all the time. I can't seem to help it. It must bore you terribly."

"Not at all," said Mrs. Appleyard. "It's very natural. Scotland is the Vermont of Europe, I always say. Do quote me when you get back."

Marion laughed and promised to make this view of Scotland known in the Highland glens.

There is always a high point in any festival. The Appleyard Center Community Supper now reached it with the appearance of two tall white-clad figures. Among the other guests they seemed like visitors from another planet. Margaret Beaufort's beautifully plain white linen suit from Bergdorf Goodman's made flowered prints and peasant skirts something you might see in Woolworth's on a Saturday afternoon. Even Mrs. Appleyard looked apprehensively at her lilac Palm Beach suit, fearing that some enemy might have printed it with petunias. Like every other woman present she wished she had worn different shoes, even if they hurt.

The men, in the face of Barton Beaufort's white linen suit and black bow tie, tried valiantly to improve their appearance. Some tucked in the tails of flannel shirts. Others pulled in their belts. Those who had ties fingered them nervously and tried to pretend that their wives had bought them. They would like to have Barton believe that they wore lightly dressed mermaids and motifs from Picasso's "Guernica" in deference to feminine whim.

Mrs. Appleyard, having invited them, knew that these were not deities from a Greek myth but just the Beauforts. It was true that they wrote Broadway successes with pens mightier than rapiers; yet in Vermont they were delightful neighbors, kind patrons of strawberry festivals, donors of chunks of salmon from the Gaspé, appreciative consumers of such basic simplicities as Quiche Lorraine and Mrs. Appleyard's oatmeal cookies.

Barton had brought a unique contribution to the supper, a box of hand-painted peppermints. He had spent an entire day with vegetable colors and tiny brushes embellishing white mints with four-leaf clovers and maple leaves. There were also suitable Vermont sentiments such as *The Granite Center of the World, More Cows than People* and *Make it Do.*

These peppermint miniatures were such rare works of art that Mrs. Appleyard did not distribute them to the general public but awarded them like medals to the workers. There was a general sentiment that they were too pretty to eat. Perhaps some are still in existence, rapidly becoming pedigreed antiques.

Before long — for even Community Suppers come to an end sometime — the last dish was washed, the last paper cup picked up from the lawn, the last of the coffee drunk (to save it). The Carriage House regained its air of peaceful shabbiness. The trampled grass began to grow again. It was so still that Mrs. Appleyard could hear the brook and the wings of a moth in the larkspur pretending to be a hummingbird. Pink roses were still pink in the glow from the west. The moon came up over East Hill and gilded the white ones.

A blue heron, carefully imitating a Japanese heron painted on silk, flew across the pond and up into the Lady Elm. Mrs.

Appleyard heard an imprudent fish leap and saw the heron fly down and catch it.

I must remember to make more jellied salmon next year, she thought, and slipped serenely into sleep.

Items from the Menu

Fish Casserole (A.R.A.)*
Spaghetti Loaf* with Mushroom Sauce*
Quiche Lorraine*
Jellied Salmon (p. 71)
Baked Beans (I.O.)*
Green Beans Vinaigrette (p. 46)
Green Garden Casserole*

Corn Pudding†
Glazed Beets*
New Potatoes and Peas in Cream (p. 74)
Jellied Salads*
Green Salad (p. 86)
Parker House Rolls (M.F.)*
Cakes: Angel, Sponge, Chiffon,* Layer
Coffee
Souvenir Peppermints

Fish Casserole (A.R.)

3 pounds halibut or any white dry fish (not oily like mackerel)	1 cucumber, cut in thin slices
	a dozen capers
	2 green peppers, cut in thin rounds
2 lemons, cut in thin slices	

In a greased loaf pan lay the ingredients in layers, in this order, fish, dotted with a little butter, lemon, cucumber and pepper slices, a few of the capers. There should be enough for three layers. Pour half a glass of dry white wine over it and bake in a slow oven, 275°, until the fish is tender.

Spaghetti Loaf

½ cup cooked spaghetti
1 cup light cream from the top of the bottle
1 cup bread crumbs, soft part of Pepperidge Farm Bread
¼ cup butter
½ cup sharp cheddar cheese, grated
1 medium onion, minced

2 tablespoons green pepper, chopped
1 pimento, cut into thin slices
3 eggs
1 tablespoon parsley, chopped fine
½ teaspoon thyme, chopped fine
salt to taste

Put butter, crumbs and seasonings in a bowl. Scald the cream and pour it over them. Mix well and stir in the cheese. Add the eggs, well beaten, and the spaghetti. Put the mixture in a well-buttered loaf pan. Dot more butter over the top. Set in a pan of hot water and bake at 350° till firm, about 45 minutes. Turn it out of the pan, slice as you serve it with mushroom sauce.

Mushroom Sauce

Cicely Bradshaw and her mother possess a sort of sixth sense about mushrooms. They think where and when they would grow if they were mushrooms and then go there on the right day and there the mushrooms are. Their shining white caps may gleam like beer cans to the uninitiated but both these mushroom fanciers can spot the difference at 45 m.p.h. They keep their pet fields a secret, even to some extent from each other, and have been known to meet unexpectedly in some upland pasture ten miles from home each equipped with a long sharp knife. So far they have not used these knives for anything more hostile than slicing off the mushroom caps, but who knows what might happen if some outlander intruded upon their privacy.

Actually privacy is difficult when you are picking mushrooms. Mrs. Appleyard and her daughter are not interested in any mushroom except *Agaricus campestris*. This is a fungus of strong character. It will not grow in a piece of ground that is shaded by anything taller than a stalk of white clover. The pasture has to be nibbled down, preferably by horses, and is usually on a sunny slope open to fresh air and city folks.

Yet one year recently these ladies stopped counting when they had frozen, eaten or given away a hundred pounds of mushrooms. They were both out in a well-ventilated pasture last year in the position of the mushroom gatherer—head down, knife in hand—when a large scarlet automobile coasted along the road and eased to a stop.

"Keep your head down," Mrs. Appleyard advised her daughter. "They will think we are peasants—old leech gatherers."

A vibrant male voice from the red car called out: "Hi, Cicely, I knew you by the chopsticks in your hair."

Mrs. Appleyard nominates this simple declarative sentence as one of the most peculiar of the year. Fortunately the owner of the red car is far too busy composing intricate 12-tone jazz to give his attention to mushrooms.

It is a fact that Cicely's dark hair is secured by chopsticks, a style that is spreading so rapidly that she will soon have to initiate something else — old stove lighters perhaps.

In the meantime there is plenty of mushroom sauce in Mrs. Appleyard's freezer, made as follows:

2 pounds mushrooms, caps and tender part of stem only	2 tablespoons flour
	salt and pepper to taste
1 small onion, minced	sherry — if used
3 tablespoons butter	1 cup light cream
pinch of nutmeg	

Wash but do not peel the mushroom caps. Slice the larger ones longitudinally. Leave the button size whole. Fry the onion in the butter till it is straw colored. Add the mushrooms. Cover, and cook till they are tender. Sprinkle the flour and seasonings over them and stir into the butter and juice from the mushrooms which will be in the pan. When thoroughly blended, add the cream, stirring it in slowly, and cook over low heat for 5 minutes. If you like a little sherry in it and are going to use the sauce right away, this is the time to do it — about one tablespoon. If you are going to freeze the sauce do not add the sherry for a couple of years, until you thaw out the package.

Quiche Lorraine

There are probably as many ways of making this as there are cooks. Here is Mrs. Appleyard's version. For six people you will need:

Enough light flaky pastry (p. 93) to line a 10-inch Pyrex pie plate.

1 cup real dairy cheese — New York, Wisconsin, Vermont, coarsely grated.

12 slices of bacon	nutmeg, sugar, cayenne, black
4 eggs	pepper, salt to taste
2 cups light cream	¼ cup chopped chives

Line the pie plate — it should be 1½ inches deep — with your Two-Thousand-Layer paste. Crimp it handsomely around the edges. Prick the bottom lightly with a fork in several places. Put it in the refrigerator for at least 10 minutes. Light the oven — 400°. Fry the bacon until it is crisp but not overcooked. Break it into small pieces and scatter it over the bottom of the pie dish. Sprinkle the chives over this. Beat together the eggs and cream, add the cheese and the seasonings. Bake for 10–15 minutes at 400°. Reduce the temperature to 325° and bake until a silver knife will come out clean from the middle — 25–30 minutes longer. The top should be golden brown, so should the pastry. The bacon and chives will come to the top.

Variations: Finely chopped onions may be substituted for the chives, not more than a teaspoonful.

A little chopped parsley may be sprinkled over the top just before you bring it to the table.

Omit the cheese. Fry a thinly sliced onion golden brown

in the bacon fat. Add a pinch of marjoram and spread the onion over the bacon.

Omit the bacon. Use the cheese and two onions sliced and fried in butter.

Green Garden Casserole

Mrs. Appleyard belongs to the generation that looks with a certain amount of suspicion upon the casserole and not perhaps without justification, for there is no doubt that a casserole can, and does, contain pretty nearly anything. If there are substances you feel strongly about, such as monosodium glutamate and cornstarch — but there, there, calm down, Mrs. Appleyard! Here is one containing none of these things. It hasn't any imitation brick siding or Tiffany glass either. For six people:

1½ cups cold cooked chicken, cubed	a few sprays of watercress and parsley
2 onions, thinly sliced	2 tablespoons butter
½ pound mushrooms, sliced	1 cup cooked broccoli
1 cup cooked spinach	1½ cups sour cream
1 cup mushroom stock from stem and peelings	1 cup chicken stock
a few spears of chives	1 tablespoon lemon juice
1 cup cooked rice	½ cup bread crumbs
	an extra tablespoon butter

salt to taste

Sauté the onions in 2 tablespoons of butter until they are pale yellow. Add the mushrooms and cook slowly till they are tender. Put the cooked spinach, mushroom and chicken stocks, sour cream, watercress, parsley, chives, lemon juice into the electric blender. Run it until everything is smoothly blended, about a minute. Pour this green mixture over the mushrooms and onions, add the chicken, the broccoli and the rice. Put it into your best Dutch iron casserole, sprinkle with bread crumbs, dot with butter. Bake at 375° until the top is well browned — 15–20 minutes.

Baked Beans (I.G.O.)

Soak 8 cups of soldier beans for several hours, although beans do not need so much soaking these days as formerly, and it is not necessary to do it overnight. Parboil them. Take your bean pot and put in 1 pound salt pork in chunks, 1 pound brown sugar, an onion, quartered, some dry mustard, salt and pepper. Bake in a slow oven, covered, until they are done. Don't let them dry out. This is as near as a good cook can get to telling you how she makes beans fit for a queen. Soldier beans have a little soldier down one seam. Around Appleyard Center they are preferred to all others for baking, far above pea beans, red kidney beans or yellow-eyes. A few people use maple syrup in place of brown sugar. For a big supper they are often baked in a wide enamel dishpan, round or oval, so they can be heated up easily and served readily at the table. No covered-dish supper would be complete without them.

Glazed Beets

Use beets that are young and tender. One of the great advantages in doing so is that then you are not confronted with them when they are old and tough. Some long winter evening when the loud howling of the wolves is heard between the icicles, Mrs. Appleyard will tell how she and Venetia Hopkins made beet wine. But not tonight.

Cook the beets in plenty of water. Slip them out of their skins, slice them and set them where they will keep warm. There should be about two cups. Cook the beet juice down until you have one cup. Soak 1 tablespoon minute tapioca in ¼ cup beet juice for 5 minutes. Add 2 tablespoons lemon juice, 2 tablespoons red wine, salt and pepper to taste. Stir this mixture into the cup of beet juice. Cook till it starts to thicken. Add the sliced beets. Serve as soon as they are hot, with the sauce poured over them.

Jellied Salads

SHRIMP AND COLE SLAW

1 package Lemon or Lime Jello	1 cup finely shredded carrot
1 cup mayonnaise	1 cup small cleaned shrimp
1 cup finely shredded cabbage	½ cup crushed pineapple

Prepare the Jello according to the directions on the package. When it is partly chilled stir in the mayonnaise, cabbage, carrot and pineapple. Rinse a ring mold with cold water or brush with oil. Put in one quarter of the mixture. Distribute the shrimp around the ring. Fill with the remaining mixture. Chill, turn out of the mold, and arrange on platter with leaf lettuce.

GRAPE JUICE AND FRUIT

1 package Grape Jello
3 cups fruit cocktail or the equivalent in fresh cut-up fruit except fresh pineapple

½ cup walnuts, chopped
1 can concentrated grape juice

Prepare the Grape Jello according to the directions on the package, substituting the concentrated grape juice for part of the required liquid. When partly chilled stir in the fruit and nuts. Place in fancy mold, complete chilling and unmold on glass platter. Serve with mayonnaise into which ½ cup whipped cream has been stirred, also a little sugar.

Parker House Rolls (M.F.)

For 2½ dozen — Time 15 minutes, oven at 400°
3¼ cups bread flour (Occident) sifted

1⅓ cups milk
1 cake yeast
3 tablespoons sugar
1 teaspoon salt
3 tablespoons shortening

Scald milk and cool until lukewarm. Dissolve yeast and sugar in ⅓ cup of warm milk. Sift flour before and after measuring. Combine dissolved yeast and sugar and salt with the remainder of the milk. Add one half the flour and beat thoroughly. Add melted shortening. Add remainder of flour gradually and beat thoroughly after each addition. Turn onto lightly floured board and knead until smooth and elastic. Place in bowl and cover and allow to rise in warm place, 80°–85°, until double in bulk, about 1½ hours. Punch down and let rise again.

Shape into rolls, rolling the dough to ¼ inch thickness. Cut with biscuit cutter. Crease through center. Spread one half with thin layer of butter. Fold one half well over the other half. Place about ½ inch apart on greased baking sheet. Allow to rise until very light, about 45 minutes. Bake in moderate oven.

Orange Chiffon Cake (M.G.)

Sift together in one bowl:

2¼ cups Softasilk or 2 cups Gold Medal flour
1½ cups sugar

3 teaspoons double acting baking powder
1 teaspoon salt

Make a well in the center and in it put:

½ cup salad oil
¾ cup cold water
flavoring — 2 teaspoons vanilla
or 2 teaspoons almond or 2
teaspoons lemon rind

Mix well. Set your oven at 325° for a 10-inch tube pan, or at 350° for a 9 x 13 pan. Beat 1 cup egg whites in a large bowl with ½ teaspoon cream of tartar until very dry and stiff. Fold the yolk mixture very gently into the whites. Pour into ungreased tube or oblong pan. Bake the tube cake for about an hour at 325°, the oblong one at 350° for 45–50 minutes, or until the top springs back when pressed.

Slice a cake made in the tube pan in three horizontal layers and fill with the following:

Rich Orange Filling

In a saucepan put:

1 cup sugar

4 tablespoons cornstarch

½ teaspoon salt

1 cup orange juice

2 teaspoons orange rind — optional

1½ teaspoons lemon juice

2 tablespoons butter

(orange juice frozen concentrate can be used in place of juice and sugar)

Bring to a rolling boil and boil 1 minute, stirring constantly. Chill well before using.

Frost the cake with a 7-minute boiled icing and decorate with some of the orange filling spooned over the top. This is a delicate cake and should be served right after it is baked.

Chocolate Icing (M.L.G.)

For a vanilla- or almond-flavored chiffon cake use the following icing:

Melt together 4 tablespoons butter and 4 squares chocolate. Blend in 2⅔ cups sifted confectioners' sugar and ⅓ teaspoon salt. Add 6½ tablespoons heated milk and 1¼ teaspoons vanilla. Beat till smooth and glossy.

August

A Bounty of Beans

M<small>RS.</small> A<small>PPLEYARD</small> in a burst of shallow optimism picked
up the telephone with the idea of making a call to Cicely.
She wished to discuss some Henry James characters with whom
she and her daughter were currently involved. She forgot that it
is easier to call Paris from a pay station than it is to get East
Alcott from an eight-party line. There was as usual a deceptive
silence during which she hoped to hear the languid voice of the
operator, in case she was not out having a cup of instant coffee.

What's instant about it? Mrs. Appleyard wondered. Certainly
not the consumption time.

Then she heard The Sigh and realized that she was listening to a conversation. The Sigh is a standard part of an eight-party line causerie. It follows a silence and precedes a statement. In this case the statement was: "My beans have come on awful sudden."

Mrs. Appleyard put down the receiver in dismay, for well she knew that when one bean ripens, all ripen. Every year she studies the seed catalogue with the idea of growing beans so that they will be ready at convenient intervals. The beans in the catalogue know how to accomplish this. They are literate, educated beans. They ripen in sixty-three days, in sixty-eight, in seventy-two. You can plant all the kinds the same day and count on a two-week span of perfect green pods, tender and delicious.

That must happen in some effete southern state such as Massachusetts. Transported to the rugged air of Vermont, threatened by late frosts in June and early frosts in August, scorched by July suns, soaked by cloudbursts, beans pay no attention to what it says on the package. They know they must achieve their destiny before it is too late. They keep right on growing by moonlight if necessary, by fireflyshine or aurora borealis. There is no use planting them at different intervals either. They know better than you do when they are ready for the freezer.

Beans must be dealt with like small children in a tantrum — kindly, firmly and at once. You must eat them, freeze them or give them away. The last is the hardest because practically everyone else is in the same dilemma. However, there are always a few people who are strong-minded enough not to have gardens. No doubt these hardy targets for horticultural benevolence privately throw away a good many vegetable donations, but this must be considered their own affair.

Never question the contents of your neighbor's compost heap or casserole. (Quoted by permission from *Mrs. Appleyard's Condensed Wisdom*, p. 398.)

Having frozen enough beans in their time to make, if carefully packaged, piled and frozen, enough igloos for an Eskimo supermarket, Mrs. Appleyard and Patience have developed what they regard as a good box of beans.

Boil the beans ten minutes, Mrs. Appleyard says. It is not necessary to cook all the water away. Pour it right into the package with the beans. It will help to keep them from drying out. When you finish cooking them — next year, two years from now — it will serve as the water in which you cook them. You need then put only a quarter of a cup of boiling water into your saucepan, just to start the thawing process as quickly as possible.

To get back to getting beans ready for the freezer: when your ten minutes are up, have a large pan of cold water ready and set your pan of hot beans into it to cool for five minutes. Then put the beans into the package, label and date it and into the freezer with it. Remember to set your freezer at sharp freeze before you start on one of these bean-freezing orgies. If it is at its coldest setting and if you put in only one package at a time, a good many can be safely frozen during the course of a day, about all you will be able to cut, probably. Keep the freezer set at sharp freeze for the next few days because you are going to be busy with that knife. At the end of that time you will never wish to see another bean, but by Thanksgiving time you will feel differently.

When you start cooking your beans for the Thanksgiving dinner, put a quarter cup of water into a saucepan. When it boils add the beans. Cover. After four minutes uncover and add butter. They should finish cooking in about three minutes more. The water will have cooked out; the beans will be crisp and tender. Never put soda in beans. All right, it does make them green but it also kills the vitamins and the flavor.

Mrs. Appleyard and Patience do peas by substantially the same method. They pick only enough for one or two packages at a time, shell only enough for one package, cook them in just enough water to cover them for about four minutes, package them in the water in which they are cooked, and freeze them as you do the beans. When serving them Mrs. Appleyard starts them cooking in two tablespoonfuls of boiling water. They need only two or three minutes cooking after they start to boil. Add butter the last minute. It speeds up the cooking process. This applies to the beans too.

It is almost impossible to tell these peas from peas actually fresh from the garden. That is assuming that they were young and tender when you picked and cooked them, and that Patience has marked them A plus. Mrs. Appleyard has said this before but she repeats it here because it is a fact often forgotten: you are not going to get anything out of the freezer better than what you put into it.

These frozen peas are so precious that she never serves them except perfectly plain with butter and possibly a very little thick cream. Beans however are more plentiful by far, and she has several different ways of serving them: beans with mushrooms, beans with croutons, beans and potatoes with onions, cream and beef cracklings, wreath of beans around a cauliflower, with Hollandaise sauce, beans with cream, sprinkled with parsley and crisp crumbled bacon.

Let the beans come on!

You might just as well, Mrs. Appleyard says, accept this simultaneity of beans as you accept the Precession of the Equinoxes, get out your sharpest knife and go to work. Whether the resulting packages will contain a reasonable facsimile of beans or whether they will shelter chunks of brownish-green blotting paper will depend a good deal on how you cut them. You might just as well, she says, leave them on the vines as break them into pieces and throw them into brine. This is the method worked out by Patience Barlow, who not only dominates the bean freezing session (Mrs. Appleyard is just an extra pair of hands) but who conscientiously labels the packages with grades ranging from B to A plus. They begin by cutting the beans as thin as possible on a long diagonal. This may be done with scissors or with a gadget designed for the purpose. Mrs. Appleyard prefers a French vegetable knife and a cutting board. Patience deftly whittles them in the air with a skill all her own.

They do only enough for a package at a time, add them to a pan containing only just enough boiling water to cover them. No salt. It only toughens and discolors them. It can be added just before they are sent to the table months later.

MENUS FOR DINNERS IN GREEN BEAN SEASON

Hot Clear Beet Soup*   Toasted Montpelier Crackers
Roast Beef*   Yorkshire Pudding (p. 221)
Roasted Potatoes in the Pan
Cauliflower and Green Beans Hollandaise *
Peach Short Cake
Coffee

Clear Mushroom Broth   Melba Toast
Roast Lamb *   Roasted Potatoes in the Pan *
Currant Jelly

Green Beans with Sour Cream Sauce*
Deep Dish Apple Pie   Hard Sauce

Hot Spcied Tomato Juice (p. 16)
Cheese and Chutney Appetizers
Stuffed Mushroom Caps *
Smothered Veal*
Green Beans with Cream Beef Cracklings *
Corn, 20 minutes from Garden to Table
Chocolate Icebox Cake*

Hot Clear Beet Soup

4 cups clear beet juice	1 onion, sliced thin
1 can consommé	2 tablespoons instant tapioca

2 tablespoons sherry

Combine the beet juice and the consommé. Mrs. Appleyard hopes you saved the juice when you cooked your last batch of beets for vegetable salad. If you did not, you have her permission to be extravagant and pour it off cans of beets until you have enough. What you do with the beets is your problem. Slice the onion very thin and pour the beet juice and consommé over it. Do this an hour before dinner. Soak the tapioca in some of the beet juice. When you are ready to serve the soup, strain out the onion, add the tapioca and cook gently for three minutes. Add the sherry. Serve with sliced lemon in the plate and pass sour cream with it.

Roast Beef

It was recently called to Mrs. Appleyard's attention that she has never told a hungry world how to roast beef. The truth is she supposed that everyone knew how. Until people began to ask her, she had forgotten that a whole generation of housewives had grown up who had never been exposed to anything more exacting than a pound of hamburg.

During that period Mrs. Appleyard, always ready to try anything new, has experimented with the constant-temperature method and has now gone back to searing a roast and basting it. However, as a concession to modernity she uses a meat thermometer. If you have ten or twelve dollars worth of beef in the oven it helps your morale considerably to be able to read a device that tells you when it is done. She also uses one of those basters that looks like a giant medicine dropper. This is also a great help. However, there is no method that will free you completely from responsibility. You still must calculate the approximate time of cooking before you ever put the beef into the oven so that you will know when to cook the rest of the dinner. Be sure you know accurately what the roast weighs.

For roasts with the bone in, allow:
For rare: 13–15 minutes to the pound
For well done: 18–20 minutes to the pound
For roasts without bones allow:
For rare: 15–18 minutes to the pound
For well done: 20–22 minutes to the pound

Begin with the oven at 450°. Rub flour all over the roast and well into it. Insert the thermometer. Don't let it touch the bone. Put the meat into a large roasting pan big enough to hold the roast comfortably and leave room for the potatoes. Do not cover the pan. Dredge more flour over the beef, letting some fall into the pan. When this begins to brown, as it will do in about 20 minutes, reduce the heat to 300° and start basting.

Mrs. Appleyard likes for basting some hot broth made by simmering beef bones with a carrot, an onion, a branch of celery, a few herbs, a dash of cinnamon, a pinch of nutmeg, but plain water sometimes has to do. The gravy, in case you make it, will not be quite so good but the flavor of the meat will not be changed to any extent. She likes the gravy that runs out of the meat best herself and so, she notices, do a great many other people. Anyway, for the first few bastings — do it every 15 minutes — you will need to add some liquid to the pan and it should be hot. When the fat begins to run into the pan, it will not be necessary to add any more liquid until you make the gravy. When you do, use some more of the hot stock. If Mrs. Appleyard said what she thinks about gravy makers and monosodium glutamate and so-called bouillon cubes, this book would not be allowed to go through the mails. She forbears.

When the thermometer reads just exactly what you wish it to say, take the pan out of the oven *at once*. Remember that the meat, especially if there are bones acting as heat conductors in it, will go on cooking inside after you have taken it out of the oven. If your guests are a little late it is better to take it out ahead of time, cover it, let it stand until you are ready to serve it, then return it to the oven for a few minutes.

By this method the fat will be brown and crisp. There will be some well done slices for those who like it that way. The inside will be tender and juicy. There will be plenty of dish gravy.

Perhaps the most valuable piece of advice Mrs. Appleyard can give you is about carving: never let a man less than sixty years old do it unless he has a diploma from a certified carving school embossed on his shirt front. Youth is a wonderful thing but an ability to carve is not one of its attributes. Mrs. Appleyard thinks carving should be done by men — a strong, just and generous sex — but it is an art and they should study it. Cutting up frankfurters for the nursery school set and serving casseroles are not suitable preparation for this task. Your husband needs a good book and something to practice on before he carves in public. He also needs a well-tempered steel knife and the ability to make and keep it sharp.

Roast Potatoes around the Meat

Parboil potatoes in their skins for twenty minutes. Run cold water over them. Peel them. Cut them in halves. Melt some beef fat — you are supposed to save it and have a jar in the refrigerator — or some butter in a frying pan. Turn the potatoes over in this until they are buttered all over. Put them into the pan with the beef. Baste them when you baste the beef. Turn them occasionally so they will brown evenly. This takes about 45 or 50 minutes, depending on the size. They should be crisp and brown outside and fluffy inside.

Cauliflower and Green Beans Hollandaise

This is simply a perfect head of cauliflower, cooked until it is just done but will still hold its shape (Mrs. Appleyard cooks hers in a steamer) and surrounded by a garland of green beans thinly sliced. The beans are dotted here and there with tiny croutons carefully browned and crisped in butter. The cauliflower is covered with Hollandaise sauce. Since the cauliflower takes longer than the beans, start it first. And since the Hollandaise is difficult to keep hot without curdling, make it last. Mrs. Appleyard has printed the rule for this so many times (in *Mrs. Appleyard's Kitchen* to mention one place) that she will not repeat it here.

Roast Lamb

Mrs. Appleyard uses the same method for roast lamb as for beef. (See p. 131). Because of the difficulty of procuring skilful carvers — she is definitely not one herself — she usually has the lamb boned. She brings home the bones and trimmings and makes broth for basting from them. For some reason more people seem to like brown gravy with lamb than with beef, so she usually makes it, as soon as the meat and potatoes are on her big well-and-tree platter. First she browns some flour in a frying pan, working it into the flour and fat already in the pan. Then she pours on some of the hot broth, blends it well, lets it cook a minute or two, strains it into the gravy boat.

For lamb that is to be just pink in the middle she allows 18 minutes with the bone in; without the bone 20 minutes to the pound. If it is to be well done she allows 22 minutes to the pound. These are approximations for guidance in timing the whole meal. The thermometer will give the final and correct answer.

Green Beans with Sour Cream Sauce

Mrs. Appleyard thinks wistfully of the time when you got sour cream by skimming it off ten quarts of milk which was standing around in the back buttery. However, modern soured cream is more generally available than that butter-colored stuff that comes off the pans with the scarlet edges. It's good too.

Here's a sauce that goes well with poached salmon, with fish mousse or with asparagus, or green beans, as in this case.

Sour Cream Sauce

3 egg yolks
½ tablespoon vinegar
what seasonings you like — salt, pepper, paprika
1 cup sour cream
½ tablespoon lemon juice

Put the vinegar and lemon juice into the top of a double boiler, beat in the egg yolks, then the cream, a third at a time. Remove at once from the heat and serve with green beans.

Cheese and Chutney Appetizers

rounds of bread toasted on one side
¼ pound butter
½ pound dairy cheese, grated
½ cup Mrs. Appleyard's Chutney (p. 103)
1 tablespoon finely minced onion
a little Worcestershire sauce if you like it

Butter the bread on the toasted side. Mix the rest of the ingredients and spread the rounds of bread with the mixture. Put them on a baking sheet and bake them at 375° until the cheese melts — about five minutes.

Stuffed Mushroom Caps

Raw mushroom caps, mouthful size, filled with cream cheese, thick cream, chopped chives and minced parsley and dusted over with paprika.

Smothered Veal (For 6) (V.H.)

2 pounds of veal, cut from the leg in inch-thick slices and cut into neat pieces, 2 x 3 inches. (Save the trimmings for Veal and Ham Pie or Pâté)

1 cup flour seasoned with pepper, salt, a little oregano, marjoram, rosemary — or what you like
4 cups hot water
2 good-sized onions, finely sliced

2 tablespoons butter
1 cup thin cream or top of the bottle
2 tablespoons white wine
2 tablespoons minced parsley
2 tablespoons chopped chives

Fry the onions in the butter until they are light yellow. While they are cooking put the seasoned flour in a bag and shake the pieces of veal in it until they are well coated. Remove the onions temporarily from the pan and brown the veal until it is crisp on both sides. Put the onions back with the veal, pour the hot water over and let it simmer over a very low flame until

it is tender — about an hour. Longer will do no harm but replace the water occasionally. It should not cook dry. When
it is tender, add the cream and let it cook a minute. Then stir in
the wine. Mrs. Appleyard uses her biggest scarlet and ivory
frying pan for this and brings it to the table right in the pan
with the parsley and chives sprinkled over the top.

Green Beans with Cream and Beef Cracklings

Prepare the cracklings beforehand (p. 75). Slice the beans
on the long diagonal. Cook them in rapidly boiling water, not
too much of it, and when it has cooked away, add a little very
thick cream. Before serving them heat the cracklings briefly,
skim them out of the pan, using a spoon with holes so you will
not get any fat with them and sprinkle them over the beans.

Chocolate Icebox Cake (P.K.)

One of the nice things about giving Kitchen Privileges, Mrs.
Appleyard says, is that someone is always making something in
your kitchen. You may, for instance, open your refrigerator
and find a Pyrex loaf pan in it lined with waxed paper with the
paper neatly folded over the top. The contents are a mystery
and remain so until Phyllis unveils her mother's Chocolate Icebox Cake.

¾ pound chocolate bits	6 large (or 7 small) eggs
4½ tablespoons hot water	1 teaspoon vanilla
3 tablespoons powdered sugar	1½ dozen lady fingers
½ pint cream, whipped	

Melt the chocolate bits over hot water with the hot water and sugar. Add the egg yolks lightly beaten and cook over hot water until the mixture thickens and coats the back of the spoon. It takes about seven minutes. Remove from the fire and let it cool while you beat the whites stiff but not dry. Add the vanilla. Fold in the whites.

Line a Pyrex loaf pan with wax paper, leaving enough at the ends and sides to fold over the top. Line the pan, bottom, sides and ends with lady fingers. Put in half the chocolate mixture; lay some more lady fingers on top of it. Add the rest of the chocolate and finish with lady fingers. Fold over the paper. Put the pan in the refrigerator for at least 4 hours. When you serve it turn the loaf out of the pan and frost it with whipped cream. Deadly, but *good!*

Gourmets on Safari

F ROM THE BEGINNING Cicely was a puzzle to the Beauforts. Presumably well educated, since she had been to Bryn Mawr, fond of reading to the point of vice, why was she not also well informed? Her refusal to read the *New York Times* every day, like other normal people, quite shocked them. It was not until the expedition to Catamount Brook that they finally found a satisfactory classification for her.

Cicely, they told Venetia Hopkins, at whose house they had been staying, was a Shakespearean nature sprite.

Just what this meant Cicely was never quite sure, but it clearly made the Beauforts happy to have found a pigeonhole for her. Nature sprites obviously had little time for newspaper reading. They were more in the line of inspectors of sunrises, guardians of lady-slippers, cherishers of semi-precious stones.

The Beauforts were fond of picnics and when Cicely volunteered to conduct them up Catamount Brook to a certain series of pools they accepted agreeably. The date was set and at the last moment a family of friends from New Hampshire who were calling on the Beauforts joined the party. The Daltons were advertised as hearty lovers of the outdoors, but their reaction to Catamount Brook confirmed Cicely's private conviction that New Hampshire is a rather decadent state.

It had been decreed by the Beauforts, and accepted by Cicely, that there were to be no paper plates and cups on this picnic. The Beauforts lived with an elegance so thoroughgoing that one could not imagine them using anything made of plastic, let alone paper. Thus a complete service for twelve in silver and crystal was to be transported up the mountainside, along with the various items on the menu. Barton Beaufort made himself responsible for the wine.

The departure of the picnickers from Appleyard Center was uneventful, except that Cicely forgot the large pan of Gazpacho over which she had been working for two days and had to go back three miles to get it. She found the party gathered at the foot of the trail. As Barton had brought along the Sunday edition of the *New York Times* no one lacked for reading matter, and the children were picking flowers in the overgrown hayfield.

The first part of the climb offered no special problems, although some of the cartons, containers and baskets in which the meal was packed had to be redistributed several times along the way. It was not until they reached the point where it is necessary to leave the trail and descend Catamount Brook itself that difficulties began to arise.

The mountain range of which Catamount is the northernmost peak is made of a mica-laden metamorphic rock. Rough garnets can be found in the upper ledges. The brooks that leap down its sides are icy, green in their pools, white and rushing in their more level stretches. Spring freshets have tumbled boulders of all sizes down their courses, along with uprooted trees and smaller driftwood. It is not, to say the least, easy going on Catamount Brook.

The Bradshaw children, born and bred in this briar patch, leapt like chamois from rock to rock, except for Camilla, who rode alternately on her mother's back or on her hip. But the Dalton children cowered and whimpered at the top of each ledge and had to be lowered from adult to adult along with the provisions, the cutlery, the napery and the wineglasses.

When Cicely came to the goal of the picnic, a deep emerald pool fifteen feet long with a sandbar at the lower end where they could all comfortably sit and eat, she plunged in and swam its full length. Perhaps it was this gesture as much as anything which pinned the nature sprite label on her. No one followed her example. One of the Dalton children was crying now and its mother did not know whether to comfort it or drown it.

Finally all the animate and inanimate essentials were assembled on the sandbar. Barton set the bottles of Liebfraumilch to cool in the brook and began carving the ham in delicate slices. Cicely ladled the Gazpacho into brown pottery bowls. There was French bread and butter and the children were allowed to make sandwiches if they wished.

For dessert an angel cake came out of its pan and a pot-pourri of fruit in red wine — peaches, canteloupe, white grapes, rasp-berries, orange sections, flavored with mint from Cicely's gar-den — from a Thermos container. The Liebfraumilch was served throughout the meal in appropriate glasses. Slowly the capacity of food and drink to soothe and calm exerted its cus-tomary spell. Even Mr. Dalton regained a measure of peace of mind after his ordeal — it was he who halfway down the brook had refused to go any farther, saying he had never liked the out-doors anyway. Barton had to coax him down the last ledge with a glass of Liebfraumilch.

The way home was reasonably easy, though occasionally a marshy trickle had to be forded. Only one of Venetia's wine glasses had slipped into the pool and could not be retrieved, though Tommy Bradshaw tried diving for it. The water was so clear that they could see it, deceptively within reach.

"An unusual form of libation," said Barton, emptying the last of the wine bottles into the pool. "I doubt if they often get the glass too."

Cicely felt that Englishmen who dressed for dinner on desert islands had nothing on the Beauforts.

MOUNTAIN MENUS

Gazpacho *
Ham — Harrington's Cob-smoked
French Bread   Sweet Butter
Angel Cake
Pot-pourri of Fruit in Red Wine *
Liebfraumilch
Cornish Pastries *

Salad in the Hand — carrot sticks, hearts of celery, radishes, raw broccoli, raw cauliflower — blue cheese dip
Tomato Juice
Green Ripe Olives
Apricot-Nut Bars *

Gazpacho

4 tablespoons mixed chopped fresh herbs, such as parsley, dill, chives, basil, marjoram, savory
6 large ripe tomatoes, skinned and chopped

2 cloves of garlic, chopped fine or pressed
2 big sweet peppers, quartered and chopped fine

With a potato masher crush the whole mixture and add gradually juice of 2 lemons and 1 cup olive oil, until the mixture is a paste. Stir in 6 cups homemade chicken stock. Season to taste with salt and ground black pepper. Add 2 cups cucumbers, peeled, seeded and chopped fine, also 1 Bermuda onion and 2 hearts of celery, chopped fine likewise. Chill 4 hours before serving. Serves six.

Pot-pourri of Fruit in Red Wine

Cut up 4 fresh peaches, 1 canteloupe. Add one package frozen raspberries, one package frozen strawberries, one large can orange juice — frozen concentrate, 1 cup seedless grapes. Add ½ cup honey, 2 tablespoons finely chopped mint leaves,

½ teaspoon mint extract, 2 cups dry red wine. Stir together and chill. Prepare at least 2 hours before serving. Serves six to 8.

Cornish Pasties

Prepare enough pastry for a two-layer pie — this will make six good-sized pasties. Roll out and cut 6-inch circles. Chop 1 pound good stewing beef — chuck or bottom round — into small cubes, ½-inch square. Include some fat. Chop coarsely 3 carrots, 2 medium onions, a little turnip if you like it, and 3 medium potatoes. Mix the meat and vegetables in a bowl, salt and pepper them lightly. Put some of the mixture on half of each circle. Dot with butter. Be generous but leave an edge; fold the other half of the circle over and pinch it well together. Prick holes in the top. Place on baking sheet and bake at 400° until done. The pasties will be browned top and bottom. It will take about an hour. Reduce the heat the last third of the baking time. Cool the pasties and eat them cold in the hand.

Apricot-Nut Bars

½ cup flour	1 cup light brown sugar
½ teaspoon salt	½ cup almonds, chopped
1 teaspoon baking powder	1 cup chopped apricots
2 eggs	1 teaspoon almond extract

Stir together flour, salt and baking powder. Beat the eggs; beat in the sugar gradually; stir in the nuts, apricots and almond extract; stir in the dry ingredients. Spread in 8 x 8 pan well greased. Bake in moderate oven — 350° — about 30 minutes or until surface springs back. Cut at once into squares and roll in powdered sugar. Makes 16.

The Corn is Yellow

Fᴿᴏᴍ ᴏɴᴇ ᴘᴏɪɴᴛ of view the year 1955 was a grim one. This was the year the crows pulled up all Mrs. Appleyard's corn. They were not particular about varieties: Golden Bantam, Midget Marvel, Gold Cross, Sugar and Gold, all were acceptable to their shiny beaks. Roger Willard planted the corn again. The next week a spring freshet, mistaking the vegetable garden for a river bed, washed most of the corn seed down into the witch grass at the bottom of the slope. It was replanted. What corn came up reared its head just in time to be met by a frost.

Naturally under such conditions ingenuity was necessary if Mrs. Appleyard was going to carry on the proud tradition left to her to maintain by generations of her husband's ancestors: that in August you eat corn. She was subjected to the indignity of buying corn, thus putting a blot upon her bright escutcheon, for it was an old Appleyard maxim that corn is not fit to eat unless it reaches the kettle no more than twenty minutes after it is picked. However, there are ways to serve it besides on the cob with plenty of butter, ways in which the elusive sweet freshness of the corn would be obscured anyway by other flavors.

It was rather relaxing not to have to start freezing corn as soon as the last bean was in its neat blue and white checked package. There is no use, Mrs. Appleyard says, in freezing it except from your own garden: you might as well save your energy and buy Golden Bantam next winter in a can.

Saved-up energy is something like the daylight you save every summer, or like champagne at the bottom of the bottle. Unless it is used at once the fizz goes out of it.

"Are you in a mood to experiment?" Mrs. Appleyard inquired of Patience Barlow.

Patience guessed she was. What else could she say? She looked slightly apprehensive, however. She was thinking perhaps of the time Mrs. Appleyard decreed that they would have something to eat every day for a week that they had never cooked before. That was the week they had Crêpes Suzette, Lobster Thermidor, Lady Baltimore Cake, Roast Lamb with anchovies, parsley and watercress, Shoofly Pie, Vol-au-Vent of Sweetbreads with mushrooms. That was all: just six items. There are, to be sure, seven days in a week. On the seventh day both ladies ate milk toast — not just ordinary milk toast with ordinary Jersey milk, mostly cream — with skimmed milk.

Mrs. Appleyard's daughter Sally Roland drove over from Roland Hill and found her mother flanked by handwritten cookbooks, busily making notes and murmuring a sort of tribal incantation containing such terms as Aunt Anne's Corn Fritters, Cousin Charlotte's Corn Pudding, Grandmother's Chowder,

Seraphina's Pancakes . . . casserole . . . omelet . . . Amanda's Smothered Chicken.

"This should be set to music," Sally suggested, for August is not only the corn season in Appleyard Center. It is also the season when the Music School makes Roland Hill resonant. Roland Hill once had an Institute of Arts and Letters, but after a while it was decided that one type of genius was enough. Mrs. Appleyard has a strange untutored liking for music and a great affection for mus'cians. She says that if the different nationalities in the United Nations co-operated the way musicians from different nations do in a symphony orchestra, all our political problems would be solved. Suppose the first cellist doesn't like the second flute. He doesn't play out of tune just to spite him.

Sally said she understood that not all musicians were devoid of egotism.

"Robin Viereck told me a story about two old fiddlers," she said. "One of them said to the other: 'Bill, you tune your A a little mite sharper than mine. Then they'll know there's two of us playing.'"

"That," said her mother, "was just an honest Vermont way of being sure that the customers knew they were getting their money's worth. Only probably most of them were like me and wouldn't know the difference. Patience, I think that chicken needs smothering, and if there's any left we'll make Seraphina's casserole tomorrow. Sally, you'd better come over this evening and bring some people to sing rounds. Cicely's coming, with Alice Richards and Eleanor Davenport and the Hiltons. Read this rule of your Great-aunt Amanda's. Doesn't it sound good?"

Sally read it and announced that she saw only two defects in it. There wouldn't be any left for a casserole and no one could possibly sing after they had eaten it.

"They can sing out of tune," her mother said placidly. "Then we'll know they're all trying."

MENUS

Supper for Singers

Smothered Chicken with Corn *
Green Beans with Croutons and Crisp Bacon
Cheese Biscuits
Soufflé in a Double Boiler *
Foamy Sauce *

Supper for the Family on a Cool Evening

Vermont Cheese Soup with Corn *
Graham Sour Milk Bread *
Peach Upside Down Cake, Vanilla Ice Cream

Dinner for Mountain Climbers Who Had Sandwiches for Lunch

Chicken Pie
Glazed Carrots *
Succotash — Shell Beans and Corn
Lettuce Salad
Raspberries with Cream
Brownies

Smothered Chicken with Corn

For eight:

2 broilers cut into 8 pieces, wing
tips off
4 tablespoons chicken fat
2 cups chicken stock (make this
the day before)

corn cut from 6 large ears of
Golden Bantam
minced parsley
2 tablespoons butter

Put the flour, seasoned as you like it, into a bag. Put in the
pieces of chicken and toss them until they are thoroughly
floured. Melt the chicken fat and the butter in a large frying
pan and cook the pieces of chicken in it, 5 minutes on a side.
Add the chicken stock. (Mrs. Appleyard makes it from the
neck and wing tips simmered with carrot, onion and celery.
She adds any stock left over from boiling fowls. A package or
two of this in the freezer is handy to have, she says). Cover
the pan and let the chicken cook half an hour longer on very
low heat. Turn the heat up, add more stock or water if necessary. Put in the cut corn, and cook till the corn is done, about
15 minutes. Sprinkle with the minced parsley and serve.

Soufflé in a Double Boiler

This is a little less strain on the nerves than an oven-baked
soufflé as it can be left for a short time over hot (not boiling)
water to keep warm if necessary.

4 egg whites
3 tablespoons orange marmalade
(or 3 tablespoons sweetened

apricot pulp, grated rind 1
lemon)
4 tablespoons sugar
grated rind 1 orange

Beat the egg whites until they make stiff peaks but are not dry. Mix sugar, marmalade and rind well together and fold gently into the egg whites. Butter the top of a double boiler. Put in the mixture, cover, and cook for one hour over water that is just boiling.

In the meantime make Foamy Sauce, using the egg yolks. When the time comes to serve it, turn the soufflé out on a serving dish, pour the sauce over it. Mrs. Appleyard likes a few chopped blanched almonds sprinkled over it but this is not necessary.

Foamy Sauce

½ cup butter
1 cup powdered sugar
yolks of 3 eggs and 1 whole egg

2 tablespoons sherry or brandy
or 1 teaspoon vanilla or ½
teaspoon almond

This has to be made at the last minute, but the butter, softened slightly, the sugar and flavoring may be combined beforehand and put in the top of a double boiler. When the time comes to serve it, beat the egg yolks and egg well, add them to the butter and sugar mixture and cook over hot water, beating all the time, until the mixture thickens. It takes only a few minutes.

The great advantage of this sauce is that someone undoubtedly clears the table for you while you are making it. Mrs. Appleyard graciously accepts this service provided it is clearly understood that no plates are stacked before rinsing. A plate that has, for instance, Hollandaise on the bottom as well as the top has an unfortunate effect on this lady's disposition.

Everybody's disposition is pretty good when the sauce is ready.

Vermont Cheese Soup
(FOR A COOL EVENING)

Mrs. Appleyard likes to make this soup with cheese from the neighboring town of Cabot, but she admits that it can be made using real dairy cheese from New York or Wisconsin. She would rather not discuss the topic of processed cheese since the subject has an unfortunate influence on her blood pressure. She simply states, more in anger than in sorrow, that she hopes everyone who likes it has a piece of aerated plaster of Paris bread to eat with it.

She begins her soup by cutting finely:

½ cup celery	½ cup onion
½ cup carrots from the garden	½ cup green pepper

These she cooks gently in ¼ cup butter or chicken fat till the onion is tender and pale gold in color. Then add 2 cups chicken stock and let it simmer.

While the vegetables are cooking she makes this sauce:

6 tablespoons butter	1 quart rich Vermont milk or
6 tablespoons flour	3 cups ordinary milk and 1
salt and pepper to taste	cup cream
1 cup grated cheese	

Melt the butter. Blend in the flour. Reduce heat; blend in the milk and cream. Add cheese and seasonings — salt, pepper, a pinch of mixed herbs. (Mrs. Appleyard doesn't add anything.) The vegetables should not be mushy but slightly crisp so by the time the sauce is ready you may put the two mixtures together into your best Dutch or Swedish enameled iron dish to heat. Stir and serve. *But* in corn season add just before serving a cup of Golden Bantam Corn cut from ears cooked 10 minutes.

Brown bread sandwiches are good with this or a long loaf of French bread cut part way through, spread with garlic butter and heated, or Graham Sour Milk Bread.

Graham Sour Milk Bread

Every now and then Mrs. Appleyard has a yearning for the kind of Graham bread her grandmother used to make. The secret was never written down. Apparently in those times everyone knew how to make it, just as before 1840 everyone knew how to design and build an attractive, comfortable durable house. The houses and the bread were both so simple that it seems to have been assumed that there was no mystery about either worth investigating or recording. Mrs. Appleyard has done little about the houses, merely gritting her teeth and groaning loudly when she sees another innocent structure being covered with imitation brick siding, but she keeps chasing a dream called Grandmother's Graham Bread.

She doesn't expect it to come true and she offers this formula as merely a reasonable facsimile and to make it easier for her own descendants to recapture their grandmother's cooking.

5½ cups Graham flour
¾ cup sugar
3 teaspoons soda
1½ cups molasses
3 cups white flour

1½ teaspoons salt
3 teaspoons baking powder
3 cups sour milk (part cream if
  possible)

Mix and sift dry ingredients. Stir in first the molasses, then the sour milk. Beat well. Put into greased pans, filling them two thirds full and bake for one hour. Start at 375° and when the loaves are well risen, reduce the heat to 350°.

Glazed Carrots

Carrots pulled out of the garden and cooked within half an hour are a very different item from the blasé vegetable, homesick for California or Texas, sulking in a ventilated plastic bag, that is commonly found in our larders. They are good cut into matchstick pieces and eaten raw, good grated raw with onions and cabbage as salad, good sliced paper thin and sautéed in butter and then simmered in water, especially good, Mrs. Appleyard thinks, glazed. She allows two small carrots for each person.

12 small carrots
1 cup hot water
3 tablespoons light brown sugar
1 teaspoon lemon juice

1 onion, minced
3 tablespoons butter
¼ teaspoon nutmeg
2 tablespoons chopped mint

salt to taste

Scrub the carrots, slice them. Sauté them and the onion in the butter. Add the water and sugar, cover, simmer 10 minutes. Uncover and cook 10 to 15 minutes longer. Add the lemon juice, nutmeg, salt if you like it. By this time they should be nicely glazed. Add the mint (or substitute parsley or chopped chives) and serve. Maple syrup or honey may be substituted for the brown sugar. Serves six.

Appointment with Orion

Moon-viewing, Cicely reported to her mother and sister one temperate August evening, is much esteemed among the Japanese. Congenial groups of people meet at certain well-favored spots to watch the moon rise. They take along special foods such as hot rice wine, bean curd, pickled radishes . . .

"A most aesthetic sort of picnic," said Mrs. Appleyard, who was stretched out on her red and white quilt, entertaining her daughters at an informal soirée. "Shall we greet the harvest moon with pumpkin pie and new cider?"

"I wasn't thinking so much of saluting the moon in this fashion. Have you had your appointment with Orion yet?"

Cicely referred to Mrs. Appleyard's well-known fondness for getting up in the black crispness of late August nights in order to see Orion haul himself over the eastern horizon for the first time since he vanished in the west the previous spring.

"Well, no," said her mother. "I've been sleeping particularly well lately. But it is just about time for him to appear."

"I challenge you to Orion-viewing, then," said Cicely. "The loser has to bring suitable refreshments to the winner's house."

"No matter what the hour?" Mrs. Appleyard gave a slight moan.

"No matter what the hour," said Cicely firmly. "The one who sees Orion first will telephone to the other, and the loser will then turn up as soon as possible with the appropriate picnic materials."

"I'm leaving at the end of the week," said Sally hastily. She had come over from Roland Hill for a brief holiday from the music school. "Please don't include me in your riotous goings-on. I am sure the night air would not agree with what ails me. I might even sneeze." As Sally often sneezed thirty or forty times when she got started, this was no mean threat.

"We wouldn't dream of exposing you to a sneeze. Anyway, no one should come who doesn't want to. It would spoil the single-minded rapture of the viewers." Cicely uncoiled herself from the small red chair and prepared to depart. She is not one of those who say "I must go" and then hover for half an hour on the doorstep.

"You don't suppose the ringing of the telephone about 3 A.M.

will dislocate the neighborhood?" asked Mrs. Appleyard. "Otherwise I accept your challenge. Cheesecake, perhaps, at thirty paces?"

"Aline Pocock is the only one who will lift her receiver. She told me once she never had time to listen in during the day, but at night she just couldn't resist those long-distance rings. It will certainly give her something to ponder if she hears that Orion has come to town."

Cicely was at the door now. "Just the right sort of night," she added. "I had better get right home. I don't want to be caught without suitable star-viewing materials."

It was not that night, however, but one several evenings later that the telephone by Cicely's bed began its insistent five-beat ring. She struggled up out of sleep to hear her mother's quietly triumphal tones announcing: "The password is Orion."

No one on the party line could possibly have had time to hear this one-sided conversation, Cicely thought, as she struggled into a skirt and sweater, slipped on her sandals and went to the kitchen to pick up the picnic basket which had stood ready for star-viewing since the evening the challenge had been issued. It was the same tea basket that had accompanied the Bradshaws and the Appleyards on their tour around England in the late 30's. They would not need the spirit lamp, but Cicely filled the Thermos with a spiced fruit punch made with a mild tea base, to be served hot. In the sandwich box she put star-shaped cookies of rich, buttery shortbread and larger star-shaped sandwiches of her own version of Anadama bread filled with cream cheese, chives from her kitchen doorstep and a little grated carrot. There were a couple of pieces of preserved ginger in a twist of silver foil to complete the menu.

By the time Cicely had driven from Birch Hill to her mother's house at Appleyard Center Mrs. Appleyard was out on the porch in her ancient camel's-hair dressing gown. The light was on in the summer kitchen and a small fire was whispering in the Glenwood heater.

"You were quick," said Mrs. Appleyard as she greeted her daughter. "I didn't expect you for five minutes at least. See, our friend has pulled himself head and shoulders above the sugarplace." The slow beat of late cicadas blended with the steady roar of water over Mrs. Appleyard's dam in the pasture brook. Cicely went in to heat the spiced tea and came out again with one of her mother's bird-of-paradise painted trays set with Wedgwood.

"I wish I had a *sake* bottle and little white cups," she said. "You will have to imagine that this is rice wine. I didn't have time to pickle any radishes either."

They sat on the porch for nearly an hour, sipping, talking, nibbling and watching, till the stars began to fade in the first gray light of dawn, and the birds began to stir in the syringa bushes. With the first light wind of the day Cicely began to sneeze.

"I hope I am not allergic to Orion," she managed to say as she rummaged for a Kleenex. "Sally was most prophetic."

"Leave everything and go right home," said her mother hospitably. "I'll see you next year."

MENUS FOR STAR-VIEWING

Cicely's
Hot Spiced Fruit Punch * (D.M.)
Shortbread

Cream Cheese and Chives Sandwiches on Anadama Bread *
Preserved Ginger

Mrs. Appleyard's
Hot Sanka in a Thermos
Thin Scalded Johnny Cake *
Watercress Sandwiches *
Madeleines, Soft Chocolate Frosting *

Hot Spiced Fruit Punch (D.M.)

Boil 5 minutes: 1 teaspoon allspice
2 cups sugar   Add 4 rounded teaspoons tea
2 cups water   12 whole cloves
            2-inch stick of cinnamon

Cover. Let stand ten minutes. Strain. Add: 1½ cups orange
juice, ¾ cup lemon juice, 4 quarts water. Heat and serve.
Serves twelve.

Cicely's Anadama Bread

½ cup yellow corn meal   ½ cup molasses
2 cups boiling water   1 yeast cake
1 teaspoon salt   ½ cup lukewarm water
3 tablespoons lard or bacon fat 1 teaspoon sugar
            5 cups sifted flour

Sprinkle the cornmeal slowly into the rapidly boiling water;
cook 5 minutes, stirring all the time. Add salt, shortening, molasses; cool to lukewarm. Dissolve yeast and sugar in lukewarm

water. Add 2 cups of the flour and beat well. Add the rest of the flour or enough to make a stiff dough. Knead well; let it rise till double in size. Shape two loaves, let rise again and bake at 375°. This bread has an unusual flavor and is good eaten plain or with some sort of cheese.

Thin Scalded Johnny Cake

1 cup corn meal, yellow or white
1 cup boiling water — more if needed
2 tablespoons butter

extra butter, about 2 tablespoons
salt to taste
Crisco for greasing pans

Light the oven — 475°. Put the corn meal, butter and the salt into a bowl. Bring it close to your rapidly boiling water. It should be as hot as possible when it strikes the meal. Pour the water over the meal a little at a time, returning the saucepan of water to the fire after each addition. When the butter has melted and the meal has absorbed all the water it will take, put small lumps of the batter on a greased baking sheet and spread them out as thin as you can. Use a broad round-ended knife or a spatula for this and dip it into hot water from time to time. Put a dot of butter in the middle of each cake. Bake until they are brown — about 10 minutes. It is perhaps unnecessary to say that when Mrs. Appleyard looks at them at the end of 5 minutes and finds that they do not look buttery enough, she adds some more. Remove the cakes from the sheet with a spatula as soon as they are done. Immediately. You may break some but such manavelins make agreeable eating. They are best when served hot but they are good cold too and will keep crisp for some time in a closed tin box. They can always be reheated briefly but there are not usually enough left to have this problem arise.

Mrs. Appleyard does not plan to stop and reheat them when she goes constellation-viewing at dawn next year.

Watercress Sandwiches

It must be a great surprise to watercress, Mrs. Appleyard thinks, to find itself one minute growing where Venetia Hopkins' spring runs into her brook and ten minutes later being suddenly made into sandwiches and seasoned with garlic and horseradish. Then, because there was some left, being sharp-frozen in her deep freeze, remaining inert until she prudently thawed them out one evening she thought Orion might be planning an early morning visit. What a peaceful pastoral life this innocent vegetation lived until Mrs. Appleyard found out it was there.

Unluckily for the watercress, there had been a food sale and there was a lot of homemade bread on hand that responded pleasantly to being sliced thin. There was Green Mayonnaise (p. 73) which had been made in the electric blender with 2 cloves of garlic and a dash of horseradish added to it. Also there was sweet butter soft enough to spread. Mrs. Appleyard cuts the cress up with scissors and mixes it with the mayonnaise.

She says you can make the sandwiches very satisfactorily even out of watercress that did not grow among mint and for-get-me-nots at the edge of a brook that runs past seven elms with orioles in them. Sadly we admit that this is probably true.

Madeleines

4 eggs	½ cup butter, melted
1 cup sugar, sifted	1 teaspoon vanilla
1 cup cake flour	1 teaspoon baking powder
powdered sugar, or whatever frosting you like	

Mrs. Appleyard had forgotten all about madeleines until she saw an unusual cake pan among Venetia Hopkins' baking tins.

"What is this wonderful heavy pan that seems to have sea shells pressed into it?" she asked. Venetia said it was a madeleine pan, from France.

"You know — the cake Proust dipped in his tea," she added.

"May I make some?" Mrs. Appleyard asked. "Then we can dunk them in our tea and perhaps pretty soon we'll remember enough fascinating circumstances so we'll each write a seven-volume classic."

Venetia supplied suitable encouragement to this project and Mrs. Appleyard got a copy of her own cookbook off the shelf —it was standing, she noticed proudly, right next to Escoffier — and went to work.

"It says here that they are easy to make," she reported confidently, for she had a childlike trust in printed words, even her own, especially after she had corrected and improved them. She did just what the book said. She dusted the pans lightly with flour. She lit the oven — 400°. She melted the butter but did not let it boil. She sifted the flour, measured it, then sifted it with the baking powder three times more. She sifted the sugar, beat the eggs well, and beat the sugar into them. Then she added the melted butter and beat it into the batter with the vanilla. Last of all she stirred in the flour. She filled the pans half full of batter, set them in the oven and baked the cakes until they sprang back when touched in the middle, about 15 minutes. There were two dozen.

She frosted some and sprinkled the others with powdered sugar. These were the ones she and Venetia dipped in their tea that afternoon. Perhaps fortunately, no literary trances in seven volumes have followed this experience.

Can there be something wrong with the rule?

Venetia says they tasted all right but perhaps some secret ingredient was lacking. If anyone can supply its name Mrs. Appleyard will be most grateful and promises not to publish it in her revised edition, but just to write it in the margin of her own copy. She uses a rather faint tired pencil. How does she always happen to have one — and an unco-operative pen — on hand? Well, that's her secret.

Soft Chocolate Frosting

1 teaspoon instant coffee, dissolved in 1 teaspoon hot water
1 square Baker's Chocolate
1 egg, beaten
1 tablespoon butter, creamed

1 teaspoon vanilla
1½ tablespoons thick Vermont cream
2 cups confectioners' sugar, sifted

Add the chocolate to the coffee and cook over hot water until the chocolate is melted. Beat the egg and stir the melted chocolate into it. Add the softened butter and beat in the sugar gradually. Beat in the cream and the vanilla. Spread on the cakes — they should be cool. Decorate with pecan halves or scatter chopped walnut meats over them.

September

Goodbye to a House

ONE OF THE most unusual occasions that Cicely and Mrs. Appleyard have ever attended was a farewell party for a house. It occurred early in September, at the season when those who have spent the summer in rented houses are suddenly persuaded that their lives will be incomplete unless they own a century-old Cape-Cod-Vermont-style farmhouse with superb view and inadequate water, like all the rest of the summer colony. (Winter residents have traded view for water in a spirit of necessitous compromise, though some more fortunate, like Cicely and Geoffrey Toussaint, are blessed with both.)

Barbara and Frank Larned were most notably infected that summer with the need to link their fates with that of Appleyard Center. They were handy with maps and found their way along the web of back roads with enviable skill. Cicely suggested for them Louis Lombard's faded yellow house and foaming trout brook, but somehow, Bar said regretfully, it did not speak to them. The murmur of the brook could not overcome the small sad voice of a house in shadows, sturdy and straight though it was. Perhaps too many people had been lonely there.

It had not been necessary, therefore, to explain to the Larneds that on Saturday nights this particular house was the unwilling target of high-spirited drivers trying to get home from Saffords' Barn Dance, and that quite often one or more cars did not make the curve by the bridge and landed in Louis' dooryard, requiring chains, shovels and occasionally bandages and sheriffs.

The relations of houses with people are as complex as those of human beings with other human beings. The Larneds found for themselves a house which spoke a language they understood and it was love at first sight. But, alas, someone else had found the beloved beautiful, a Frenchwoman (from Paris, France, said Roger, as usual the fount of information and misinformation, distinguished in this way, no doubt, from Paris, Maine), who was going to raise cats, chickens and canaries and live there all the year round. She was variously described as a widow-woman and as a wife whose husband traveled a good deal. Time would tell.

The house was the old Bass place, part of the Bass family for more than a hundred years. It hurt Cranston and Lily to the quick to have to sell it, but sell it they must, for it had stood empty for three years and they could only come for an occasional weekend. Cranston could farm no longer and they had to live in a village near work for Lily — she was a fine teacher. As for Cranston's sister, Sara — it was understood that she did not care for the idea at all, and probably would not come again unless they kept the grove of birches that startled the eye each time it came into view.

Sara had always reminded Cicely and Mrs. Appleyard of Emily Dickinson. She was not only a poet, she was poetry itself, a flame in a tiny lamp. Ferns were her friends; she talked the language of birds readily, more shyly and hesitantly that of human beings, so that she took refuge in music and in reading when she was not out walking through the birches, or testing one of the Bass farm sunsets against some inner standard.

The Bass house and its setting spoke loud and clear to the Larneds. There was even the perfect place for a studio-workshop for Frank in the shape of a little old schoolhouse just across the road. They kept going back to the isolated hilltop and its widespread mountain prospect with a wistfulness which appealed greatly to the Bass family, who said frankly that they would have much preferred it if the Larneds could have had the house. Oh, they liked Marissa Peckham well enough, but she was different somehow; the Larneds were much more their kind of folks. Still, Mrs. Peckham had claimed the house first.

Cicely, as real estate agent, a role she occasionally adopted for the fun of it, though she generally described herself as more of an anti-real estate agent, was somewhat involved in the proceedings. Thus it came about that she and Mrs. Appleyard were climbing a steep stretch of abandoned road one sunny quiet afternoon early in September, their goal the last appearance of the Bass farm as such.

The Larneds had already arrived when Cicely and her mother came up the last almost perpendicular slope. So had Mrs. Peckham, a bright-eyed dark-haired woman who looked far too slender to survive a Vermont winter all alone in a big house four miles from the village and with no close neighbors. As the Larneds had been to Paris, France, they were able to converse with their triumphant rival about their affection for her native city.

In a minute or two the Basses appeared with materials for a tea which could certainly be called High. For the last time Cranston brought in wood from the shed and Lily made a fire in the polished black stove. The old kettle hissed and hummed. Cicely noticed that like the Appleyards they kept marbles in it to keep the hard water from encrusting it too deeply. You could hear them roll when Lily lifted it to fill the painted earthenware teapot that Mrs. Appleyard had admired for some years.

On the round walnut table was spread a fringed damask cloth; pink luster cups were set out with thin silver spoons beside them. There were plates of chicken sandwiches made with fine-grained white bread. There was a special apricot preserve with a mysterious flavor. Finger lengths of fruit cake, moist with fruit, starred with nuts, lay on a Sandwich glass plate. A many-layered, maple-frosted cake stood beside it. Hot toasted and buttered Montpelier crackers came in relays from the wood stove to serve as base for the apricot preserve.

After the teapot had been filled and emptied several times and the guests could hold no more, Mrs. Bass asked each one to choose something from the house as a remembrance. Mrs. Appleyard, too ladylike to ask for the painted teapot, chose a pair of carved walnut brackets. Cicely asked for the round blue-spotted covered butter dish. The Larneds cherished a plaster of Paris cat with an Egyptian smile. To Mrs. Peckham the Basses left all kinds of furniture, including a large number of beds.

"Perhaps she is going to have other guests than those in feathers and fur," suggested Cicely as she and Mrs. Appleyard and the Larneds strolled along the firm grass-centered road for a last look at the ghostly stems of the birches.

"I prophesy that she won't last out the first winter," said Mrs. Appleyard. "The cats will eat the canaries, she will eat the chickens, and solitude will eat her."

Time would tell.

MENU FOR A FAREWELL TEA

Chicken Sandwiches on Homemade Bread *
Montpelier Crackers Toasted and Buttered
Apricot Preserve
Fruit Cake
Maple Layer Cake *
Tea

Bread (W.H.)

A generation brought up more and more on bread made of plaster of Paris, old absorbent cotton and almost edible sponges has duly revolted and makes its own bread. Cicely notes that almost as many men of her acquaintance are skilled breadmakers as women. She has extracted the secret of his success from the best baker (amateur) that she knows. Herewith his directions. He says:

I make this with an electric mixer, but I've done it on occasion without; doesn't seem to make much difference.

For two pound and a half loaves:

Dissolve one or two envelopes of dry yeast (two to make it faster) in two cups of lukewarm water.

Add enough dry-milk powder (varies according to the brand) to make a pint of milk. Mix it until it dissolves. Add two tablespoons of margarine or butter. Add an egg. Then two tablespoons of sugar, one tablespoon of salt and four tablespoons of honey. If you've kept the mixer going, you can then start adding flour, otherwise get this all mixed first.

Use from six to seven and a half cups of King Arthur unbleached all-purpose flour. With the mixer you can put in about three cups of it before the batter starts to climb the beaters; then I take out one beater and continue to mix at low speed plus a rubber scraper. The last cup or so of flour you have to knead by hand.

The dough tends to be sticky (honey and egg) but don't make the mistake of adding too much flour in an attempt to overcome this, or you'll get too dry a loaf. Kneading — ten to fifteen minutes — will get rid of some but not all of the stickiness.

Let the bread rise in a bowl greased with Crisco or something similar, over a pan with hot water in it, out of drafts. (The cover can be a dish towel.) It will double in size in anywhere from an hour to three or so, depending on such things as warmth, humidity, the collusion of the planets, and your own impatience. When it is about twice its original size, punch it down, fold the edges to the middle, and turn the lump over. Let it rise again. It's a lot quicker the second time — usually.

Then make loaves. There are lots of ways. A simple one is to divide the dough into four parts, knead each one into a ball, and put two such balls into each greased loaf pan. More complicated (but some people say it makes a smoother loaf) is to flatten it out, fold it in thirds, flatten that out, fold it in thirds and so on. When I get the loaves made, I puncture them all over the top with a fork, which is supposed to let out air bubbles (maybe it does) and makes a nice pattern. Then the loaves have to rise till they're double in size (an hour or so), again covered and in a warm place.

I preheat the oven to 375°, put in the bread and set the timer for ten minutes. When it buzzes, I cut the thermostat down to 325° and set the timer for half an hour. Look at the bread sometime around the twenty to thirty minute mark and if it seems to be too brown, turn the thermostat to 300°.

Take the bread out, and out of the pans. Cool it on a wire rack. While it's still hot (just as soon as you get it on the rack) brush the tops of the loaves with Mazola or melted butter.

That's the story. One note: probably because of the honey, this bread keeps very well, especially if it's airtight-wrapped in wax paper and kept in the refrigerator.

Cicely can vouch that this makes a fine-grained sweet-tasting loaf, that cuts well, toasts well and tastes — well, like bread.

Apricots

Mrs. Appleyard has not yet focused her crystal ball so that she has been able to report just what is it that makes the Bass apricot preserve so particularly excellent — Cicely suspects lemon peel and a little almond extract are involved — but she has some suggestions about how to use apricots. It became necessary for her to be ingenious about apricots because she had fallen absent-mindedly into the habit of saying to herself in the super-market: "I ought to have some apricots in the house," and putting a package into her wire basket. When she was confronted one day with five packages on her cupboard shelf, the idea dawned on her gradually that she had better use some of them. These were some of the ways:

Apricot Sauce

An electric blender is a great help in making apricots into pulp. Use dried apricots, the tenderized kind (Mrs. Appleyard hates the word and all its sisters, cousins, aunts and brothers-in-law!). Follow the directions on the package but do not drain off the water. The blender works better with water. When the apricots are tender, put them into the blender. Do not put too many in at a time but do them in rather small batches, using part of the liquid each time and running the blender about 2 minutes. You now have a fine bowl of pulp to use as you like.

For Apricot Sauce, take:

1 cup apricot pulp   juice and grated rind of half a
½ cup sugar   lemon

Stir the sugar with the warm apricot pulp until it is thoroughly dissolved. Add the lemon juice and the rind. Taste it and add more sugar if you like it very sweet. Serve it as sauce for orange sherbet or vanilla ice cream.

Apricot Soufflé

3 tablespoons butter	1 tablespoon butter extra
1 cup milk, scalded	¼ cup flour
⅓ cup sugar	½ cup apricot pulp
a little vanilla or almond extract, or both, or neither	5 eggs, separated

Melt the butter, turn off the heat and rub in the flour. Light the oven: 350°. Put the extra tablespoon of butter in a heat-proof glass dish and set it into a pan of warm water in the oven. Stir the scalded milk into the butter and flour mixture. Do it slowly, stirring all the time so there are no lumps. (If there are, you must strain them out.) Cool the mixture slightly. Add the apricot pulp mixed with the sugar and flavoring. Beat the egg yolks thick and lemon-colored and mix in thoroughly. Beat the egg whites stiff and dry. Fold gently into the mixture. Mrs. Appleyard does it with what Venetia Hopkins calls the Spendthrift's Enemy — a rubber scraper. She uses it also to heap the mixture lightly in the warmed dish.

Put the dish back in the pan of water. You should put a rack or the top of a Crisco can under the soufflé. Bake it at 350° for 20 minutes on the lowest shelf of the oven. Then reduce the heat to 325° and transfer the dish to the upper shelf. You may breathe while you do this, but not hard. The soufflé is done when it no longer hisses when you listen to it. This will take another 25 minutes. Perhaps a little more. As in the case of every other soufflé, the customers must wait for it, not the other way. They usually seem perfectly willing, Mrs. Appleyard says.

Apricot Soufflé in the Double Boiler

For a change Mrs. Appleyard sometimes makes the less nerve-racking kind of soufflé like the orange kind (p. 148). She uses apricot pulp sweetened and flavored with almond instead of the orange marmalade.

Apricot Rolls

At the time there was a large bowl of apricot pulp in Mrs. Appleyard's refrigerator she received from one of her favorite philosophers a package containing sugary apricot-flavored rolls apparently constructed of thin sheets of apricot. They came from Charleston, S.C., where the philosopher, who just to make things confusing is delightfully feminine in the French marquise style and is called Sheldon Beauregard, says they are called Peach Leather. By the time Mrs. Appleyard got this information and an invitation to join the Pythagorean Society, she had already made a pretty good facsimile. This is how.

    1 package (11 ounces) dried quick-cooking apricots
    1 cup sugar
    extra sugar for rolling — about a cup

Cover the apricots with water and cook them until they are quite soft, 15 to 20 minutes. Either drain most of the water off and put them through the meat grinder, using the finest cutter, or make them into pulp in the electric blender (p. 170). What you want is a fine, smooth apricot pulp, not too wet, not too dry. Light the oven — 450°. Add the cup of sugar to the apricot pulp. Put the mixture into an aluminum saucepan and stir it over a low flame until the sugar is melted. Now spread it as thin as possible on ungreased cooky sheets or in very shallow cooky pans. Half the amount given will cover two 10 x 14 sheets. It should be spread so thin that you should see the metal through it as if you were looking through colored cellophane. When it is as thin as you can possibly get it, put the sheets into the oven. After 5 minutes reverse their positions in the oven, upper one on the lower shelf, lower one on the upper shelf, turn off the heat and leave them to dry overnight.

In the morning the pulp should be dry enough to roll. If it is not dry enough so that it can be lifted from the pan with a spatula and hold its shape, light the oven again for a few minutes, turn it off and leave the pans for another half hour. The pulp should feel just slightly tacky. It should be a little less sticky than Scotch tape and not much thicker.

Now score it neatly with your spatula into 2 x 3 inch pieces. Sprinkle it all over with sugar. Put some more sugar on a shallow plate. Spread wax paper over the table before you begin. This is a sit-down job. Mrs. Appleyard, never fond of doing one thing at a time if two are convenient, places herself in front of a window where she can see blue jays battling over the smörgåsbord she has prepared for their entertainment and hers.

With the spatula remove the apricot oblongs and lay them one at a time, unsugared side down, in the plate of sugar. Roll them as tightly as you can in the sugar. Have a candy box lined with wax paper ready. Pack the rolls in neatly, sprinkling sugar between the layers and separating the layers with wax paper.

If you like apricots, Mrs. Appleyard is pretty sure you will like these.

Prune Tortoiseshell

No sooner had Mrs. Appleyard conquered the apricot rolls than it occurred to her that prunes might be treated in the same way. So she took:

1 pound quick-cooking prunes	½ cup sugar
juice and thin peel of half a lemon	more sugar for rolling, about 1 cup

Simmer the prunes until it is easy to remove the pits — about half an hour. Then use exactly the same method as with the apricot roll-ups in the preceding recipe. You may roll them around blanched almonds or toasted almonds, Mrs. Appleyard says. She adds that she sees no reason why strawberry pulp shouldn't be treated the same way. After all, even if the strawberry season was over, there were still strawberries in the freezer. And wonderful peaches from Virginia in the market.

"You've done enough," Patience Barlow said gently but firmly.

She was washing the pans and it seems Mrs. Appleyard had left one of them in the oven too long. It was covered with a substance that could have been made into a tortoiseshell cigarette box without not much more trouble than it took to get it off the pan. It would have been easy to cut the whole thing up with a hacksaw, or anyway with an acetylene torch.

It was Patience who gave the confection its name.

Mrs. Appleyard sensibly decided to use the peaches in ice cream or pandowdy or shortcake. It was weeks before she rolled anything more complicated than a sugar cooky.

Strawberry Roll-Ups

However, Mrs. Appleyard could not forget her curiosity about strawberries. She did not sacrifice her own Appleyard Center strawberries but used:

1 12-ounce box of frozen straw-   sugar for rolling, about ¾ cup
  berries

She thawed the strawberries, poured them into the electric blender and ran it until they were thoroughly puréed. The resulting pulp was rather moister than the apricot or the prune pulp so she poured it into a shallow aluminum pan. It would have run off a cooky sheet. She distributed it evenly simply by tipping the pan from side to side, put the pan into the oven at 450° and turned it off after 5 minutes. In the morning the pulp was still too sticky to handle so she lighted the oven again at 250° and turned it off after 5 minutes. In about half an hour the pulp was tacky enough but not too sticky. She marked it into 2 x 3 inch oblongs and got them off the pans.

During this period she was heard to murmur a few rhetorical questions such as: "Why did I get mixed up in such an affair again?"

However, she felt much better pleased with the world when she had sugared, rolled and packed them and had tried one that was slightly frayed around the edges. She served them for dessert the next day with cream cheese, broken up with a fork and with thick Vermont cream stirred into it. About that time, Cicely reports, Mrs. Appleyard was heard telling her friends that it really was no trouble at all.

Ho! Hum!

Stirabout Maple Cake (L.P.)

1 egg	1 cup soft maple sugar
1 cup sour cream	½ teaspoon soda
2 cups flour	1 teaspoon cinnamon
¼ teaspoon nutmeg	½ teaspoon salt

Light the oven — 375°. Sift the flour four times with the dry ingredients. Beat the egg. Beat in the maple sugar. Stir in the sour cream and the flour mixture. Bake in two greased layer cake pans until the cake shrinks from the edges and springs back when pressed with the finger — about 20 minutes.

Frosting

Into a measuring cup stir together ⅓ cup sugar and ⅔ cup maple syrup. Cook this slowly to soft-ball stage. Use a candy thermometer and don't turn your back or it will be all over the stove. Mrs. Appleyard christened her new gas range in this sweet and expensive way. "What gas range is this?" asked Cicely as she unthinkingly typed these words. "Did you win it in a contest?" "Oh," said her mother airily. "I'm thinking of entering the Sillsbury Baking Contest. The least you can get is a new stove. Or perhaps Our Book will be so successful . . . " "This is the first I've heard of writing up stoves before they are installed," said Cicely. But she let the sentence stand. She is a dutiful daughter, and besides there was a strong likelihood that by the time the book was printed, a splendid gas range would indeed grace the Summer Kitchen. Cicely had watched her mother operate for some years and knew that her lightest word could bring about astonishing results though not always just those she had planned on.

Back to the frosting, which is about to boil over. Beat 2 egg whites well. Pour on the cooked syrup gradually and keep beating until the frosting is cool. If the frosting strikes you as too sweet add a pinch of salt to your beaten egg whites. Use this on top of the cake and between the layers. Decorate with pecan halves, or with butternuts.

Labor Day Dance

THE LABOR DAY WEEKEND is a complicated one in Apple-yard Center, what with the theatrical producers dashing up from Broadway for a last breath of fresh air before sealing themselves hermetically in theaters and smoke-filled rooms, the Music School geniuses getting ready for Carnegie Hall and children needing new shoes and haircuts before school starts. No motion picture camera can do justice to its various activities.

Mrs. Appleyard gives some of the haircuts and pays the customers according to the quantity of hair involved and how still they sit. Tommy Bradshaw received fifty cents for almost enough hair to stuff a small pillow. Extravagantly Mrs. Apple-yard swept it off the porch and into the asters, where, she states, chipping sparrows will find it next year if they need it.

Hair is an interesting substance, she says. It varies not only in color but in diameter, texture, curliness and how it grows. She has had ample opportunity to observe these variations since she cut both her sons' hair until they went to college, and that of any friends they brought home. She did not pay that generation so she feels it is only fair that she should occasionally make use of the information thus acquired in one of the mystery stories she writes.

She has been working lately on an item called "Death of a Dancer." Inspired perhaps by this title, she decided to add to the Labor Day complications by giving a dance. She chose the ballroom of the old tavern at Roland Hill for this festivity, and enlisted her daughters' co-operation. Mrs. Appleyard has a peculiarity. She likes to give parties but hates to give invitations. Her bargain with her daughters stipulated that she would engage the musicians, put new candles in the sconces, supply punch, oatmeal cookies and similar innocent refreshments, while they would invite about forty people. This arrangement was perfectly harmonious and resulted in sixty-six guests answering to the scrape of Robin Viereck's fiddle.

He, of course, was the most important guest, and Mrs. Appleyard went in person to invite him. Music is only a sideline with Robin. His real interest is goats. Mrs. Appleyard was welcomed by a delegation of Nubians of distinguished lineage. For all she knows they may be descendants of the original goats that people had to tell the sheep from. Robin gets sixteen quarts of milk from them, he told her.

"Where do you sell it?" Mrs. Appleyard asked.

"Well, I don't have much luck selling it," Robin said. "I drink what I can and the rest I run through again. It gets real strengthening after a while. If I'd only begun drinking goats' milk about seventy-eight years ago I'd have been pretty rugged by now. Probably."

Evidently the goats throve on their own milk. That is, if activity means anything. When Mrs. Appleyard came out there were five Nubians on her new car: one on the hood, one on the luggage compartment, and two on the roof. With the towering white cloud-mountains in the sky, the cold blue mountains below, the rocky hillside, the green lake and Robin's brown cottage tucked under the hill, the effect was charmingly Swiss.

"Lucky I keep them manicured," observed their owner. "Just start the motor — they'll jump."

Mrs. Appleyard was relieved to learn that her car would not be scarred or permanently decorated in the style of a Swiss alp. She started the motor. There was a noise of dancing hooves. Lithe sleek brown forms filled the air around her. A buck reared up at the window and tried to get in the front seat with her.

"He likes you," Robin said.

Indifferent to this compliment, Mrs. Appleyard raised the window hastily and drove off.

She stopped at the store for her mail. As she came out she was affectionately greeted by the Nubians. They had strolled down for their mail too, she supposed. They stepped on her feet and seemed delighted to see her. So did a large hissing gander and his long-necked family.

"Goats and ganders adored her," murmured Mrs. Appleyard, making her way through this crowd of admirers. She was carrying three gallons of ice cream — vanilla, butter pecan and banana almond. Or perhaps they just like ice cream, she thought honestly. I wonder if they'll come to the party.

Mrs. Appleyard's pastoral popularity was ephemeral. Not a

Nubian appeared in the ballroom of the Tavern. The first footsteps were those of her grandchildren, who came early to polish the floor. They scattered something called Spangles out of a box and slid over it screaming happily until the place was like a skating rink. The room was lighted by a pink glow from the west and a yellow moon from the east. It is a long room with small-paned windows along three walls and a fireplace at each end. Old chairs and benches in soft yellow line the gray and green walls, on which hang old portraits and prints and tin candle sconces.

Mrs. Appleyard had put new candles in the sconces, an exercise during which she usually calls down a short blessing upon the memory of Thomas Alva Edison. Candlelight is picturesque, and, if you are over twenty-three, merciful. Still, after you have dealt with forty-two candleholders of different types, it is restful to know that there is an invention by which you can turn a switch and have a light come on that neither smokes nor drips wax upon the Steinway.

The dance followed the standard pattern for such festivities. At first it was a problem to get anyone on the floor. Later the question was how to find enough space on it for all the dancers. Distinguished guests with high I.Q.s and several degrees stumbled and confused their left hands with their right, while small children executed complex maneuvers with skill and style. Mrs. Appleyard was much pleased to be led out upon the sea of glass by a young gentlemen about three fourths her height, half her weight and one sixth her age.

"Did you have a good dance with Robert?" Tommy Bradshaw asked her.

"Yes, indeed, he dances very well," his grandmother said.

"I thought you'd like it. I told him to ask you," Tommy said.

Mrs. Appleyard has heard of brothers getting partners for their sisters, but this is the first example she knows of a grandson saving his grandmother from a wallflower's fate. She now turned her attention to the refreshments. One of the problems is to be sure that hollow-legged boys do not eat up everything before the less enterprising grownups appear. Mrs. Appleyard has a partial solution for this difficulty. She supplies at least five kinds of ice cream from the freezer and encourages the younger set to make their own cones in any wild combination of flavors that fancy dictates.

This is simply a delaying action. It does not mean that the younger guests will be indifferent to oatmeal lace cookies and fudge cake. It is just hurling the wolves something from the sleigh to distract them for a while.

"Ah," said Anstiss Baxter as she was offered a plate of meringues, "this is one of the items where to get one you have to show your birth certificate to prove you are over twenty-one."

This seemed like an excellent idea to Mrs. Appleyard. She plans to put it into practice another evening.

MENU FOR LIGHT REFRESHMENTS
DURING INTERMISSION

Ice Cream Bar *
Labor Day Punch (p. 54)
Oatmeal Cookies ‡
Walnut Cake *
Angel Cake (p. 33)
Brownies ‡
Fruit Cake ‡

Ice-Cream Bar

If she really had a bar it might be better, Mrs. Appleyard thinks, but as it would have to be twenty feet long to accommodate the ice-cream eaters perhaps it is better to keep on with the somewhat battered oval table in the Winter Kitchen. On this she puts four kinds of ice cream — vanilla, chocolate, maple walnut and black raspberry, for instance — the kinds they tell her at the Co-op are the popular favorites of the moment. She also puts out bowls of crushed strawberries or raspberries, chocolate sauce, maple syrup, chopped nuts. The possible combinations are difficult to estimate mathematically and of a kind calculated to make anyone over fifteen years old turn pale. The ice-cream fanciers, however, are not even slightly jaded by this simple type of hors d'oeuvre but are soon ready to get to work on any oatmeal cookies overlooked by their seniors and then dance quadrilles with renewed vigor.

Walnut Cake (L.P.)
(No Flour)

1 pound walnuts weighed in the shell	6 eggs, separated
	1 cup powdered sugar
1 teaspoon baking powder	

Shell the walnuts and grind the meats. Add the baking powder. Light the oven — 375°. Beat the egg yolks, beat in the sugar, stir in the nuts. Whip the whites until they are stiff but not too dry and fold them into the mixture. Bake in two layers until the cakes shrink from the pans and spring back in the middle when touched. Cool and just before serving put whipped cream or mocha cream filling (p. 18) in between or on top. Or serve it cut in squares from a square pan, with whipped cream. Plan a light breakfast.

Ladies' Luncheon

THE INSTITUTION of the Ladies' Luncheon is one of the most pleasant in Appleyard Center and environs. This is partly because it takes place, as a rule, during the latter half of September, at a time when a mellow glow hangs over landscape and inhabitants alike: a mental glow arising from having cheated the frost of the last of the tomatoes and zinnias, completed another summer without disaster, said goodbye to the summer people fondly yet firmly; an interlude of relaxed peace before the first onset of winter.

Partly too because an assemblage of ladies has a flavor all its own and gives scope for a kind of social commentary not quite suited to mixed gatherings. So when Venetia Hopkins gave out invitations for a luncheon party in the third week of September, the Appleyard ladies knew they could look forward to elegant food in superior company.

Cicely was the last to arrive at the lunch party, driving up with a flourish and clatter in the 1931 Model A Ford that made her feel more like a fresh girl of twenty than the riper woman of forty that she really was. As she entered Venetia's comfortable kitchen she realized, however, that she could keep the illusion of youth for the afternoon, for none of the other ladies was under sixty, and some would not see eighty again.

All shades of gray hair were represented and all kinds of permanents, some more obviously homemade than others. Venetia and most of the rest had got out their tweeds for the occasion. In Vermont there are only about two weeks out of the year when it is comfortable to wear a tweed suit. This was the September tweed week; the other had come in early May. The Duncan sisters, however, had worn their gayest legislature silks.

"I don't know," said Daisy, settling her crocheted stole, "why I came out in this flimsy dress and a straw hat and dirty gloves." As always she looked as bright and neat as a small chickadee poised over sunflower seeds on a winter feeding tray. Fiona had her customary air of an efficient countess. Beatrice as usual reminded one of Einstein. Geoffrey Toussaint had a theory that all old ladies look like either Einstein or Thomas Jefferson, and Beatrice certainly bore him out.

"I often get real mean," she was murmuring. "Oh, you should just see how mean I am when I'm at home. Of course we all get that way sometimes. I wish I could go to Boston this winter and get a little room and just paint and paint and not have a soul tell me what to do." Cicely liked this picture of Beatrice imitating Gauguin in a Vermontish and feminine style. She wondered what the artistic bohemians of Boston would make of Beatrice's innocently fateful paintings.

The guests were helping themselves to Shrimp Jambalaya,

which bubbled in a huge frying pan on the shiny black stove, and to the hot rolls that had come from the Covered-Dish Supper at Appleyard Center, having spent a quiet two months in Venetia's freezer. They were Maria Flint's best and they tasted perhaps a little better even than when they were first baked. The freezer, brimming with summer souvenirs, had also yielded mushrooms picked in early August in Solon Marsh's back pasture. Watercress for the salad had been gathered by Venetia from her brook, and her special dressing was now soaking delicately the avocado slices, tomato quarters and mild onion rings that shared the enormous wooden salad bowl with late lettuce from her garden.

A happy luncheon silence had fallen over the company, and Cicely, who could always eat with greater expedition than anyone else, was the first to lift her head and take a long look at her fellow guests. This was strictly county society, she thought. Angela Thirkell should be here. As often happened she heard her mother begin to describe, across the room, how she had actually met Angela Thirkell during the past winter at a literary tea in Boston. This sort of extraverbal communication between Mrs. Appleyard and her eldest daughter might have become embarrassing over the years if they had had anything they wished desperately to conceal from each other.

Marietta Cushman from over the mountain seemed at first glance quite conventional. Yet she was actually one of the liveliest and most adventurous of the ladies, willing to patronize unpopular though worthy projects, which thus became acceptable in her village. She was a cousin of the Duncans, and both sides were pleased to acknowledge the relationship.

Cicely suspected that she herself was probably related to Marietta too. When she had first come to live in Appleyard

Center she had enjoyed discovering a new cousin each week and telling the children as they roamed around the countryside that such and such a house was inhabited by relations; but it was an old story by now, and it seemed more entertaining now to sit by, knowing you were connected with two thirds of the people in the room while neither side was in any particular hurry to claim the relationship.

"Are you very philosophical, Cicely?" a soft insistent voice asked at her elbow. It was fragile, earnest Cathie Winston, dim-sighted and poetic. What she might mean by her question bewildered Cicely for a moment, her thoughts having flown at once to Plato and Aristotle and beyond them to the pre-Socratics much mentioned by her sister Sally Roland on her last visit to Appleyard Center. Cicely held in considerable respect anyone on intimate terms with these philosophical heroes. However, it appeared that Cathie meant merely to inquire whether Cicely minded when her children screamed at her and called her names, and was reassured when Cicely told her she did not mind these assaults in the least and was able to give as good as she got.

It was time for dessert: Venetia's traditional plate of brownies, dark and melting, and a white cake dripping with icing and patterned with nuts, as well as pistachio ice cream and chocolate sauce.

"I'm thinking of selling my house," announced Lois Prince in ringing tones from across the room. "I'm tired of Mountain View, tired to death of it — I'm going far, far away."

"Oh, where?" asked Cicely with interest, for she was one of those who feels the departure of each train or bus a mortal wound if she is not aboard, and she was at once imagining Lois striding through a Turkish bazaar or banqueting on a Tahiti beach.

"Well," said Lois pensively. "I had thought of Great Barrington."

Cicely moved into the kitchen again, yielding her place on the comfortable yellow sofa to Mrs. Appleyard. A second cup of coffee was most welcome and she drank it sitting next to Rachel Benson who had exiled herself to the end of the kitchen table for spilling salad dressing down the front of her new blouse.

In spite of the misplaced condiments she looked fashionable and feminine as she remarked to Venetia: "Yes, I like to have something planned ahead. I've got twenty-five feet more of stone wall to lay, come spring. I've done fifty this summer. Any time I miss the Garden Club back in Ashtabula I go out and lay a couple of feet. I just *love* slate stone. The only trouble is that when Caspar Prout comes to fix the underpinning where it gets heaved by the frost he tries to borrow slate off my wall. That I will *not* have. He painted the ceiling of my porch blue, too, when I was home visiting mother in Ashtabula. I never could stand blue."

Cicely gazed at the pretty blue blouse which was now decorated with a trail of French dressing (plenty of garlic). She hoped Rachel would get a new blouse of a color she liked better and that she would stick to her guns, or rather her slates. They would make handy weapons if it came to a showdown.

The party was beginning to break up now. Mrs. Appleyard was collecting her mink scarf and arranging the heads and tails so that they lay in the proper directions. With her gray-blue suit she was wearing what is called in the local accounts of weddings matching accessories of cherry red — neat red calf shoes, a red sailor hat and a handsome red handbag that Cicely had given her last Christmas.

Cicely took great pride in her mother's chic appearance. It

had taken a good deal of frankly critical handwork on the part of Mrs. Appleyard's children to achieve this result. There was still a slight tendency for her slips to show, but perhaps in time this too would be corrected. Meanwhile they were extremely pretty slips. Cicely hoped that her own daughters would take an equal interest in seeing that she was well turned out. Till they reached the age of the cold eye and the tactful gibe she was quite happy in her unmatched stockings, slightly scuffed shoes and a five-year-old suit.

Jason Teasdale had already knocked discreetly at the kitchen door to let his wife know that he was waiting for her. He had strict ideas about when parties should be over and was one of the world's promptest men. When he said he would come at three o'clock he would always appear at two forty-five.

What a lot of women there were, Cicely thought, who had never learned to drive cars, and quite a few of them were able to press their husbands into service as chauffeurs when the husbands would much rather be out planting apple trees or investigating the habits of muskrats. Such women were notably competent, strong-minded and eloquent.

Cicely admired the skill with which these ladies managed their spouses, but she doubted if she could ever achieve the same effect. Tom was away so often on his architectural affairs that she had had to learn to thaw pipes, put on storm windows, shovel driveways and respond to the thousand and one emergencies that beset the country dweller in the electric age. It was too late in life for her to achieve fragility.

In another century, Tom told her, she would undoubtedly have been driving a covered wagon to California, repelling attacks of Sioux and Shoshone and shooting buffalo. Having driven twice across the continent near one of the emigrant routs and having seen the tracks in the Utah desert worn by the heavy wagons, having crossed Donner Pass and brooded on the disaster of the Donner Party, Cicely often wondered whether she would have had the courage to keep her children alive on a diet of ... but this line of thought was surely not complimentary to Venetia's delicious luncheon menu.

With the departure of the Countess of Overbrook (Vera Teasdale) on the arm of the Earl (his other arm managing with the deftness of long practice her deck chair, her lapboard and her special cushion) the party swiftly disintegrated until only Cicely was left to assist Venetia in putting away the remains of the meal, and, greatest of pleasures, to talk over the party, which she duly pronounced a success against all Venetia's hesitations about the casserole, her worries over the salad dressing and lamentations as to the height of the layer cake.

Cicely took all these protestations for what they were worth. Not everyone, she knew, purred blandly over the success of a meal in a mood of self-deserved congratulation, as she and her mother often did. Some needed reassurance, so Cicely dealt it out honestly and generously, and at last got Venetia to agree that, yes, everyone did seem to have had a good time.

MENU FOR A LADIES' LUNCHEON

For six:

Paella *
Parker House Rolls (p. 122)
Marinated Mushrooms *
Watercress, Avocado, Tomato, Onion Ring Salad
Brownies ‡
Walnut Cake (p. 182)

Paella (V.H.)

For six:

1 fowl, boiled and the meat removed from the bones
2 tablespoons fat from the fowl
4 cups stock from the fowl
2 small onions, minced
meat from 4 pork chops
½ pound pepperoni sausage, skinned and sliced
½ pound rice, washed in 12 changes of water
2 packages of frozen peas or 3 cups fresh peas

½ cup white wine
seasonings: a bit of bay leaf, 4 cloves, salt to taste, pepper from the grinder, ¼ teaspoon powdered saffron, 1 tablespoon chopped parsley
1 can pimentos (4 pimentos), cut in strips
1 pound lobster meat, fresh if possible (or frozen)

This must be made in a large frying pan and brought to the table in the pan.

Cut the pork into small cubes and fry it in the chicken fat till it is tender. Add the onion and cook till it is pale yellow. Add the stock, the white wine, the seasonings (except saffron and parsley) and, when the stock boils, the rice. Add the chicken and cook gently till the rice is done — about 20 minutes. In the meantime, cook the peas. When the rice and peas are ready, sprinkle saffron over the rice and stir it in. Now over the top arrange the pieces of lobster meat, the peas, pimentos and sausage in a handsome red and green design. Sprinkle in the parsley. Cover the pan just long enough to heat the lobster through, and bring to the table amid shrieks of admiration. There are probably as many ways of making this as there are cooks and you might find clams, shrimps, oysters, artichokes or bacon lurking in it here and there. Mrs. Appleyard can

vouch for everyone wanting a second round of the above
version.

Marinated Mushrooms

Peel and trim 1 pound of small mushrooms. Boil them in
water to cover, slightly salted and with the juice of a lemon
added. Boil in another saucepan: 1 cup vinegar, half a clove of
garlic, 1 bay leaf, a pinch of thyme, 1 teaspoon salt, some
freshly ground pepper and 2 spring onions, finely cut. Cool
this mixture and take out the garlic. Then add ¾ cup olive
oil. Drain the mushrooms well and put them in a deep bowl.
Pour the dressing over them and let them stand in it several
hours until well chilled and blended. Serve them in a shallow
dish, sprinkled with chopped parsley and basil, finely cut.

October

The Bake-Off

IT ALL BEGAN with the Surprise Cheesecake. This confection, made according to Mrs. Appleyard's favorite formula, surprised that lady more than anyone. It happened that it was her turn to entertain the croquet players. Naturally she tried to plan the perfect menu. She wanted it to be simple, in a sinister and exotic way, fitting for guests about to engage in this ferocious sport. Yet, she felt, the meal should end with something soothing enough to discourage actual mayhem upon the greensward.

Ice cream seemed too innocent, not to mention a little too

cool for Indian summer. She toyed briefly with the idea of Baked Alaska, as suiting the bitter-sweet, hot-and-cool character of this her favorite season. The oven, however, had recently developed a morose habit of refusing to light and then changing its mind suddenly. Only yesterday it had blown Mrs. Appleyard, that thistledown cook, across the Summer Kitchen and part way into the woodshed. Certainly she would expose neither herself nor a fragile meringue to such temperamental behavior.

"We'll have cheesecake," she told Patience Barlow, handing her a list of ingredients suitable for a safari by the Swiss Family Robinson. "I think we have everything on hand," she added, and got to work on a project concerning Boeuf à la Mode.

By the time she had put the beef away to jelly, the cheesecake emerged from the oven, wreathed in flaky pastry, quivering slightly in the center, brown but not too brown — a handsome sight. As Mrs. Appleyard consumed her sanitary lunch of cold boiled rice garnished with prunes, she wished she could eat about a square foot of cheesecake. Of course she restrained herself. When dessert time came that evening, she was delighted to have several of her guests state that they had never tasted anything like it and ask for the rule. Balls were clicking furiously on the lawn for the final round before she got round to trying it herself.

She had never tasted anything like it either!

This was no ordinary cheesecake, suave, sweet and serene. This was cheesecake with a tang. It had a faint suggestion of Welsh rabbit or of cheese fondue, only with the cool and creamy consistency of cheesecake. It was to ordinary cheesecake, she decided, as Berlioz is to Schubert.

The embattled croquet players, Mrs. Appleyard reflected as

she cut herself another slice, were not the only ones who would
like the rule. She'd like it herself . . .

The mystery was explained when she went to get cream for
the coffee. The bowl of cottage cheese that ought to have been
in the cheesecake was right next to the cream. The fine chunk
of Vermont Cheddar, destined for Cheese Soufflé the next day,
had vanished. Mrs. Appleyard leaped immediately and correctly
to a conclusion about where it was: in the cheesecake, of course,
imparting that subtle and racy flavor.

"Nonsense," she said the next morning when Patience Barlow expressed sorrow at the transposition of cheeses, "this is
one of the discoveries of the age. We'll enter it in the Sillsbury
Bake-off and you shall go to New York, stay at the Waldorf,
and win a new gas stove and $25,000. Or anyway a stove," she
added prudently, for after all she is a New Englander and therefore subject to these attacks of moderation.

Patience Barlow is even more restrained. She refused to be
dazzled by Mrs. Appleyard's lyric description of the new
stove. She admitted they could use it, *but* . . .

"I guess you'd better be the one to go," she said firmly.

So that was how Mrs. Appleyard happened to find herself
on television, baking cheesecake in a peach-colored stove in a
Louis Seize ballroom. There she was in the pale blue smock
Patience had made for her. She had on her comfortable shoes,
the blue suede ones. She was glad she had bought new laces
for them. The extra knots in the old ones had become rather
tired looking.

Crystal chandeliers shot spectrums above her head as she
deftly blended cheese and cream. She was slightly hampered
in her motions by a large spray of white and purple orchids.
A young man had just pinned them to her shoulder. He looked

like Cary Grant, only smaller, and he had on a pale giraffe-colored linen suit with an orange cummerbund.

"This program is being broadcast in compatible color," he told Mrs. Appleyard. "You should have cherries and chopped chives on your cake."

"What's compatible about that?" Mrs. Appleyard asked, but he had already slithered off and was mounting camellias on a black velvet shoulder. Its owner was baking mushroom short-cake. There were two orchestras competing with the roar of the Waring Blendors. One was playing the part of Berlioz's *Romeo and Juliet* where the young Capulets are going home from the ball. The other was weaving through Schubert's "Trout Quintet." Mrs. Appleyard thought they rather slurred some nuances by eating cucumber sandwiches as they played.

"But I suppose they know best," she said generously.

She put her cake in the oven and joined the croquet game. The wickets, she noticed, were made of spun sugar. Her smallest granddaughter was crawling through one and eating another. This reminded Mrs. Appleyard of another croquet game some-how. Except that there were flamingos in that one and hedge-hogs for balls, which was obviously foolish. These balls were made of popover batter.

"Just sign the receipt," said the Cary Grant young man in the heavy black spectacles, handing her $25,000 in chocolate wrapped in gold, a jade green stove neatly set with emeralds, and a chinchilla apron. "The tax will be $26,000. You can pay as you leave."

Was Mrs. Appleyard glad to wake up and find that it was a Phantom Bake-off? Will she ever get a new gas stove? (The emerald-studded one would have done so nicely for the Princess to make curry on at her next visit.) Will Patience Barlow try

Mrs. Appleyard's idea for Dream of Mushroom Shortcake?
Tune in any time, and if you hear the answers, please let
Mrs. Appleyard know.

Surprise Cheesecake

Enough Two-Thousand-Layer pastry to line a 10-inch pie
plate.

½ package Lorna Doone short-   ¼ cup melted butter
bread rolled into fine crumbs

Or — if you have no pastry on hand — use a 9-inch spring
form mold and roll fine:

2 packages Lorna Doones and   1 tablespoon Spry for greasing
use ¾ cup melted butter   mold

For the cheesecake mixture:

½ cup sugar   4 eggs
1½ teaspoons grated lemon rind   3 tablespoons lemon juice
½ cup flour   1½ pounds soft Cheddar cheese
2 8-ounce packages cream   not too mild
cheese   1 cup heavy cream
4 ounces blanched almonds

Line the plate with pastry or mix the shortbread crumbs with
melted butter. Save out ¾ cup of the crumbs to sprinkle on top of
the cake. Grease the spring form mold with Spry and press the
rest of the crumb mixture on the bottom and sides of the mold.

Now light the oven — 325°. In the electric mixer beat the eggs at speed 3 until light. Beat in sugar until mixture is creamy, then lemon juice and rind. Then add Cheddar cheese, rather coarsely grated, cream cheese in small lumps. Keep beating and add the flour gradually. Increase speed to 6 (whipping cream) and beat 2 minutes. Add cream. Beat until smooth — about 1 minute. Do not overbeat. Pour into lined plate or mold. Sprinkle with crumb mixture. Decorate with blanched almonds. Bake 1 hour at 325°; turn off the oven and let stand 1 hour longer. Chill well. Serves twelve.

Try and Try Again

CICELY was always glad that it was to the members of the Book Club that she had decided to serve Croque-bouches. She did have better sense, she hoped, than to try something both new and difficult on a group less generous in spirit. She had seen the recipe for this rare treat in the Sunday magazine section of a reputable newspaper. Its difficulty appeared to lie chiefly in the construction of the pyramid of glazed and filled cream puffs on their base of pastry. The recipes for the various parts did not seem impossible by themselves.

Book Club fell on alternate Thursdays. Perhaps it was partly because Cicely had to produce the program for the evening as well as the refreshments that her attention wandered during the preparation of her *pièce de résistance*. Somehow Sophocles and cream puffs did not mix; Oedipus and puff pastry were antithetical. Thoughts on Greek drama kept drifting between her and the candy thermometer.

She began the Croque-bouches early Thursday morning, intending to set the parts away to be assembled after supper, since the recipe said that it should be served quite soon after it was made. Lucky that she did, for trouble began at once with the pastry base. Cicely had achieved a light hand with yeast dough, but she had never reached the mastery of pastry that her mother and sister possessed. Try as she would, the mixture stuck to the board, the rolling pin and to her, until in frustration she gave the whole grimy mess to Camilla for doll pies and substituted a pastry mix, usually reliable and guaranteed to resist the most brutal treatment.

The resulting pastry base was acceptable, though scarcely of the required thousand-layer variety, and Cicely started on the cream puffs. Some slavish streak made her follow the magazine's recipe for them rather than her own familiar and successful one. She was still doting enough to believe that a newspaper which printed the truth would also have infallible recipes. The low-lying pancakes which greeted her when she opened the oven door were enough to shake the most sanguine soul. When the Bendix with a grinding rattle and groan burned out its main bearing shortly thereafter, Cicely knew that this was one of Those Days.

Grimly she called the plumber and kicked the pile of wash she had planned on finishing that afternoon behind the stove. A second batch of cream puffs were just high enough to admit a knife. This used up all the eggs, since four were reserved for the pastry cream. Hens had recently grown weary of laying, and the store was all out of them till the morning.

She should have known better, Cicely told herself, than to try the pastry cream at all, after this multiple warning. It curdled, and then when she tried to coax it back with more cream it refused to thicken. Fortunately she had a vanilla pudding on the emergency shelf, and by some miracle did not scorch it. After whipped cream had been beaten into it, it looked quite respectable, but of course there would be no mistaking that heavily synthetic flavor of vanilla.

Now for the glaze. The cooking of the sugar syrup coincided with the plumber's arrival — Cicely is one of the few people in Appleyard Center who can send for a plumber and get him the same day; naturally she takes this as a personal tribute — and in the course of visiting with Mr. Harmon in the cellar she let the syrup crystallize when it should have remained golden and syrupy. Of course it is much more important to be on good terms with your plumber than to keep an eye on the candy thermometer, and Mr. Harmon always had a tale or two to tell that she did not like to miss. Thus it was that they were both in the cellar when the boiler sprang a large leak.

Cicely always considered this one of the most fortunate parts of the whole day. Handy though she had become with tools, she could not have staunched so large a leak with chewing gum or electrician's tape. She abandoned the making of syrup till later in the day and gave heed to Mr. Harmon while he explained how long it would take to get the necessary parts from Burlington for the Bendix. The boiler he could replace tomorrow; meanwhile there would be no hot water.

By now Cicely knew that she should never have embarked on so vainglorious a creation as the Croque-bouches, led astray by the fetching name and impressive picture. She made a package angel cake of the sort that is almost impossible to tell from a homemade one, except that it is usually better, and called it a day at the cookstove. The prospect of no hot water for washing up did not encourage her to continue her experiments, so she cooked the crystallized syrup over with water to thin it; not a success, she noted mentally, but it could hardly matter now.

The children's supper was early and sketchy, served from the stove to save dishes. Blessing the invention of television as she settled them in front of the set, Cicely attacked the final assembly of the Croque-bouches. It was worse than she had imagined. The cream puffs had sunk even lower since she took them from the oven and it was all she could do to find room for any of the filling. When she piled them on the pastry base they should ideally have risen like a veritable Matterhorn of crispness; instead they lay limply upon one another like old sponges and what filling had got in promptly ran out. The glaze was thin and weak instead of golden and robust. Finally she had to transfer the whole creation to a bowl instead of the glass platter she had planned to use.

The ladies of the Appleyard Center Book Club were friends indeed that night. They ate the Croque-bouches and even pronounced it good. Cicely had exhibited it more as an object lesson for herself than as part of the refreshments. Happily the rest of the evening made her feel, as always, that she loved the human race and particularly that part of it which had chosen to live within five miles or so of Appleyard Center. Why this was she could never quite say, except that the half-dozen women, some older, some younger than she, who met together during the winter to read poetry or plays, somehow gave each other stimulus, affection and support of a kind that rarely existed between two friends, let alone six or seven.

By the time Cicely had had her second cup of coffee she could feel at one with the world again, not a storm-tossed, star-crossed particle kicked around by the elements, mocked by machines and materials. As a sign that she felt better she took another piece of angel cake. Perhaps after all she would not write that tart letter canceling her subscription to the *Sunday Clarion*.

Cicely feels somewhat bitter still about the Croque-bouches and pettishly refuses to give the rule. Mrs Appleyard has kindly supplied a rule for Cream Puffs that is not stylish, but reliable.

Cream Puffs

No one has ever improved on the classic rule for cream puff batter. Mrs. Appleyard hasn't tried to do so and doesn't intend to, but she has a suggestion about adapting it to modern equipment that she hopes may save you some energy — as it has her. The rule for the batter is, as usual:

½ cup butter	1 cup boiling water
4 eggs	1 cup flour

Bring the water to the boiling point in a quart saucepan. Add the butter immediately. As soon as the mixture boils again dump in the flour all at once. Remove the pan from the heat and stir hard until the mixture leaves the sides of the pan.

There is always a moment when it seems as if it were never going to do this, but be brave — it will. Light the oven — 375°. Now transfer the batter to the large bowl of the electric mixer. Set the dial at the speed for creaming butter. Break the eggs in one at a time, beating half a minute after each addition and scraping the batter in toward the beaters carefully with a rubber scraper, known to Mrs. Appleyard as the Miser's Delight — one of the few items that used to cost ten cents and still does. Beat at least one minute after the last egg is in. Put the batter by spoonfuls on a large cooky sheet. If you have a steady hand and eye you may be able to get a neatly spaced design of twelve puffs. Mrs. Appleyard, to her shame be it said, often ends up with nine, some larger than others. Bake them for half an hour. Then turn the pan so they will bake evenly, reduce the heat to 325°, and bake until there are no iridescent bubbles left on them — about half an hour longer. If you have any doubts, remove the smallest and least symmetrical one and see what happens. If it is not done, it will soon collapse like a weary popover. If it holds its shape, the others can come out too.

The ways of filling them, Mrs. Appleyard generously leaves you to decide for yourself. Her customers usually seem pretty well satisfied with vanilla ice cream inside and chocolate sauce outside. However, just to keep her public mentally active, she has been known to include such substances as crabmeat or lobster salad. She had a caviar and sour cream phase too, small puffs for this. She says her Pâté Maison (p. 213) tastes pretty good in them too.

While she is on the subject of labor-saving in the cream puff zone, she will just mention, her face reddening slightly, that her attempt to make the batter in the electric blender resulted in a catastrophe of considerable proportions. She still bears a scar from contact with one of the knives — so does the Spendthrift's Enemy, the rubber scraper. This was incurred in the line of duty while extricating a certain amount of a very adhesive mixture. The puffs turned out to be an exercise of making molehills out of mountains but the bluejays were crazy about the result. So never mind!

MENUS FOR A READING CIRCLE

Angel Cake with Raspberry Cream*
Coffee

Apple Pie with Ice Cream*
Tea or Sanka

Oatmeal Shortbread*
Hot Chocolate

Orange Bread*
Fruit Punch

Shortbread*
Chocolate Crisps*

Cicely's friends are not only sympathetic and supporting in time of disaster, sympathetic and jubilant in time of triumph. They are good cooks too. The menus to accompany literary evenings were contributed by them. She leaves the reader to decide whether the angel cake or the apple pie goes better with Chekhov, the oatmeal shortbread or the orange nutbread with Sophocles. All she does is to warn you that coffee on top of *Hamlet* can lead to a thoroughly sleepless night.

Angel Cake with Raspberry Cream (E.B.F.)

1 Angel Food Cake (see p. 33), sliced horizontally in thirds. Dissolve 1 package plain gelatin in ¼ cup cold water. Bring to a boil the juice of 2 packages frozen raspberries and add to the dissolved gelatin. Put the berries in the mixture, place in refrigerator and allow to stiffen. Whip ½ pint heavy cream and fold into the gelatin mixture. Spread the mixture between the layers and on top and sides of the cake. Serve right away.

Apple Pie with Ice Cream (E.C.H.)

Pastry: For a 9-pie dish

2 cups Gold Medal sifted flour
1 teaspoon salt
⅔ cup and 2 tablespoons shortening — Fluffo if you like a golden look to the pastry, otherwise Crisco
4 tablespoons water

Filling:

7 cups sliced apples — 1 cup sugar and 1 teaspoon cin-
    Wealthys are good   namon

Dot with 1½ tablespoons butter and bake the pie at 425° for 50–60 minutes. Serve with a scoop of ice cream on each piece.

Oatmeal Shortbread (S.P.M.)

3½ cups oatmeal
⅔ cup sugar
¼ cup flour

1¼ sticks butter or margarine
½ teaspoon salt
1 teaspoon vanilla

Work all ingredients together in a bowl. Have 9 x 13 x 2 pan thoroughly floured and buttered. Put mixture into pan and press down firmly. Bake in moderate oven (325°) about 30 minutes or till lightly browned. Remove from oven and cool about 10 minutes. Cut into squares.

Scotch Shortbread (P.B.H.)

½ cup confectioners' sugar
1 cup butter
2 cups sifted bread flour

¼ teaspoon salt
¼ teaspoon baking powder

Cream the butter, add the sugar and blend thoroughly. Mix salt and baking powder with flour, sift again. Blend with the creamed mixture by hand till thoroughly mixed. Roll ⅓

inch thick. Prick all over with a fork. Bake on a greased sheet 20 minutes at 375° or until delicately brown. If you have them available, press the mixture into small Swedish molds, prick and bake.

Chocolate Crisps (P.B.H.)

1 package Nestlé semi-sweet chocolate bits or your favorite brand

2 cups Kelloggs' K cereal (full of protein)

Melt chocolate in top of double boiler. Remove from the stove, add K cereal. Stir in carefully. Shape teaspoonfuls on wax paper. Chill at least half an hour. You might add ½ teaspoonful instant coffee for the sake of variety.

Orange Bread (E.H.D.)

3 cups sifted flour
1½ cups sugar
3 teaspoons baking powder

3 tablespoons butter
1 egg
1 cup milk

1 cup ground orange rind

Simmer the orange rind in water to cover. When tender, remove white part and grind the remainder in food chopper. Make the batter in the usual way, but let it stand ½ hour before putting into oven. Bake in a loaf pan at 350° for 1 hour and 20 minutes.

Last Party of the Season

It is a common delusion on the part of summer visitors to Appleyard Center that when they go away life stops. Actually, of course, from the point of view of the winter residents, life begins. It refreshes their spirits to know that they are no longer referred to as "natives" by — if one judges by those brightly flowered skirts and shirts, those fluttering scarves, those clanking beads and bracelets — peasants from Lower Scythia.

Neatly and fashionably dressed in their basic black dresses, their charcoal-gray suits, Vermonters carry on their own lives. They raise money for the Red Cross and the March of Dimes. They buy shining cars, larger and handsomer cars than the out-of-state vehicles they have been pulling out of ditches all summer.

They stop pasteurizing milk and begin reading books from the Book Wagon. They organize Chicken Pie Suppers and variety shows for the benefit of the Hot Lunch Program. They drive fifty miles over frozen ruts, through sleet and slush, and down ice-glazed hills to listen to the Vermont Symphony. A good many of them go to Florida, where they take a kindly interest in quaint native customs of which they will have good stories to tell when they get back, come cowslip time.

Mrs. Appleyard knows all these things, for she sometimes invades the winter privacy of the hills. She realizes that when she goes away she takes with her just her own life, not anyone else's. Still, as she hides the key in the usual place, sees Roger Willard taking in the mailbox, hears the gate click behind her, looks back at the weathered blue shutters so neatly closed, even she feels that parties are over. Naturally she is wrong.

Before she has crossed the Connecticut, the mice have given a series of small exclusive dances in her miniature rooms. In the Salem dining room, the one with the lacquer cabinets and the Chinese rug, they have knocked over three Queen Anne chairs, a candlestand and a silver bowl of fruit. In the Vermont room there is pewter on the floor. There would be cider too if there had been a quarter of a teaspoonful in the cider jug.

Refreshments consisting of flowers from the garden outside the French windows were served in the living room of the Great Porcupine Island house. As usual one domestically inclined mouse has tried to take up knitting again. She has already been into Mrs. Appleyard's pantry to pick out a suitable ice-cream cone for a bassinette. She has no better luck than usual at finishing that baby blanket and the ball of wool — as usual — is under the maple bed in the room with the stenciled walls.

MENUS FOR FROSTY EVENINGS

As Mrs. Appleyard does not have access to the mouse family's private manuscript cookbooks and file of appropriate menus she offers some of those she uses herself at this season.

Broiled Flounder Fillets* with Lemon Butter*
Broiled Tomatoes*
Shell Beans and Mushrooms*
Popovers
Apricot Almond Trifle*

Pâté Casa Blanca*   Melba Toast
Risotto*
Tomato Sauce*
Onion Relish*
Autumn Garden Salad
Apple Pie with a Tang*
Coffee   Red Wine

Porterhouse Steak, Planked*
Mashed Potatoes
Broiled Tomatoes (p. 211) and Mushrooms
Fried Onions
Yorkshire Pudding*
Prunes in Jelly*
Brownies‡

Broiled Flounder Fillets

Allow 2 fillets for each person. Squeeze lemon juice over them, paint them with a pastry brush with melted butter. Do this on both sides and fold them neatly. Do not roll them: they should lie flat. Lay them in a shallow buttered pan and slide it under the broiler. Broil on both sides until they are delicately brown, about 3 minutes on each side, but this will depend on the thickness of the fillets, distance from the flame and your broiler. They should not dry out, but be thoroughly cooked, yet tender. Remove to a hot platter and spread over them the following sauce. For six fillets:

Lemon Butter

¼ cup butter	1 teaspoon chopped parsley
grated rind of 1 lemon	1 teaspoon chopped chives
2 tablespoons lemon juice	

1 teaspoonful of your favorite fresh herbs, minced (Mrs. Appleyard likes small amounts of chervil, tarragon, thyme and basil, but choose your own)

Cream the butter, add the lemon juice, rind and herbs. Mix well. Do not melt it. Let the hot fish do that.

Broiled Tomatoes

After the first frost has come it is a pretty sight to see the window sills of white houses decorated with ripening tomatoes rescued the night before.

Now there is the problem of what to do with them. Small, almost ripe ones are good cut in halves, the ends sliced off so they will rest evenly on the pan and broiled. Make some garlic butter. Combine it with fine bread crumbs. Cover the tomatoes rather thickly with the mixture; dust over some grated cheese. Slide the pan under the broiler and cook till the cheese is melted and the crumbs start to brown.

Shell Beans and Mushrooms

One of the happy coincidences of life in Vermont is that in years when there are mushrooms they appear just about when the shell beans, the ones with the carmine splotches on the pods, are ripe.

For six people allow:

2 cups beans, after shelling	1 tablespoon flour
1 pound mushrooms, caps only	1 cup light cream
1 onion, minced	½ cup mushroom stock
2 tablespoons butter	

Seasonings to taste — Mrs. Appleyard uses a little freshly ground pepper and ¼ teaspoonful nutmeg.

This is better to fix ahead of time as it benefits by standing awhile and blending. Cook the beans until they are almost done, about 25 minutes. Start the onion cooking in the butter slowly, until it is pale yellow. Peel and slice the mushrooms. Put on the stems and skins to simmer in hot water. Add the sliced mushroom to the onion and cook until both are tender. Sprinkle in the flour and seasonings and blend them with the butter. Turn off the heat. Blend the cream in carefully. Pretty soon the beans will be cooked. Add any water left in them to the mushroom stock and cook it down to half a cup. If you have been saving a little beef or chicken stock this is a good place to put it. Add the beans to the mushroom mixture. Add the mushroom stock when it is ready. Set the pan aside. Reheat the mixture just before you serve it.

Apricot Almond Trifle

12 ladyfingers, split
1 cup apricot pulp, sweetened
1 cup sugar
3 eggs
1 teaspoon almond extract

4 ounces almonds, blanched and peeled
1 cup thin cream
2 tablespoons soft butter
2 tablespoons candied fruits, diced

Split the ladyfingers and spread them with the sweetened apricot pulp. Put them in a glass bowl in which you will serve the trifle. Put the blanched and peeled almonds into the electric blender. Add the cream and run the blender until the almonds are finely cut. Add the sugar, eggs, flavoring and run until the mixture begins to thicken. Add the butter in small pieces and run the blender until everything is well blended. The mixture should be like thick custard. Pour it over the ladyfingers and decorate the top with candied fruit. Chill the trifle in the refrigerator for several hours.

Mrs. Appleyard has varied this by arranging apricot rolls (p. 172) in between the ladyfingers and by adding toasted almonds to the top decoration just before serving.

She says that the blender is a convenience, not a necessity. The almonds can of course be chopped by hand and the rest of the mixture may be done simply with an egg beater, or an electric mixer.

Pâté Casa Blanca

It was a bright October day, the kind of day Mrs. Appleyard would have said it would not have been possible to improve. This one, however, was made even more memorable than usual by the gift of some wild ducks. Mrs. Appleyard promptly cooked them according to the method advised by the donor. They were allowed to glance at the fire briefly and only the breasts were eaten. Fortunately the next day was cold, dank and dingy — just the right day to stay indoors and make pâté.

Mrs. Appleyard began by taking the meat off the carcasses and cutting it into small neat cubes. She put the bones, the livers and gizzards on to cook in cold water with a carrot, a branch of celery, two onions, herbs and spices. She says the quantities of the seasonings should not be large but she likes several kinds: small pinches of cinnamon, nutmeg and allspice, three cloves, three *chile tepines*, a minute piece of bayleaf, a very little oregano, rosemary and marjoram. Peppercorns may be added during the last 10 minutes. This simmered for 3 hours, during which time Mrs. Appleyard stenciled a tray she had been planning to restore to life ever since she first noticed it in 1912. Apparently she has some tortoise ancestry back somewhere in her pedigree.

When the tray had progressed to a stage where its original owner might possibly have recognized it, the remaining scraps of meat had fallen from the bones and the broth had cooked down to 2 cups. The stock was chilled. This was the kind of day you could chill anything just by setting it outside on the porch table. While it was cooling, Mrs. Appleyard chopped the scraps of meat, liver, gizzard, two chicken livers she had saved for just such an emergency, and a pound of Colburn's Montpelier sausage meat all together. She also rolled out dry Pepperidge Farm bread into crumbs. Somewhere about this time she remembers eating some lukewarm rice and four prunes.

By this time the stock had jellied and the fat had risen to the top. She skimmed off the fat and carefully coated an oven-proof bread pan with it; then dusted fine crumbs all over the fat. She states that she had a cup and a quarter of crumbs and that they were as fine as sand from the Sahara. Three quarters of a cup of crumbs, the jellied broth and two well-beaten eggs were then added to the meat. Last of all she added a small onion chopped very fine, almost to a pulp, and the cubes of duck, mixing them well into the mixture. She added in a wistful tone that she would have put in truffles if she had any.

She lighted the oven — 250° — put the mixture into the pan, coated the top of it with the remaining ¼ cup of Sahara bread crumbs, dotted it with the rest of the duck fat, covered the dish with chef's foil, and set it on a rack in a pan of hot water in the oven. She baked it 3 hours.

During this period she put her feet up and read a good book. (*The Eustace Diamonds* by Anthony Trollope, in case you were thinking of asking; has no opinion as to whether Trollope would have liked the pâté. Standish Appleyard did and that is endorsement enough.)

"You had better list the ingredients," said that gentleman. "I might feel like making one sometime."

Mrs. Appleyard, delighted with this display of interest, did so:

½ cup cubed duck meat
1 cup minced duck meat, liver, gizzard
1 carrot, 2 onions, 1 branch celery
herbs and spices, your own assortment, small amounts

2 cups jellied stock
2 chicken livers (raw)
1¼ cups fine bread crumbs
2 eggs
1 small onion finely minced or grated

Risotto

There are as many ways of making risotto as there are combinations of things in the icebox. You might, for instance, find:

3 chicken livers	half a can of pimento
a cup of chicken stock	a few mushrooms
half a green pepper	1½ cups cooked rice

Mrs. Appleyard hopes you also have two onions, and some parsley. Start heating the rice in the chicken stock while you mince the onion and slice the pepper, pimento and mushrooms. If you have chicken fat on hand cook the onion in it until it is golden brown, or use butter. Then add the pepper, pimento and mushrooms and cook them until they are tender. If you have a little chicken and a few green beans you may add them to the rice at this point. Now mince the parsley. Add the contents of the frying pan to the rice mixture. Cook the livers in a little more chicken fat or butter. Cut them into small pieces and add them to the rice. Sprinkle the parsley over it before you bring it to the table. The whole process has taken about 15 minutes and the icebox is gratifyingly neat. The risotto will not be correct unless the rice has absorbed the stock so that it is neither wet nor dry — just nicely moist.

Tomato Sauce
(To go with Fish or Meat)

1 pint tomatoes, peeled and chopped, measured after chopping
1 clove of garlic

2 onions, sliced
1 green pepper, minced
2 tablespoons minced chives
salt and pepper to taste

Put the tomatoes, their juice, the onion and the garlic into the electric blender. Run the blender until the tomatoes are well puréed. Strain out the seeds. Add the pepper, chives and seasonings. Serve cold.

Onion Relish (V.H.)

1 medium onion, sliced
grated rind and juice 1 lemon

2 teaspoons sugar
pepper from the grinder

Mix together and let stand one hour before serving. Good with cold meat, hamburg, broiled fish.

Apple Pie with a Tang and Cross Bars

Of course no apple pie is better than the classic kind — light flaky pastry enclosing tart New England apples newly picked, sugar just darkened with cinnamon, nutmeg, 2 cloves, a whisper of grated lemon rind, and a few dots of butter. Still, when there are no apples left and you come across a package in the freezer that says "Dutchess Apples in Syrup" you might like to try this.

She makes the pastry beforehand (p. 93) and puts it into the refrigerator to chill while she is thawing out the apples. Mrs. Appleyard believes this is an illustration of a law of thermodynamics. Something about everything getting to be the same temperature. Naturally such speculations should not keep you, if you have to use apples with their skins on, from peeling, coring and slicing seven or eight of them and poaching them until soft but not mushy in the following syrup:

½ cup sugar
¼ cup water
4 tablespoons maple syrup

Cool slightly and add 1 tablespoon lemon juice, 1 tablespoon orange juice, grated rind of 1 lemon and 1 orange, 1 tablespoon orange cordial. (Mrs. Appleyard makes this by pouring brandy over thin orange peel and adding sugar. You could also get it out of a bottle.)

Now put the seasoned apples into a baking dish and put the crust on in strips. Finish the edge with a ribbon of pastry made by twisting two strips together. Bake at 450° for 15 minutes and then reduce to 350° and bake until the pastry is well browned — about 20 minutes longer.

Porterhouse Steak, Planked

Mrs. Appleyard is the fortunate owner of an oak plank big enough to hold a steak of noble proportions, a wall of mashed potato and a rug of vegetables. However, the plank is not really necessary. The various items can be cooked separately and arranged around any platter large enough to hold them comfortably and leave room for carving the steak. There are also aluminum well-and-tree pans that go right under the broiler and can be set on a larger platter for serving.

However you serve it, it is still steak and should be treated with respect. Mrs. Appleyard does not respect any steak less than two inches thick. There are, of course, different tastes about steak. If you like yours well browned outside and tender, juicy and reddish pink inside, here is how Mrs. Appleyard achieves that purpose whether the steak is planked or merely broiled. She cooks partly by ear. A steak not only looks and smells done but it sounds done, she says. There is a certain vibrant purposeful hiss and fizz from a steak that is ready to eat. Listen for it and train your ear to it.

To keep the juice where it belongs, inside the steak, instead of letting it run out and dry up, Mrs. Appleyard begins by searing it on both sides. The searing time depends somewhat on the size of the steak — that is, its whole area, its thickness, its temperature. For a large steak, one weighing somewhere near three pounds, cool from the refrigerator (not the freezer) she allows two minutes on each side. By the time it is seared on both sides she knows by sight, smell and sound how long the rest of the cooking will take. As she turns it back to the first side she is usually heard to say in her crystal ball tone: "This needs five minutes on the first side and four on the second," or some such occult remark based on a mysterious type of inferential calculus, and then she adds crisply: "Platter ready at seven-five."

In figuring when the steak will be ready to serve she includes the time spent turning it. A clock with a moving second hand is a great help, she says.

The schedule for a 2¾-pound steak will run about like this.

Close to the flame:
 Side A: 2 minutes
 Turning: 1 minute
 Side B: 2 minutes
 Turning: 1 minute
Slightly farther from the flame:
 Side A: 5 minutes
 Turning: 1 minute
 Side B: 4 minutes

 Transfer to platter: 2 minutes
 Total time: 18 minutes

 Please note that Side B will always receive just a little less time than side A. That is because it actually received some cooking from the heated broiler underneath, although it is side A that first faces the flame. If you expose side B as long as side A, your steak will be overcooked. If you get into the habit of listening to it while it cooks you will hear that this is so as well as taste it later.

 This schedule is for any steak. For one to be served on a plank the principle is the same up to the second cooking of side B. At this point you transfer the steak, turning side B uppermost, to your well-oiled plank. Quickly heap fluffy mashed potato around the edge and arrange in between it and the steak mushroom caps dotted with butter, sliced tomatoes already partly cooked and covered with buttered crumbs, little heaps of partly fried onions. This will take at least five minutes and as your steak cannot help losing a little cooking momentum you will probably have to give it five minutes under the broiler instead of four for a plain steak. This would make a five-minute difference in the total time, which would then be 23 minutes instead of 18.

However, since no two steaks are exactly alike, this is only, Mrs. Appleyard says, a slightly more definite guide than any she was ever given. The great thing is to train your ear to know when the steak is done as *you* like it and to be sure that each side gets two turns at the flame. Mrs. Appleyard thinks a steak, either plain or planked, looks handsomest with plenty of crisply curled parsley around it.

Spanish Steak Sauce

Cicely cannot resist putting in her favorite sauce for steak: Melt half a cup of butter in the broiler pan after you cook the steak. Blend 1 tablespoon ketchup, 1 tablespoon paprika, ½ teaspoon mustard and ½ teaspoon sugar in a cup. Add this to the melted butter, also a clove of pricked garlic. As the sauce begins to bubble — you have put the pan on a burner on medium heat — turn down the heat, remove the garlic and add 2 teaspoons vinegar, stir vigorously and remove from the stove at once or it will separate. Serve at once with the steak.

Yorkshire Pudding

Mrs. Appleyard used to think that you couldn't have Yorkshire Pudding unless you had roast beef. Suddenly it dawned on her one wakeful night when she was brooding on various subjects, that this was not necessarily so. Serve it with hamburg, she says: it needs it more than roast beef does and you have your oven free to bake it at just the right temperature. Also she says that you can make it better in the electric blender or the electric mixer than you can by hand. She saves beef fat from a roast or steak or gets a little suet from the butcher and tries it out. This she puts into a nine-inch heavy iron enameled frying pan so that it is half an inch deep. The batter is the traditional one:

1 cup milk	1 cup flour
3 eggs, well beaten	salt to taste

Light the oven — 400°. Add the milk slowly to the flour sifted four times, beating as you do it. Beat the eggs in one at a time. (In the electric blender you dump everything in and whizz! It's done!)

Bake until it is well risen — 15 to 20 minutes. Reduce the heat to 300° and bake 15 minutes longer when it should be light, crisp and a pleasing deep amber in color.

Prunes in Jelly

½ pound quick-cooking prunes	grated rind 1 lemon
¼ pound almonds, blanched	2 cups juice from prunes (hot)
2 envelopes plain gelatin	½ cup cold water
½ cup lemon juice	¼ cup sherry
¼ cup sugar	

Cook the prunes until they are tender and the pits can be easily removed. Substitute a blanched almond for each pit. Arrange the rest of the almonds at the bottom of heat-proof glass custard cups which have been rinsed out with cold water. Soak the gelatin in cold water ten minutes. Add the hot prune juice. It should be almost boiling. If you haven't enough, add boiling water. Stir well. Cool slightly. Add the sugar, lemon juice, rind, and sherry. If you do not care for sherry, substitute orange juice or water. Taste it. Add more sugar if you like it very sweet. Pour a little of the liquid into each mold. Let it cool until it begins to set, then pack in the prunes. Pour in the rest of the liquid. Chill in the refrigerator. Serve with the kind of Vermont cream that is so annoying that you have to get it out of the jar with a spoon.

Variation: Use apricots instead of prunes. Increase the sugar to ⅔ cup. More if you like it very sweet.

The Summer Kitchen

IT'S HIGH TIME," said Mrs. Appleyard rather sternly to her daughter, "that you got your part of this book written."

She was speaking on the telephone to Cicely at the time and as they were a couple of hundred miles apart and it was midnight or thereabouts they were having a comfortable uninterrupted conversation of a sort that was quite impossible at closer quarters or during the day. Anyone who thinks Vermonters are a taciturn race had better try getting the line after the dishes are done any morning in the week.

"I know," said Cicely. "I wish I were a stronger character. I need something to set me off."

A few weeks later Cicely received a firm but kindly note saying that the manuscript for *The Summer Kitchen* should be finished in two weeks' time. As she was due to leave for New York the next morning where she had, in a moment of giddy courage, undertaken to show the city to thirty-one adolescents including, worst folly of all, her own eldest daughter, she was not in a position to write any books that week.

By the time she got home it was May. The sort of controlled chaos usually characteristic of her establishment had got a little out of hand. The caretaking young couple had broiled steaks in the fireplace and dropped them on the new floor along with their cups of coffee — that, at least, was Cicely's archaeological research. Two lambs had been born and one had died. The other had to have its tail removed, a problem handily solved by the use of a cutter for chewing tobacco. Tommy Bradshaw had bought it at an auction three years before, saying that it would come in handy. Cynthia needed a dress for a dance so Cicely spent an evening sewing, winding up with hemming a skirt four yards around. This left her cross-eyed the next day, a poor state for typing.

Carpenters and plumbers drifted in and out, engaged in remodeling the kitchen. Cicely discovered that if she shut herself away upstairs in a quiet room she suffered more interruptions than if she stayed downstairs where she could be easily consulted about the proper position of windows and appliances. Also the children could more easily ask her for something to eat when they got home from school and she could more briskly tell them to go and open a can of soup. During the writing of so elegant a cookbook the meals at Sky Farm consisted largely of hot dogs scorched on the gas burners, brownies, cold cereal, potato chips, popsicles, fudge and raw carrots.

The table on which she wrote was within happy hearing

distance of the television set. Occasionally she would find that she had written Honolulu for Hamburger or fabulous for frying pan as certain voices penetrated the veil of concentration that she was able most of the time to maintain between herself and the real world. On the table curious still-life formations began to collect. Over and under the recipes, carbon paper, filing cards and scraps of yellow paper essential to the book, drifted teddy bears and newspapers, coffee cups and fish hooks, unsorted laundry and report cards, patterns for ballet costumes, unread magazines, unpaid bills, saltines and binoculars.

"If only . . . " Cicely would begin to complain to her hard-hearted co-author. "If only Tommy hadn't had to go to the hospital with mysterious spots, I should have been finished yesterday. I feel like a prisoner."

"Nonsense," said her mother briskly. "You know you prefer it this way. If it wasn't Tommy's spots it would be somebody's tonsils. Have you written about the Covered-Dish Supper yet?"

"Camilla was singing all this morning — 'Come down from your ivory tower — come down from your ivory tower.' What do you suppose she meant?" Cicely asked.

"Don't change the subject," admonished her mother. "I shall be up Saturday so you had better get into high gear. Your work habits are deplorable, but I love you just the same." And she hung up, feeling as usual that there was something faintly vicious about long-distance telephoning.

I will finish on Mother's Day, said Cicely to herself. Sunday is a nice quiet day and I can work all the time. Meanwhile Mrs. Appleyard supplied her with page after page of beautifully illegible manuscript which only the two of them could decipher.

On Sunday Cicely began the day by going to clean the

church. She had forgotten that it was her turn. Then she had to arrange for the sheep to go to be sheared. Next there were cupcakes to be made for the farewell tea for the minister and his wife. She overestimated the size of the pans and all the lids came off, so she stuck them together with frosting and called them filled cookies. Camilla had a nosebleed and came dripping through the hall.

"Go away, you Stone Age woman," she said to Cicely. "You wish I was dead."

It was time to go to choir practice. Bach made her feel better but it didn't get her further on with her typing. The farewell tea went smoothly. There were enough cupcakes without Cicely's. Her daffodils shared in the decorations. She sniffled happily during the speeches. This was one of the days on which she loved everybody. If only . . .

Sunday was going fast. The pile of typed sheets grew higher. Mrs. Appleyard and Venetia Hopkins invited Cicely to supper.

"I can eat or type," she said, "but not both."

She accepted on the grounds that a last consultation was needed. This produced, as she feared, seven more recipes to type out. The manuscript had got into the dangerous stage in which the two authors kept writing in remarks to each other not originally intended for publication.

"This must stop," said Cicely, and she piled her various papers into a cardboard box and went home. A moon as thin as a shaving hung impossibly large above her yellow house, looking like a Hollywood-scale sign for a New Moon Café.

As she typed the last words of the last section of the last chapter the telephone rang. It was Cynthia. She wished to be fetched home from where she was visiting. Also she had seen a bathing suit she needed terribly. Everybody was buying a bathing suit.

"Won't you even discuss it?" Cynthia asked.

"No," said Cicely suddenly. "This is *Mother's* Day. And I'm coming down from my ivory tower." She hung up before Cynthia could reply, laid the last sheets of manuscript on the proper pile and began to sort the laundry. The cat asked to be let in and the dog to be let out.

How difficult it is to be literary, she thought. Life keeps breaking in. Or is it out? (Luckily it's both, says Mrs. Appleyard.)

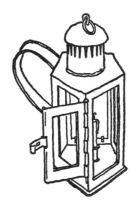

Index

The
Winter Kitchen

Mrs. Appleyard's Winter Kitchen

LOUISE ANDREWS KENT
AND
ELIZABETH KENT GAY

DECORATIONS BY ROBERT MACLEAN

Keats Publishing, Inc. New Canaan, Connecticut

To

PATIENCE BARLOW

who stencils walls,
makes miniature furniture, cooks and
paints on velvet with Mrs. Appleyard
and who says she wonders
what will happen next

Acknowledgment

SOONER or later most of us repeat our conversation and those of us who enjoy cooking give away the receipts for our favorite dishes more than once. Mrs. Appleyard is no exception. One of the pleasantest opportunities she ever had to talk about cooking was in the pages of the *Ladies' Home Journal*. She and her daughter are grateful for being allowed to use, in *The Winter Kitchen*, some material that has appeared in the *Journal* in a different form and they thank the editors for inspiring them in the first place.

Appleyard Center is an imaginary place with real people, sometimes imported from a long distance, in it. Mrs. Appleyard only wishes that they were always there.

She says that any attempt to apply the geography of Kents' Corner to the Appleyard Center landscape will only make you dizzy.

Contents

Contents

NOTE

* *Indicates recipes printed in this book.*

† *Those found in* The Summer Kitchen.

The Winter Kitchen

Mrs. Appleyard has had a winter kitchen for years but it is only recently that she became a winter person. She realizes with humility that she will never be the genuine seasoned article: she didn't start soon enough. However, she can no longer be classified with City Folks or Summer People and be lightly dismissed from consideration.

There she is, a solid fact, in the costumes well known over the years in Woodbrook Green, Massachusetts. Appleyard Center is now becoming acquainted with her two fur coats, one long, one short. (They can both be mistaken for mink at quite a distance.) It recognizes easily that Burberry raglan, known as

Old Ironsides or the Family Disgrace, the hats, veterans of many a symphony concert, the violet suit, the velvet and fur boots. These exterior decorations are becoming as familiar to Appleyard Center as the orange snowplow or evening grosbeaks eating sunflower seeds or petunias in the store window.

Mrs. Appleyard was surprised and delighted to find that petunias that had been a white ruffled cascade all summer would blossom all winter too. They would not do it for everyone, but any plant Mary Angell puts in the store window always thrives. To have a green thumb and to be able also to run a cash register with speed and accuracy is a combination of abilities much admired by Mrs. Appleyard. She knows an author who has trained a poodle in manners suitable for the court of Louis XIV and who also inspires perfect cooking in her cook. This is harder than improvising something yourself, she says. She also has a relative, her daughter Sally as a matter of fact, who plays field hockey and lacrosse, teaches Greek, is capable of being the whole alto section in a cathedral choir, performs agreeably upon the flute and deals competently with sweetbreads and mushrooms. Who said this was an age of monotonous specialization?

The store window at Appleyard Center is a sort of club. Neighbors bring in geraniums or begonias that have been sulking at home and they cheer up instantly. People also leave copies of the *Saturday Review* and *The New Yorker* in the window in case someone hasn't seen them. Mrs. Appleyard may often be found among the petunias on a sunny morning waiting for the mail and working on a Double Crostic. If there were only a cracker barrel, she'd be a philosopher, she says.

Her own house has no central heating so she has shut it up for the winter. Like a sharp sword sheathed in ice, the cold hangs in the ten bedrooms, in the two kitchens and in the period bathrooms. The living room with the birds on the walls and the map room are full of porch furniture. Loaves of fruitcake soaked in brandy are mellowing for next summer in the pantry. The furniture of miniature rooms is packed away so that mice will have plenty of space to dance. Shutters are closed. They were green not long ago but rain, snow, and the white light of winter are turning them blue. No wonder, thinks Mrs. Appleyard, blowing on her fingers.

She was delighted when her daughter Cicely suggested that some rooms in her house near the store could be made into an apartment. There is nothing she likes so much as changing the sizes and shapes of buildings. The southwest corner of Cicely's house soon sprouted bay windows that catch every ray of sunshine. Shelves for china appeared in surprising places. An electric unit that could do everything but plan menus suddenly lurked in a strategic corner. Before anyone could say Pouilly Fuissé Château Latour 1939 (pronounced in Vermont Polly Fish) the stove had burned the bottom out of Mrs. Appleyard's new double boiler. The makers of the stove had prankishly marked the front burners "R." Cicely, a woman of decision, definitely not the type to tolerate the orders of misplaced robots, snatched off the handles and transferred them so that the front burners are now marked "F." It took a little while for Mrs. Appleyard to learn that they meant what they said. She still keeps posted a notice lettered in her early Chaucerian hand. It says:

Questions for Morons

Which burners do you think you turned on?
Which did you really turn on?
Do you think you turned them off?
Which?

Thus equipped she has gone into action. Every now and then something she has cooked turned out pretty well, as she might have said in Massachusetts, or not badly — as she has learned to say now that she is a Vermonter. In the *Winter Kitchen* she reports some of her less disastrous experiments.

Every now and then someone from effete tropical Massachusetts writes to Mrs. Appleyard and says: "So you live in Vermont, in the country all winter now. How wonderful!"

Yes, it's wonderful — that anyone survives it. If you yearn for clean air, clean snow, water that tastes like water, birch logs blazing in the fireplace, new-laid eggs and Vermont turkeys, it is well to realize that you have expensive tastes. Clean air is delicious but at twenty below zero it has to have the chill taken off it before you can breathe it comfortably. Snow has to be shoveled not only off the front steps and a bit of sidewalk, as in the city, but off roofs and porches. It has to be plowed with a tractor so the oil man and the gas man can make frequent visits to their tanks. It must be plowed away from the garage in time for the snowplow to thunder along sending plumes of snow towards the stars and plow you in again.

Water runs downhill — except in winter. This statement can be the basis for the conversation of seventeen people for a whole evening. Mrs. Appleyard will not report all the reasons and suggested remedies. As evidence that the problem is a real one she will simply quote a neatly written notice from the bulletin board in the store: "Since our water will not run till spring, we would like to arrange for baths and will be glad to pay for expense and trouble."

As to those blazing birch logs: city folk think that wood grows on trees. Well, so it does and it stays right there unless someone cuts the tree down, saws it into four-foot lengths, splits it, cuts it the length you want and piles it where it will dry. A year later you can carry it into your woodbox. It costs rather more than burning oil but the smell of the smoke and the look of the flames are worth it, especially if some other tree falls on the power line some zero night and your thermostat stops working.

New-laid eggs are delicious and every now and then some are laid in a Vermont henhouse in winter. In Appleyard Center local ones can be bought and they are the right color, a warm brown like some Vermonter who has been in Florida all winter. However, in other shops they are more likely to come from some Connecticut chicken hotel where the lights blaze all night long and the eggs are white. They pay extra for white eggs in New York, Mrs. Appleyard understands. She thinks this is splendid and hopes all white eggs will go there.

Vermont turkeys are wonderful, just as good as you think. When some of Mrs. Appleyard's favorite neighbors came to their summer house from Salt Lake City for Christmas, they immediately set out shopping for a turkey. Because of the size of the oven, the roasting pan and the family it had to be of special dimensions. It was an excellent bird and bore upon its broad breast the announcement that it was a Product of Utah. Few Vermonters have ever tasted a Vermont turkey. To meet one socially is like getting into an exclusive club. You put your name down on a list. July is a good time to start. It helps if you have a couple of sponsors whose ancestors came to Vermont over a blazed trail before 1800.

Until a few years ago you could pick your own wild cranberries from a bog near Cranberry Meadow Pond: if you got there first, that is. With industry, a flexible back and perfect eyesight you could collect perhaps two quarts. However, the beavers have now been at work and unless you are a talented skin diver you had better get your cranberries in a package from Massachusetts.

One pleasant thing about living in the country is to bring in your own Christmas tree and make wreaths with your own evergreen and cones and berries. Cicely Bradshaw bought a woodlot to be sure of getting these materials. The tree this year was handsome and cost, before trimming, about a hundred dollars, Cicely figures.

When she had spent her first winter in Vermont, Cicely started to collect material that would help other winter amateurs. She filed the information in an envelope labeled "How to live in the country and not make a fool of yourself." After ten years she gave up the idea of writing on this subject. It is not possible, she says.

Her mother knows Cicely is right. That is why she is writing so rapidly about winter before she knows too much about it.

October

How Far Down?

I F Mrs. Appleyard believed the calendars she has received from affectionate insurance companies and plumbers, she would expect winter to begin in December. In Vermont this is non-sense. Even in September, Vermonters begin to say to each other in somber tones, "It won't be long now." Sometimes they add suspiciously, "But perhaps you like it."

Mrs. Appleyard hastily repels the suggestion. She says she likes snow in pictures and to look at while she is indoors with a good fire going. She adds that she does not wish to shovel it, walk in it or drive in it. This is the Party Line and is greeted with polite groans of approval. It is however timidly admitted that the storm in the first week of October was kind of pretty. Indeed it was.

In order to achieve this particular effect, you first arrange to have all the maples turn their most brilliant colors. This happy combination of crimson and plum color, peach and scarlet, gold and vermilion is not arrived at, as city folk are apt to think, by any casual night of frost. It is a process of ripening that takes place first on the sunny side of a tree as it does on the sunny cheek of a peach or an apple. It has been prepared for ever since spring by the correct amounts of sunshine and rain, delivered at the right time, and in autumn by warm days and cool nights. A light touch of frost helps, but a sharp frost scorches the leaves and makes them fall with either wind or rain.

This year everything had worked together for good. Elms were great golden wineglasses, maples had turned into rainbows without a leaf lost, birches and poplars were still delicately green just spangled with gold. Beeches were orange and bronze. Over them one night snow sifted quietly down. The next morning the hills were a sight not easily forgotten. The snow was not deep. On hayfields and lawns the grass underneath gave it a strange greenish tone as if northern lights were flickering over it.

Yesterday it would have seemed impossible for the leaves to be more brilliantly scarlet and yellow than ever. Yet they were. Officially it had stopped snowing when Mrs. Appleyard first looked out but the air was still quivering with tiny prismatic particles between her and the sun. She turned and looked down the valley. Stretching from one hill to the next, rising out of maples, descending into elms and firs was — not a rainbow — a snowbow, a complete arch of color.

It was sharper and clearer than any summer rainbow. As she watched, a second arch grew below it.

"This is too much," Mrs. Appleyard said to Cicely.

"Not for the foliage festival," her daughter said firmly. "If we could just keep it there for the photographers for a week — "

"No one would look at it," her mother said. "They'd just think it was a travel poster."

"Well, we needn't worry," Cicely said. "It's fading."

In a moment both bows were gone, but during the morning there was another change in the color pattern. Slowly, gently, leaves began to fall from the trees, making pools of color on the snow, like mirrors reflecting the crimson or gold above. It happened on every hill, changing the distant ring of mountains from blue violet to deep amethyst. Except on the highest hills the snow melted fast and the mirrors under the trees became neatly arranged Persian carpets.

By this time, Cicely and her mother were on the road, bound for the Dowsers' Convention. This is, Cicely considers, the high point of the Foliage Festival. There is the fascination of seeing the dowsers at work, a handsomely arranged landscape with the White Mountains shining in the distance and one of the best dinners served anywhere. Cicely is an expert on community meals and her mother was more than willing to accept her guidance.

When they arrived, the dowsers were already at work. They were walking across a bright green field, still with snow lying in the shadow of its southern stone wall. The dowsers' ages ranged from eight to eighty. Their dowsing rods were as varied. Mrs. Appleyard saw forked twigs of apple, of cherry, of willow. There was one of maple with crimson leaves still fluttering on it. There were rods of aluminum and of stainless steel. Their owners wore quilted jackets of scarlet silk, mackinaws with the tartans of Scottish clans, old football sweaters, caps of many colors, new dungarees as stiff as boards or old ones mellowed to the color of an ancient wheelbarrow.

Mrs. Appleyard noticed a pair of gray flannels and a tweed jacket with leather patches on the elbows. Have college professors taken up dowsing? — she wondered. There were also some flowered prints. These were showing under the coats of some rather large ladies. One was using a turkey wishbone for a rod. They were, Mrs. Appleyard noticed with regret, doing a good deal of giggling. Can her sex take nothing seriously?

Most of the men had that splendidly cleanshaven look of those who meet the razor once a week. There were, however, two who displayed thick prickly stubble, one a sable — or perhaps a fox — silvered, the other the color of a new horse chestnut. Mrs. Appleyard heard them agreeing that the stick worked its best if you had at least a week's beard. Happily adding this thought to her collection of reasons men give for not shaving, she admired their man-made fur and also the silky curly brown beard of a young dowser in sandals, Bermuda shorts and a Mexican poncho. His stick — dowsers, she learned, don't talk about rods — was of silver.

It seemed to work neither better nor worse than other sticks. As the men crossed the field their sticks seemed to turn at about the same point. Each marked the spot with a wooden tab on which was his number. He also handed the judge a card on which were his number, name and an estimate of how far down the water was and how many gallons a minute it would run.

Of course Mrs. Appleyard had her favorite candidate, a spry gnarled dowser with wonderful deep wrinkles. Seen in profile he seemed to have been carved out of an old chopping block but when he looked in her direction, she saw that he had gentle, faded blue eyes, the color of his dungarees and a smile as genial and toothless as a five months old baby's.

Mr. Stanford — that was his name — held his applewood stick lightly and not very high. It seemed to drop lightly rather than wrench itself over. Everything about him seemed easy and natural. Other men wrestled with their sticks, talking to them all the time. Most whispered or muttered but one could be heard across the field.

"Here? Is it here? To the left a foot? Yes! Yes! How far down? Ten? No. Eleven? No. Too far? — Oh, ten and a half? Good! How many gallons? You don't want to tell? Come on — two gallons? Three? Four? Too many? Three and a half? Good! *Good!*"

He mopped his forehead, sweating in spite of the cold breeze, and showed how the bark had twisted from the forked ends of the stick.

"It's nonsense, isn't it?" a man near Mrs. Appleyard said.

The one next to him answered, "No, not really. I don't have the power but I tried it once with a man who had. I was on my own place, close to where I knew there was an old well. I walked across it, holding the stick. Nothing happened. I said 'It's just about here, I know' and when the dowser put his hands on my shoulders, I felt something like an electric charge run through me. The stick seemed to fight to turn in my hands. When it dropped, the bark twisted off just like that one there and the palms of my hands were sore for a day. They'll start digging now, I guess."

In the background was a large machine rather like a dinosaur. It was painted a cheerful orange to harmonize with the blazing hills and it was called a backhoe digger. It began lumbering into position, for all the dowsers had had a turn. Even the lady with the turkey wishbone had teetered across the field on her pointed heels and her friends had clumped across in their plastic overshoes.

"We'd better go to dinner," Cicely said. "It will be ages before they get the digging done."

Dinner was in the town hall across the green from the church. The food was served in cafeteria style and you paid for each item. Choosing among the delicacies offered was quite a strain on the nervous system.

The menu was written on a blackboard:

Black Bean Soup*
Baked Ham   Lobster Newburg   Roast Turkey
Potato Salad   Tossed Salad   Jellied Fruit Salad
Hot Rolls   Popovers*
Apple Pie   Cranberry Lattice Pie*
Coffee   Tea

Mrs. Appleyard does not know how all the items were made but she used her mental dowsing stick on the ones she chose and gives her diagnosis.

Black Bean Soup

1 pound black beans	¼ teaspoon thyme
2 quarts water	1 onion, sliced
hambone	1 stalk of celery, cut fine
½ teaspoon garlic powder	3 tablespoons butter
¼ teaspoon allspice	1½ tablespoons flour
4 whole cloves	6 tablespoons sherry
1 bay leaf	2 lemons
3 hard-boiled eggs	

Soak the beans overnight with the water. In the morning put them on to cook with the hambone and the dry seasonings. Slice the onion and cut up the celery and sauté in a tablespoon and a half of the butter. Add them to the soup and simmer it four hours. Add hot water from time to time. When the beans are soft, strain off part of the liquid and set it aside, remove the hambone and the cloves, put the rest of the mixture through the blender and run it till it is smooth. Make a roux of the rest of the butter and the flour, add the liquid slowly, stirring well over very low heat. Cook it two minutes, add the bean purée. Some people add 2 tablespoons of tomato ketchup at this point. It gives it a good color, Mrs. Appleyard admits, but she prefers hers without. The soup is now ready but it may be kept in a double boiler until you are ready to serve it. Have the plates very hot. In each one put 1 tablespoon of sherry, two slices of lemon, three slices of hard-boiled egg. Pour the soup over. Serves six.

Popovers
(FOR 12 POPOVERS)

1½ cups milk   1 tablespoon butter — extra butter for pans
3 eggs   1½ cups flour, sifted three times
                   ½ teaspoon salt

Mrs. Appleyard knows that popovers can be made successfully by starting them in cold ungreased pans in a cold oven, only they are made by someone else. She has tried both the hot and cold methods and has better luck with the hot one. It's like dowsing: you have to follow your luck.

Use round iron pans or set ovenproof custard cups on a cooky sheet. Put half a teaspoon of melted butter in each cup. Light the oven: 450°. Set in the pan or sheet of cups. Now here is Mrs. Appleyard's contribution to popover lore. You are told to fill the pans half full and this is harder than it sounds. To get twelve pans all with the same amount in them is, in Mrs. Appleyard's experience, a most coincidental event. However, it is possible — if you have a measure. Mrs. Appleyard has one: it is a wooden tab intended as a marker for young plants. She has ruled a line on it at the height of half a popover pan and now even she can produce them of a uniform height and brown crisped effervescence.

Put all the ingredients milk, eggs, butter, flour measured after sifting with the salt into the blender. Blend for three minutes. If any flour has stuck to the side, push it into the batter with a rubber shaper.

Using your measure, fill each pan half full. Return the pans or cups to the oven. Bake 30 minutes. Reduce the heat to 350° and bake 10 to 15 minutes longer. Remove from pans. Make tiny slits in the side with a sharp knife. This lets the steam escape. Turn off the oven. The popovers not used immediately may be kept hot for a time without getting soggy. Good luck to you!

Cranberry Lattice Pie

2 cups cranberries   ⅔ cup water
1 cup sugar

Put cranberries, water and sugar in that order into a saucepan. Cook till the berries all pop — about ten minutes. Cool while you line a pie plate with pastry and cut strips for the lattice. Light the oven: 450°. Put the cranberries into the pie shell, put on the lattice, the first strip going north and south and the next east and west and so on until the pie is covered. Moisten the edge of the crust a little, using a pastry brush, so that the lattice strips will stay in place. Bake for 10 minutes at 450°. Then reduce heat to 350° and bake until the crust is well browned, about 30 minutes longer.

The digger was nearly ten feet down when they got back to the field. Already many dowsers had been eliminated from the contest. Not a drop of water was running into the hole. The greatest depth guessed was twelve feet eight inches. Mr. Stanford told Mrs. Appleyard so.

"I calculated two gallons at ten and a half feet," he confided to Mrs. Appleyard in a wonderful soft deep Vermont voice several sizes too big for him. Vermont men often have such voices. The shrill nasal ones are employed by women to keep the soft-voiced men up to their work.

Mr. Stanford added: "I guess it just wasn't my day but there's water there somewhere, I vum."

"Twelve feet eight inches down, I swear," said the man in the poncho. "No question about it."

How much nicer "I vum" sounds than "I swear," Mrs. Appleyard thought in a spirit of pure partisanship.

Even if Mr. Stanford could not win, it was a wonderful day. The sun was warm now on the red and gold hills and on the purple Vermont mountains behind them. In the distance the White Mountains were like silver clouds and the clouds were like floating mountains.

"Yes," Mrs. Appleyard heard the lady with the turkey wishbone say, "it was worth coming just for the dinner." She named a town in the southern part of the state. No backhoe digger shall drag this dishonored name from Mrs. Appleyard. "Down at —— they had, you may not believe me if you don't care to, *they had a caterer!*"

"No!" said her friend in a tone of deep shock. "What did they serve?"

The awful details are still unspoken, for just then it happened.

Water began to gush into the hole.

"Four veins — no, five. I snum!" Mrs. Appleyard heard Mr. Stanford say happily as the digger raised its long neck and clanked off.

But when the measuring was done — you guessed it, so did Mrs. Appleyard — it was ten feet seven inches down and a gallon and six ounces a minute and Mr. Stanford's guess was the nearest. So he had a prize in a wallet and a free dinner — he took the ham, which he pronounced excellent, and the apple pie — and his name will forever be engraved upon the Dowsers' Cup.

"Did you see the snowbow this morning?" Mrs. Appleyard asked him.

Mr. Stanford forked in potato salad and nodded happily.

"I believe one end came right down in this field," Mrs. Appleyard said.

"I vum!" said Mr. Stanford.

Musical Cooks

DURING October Mrs. Appleyard still stayed in her own house, stoking her Franklin stoves by day and the stove in her winter kitchen both by day and by night. This art object is perhaps a hundred and twenty years old. In decorating it no pains were spared. It has cherubs' heads, egg-and-dart molding and acanthus leaves on it. There is a grating in front that opens and shows the fire. On top is an interesting piece of metal that looks as if it had been crocheted in a hurry by some absent-minded giantess. Lift it and you'll find a practical flat top with a stove lid, a splendid place to keep a soup kettle going.

The pipe from the stove wanders through the house, warming the dining room and the bedroom above it slightly. It keeps the bathroom thawed so you can't skate in it and even takes some of the chill off Mrs. Appleyard's bedroom. It is perhaps the most effective heating device ever invented — if you keep stoking it. Luckily Mrs. Appleyard has an ankle-length camel's-hair dressing gown, just the costume for night stoking. The story that her scarecrow wears it in summer is simply not true — yet.

Fortunately there were some warm days in October and it was on one of these that the music room was christened. Two years ago Mrs. Appleyard had the good luck to have a few days of comfortable illness. Cicely, instead of sending flowers, asked her mother if she would like the door of the Remember Appleyard house to use anywhere. The door is a beautiful one, the kind that has two large crosses and panels of several sizes. The pine of which it is made has been furrowed by storms since 1797. At that time it was impossible for Americans to build anything badly proportioned. Ash houses, smokehouses, sawmills, corn barns were all just right. Exactly when people acquired the taste and skill necessary for making everything just wrong, Mrs. Appleyard is not sure but she sees the results — the brick siding that imitates the most hideous bricks, the windows sullenly lurking under the eaves of little houses, the artificial stone of many colors.

"Say no more," said Cicely. "Remember your blood pressure."

Mrs. Appleyard obediently thought about the old door.

"A door," she said after a while, "can't just be nailed on the outside of a house for an ornament. It has to open into something. I think I'll make the woodshed into a music room."

The room, she explained, as she began to draw pictures of it, would be just for chamber music and playing Hi-Fi records. Cicely was relieved. She had seen her mother's Steinway inserted into the ballroom of the Museum with about a quarter of an inch to spare and she remembered the last time a piano was taken out of there, the wreckage was extensive.

Besides, she thought, this may be fantasy.

Of course she knew very well that a plan of her mother's is about as fantastic as a load of gravel. The next time she tried to make a telephone call, always an interesting project on an eight-party line, she heard her mother buying the silver-gray boards and the beams of an old barn.

"Roger Willard will be right over to get them," she told the owner.

When Cicely next saw her mother she was drawing the plans, using the same method she follows when she designs her miniature rooms. She uses sheets of thin cardboard cut on the scale of an inch to a foot. There is a sheet for each wall, one for the ceiling and one for the floor. She colors them, draws in the things she intends to hang on the walls, even shows the rugs and where the couch is going.

It took Roger Willard some months, but at last the music room was almost ridiculously like the patterns. There were the gray boards and the bluish green of the mantelpiece, a color suggesting that Mrs. Appleyard had made a raid on Williamsburg and escaped with a sample of woodwork. The bookcases were there with gilded hollow half circles over them made from an old chopping bowl. The Hi-Fi, FM and TV were chastely hidden in cupboards of gray boards. The Franklin stove was sending real smoke up the chimney and suprisingly little into the room. The cupboards beside it were full of wood and could be filled again from outside. Small-paned windows on two sides and the fanlight over the door caught sunshine all day long.

The fanlight was not exactly like the drawing. It was an improvement. Picking out her favorite hardware store to give them a nice piece of business, she showed the picture to the manager and asked if he could order one like it for her.

Well, he guessed he could but he didn't see much sense in it. There was one up over his garage that he figured would come pretty close to fitting.

That would be fine, his customer said, and could she buy it?

Well, the owner guessed not. No good to him. Most of the glass out of it. All cobwebs, no paint, but if the customer wanted to have such a piece of junk fixed up, she'd be welcome to it.

So there it is, making patterns like the spokes of a wheel on the hooked rugs, just right for the old door below it and giving Mrs. Appleyard, every time she looks at it, an extra reason for liking to be an adopted Vermonter.

The design around the door was copied from an old house fifty miles away. Mrs Appleyard saw it one day when she was at a Book Fair pretending to be an author and not a master builder. Luckily she had a pencil and the back of an envelope handy. Roger Willard carved the pattern. He used a set of tools that Mrs. Appleyard once tried for about twelve minutes twenty years ago. She then cleverly decided not to be a wood carver. She did make the plaster ornaments on the mantelpiece and above the doors. She used something she calls the lost-wax process. Someday when she is feeling strong and sadistic she is quite likely to tell how she did it.

With Patience Barlow's help she made the curtains. They look rather like Fortuny copies of old Italian brocade. The background is a greenish, grayish blue and the pattern is in dull

gold and Venetian red. Two large stencils were used and it took
Mrs. Appleyard and Patience about three weeks before the curtains were finished. During this time these ladies enthusiastically
gave up cooking. Perhaps Mrs. Appleyard ate something besides
cucumbers and yogurt but she can't remember what it was.
Patience did cook herself an occasional hot meal — tea and cinnamon toast. The cooky jar was emptied and not replenished.
Hungry grandchildren came and clinked the lid and looked re-
proachful. Friends to whom Mrs. Appleyard had said "Do drop
in to lunch sometime" dropped in, saw every available table covered with newspapers, brocade and coffee-can covers containing
gold and Venetian red, took a long breath of oil and Japan drier
and dropped rapidly out again.

Yet there came a day when Mrs. Appleyard could think of
nothing more to do for the room — except give a party for it,
of course. The idea for it came when she heard a group of her
favorite musicians agreeing that they would rather cook than
play their instruments. Then one of them asked Mrs. Appleyard
when she was going to christen the music room.

"Tomorrow night while you are still here," she said. "And
every one of you must either cook or play. I promise not to
play my accordion," she added. "Now tell me what you are
going to cook so I can have the right things for you."

The resulting list began with a small cabbage, which Mrs.
Appleyard acquired from her own garden, and ended with a
quart of fine white Burgundy, which she produced from her
own cellarway if not from her own vineyard. She did have to
go to town for some of the items between. The only thing
missing from the market was fresh mushrooms. She planned to
substitute some cans she keeps for such emergencies but on the
way home she stopped at an appropriate pasture. It had two
palominos in it, looking especially decorative against a back-

ground of flaming maples and deep blue sky. It also had mushrooms pushing up shining ivory umbrellas through grass that was still green, so the menu was safe.

When she got home Roger Willard was putting a small fir tree on the roof to show that the music room was finished and Patience Barlow was arranging autumn bouquets in big stoneware jars. They and others who had worked on the room were all invited to the party.

All the cooks were men. The women preferred to stick to their cellos and violas. There was probably psychology mixed up in this, Mrs. Appleyard thought, but she was much too busy to unmix any of it. After all, men cooks always need a kitchen maid. By being one on this occasion, Mrs. Appleyard was also able to be a gastronomical spy and find out their secrets. Not that they were unwilling to share them but their instructions were of the "take a little of this and some of that and cook it till it's about right" style. Mrs. Appleyard, whose only virtue as a cook is that she writes down promptly how she did something that came out right, had her notebook handy and used it.

Everyone seemed happy. A group in the music room played the Brahms Clarinet Quintet three times. Roger Willard was sitting down — a posture unusual for him — listening to Mozart in the living room. Other guests relaxed on the porch and breathed in the prophetic smells of supper. There were lights coming from the barn where people were looking at the miniature rooms and from the carriage house where someone was reading a mystery story and from the corn barn where others were sitting around the fire.

In the kitchens every stove was in use. A violinist, whose reddish curls began to stand up all over his head as the steam rose, was making cabbage soup on the cherubs'-head stove. A very tall pianist, working at an electric stove, was simmering broilers in white Burgundy and could he have another half pound of butter, please? In the summer kitchen a cellist was getting ready to bake coffee cake. He had arrived with his bowl of raised dough, tenderly wrapped in damask napkins and a pink knitted blanket. He was now dipping pieces of the dough into a mixture of preserved fruits and spices and dropping them into an angel-cake tin. He looked much more nervous than he did when Mrs. Appleyard heard him play Dvořák's Cello Concerto. She assured him that they would find a quiet, calm, warm place for the final rising of his coffee cake. She thought near the Franklin stove in the library might be the best. The flautist was busy with the salad.

Why, Mrs. Appleyard found time to wonder, do people say "flautist" which is such an ugly word instead of "flutist" which is a pretty one?

Just to be embarrassing, she supposed and decided to call this one, who was small, impish and rather like Puck in *A Midsummer Night's Dream*, a flutist. He asked her for a garlic press. Mrs. Appleyard brought it to him and they had a congenial talk about garlic. The flutist said it was good for relaxing tension and he always liked some before playing the flute. Mrs. Appleyard, fascinated with this musical secret, contributed the information that Marco Polo said the natives in the Himalayas gave their ponies garlic so they could breathe well in the thin air of the high mountain passes. She then passed on to the oboist who also wanted garlic and a sharp-tined fork with which to score the outside of a cucumber. She gave him both and put her own contribution, a chocolate icebox cake which she had just been decorating with whipped cream, into the refrigerator.

The menu resulting from these activities was:

Cabbage Soup*

Fish Mousse, mushroom sauce   Coq au Vin*

Spaghetti with Meat Balls

Coffee cake*

Tossed Salad   Cucumber Salad, Yogurt dressing*

Chocolate Icebox Cake†

Coffee   Pouilly Fuissé

Ice cream and oatmeal cookies for the children many of whom turned out to be over twenty-one.

The meal was planned for seven o'clock and was served right on time at eight. Mrs. Appleyard never could remember just how many people ate it but there was plenty — just exactly plenty — and not enough left over for a blue jay on a reducing diet. Music was laced in and around the supper with wood-smoke and people laughing. After it was all over, and with the assistance of a couple of poets she had washed the dishes, she realized that all she had eaten was cucumber salad. But after all she had heard the Brahms Clarinet Concerto in her own music room. She can eat another day.

Cabbage Soup

2 pounds beef chuck, cut in inch cubes	½ teaspoon mixed spices
bones from beef chuck	2 pounds tomatoes
2 pounds chicken necks and wingtips	6 potatoes
3 quarts water	1 stalk of celery
½ teaspoon mixed herbs	2 onions, minced
4 tablespoons fat from stock	

Put the beef, the bones and the chicken necks and wingtips into a deep kettle with the water. Add the herbs and spices and let it simmer for 2 hours. Skim it from time to time to remove as much of the fat as possible. While it is cooking prepare your vegetables. Peel the tomatoes by holding them over gas flame until the skin cracks. You need a wooden-handled fork for this. If you don't have one, plunge the tomatoes briefly into boiling water. Cool them and cut them into eighths. Peel the potatoes. Small new potatoes freshly dug were used in this soup but potato balls made from larger ones will do or half-inch dice. Cut the celery fine and mince the onions. An hour before serving time remove the bones from the soup. Sauté the celery and onions until the onion is transparent in fat from the stock and add them to the soup. Then in the same pan sauté the cabbage for 5 minutes. Add it to the soup. Add the potatoes. Cook until potatoes are done — about 2 to 5 minutes. A short time before serving add the tomatoes. They should keep their shape. Rinse out the frying pan with some of the soup to get all the flavor. Salt to taste. Serve it in a large brown bowl. For ten.

Coq au Vin

1 cup chicken stock	parsley
2 three-pound broilers, cut in four pieces, wingtips removed	4 tablespoons flour with ½ teaspoon poultry seasoning
1 onion, grated	½ pound butter
1 pound mushrooms, sliced vertically	2 cups dry white wine
toasted French bread	

Begin by making stock of the wingtips and necks of the chickens. Cook it down to ½ cup. Cool and skim off fat. Grate the onion. Slice the mushrooms, caps only. The stems may be added to the stock. Cut the parsley fine. Mrs. Appleyard does this with scissors, rather than cutting it on a board with a knife or chopping it.

Put the flour and seasoning into a large paper bag and toss the pieces of chicken in it till they are well coated. Melt but do not brown the butter in a large iron frying pan. Brown the pieces of chicken on both sides and transfer them to a large fireproof baking dish. Set them into a 350° oven to finish cooking for 20 to 30 minutes. Cook the onion in the frying pan until it is transparent. Add the mushrooms and sauté them 3 minutes. Add the chicken stock and cook two minutes longer. Add this sauce to the chickens. Rinse out the frying pan with the wine. Simmer it, stirring well to get all the flavor. Add salt to taste. Pour it over the chicken. Sprinkle over the parsley. Serve with French bread to mop up the sauce. For eight.

Coffee Cake

Use a package of hot roll mix for this. Follow directions for first and second risings.

Mix 2 cups sugar, ¼ pound mixed candied fruit, ¼ pound each of currants, seedless raisins and walnuts, ¼ teaspoon nutmeg, ½ teaspoon cinnamon. Butter an angel-cake tin well. Tear off pieces of dough. Dip them into the sugar mixture and pack them lightly into the angel-cake tin. Cover and let it rise till double its bulk in a warm place. Scatter with what is left of the sugar mixture. Dot with butter.

Bake at 375° for 25 minutes. Reduce heat and bake until delicately brown, about 15 minutes longer.

Cucumber Salad, Yogurt Dressing

2 large cucumbers	2 tablespoons scissored parsley
1 bean of garlic	1 cup yogurt
¼ teaspoon white pepper	½ teaspoon paprika
salt to taste	mint leaves

Peel the cucumbers. Score the sides deeply with a sharp-tined fork. Slice them paper-thin. The scoring indents the edges of the slices. It isn't necessary but it looks attractive, Mrs. Appleyard thinks. Add the garlic, put through the press, the pepper, salt and the parsley to the yogurt. Toss the sliced cucumbers in the mixture. Sprinkle over the paprika. Decorate with small sprays of fresh mint leaves.

Harvest Supper

ONE OF Mrs. Appleyard's favorite parties is the Harvest Supper. It is given by the PTA to raise money for the hot-lunch program. The school Halloween exercises are part of the entertainment. The combination gets people together in an atmosphere of warmth and relaxation. Summer residents, who have come for a last weekend to shut up their houses, appear. Neighbors come from around the county for what is known as an excellent meal. Children can come for half price. A child of the right size and shape often eats twice as much as his father so this is rightly regarded as one of the bargains of all time. The stage of the Community Hall is decorated with tall cornstalks and pumpkins and bright leaves cut out of paper. The real leaves are all off the trees now. There are great piles of them, fine for rolling and rustling in, near the schoolhouse. All the brilliant reds and yellows have turned to the same dull pinkish tan. Oaks still show color but they are rare in this part of Vermont. Every year what Mrs. Appleyard thinks are evergreens prove to be nothing of the sort. They are larches. First they turn an olive-gold green, next — briefly — they are spires of bright burnt orange, and then, just before the needles fall, they are the color of cinnamon toast. There is an enormous old larch near one of Mrs. Appleyard's favorite houses, an old brown house suggesting kinship with the House of the Seven Gables though a century younger. It has enough gables, if you count the dormers, and a dark roof almost the color of the clapboards. The big larch twists up above the end of the house and its needles fall on the roof, edging the dark shingles with bright gold. Even after the zinnias and dahlias have frozen, the house, with pale blue smoke curling out of the big chimney, the one with the secret staircase around it, looks warm and welcoming as it must have to slaves on their way to Canada a century ago.

Frances Ward, the owner of the house, will be at the party tonight. She will bring her violin and she will fiddle for dancing after supper. She also plays Bach and Corelli but tonight she will be fiddling. The technique is different. Not every violinist can also fiddle the "Devil's Dream" with properly controlled wildness or inspire the dancers of "Money Musk" to be both stately and gay. Luckily Frances can and after supper and the Halloween Exercises there will be plenty of dancers on the floor. They will be sustained by the following menu:

Baked Beans*   Red Flannel Hash*
Succotash Casserole†   Fish Balls*
Harvest Vegetable Salad*
Brown Bread*   Mustard Pickle
Watermelon Pickle
Squash Pie   Cranberry Apples*
Coffee

Baked Beans

One of the first things Mr. Appleyard did when he had married his wife was to carry her off to a lonely island where they spent a week cut off from the mainland by waves like Vermont mountains and fog like potato soup. During this happy time he began converting her into being a Vermonter by breaking the news to her that he regarded beans as baked in Boston as food unsuitable for human beings.

His bride, who up to that moment had never even boiled a kettle of water, solemnly promised that the shadow of a pea bean should never cross her husband's plate. She learned that there were beans called soldier beans and others called yellow eyes. Either, Mr. Appleyard said, might be used — on the whole he preferred yellow eyes — so long as the pork with them was streaky fat and lean and if they were flavored with maple sugar, not with molasses.

Mrs. Appleyard began to realize that married life was a serious affair. By the time she reached their apartment on Beacon Hill she was able to inspire her cook, who was even more ignorant than her mistress, into baking beans that were not tough, slippery, and pallid and made unpalatable to a Vermonter by a weird mixture of molasses and tomato sauce.

Here is how Mr. Appleyard liked his beans:

Appleyard Center Baked Beans

2 quarts yellow eye beans	1 tablespoon dry mustard
boiling water	½ teaspoon ginger
1 onion	1 teaspoon ground pepper
1 cup granulated maple sugar	salt to taste, perhaps 1 teaspoon
1 pound streaked salt pork	

Cover the beans with cold water and soak them overnight. In the morning strain off the water. Cover them with boiling water and simmer until the skin wrinkles when you blow on a tablespoon of them — about 20 minutes. Drain. Put a layer of beans in the bottom of a beanpot. Add the onion. Mix the dry ingredients and scatter them in as you add the rest of the beans. Score the rind of the pork deeply. Bury it among the beans so that the scored edge just shows. Fill the beanpot with boiling water. Cover. Bake 6 hours, at 300°, adding water from time to time. Uncover. Bake until beans are done, golden brown, tender but not mushy — about half an hour longer.

These beans have a texture and flavor a little like chestnuts. Granulated maple sugar is now so hard to get that Mrs. Appleyard has used light brown sugar, a cup of it with an added tablespoon of white sugar, with pretty good results or anyway no open disapproval from her Vermont gourmets.

If, like Mrs. Appleyard, you like beans but are denied the privilege of eating salt or salt pork, you might like to try this version. She sometimes carries her own private unsalted casserole of this or that to a community supper and usually finds friends who share it.

Mrs. Appleyard's Own Baked Beans

2 cups yellow eye beans
⅛ pound butter
¾ cup light brown sugar
1 teaspoon granulated sugar
¼ teaspoon ground pepper
1½ teaspoons dry mustard
bit of bay leaf, scalded in
   water and removed

pinches of rosemary, basil,
   marjoram, orégano, curry
   powder, nutmeg
1 onion, minced
2 beans of garlic, crushed
1 cup light cream
¼ pound beef suet in
   ½-inch cubes

1 tablespoon brown sugar (extra)

Soak and parboil beans as above. Mix the butter, sugar, dry seasonings, onion and garlic and combine them with the beans. Put them into a small beanpot or into a casserole with a tightly fitting cover. Bake covered for 6 hours at 300°. Try out suet cubes until golden brown. Drain. Uncover the beans. Pour in the cream. Stir beans so that different ones are on top. Scatter suet cubes over the beans. Sprinkle over the extra brown sugar. Cook ½ hour or until the beans are tender and have absorbed most of the liquid. Serves four to six.

Red Flannel Hash
FOR SIX

Some dishes are causes, others are results, Mrs. Appleyard says. Red flannel hash is the result of a New England boiled dinner and, Mrs. Appleyard thinks, the best part of it.

There are three important points about any hash. Always chop it in a wooden bowl, not too fine. Do not use cooked potatoes — cook them especially for the hash. Have twice as much potato as you do meat. In red flannel hash be sure you have plenty of beets to give it color. Mrs. Appleyard does not include cabbage in her hash. She thinks it tends to make it slippery. However she does not insist on this point. If you like it, go ahead.

For a large frying pan:

4 tablespoons beef suet in ¼-inch cubes	3 cups of vegetables from boiled dinner: carrots, lima beans, turnips, beets, chopped not too fine
1 tablespoon onion, finely minced	
1 cup of meat, chopped	1 cup stock from boiled dinner, simmered down to ½ cup
6 cups of freshly boiled potatoes, chopped in small cubes	

Try out the beef suet in a large iron frying pan. Skim out the cubes. Drain. Add the minced onion and cook over low heat till straw-colored. Mix the meat, potato and vegetables well and add them to the pan. Stir briefly until fat and onion combine with mixture. Add the stock. Turn heat as low as possible. Smooth mixture but do not mash it down. Cook it until it begins to brown around the edges — about 40 minutes.

Have a large hot platter ready. Physical strength is now necessary. The frying pan is hot and heavy. With a spatula carefully loosen the hash all around the edges. Make a deep crease with the spatula across the hash at right angles to the handle. Now take a holder and bravely grasp the handle of the pan in your left hand. Tip the pan and fold the top half of the hash over the lower half. Run the spatula carefully under the lower half to be sure it is free from the pan. Place the platter over the pan. You'll need another holder at this point. Invert pan and platter. The hash will drop out and be like a glazed brown omelet with red edges. Sprinkle the suet cracklings over it. Put sprays of parsley around it. Mrs. Appleyard hopes that after you have lived dangerously with the hot pan and platter you will enjoy it.

Fish Balls (M.O'M)

Never having fried anything in deep fat in her life, Mrs. Appleyard falls back upon the wisdom of the good angel who helped her in her kitchen for seventeen years, told the children about leprechauns, played them the record of "The Two Black Crows" and taught them manners by example. She has since used her wit, charm, philosophy and just plain goodness on her own children and still has a supply on hand for her grandchildren. Do they appreciate their good luck? Mrs. Appleyard hopes so.

In the Appleyard family it was a grave misdemeanor to form fish balls into firm cakes. If you like them that way, better get them out of a can and relax. The Appleyards like them light, fluffy and as prickly as porcupines. This happy result is achieved this way.

2 cups of raw potatoes, diced	1 teaspoon butter
1 cup of uncooked salt codfish, picked fine	pinch of ground pepper
	1 egg, well beaten

Freshen codfish as directed on package. Have water boiling in saucepan. Add diced potatoes and codfish picked in small pieces. Cover. Cook till potatoes are soft. Drain well. This is important. Unless fish and potatoes are well drained as soon as they are cooked they will not hold together well while frying. Cover. Shake over low heat until well dried. Now, using a pastry blending fork, mash and beat the fish and potatoes until they are very light. Add butter and pepper. Beat in the beaten egg. Have fat heated to 375°. It should be about two inches deep. Dip a tablespoon into the fat, then spoon up lightly some of the mixture and drop it into the fat. Fry it one minute. Fry five at a time. Drain on paper towels. Reheat fat and fry another batch. Serves six.

Fish Hash

This seems the right place to mention that the same mixture used for fish balls also makes fish hash. This is how Mrs. Appleyard's grandmother made it. Six slices of salt pork were cut in quarters and fried gently until a delicate golden brown. The pork was removed and drained on brown paper. The fat was left in the pan — an iron frying pan, medium size. The fish hash was carefully browned like the Red Flannel Hash above, removed from the pan in the same way and garnished with the salt pork cracklings. This served six people. Of course they also had oatmeal, thick cream, eggs, three kinds of hot bread, plenty of fruit and a lamb chop if they preferred it to the hash so they would usually say yes when asked by their hostess if they had "made out a breakfast."

Harvest Vegetable Salad

This varies according to what vegetables are available. Occasionally, when frost delays, lima beans ripen before they are frozen to a mush, and tomatoes, picked not quite green, turn red on Mrs. Appleyard's windowsills. This was such a year: there was even oak leaf lettuce left in the garden to put around the edge of a huge wooden chopping bowl. In the center was a small yellow bowl containing mayonnaise mixed with sour cream. Around it were a ring of cooked beets cut in cubes, one of cooked sliced carrots, another of raw broccoli flower heads alternated with raw cauliflower flowerets. Green beans, frozen in August, made another ring. Then more beets, more carrots, finely cut celery and here and there a little heap of asparagus tips frozen in June or peas, marked A+ by Patience Barlow when she put them into the freezer in July.

French dressing has been poured over all the vegetables, parsley and chives have been snipped with a scissors and scattered here and there. Mrs. Appleyard gets the same pleasure out of one of these arrangements that she does out of painting a dish of fruit on velvet. She says it's less trouble: you don't have to frame it or hang it on the wall.

Brown Bread

Mrs. Appleyard heard the other day of a man from Texas who sends to Vermont to have brown bread without raisins made for him and flown west. If she knew his name she would ship him a loaf of hers as a tribute to a congenial spirit. She doesn't like raisins either, at least not in brown bread. Plum pudding or fruitcake or mincemeat she considers suitable situations for this nutritious fruit.

For two loaves:

1 cup rye flour	1 ¾ cup sweet milk
1 cup stone ground whole wheat flour	¾ cup molasses
	¾ teaspoon soda
1 cup stone-ground cornmeal	¾ teaspoon salt

If you have thick sour milk on hand, use 2 cups of it instead of the sweet milk and increase the soda to 1 teaspoon.

Sift dry ingredients thoroughly. Mix the milk and molasses well together. Make a hollow in the flour mixture and pour in the milk and molasses, beating it in well as you pour. Put the batter into tall, tightly covered greased tins. The easy way to get these is to inherit them. Sometimes they turn up at auctions. Do not fill tins more than two thirds full. Place them on a rack in a tightly covered kettle or use your covered roaster. Steam 3 hours. Start with plenty of boiling water as the bread will cook more evenly and quickly if you do not have to replace water during the steaming process. At the end of the 3 hours, remove tins from water, uncover them. Place them in the oven at 300° for ten minutes so the bread can dry a little. Of course the usual place for this bread is with baked beans, but don't forget that when cold it makes delicious sandwiches to go with any kind of shellfish. Slice it very thin and spread it either with sweet butter or first with butter and then with a mixture of cream cheese and horseradish.

Cranberry Apples

8 fine tart apples	2 cloves
2 tablespoons lemon juice	2 cups sugar
pinches of nutmeg and	2 cups water
cinnamon	2 cups cranberries

Wash, peel and core the apples. They should be perfect but not too large. Brush them with lemon juice and set them in a cool place while you cook the peel and cores in water seasoned with the spices. Also mix the sugar and water and bring it to boiling point. Add the cranberries and cook until they all pop. Put the apples in a shallow heat proof glass baking dish, lightly buttered. Fill centers of apples with the popped cranberries and pour 1 tablespoon of the cranberry juice over each apple. Set the dish in a 350° oven and bake. Apples should keep their shape. Now mix juice from the apple peelings — there should be ½ cup — with the same amount of the cranberry juice. Use this mixture to coat the apples as they cook. It will slide off but keep spooning it over every 10 minutes during the baking. This may take 40–50 minutes according to the kind of apples used. When they are tender, put them into a serving dish. Add a little of the cooked cranberries to any that do not look well filled. Pour all the juice in the pan over them. Chill.

These may be eaten as a dessert or used as a garnish with roast turkey, duck or goose. Grated orange rind may be sprinkled over them if you like.

After supper the children, who had been well brushed and polished for the occasion, began decorating their faces to make goblins, elves and witches of themselves. There were some of the most benevolent-looking witches Mrs. Appleyard had ever seen, including the head one who was her granddaughter Camilla. This is high promotion for Camilla: she was always an elf before. Now she is beaming because she has a broomstick and a black pointed hat with stars on it. She also wears her new glasses becauses she is a nearsighted witch as well as a genial one.

With the help of her assistant witches she casts a spell with great efficiency and the children, who have been happily dancing around the stage, are all frozen into uncomfortable positions. They have, it seems, pains in their midriffs, teeth and ears and toes. Camilla puts down her black cat, which walks among the frozen figures with a good deal of satisfaction. Perhaps, like some of the mothers, it wishes it too had a magic wand and could get peace so easily. However, the moment of quiet is soon over. A golden-haired good fairy appears. The children are unfrozen. Camilla snatches up her cat and hurries off on her broomstick. She is followed by her goblins and elves who deliver a few sly pinches and tweaks as they go. One has the impertinence to pull the good fairy's yellow curls. There is loud applause from the parents, who tell each other kindly and sincerely how well each other's children did. Of course they know whose child did the best.

Even grandmothers, Mrs. Appleyard thought as she happily listened to Frances Ward tuning her fiddle for the dancing, have a right to an opinion, I suppose.

November

Bridge Party

IT WAS a distinct surprise to Mrs. Appleyard's friends when she announced that she was going to give a bridge party. Philanthropic considerations had led her, in 1912, to give up playing this interesting game. She was the kind of player who always held poor cards — or did they just seem so when she held them? Her intentions about keeping her mind alert were good but somehow her thoughts would drift to her trousseau — this was when she was engaged to Mr. Appleyard — or to the island they were going to on their wedding journey or just to Mr. Appleyard.

There came to be a tone of well-bred patience in her partners' voices. It is not true that the term "dummy" was invented just for Mrs. Appleyard — that was simply a rumor — but it certainly suited her admirably. So well, in fact, that it took her some time to realize that when her friends asked her to make a fourth "just to help out," she would be rather more helpful if she stayed at home and read a good book.

Luckily Mr. Appleyard was not a bridge player. He preferred squash rackets, cowboy pool, golf, poker, tennis or chess. So they were married and lived happily for a time that now seems short to Mrs. Appleyard though it was more than thirty years. She became rather an attentive chessplayer but she has never gone back to bridge. She has sometimes been invited to play but not by anyone who knew her in her youth. The game is really complicated now, she hears.

"Of course she can't really be meaning to play herself," her friends exclaimed uneasily when they heard she was giving a bridge party.

They were right. It was a different kind of party and indeed a different kind of bridge, a covered one, in fact.

It was Cicely's idea really.

"The town is going to take down the East Hill Bridge and widen the road there. I think they would give it to you if you'd take it away," she told her mother.

Mrs. Appleyard, who was feeling a little let down because she had moved into her new apartment at Cicely's for the winter and everything was perfect, brightened up at once.

"I could put it across the brook," she said. "Roger told me that my old one needs rebuilding. It would probably be an economy to have a covered one."

"Of course," said Cicely who is the same kind of economist as her mother and President Kennedy and other people with vision. "Let's go and look at it."

The covered bridge was a great favorite of Mrs. Appleyard's. When she had foreign visitors, she used to entertain them by taking them to see it, telling them that it was the smallest one anywhere around.

The visitors had usually been shown the widest rivers, the tallest buildings and the busiest street corners in the world. Sometimes they had seen a mountain with the largest possible letters painted on it. (HOLLYWOODLAND, it says.) They seemed to enjoy the change of scale.

Mrs. Appleyard liked the bridge best when the elms along the river were arches of gold and maples blazed on the hillside above it. On this November morning the sky was dingy with cold, sullen gray clouds. The pastures were lion-colored with dark manes of bare maples. Mountains were a wall of dark steely blue. They seemed to have moved in closer since yesterday. Still, even in these forbidding circumstances, the bridge looked attractive.

"Cozy," said Mrs. Appleyard. "I'll have a few electric outlets put into it and we'll have tea there summer afternoons while the children are swimming. It will be shady and well ventilated at the same time."

Even if November had been a grass-growing season, no blade would have increased in height under Mrs. Appleyard's feet. She talked to the selectmen, who did not see any reason why she couldn't have the bridge — probably. (Vermont for "yes.") So long as she took it pretty quick. They planned to start work that week. She talked to Roger Willard who thought likely, he guessed, maybe it could be moved and he would get estimates.

When Cicely next saw her mother she was happily at work with pencil and paper making out a list of guests and a menu for the bridge opening. She had a picture of the inside of it showing the kingpost trusses and a harvest table heaped with food.

"You mean you plan to start cooking there in November?" Cicely asked.

"If it's Indian summer," her mother said. "If it snows, we'll eat here and just go and look at it. Anyway I've planned to cook things here and carry them down. I'll keep them hot on that wonderful heating tray you gave me. There's lots of watercress in the brook. I'm only asking eight people besides you and me," she added virtuously.

Her daughter said she hoped her mother would keep the number at eight.

"The last time you said that," she pointed out, "there were seventy-three."

"That was just for dessert," her mother said hastily, "and I didn't know a good many of them."

"If that makes it any better," Cicely said. "How can you be sure there won't be people around you don't know this time?"

"Foliage is over and skiing hasn't begun," Mrs. Appleyard said. "I'll read you the menu," she added, since the subject seemed to need changing.

Cream of Watercress Soup*

Seafood Croustade*   Cold Baked Ham

Hot Brown Bread (p. 34)

Orange, Avocado, Onion and Watercress Salad

French Dressing

Brown Betty*

Vermont Cheese   Crackers

Cider   Jug of Red Wine

Coffee

"What, not a vintage wine?" inquired Cicely.

"Not out of paper cups," her mother explained.

They did not drink out of paper cups. No electric outlets were put in the bridge and they did not eat in it. By the day of the party it was being burned where it had always stood.

"I suppose we might go over and cook hot dogs there when they burn it," said Mrs. Appleyard.

This was the day Roger Willard brought the news that moving the bridge would cost a substantial amount suitable for sending a man to the moon, about as much as it would cost to send Tommy Bradshaw to college, a purpose for which these ladies had been saving up for some years.

"We might give up sending him to college," Cicely suggested. "He always says his teachers are dopes. Perhaps he'd do better as a self-made man."

"I don't care for them much," Mrs. Appleyard said. "They always seem so pleased about it. As if everyone weren't self-made really. Only the educated ones are sometimes humble enough to know they had help. I'll tell the guests that the party will be here in the evening instead of at noon," she added.

"Why not at noon?" Cicely asked.

"Because," said Mrs. Appleyard, "evening is a better time for bridge. And as I've been pretty economical this week, I am going to buy you two card tables each with four unspavined legs."

The party was a great success. No one came except those invited. The tables were splendidly sturdy. Venetia Hopkins and Mrs. Appleyard played chess. An extra bridge player had been asked so that Cicely would not have to help by making a fourth. She was able to keep an eye on the Brown Betty and keep up her reading average of two books a day. Mrs. Appleyard's is only one but then she has to write one occasionally and that cuts into her reading time.

A cold rain fell all day. Cicely kindly made no reference to Indian summer. About the time the guests went home, the rain stopped and clouds blew away from the moon. The wind from East Hill brought a smell of wet wood smoke with it.

In her mind Mrs. Appleyard followed the course of the brook, in full flood tonight, down to her own pond. Suddenly it was spring. Purple iris and blue forget-me-nots edged the pond. The waterfall foamed so loud that she could hardly hear the wood thrushes calling. Suddenly, below the tall green wine-glass of the lady elm something rose out of the dark cedars, a silvery gray shelter from rain, from hot sun, from snow.

Well, thought Mrs. Appleyard, this one can't be burned or carried away by floods. I'll always have it now.

Mrs. Appleyard did most of the cooking for her bridge party the day before it took place. Since she had chicken stock on hand and watercress in the brook she began by getting them together.

Cream of Watercress Soup
FOR EIGHT OR TEN

1 quart fresh crisp watercress, carefully washed	pinch of nutmeg
	pinch of cayenne pepper
1 quart chicken stock	salt to taste (perhaps 1 teaspoon)
3 tablespoons butter	3 cups rich milk
3 tablespoons flour	1 cup thin cream
3 egg yolks	

She makes the stock with veal bones — 2 or 3 pounds, the carcass of a roasted chicken with any meat that clings to it,

4 carrots, washed and sliced, 2 onions sliced, 2 stalks of celery cut fine, celery tops, a tablespoon of snipped parsley, pinches of basil, rosemary and orégano. She uses a large kettle, puts in 2 gallons of water, cooks the stock over low heat for 4 hours. It should cook down to about 2 quarts. She strains and chills it, skims it when it is chilled. It ought to be stiff enough to skate on, she says, and adds that having it on hand is very sustaining.

Put the washed watercress and a cup of the stock into the blender and let it run till you have a smooth bright green purée. Melt the butter, rub in the flour mixed with the seasonings, cook until smooth, about a minute. Remove from heat, stir in the other 3 cups of stock a little at a time. Stir in the purée. Cook over hot water 15 minutes. Scald the milk and cream. Stir them into the watercress mixture. When you are ready to serve the soup, beat the egg yolks. Add some of the soup to them, a little at a time, stirring well, until you have about a cup of egg mixture. Stir this into the soup. Cook until the egg yolks thicken, about 2 minutes. Do not cook too long or it will curdle. It may stand over hot but not boiling water until it is ready to serve.

Mrs. Appleyard likes Euphrates sesame seed crackers with it.

Croustade of Seafood
FOR EIGHT OR TEN

The croustade was also made the day before. It is simply a loaf of home-baked bread, baked according to Andrea Morini's rule but in a round enameled iron casserole instead of in a regular loaf pan. On the afternoon of the party Mrs. Appleyard sliced off the top of the round lightly browned loaf and removed the soft part of the bread. (Don't worry about its being thrown away. She dried it and used it for stuffing another day.) She then buttered the inside of the croustade and the inside of the lid with softened sweet butter. Just before she filled the croustade she set it into a 350° oven to heat for about 5 minutes while she was making the filling.

Seafood Filling

Seafood, flash-frozen as it leaves the ocean, is often better than fish in fish counters, which is often, Mrs. Appleyard regrets to remark, frozen anyway, though partly thawed to an uninteresting limpness. Fish is really mostly water, held together by a few bones. When it thaws, liquid runs out of it leaving it dry and tasteless. Unless you caught it yourself, fish straight from your freezer has the most flavor and the best texture.

For a large croustade, use:

¼ pound butter	½ pound shrimp, peeled and
2 cups light cream	deveined
1 teaspoon paprika	½ pound scallops
¼ teaspoon nutmeg	½ pound oysters
salt to taste	1 pound fillet of haddock, cooked 7
4 egg yolks, beaten	minutes in rapidly boiling
1 pound lobster meat,	water and flaked
cut up, not too fine	4 tablespoons sherry
	2 tablespoons brandy

Use a large enameled iron frying pan. Melt the butter over low heat. Scald the cream and the dry seasonings. Add some cream to the beaten eggs and then the egg mixture to the cream. Add all the fish to the melted butter. Toss over medium heat, till the edges of the oysters start to curl, about 3 minutes. Add the cream and egg mixture. Cook till it thickens and the sauce coats the back of the spoon. At the last minute add the sherry and brandy. Fill the croustade. Serve.

Guests cannot eat this standing up with a fork. They need a table and knives for cutting. Mrs. Appleyard has some small tables that look like Vermont verde antique marble and seem to be about as strong. They are cheering to men, who would be miserable sitting down with plates in their laps. Of course that harvest table in the bridge would have been even better but then — well, let's not brood about it. Think about the salad.

Avocado Salad

This is one of those combinations for which there is no definite rule. Perhaps you prefer it without the onion. In any case it should be mild onion and sliced very thin. Slice the avocado and put it in the bottom of the salad bowl. Squeeze lemon juice over it and cover it with sections of grapefruit and orange and the onion so that it will not turn dark. Since there is plenty of fruit juice in the bowl your dressing should be only oil mixed with whatever seasonings you like. Mrs. Appleyard sometimes adds a little ginger, besides mustard and paprika, and decorates the bowl with a little crystallized ginger. She sometimes puts chicory around it but she likes watercress best.

Brown Betty

In a moment of enthusiasm and forgetting that she is now a kind of Vermonter, Mrs. Appleyard labeled this in her notebook "Perfect Brown Betty." She apologizes for her excitement and says it's pretty good, especially when made with her neighbor's McIntosh apples.

2 cups cubed homemade bread (no crusts)
3 cups pared and thinly sliced apples — 4 large Macs or 6 medium
1 cup white sugar   2 tablespoons butter, in small dots
½ teaspoon nutmeg   grated rind and juice
¼ teaspoon cinnamon   of one lemon
⅛ teaspoon cloves   2 tablespoons butter, melted

Into a straight-sided buttered baking dish, a French soufflé dish or a Swedish enameled iron dish that will hold 1½ quarts, put a layer of your cubed bread. Mix apples, sugar and spice and cover bread with a layer of it. Dot with butter, add a little lemon juice and rind. Put in more layers, alternating bread and apples, till the dish is well heaped. Finish with the cubed bread. Pour over the melted butter. Cover. Bake at 375° for half an hour. Uncover. Bake until apples are tender and crumbs are brown — about half an hour longer. Serve at once with thick cream or vanilla ice cream. Like a soufflé, it will collapse if it stands.

Deer Season

WHEN deer season began, November ceased to be a quiet gray month. Men who wore dull grays and browns the rest of the year happily blossomed into crimson shirts checked with black, into turquoise quilted jackets and tartans never seen by any Scot. Scarlet caps covered the bald spots of bankers as they strolled the streets of Montpelier with guns under their arms. Business sagged into its annual lethargy. Lawyers, doctors, merchants, chiefs had all gone hunting. Also, more inconveniently, had garage men and plumbers. So, Mrs. Appleyard supposed, had rich men, poor men, beggar men, thieves. Also, she thought, with the tingle of the spine that means a mystery story coming on — murderers.

She did not mean the slayers of ten thousand deer but those of the other hunters who are found dead in the woods every year in their bright caps and shirts. Some of these killings are accidental, she supposes. However she realizes that most of the guns she sees will kill neither men nor deer. What most men like about Deer Season is getting out in the woods with their sons and brothers. They are having the happiest hours of the year and they will hurt no one as they take part in this American ritual.

Some of their ancestors came to this country for religious and political reasons but others came because they were eager for land and for the freedom to go hunting. In England the killing of a deer was a privilege of the rich and well fed. The poor and hungry could be hanged for it. If you were a thirteen-year-old juvenile delinquent, you could also be hanged for stealing a silver spoon. Or on the other hand you might be sent to the colonies and become the distinguished ancestor of dashing deer hunters. No matter if you were a colonial governor and were painted by Copley, when she heard your gun go off, Mrs. Appleyard would be pro-deer.

The morning deer season started, Roger Willard came to tell her about the big buck whose tracks she had often found near her pond. Once she had seen him on the hill at sunset, rearing up against a silver-green and orange sky to eat wild apples off one of her trees. One day she was walking near the old cellar hole, the site of the first house in Appleyard Center. There are scraggly lilacs there and Lombardy poplars and bright red roses and apple trees, descendants of those planted a century and a half ago. There was also the buck and he nearly knocked Mrs. Appleyard down as he cavorted out of the cellar hole and into the woods.

"This morning," said Roger, "I got to your house about seven. The road was full of cars with guns sticking out the windows. New York cars — quite a few of them."

There is no way to report exactly the tone in which Roger said "New York cars." It is somewhat as if he said "rattlesnakes," accepting them as a manifestation about which nothing could be done.

"A couple from Massachusetts," he added more tolerantly. After all Massachusetts is in New England and Mrs. Appleyard used to live there. "They were parking cars just about any-where and beating it for the woods. I went round back of the barn to see if the buck had left tracks around the pond and there he was, flat up against the barn, watching those Yorkers. You know the red paint on the back of the barn has faded and worn off in spots and he kind of melted in it. There was a little mist rising off the pond — that helped some too, I guess. Anyway they didn't see him and I swear he looked as if he were laughing at them. Either he didn't see me or he knows the difference between a gun and a Stillson wrench. He didn't hurry a mite, just watched the Yorkers stravaging off into the woods, guns and plaid pants and red caps and all. Then he had a good drink out of the pond and went along, not very fast, to the old cellar hole, having a nap there now, I wouldn't wonder. You think I ought to paint that side of the barn? There's still some Venetian red in the barrel."

"No," said Mrs. Appleyard who was delighted to think of the buck using this background for protective coloration while the Yorkers, armed to their dentures, trudged through the woods.

Of course, to do them justice, many of them spent much of the day sociably drinking by the roadside. She saw one trio playing a few hands of bridge. Or was it poker? Not having been asked to make a fourth, she is not sure but she feels that the practice should be encouraged.

She toyed with the idea of putting her outdoor fireplace at the disposal of hunting parties. For a price, naturally: to raise money for the PTA. She would have gourmet foods and vintage wines on sale, pine tables for eating or bridge, a supply of crossword puzzles, paperbacks of her own mystery stories and cots with tartan rugs.

That will keep them out of the woods, she thought, and went on to plan some good sleep-producing menus.

The Elizabethans served the right sort of meal. Once when the Earl of Leicester entertained the Queen, there were two hundred courses. One was lamb "cooked to resemble venison." I might give the hunters collops of lamb, thought Mrs. Appleyard. There wouldn't be time to make imitation venison pasty. I'd let them cook the collops themselves. I'd have chefs hats for them — plaid, of course. "Now," I'd say, "just take some currant jelly — "

At this point in her meditation, the telephone rang.

It was Venetia Hopkins reporting that her gun had brought in a haunch of venison. She did not mean that she had killed a deer. She can't even bring herself to shoot a woodchuck that has just eaten most of her green peas. In deer season, Earl Lester (not related to Queen Elizabeth's friend) borrows her gun, a very fine one, and if he gets his deer, he gives Venetia a piece.

Mrs. Appleyard rather likes the phrase "his deer." It suggests that a large buck has Earl's social security number tattooed on it and is leaping around waiting for Earl to shoot it.

"I'll hang it till the weekend and if you'll come over and help cook it, we'll have a party."

Mrs. Appleyard, who is inconsistent enough to like to eat venison when it has become an impersonal piece of meat, says: "Fine. We'll cook it to resemble venison. I'll be right over to plan the menu."

MENU FOR DEER SEASON

Celery   Olives   Radishes
Clear Beet Soup†
Roast Venison, Currant-Orange Sauce*
Kasha with Mushrooms*   Green Beans, Garlic Croutons*
Red and Green Peppers, Sautés*
Lemon Soufflé*   Foamy Sauce*
Charmes Chambertin 1953

Roast Venison

Not being obliged to make lamb masquerade as venison, Mrs. Appleyard cooked the venison as she would lamb. It had been hanging for two days in the freezer room. It stood there for two days longer in the covered roaster with the ventilators in the cover open. It weighed 4¼ pounds, all clear meat, no bones. Mrs. Appleyard, after a brief glance into her crystal ball, decided to cook it at 250° and allow 25 minutes to the pound or until the thermometer she had inserted in it registered 145°. She rubbed it all over with melted butter, dusted it very lightly with flour seasoned with pinches of mixed herbs, cinnamon and nutmeg, put it uncovered on a rack in a pan in the oven and left it alone for an hour and three quarters. She says a hot oven dries and toughens venison.

If you feel in the mood to take more trouble and have an eight-pound roast here is another method.

Marinate it for two days in the covered roaster. Pour around it: 1 quart of red wine (Zinfandel), 1 quart fizzy cider.

Add:

6 cloves	5 cloves garlic, put through press
1 teaspoon each, allspice, nutmeg and cinnamon	1 teaspoon mixed herbs, thyme, rosemary, orégano
3 onions, sliced thin	3 cups carrot sticks
	bay leaf

Turn it twice each day. Remove from marinade. Cover it with seasoned flour and slices of beef suet. Put it on a rack in the roaster. Put about a cup of the marinade in the pan. Add more as it cooks away. Cook uncovered at 250° to 145° if you like it rare, about 4 hours for this size piece, or to 155° if you

like it better done but do not overcook it. Gravy may be made
from the juice in the pan. Brown 2 tablespoons of butter, work
in 2 tablespoons of browned flour, remove from heat. Stir in 1
cup of the hot juice from the roaster. Add ½ glass of currant
jelly.

In either of these methods if the roast does not look brown
enough to suit you, run it very briefly under the broiler. Let it
cool slightly while the soup is being eaten. It carves better if it
is not hot from the oven.

Currant-Orange Sauce

1 cup red wine	juice of 1 orange
1 tablespoon thin orange peel, finely cut	½ cup orange marmalade, made from Seville oranges
1 tablespoon thin lemon peel, finely cut	1 glass currant jelly

Mix the wine, orange and lemon peel and orange juice. When
it boils, add the marmalade and the currant jelly and stir until
they melt. Set aside in a warm place until it is needed.

Kasha with Mushrooms

Kasha is one of Venetia's specialties. It is a confusing vegetable to many people. Mrs. Appleyard looked it up in the dictionary and found it defined as barley groats. You may use
groats if you like. Follow the directions on the package. The
kind Venetia used, however, is a kind of cracked wheat. She
buys it from a Syrian shop where they part with it suspiciously.
Apparently something — possibly her blond hair and blue eyes
— make them think she is not a Syrian. She always feels slightly

nervous while buying it, as if a real Syrian might come along and, with one imperious gesture, make her hand it over.

Sometimes she uses a kind packaged under the name of Wonder Wheat or some misspelling of that name. The package contains an envelope full of herbs and spices. It is the opinion of both Venetia and Mrs. Appleyard that these condiments should be discarded or perhaps they could be used to melt snow off the front walk. The charm of kasha is that its own delicate flavor absorbs and complements other flavors. Mrs. Appleyard sometimes buys whole-grain wheat and grinds it herself. This sort of kasha has to be soaked in cold water for 2 hours before the first cooking.

Whatever kind you use, cook it for 5 minutes over high heat, strirring it constantly. Use about 2 cups of water to one of kasha. Then cook it over boiling water for at least half an hour. Turn off the heat and leave the kasha over the hot water. Just before you serve it, set the water under it boiling for 5 minutes.

The mushrooms used with it were caps only, sliced vertically, tossed in butter with finely minced onion for 5 minutes and added to the kasha before its last 5 minutes of cooking. For eight people allow a quart of cooked kasha, half a pound of mushroom caps, a teaspoon of minced onion, two tablespoons of butter.

Green Beans with Garlic Croutons
FOR EIGHT

The beans were Mrs. Appleyard's own frozen beans from her garden. Packaged French-cut frozen beans may be used.

2 packages beans	garlic croutons
½ cup heavy cream	2 tablespoons sour cream
salt, pepper paprika, to taste	

Cook the beans in the top of a double boiler in a small amount of boiling water, about 2 tablespoons to a package. Keep stirring with a fork so that the ice in them will melt as fast as possible. After 6 or 7 minutes, the water should have all cooked away. Add the sweet cream. Set the beans over hot water until serving time. They improve while standing.

In the meantime make the garlic croutons. Cut 3 slices of homemade bread or Anadama white bread into quarter-inch cubes. Toss them in 3 tablespoons of melted butter until they are delicately browned. Sprinkle them with 1 teaspoon garlic powder. Set aside in a warm place. At serving time add the sour cream and seasonings to the beans. Put them in a hot dish. Serve with the croutons sprinkled over them.

Red and Green Peppers, Sautés

Plain green peppers will do but if they are partly ripe, showing some red and orange, they look cheerful. Allow half a good-sized pepper for each person to be served. Split the peppers, carefully clean out seeds and white pulp. Cut the peppers with scissors into long narrow strips. Toss these in melted butter or in part butter and part cooking or olive oil until the edges are brown. Do not overcook. They should be slightly *al dente*. Venetia cooks them in a scarlet and ivory frying pan and serves them in the same pan.

Lemon Soufflé
FOR EIGHT

The lemon soufflé went into the oven when the guests sat down to eat their soup. It takes only a few minutes to mix it and this Mrs. Appleyard did while Venetia was serving the soup and persuading the guests to stop admiring the table and sit down.

This soufflé needs a large straight-sided dish, or two smaller French soufflé dishes will do. In either case before you start beating your eggs, light the oven at 325° and set into it a large dripping pan with a rack in it and about an inch of hot water. Mrs. Appleyard, earlier that day, had made a collar of wax paper to extend the height of the soufflé dish. She uses paper clips to fasten it.

No — she says in response to an impertinent question — she has never found a paper clip in the soufflé but try Scotch tape if you like.

The ingredients are:

8 eggs separated in two bowls,   2 cups powdered sugar, sifted
the yolks in the larger one   4 tablespoons lemon juice
grated rind of 2 lemons

Beat the egg whites stiff. Beat in, a tablespoon at a time, a cup of the sugar. Without washing the beater, beat the egg yolks till thick and lemon-colored. If you use an electric mixer you can get an assistant to beat the yolks while you do the whites. Add the lemon juice and rind to them, still beating. Beat in the rest of the sugar. Fold in the whites. Be gentle but thorough.

Put the mixture into the soufflé dish. Clip on the paper collar. Set the dish on the rack in the pan of hot water in the oven. The soufflé should be ready in 40–50 minutes. This will serve eight generously and how else do you want to serve them?

Foamy Sauce

Mrs. Appleyard has the ingredients for the sauce all ready and when dessert time comes, she makes it. While she performs this congenial task, the guests clear the table. Guests are wonderfully well trained these days. Mrs. Appleyard thinks that one of the happy features of modern times is that no impatient retainer is breathing hard down your neck, ready to snatch your plate before you have finished. Miraculously, on this occasion both soufflé and sauce are ready when the guests are back in their places.

The sauce consisted of:

½ cup butter, creamed	3 egg yolks
1 cup powdered sugar	1 teaspoon vanilla
2 tablespoons sherry or rum if you prefer	

Have the butter already creamed in the top of a double boiler. Mrs. Appleyard uses rather a deep one into which the eggbeater fits well. Set the butter over hot, not boiling water. Beat in first the sugar, a little at a time. Then beat the egg yolks well and add them. Keep beating. Add the flavorings. Beat some more. At the end of 7 minutes, if you arm is still working, the sauce should be light and foamy. Have a warm pitcher that pours well ready. Scrape every drop of sauce into it with what Venetia calls a spendthrift's enemy. Mrs. Appleyard calls it a miser's friend. Actually, if we are going to be literal, it's a rubber scraper.

This dessert was so popular that after the first refined screams of excitement and a few manly growls of approval, it was eaten in a sort of trance. A cook's best compliment, Mrs. Appleyard thinks.

Thanksgiving

It seemed to Mrs. Appleyard that the guns had hardly stopped cracking for deer season when Thanksgiving arrived. She and Cicely served a co-operative meal. The turkey, mashed potato and the giblet gravy were cooked in Cicely's large kitchen. The pies, the vegetables and the cranberry sauce were cooked in Mrs. Appleyard's apartment. By Thanksgiving time she had become so congenial with her new electric unit that she often turned on the proper burners at the right speed and also got them off again without scorching anything.

She still feels rather as if she were piloting a jet plane and it continues to be a happy surprise that the refrigerator and the oven work side by side in perfect harmony, the same current keeping the ice cream cold and the oven hot. She also feels that people smart enough to think up such comfortable co-operation ought to be able to stop shaking fists full of bombs at their neighbors.

"We could just turn it over to the women, I suppose," said her grandson, Tommy Bradshaw, with just a slight tone of skepticism in his voice, "but who will make the pies?"

"I'd trust Mrs. Roosevelt and Mme. Khrushchev to take care of the bombs," Mrs. Appleyard said. "I daresay neither of them has a really light hand with pastry," and she went on rolling out hers. Perhaps this is as good a place as any to tell how she treats that substance.

2000-Layer Pastry

If you like your pastry pale, tough and tasteless, do not follow this rule, which produces a sort of puff paste, tender, brown and flaky. It is easy to make and is better made by amateurs than by experienced pie makers, who are inclined to thump with the rolling pin. You ought not to hear pastry being rolled out, Mrs. Appleyard says.

She learned this method from her grandmother. Her own contribution is a mathematical one. An essential feature of the process is that you keep cutting the rolled pastry into three pieces, turning your board 90 degrees, piling the pieces on top of each other and rolling the paste out again. The first time you do this, you have three layers, the second nine. They increase in numbers so fast that if you cut, pile, turn and roll seven times, you produce 2187 layers. This is enough, Mrs. Appleyard thinks. She has had approximately 20,000 on occasions and once, out of curiosity, she rolled it out ten times which produced — if her arithmetic is correct and please check it and let her know if it is — 59,049 layers. It did not seem to make much difference in the result.

Take:

4 cups all-purpose flour, sift it 3 times. Measure it. Use what is left beyond 4 cups for flouring your pastry board and rolling pin.

Extra flour for rolling out, as little as possible. Use a pastry-board cloth and rolling-pin cover if you have them or put lightly floured wax paper between rolling pin and paste.

1 cup butter, very cold   1 cup lard, very cold
1 cup ice water

Chill beforehand your water, chopping knife and spatula.
Mrs. Appleyard keeps a large wooden chopping bowl in her
freezer room and uses it to mix her paste in but she has managed
with a large chilled pottery bowl.

Put the flour, butter and lard into your bowl. Chop until
butter and lard are well distributed through the flour in pieces
no bigger than your little fingertip. Add half a cup of the ice
water, all at once. Work it well in with your chopper. Add the
other cup. Work it in. You now have your paste. Get it out of
the bowl and on your floured board with your chopper and
spatula.

Roll paste out gently into an oblong about twelve inches long.
Cut it in three pieces. Lay end pieces on top of middle one.
Turn the board ninety degrees. Roll out paste again, never
touching it with your hands, until you have repeated the process
seven times. You now have 2187 layers of cold air trapped in
the paste.

Mrs. Appleyard now cuts it into chunks the right size for
the pies she is planning to make, wraps each piece in wax paper
and shapes it into a ball as she wraps it. This is the nearest she
comes to touching the paste with her hands. She puts the balls
of it into the refrigerator and takes them out the next day and
rolls them out as she needs them.

When the heat of the oven suddenly strikes the cold air
trapped in the paste, the air expands making the pastry rise to
puffy lightness.

After the dinner had been cooked and served from the two
kitchens, Cicely and her mother agreed that neither felt as
if she had done anything at all. They decided that no house is

complete without a kitchen unit in the living room. That is if there is also a living unit in the kitchen, not to mention a table long enough to seat twelve people in front of a big fireplace. Cicely's house provided all these items as well as a red damask tablecloth faded to the color of old Italian brocade for the table, white openwork compotes for mounds of fruit, white ironstone plates and platters embossed with sheaves of wheat. Her mother produced old blue Canton to serve pie on.

The guests were Hugh Appleyard and his family. They have come home from Brazil, where they found a suitable place for the new capital, and are now turning their attention to the United States. Now that Nicholas (eleven months) has joined the organization his grandmother feels sure that the streets of Boston will be cleared of automobiles and given back to the cows, that cities she is too polite to name will have water suitable for drinking, that unspoiled Vermont will remove car graveyards from the lush green foreground of its best mountain views and that our nation's capital will be moved to Colorado. Just give Nicholas time — he certainly has the energy.

THANKSGIVING MENU

Cream of Spinach Soup*
Montpelier Crackers, Split, Buttered and Toasted*
Roast Turkey with Link Sausages*
Chestnut stuffing   Giblet Gravy*
Whole Cranberry Sauce
Green Beans with Mushrooms*   Glazed Carrots†   Mashed Potato
Pumpkin Pie*   Mince Pie*
Vanilla Ice Cream   Cabot Cheese
Coffee   Cider   Pouilly Fuissé Latour 1955

Cream of Spinach Soup

Make this just as you make the Cream of Watercress Soup (p. 44) substituting spinach for the cress. It may be made the day before you serve it all except for the addition of the egg yolks. Reheat it in a double boiler and add the beaten yolks just before you serve it.

Toasted Montpelier Crackers

As Mrs. Appleyard said in *The Summer Kitchen,* she uses the real names of products when she thinks it will help her readers. These crackers have been made by Cross in Montpelier since 1828 and the standard has never been lowered. They may be ordered through the Maple Corner Store, Calais, Vermont. Receipts for using them are on the box. They are fragile and you may find a few crumbs. Use every single one in meat loaf, stuffing or with bread crumbs in au gratin dishes.

When you use them with soup simply split them, butter them generously and put them under the broiler four inches or more from the flame. Remove them, a few at a time, as soon as the butter is a pale golden brown and move the others towards the spot where they brown the most quickly. They should not be dark brown. This takes only a few minutes so watch them all the time. It may be done in the oven but Mrs. Appleyard thinks it is easier to get the right shade of pale gold under the broiler where you can see what's going on all the time. In any case do them ahead of time. They are better if they stand and cool for a while. Of course Mrs. Appleyard has scorched her quota, but the chickadees that come to her feeder relish every crumb.

Roast Turkey

This was a Vermont turkey and just as broadbreasted as if it had come from New Hampshire, New York or Utah. It weighed, ready to stuff, about fourteen pounds. It had never been frozen and it had been kept not in the refrigerator but in a cool room for two days in a covered roaster. Whether a turkey has been frozen or not it is important to have it at an even temperature all through before you stuff it. Be sure to get the giblets and neck out of a frozen turkey as soon as you can so that there will not be an icy spot left in the center. Cooking and mincing the giblets for gravy is something you can do the day before the turkey is to be roasted and you will be glad you got the task out of the way.

Cicely allowed 22 minutes to the pound at 275° and she cooked the turkey uncovered on a rack in a dripping pan until the meat thermometer, thrust into the second joint close to the body, registered 185°. She figured that it would need about 5 hours cooking time. During the last 2 hours she draped links of sausage over the turkey. She had already brushed it all over with melted butter before she put it into the oven. The sausages help to baste it and are delicious themselves with this long slow cooking. When a turkey was thus decorated, Mrs. Appleyard's English father used to call it the Alderman in Chains.

This alderman had enough parsley around it for a wreath for a winner in a Greek race. That's what they used — parsley.

καλὰ σέλινα means beautiful parsley. Mrs. Appleyard, who is teaching herself Greek in her spare time, learned this just in time to tell it to her grandchildren, who brought her an enormous bunch of parsley from her own garden. They promptly offered to make her a wreath of it but she decided that on the whole it would be more becoming to the turkey.

Chestnut Stuffing

Cicely and her mother had stuffed the turkey the night before. Mrs. Appleyard has recently learned a fact of life that she wishes she had known long ago. It is not necessary to shell chestnuts. They come in cans, all cooked. Or — if you are lucky enough to have a good Italian grocery at hand — you can get dried ones. You soak them overnight and cook them until they are soft. Either way is so much easier than that routine of cutting crosses on the shells, of toasting and tossing the nuts in a buttered frying pan that chestnut stuffing is no longer a hard-fought battle.

For this batch Cicely allowed:

3 cups bread crumbs, made of homemade bread, dried and rolled into rather coarse crumbs
1 teaspoon mixed herbs
½ pound sausage meat
24 chestnuts, each broken into 4 or 5 pieces

1 cup Montpelier cracker crumbs
1 small onion, finely minced
2 eggs, lightly beaten with ½ cup milk

Mix all together. *Never* taste it after you have put in the raw sausage meat. There is still such a thing as trichinosis in the world. Cicely likes a dressing that is rather dry in texture. Add more milk if you like yours moist. You may also use ¼ lb of butter, melted, if you prefer it to the sausage meat.

This is a very lightly seasoned dressing because otherwise you would not taste the chestnuts. If you are not lucky enough to find them, this may be made as a plain dressing in which case you would probably increase the amount of herbs. Remember that the sausage meat has sage in it and that will supply part of the flavor.

Cranberry Sauce

The Appleyards like cranberry sauce with the berries popped and not strained. Mrs. Appleyard buys Massachusetts cranberries and cooks them exactly the way it says on the package. For eight people she uses two packages and cooks them the day before they are to be served, heaps them in her best Sandwich glass compote and sets them in a cool place.

Giblet Gravy

The day before you plan to make the gravy, simmer the gizzard, heart and neck until they are tender, 2 or 3 hours. The last 20 minutes add the liver. Mince all the meat fine, discarding bones and gristle. Use a wooden bowl and a chopping knife. Set the chopped giblets in a cool place. Save the water in which they were cooked in a separate bowl.

The next day when the turkey is almost cooked, take:

4 tablespoons of fat from the roasting pan	pepper from the grinder
1 small onion, finely minced	paprika, salt to taste
minced giblets and meat from neck	2 cups stock from giblets
4 tablespoons flour	2 cups rich milk
	2 tablespoons finely scissored parsley

In a large iron frying pan put the fat and sauté the onion in it. Add the minced giblets and cook over low heat stirring constantly until the mixture begins to brown. If it has absorbed all the fat, add another tablespoonful. Mix flour and seasonings and sprinkle over the mixture, blending them in well. Add gradually, while stirring, the stock. When the mixture begins to thicken, blend in slowly the milk. (In the city use 1 cup milk and 1 cup thin cream.) This may now stand until you are ready to serve it. Heat it up, put it in hot bowl, sprinkle parsley over it.

Green Beans with Mushrooms
FOR EIGHT

2 packages frozen French-cut beans	1 tablespoon flour
1 teaspoon minced onion	½ teaspoon paprika
2 tablespoons butter	salt to taste
½ teaspoon nutmeg	½ cup cream
1 pound mushrooms, caps cut vertically, stems sliced thin	2 tablespoons sherry (optional)

Every now and then Mrs. Appleyard tries to have a Thanksgiving or Christmas dinner without this vegetable but her grandchildren, hardened gourmets when still in their high chairs, protested. Make these ahead of time and keep them in a double boiler till they are needed. They improve with standing.

Cook the beans in a small amount of water until they are tender but not mushy. Do not overcook. Put them in the top of a double boiler. Sauté the onion in the butter till it is straw-colored. Add the mushroom caps and stems and cook 4 or 5 minutes, stirring well. Sprinkle over the flour mixed with the seasonings, blend it in. Do this over very low heat. Add the cream, let it get hot but not boil. Add the mixture to the beans and stir well.

Just before serving reheat, add more cream if necessary. Add the sherry. Serve.

Variations on a theme:
Perhaps this is as good a place as any to mention that this combination of mushrooms, onion, butter, cream and seasoned flour may also be used with:

Broccoli	Lima Beans
Brussels Sprouts	Shell Beans

Mix the mushroom sauce — that's what it really is — with the cooked vegetable. Let the mixture stand over hot water till needed. Mrs. Appleyard likes the flavor of sherry with the green beans and lima beans but not with the other vegetables. You may like them all better without.

THANKSGIVING PIES

In Mrs. Appleyard's youth her grandmother always had a large chicken pie as well as the turkey. There used to be three other kinds of pie too. Mrs. Appleyard has fallen far below this standard. She considers chicken pie an event in itself and she made only two kinds of pie for dessert — mince and pumpkin.

Mince Pie

If you have a large hungry family, a big covered crock and a cool place to keep it in, it is worthwhile to make mincemeat yourself. Do it at least a week before Thanksgiving. It mellows

as it stands. Vermonters sometimes use venison for the meat but
beef is excellent in it.

3 pounds round of beef, simmered till
tender, about 5 hours and
chopped, rather fine
1 gallon fizzy cider
Tart apples, twice as much bulk as
you have meat, measured after they
are pared and quartered and after
the meat is chopped
1 pound suet, chopped
1 pound citron, chopped
¼ pound each candied orange and
lemon peel

2 pounds seedless raisins
2 pounds currants
1 pound seeded raisins
1 tablespoon cinnamon
1½ tablespoons nutmeg
¼ teaspoon clove
2 teaspoons allspice
1 tablespoon extract of lemon
2 lemons, juice and grated rind
3 cups brandy
2 pounds sugar
1½ cups stock from meat

When you chop the meat, remove any pieces of gristle. Do
not put meat through the grinder. Use a wooden bowl and a
real chopper. While you are chopping the meat let the water
in which it was boiled cook down so that you have about a quart
of good stock. Also put the cider on to cook until the gallon
cooks down to 2 quarts. Measure the chopped meat. Fix twice
as much chopped McIntosh apple. Chop and mix in the suet.
Moisten the mixture with a quart of the cooked cider. Cook the
citron and peel in the other quart for ten minutes. Strain. Add
them to the meat. Add currants, raisins, spices, lemon extract,
lemon juice, rind and sugar. Add the meat stock. Put the whole
mixture in a heavy kettle. Cook for 2 hours over very low heat.
Stir carefully from the bottom now and then. Moisten occasionally with the rest of the cider. During the last half hour the
mixture should be thick enough so it will absorb the brandy. Do
not add the brandy if the mixture is too moist. As it stands it
should dry slightly and absorb the mixture. Add more brandy
if needed just before you make the pies.

If you do not feel in the mood for this adventure you have Mrs. Appleyard's permission to do what she plans to do this year: buy S. S. Pierce's mincemeat, heat it slightly and add some brandy the day before you use it. Cover and let it stand in a cool, not cold, place overnight.

Actually if she were not writing this book she would be making mincemeat herself. She says there is something restful about it. During much of the process you can be writing letters, making a miniature Chippendale chair, reading Gibbon's *Decline and Fall of the Roman Empire* or just watching evening grosbeaks eating sunflower seeds. Mince pie contains everything necessary to the nourishment of the human system. So do sunflower seeds, but on the whole Mrs. Appleyard prefers mince pie. The house smells wonderful and breathing the spicy steam from the cooking mincemeat is good for you.

"In what way?" inquires one of her grandchildren, a scientific type.

"It's good for — well, for sinus trouble," Mrs. Appleyard says.

"But you don't have any," objects her relative.

"That's why," his grandmother says firmly and goes on to the subject of

BAKING MINCE PIES

You have plenty of pastry on hand, of course. It may be in a package, in which case follow directions exactly and you will get a perfectly edible pie in which Mrs. Appleyard wishes she could take more interest.

She herself has suitable portions made the day before (as on p. 60) in the refrigerator. They are wrapped in wax paper. The larger balls are for the bottoms of double crust pies or for pie shells. The smaller ones are for top crusts.

Flour your board slightly, also your rolling pin. Gently roll
out a circle of paste at least an inch larger than your pie tin. Add
a few extra dots of butter. Place your tin face down on the paste
and mark a circle an inch larger than the tin around it. Cut out
your circle. Save the scraps left over. Touch the paste with
your hands as little as possible. Using a cold spatula and pancake
turner, fold your circle in quarters, and lift it to the pan. Unfold
it. Press it against the sides of the pan. You'll have to use your
fingers for this. Put the lined pan into the refrigerator while you
roll out the top crust. Chill the scraps too. Now roll out one
of your smaller balls. Fold in quarters. Snip it with scissors in
three places to make gashes through which steam can escape.
Light the oven: 450°. Fill the pan generously with mincemeat.
It will settle while cooking. With a pastry brush, moisten the
edge of the lower crust with ice water. Put on the top crust.
Fold the lower edge up over the top edge and press crusts lightly
together with a fork. Return pie to the refrigerator for 5 minutes while you roll out the scraps you saved. Cut the rolled paste
into strips. Twist two strips together and lay the twist around
the edge of the pie. Make a bowknot of any pieces left and lay
it on top of the pie.

The whole thing is going to puff and brown delicately and
melt in the mouth. It is not going to remind anyone of our great
and admirable plastics industry.

Start the pie on the lower shelf of the 450° oven and bake 30
minutes. Move it to the top shelf. Reduce heat to 350°. It may
take another half hour to brown it enough. Serve it hot with
vanilla ice cream and wedges of Vermont cheese. If there is
any left, it's also good cold.

Mrs. Appleyard has been known to bake a mince pie the day
before and have it cold and also have one hot. The cold pie was
a tribute to Mr. Appleyard's ancestors who brought plenty of

frozen pies with them when they came to Vermont from Massachusetts with an ox team over a blazed trail.

It took Mrs. Appleyard about a quarter of a century to realize that she could have her pie hot if she liked and that the operation Deep-Freeze customers could enjoy theirs too. She also learned from Mr. Appleyard's mother how to make

Pumpkin Pie Filling

This is also something that you do the day before you are going to bake your pie.

Mrs. Appleyard likes to use fresh pumpkin from a small sweet "pie" pumpkin from her own garden. She says this is largely a sentimental idea and that to be perfectly honest she can't tell it from canned pumpkin properly treated.

The treatment consists of buttering a large iron frying pan and cooking the pumpkin pulp — either freshly steamed or canned — until the natural sugar in it caramelizes and it is a deep golden brown in color. It should be as dry as mashed potato. This process takes your complete attention: no chess, no bird watching, please. Stand right there and, with a large wooden spoon, turn the pumpkin over and over so that every part of it comes in contact with the hot pan from time to time. Do it over medium heat. You are trying to make it a uniform brown not a kind of palomino with black spots.

From time to time steam will puff out of it. Stir those steaming spots well from the bottom. Drying out pumpkin in the oven is not a substitute for this top-of-the-stove process. In the oven the pumpkin just dries on the outside and is still moist inside. It takes only about 20 minutes to cook 2 cups of watery pumpkin down to the 1½ cups of the dry golden substance that you need for baking two pies.

Mix:

1½ cups caramelized pumpkin	1 cup cream
2 tablespoons flour	1 teaspoon cinnamon
1 cup sugar	½ teaspoon ginger
1 teaspoon butter	½ teaspoon nutmeg
3 cups rich milk	2 eggs

Put the cooked pumpkin into a bowl. Sprinkle it with the flour. Add sugar. Stir till the flour vanishes. Butter a saucepan. Pour in the milk. Scald it but do not let it boil. Add the cream and the seasonings. The Appleyards like it lightly spiced so that they can still taste the pumpkin. Increase the seasonings if you like the pumpkin concealed by a dark smog of spice. Add clove and allspice, chile tepines and curry powder for all Mrs. Appleyard cares — it's your pie, isn't it? ("Relax," says Cicely at this point.)

Her mother relaxes and says that you mix the sugar with the pumpkin, pour the hot milk and cream and spices over the pumpkin mixture and then add the well-beaten eggs.

You are supposed to have two pie shells ready. (For pastry see p. 60.) They should be nicely fluted around the edge or with a braided strip laid all around the edge. Do not fill the shells too full: three quarters of an inch is about right. The filling will expand slightly in baking. Bake only what you will use that day. Both filling and pastry will keep in the refrigerator until you need them. Put one-inch strips of gauze, slightly moistened, around the edges of the pies. This will keep them from browning too fast before the filling is cooked.

Bake in a preheated oven at 450° for half an hour. Reduce the heat to 325° and bake them until the crust is well browned and they just shake in the middle when moved — about 15 minutes longer. Or test the filling with the blade of a silver knife, delicately inserted. When the pies are done, it comes out clean.

Old Home Day

Just because Mrs. Appleyard has officially changed her residence from Woodbrook Green in Massachusetts to Appleyard Center in Vermont it does not mean that she feels no responsibility for her native state. She still has to check up on the Symphony from time to time, visit the gentlest yet firmest dentist in the world, have the heels of her shoes made straight and her hair made crooked and buy a hat that will be like her other hats, yet different. Accordingly she was much gratified when the McNabs asked her to visit them for a few days. The people who bought her house were delighted to take the McNabs along with it and give them kitchen privileges so she would be a visitor in the house where Washington once slept.

When she finished packing her car the contents may safely be called unique. Who else travels with seven favorite cookbooks, frozen vegetables from a Vermont garden, a Burberry coat thirty-three years old, four pens with which no one else in the United States including Puerto Rico can write, eight pounds of fruitcake, Volume Two of the *Decline and Fall of the Roman Empire*, materials for making tinsel pictures and a large box containing what are simply called The Papers?

These are filed according to a system peculiar to their owner in envelopes of various shapes and sizes. Seeing them, librarians shudder briefly and then brighten up, for they remember that Mrs. Appleyard once thought of joining their profession — but didn't. If she had, some library, like her box, might contain an envelope marked "Ideas — not for anything special." Perhaps the escape was not narrow but it was certainly fortunate.

There was a light frost, crystallized dew really, the night before Mrs. Appleyard started south. It steamed off the sunny sides of fence posts and telephone poles but lay in the shadows of pointed firs marking their silhouettes in silver on the lion-colored grass. Fir trees themselves had their own dark needles pointed with sparkling needles of hoarfrost, each one a rainbow. Every blade of grass, every dried stalk of mullein or golden rod or milkweed was its own private prism, its own burning glass.

Burning, she thought. Something has really burned.

She saw through smoke the blackened shell of a barn. Hay bales still steamed. Tools saved from the fire had been hastily piled in an untidy heap. A few desolate cattle stood near it quietly and their owner stood hopelessly looking at them. His hands were thrust into his pockets. His coat collar was turned up against the raw, smoky air. The place used to look like a Currier and Ives print. Now it was Vermont Tragedy, one too often repeated. The owner might collect insurance, but the life that had gone into building up his farm was blowing away with the smoke.

The two hundred miles of road slipped quietly away. The car seemed to know every turn. It was only two o'clock when it stopped in front of the square white house on Woodbrook

Green. Mrs. Appleyard gave a brisk look around the green and saw that everything was normal: small boys scuffled in the sport locally known as pig-piling or hung upside down on gates. Small girls told them what they ought to be doing. This display of wisdom was checked by the appearance of Mrs. Appleyard. Both sexes converged on her car and began to unload it. Soon a train of native bearers had carried everything to the front porch and sat there eating Vermont apples.

They dashed back to the green as the sightseeing bus zoomed past the statue of General Washington. Visitors who come to see the sights of Woodbrook Green are innocently unconscious that to young Woodbrookians these foreigners are one of its sights. Their numbers, costumes and cameras are carefully checked. Their habit of glancing listlessly at the church steeple and appraising it as "cute" is noted for imitation later. Their questions are politely if inaccurately answered.

Mrs. Appleyard looked on in pleasure. Like the visitors she had forgotten that she too is one of the sights. Suddenly one of the group left the shadow of Washington's horse and plunged across the green. In no time at all she had Mrs. Appleyard's hand in a warm, adhesive clasp and was saying: "When the children told me who you were, I just had to come and tell you how I *love* your books. I always feel so *safe* when I'm reading one."

Mrs. Appleyard, who writes what she has always supposed was a spine-tingling type of mystery story, was not quite sure if she had received a compliment. However, like any author, she was made happy by the idea that people read her books or indeed used them for any purpose — to keep a door open, hold up other books, hold down papers, prop up a window. Everything that wears a book out is good. Sometimes a reader loses a library copy and has to replace it. Mrs. Appleyard gazed in a benevolent glow at the possible consumer of literature and thanked her for her kind words.

"What are you writing now — or is it a secret?" her reader asked coyly.

"Just a cookbook and I really must unpack the manuscript," Mrs. Appleyard said, detaching her hand before writer's cramp set in.

"Now don't put any arsenic in the soup!" said her reader, shaking a finger as she started back for the bus.

This piece of advice gave Mrs. Appleyard several ideas but she decided not to file them in that mysterious envelope. She merely picked up the box containing The Papers and made her entry, an easy matter since on Woodbrook Green no one locks doors. She could hear that someone was exercising kitchen privileges.

The dishwasher was making a noise like waves dashing against a lonely lighthouse in a northeast gale. The whistling kettle whistled. The blender was blending and the mixer was mixing. The washing machine groaned under its load and disgorged the soap it did not need upon the floor. It looked as if it were standing in a meringue. Stewart McNab (eighteen months) had paved a section of the floor with muffin tins and was filling them with soapsuds. This takes good co-ordination but Stewart is a remarkable child, as indeed, by some coincidence, are all Mrs. Appleyard's grandchildren, legal and adopted.

The kitchen was deliciously perfumed with chocolate. Three layers for a cake were cooling on the table. The beaters of the mixer were darkly immersed in fudge frosting. Moira McNab, who was operating the mixer, had her back to the kitchen and her face to the window and such chrysanthemums as had survived the dimpled hands of young nature lovers.

It was one of them, Stewart McNab in fact, who first saw

Mrs. Appleyard. Having no bagpipe handy with which to greet her, he picked up a roll of aluminum foil and blew a loud and soapy blast through it. Moira spun around and found Stewart and Mrs. Appleyard happily beaming upon each other. With his bright red cheeks and bright brown eyes, Stewart could be used to advertise any brand of soap or cereal. As if to prove it, he flung himself in his new shirt of the McNab tartan right into the suds-meringue and came up with a package of bite-sized crunchy rainbow goodness which he offered to Mrs. Appleyard.

Both she and Moira were laughing by this time.

"I'm sorry you have such a noisy welcome," Moira said, turning off some of the instruments of the orchestra.

"I love it," Mrs. Appleyard truthfully stated. She added, to Stewart, "Bhan oidhch an oidche na'm bu ghillean na ghillean," and received a suitable reply through the aluminum trumpet.

In case you have not brushed up on your Gaelic lately, this remark — Mrs. Appleyard says — means: "The night is the night if the lads were the lads." It refers to the time when some McNabs, always an active, decisive clan, it seems, were planning an outing to cut some of their neighbors' heads off. As they were discussing the matter over a haggis with usquebaugh, the McNab of that ilk said to his twelve sons, "Bha'n oidch' an oidche na'm bu ghillean na ghillean" and of course the night *was* the night and the lads were the lads so the story had a happy ending — for the McNabs anyway. Judged by Stewart's appearance, they must have been a fine sight in their tartans of orange red and reddish orange and two shades of green, with their sporrans and their dirks and sprays of heather stuck in their bonnets.

I ought to make Stewart a sporran, Mrs. Appleyard thought. I wish I hadn't let that coonskin coat get made into so many

Davy Crockett hats when they were in style. It would have been just the thing.

"One or two of the neighbors are coming in for dessert tonight," Moira said.

"You mean I'm going to get some of that chocolate cake — wonderful!" said Mrs. Appleyard. "I brought some white fruit-cake. It doesn't keep as well as the dark kind so we'd better use some tonight. It would be too bad if it spoiled. What can I do to help?"

Moira said that there wasn't a thing. She would mop the floor and they'd have supper early so she could get Stewart to bed and then Mrs. Appleyard might like to rest. Mrs. Appleyard realizes that nothing makes a visitor so popular as taking long rests and she was so tired after her drive that, soothed by a few paragraphs of Gibbon, she went sound asleep. Two hours later she became conscious of people being very quiet in the front hall and of doors being carefully shut. Such stillness is always peculiarly resonant so she got up and was dressed when Moira knocked at her door.

The pseudo silence suddenly ceased. Mrs. Appleyard emerged from her room into waves of talk and laughter and firelight, into a delicious blend of coffee, Chanel No. 5, hot chocolate sauce and white wine punch. Everywhere she looked — in the North Parlor and in the library, in the kitchen where men, true to the prerogatives of their sex, stood in all seven doorways while wives dodged around them, in the dining room where candlelight glowed upon a galaxy of desserts — were graduates of her kitchen and its privileges.

For a moment it was touch and go whether Mrs. Appleyard would burst into tears or not. Fortunately the Carroll twins hurled themselves out of the crowd and fell upon her just in time so that she banged her ankle bone sharply against a fine old Boston rocker. A combination of pain, joy and surprise — the twins were supposed to be in Oregon — braced her to reveal merely joy.

She took a long breath and rapidly decided which was which. Yes, Sam had an extra dimple and Pete a small scar on his forehead acquired in a fall down the front stairs, so she attached the correct names to them. Always an original thinker, she did not mention that they had grown even though their blond crew cuts and blue eyes were unexpectedly high in the air.

Sam said: "I remember that dress."

So did everyone who had known her five years, Mrs. Appleyard supposed. Her friends often say: "I always liked that dress," in a way that seems to imply that they must have seen the design in *Godey's Lady's Book* for 1868.

Pete Carroll, more contemporary in mood, said politely, "And I love your shoes."

So does Mrs. Appleyard.

It was a happy day when she discovered Celestial Swans ("the shoes of featherdown that float or fly"). They are comfortable, they are chastely chic, they build morale. It is obvious that the feet in them belong to a Republican, an Episcopalian (occasionally a Unitarian), to a Friend of the Symphony, to a reader of the *Atlantic Monthly* (through bifocals), to a member of the Horticultural Society, to an admirer of Picasso (she thinks he's modern) and to a member of the English Speaking Union. It is not true that she had to show her birth certificate to the salesman. Why should she when on her wrist is a gold chain dripping with little gold disks with her grandchildren's initials and birthdays on them? She sees her dentist twice a year. She does not know a psychoanalyst. She owns a Vermont tweed suit and a scarf made of five minks. One of them, in the battle of life, has probably lost an eye.

Celestial Swans come in many colors and textures. Mrs. Appleyard could have exhibited a fine variety but she chose the sedate well-polished blue pair with the silver buckles. She was much pleased when the twins got down on the floor and tried to see their faces in them.

Their mother, Allison Carroll, detached them from this task and led Mrs. Appleyard to the dessert table, so she could see it while it was a still life. They were none too soon. Blades of shining silver already approached the succulent array of cakes, tortes, cheese cakes and trifles. There was ice cream and sauces to put on it, but ice cream had changed its social position in Mrs. Appleyard's lifetime. It no longer sits coldly upon the pinnacle of gastronomy.

She can remember when it came only from a well-known caterer's and so seldom that special plates were used for it. When the first plate was set down, the children all began to shiver and start their teeth chattering. Their favorite kind was macaroon with orange sherbert. Macaroons baked within an hour came along with it. This combination was eaten in what was known as the ice-cream silence.

Soon dawned the day of the home hand freezer. People followed rules from Philadelphia or the White Mountains, happy places where the inhabitants were supposed to live chiefly upon this delicacy. The result of several hours' cranking came to the table in a sturdy cylinder skidding around in a blue Canton dish. On top of it was a tiny upward-pointing finger of ice cream showing where the crank was while the freezer had been whirled for an hour in ice and salt. Sometimes ice cream tasted of salt but children ate just the same.

Mrs. Appleyard's father used to say: "Those children would eat glue if you froze it!"

Actually, the truth of this remark was not tested until his

great-grandchildren's youth. By that time ice cream contained little of such indigestible substances as cream and fresh fruit. It is now often constructed of good health-giving milk solids, gelatin (a form of glue), dried eggs, emulsifers, cornstarch, lecithin with artificial colors and flavors. These are guaranteed by the United States government, which seems to know a lot about such things, if that's any virtue.

However, it is still possible to buy ice cream made out of cream. There are a few things that the atomic age has not yet spoiled. Mrs. Appleyard hereby confers a gold medal on a few of them: Howard Johnson's ice cream (her favorite is pistachio), Bailey's coconut cakes, Baker's cooking chocolate, Gilchrist's golden macaroons (still baked fresh every hour), Underwood's deviled ham, Royal Riviera pears and Cross's Montpelier crackers. This being a beautiful morning when blue and white snow is bright under a white and blue sky, when maple trees are fans of white coral lightly dusted with crushed diamonds, when pointed firs are white pyramids outlined with invisible green, she is in a pleasant mood and she is not going to mention what has happened to a lot of other foods: just read the labels for yourselves.

With this sinister and sadistic suggestion, she turns her thoughts again to the dessert party. It is a good kind of party, she thinks. Neither hosts nor guests have to give their children knockout drops so as to be there in time: they can bring them along. If it is a co-operative party, like this one on Woodbrook Green, no one has to work very hard although it is evidently a point of honor, Mrs. Appleyard observes, that the desserts should be handmade and not in any blithe fifteen minutes. The kind made out of a package and tasting like the package was conspicuously absent from the table.

"I feel as if I were at a party in a Jane Austen story," Mrs. Appleyard stated. "Syllabubs, quivering jellies, trifles, floating island! Who could ask for anything more?"

Indeed she found it necessary to ask for less. A real helping of all these delights would have run to 5000 calories, she estimated roughly. By special permission she was allowed to pave her plate with a mosaic of small cubes of many colors. With plenty of white wine punch this menu was stimulating at the moment and soothing later.

DESSERT PARTY MENU

Almond Ring*   Upside-Down Caramel Custards*
Glazed Strawberry Cheese Cake*   Pistachio Marron Trifle*
Floating Island*   Fudge Layer Cake with Marshmallows*
White Fruit Cake*   Coffee

Almond Ring

Mrs. Appleyard has given out this information before but as she is still asked for it, she repeats it here. She is proud indeed of the alumna (Woodbrook, K.P. '58) who succeeded in turning out a perfect ring in spite of three children and a thesis to type for her husband.

Spry for greasing mold	1 cup sugar
2 Zwieback rolled very fine, sifted, rolled again	6 ounces almonds, blanched, chopped fine or ground
whites of 5 large eggs	through medium cutter
1 teaspoon almond extract	of grinder
8 candied cherries	

Use a circular mold that will hold a quart. Don't use a fluted one or you will rue the day. The mold should be perfectly smooth. A glass one is best but they are not easy to find. Begin by greasing the mold thoroughly with Spry. There must be no bare spots. *None.* Not *any.* (Is that clear?) Pour in your powdered Zwieback and tip the mold around till every bit of it is coated. Light oven: 325°. Beat egg whites to a good froth. They should be slippery and sticky rather than fluffy. Add almond extract. Fold in alternately sugar and chopped almonds. Pile lightly and evenly and bake for ½ hour or till the top looks like a macaroon. Remove from oven. Press cherries lightly on top. Let stand exactly one minute. Loosen with spatula around the outside edge, pushing spatula gently underneath as far as it will go. With a thin flexible table knife, loosen it carefully around the inner edge. Invert the ring at once on a cooky sheet. Even with the most careful handling, you may find that a small piece has stuck to the mold. Grieve not but tailor it back into place neatly. Now invert the ring again on your serving plate. This will bring it macaroon and cherry side up. Mrs. Appleyard sometimes blanches and browns a few extra almonds and alternates them with the cherries. With it she serves in a separate bowl vanilla ice cream with frozen peaches and raspberries but other flavors go well with it too.

Fudge Layer Cake with Marshmallows

It seems pretty unfair to Mrs. Appleyard that her daughter Cicely first advised her to go on a diet and then asked her to write the rule for "that chocolate cake — you know, the one with the marshmallows lurking under the frosting." Mrs. Appleyard knows all right and it would not take much persuasion to get her to put on her cherry-colored smock and start baking

one of the things; not to mention retiring into a corner immediately afterwards and eating most of it.

Ah well! Into each life some rain must fall and out of each
life a certain number of chocolate cakes had better fall too.
Just be sure this one lands right side up.

2 cups cake flour, sifted before measuring	3 egg yolks, well beaten, large eggs
3 teaspoons baking powder	1 teaspoon vanilla, or — if you'd rather, 3 drops of peppermint
4 squares Baker's chocolate, unsweetened: melted with 2 teaspoons water over hot water	½ cup butter
1 cup brown sugar	1 cup white sugar
1¼ cups milk	3 eggs whites, beaten stiff
	24 marshmallows

Light oven: 350°.

Sift flour three times with the baking powder. Grease two
9 × 9 layer tins. (Increase quantities by one half if you make
three layers: use five small eggs.) Flour pans very lightly, just
the thinnest veil. To the melted chocolate add the brown sugar,
half a cup of the milk and two of the egg yolks. Cook this mixture over hot water stirring all the time till it is like thick custard.
Remove from heat and cool. Add flavoring. Cream the butter
and the white sugar, add the remaining egg yolk, well beaten,
with the rest of the milk, add the cholocate mixture alternately
with the flour, beating well. Fold in the stiffly beaten egg
whites. Spoon lightly into the pans and bake until it shrinks
from edge of the pan and springs back in the middle when
touched with the finger — about 35 minutes.

Remove from pans. Pave each layer neatly with marshmallows which you first cut in halves horizontally and dip briefly
into cold water. While the cake is cooling and amalgamating
itself with the marshmallows, make:

Fudge Frosting

⅓ cup light cream	2 tablespoons butter
4 squares Baker's unsweetened	1 teaspoon vanilla or 3 drops of
chocolate	peppermint extract
1 egg	2 cups confectioner's sugar

Put the light cream and the chocolate in the top of the double boiler and stir until chocolate melts. Cool to lukewarm: stir in the egg unbeaten. Beat in the butter. Add the flavoring. Add the sugar, 2 cups, or more if necessary to make it the right consistency to spread. Put the layers of the cake together — they should be almost cool. Have triangles of wax paper on your serving plate. Place the cake where the points meet. Swirl the frosting over the cake. Remove the papers. No doubt someone will be at hand to lick the surplus frosting off them and scrape the pan.

If you flavor the cake with peppermint, you might like to try covering the layers with white peppermints instead of marshmallows.

"Couldn't they be any other color?" inquires one of Mrs. Appleyard's grandsons.

They could indeed, a whole rainbow. However, if Mrs. Appleyard gets absent-minded about that diet, they will be white. Marshmallow or peppermint, pink, yellow or green, if it is half as good as Moira McNab's masterpiece, all will be well.

Upside-Down Caramel Custards

FOR SIX CUSTARD CUPS

1 cup white sugar	4 eggs, well beaten
1 quart milk, part cream	1 teaspoon vanilla

Put a few drops of water in each cup. In an iron frying pan, caramelize the sugar over medium heat. Have the milk and cream heating over hot, not boiling water. Do not scald the milk or you will have trouble when you add the caramel. Be sure to stir caramel thoroughly and get all the lumps out of it. It should be a rich dark golden brown syrup. Put a little into the bottom of each cup. Add the rest very slowly and carefully to the warm milk. If you are not careful, it will foam up and go all over the stove. (How did Mrs. Appleyard find out this interesting fact? We can't imagine.) Stir well. When there is no undissolved caramel in the milk, set the mixture aside to cool while you beat the eggs. Beat them well, then pour the caramel mixture over them and beat some more. Add the vanilla. Light the oven: 350°. Put a rack and some hot water in a baking pan. Fill the custard cups. Set them on the rack. Bake until custard is set — about 25 minutes. If you put the mixture all in one dish it will take almost an hour to bake. Serve cold. The caramel makes the sauce for it.

Glazed Strawberry Cheese Cake

1 cup wheat germ, mixed with	1 8-ounce cream cheese
½ cup sugar	4 eggs, separated
¼ teaspoon nutmeg	1 tablespoon flour
1 pint cottage cheese	1 cup sugar
½ cup light cream	1 large box frozen strawberries,
½ cup heavy cream	defrosted
2 teaspoons vanilla	1 glass currant jelly
1 tablespoon instant tapioca	

Use a 9 × 13 Pyrex oblong dish. Butter it well and coat it with the wheat germ mixed with the ½ cup of sugar and the nutmeg. Save about ⅓ of the mixture for topping.

Light oven: 300°.

In the mixer put the cottage cheese and the light cream and beat till smooth. Add the heavy cream, vanilla, cream cheese, egg yolks, flour and sugar and blend well by hand. Beat egg whites stiff but not dry and fold them in gently.

Put mixture in the coated dish. Top it with the remaining wheat germ mixture. Bake one hour. Cool.

For the glaze:

Strain 1 cup of juice from the defrosted strawberries. Add 1 glass currant jelly and cook till jelly is melted. Add instant tapioca. Cook over hot water till clear — about half an hour. Cool until it begins to thicken. Top cheescake with the drained whole berries. Add glaze spooning it over each berry. Chill.

Pistachio Marron Trifle

2 dozen lady fingers	½ cup candied fruit (orange
½ cup currant jelly	peel, lemon peel, citron)
24 marrons in syrup	½ cup peach brandy
12 almond macaroons	½ cup pistachio nuts

Custard:

6 eggs	4 cups scalded milk
½ cup sugar	1 teaspoon almond extract

Raffetto's marrons either in vanilla or brandy-flavored syrup were as good as ever last time Mrs. Appleyard had them. However, at the moment she has taken to making her own and she tells how on p. 291. The pistachios are shelled. She mentions this because a very sophisticated and elegant friend of hers encountered them in the shell and almost wrecked one of the extremely efficient homegrown set of teeth that she has had for a certain number of years. Her host, hearing the crunching sound, commented admiringly: "I would certainly like to see what you would do with a peck of steamed clams in the shell."

Mrs. Appleyard makes her own peach brandy but perhaps you spent your summer in some more intellectual way such as sailing your boat or trudging through the Louvre, so she advises you to buy a bottle. She says it's better than hers anyway. Or a little Cointreau will do.

Make the custard first so it will be cooling while you arrange the trifle. Beat the eggs until yolks and whites are well blended. Use a wire whisk or a fork. Beat in the sugar. Pour the scalded milk over the mixture, stirring all the time. Cook over hot but not boiling water until the mixture thickens. This takes about 10 minutes and the mixture must be stirred often from the bottom of the pan. Remove it from the hot water as soon as the custard coats the back of the spoon. It will curdle if it is left too long. Add flavoring. Chill. The friend whose trifle Mrs. Appleyard is describing colors the custard delicately with a little green coloring. She says this makes it taste more like pistachio. Mrs. Appleyard does not guarantee this psychology but says that the trifle looks very handsome in a big glass and gold bowl.

Arrange lady fingers thinly spread with currant jelly around the inside of the bowl. Put in a layer of marrons, quartered, six macaroons cut in eighths, some of the candied fruit. Mix the syrup from the marrons with the peach brandy or Cointreau and sprinkle it over everything, put in another layer of ladyfingers and repeat the process till the bowl is filled. Pour the custard over everything and sprinkle the top with the pistachios. Set the bowl in a cold place for several hours. Whipped cream may be used as a decoration for the top just before serving but it isn't really necessary.

Floating Island

This innocent dessert used to be a favorite with children. Could it be that children were more innocent than they are now? At present it seems to be grownups who like it. This should be served in a large rather shallow bowl so there will be room for plenty of islands.

Meringue:

8 egg whites	1 quart milk, scalded
⅓ cup sifted granulated sugar	½ cup sugar
½ teaspoon vanilla or almond	

Custard:

scalded milk from the meringue recipe	8 egg yolks
½ teaspoon vanilla or almond	½ cup sugar

Make the meringue first. The egg whites should be cold and put into a well-chilled bowl. Beat them to a stiff froth and beat the ⅓ cup of sifted sugar into them. Put the milk into a shallow pan, add the vanilla and half a cup of sugar, let it come to a boil. Drop in heaping tablespoons of the meringue. Use half of it and poach the "islands" over low heat for 3 minutes on each side. Remove them with a skimmer and drain on a paper towel. Repeat with the other half of the meringue.

Now the custard:

Mrs. Appleyard has heard from several readers that the remark "coats the back of the spoon" annoys them. They say they can't tell where it is coated and that it makes them nervous. Anyone in this critical mental state, Mrs. Appleyard says, had better use a candy thermometer and cook the custard to 175°.

She herself finds the back-of-the-spoon technique less nerve-racking, says it makes her feel more like a Norn or a wise woman of the tribe. Well, everyone to her taste. Use the milk in which you poached the meringues. Taste it. Add more flavoring if needed. Strain it through a very fine sieve on the beaten egg yolks. Put the mixture into the top of a double boiler. Cook it, stirring carefully until it coats — excuse it, please: to 175°. This happy moment might occur in about 5 minutes. Pour it into that cool shallow bowl. Mrs. Appleyard uses a Chinese one with green and yellow dragons on it. Put on the islands. Sift a little sugar over them. Chill till serving time.

White Fruitcake (S.H.L.)

½ pound each candied citron, orange peel, lemon peel, and cherries
½ pound pitted dates, cut fine
2 pounds seedless Sultana raisins
½ pound dried figs cut fine with scissors
1½ pounds blanched almonds, slivered (keep 24 whole for decorating)

juice and grated rind of two lemons
2 teaspoons almond extract
½ cup brandy
1 pound each of butter and sugar
4 cups flour
12 eggs
½ teaspoon nutmeg

Put fruit and almonds in a bowl. Pour lemon juice and rind, almond extract and brandy over it. Let it stand while you cream the butter very smooth and work in half the flour. Separate the eggs. Beat the yolks till lemon-colored and beat in the sugar. An electric mixer is a great help in such a project. Light the oven: 300°. Sprinkle the rest of the flour and the nutmeg over the fruit mixture. Beat egg whites stiff. Combine in a large bowl the flour-butter and egg-sugar mixtures. Fold in alternately the floured fruit and the egg whites. Put into greased and lightly floured tube pans. Bake till testing straw comes out clean, about 4 hours. If in one large pan without a tube, it will take longer — perhaps 5 hours. Reduce heat if it browns too quickly.

This is perhaps the right moment for Mrs. Appleyard to express her opinion on the subject of straws for testing cake. A dry clean straw is undoubtedly the best cake tester but where do you get them? The old-fashioned way was to pull one out of a broom. It was washed perfunctorily or not at all. Mrs. Appleyard has seen this method practiced but it never appealed to her.

Luckily her garden — a rather elaborate name for her two hollyhocks, phlox of many colors, chiefly magenta, and such cinnamon pinks as the deer left during November — grows a sturdy variety of grass, Tall Timothy, to be exact. Only the toughest kinds of plants can survive Mrs. Appleyard's inky thumb. She harvests her Tall Timothy with care, leaving plenty for next year, peels it and dries it. It is not only cleaner than a broomstraw — it is straighter, smoother and stronger. She also uses it for picture moldings in her miniature rooms when she has to frame anything. She never sweeps anything with it. She keeps it in a red glass vase from the Chicago World's Fair of 1892, right above the kitchen sink. Help yourself, any time.

December

Apartment Warming

WHEN she used to live alone in the house on Woodbrook Green, Mrs. Appleyard's friends were always telling her she ought to move into a nice little apartment. They did not approve of her version of living alone, which was to fill the house with medical students and their wives and give them kitchen privileges. It is true that two charming young couples "without encumbrance," as landlords so kindly put it, came to live with her when the men were medical students and that when they went away, as competent and impressive doctors, they took with them seven active children including twins. No doubt an apartment would have been more peaceful but not nearly so much. fun.

One mathematical fact not always understood by the general public, though it's really very simple, is that as soon as a child can crawl it begins to make friends. Modern children are bright and frighteningly healthy with vitamins and anti-this-and-that shots and all that good advice from Dr. Spock and they begin to crawl early. So if you have seven children on the lawn you soon have fourteen. And then more. It gets to be rather like that 2000-layer pastry of Mrs. Appleyard's. Only the numbers increase faster because mothers come too.

It is only fair to say that some of them simply dash in ana state: "You wouldn't mind my leaving Archibald here, I hope," and, pausing not for a reply, make a beeline for the League of Women Voters while Archibald is still hitting high C. It is remarkable, Mrs. Appleyard says, how quickly a child stops screaming after his mother has gone; how soon he turns to snatching up any flowers imprudent enough to open their petals that morning.

Of course in December he is more likely to be whanging a fire engine against a Chinese cabinet. It was in spring that someone heard Mrs. Appleyard utter the inhospitable wish that tulips had thorns. She says that in a leisure moment (when was that, Mrs. Appleyard?) she has designed a childproof garden, bright with rugosa roses, cactus, barberries and thistles, those large thistles with the very long spines. When it was pointed out to her that she was the one who was so good at pulling out thorns with tweezers, she invented the Child Picker.

This machine is rather like a cotton picker, only larger and stronger of course because children are so hard on machinery, which would pick up small flower snatchers and drop them into a child pound. One wall of this enclosure would have a row of buttons on it. The child would be able, by pushing the proper ones, to get chewing gum, chocolate bars, lollipops, Mrs. Appleyard's oatmeal cookies and other soothing and adhesive substances.

Traces of these could be removed by his mother when she returned from her civic work. Luckily for such a project, Mrs. Appleyard had a coronary and put in a downstairs bathroom. Several of the mothers of Woodbrook Green say they don't see how they ever got along without it.

The Child Picker would also have an attachment for removing velocipedes, tricycles, scooters and stuffed tigers three feet long from steps, walks and porches. Mrs. Appleyard says there would be a fortune in such a machine. Questioned closely, presumably by someone who wanted to get in on the ground floor as to just how stock in the Child Picker would compete with — say — that of a breakfast cereal loaded with tranquilizers, she replied that mothers would pay well to get the children back, or anyway the velocipedes.

"Why would they?" asked her possible financial associate who just happened to be the father of some of the stickiest of the children who were riding around in circles screaming.

He seemed to have a point there so Mrs. Appleyard took up painting on velvet.

She had always said she would sell the house on Woodbrook Green when the right people came along. After she had been leading her pleasant communal life for ten years, the right people did and soon afterwards she arrived in Appleyard Center preceded by a van containing a number of things. She had wondered how the truck would get into her yard. It turned out to be quite simple, really. The driver backed the trailer in knocking down two gateposts and plunged across the lawn, which was like green velvet only mushier, making its own road.

The men then swiftly put the furniture into the carriage house, dropping an eighteenth century girandole here, a Chippendale mirror there and drove back to Massachusetts.

Mrs. Appleyard was now a year round Vermonter.

As soon as she had mended the mirrors, using the lost-wax process to replace some eagles, which she thinks must have been eaten by the movers, she began to plan her apartment.

In summer rugged Vermonters sleep under blankets and send annoying postcards saying so to such tropical spots as Boston. Really prudent residents use electric blankets, with a few un-wired ones at hand in case the current goes off. Naturally every summer night Mrs. Appleyard thought of winter and she joy-fully accepted Cicely's invitation to have an apartment in her warm house. There were two bedrooms and a bath and her mother, she said, could do whatever she liked with them.

Seeing her mother's eyes flash with delight at this remark, Cicely was not much surprised one morning to find Roger Willard making a large hole in one wall of the house.

"Your mother says this is going to be a sun trap for her bed-room," Roger informed her. "There's going to be one in the living room too. Bay windows, I call 'em."

Roger also insulated floors and covered them with cork tiles, painted woodwork white and walls a delicate sea-blue-green, built shelves for china and cupboards for saucepans. He also told Mrs. Appleyard what programs to watch on TV and gave her some useful suggestions for baking drawn from his experience as an army cook. ("Take 100 pounds of flour, 58 pounds of water and a pound of yeast . . .") He also found what was wrong with the power steering of her new car ("some dope put the cover on crooked when he checked the oil") and fixed the antenna of her FM radio. Nor is this all, but perhaps it is enough to show why Mrs. Appleyard enjoys his company.

Naturally he was present when her electric kitchen was put in place. This ingenious device has three burners, an oven, a broiler, a double sink and a refrigerator with a freezer compartment all in about the same space occupied by an ordinary chest of drawers.

She planned a menu for her apartment-warming that would demonstrate its happy versatility.

Seafood Chowder*   Toasted Montpelier Crackers
Ham Mousse*   Mustard Sauce*
Corn Pudding*   Tossed Salad (p. 147)
Deep-Dish Apple Pie*   Vanilla Ice Cream
with Vanilla Ice Cream   or   with Chocolate Sauce*
Coffee

She was up early the day before the party. She was planning to make the Ham Mousse, the pastry for the pie and the chocolate sauce. She has recently worked out a way to make it so that it can either be heated up or served at room temperature. It does not get sugary and too thick but stays so it can be poured easily if you just keep it on top of the stove where your grandchildren can get it when necessary.

She had even got out her package of chocolate and had found — as Cicely deduced later — that she didn't have enough. That indeed was as far as the preparations for the apartment warming went.

It was a wonderful day as she started for River Bend, a day with the mercury almost touching zero and a coating of fresh diamond dust over snow that had been melting the day before. Every tree had its shadow sharply cut out of thin blue glass lying on the ground below it. Barns glowed red against the snow. The ring of mountains was a dark blue wall, white topped against the cloudless sky. At the schoolhouse the new flag with its fifty stars looked brighter than any flag Mrs. Appleyard had ever seen as it echoed the red, white and blue theme in its own key. Blue jays flashed screaming across the snow. The sun was bright on the heads of a flock of red polls.

The Appleyard Center roads were freshly sanded but as she crossed the town line she found glare ice. She slowed to a cautious crawl keeping far to the right, close to the snowbank. She had almost reached the top of the long hill that twists for two miles down into River Bend when a truck came speeding towards her in the middle of the road. The driver had room to pass but he jammed on his brakes and skidded towards her in a fierce deadly curve.

So Mrs. Appleyard spent the evening of her apartment warming in her favorite hospital. She had a poached egg for supper and some excellent prunes. In a few days she and her cracked ribs returned to Appleyard Center. Her car was demolished so she has not been back to River Bend yet to get the shrimps for the chowder. However, since this is a cookbook and neither a clinical study nor a report to the State Police, she supposes there is no reason why she should keep secret the way she makes the dishes on her menu.

Seafood Chowder

FOR EIGHT

¼ pound beef suet
3 medium onions, minced
6 medium potatoes, sliced thin
½ teaspoon garlic powder
1 teaspoon mixed herbs
¼ teaspoon nutmeg
1 teaspoon paprika
3 pounds haddock fillets, frozen
2 tablespoons flour

3 tablespoons cold water
8-ounce tin of frozen lobster
1 pound shelled, cleaned and
   frozen shrimp
2 8-ounce tins of minced clams
3 cups rich milk
2 cups light cream
sliced lemon
Montpelier crackers

An electric skillet is good to make and serve this in but a big gaily colored enameled iron frying pan will do.

Cut the suet into very small dice and try them out in the frying pan over low heat until they are crisp and a light golden brown. Remove them with a skimmer and drain them on brown paper till you need them. Cook the minced onions in the fat until onion is transparent and straw-colored. Pare the potatoes. Slice them less than a quarter of an inch thick. Pour 1½ quarts of boiling water into the skillet. Put in the potatoes and mix them well with the onions. Sprinkle in the seasonings, except the parsley. Lay in the haddock fillets cut into 4-inch pieces. Cover pan but let some steam escape. Cook about 15 minutes. Water should cook down to about a quart. Now turn off heat. Put the flour in a cup. Add the cold water to it, stirring till smooth. Salt to taste. Strain it through a fine strainer into the mixture. Stir it in well.

The basis of your chowder is now ready and you may set it aside in a cool place to mellow. Several hours will do no harm. Just before you serve it, heat it to boiling point and add the lobster and shrimp, which have slowly defrosted in the refrigerator. Cut the largest pieces of the lobster in medium-sized pieces. Leave shrimp whole. Add the minced clams. Check the time. When liquid boils again, cook mixture 5 minutes. Heat milk and cream so they are just scalding. Add them to the mixture. Taste it and add more seasoning if you like. Do not let the chowder boil after you have added the milk or it will curdle. Put in the suet cubes. Add the minced parsley.

Pass the lemon slices and Montpelier crackers, split, well buttered and delicately browned with it.

Ham Mousse
FOR EIGHT

1½ tablespoons plain gelatin	¾ cup cream
2 tablespoons cold water	2 teaspoons dry mustard
¾ cups hot water	1 teaspoon horse radish (optional)
3 cups ground ham	⅛ teaspoon cayenne

Soak gelatin in cold water 5 minutes. Dissolve in hot water, stirring till it is free from lumps. After grinding the ham — be sure there is no gristle or fat in it — pound it in a mortar till it is smooth. Add gelatin and the seasonings. Whip cream till stiff and add it. Have a mold ready with cold water and ice cubes standing in it. Empty it and put in mousse. Chill in refrigerator for at least 3 hours. When unmolding, set the mold for about 10 seconds into hot water, wipe dry and invert it on serving plate.

Mustard Sauce (C.B. & M.C.)

1 pint heavy cream	salt to taste
½ cup sugar	⅔ cup vinegar
4 tablespoons dry mustard	2 egg yolks

Heat half the cream and the sugar over hot water. Add mustard and salt mixed with the vinegar. Beat egg yolks slightly. Add some of the sauce to them, about 3 tablespoons, one at a time, mixing well. Add the egg mixture to the sauce. Stir it in carefully and cook until it thickens slightly — 2 or 3 minutes. Cool. Before serving, whip the remaining cream and fold it in.

Everyone will say: "*What* makes this mustard sauce so delicious? So much better than mine?"

Mrs. Appleyard, having asked these questions, has gratefully received the directions above.

Corn Pudding

This is best of all made from corn picked fresh from the garden, but either corn from the freezer or whole Golden Bantam from a can may be used successfully.

6 tablespoons melted butter	3 eggs
¾ cup cornmeal	2 cups rich milk
1 cup boiling water	2 teaspoons baking powder
1 cup corn	

In a baking dish that will hold a quart and a half — Mrs. Appleyard likes an old brown Bennington one best — melt 2 tablespoons of the butter. Scald meal with boiling water, right from the kettle. Stir it well with a spoon with holes so there will be no lumps. Add the rest of the butter. Stir till it melts. Beat eggs lightly, add the milk and beat some more. Add the baking powder, beat the mixture into the cornmeal. Add the corn, cut from the cob, or slightly thawed if frozen, or drained if in a can. Stir well. Have the oven ready at 375°. Put the mixture into the warm, buttery baking dish. Bake 35–40 minutes.

Reduce heat to 350° after the first 10 minutes. It should be golden brown on top and have a brown crust on the bottom of the dish.

Mrs. Appleyard likes it cooked so that the center is still rather soft. Other members of the family cherish the brown crust especially but they seem on the whole rather amiable about eating it the way they get it.

Deep-Dish Apple Pie

Make 2000-Layer Pastry (p. 60) the day before you plan to make your pie and set aside a ball of it of suitable size to cover a large dish. This is Mrs. Appleyard's favorite apple pie. There is no problem about the under crust being properly baked because there isn't any. If you choose a dish about twelve inches across and not too deep — three inches perhaps, you get a good proportion between apple and pastry.

2 cups sugar	12 tart Vermont apples
1 teaspoon cinnamon	1 tablespoon butter
⅛ teaspoon cloves	juice of ½ a lemon
1 teaspoon nutmeg	½ teaspoon grated lemon rind

Mrs. Appleyard suggests that you measure the spices carefully and mix them evenly through the sugar. She says it's better not to use any than to scatter them casually about. Perhaps you may prefer different proportions of nutmeg and cinnamon but anyway measure them and don't overspice. You should be able to taste the apples.

Pare the apples. Quarter them. Remove cores and seeds. Slice rather thin. Butter the dish well. Put in a layer of apples, sprinkle them with spiced sugar, repeat layers of apples and sugar till the dish is full. Dot the top layer of apples with butter, sprinkle with lemon juice and rind and any sugar there is left. Apples should be well heaped up because they will settle.

Roll out the pastry gently and cut a circle of the size needed, a little larger than the dish. Moisten the edge of the dish slightly. Fold the circle of paste in quarters, gash it with scissors. Lay it on the dish, centering it carefully, and unfold. Pinch the paste into a neatly fluted border. Take any scraps of paste left and roll them out into an oblong. Cut this into narrow strips. Twist them into a chain and lay it around the pie just inside the fluted edge. Mrs. Appleyard uses the last scraps to make bowknots. She makes two loops and lays them on one side of the pie, then two tails with the ends cut diagonally and a piece across the middle to conceal the place where ends and loops join. Then she makes another for the opposite side of the pie. When the paste rises and puffs, it looks as if the bowknots had really been tied.

After indulging in this innocent pastime, she chills the pie for a few minutes while she is heating the oven to 450°. Put in the pie. After the first 10 minutes reduce the heat to 425° or less if it seems to be browning too quickly. Bake it until it is puffed and delicately brown. Serve it either hot with vanilla ice cream or cold with cheese.

Perhaps someone doesn't eat pie. Mrs. Appleyard with her genial Puritan inheritance can hardly understand this but there are such cases. If one arises give the customer some of the ice cream and

Chocolate Sauce

4 tablespoons butter	1 cup hot water
4 squares Baker's unsweetened chocolate	2 cups sugar
	2 teaspoons vanilla

In the top of a Dutch iron enamel double boiler, put the butter and melt it over low heat. As it melts, add the chocolate and stir till it is melted. Add gradually the hot water. Then stir in the sugar. Cook over low heat, stirring all the time, until every grain of sugar is melted and the sauce thickens — about 5 minutes. This will keep at a good consistency over hot, not boiling, water for some time and will keep so that it can be poured at room temperature. Just before you serve it, add the vanilla.

Well, you can see that Mrs. Appleyard's intentions about her apartment warming were good. If she gets a new car and road conditions seem favorable, she still intends to go to town and get those shrimp and make some chowder.

Candlelight

PERHAPS Appleyard Center is not really busier at Christmas time than New York or Boston. Probably, Mrs. Appleyard admits, it just seems so. Everyone is taking part in the holiday. They are all cutting their own Christmas trees, hauling their own Yule logs, making their own wreaths. When you hear Christmas carols, it is not because they have been piped into a shop to promote customer acceptance: the 4-H club is practicing them, sometimes more than one at a time. The sound of sleigh bells is rarer than in New York, where they are broadcast from every shop in magnificent silvery peals, but when you hear them, they are real sleigh bells, two at least, and they are on a real horse. He does not look much as if he had dashed out of a Currier and Ives print and the bells have a deliberate, almost serious sound. He is a sedate brown horse with a thick winter coat. It harmonizes well with the ancient buffalo robe that his master has wrapped around himself and the boys.

Less in period are the boys in their cowboy suits. Davy Crockett hats and guns in belts hardly seem to Mrs. Appleyard appropriate symbols for a New England Christmas but of course, she says, our culture is a complex one, and if it had been left to the passengers on the *Mayflower* we wouldn't have Christmas at all. She notes with pleasure that the boys are as red-cheeked and bright-eyed as if they came out of an advertisement for one of the tastier forms of toothpaste and that they have their skating boots with them. Frank Flint has dammed up the brook back of his house and the water has spread out and frozen into a pond that looks greenish blue against the snow. Shrill screams are coming from it, making it sound rather as if blue jays were skating, but it is only happy children. Girls do most of the screaming. A pond full of boys never sounds quite so excited.

It reminds Mrs. Appleyard of Rockefeller Center — it's so different. No one is waltzing to "The Beautiful Blue Danube." No one is looking on. Everyone is scrambling over the ice in white jackets and red ones, white boots and black ones, caps, mufflers and mittens of all colors. None of these costumes was designed by *Vogue* but the occupants don't seem depressed about it.

Close to the pond is Frank's red barn. In the barnyard a big bay horse, a small white and brown pony and some Black

Angus heifers are out in the winter sunshine. Their winter coats look as thick and plushy as if they had been woven on one of those machines that make mink by the yard. They seem to be quietly enjoying the skating. Dogs of course are skating too, or anyway pretending they are as they run and bark among the skaters. There are three Norwegian elkhounds, two bandy-legged beagles and a golden cocker. A black saddle horse and a silvery gray burro are hitched to the fence. The burro is adding his braying laugh to the noise from the pond. The horse preserves a dignified silence.

The sun slipped suddenly behind the hill, leaving snow glowing on the mountaintops and turning white birch trunks pink. The moon's coppery gold disk floated up out of Frank's sugar place.

It's going to be a fine evening for the carol singing and for the Davenport's Open House, thought Mrs. Appleyard. I must go and pack my marzipan.

When they got to the church, Fairfield Davenport already had fires going in both the iron stoves that send their long pipes stretching through space and warming it. The stoves were a modern improvement made about 1830. Up to that time people used foot stoves with coals in them or — even more primitive — a freestone in a wooden box with holes in it. You heated the stone in the brick oven and carried it to church in a box. Mrs. Appleyard rather wished she had brought Remember Appleyard's freestone. The fact that heat rises occurred to her.

The old square pews were beginning to fill with people dressed in their warmest clothes. Like the cattle in their winter coats, they looked a size or two larger than usual. Candles lighted the church warmly downstairs and their reflections sparkled in the many-paned windows in a pattern of black and white and gold. Above the high pulpit was a misty, smoky twilight.

Through it Mrs. Appleyard could just make out the letters on the wall: "Remove not the ancient landmark that our fathers have set."

Most of the woodwork in the church is of unpainted pine that has mellowed to a soft brown, but the pulpit, the top edges of the pews and the gallery are all painted a misty blue rather like the smoky air above them. The last time it was painted was before Mrs. Appleyard was born. Her husband, then ten years old, remembered how he and his father, as a gift to the church, mixed blue paint as near as they could to match the old and made everything fresh and clean. An earlier generation of Appleyards had hewed timbers for the building and sawed primeval pines into boards for the pews.

They certainly, Mrs. Appleyard reflected, chose the hardest pine they could find.

The seats were now well filled. Joyce Madden sat down at the organ and the carol singing began. The service was a simple one. Fair Davenport read the Christmas story from St. Luke, pausing often for an appropriate carol. Most of them were sung by the whole congregation but there were some for the choir alone. Mrs. Appleyard however sang them all but not so anyone could hear. She is, fortunately, an internal singer. Every word and note is clearly formed in her mind but the outer voice is someone else's, one of her grandchildren's perhaps or a daughter's or a neighbor's. She knows them all as well as if they were woodwinds in the Symphony, piccolos, flutes, oboes, clarinets and the loud bassoon.

After the singing in the church was over, the 4-H Club and a few valiant parents went singing around the village. They walked to the very edge of it where Robin Viereck lives with only his Nubian goats and his fiddle for company. He came out onto the porch with his fiddle and played while they sang. The goats came out too and tap-danced to "God rest ye merry, gentlemen." When the carols were over he struck into "Portland Fancy" and everyone square-danced in the snow.

Back in the Davenports' big red house the ladies of the village were helping Eleanor unpack and set out the different things that had been brought to the Open House. Eleanor herself must have been working for days to make the wonderful display of sugar cookies in all the Christmas shapes — stars, trees, angels, sheep and shepherds. She had made brandy balls too and tiny meringues; not to mention, of course, feeding her family, making the house beautiful for company and conducting choir rehearsals. By the time the carol singers began stamping snow off their boots, the long table was ready. These were some of the things on it.

> Sugar and Spice Cookies* Pecan Brandy Balls*
> Oatmeal Lace Cookies* Marzipan Fruit*
> Dark Fruitcake* Swedish Cookies* Baked Fudge Brownies*
> Hot Spiced Cider* Coffee

Sugar and Spice Cookies

From the following rule, Eleanor Davenport confided to Mrs. Appleyard, she had made ten dozen cookies.

2½ cups flour	1½ cups sugar
½ teaspoon nutmeg	2 eggs
pinch of allspice	½ cup flour for rolling out,
1 teaspoon cinnamon	less if possible
¼ teaspoon cloves	2 tablespoons cream
½ teaspoon baking powder	pink and green sugar for
1 cup butter	sprinkling

Make the cookies in the mixer. Do not substitute anything for the butter or neither flavor nor texture will be right. Sift the flour three times. Measure it, sift it again with the spices and baking powder. Cream the butter, add sugar gradually, beating all the time. Mix eggs and cream together and beat them in well. Stir in the spiced flour. Chill the mixture one hour. Light oven: 375°. Remove enough dough for a batch of cookies. Keep the rest chilled. Roll it out using as little flour as possible. (Mrs. Appleyard finds it helpful to cover the rolling pin with a paper towel. She fastens it on with Scotch tape.) Cut the cookies in fancy shapes. Put them on a buttered baking sheet. Handle them with two spatulas. Sprinkle some with green sugar, some with pink. Bake about 8 minutes. Do not over-bake.

Pecan Brandy Balls (N.F.L.)
MAKES THIRTY-TWO

½ cup butter	1 cup pecans, finely chopped
¼ cup granulated sugar	1 tablespoon brandy
¾ cup flour	½ cup confectioners' sugar

Cream butter, beat in sugar, flour, nutmeats. Add the brandy. Light oven: 300°.

Press mixture into a square pan 8 × 8. Cut it into 32 pieces. Make each piece into a ball. Sugar your hands lightly with confectioners' sugar while you do this. Put the balls on a lightly greased cooky sheet. Bake 30–35 minutes. They should not brown except where they touch the pan. Remove from the oven. While they are still warm roll them in confectioners' sugar. Cool. Roll them in confectioners' sugar again, using extra if necessary. Keep them in a tightly covered tin box between layers of wax paper. These keep well, so they can be made two

or three days before they are used. They do not, however,
Mrs. Appleyard notices, keep well at the party. So make plenty.

Oatmeal Lace Cookies (P.B.)

As soon as Mrs. Appleyard saw these she realized that her
friend Patience Barlow had been at work. Mrs. Appleyard invented the formula for these about a quarter of a century ago.
With her grandchildren's interests at heart she still makes an
occasional batch. Some of them are larger than others. Some
are usually slightly scorched around the edges. It is Patience who
turns them out uniform in size and shape and of a golden lacy
color and texture that Benvenuto Cellini might have equaled if
he'd felt in the mood and had enough gold on hand.

Mrs. Appleyard was recently given a present that she is
much pleased with, a copy of the latest edition of *Clara Carpenter's Cook Book*. For Clara Carpenter, Mrs. Appleyard feels
a kind of awe and veneration. Mrs. Appleyard — it seems hard
to believe this — was a small child once and her grandmother,
Mrs. Elmore, went to Miss Carpenter's cooking school.

The food that emerged from Mrs. Elmore's kitchen, which
had a polished range rather like a baroque pipe organ, a sink
of Vermont soapstone and tables covered with red and white
damask, was excellent but then, according to Mrs. Appleyard,
it was so before Mrs. Elmore ever crossed Miss Carpenter's
threshold. Apparently Miss Carpenter conferred a sort of mystic
Phi Beta Kappa upon her graduates. The possession of it enabled
them to sit serenely at Louis Quinze tables in their libraries with
sunlight, tempered by stained glass, falling upon rubber plants
and marble busts. They were dressed in black satin basques
trimmed with velvet and jet. Their caps were of velvet

and rose-point lace. They read the works of W. D. Howells and Mrs. Humphry Ward while in their kitchens young ladies who had recently been treading the heather in the highlands broke Lowestoft cups and made Lobster Newburg and vol-au-vents of chicken and oysters under Miss Carpenter's inspiration.

Mrs. Appleyard admits that this picture is slightly idealized. Her grandmother was supposed just to relax among the bric-a-brac. Her daughters considered that at her advanced age (about five years younger than Mrs. Appleyard's at present) this was how she ought to spend her time. Actually, as soon as her daughters left the house to attend to their whist, charities, golf and music Mrs. Elmore would put on a layer or two of aprons and interpret Clara Carpenter to her minions. Moreover it was she who rolled out the pastry for vol-au-vents.

Miss Carpenter's cookbook was a dingy green volume then. Now it has burst into pale pink and turquoise blue. Mrs. Appleyard was much flattered to find included in it, though without mentioning the source, her rule for oatmeal lace cookies exactly as it was given in a book called *Mrs. Appleyard's Kitchen* in 1942: not exactly fame but certainly a nice tribute.

Time however has marched on and that's not exactly how Patience Barlow and she make the cookies now. They have kept experimenting and this is their present formula.

1 cup butter, melted	2¼ cups regular rolled oats
2¼ cups light brown sugar	1 tablespoon flour
1 tablespoon white sugar	1 egg slightly beaten
1 teaspoon vanilla or, if you prefer, ½ teaspoon almond extract	

Before you begin to mix them please note that: quick-cooking oats will not do. You can get regular ones if you insist. The sugar must be light brown. It may be called Golden Brown on the package. That is all right but dark brown will not do. Use butter: margarine will not do. Don't try to make half the rule unless you beat the egg, measure it and use half of it. A messy business and what do you do with what's left? Throw it away? Not in New England. (It seems rather elaborate to get a veal cutlet, so you can dip it in egg and then in crumbs, doesn't it?) Anyway you'll be sorry you did not make the whole batch. They keep well in a tightly closed box between layers of wax paper. Don't try to make them on a hot, humid day with a falling barometer. A clear, crisp blue and white morning is what they prefer.

In a saucepan large enough to hold the whole mixture, melt the butter over low heat. When it starts to froth a little, stir in the sugar, brown and white. Remove pan from heat. Stir in the oats and the flour. Let the mixture cool for at least 5 minutes. This is important. Add the beaten egg and vanilla. Light oven: 375°. Set the mixture in a cool place while the oven is heating and while you fix your pans.

Patience Barlow has baked these circles of golden lace on various kinds of cooky sheets. Heavy ones are best, she says. Better still are old-fashioned iron dripping pans. Grease them lightly with the paper the butter was wrapped in and a small amount of butter. After the first batch is baked it will not be necessary to grease the pans again. Mrs. Appleyard used to keep three pans going. She now finds that two will serve to keep her mentally active.

Put the mixture on the pans by teaspoonfuls, pushing it off the spoon in small circular lumps, leaving plenty of room for the cookies to spread. Seven or eight is about all most pans will take. Fill a second one as soon as the first is in the oven. It takes about 7 minutes to bake them. Watch them carefully. They should be deep golden brown on the edges.

Getting them off the pans needs a little deftness. Let them

stand one minute. Use a spatula and a small pancake turner. Keep testing the edges with the spatula. When the edge of a cooky turns up easily, slide the pancake turner under it and remove it to a large platter. Don't put cookies on top of each other. As soon as they are completely cool, put them in a large tin box with a tight cover with layers of wax paper between and try to hide it from your grandchildren till dinnertime. This rule makes about fifty-two cookies but the smell usually attracts volunteers who are glad to help by eating any that are scorched or broken. If you get forty-six into the box, you have done well.

Marzipan Fruit

Last year Mrs. Appleyard made marzipan fruit for her grand-children. This year they took over the shaping and coloring of the fruit so all she had to do was to supply the marzipan. She made it the day before it was to be used.

The ingredients are:

2 6-ounce packages shelled almonds	3 egg whites, unbeaten
3 cups confectioners' sugar	1 tablespoon soft butter
¼ teaspoon cream of tartar	3 teaspoons pure almond extract
extra confectioners' sugar	

Blanch the almonds. Skin them. Dry them on cooky sheets covered with paper towels in a 250° oven for 15 minutes. Put them on fresh paper towels and let them cool. They must be thoroughly dry. Grind them. This can be done by putting them through the finest attachment of your meat grinder. Mrs. Apple-yard prefers to use her small active Dutch coffee grinder. It makes a noise like a jet plane and reduces a handful of almonds to dry powder in 15 seconds. You can do only a small amount at a time but in a few minutes you will have about 3 loosely packed cups of almond powder.

Now mix the remaining ingredients into what is really un-cooked fondant. Sift the confectioners' sugar with the cream of tartar. Work in the egg whites one at a time, add the butter and the almond extract. Then mix in the powdered almonds. A pastry blending fork is a good tool for mixing the fondant. Next dust a board with confectioners' sugar, dust your hands lightly with sugar and knead the marzipan thoroughly. It should be quite stiff. Wrap it in wax paper and chef's foil and set it in a cool place.

Next day fix your palette of vegetable coloring — Mrs. Apple-yard uses a large white platter for this — and get out your paint-brushes, which should be kept especially for this purpose. Have at least three brushes and three glasses of water to wash them in. Change the water frequently so that your colors will stay clear. Put first on your palette red, yellow, green and violet. Mix orange (red with yellow), carrot color (yellow with a touch of red), pear color (green with a very little red), brown (red and green), strawberry color (red with a touch of yellow).

Shape the marzipan into apples, pears, bananas, strawberries, carrots, peaches, peapods — half open and showing the peas — and potatoes.

Have at hand whole cloves, bits of candied angelica for leaves and strawberry hulls and a mixture of sugar, cocoa and cinna-mon to roll the potatoes in. If angelica is not available, cut the strawberry hulls out of heavy green paper. In either case fasten the hulls on with the small ends of toothpicks dipped in green or brown coloring. Toothpicks are also useful in modeling.

Apples. Dilute yellow coloring and paint them all over. Put a little green around the stem end. Paint one cheek red. Add a few red stripes. Use a clove for the blossom end.

Pears. Dilute yellow and paint all over. Paint one cheek with your pear green and touch the other with red. Use a clove for the blossom end. Fasten on leaves with a brown stem.

Carrots. Paint with carrot color. Touch top with green. No leaves or stem.

Tangerine Oranges. Make little pits all over the surface with the fine point of the toothpick. Paint deep orange color all over. No leaves or stem.

Peaches. Paint yellow, not diluted. Paint one cheek with red just touched with violet. Fasten on leaves with brown stem.

Bananas. Paint with diluted yellow. Stripe and dot with brown and touch end with green.

Peas. For both the partly opened pod and peas inside, use diluted green.

Strawberries. Paint all over with strawberry color. Dot with green seeds. Fasten on hulls with green toothpick stems.

Potatoes. Make depressions with the blunt end of the toothpick. Touch these with brown. Do not paint the rest of the potato, but roll each one in the sugar, cocoa and cinnamon mixture.

Mrs. Appleyard packs assortments of these art objects in strawberry baskets lined first with chef's foil and then with crumpled green tissue paper. She says you can produce a basketful rather quickly, if you organize your workers so that one makes potatoes, for instance, and another specializes in strawberries. However she never seems to have much luck with the assembly line technique, partly perhaps because she doesn't much like to practice it herself. After all, Christmas is hardly the time when an overseer should march up and down among the workers cracking a whip. Her marzipan factory will probably remain inefficient.

However, the results look gay and taste good, the way they did when she was a child. This is not true of the handsome basket she bought for models. By a strange coincidence marzipan made of cracker crumbs, flour, dried egg whites, corn syrup and artificial flavoring does not taste like the real thing. Obviously Mrs. Appleyard has been indulging in the morbid pastime of reading labels on packages. Let us turn to happier things such as

Dark Fruitcake

Mrs. Appleyard ate a piece of fruitcake and said to her daughter, "Why, this tastes like my grandmother's Huckleberry Gingerbread!"

"That," said Cicely, "isn't really so very peculiar. Your granddaughter Camilla made it from your grandmother's rule."

Mrs Appleyard never felt prouder than when she thought of Camilla at eleven years old mixing the following ingredients:

4 cups sifted flour	½ teaspoon soda
1 pound seeded raisins	1½ cups butter
1 pound currants	3 cups sugar
¼ cup citron	6 eggs, separated
½ cup walnut meats (optional)	½ cup dark molasses
1 teaspoon nutmeg	1 cup milk (or ½ cup strong
1 teaspoon clove	coffee and ½ cup brandy)
2 teaspoons cinnamon	

Sift flour. Measure it. Flour fruit and nutmeats (if used) with half a cup of it. Sift the rest three times with the spices and soda.

Cream butter, work in sugar, sifted. Beat well. Add egg yolks, beaten thick. Mix molasses with whatever other liquid you use. (Mrs. Appleyard uses brandy and coffee.) Add liquid alternately with the flour. Add the floured fruit. Beat egg whites stiff and fold them in.

Bake in a large round graniteware pan, lined with buttered brown paper and waxed paper for 3 hours at 275° for the first hour and at 250° the rest of the time. Have a pan of water on the bottom of the oven. This keeps the bottom of the cake from cooking too quickly. You may also bake it in separate loaf pans. It will not take quite so long. The cake should shrink from the sides of the pan and one of Mrs. Appleyard's special cake testers should come out clean.

Baked Fudge Brownies

For a 9 × 13 pan:

1½ cups butter (3 sticks)	3 cups sugar
6 squares chocolate	1½ cups flour
¼ cup warm water	6 eggs, lightly beaten
3 teaspoons vanilla	extra sugar (about ¼ cup)
1 8-ounce can walnut meats, broken	

Melt butter, add water, chocolate. When chocolate is melted and well mixed with the butter add the sugar, beat well, cool. Flour the nuts with ½ cup of the flour. Beat eggs with wire whisk so that they are well blended. Light oven: 350°. Add eggs to the chocolate mixture, beating well. Add the flour and the nuts. Put the mixture in a lightly greased and floured pan. Scatter the ¼ cup of sugar over the top. Bake until it shrinks from the pan, is crusty on top and firm to the touch in the center:

about 40 minutes. Do not overbake. Chill. Mark into 48 squares. Do not try to remove brownies from the pan until they are really cold.

Swedish Cookies

To make these get a Swedish cooky press and follow the rule that comes with it exactly. Mrs. Appleyard thinks this piece of equipment well worth having. The cookies are delicious and a large number can be made in a comparatively short time, much more quickly than if they are rolled and cut.

Spiced Cider

To a gallon of cider allow:

a 4-inch stick of cinnamon	⅓ teaspoon allspice
12 whole cloves	½ teaspoon cinnamon

Let the cider stand with the spice in it for at least half an hour. Bring it to the boil in a large kettle but do not boil it. Ladle it into pottery mugs. A gallon serves sixteen.

The stamping of snow off feet, the piling of overshoes in the woodshed and the heaping of coats on a big harvest table kept up for a long time. So did the sampling of refreshments and the laughter and talk around the fire in the back parlor. The doors of the front parlor were still closed. At last Fair Davenport slipped away. Eleanor turned off all the lights. Only one candle and the flickering fire lighted the room as Eleanor sat down at the piano.

People stopped talking and all eyes were on the folding doors. As they opened, everyone took a long breath. You could smell the tree before you saw it, breathe in the scent of balsam warming in the glow of a hundred candles. The tree filled half the room. The silver star at the top almost touched the ceiling. The branches were as dark and fresh as if it were still standing in the woods. Some of the mysterious darkness of the woods came into the room with it. There was nothing on it but the silver star and the candles. Their sparkling light deepened the shadows.

Eleanor began to play "Silent Night." Voices joined in; a few, then more, then everyone was singing. Even Mrs. Appleyard murmured almost audibly, "Sleep in heavenly peace," and felt that she would. The candles burned only till the carol was over. Fairfield put them out before they came too near the prickly resinous needles. The tree was so beautiful, Mrs. Appleyard thought, partly because — like a sunset, an eclipse of the sun or a rainbow — its moments were so few. A whole city of electric lights could never give the same sense of wonder.

Outside it was so clear that the sky was blue behind the floating moon. Crisp snow squeaked under people's feet. Smoke from the Davenports' Yule log, part of a big sugar maple, rose straight into the blue air, a column of silver. Loops and sprays and wreaths were dark against the white houses of the village. Lights were bright on trees in the windows and trees outside in the snow.

Christmas had begun.

Bradshaw Christmas

Cicely Bradshaw's Christmas celebration is a mingling of so many traditions that it made Mrs. Appleyard dizzy when she tried to diagnose where they all came from. Her own childhood had provided well-stuffed stockings with tangerines in the toes and the hiding of presents, sometimes in such strategic places that they were not found till spring. She used to help to hang wreaths of holly in the windows and Christmas was not legal unless there were branches of holly back of the copy of the family Gainsborough and other favorite pictures. No tree. Trees were not English and Mrs. Appleyard's father was.

It was from the Appleyards that the custom of cutting your own tree from your own land reached the Bradshaw family. Mr. Appleyard used to have one shipped from Appleyard Center to Woodbrook Green and Mrs. Appleyard recognized on Cicely's tree some of the ornaments that he used to hang on the branches. She was however unprepared for everyone in the Bradshaw family having his own small tree besides the big one. "Everyone" includes Eric, the Norwegian elkhound, Laddie, the golden cocker, and the two tortoise shell cats. One of the trees was a rubber plant embellished with sprays of silver leaves. There was a crystal tree sparkling with emeralds, rubies and sapphires. Another one turned its tinseled branches and played what Mrs. Appleyard rather thought was "Silent Night." It was made in Japan and its maker had a different opinion: "Tune — Holly Night," the label on the bottom said. This was the canary's tree. He accompanied the tune — whatever it was — with valiant trills.

Mrs. Appleyard had introduced the crèche into their family Christmas and she was glad to see that the Bradshaws had one too. Not all her innovations became traditions. One year, inspired by *Life* Magazine, she had bought a large number of soda straws and had threaded yards of string through them to construct for Cicely an icosahedral star. Rather to her surprise it came out looking much like the picture, but it did not become a permanent feature of the Bradshaw Christmas. Mrs. Appleyard is willing to bet a certain number of soda straws, enough to make another star, in case you are interested, that she is the only reader of *Life* who made an icosahedral star and had it eaten by a Norwegian elkhound. Somehow Eric's tree, so neatly trimmed with dog-biscuit bones, was not enough for him. Dogs, Mrs. Appleyard remembered from her youth, used to like chewing string on Christmas day. Eric certainly chewed the most string of any dog she knows.

Homemade wine from dandelions, elderberries, choke-cherries — each brewed in its season — were her granddaughter Cynthia's contribution to the Christmas festivities. There was even a rich fruity old port (several weeks old) made from Mrs. Appleyard's own beets. But who, she wondered, introduced the gingerbread house into the family? And how did fifteen-year-old Jane instinctively know how to make it? At fifteen Mrs. Appleyard had never even made fudge. She is lost in wonder, love and praise at the ease and deftness with which her granddaughters carry out such projects.

Cicely says that it's perfectly natural: that the children always helped her and that after a while she left it to Cynthia and that when she went to college, Jane took over.

"And I'll make it when Jane goes to college," said Camilla who at the moment was building a house out of lumps of sugar stuck together with pale blue mortar. Mrs. Appleyard has no doubt that Camilla will become a gingerbread architect at a suitable time.

While the gingerbread house was being baked, Mrs. Appleyard attended to her own Christmas tree. Earlier in the year she had been reading *Buddenbrooks* and she was charmed with the description of their Christmas tree, which was trimmed with white lilies and white candles and tinsel. As soon as her tree, a small but perfect balsam, was brought in, she started to town to find the lilies. She already had plenty of tinsel and a string of tiny white electric candles with white bulbs. Cynthia, who had a sort of built-in divining rod where her mother's tastes are concerned, had given it to her. Mrs. Appleyard had seen sprays of lilies, straight from Hong Kong, in the supermarket. The only trouble is that the days had drifted happily by since she had seen them. In fact when the manager told her that there had been none since Easter, she realized that of course he was right. She bought an armful of white roses.

The sun had gone down by the time she had finished trimming her tree and it was dark in the bay windows where the tree stood on an old chest of fiddleback maple. When she turned on the lights the tree seemed to blossom suddenly with stars and silver and roses. Even if the Buddenbrooks would not have recognized its ancestry, they might, she thought, feel a sort of magic about it, something that said, "All is calm — all is bright."

When she turned it on for the family there were gratifying shrieks of surprise and Cicely conferred the supreme compliment by announcing: "This must be a tradition from now on."

Mrs Appleyard did not plan to compete with the tremendous meal the Buddenbrooks always had at Christmas. She could not remember the details and someone had borrowed (courteous for stolen) the book. She knew there was carp simmered in red wine but she did not quite see how she was going to get a carp.

At Christmas time there was fishing through the ice going on only a quarter of a mile away but this is not, Mrs. Appleyard feels, a womanly occupation. Men, she thinks, fish through the ice more to get away from women than for the sake of the fish they catch: she will not intrude upon their icy privacy. Not even if some one had stolen carp from Versailles and domesticated them in Crystal Lake would Mrs. Appleyard be present when a red flag ran up to announce a catch. Making plum pudding in a warm kitchen is more in her line. There must be plenty because something delightful had happened. Hugh and his family, all six of them, were coming and also Henry and Valerie Haddam, summer neighbors, had driven east for Christmas and would come to dinner.

"So that will make fourteen of us," Mrs. Appleyard said. "What shall we have so that it will be like Thanksgiving only different? I love having two kitchens, and with so many people there'll be lots to help so it will be easy. Shall we have a boar's head? Or a suckling pig? Or shall I try for a turkey as good as the last?"

It was decided that turkey is best for a family party. This is the menu they built around that now domestic bird.

Peanut Butter and Bacon Appetizers*
Stuffed Celery*   Chicken Liver Pâté — Melba Toast*
Sesame Seed Crackers
Roast Turkey (p. 64)   Giblet Gravy (p. 66)
Cranberry Apples (p. 35)   Candied Sweet Potato*
Mashed Potato   Cauliflower and Green Beans*   Hollandaise*
Plum Pudding*   Hard Sauce*
Cynthia's Dandelion Wine*

Stuffed Celery

For the filling: equal amounts of cream cheese and Swiss
Colony Blue Cheese blended together with enough light cream
to make the mixture soft enough. Use only the best and crispest
stalks. Save the rest and the tops for soup. These can be made
ahead and kept in a cool place till needed. One thing you can
say for old-fashioned Vermont houses — there are always plenty
of cool spots in them. The remarkable thing is that there are also
warm ones.

Chicken Liver Pâté — with Melba Toast

You need a blender to do this. You can, of course, put the
livers through the finest attachment of your meat grinder and
pound them in a mortar but Mrs. Appleyard rather doubts if
you'll feel like doing that two days before Christmas. Better
forget the whole idea and buy some French pâté de foie gras or
Sell's Liver Pâté, one of those things she likes to mention that
keep the same quality over the years.

For the Melba toast, which can be drying out while you are making the pâté:

Trim the crusts off homemade bread sliced thin. Cut the crusts off. Cut each slice into four triangles. Put them in large pan into a 200° oven and leave them until they are light golden brown, dry and crisp. It takes about 2 hours.

For the pâté:

1 package (8-ounce) frozen chicken livers, defrosted several hours in the refrigerator
¼ teaspoon mixed herbs
½ teaspoon white pepper
1 teaspoon minced onion
2 tablespoons butter, extra, for sautéing

½ cup chicken stock (or water)
2 tablespoons butter, softened
¼ teaspoon nutmeg
1 teaspoon sugar
½ pound mushrooms (use caps only) chopped rather fine

Melt butter. Sauté mushrooms until tender. Remove them and keep them until later. Sauté the onion one minute. Add more butter if needed. Add livers, defrosted so they can be easily separated. Cover tightly. Cook over medium heat 3 minutes. Uncover, turn livers over, cover again and cook 2 minutes longer.

Into the blender, put water or stock, seasonings, softened butter, the livers and all the scrapings from the pan. Blend until smooth. Mrs. Appleyard does it three times, a minute at a time. It should be like very thick cream. It will stiffen as it chills. Stir in (do not blend) the chopped mushrooms. Mrs. Appleyard uses a small rubber scraper to get the pâté out of the blender and she packs it in a wide-mouthed jar such as a peanut butter jar. After it has chilled for several hours it will be just right to spread on the Melba toast.

Peanut Butter and Bacon Appetizers

These are for the children. Appetizers is an inaccurate description. Actually they are more like something thrown to a pack of hungry wolves to placate them.

Cut rounds of Pepperidge Farm bread with a small cooky cutter. The corners make excellent bread crumbs. Toast the rounds on one side lightly and then spread them generously with real peanut butter. You make it — surprise! — out of peanuts. Did you ever read the label on a modern jar of peanut butter? Well, don't let Mrs. Appleyard spoil your Christmas. If you don't feel like grinding peanuts yourself, you can buy the old-fashioned kind from your nearest Co-op store, pure peanut butter with no homogenized oil added.

Cut bacon into small squares. Cook them slowly till they are translucent. Put the canapés on a cooky sheet. Top each one with a square of bacon. Just before serving time, put the cooky sheet under the broiler and cook them until the bacon is crisp — 2 or 3 minutes. Watch them — the charcoal stage arrives rather quickly. Serve hot.

Cauliflower and Green Beans (O.H.P.)

Festive looking is cauliflower in a wreath of green beans. Begin by making some garlic croutons. Cut 3 slices of homemade bread into small cubes. Brown them in 2 tablespoons of butter, sprinkle with ½ teaspoon of garlic powder.

Cook a perfect head of cauliflower. Mrs. Appleyard does this in one of those French vegetable steamers that fold up or spread out to fit various sizes of pans. The pan must be covered tightly.

The cauliflower should be tender in about 20 minutes of steaming unless it is very large. Test the base with a sharp vegetable knife. It should go in easily. For a large number of people it is better to do two good-sized heads.

At the same time cook frozen French-cut beans. Allow two packages to a large head of cauliflower. Cook them in a small amount of water, which should be boiling when you put in the beans. Cover them at first. After 3 minutes, turn them over so that the frozen top parts will have a chance to melt. Cook another 3 minutes. When all the ice is melted, add 2 tablespoons of butter and cook uncovered until all the water cooks away. Watch them carefully. They will be done in 2 or 3 minutes. Remove from heat, cover and let them stand until you are ready to serve the cauliflower. Put it on a hot circular dish. Reheat the beans briefly and make a wreath of them around the cauliflower. Scatter the croutons over them. Serve with Hollandaise.

Hollandaise Sauce

½ cup butter	1 tablespoon lemon juice
yolks of 2 large eggs	½ teaspoon grated lemon rind
pinch (⅛ teaspoon) of cayenne pepper	

This sauce, Mrs. Appleyard says, is usually considered hard to make but if you follow directions carefully it is really less trouble than most sauces. To make it you need courage and a French wire whisk. If you have a stove where you can absolutely trust your flame to produce the lowest possible heat evenly and steadily, you may make it over direct heat. Mrs. Appleyard, who is brave but not rash, does it in the top of a double boiler over hot, not boiling water.

Use only the best butter. Divide it into 3 pieces. Put the egg yolks, unbeaten, the lemon juice and rind and the cayenne into the top of the double boiler over the hot water. Start beating with your wire whisk and add the first piece of butter. Keep beating and as the butter melts, add the second piece. The sauce will start to thicken. As the second piece of butter disappears add the third one. Here's your danger point. Just as this last piece of butter melts — keep on beating all the time — remove the sauce from the heat. It will curdle if it's left a minute too long. Don't have hysterics if it does because it can be brought back by beating in a little cream — a teaspoonful or more. Be sure the cream is well chilled. Put the sauce into a warm, not hot, bowl and serve it immediately.

Sweet Potatoes, Candied and Brandied with Cashew Nuts

Allow one medium-sized potato for each person to be served. Parboil 20 minutes. Mrs. Appleyard does this in a vegetable steamer. Peel potatoes. Slice them lengthwise in halves. For eight potatoes allow ¾ cup brown sugar, ⅓ cup hot water, ⅓ cup brandy, ½ cup cashew nuts, 2 tablespoons butter. Melt the butter in a large iron frying pan. Add the brown sugar and hot water and cook until the syrup is quite thick — 2 or 3 minutes. Put in the potato slices, cut side down, and cook them gently in the syrup 3 minutes. Turn them over. Baste with the syrup. Set the pan into the oven at 350° and cook until the potatoes are tender and the syrup thick, about 30 minutes. Sprinkle brandy over them and the cashew nuts, broken. Put pan over the heat for a minute and let the syrup boil up. Arrange potatoes on a hot serving platter, pour syrup and nuts over them.

Sherry may be used instead of brandy or both may be omitted. Peanuts or pecans may be used instead of cashews.

Plum Pudding (A.C.R.)

This pudding is made several weeks before Christmas. It keeps well in a cool place right in the molds in which you steamed it and needs only a short period of steaming when you serve it.

2 cups dried French bread crumbs
1 pound beef suet, ground fine
½ pound almonds, blanched and ground
½ pound citron, diced
½ pound seedless raisins
¼ pound candied cherries
½ pound currants
1 teaspoon each of cloves, cinnamon, allspice
½ a nutmeg, grated (1 teaspoon)
2 tablespoons rose water
juice of 1 lemon
1 cup sherry
2 tablespoons rum
10 eggs
2 cups sugar
1 cup flour

Dry the French bread, using the inside of the loaf only, and roll it into very fine crumbs. Mix it with the suet, ground almonds and the fruit. Sprinkle the spices over the fruit. Pour over the rosewater, lemon juice, sherry and rum and let it stand overnight. (Rosewater is not easy to find now but you can still get it from S. S. Pierce.) The next day separate the eggs, beat the yolks till they are thick. Beat in the sugar. Beat the whites stiff but not dry and fold them into the yolks, then fold the whole mixture into the fruit mixture. Scatter the flour over the whole thing and fold it in.

This makes several small or two large puddings. Steam them in coffee cans, brown bread tins, melon molds, anything that has a tight cover that fits over the can. Most modern cans unfortunately either have a cover that is damaged when opened or a projecting edge that makes it impossible to get the pudding out intact. A melon mold is really the best container.

Butter the molds well. Fill them not more than two-thirds full. The pudding expands as it steams. Set the molds on a rack in a large kettle with a tightly fitting cover. Pour in boiling water almost to the level of the rack. Steam the puddings 5 or 6 hours, replacing water as needed.

In serving hers Mrs. Appleyard likes to decorate it with a sprig of holly. Luckily she has friends in Corvallis, Oregon, where the handsomest holly grows, so when she had steamed the pudding long enough to reheat it — about half an hour — she put it on a silver dish, poured brandy over it, lighted the brandy and brought it in with blue flames flickering around the holly.

Don't forget that the dish will be hot, she says. Plum pudding is not especially improved by being dropped. What made her think of this cooking hint? Well — never mind.

Luckily Camilla is a great weaver of holders. She made her grandmother some appropriate green and red ones for Christmas, so on this occasion all went well.

Hard Sauce

½ cup best butter	1 teaspoon vanilla
1 cup powdered sugar, sifted	½ teaspoon cinnamon
½ teaspoon nutmeg	

Butter should be at room temperature. Cream it. Work in the powdered sugar. Add vanilla. Beat well, using a pastry-blending fork. Put sauce into a Sandwich glass dish, swirling it around artistically. Sprinkle with spice. Chill so it will hold its shape. Remove from refrigerator a little ahead of time. It should be hard but not like granite.

Getting dinner on Christmas Day was a leisurely process. Most of Mrs. Appleyard's part of it had been done beforehand and she spent most of the day reading her new Christmas books in large intemperate gulps. She also at intervals contemplated her favorite present. It was handmade for her by Hugh's oldest son, Bruce, and consisted of a set of Napier's Bones. In case you are not very familiar with this device, you resemble Mrs. Appleyard more than you might think. It is intended to help in mathematical calculations. Its inventor also thought up logarithms. Then one thing led to another and after a while we had the slide rule and giant computers and spent our time sending chimpanzees and men in orbit and planning to send a man to the moon. No one admires our astronauts more than Mrs. Appleyard. In fact she is planning to go to tea with her cousins in Australia by capsule some day and come back on the third round. Still she wishes people would leave the moon alone and just go on happily and incorrectly rhyming it with June.

Even equipped with Napier's Bones, there is not much chance of Mrs. Appleyard's inventing anything catastrophic. All she knows about logarithms is that the log of 1000 to the base of 10 is 3. Napier figured out that it was 2.7182181828 — but someone else decided that 3 was easier to use. This view — all mathematicians will be glad to know — is heartily endorsed by Mrs. Appleyard.

Napier's Bones as made by Bruce consist of nine strips of Vermont maple, each nine inches long and an inch wide, nicely sanded and polished. They are marked out into inch squares and the multiplication tables from one to nine are neatly printed on them. All the marks are burned in with an electric pencil. Ornamental — yes, and useful too for anyone who writes cookbooks and who might want to plan a meal for six instead of for eight. Just get out your Napier's Bones.

Mrs. Appleyard came up for air between calculations and asked Cicely what time she planned to serve dinner. "We asked the Haddams for six, didn't we?"

Cicely began to murmur statistics, not simple things about three fourths of a cup of flour. For these a real computer was needed: "Tommy skiing will pick up Cynthia, five-thirty. Hugh, skating, will bring Camilla six-fifteen. Persuade eight children to brush hair, dress, wash. Turkey weighs twenty pounds. Haddams asked for six will be two hours late . . . twenty-five minutes to the pound . . . when will droppers-in drop out? . . . how long to mash potatoes for fourteen . . . extra plates . . . high chair . . . We'll serve the turkey at eight-ten," she concluded.

"Then I'll make Hollandaise, triple rule, at five minutes past," Mrs. Appleyard said and sank restfully into another book.

The house smelled wonderful — of balsam and roasting turkey and woodsmoke from blazing birch logs. The musical tree from Japan was very excitable: the slightest motion near it, such as the cats batting their catnip mice, made it twinkle out "Holly Night."

English is a confusing language: it might just as well have said "Wholly Night."

Thankful that she did not have to label a musical revolving Buddha in Japanese, Mrs. Appleyard put another log on the fire.

Cicely's computations worked perfectly. By eight-ten the dinner was ready and the family and guests were there to eat it. Candles burned on the long table, light sparkled on all the Christmas trees. The canary seemed delighted with his tree and gratefully sang an obbligato every time it tinkled. Outside the dogs were chewing the bones so neatly wrapped in Christmas paper and tied to their trees. The cats had now given up inhaling catnip and were seriously at work with their velvet paws batting silver balls. They broke only two.

Henry Haddam sat at one end of the table and served vegetables. Hugh carved the turkey at the other end.

He carves as well as his father, Mrs. Appleyard thought.
High praise.
Cynthia filled glasses with her own wine — dandelion or beet.
Ah that beet wine of 1961! What a vintage! Or is it a rootage?
Anyway it made Mrs. Appleyard's ears ring: obviously a root-
age to remember.

Cynthia's Dandelion Wine

Choose a bright warm May morning when dandelions look
up out of the grass like small hot suns. Pick 4 quarts, flowers
only. By the time you have done that you will have stood on
your head all you want to and will be willing to work in the
shade for a while.

To 4 quarts of dandelion blossoms allow:

1 gallon boiling water	2 packages frozen raspberries
juice of 6 lemons	3 pounds granulated sugar
	2 yeast cakes

Wash and scald a two-gallon crock with a cover. Put the
flowers in and pour the boiling water over them. Let them stand
in a cool place overnight. In the morning strain liquid from
the flowers, squeeze all the juice out of them through a strainer.
Put the juice on to boil with the lemon juice, raspberries and
sugar. Boil 20 minutes and pour it back into the crock. Let
cool till lukewarm, then add yeast. Cover and let the juice fer-
ment until it stops hissing — about ten days. Strain through
filter paper into scalded cider jugs. Let it stand three days to
settle. Tops should be on but not tightened. Strain once more
through filter paper into clean quart bottles. Let it stand for
another day to be sure it is clear. Filter again if necessary. If

not, cork the bottles tightly. Leave them in the cellarway till Christmas.

The Hollandaise did not curdle. The plum pudding blazed blue and was scorching hot. No one dropped the platter. The Hard Sauce was just cold enough. Mrs. Appleyard did not make the coffee, it was excellent.

It had been a perfect day, she thought: sunshine on snow, grandchildren, red carnations, neighbors dropping in, books, Jane's gingerbread house, telephone calls from distant children, Cicely, warmth, music, Hugh's family skating on the millpond, cards from two hemispheres, Double-Crostics, Napier's Bones, laughter. Who could ask for anything more?

December–January

Epact of Turkey

ONE OF THE few restful aspects of Christmas vacation, Cicely Bradshaw says, is that the children, to use an elegant phrase, eat off the turkey. The Bradshaws all, including the cats, like turkey best when it's cold. This convenient taste somewhat makes up for the fact that on any given day each of the children wishes to be driven twenty or thirty miles in a different direction. Skiing beckons one, ballet another, sacred ties of old friendship (two weeks old at least) a third. The fourth would like to shop for a new skirt "and one or two other things," a remark with sinister implications.

Such projects leave little time for cooking even if one had the inclination. Mrs. Appleyard certainly lacked it. She was perfectly happy eating yogurt with apricots and doing double crostics. Her excuse for taking up this occupation rather than writing a book or painting on velvet or cooking or shortening any of her well-known skirts is that her mind needed stretching. She also admitted that if she laughed, coughed, sneezed or even whistled, her ribs reminded her of her brief but emphatic contact with that green truck. Besides, she said, she had to entertain the insurance adjusters, dignified, cleancut young gentlemen in dark suits, plain dark ties, white shirts and beautifully polished shoes. There is something very soothing about a medium-sized black shoe in which you can see your face — in case you want to, of course.

Actually the less Mrs. Appleyard saw of hers the better she was pleased. Having her nose cracked did not improve her appearance so much as she had hoped. If it had been really broken she supposed it could have been set Greek or Roman or Early Aztec but it simply had its usual undistinguished lines with, around it, areas still faintly black and blue, not to mention yellow and green. She is definitely a type that looks better by candlelight — she hopes.

Still, even though she has not been in the mood to make the turkey into esoteric *plats du jour* in case any gourmets dropped in, she realizes that there are people who like turkey some other way than cold. For such restless spirits she suggests a few menus that will keep them occupied till New Year's.

The days just after Christmas belong, she says, neither in December nor in January. They are part of the epact, which is the excess of the solar year over the lunar months of the calendar. This is the kind of thing she learns from double crostics and she feels it is her duty to make the information readily available. What you eat during this period is, naturally, an epact of turkey — what is left over from Christmas and will, with ingenuity, last until the New Year.

You cannot be sure what time the family, working so hard at play, will get home, but you can be certain they'll be hungry. These dishes can be fixed ahead of time and served quickly. They are planned for six. If your family is larger than that, act accordingly. You will have done your duty by the turkey all the sooner and you will be able to enter the hamburger-and-hot-dog phase with a clear conscience.

I.

Turkey with Broccoli and Mushroom Sauce*
Mashed Potato Cakes*   Beets Appleyard*
Brown Betty (p. 47)   Hard Sauce (p. 130)

2.

Turkey Salad*   Tomato Conserve*
Baked Stuffing*   Spinach Appleyard*
Mince Pie (p. 68)   Vanilla Ice Cream

3.

Creamed turkey and oysters   Peas
Toasted English muffins*
Pineapple Upside-Down Cake*   Foamy Sauce (p. 58)

4.

Turkey Soup*   Thin-Scalded Johnnycake†
Tossed Salad*   Crackers and Cheese*

MENU I

Turkey with Broccoli and Mushroom Sauce

dark meat of turkey, sliced	3 tablespoons milk, rich, or light cream
cooked broccoli flowers,	4 tablespoons bread crumbs
2 pkgs, frozen	1 tablespoon butter
1 cup Mushroom Sauce (p. 169)	2 tablespoons grated cheese

Slice turkey neatly. Put cooked broccoli flowers in a lightly buttered shallow baking dish. Cover them with the turkey slices and then with the mushroom sauce to which the milk has been added. Sauté bread crumbs in butter and spread them over the sauce. Sprinkle grated cheese over the top. Do this ahead of time. When you serve it, put it over medium heat until the sauce starts to bubble, then run it under the broiler till the cheese starts to brown.

Mashed Potato Cakes
SIX CAKES

2 tablespoons butter   2 tablespoons flour
2 cups cold mashed potato made with real potatoes and cream and butter

Flour your hands slightly. Roll the potato into six balls of uniform size. Flatten them. They should be about ½ inch thick. Have the flour, seasoned as you like it, in a thin layer on a plate. Have the butter melted over low heat in a large iron frying pan. Dip both sides of the cakes in the flour. Shake off what does not stick readily. Place them in the buttered frying pan and cook them until they are well browned on both sides. This will take at least half an hour and may take longer. They will have to be moved around the pan at intervals so that they will be evenly browned. The moving and the turning are both delicatę operations, best done with a spatula and a short-handled pancake turner. Cakes should be turned only once.

Beets Appleyard

2 beans garlic, crushed	1 tablespoon lemon juice
grated rind of one lemon	3 tablespoons sugar
1 can juice from beets	2 tablespoons butter
⅓ cup red wine	1 tablespoon minute tapioca
2 tablespoons cider vinegar	1 can of shoestring-cut beets

Soak the garlic and lemon rind in the beet juice, wine, vinegar and lemon juice for one hour. Strain juice, add sugar, butter and tapioca. Cook in the top of a double boiler until sauce is thick and clear. Add the beets. Set aside till serving time. Reheat. If sauce seems too thick, add a little more wine, heated.

MENU 2

Turkey Salad

3 cups turkey, white meat, cubed	½ cup chow-chow pickles,
1 cup celery, cut very fine	finely chopped
1 cup French Dressing (p. 190)	2 sliced, hard-boiled eggs
1½ cups Mayonnaise (p. 265)	12 large stuffed olives
lettuce	

Cut the turkey into rather large cubes. Cut the celery very fine. Mrs. Appleyard does this by cutting well-washed stalks into quarter-inch strips and then cutting strips into quarter-inch cubes. She uses scissors, says this is neater than chopping and really no more trouble.

Mix celery and turkey and marinate in French dressing for at least one hour. She uses her own mayonnaise but your favorite brand will do. She also usually has some of her own pickle on hand but if it has all vanished, she uses Crosse and Blackwell's Chow-Chow pickles. In either case chop the pickle rather fine. Get Boston Market lettuce if possible. This is easier to do in New York than in Boston. It is more than likely that you will have to use iceberg, so named apparently because it has all the flavor and texture of the part of an iceberg that is above water.

Asked how the bottom seven-eighths tastes, Mrs. Appleyard froze not but replied imperturbably, "Salty and fish with just a hint of whale oil," and added a request for at least a spray or two of watercress, chicory and parsley around the edge of the salad bowl.

At serving time drain off the French dressing. Save it: there are many ways in which a little marinade can be useful. Stir half the mayonnaise into the turkey mixed with the celery and the pickle. Mask the mixture with rest of the mayonnaise. Decorate with the sliced hard-boiled eggs and the stuffed olives, also sliced. Surround with salad greens. Keep cool till ready.

(Good advice for the cook as well as the salad, Mrs. Appleyard says.)

Spinach Appleyard

Mrs. Appleyard prefers spinach out of a cellophane bag, or frozen spinach even to spinach from her own garden. She has never succeeded in washing spinach so there is no sand in it. She supposes that professional spinach washers must have enormous automatic washers in which the spinach swirls gently in a green centrifugal forest, spinning out sand as it goes. Perhaps next summer —

"Please do not try that in my new dishwasher," Cicely said firmly on hearing this speculation.

On the whole a reasonable request, Mrs. Appleyard thought, and continued to buy her spinach in cellophane.

1 teaspoon onion finely minced	2 tablespoons thick cream
2 bags washed spinach	2 tablespoons butter
¼ cup water, hot	pinch of nutmeg

Croutons:

4 slices homemade bread	2 tablespoons butter
¼ inch thick	½ teaspoon garlic powder

Begin by making the croutons. Cut the crusts off the bread. Cut it into ¼-inch cubes. Melt the butter, toss the croutons in it till they are golden brown. Sprinkle the garlic powder over them. Remove with a skimmer and set aside till needed. In the same pan put the onion and cook until it is transparent and yellow. Rinse out the pan with ¼ cup hot water. Swish it around to get all the flavor and pour it into the kettle in which you plan to cook the spinach. Chop the spinach, rather coarsely. Mrs. Appleyard does this in a big wooden chopping bowl and an old-fashioned steel chopper. There should be just enough water in the kettle to cover the bottom of it. Have it boiling hard. Add the chopped spinach. Cook it 5 minutes, chopping while it cooks. By this time it should be tender and a bright light green. Remove it from the pan to a hot dish, leaving the water. Cook this down to about a tablespoon. Add the cream, butter and nutmeg, heat and pour this over the spinach. Sprinkle croutons over and serve.

Baked Stuffing

Get this ready earlier in the day and set the dish in the oven about the time you start chopping the spinach.

Mrs. Appleyard has a habit of making more stuffing than the turkey will hold. She saves it and combines it with stuffing left in the turkey.

1 cup stuffing from turkey	½ cup hot water
2 cups stuffing (extra)	1 tablespoon butter
½ cup giblet gravy	1 egg, well beaten
1 tablespoon butter, in small dots	

Put stuffing in bowl. Mix gravy and hot water. Add 1 tablespoon butter. Cool slightly. Add beaten egg and add the mixture to the stuffing. Dot the top with butter. Bake at 375° about 25 minutes.

The exact contents of the dish can vary with what you have on hand — a little mushroom sauce, a few chestnuts or cashews or a little diced celery go well in it. Life is a lottery, so is a casserole: be valiant.

Having given this advice and also having encountered a good many casseroles where the makers had shown no hesitancy, Mrs. Appleyard wishes to make it clear that her remark was addressed to the eaters.

Tomato Conserve

4 quarts ripe tomatoes, measured whole	1 cup seedless white raisins
sugar	½-ounce stick cinnamon
3 oranges	6 medium-sized tart apples,
3 lemons	peeled, cored and cubed

If you make this in winter, substitute 2 large cans of tomatoes for the ripe tomatoes. They will be better than anything except tomatoes from your own garden.

Peel the tomatoes by holding them by a wooden-handled fork over the gas flame until the skins pop and sizzle. Peel off skin. Slice tomatoes and cut them up, not too fine. Pour off about a quart of the juice. Keep it to drink, chilled, or use as soup. If you are using canned tomatoes, use just as they come from the can.

Measure tomatoes and add an equal quantity of sugar. Slice oranges and lemons very thin. Cut slices in eighths. Use kitchen shears for this. Add the orange, lemon, raisins and stick cinnamon to the tomatoes and put them on to boil. Use a large kettle. Put the sugar into a 250° oven in a shallow pan. When the tomato mixture starts to bubble, add the heated sugar. Cook 5 minutes, stirring well from the bottom of the kettle. Cover, turn off heat. The second day, reheat and boil 5 minutes longer. The third day reheat (cheer up — this is the last time!) once more. Peel, core and cut the apples into small cubes. As soon as the conserve starts to boil, add the apples. Cook until they begin to soften. By this time the juice should crinkle when tested on a cold saucer. Stir conserve well from the bottom of the kettle always while it is boiling and especially during this last day's cooking. Remove the stick cinnamon. Put the conserve into sterilized jars. Steam them 10 minutes on a rack in a covered kettle to seal the lids.

MENU 3

Creamed Turkey and Oysters

8 ounces oysters, frozen
2 cups breast meat of turkey
3 tablespoons butter
½ teaspoon minced onion
caps from ½ pound mushrooms,
    sliced,
    or
4-ounce can of mushrooms, caps only
3 tablespoons flour

2 cups rich Vermont milk
    (known in the city as thin
    cream)
2 pimentos
1 green pepper
1 cup heavy cream
2 egg yolks
½ cup white wine
juice of ½ lemon (1 tablespoon)

½ cup chicken or turkey stock, jellied

Let the oysters thaw out gently in the refrigerator ahead of time. Slice turkey rather thick and cut it into fairly good-sized pieces. Melt butter, sauté the onion and the mushroom caps in it until onion is straw-colored. Sprinkle in flour, stir well. Reduce heat. Add the milk slowly, blending it in well. When sauce is smooth increase heat and simmer mixture for 5 minutes. Add the turkey, the pimentos cut in small strips, the green pepper cleaned of seeds and cut in very thin strips. Add the cream. Simmer a minute longer. Transfer everything to the top of a large double boiler and let stand till you are ready to serve it. Then heat mixture over hot, not boiling water. Beat the egg yolks, add wine and lemon juice, beat all together. Stir 3 tablespoons of the hot sauce into the egg mixture, one at a time, blending sauce well into the eggs and then add this mixture to the turkey mixture. Cook, stirring well for 5 minutes or until it thickens. Remove from heat. During this last 5 minutes bring the jellied stock to a boil in a small saucepan. Add oysters. Cook them until the edges curl. Add them and the stock to the turkey mixture.

Toasted English Muffins

Split muffins, butter generously, run them under the broiler. Soon done: soon charcoal too. Have this done by someone who can give all his time to it.

Pineapple Upside-Down Cake

Mrs. Appleyard's favorite weapon for this dessert is an iron frying pan large enough to hold 7 slices of pineapple. Dressier enameled pans may also be used, she admits, but most of them are not big enough.

½ cup butter	1 large can (7 slices) of pineapple
2 cups light golden brown sugar	small jar maraschino cherries

Melt butter in frying pan. Stir in sugar and melt it. Arrange the pineapple slices in the pan. Put cherries in their centers and in the spaces between slices. Add a tablespoon of the cherry liquid. Set the pan in the oven: 375°. Make the following batter and when butter and sugar mixture begins to bubble, pour it over them.

Batter:

1 cup milk	2½ cups cake flour, sifted 3 times
1½ cups sugar	and measured
6 tablespoons melted butter	2½ teaspoons baking powder,
3 eggs	sifted with flour
1 teaspoon vanilla	

Mix milk, sugar, butter, eggs and vanilla. Beat with an egg-beater until they are well blended. Beat the mixture into the sifted flour and baking powder. Keep on beating till the batter is smooth. Pour over the hot bubbling fruit and bake until a testing straw comes out clean.

Turn the cake upside down on a platter big enough to hold it. This takes courage, speed and a strong wrist. Good fortune attend you!

Serve the cake with thick cream, vanilla ice cream or with Foamy Sauce (p. 58).

MENU 4

Turkey Soup

carcass of a 20-pound turkey (it was stuffed with chestnut and sausage stuffing. The roaster contained the juices that had run out of it, thick as molasses and almost as dark)

2 onions   2 carrots sliced
celery tops and outer stalks

The day before you plan to make the soup, break up the carcass and put the bones and any meat and stuffing that clings to them into the roaster. Add wingtips, all the skin, onions, carrots, celery tops and stalks. Cover bones with water and simmer 5 or 6 hours. Strain off liquid — there should be about 2 quarts. Remove any scraps of meat from bones and add them to the broth. Chill it well.

The next day you will need:

any leftover giblet gravy	2 tablespoons flour
2 tablespoons turkey fat, skimmed from the broth	1 teaspoon burnt onion powder
1 onion finely grated	⅛ teaspoon each of pepper, clove, cinnamon, allspice
stems from 2 pounds mushrooms, sliced thin	1 teaspoon mixed herbs
	½ teaspoon paprika
1 teaspoon instant coffee	

Skim all fat from the broth. Save it. Mrs. Appleyard wants
it for the birds that come to her feeding station. They love her
cooking. One of their favorite entrées is Yorkshire Pudding
with turkey fat on it. However she will let you have a little
for the soup. Simmer the skimmed broth down to 1½ quarts.
Add giblet gravy to it. Melt the 2 tablespoons of turkey fat
and sauté the onion and the mushroom stems in it. Mix flour
with the seasonings. Sprinkle it in, blend over very low heat.
Add broth gradually, stirring well until soup is smooth. Simmer
until it thickens. Serve.

If you would rather have a clear soup, a sort of turkey consommé, omit the giblet gravy, the fat and the flour. Add 2
tablespoons of sherry.

If you like a blander soup add a cup of rich milk to the mixture just after you add the broth.

Any one of the three versions will brace you up for the New
Year.

Tossed Salad

One of the most unusual things about New York, Mrs. Appleyard says, is the tossed salad. Whether you eat at some humble
cafeteria or at a restaurant where the headwaiter makes your
teeth chatter with fear, you are awarded the same mixture of
ground-up iceberg lettuce, chicory, radishes, well-matured carrots, stringy celery and pallid tomatoes. No one has told Mrs.
Appleyard just how this gastronomic miracle is achieved, but
she knows what she would do if she had to make several tons
of it every day. She would get a large truck with a revolving
cement mixer, have it equipped with special knives and make
the salad as she drives along, handing out buckets of it to her
clients. Occasionally she would replenish the mixture with

tomatoes too far from home or determined branches of celery. In another cylinder she would make the peculiarly tasteless dressing that is always applied to the salad. Not having suitable ingredients at hand, she has not completely worked out the rule yet but she rather thinks it has a cornstarch base flavored with water, gum tragacanth, mineral oil and monosodium glutamate. A great many people in New York have high blood pressure for some reason. Perhaps she could collect statistics on that point while she was on her delivery route. She would have to be up bright and early anyway to accommodate all her customers. There must be thousands.

"What would you do the rest of the day?" inquired her daughter.

Mrs. Appleyard said that for one thing she would have to make the imitation vinegar that goes into the dressing. She had forgotten that she would need that. Then of course in the afternoon she would have to collect all the salad that had not been eaten the day before. She had never, she says, actually seen one of those wooden salad bowls empty.

"Probably," she added, glowing with creative imagination, "that's what you start with next day . . ."

No doubt she will work out the whole cycle efficiently in time. At present she is sticking to an old-fashioned method.

She takes:

4 beans of crushed garlic	½ teaspoon sugar
6 tablespoons olive oil	⅛ teaspoon cayenne
Boston Market lettuce	1 teaspoon dry mustard
romaine	½ teaspoon pepper from the grinder
fresh watercress from the brook	1 teaspoon paprika
1 tablespoon cider vinegar	1 tablespoon minced fresh parsley
1 tablespoon lemon juice	1 tablespoon chopped chives
salt to taste	

Parsley and chives both grow all winter in a sunny window if they are kept well watered.

Several hours before you toss the salad, crush the garlic and pour the olive oil over it. Wash the lettuce, romaine and watercress. Dry it between clean dish towels. Put it in the crisper of the refrigerator. Have a big salad bowl ready. Mrs. Appleyard prefers a china one. She says that wooden ones, unless they are plastic coated, are hard to keep clean. Whatever kind you use, you'll need lots of room for tossing.

Mix the vinegar, lemon juice, salt, sugar and spices in a big wooden salad spoon and put the mixture into your salad bowl. Add the strained garlic oil a tablespoon at a time, mixing well with the salad fork after each addition. Lay the spoon and fork crossed over the dressing. This is to keep the salad greens from being soaked in the dressing. Now add the greens. Tear up the romaine and the lettuce rather coarsely. Sprinkle the minced parsley and chives over them.

During the crisis just before serving time, Mrs. Appleyard appoints some conscientious guest, usually a man, and asks him to toss the salad gently at least twenty-eight times. The idea, she explains to him, is that every leaf should be coated with the dressing and that no dressing should be left in the bottom of the bowl. He almost always, whether his chief interest is basketball, golf or skiing, does an excellent job, perhaps better than could be done with a patented concrete mixer.

Crackers and Cheese

No doubt you have your favorite kinds of both. Mrs. Appleyard's are Vermont or New York State cheddar cheese aged about a year, Swiss Colony blue cheese and Borden's Liederkranz. Almost all cheese is improved by standing at room temperature a while before it is served.

She realizes that some changes are improvements. She thinks that most of her grandchildren's generation have more sense of belonging in the world than she had at their age. She knows that radio has made good music better known and appreciated than it has ever been before, and she loves to have it drifting into her room from the top of Mount Washington. She has no yearning to go back to horse-drawn vehicles. She likes drip-dry clothes and electric blankets. Still she is glad that Montpelier Crackers are the same as ever.

January

International New Year

A cook, Mrs. Appleyard says, has to be a prophet too. A cook is constantly predicting things. Sometimes the prophecies are rather simple: "We are going to have hamburgers for lunch" or "The potatoes will be done in twenty minutes." Sometimes there are more complicated situations with conditions attached: "If you bring home some trout, I'll cook them for supper with bacon." Then there are frightening moments where the voice of doom states: "If you slam the oven door, the cake will fall . . . Another minute and the toast will burn."

This type of prophet has the annoying habit of being always right. If she says there are going to be hamburgers for supper, small indeed is the chance that you will find yourself eating sweetbreads and mushrooms sous cloche with a side dish of lobster Bordelaise and crêpes suzette for dessert. Yet people tolerate her utterances, perhaps because she constantly assures them that they can count on a future even if it's only to last twenty minutes. Also it is a future where, if you do right, you can expect something good and — usually — get it: so different in this way from the home life of Job, for instance.

Of course cook-prophets are usually women. Men are more apt to look back into the past: "I never liked tripe . . . Mother made delicious cornbread . . . Where did you get the albatross for this stew? I had that for lunch."

Mrs. Appleyard knows, of course, that the best cooks are men. So are the best politicians, mathematicians and dressmakers. Unfortunately the best men are not always cooks.

Putting on a chef's hat and scorching steak in the backyard does not make the scorcher a cook any more than delivering one smashing checkmate makes a woman a chess player. It is the daily battle with fire and saucepan that makes a cook. Men cooks have one striking ability, which is always to have a kitchenmaid at hand. To her go such tasks as peeling onions, scouring burnt saucepans and washing the eggbeater. She is, lucky squaw, also allowed to grate cheese and crush garlic. And Old Man River, he just keeps cooking along.

At this moment in Mrs. Appleyard's reflections, her daughter Cicely was called to the telephone and began to act as prophet in her own right.

"Of course we will," Mrs. Appleyard heard her say. "If you'll take four, I'll take the other five. They'll help cook? Wonderful — we'll make it international. Sleeping bags on the floor, dinner for everyone New Year's Day. Mother will love it — won't you, Mother?"

Mrs. Appleyard agreed, on principle, to love blindly whatever was going on. She was quite pleased to learn that her affections had been plighted merely to having nine foreign students to dinner and that there would be only five sleeping bags to step over on the living-room floor.

"Pamela Hoyt says she'll find out what they can cook and we'll plan a menu tomorrow and I'll do the shopping," Cicely said.

"Are they men or girls?" her mother asked.

"Both."

"Fine," said Mrs. Appleyard, "we'll have some kitchenmaids."
The menu involved was:

Tarts* with Caviar or Purée de Foie Gras
Olives   Radishes   Celery
Grønkålsuppe*
Crown Roast of Lamb, Kasha Stuffing*
Tiny Onions and Peas with Mustard Sauce*
Cole Slaw   Scotch Oatcake*
Paradise Jelly*   Artichokes Hollandaise*
Baked Alaska*   Cheese Fondue*
Beer   White Wine   Red Wine   Coffee

Mrs. Appleyard contributed only enthusiasm, Paradise jelly and Baked Alaska, all American products. Cicely and Pamela with a certain amount of international diplomacy reduced the menu to things that could be cooked in Vermont and translated the quantities into American weights and measures. They persuaded the Viennese delegate that it was not practicable to serve shaslik the way his mother used to make it since she began by marinating it for three days. They soothed the Swiss delegate when he encountered Swiss cheese, so called, and convinced him that no international insult was intended. They even persuaded him to see what he could do with Vermont cheddar.

The French Cordon Bleu was charmed by a visit to the Golden Dome Market. She was happy to find real French purée de foie gras and caviar and tins of pearl onions and tiny French peas because they were familiar. She was just as pleased to find pastry in a package because it was strange. She would invent something, she said.

"My mother will love you," Cicely told her.

Of course Mrs. Appleyard did — and all the others too, and the hustle and bustle and the different accents and the sleeping bags on the floor. They were not there when she went to sleep. The students had stayed at the Hoyts' to see the New Year in. When she got up in the morning, there were two bags on the floor of her living room, which is also her winter kitchen, an all-purpose room in fact. The bags contained one blonde and one brunette, she noticed as she stepped over their feet on her way to take her bath. The blonde turned out to be the French Cordon Bleu and the little shy brown chipmunk was German. Both spoke beautiful English, embarrassingly better than American English. Mrs. Appleyard tried her French and German on them. She so delighted them by her ineptness that they were soon friends.

Gretchen was assigned to Cicely's kitchen to make cole slaw and Marie-Claire stayed in the winter kitchen. Mrs. Appleyard was delighted to observe that with a Cordon Bleu in charge the men became the kitchenmaids. She always knew there was something special about that school.

It took all day to get the dinner ready. Mrs. Appleyard took full notes on the menu. Here they are.

Hors d'Oeuvres (French)
Pastry tarts, with foie gras

Marie-Claire made the pastry according to the directions on the package. She translated them into French for Mrs. Appleyard's benefit and made the project sound excitingly exotic. She rolled the pastry out deftly and, with Mrs. Appleyard's small crimped cooky cutter, swiftly produced fluted circles and put them on a baking sheet. Then she made the same number of circles and cut holes out of the centers. She wanted the inner edges fluted too, so Mrs. Appleyard went into a brief trance and invented an appropriate instrument — a ginger-ale bottle cap with two nail holes punched in it. Marie-Claire moistened the bottoms of the tart shells slightly with a pastry brush and placed the open-centered circles on top of them. The small circles cut out were also placed on the baking sheet to be used as lids for the tarts. She chilled the tarts for 5 minutes while the oven was heating to 450°. She baked them for 5 minutes, then reduced the heat to 375° and baked them until they were puffed and delicately browned, about 12 minutes longer. At serving time she filled some with the purée de foie gras and some with caviar. This was to show that she was broad-minded and admired the Russians for whatever was admirable about them. Of course, as Mrs. Appleyard well knew, the caviar had not been nearer Russia than Gloucester, Mass., where some ingenious Americans had dyed cod roe black. Still, imitation is a compliment and with onion, sour cream and a dusting of hard-boiled egg yolk it was good enough so that Mrs. Appleyard wishes she had some right now.

Grønkålsuppe
DANISH SOUP (J.H. and B.L.)

a hambone with some meat on it	2 cups chopped green cabbage
2 potatoes	2 carrots
bunch of green onions with the tops	¼ cup chopped parsley
3 stalks of celery with the tops	3 tablespoons flour

1 cup cream

Boil the hambone until the meat falls from the bone, at least one hour. Remove bone. There should be about 2 quarts of liquid. In it put all the vegetables chopped, not too fine. Cook until they are tender, about 40 minutes. Pour cold water slowly on the flour, mixing well, and rub it through a fine strainer into the soup. Bring soup to a boil, add the cream. Cool for several hours. Reheat when you serve it. It will be quite thick. A little hot water may be added if you like.

At this time add what seasonings you like, freshly ground pepper, a pinch of mixed herbs, a pinch of cinnamon. It is supposed to be even better the next day. Mrs. Appleyard cannot vouch for this because there wasn't any left. She thinks that with garlic bread and a salad it would make a whole meal.

Crown Roast of Lamb
Vienna with help from Turkey

This rule is for eight. The international party somehow grew into sixteen so there were two roasts in Cicely's big oven.

8 link sausages
1 cup kasha (cracked wheat)
1 pound mushrooms, caps only
1 medium onion, minced
¼ teaspoon pepper
salt to taste
pinch (each) of paprika and thyme
16 rib lamb chops

3 tablespoons butter
⅛ teaspoon nutmeg
6 tomatoes, halved
3 beans garlic, crushed
1 tablespoon minced parsley
1 cup bread and cracker crumbs,
  mixed
½ cup cream

sprays of parsley and watercress

Have your butcher make the rib lamp chops into a crown. He'll like to do it. It's a nice change from wrapping hamburg in cellophane. The fat should be towards the center, and it should be cut away from the ends of the bones, leaving 1½ inches bare.

Cut the sausages in two pieces. Make a slit in the cut end of each one and slip them over the ends of the chop bones. Light the oven: 300°. For a 3-pound crown roast allow 1¼ hours for medium rare, 1½ hours for well done. If you use a meat thermometer, insert it in lean meat. Be sure it does not touch the bone. For medium (slightly pink) it should register 160°, for well done 185°. It is so difficult to insert it properly in a crown roast that Mrs. Appleyard does not use one but depends on instinct.

While the roast is cooking, make the stuffing. Cook a cup of kasha for 5 minutes in 2 cups of boiling water. Mrs. Appleyard is lucky enough to have a neighbor who grinds wheat to just the right coarseness for kasha. You may also use groats or brown rice or wild rice.

After the first 5 minutes of cooking put the kasha over hot water and cook till it has absorbed all the water in which it was cooked. In the meantime wash the mushrooms. The best for this purpose are button mushrooms of medium size. Cut off the stems at the level of the caps and slice them vertically. Cook the onion in butter until onion is straw-colored. Add the sliced mushrooms. Sprinkle them with pepper, salt to taste, paprika, and thyme. Mix them with the kasha and keep hot. Twenty minutes before serving time fill the center of the roast with the stuffing. If there is any extra, serve it separately.

The tomatoes are a garnish for the roast. Cut them in halves. Cover them with crumbs mixed with crushed garlic and dotted with butter. Bake them in a shallow pan for 20 minutes. Just before serving time pour a little cream over each one. Slide them under the broiler till the crumbs are brown — 2 or 3 minutes.

Sprinkle the minced parsley over them. Arrange them around the roast. Put a sprig of parsley on top of the stuffing and a wreath of parsley and watercress around the platter. Cicely supplied one of Sheffield silver with a gadroon edge. Her mother polished up one with a border of grapes. Both wish the donors at the time of their weddings to know that the Viennese chef considered the effect worthy of his talents.

Paradise Jelly (H.J.P.)

Europeans are not supposed to like jelly with meat, but perhaps there were enough Americans present to account for its all vanishing. Anyway it was a Dane who asked for the rule and who said he would get his mother to try it next time quinces were ripe.

6 large apples	1 quart cranberries
9 large quinces	about 2 quarts water
	sugar

Wash apples and quinces. Remove blossom ends, stems and cores. Pick over and wash cranberries. Cut up quinces and

apples, add water and cranberries. Boil till mushy. Put in a
jelly bag and let juice drain off overnight. In the morning boil
the juice twenty minutes. Skim it carefully. Measure. Add
1 cup of heated sugar for each cup of juice. Cook until it jells
when tested on a chilled saucer. Cover with paraffin — first
a very thin layer; when it hardens, another one. Put on sterilized
covers.

Mrs. Appleyard hopes you know someone who has a quince
tree and that they really grow in Denmark and that that nice
young Dane has a cranberry bog. Or perhaps he'll get mountain
cranberries from Sweden. He seemed a determined character:
she's sure he'll manage all right.

Peas and Pearl Onions with Mustard Sauce (L.V.B.)

Allow one can of very small onions to 2 cans of tiny French
peas. Drain vegetables and heat over hot water with 2 tablespoons of sweet butter. Pass the mustard sauce with them.

French Mustard Sauce

2 tablespoons butter	½ teaspoon crushed garlic
2 tablespoons flour	1 tablespoon grated Parmesan cheese
salt to taste	¾ cup light cream
a few grains of cayenne	1 egg yolk
1 tablespoon Dijon mustard au vin blanc	2 teaspoons butter (extra)

Melt 2 tablespoons of butter. As soon as it starts to foam, remove pan from fire and rub in flour mixed with salt and
cayenne. Add mustard, crushed garlic, grated Parmesan and
then the cream, slowly, stirring all the time until mixture is

smooth. Return pan to low heat and add a tablespoon of the warm sauce to a beaten egg yolk, stir well add another table-spoon of sauce, mix thoroughly and stir mixture back into the sauce. Add the extra 2 teaspoons of butter, dot by dot, and cook till sauce begins to thicken. Remove pan from heat, cover it and set it aside where it will keep warm, not hot until serving time.

Scotch Oatcake (A.L.)

It was not possible to get real Scotch oats but A. L. turned out what seemed to Mrs. Appleyard like a very fine batch by put-ting regular oats, the kind she uses in oatmeal cookies, through the grinder.

2 cups regular oats, ground	1 cup flour
¼ cup sugar	½ cup butter
2 tablespoons butter (extra)	1 teaspoon baking powder
salt to taste	3½ tablespoons water

Mix the oats and the flour sifted with baking powder and salt together. Work in the butter, which should be at room temperature, with a pastry blending fork. Add the water. Pat out the oatcake into a well-buttered round tin. Crease it in wedge-shaped pieces. Dot with extra butter. Bake at 325° until delicately browned: 10 to 15 minutes. Serve hot or cold.

Artichokes Hollandaise

Cicely did these. She washed them and cooked them in a very large steamer for about half an hour while the soup and the roast were being eaten, and made the Hollandaise (p. 127) while the table was being cleared.

There is something restful about eating artichokes and it took a long time, so long that Mrs. Appleyard, never much of a dallier, excused herself and sneaked off into her kitchen to deal with the dessert.

Baked Alaska

The day before, Mrs. Appleyard had done the basic part or — to be quite accurate — Sara Lee in Chicago had done most of the work for her by baking pound cake with real butter and freezing it for Mrs. Appleyard's convenience.

(You may make your own, if you like, p. 272.)

She had sliced the pound cakes and lined the oblong pans the cakes came in first with wax paper, then with the slices. Then she had put in quart bricks of chocolate ice cream, which were by a happy coincidence the right size, topping them with the top slices of the cake. She had then returned the pans to the freezer so that the ice cream was good and hard.

Now she covered a cooky sheet with several thicknesses of heavy brown paper on it, lighted the oven: 450° and made the meringue.

Meringue (for two loaves)

whites of 6 large eggs ¾ cup sugar
¼ teaspoon cream of tartar 1 teaspoon vanilla

Beat whites until frothy with the cream of tartar, add the sugar a tablespoon at a time, beating after each addition. Beat till it sticks to the bowl and forms peaks. Add the vanilla. Remove loaves from pans, remove wax paper, set them on the cooky sheet. Cover sides and tops with meringue. Smooth it slightly along the sides but heap and swirl it lightly and casually on top. Bake it 3 to 5 minutes, in a preheated 450° oven until the top just starts to brown. Serve at once, so it will be warm outside and cold inside. One loaf is supposed to serve eight but Mrs. Appleyard says that's a little skimpy. For the sixteen internationalists she made three loaves. All vanished. She sometimes serves Hot Chocolate Sauce (p. 103) with it but not after a dinner like this one.

Cooking this meal and in betweentimes coasting or skiing on Cicely's hill, the one bordered with white birches, gave everyone a good appetite, including Mrs. Appleyard who got most of her exercise walking between her kitchen and Cicely's. Probably she walked about three miles, she thinks. She also went out into the zero air for a while and watched the skiers.

Their tracks, as they climbed the hill, made a pattern of pale blue featherstitching against the snow. The tracks downhill were deeper and bluer. Caps and jackets were spots of bright embroidery. Camilla had the dog sledge she got for Christmas out with Eric hitched to it. He pulled it amiably and curled his handsome black and silver tail until it touched his back but he did not make much headway. Eric is more interested in dreaming of chasing elk than in supplying motive power for a sledge with bright green cushions piped with scarlet. However, he added a picturesque touch to the landscape and though this year he had no icosahedral star to chew, he thoroughly enjoyed the bones from the crown roasts.

After the Baked Alaska was finished, the skiers went out to the hill again, by starlight this time. When they came back, Jean Gebhardt made cheese fondue for them. Luckily Cicely and her mother both have electric skillets. These are ideal for making the fondue.

Vermont Cheese Fondue
FOR EIGHT

1 bean garlic, peeled
1½ cups white wine
½ teaspoon pepper
1 teaspoon Worcestershire
   sauce

2 pounds Vermont cheddar cheese
   cut in small cubes
1 tablespoon kirsch
French bread sliced ½ inch thick
   and toasted

Split the bean of garlic and rub the pan well with it. Pour in the wine and heat until it starts to bubble. Add seasonings except the kirsch. Add the cheese, lower the heat, stir until the cheese is melted and mixture is smooth. Add the kirsch. Stir well, reduce heat to below 200°. Give everyone a plate, a fork and a piece of toast and let them dip the toast into the fondue. Start the second skilletful as soon as the guests start dipping into the first one. Keep the fondue warm. The bottoms of the pans will ultimately be covered by a crisp golden crust. This is the best part of all. The more of it the customers get off with a spatula, the less trouble it will be to wash the pan.

How fortunate, Mrs. Appleyard thought, that she and Cicely had given each other an automatic dishwasher for Christmas. The kitchenmaids loved it and fed it several rounds of dishes. Orion, the canary, sang all the time to its pulsating swish. The mechanical Christmas tree joined in occasionally. The cats arranged themselves like gargoyles carved out of tortoise shell and listened politely. Eric thumped his tail in a rhythm of his own. Marie-Claire could play the piano besides being able to cook, ski and look like a porcelain angel, so till midnight carols in many languages rang through the house.

How nice to be able to go abroad without packing a suitcase, Mrs. Appleyard thought as she stepped over the sleeping bags on her way to bed. The occupants were already asleep in the light of her Christmas tree with its tinsel and starlight and white roses. What a brave old world that had such creatures in it! she thought and was asleep before she could remember what she was misquoting.

Furred and Feathered Friends

IT TOOK Mrs. Appleyard some time to recover from the international festivities. For nearly two weeks she spent most of the time reading her Christmas books. These however did not last her indefinitely. She received only fifteen and as she averaged about a book and a half a day, number of pages and density of ideas considered, the supply was soon exhausted. At one time her average was two a day but of late years she has made a conscientious effort to read more slowly. In fact the last time she reread *Gone With the Wind* it took her two days. Cicely tries to keep her mother supplied from the circulating library but she has to read the book first herself. There was a time when mothers read books to see if they were suitable for their daughters but times change and it is Cicely who carefully leaves a note tucked into some sturdy tall octavo saying: "Dear Mother, I forbid you to read this book."

This means that the book contains a larger proportion of obscenities than Mrs. Appleyard really enjoys. She goes back to Gibbon who did as he promised and, when he felt obliged to write anything improper, put it into a footnote where it was "veiled in the decent obscurity of a classic tongue." Mrs. Appleyard wishes modern authors would take up this practice which would, she thinks, encourage the study of Latin and Greek. She clings to an old-fashioned belief in the cultural value of these languages though she must admit, having glanced at some of Mr. Gibbon's footnotes, that it is possible to be as uncultured in Latin or Greek as in American.

During her reading period, as she supposes she would have called it if she had been an Oxford undergraduate, she lived chiefly on yogurt and Tiger's Milk (orange juice, brewer's yeast and delicious veal bones ground fine) with an occasional toasted cheese sandwich or a grapefruit sent to her by someone who knew exactly what she wanted. Occasionally she made a batch of candied grapefruit peel but after a time she became conscious of the fact that the peel, if placed end to end, would probably reach nearly to Florida so she gave up that sticky sport. She did however make a few candied cranberries while she was about it.

She also constructed a meat loaf, which seemed rather tasty the first six times she ate it. In fact at first she served it to herself under the flattering title of *pâté maison*. She always writes out the menu, of course, and inserts it in the rococo gilt frame she once had given to her for that purpose.

("Mrs. Appleyard," inquired her favorite editor at this point, "do you expect your readers to believe that?"

"No," said Mrs. Appleyard, "but I'm sure they'd like to.")

It was at this time that Mrs. Appleyard became so much more interested in feeding birds than in cooking for herself. At first she was embarrassed to find that her menus were no more interesting to the birds than her own were to her. Birds in Appleyard Center have so many feeders to choose among that they are pampered and blasé, she decided.

Naïvely she had expected that, like human beings, the birds would pass the word around that a charming little new restaurant, cafeteria service, had opened up back of the cedar hedge, near that sprangly old Golden Transparent apple tree; that the counter was protected from snow and rain; that sunflower seeds were exquisitely served in an emerald-green container and that all you had to do to get more was to jump on the handle. She had also supposed that possible customers would hear that the suet, handsomely set forth in silver dishes (formerly containing frozen pound cake) had a certain *je ne sais quoi* about it: pound cake crumbs in fact.

Obviously, she began to think sadly, what they were really saying was "No Cordon Bleu, she."

However one morning while she was still asleep, someone rapped sharply on her door.

"Come in!" Mrs. Appleyard said drowsily but politely.

No one came in and the rapping went on.

After a while she realized that it came not from her door but from the window near the bird feeder. She got up to look. The customer departed promptly in a great flashing of blue and white and West Point gray. He flew into the apple tree and screamed impatiently at Mrs. Appleyard who, being a woman, forgave him his bad manners because of his handsome appearance. Besides he was her first visitor. He and his fellow blue jays, sometimes there were five posing in the apple tree, had irritably snatched most of the suet by ten o'clock. They evidently resented bird watchers though all Mrs. Appleyard was doing was sitting at her desk writing a book, a quiet occupation, she had always thought; nothing obviously menacing about it. Still the blue jays may have known some other authors because every time she moved her pen they would fly off announcing: "The pen is mightier than the sword" or screams to that effect.

Perhaps they are Russian blue jays and think I am writing a sequel to Dr. Zhivago, thought Mrs. Appleyard.

This seemed unlikely. She came to the conclusion that they suspected her of being a capitalist. Little did they know how near the purchase of sunflower seeds was bringing her to bankruptcy.

However she was getting less nervous customers now so she kept her smörgåsbord running. When the Christmas trees were untrimmed, she set some of them up around the feeder and decked them with holly. Sometimes on bright blue and white mornings, the trees would be diamond-dusted with snow and chickadees with their neatly tailored black velvet caps and bibs would hop in and out among the branches before landing on the feeder. They were more afraid of the jays than they were of Mrs. Appleyard and her powerful pen, she noticed.

One morning as she sat writing, arrived a great flock of evening grosbeaks, splendidly caparisoned in yellow and white and iridescent black. Their soft voices and fluttering wings made a perpetual whispering as they found sunflower seeds and cracked them. They seemed to regard Mrs. Appleyard simply as part of the décor, a compliment of which she was humbly appreciative. A downy woodpecker, stylish in black and white with his scarlet cockade appeared. There was a pair of nuthatches, inquisitive and skeptical with their turned-up beaks; red polls and pine grosbeaks came too. At last she had a visitor well-known in Appleyard Center, a chickadee with cap and bib mottled with white as if snow had been sprinkled on him. He had a pink bill instead of black and his eyes were surrounded by white instead of black so that he had an expression like no other chickadee. He had an excellent appetite, in fact he was so hungry that Mrs. Appleyard put out the rest of the meat loaf for him and some Yorkshire pudding with melted suet poured over it. He liked it so much that Mrs. Appleyard realized that she was now in ornithological society. He came every day and neither a moving pen nor rustled papers disturbed him at his lunch.

At last, thought Mrs. Appleyard, I have a feathered friend. And I, she reflected putting on her new platinum mink hat, am a furred friend. How nice we're so congenial.

Menu for Birds and Their Watchers

Meat Loaf* with Mushroom Sauce*
Broccoli with Garlic Croutons*
Yorkshire Pudding, giant-sized*
Candied Grapefruit Peel*   Candied Cranberries*
Mince Turnovers*

Meat Loaf

1 pound ground chuck	1 teaspoon minced onion
1 pound Vermont sausage meat	pinch of mixed herbs
6 slices of bread	pinch of celery flakes
½ cup milk	½ cup dried bread crumbs
2 eggs lightly beaten	6 strips of suet
¼ cup light cream	1 tablespoon melted butter

Have the butcher put the ground chuck and the sausage meat

together through the grinder. Soak bread in milk 5 minutes and squeeze it dry. Mix together the beaten eggs, light cream, onion, herbs and celery flakes and mix with the soaked bread, then work this mixture thoroughly into the ground meat with a pastry blending fork. Butter a bread tin and put in the meat mixture. Cover the top with the dry crumbs mixed with the melted butter. Lay over the top 6 very narrow strips of suet. Bake at 350° for one hour and 15 minutes.

Note: this time is for 2 pounds of meat. A smaller quantity will do in 45 to 50 minutes. In both cases reduce the heat to 300° if it browns too quickly. Before you put the loaf on the serving platter, pour off the melted fat. Save it.

As Mrs. Appleyard is frequently heard to remark at this season, "That's for the Birds."

Mushroom Sauce

1 pound mushrooms, peeled, caps only	salt to taste
	½ teaspoon paprika
1 teaspoon minced onion	¼ teaspoon pepper
2 tablespoons butter	¼ teaspoon nutmeg
2 tablespoons flour	piece of bay leaf
1 cup light cream	1 cup heavy cream
1 tablespoon sherry	

Save the mushroom skins and stems for soup. Slice the peeled caps vertically. Sauté onion in the butter until translucent, then add the mushrooms and cook till they are tender — about 5 minutes. Remove with skimmer to top of a double boiler. Now rub the flour into the butter. Add more butter if necessary. There should be at least 2 tablespoonfuls in the pan. Remove pan from heat while you are doing this. Return it to very low heat and cook the roux for 3 minutes. Now add the light cream slowly at first, stirring well to make a thin paste free from lumps. Add the dry seasonings, including the bay leaf. Add the heavy cream. Let the sauce simmer gently but not boil for 5 minutes. Pour it over the mushrooms in the double boiler. It will be all the better if it stands for an hour before you use it. At serving time fish out the bay leaf, heat sauce, add sherry.

Broccoli with Garlic Croutons

1 package chopped broccoli	¼ cup cream
1 tablespoon butter	garlic croutons (p. 56)

Follow cooking directions on a package of frozen broccoli. It will speed up cooking time and will not injure the flavor if you allow it to defrost at room temperature half an hour before you start to cook it. Cook uncovered after it is boiling hard. If the water has not all cooked away when broccoli is tender but not mushy, remove broccoli to a hot dish and cook the water down to 2 tablespoons. Add the butter and the cream, heat well and pour over the broccoli. Sprinkle over the garlic crumbs. Serves four, stingily.

Yorkshire Pudding
GIANT SIZED

If you have a 15-inch scarlet and ivory enameled iron frying pan or a plain 15-inch iron pan, now is the time to use it.

3 cups rich milk	3 cups flour, measured after sifting 3 times
salt to taste	tried out beef suet, half an inch deep in the
12 eggs	pan

Light oven: 400°. Try out suet over medium heat. Be sure the flour is warm and dry. Have a pitcher big enough to hold the entire mixture. Use an electric mixer or your blender. Mrs. Appleyard prefers the blender. Blend the ingredients in three lots, dumping in 4 eggs, a cup of milk and a cup of flour each time. Pour the blended mixture into your pitcher and repeat the process. You blend each batch only one minute so it does not take long. If you use an electric mixer or a hand beater it takes longer. Add the milk slowly to the flour, beating all the time, and then beat in the eggs one at a time. Do not let your suet overheat. It should be hot but cracklings should not be browned.

Pour in your batter. Stand back! The fat will spit, spatter and sizzle and come up around the batter on the edges of the pan. Set the pan in the oven. Bake it until the pudding has risen well and has started to brown — about 20 minutes. Don't keep looking at it. You will only be depressed by its sullen appearance and letting cold air in on it only delays the rising. Reduce the heat to 350°. It takes about an hour altogether for a 15-inch pudding to get crisp and brown. Leave it a little longer, reducing the heat to 300° if you have any doubts. You don't want any soft and soggy spots in it.

Mrs. Appleyard first made this for her friend Venetia Hopkins who was having ten people to dinner and who was afraid there would not be enough. There was. Fortunately one of them was a poet with strong wrists developed by tennis and skiing. It was he who maneuvered the pan in and out of the oven. In case Mrs. Appleyard forgot to thank him, she does so now.

For four people use a nine-inch pan and a third of this mixture. It should cook in 45 to 50 minutes.

Candied Grapefruit Peel

Cut the peel of two grapefruit lengthwise in ¼-inch sections. Soak overnight in 4 cups cold water with 1 tablespoon salt. Drain, cover with cold water, bring to boiling point and cook 20 minutes. Drain and repeat the process several times until peel has no bitter taste. Then cook until tender, an hour or more. Drain and cook slowly in syrup made of 1 cup sugar and ½ cup water. Use a candy thermometer and cook until it registers 238°. Or you can do it in the electric skillet with the control set at 238°. Put in the peel, cook till transparent. Remove peel with a spoon with holes. Spread on aluminum foil till cool. Roll in granulated sugar. Store in tightly covered tin box.

Candied Cranberries (J.B.)

When a former colonel in our armed forces turns his attention to cooking, he really makes something unusual and good.

1 cup sugar	1 cup cranberries, the largest and
1 cup water	best of a package

Make a syrup of the sugar and water in an electric skillet with the control set at 238° or in an iron skillet over the flame. It is hard to use a candy thermometer in a shallow pan, so test the syrup by dropping a little off the spoon until it spins a thread. With a good-sized needle make several holes in each cranberry. This is so that they will absorb the syrup and also it helps them keep their shape. When the syrup threads, drop in the cranberries and cook until they look translucent. Skim them out, place them on aluminum foil to dry overnight. The next morning roll them in granulated sugar, spiced if you like with a little cinnamon. Store in a tightly covered tin box.

Syrup left from either the grapefruit or the cranberries may be used in punch.

Mince Turnovers

If you have some of Mrs. Appleyard's 2000-Layer Pastry (p. 60) left in the refrigerator, it's an easy matter to make these: that is, if you also have a little mincemeat on hand.

Light oven: 450°.

Roll out the paste into a piece ⅛ inch thick and 8 inches square and cut it into sixteen 2-inch squares. Put a teaspoon of mincemeat on each one, moisten edges, fold the squares over into triangles and press edges together with the back of a fork lightly dipped in flour. Put into a shallow pan and bake for 15 minutes. Check to see if they are puffed and delicately browned. Bake 5 minutes longer if necessary. Don't worry if the mincemeat is oozing out at the edges here and there: it tastes all the better. Serve either hot or cold: very nourishing at 10° below zero.

Use packaged pastry if you must, though the turnovers will not be so delicate as these.

Snowbound

Perhaps Icebound would be a better description but the snow came first. It fell steadily for two windless days and nights in tiny determined flakes that heaped themselves up so efficiently that even the slender gnarled branches of the Golden Transparent apple tree were piled six inches high. Maples, which had been fans of black coral against the sky, suddenly became white coral dusted with powdered rainbows. Elms were wineglasses holding bouquets of white leaves. Black twigs of white birches were whiter than the trunks. Only big pines a century old were still obviously pines, thrusting out their arms in their own pattern, carrying their burden with their old patience.

A storm like this would jam the streets of Boston or New York with crawling cars. In the District of Columbia it would occur to no one that the streets were for driving. Cars that had been freed from their owners' nerveless hands would rapidly get to look like igloos. It would be a time of peace. The only time that Mrs. Appleyard was ever offered champagne at ten o'clock in the morning was during a storm like this. She thinks there ought to be more of them. She likes to think of her Washington employees sitting at home quietly drinking champagne. No one would order nuclear tests in the atmosphere or think up any new "temporary" taxes (like the income tax for instance) or raise the postal rates again. Of course Mrs. Appleyard realizes that this is necessary. In 1912 it used to take a day for a letter to get from Boston to Appleyard Center. Now that the Post Office has so much interesting automatic equipment, it sometimes takes four days. Naturally such service has to cost more than it did when letters were sorted with a good deal of thumb-licking and carried in model T Fords. Letters have to be kept somewhere all those days so extra space is needed. Besides it is necessary to buy more automatic sorters so that the pace throughout the country will be uniform. If it would only snow oftener in Washington, it would save the taxpayer millions of dollars — or is it billions? Who knows the difference? Or cares?

Not Mrs. Appleyard certainly.

She occupies herself with important distinctions such as whether syrup is hot enough to spin a thread six inches long (240° in case you have any spinning to do) or is merely at softball stage (238°). She also likes to try to tell a skunk spruce from a fir balsam when both are pyramided with snow.

Snow can be enjoyed in Appleyard Center. It does not stop traffic. This is not because the snow is essentially different from Washington snow. Each crystal is unlike any other crystal but the substance as a whole is the same. The attitude towards it is where the difference lies. In Washington they figure that the Lord sent it and will after a while take it away. In Appleyard Center, Eric Vardon, the road commissioner, knows that if he does not plow eighty miles of road, milk will not get to market, mail will not leave, children will not get to school, their fathers will not get to work. If snow is getting deep on the roads at 5.30 A.M., that's when he starts plowing. He keeps it up till the roads are passable. And plows again the next day if necessary, adding sand and salt to taste.

In fact he is so efficient that Mrs. Appleyard heard one of her neighbors say: "Sometimes I wish I could be snowbound three-four days. I need a good rest."

So Mrs. Appleyard has not been snowbound since she became a winter Vermonter but she has been icebound. There were two clear blue and white days after the snowstorm. Then came the sleet, encasing everything in glass, every twig, every telephone wire, every pine needle. Maple trees were crystal fans instead of coral. The ski slope outside her window was a sheet of frosted glass banded with blue glass shadows of birches. It was eerily beautiful — up to the time the electricity went off.

The first thing she missed was the lights but perhaps, she thought, I need a new fuse on that circuit. She went into the bathroom. From there the house usually sounds to her rather like the *SS Normandie* in the middle of the Atlantic. She can hear the purring of the oil burner, the throb of the pump, the swish and splash of washing machine and dishwasher, clothes being softly tumbled in the clothes dryer, the hum of her own refrigerator and freezer and of Cicely's too, and the whirring of electric clocks.

The TV, often unwatched, tries to convince an unseen and unseeing audience that one kind of toothpaste is different from some other kind. The record player plays the first half of Schubert's great *C Major Symphony*. No one turns the record over so it repeats the first half with all the thumps, conscientiously. Music more varied, interspersed with announcers'

voices, terribly cultured, that drop a minor third on the last
phrase of each paragraph and mispronounce words interestingly
in many languages including their own and the Scandinavian,
drifts in over the FM radio. A kettle on her electric stove
whistles excitedly.

Now this had all stopped. Fortunately, Cicely is ready for
such an emergency. She has gas as well as electricity to cook
with, candles to light, white birch logs to burn in the big fireplace. She drew what water was left in the taps and rationed
it for drinking water.

"We could melt icicles if we need water for washing," Mrs.
Appleyard announced. "There's one as big as my arm outside
my window. I heard of someone who used them in martinis."

"How handy," said Cicely, "but why not pour the gin in the
gutter and have it ready mixed."

"Because I don't care to have gin drop on my head while I am
writing," her mother said firmly.

"I thought Roger fixed that place where the ice backs up,"
said her daughter.

"He did but that was at my left. Now that it's fixed, the water
drops on my head unless I sit at one side and catch it in my
silver mug. It takes more than an hour to fill it. Anyway it
won't run in weather like this and he's going to take down the
gutter tomorrow. I never expected to know so much about
gutters," she added. "Or electricity — oh goodness, my freezer.
Everything will melt in it. If you don't mind letting me use
your gas, I think I'd better cook everything in it for dinner.
Yours is so much bigger that if we cover it with newspapers
and a rug it will probably keep till the power comes on but
mine will soften up, I'm afraid. I'll start now while it's still
light and we can eat stylishly by candlelight."

This was what she cooked.

ICEBOUND MENU

Princess Pea Soup*   Seafood Casserole*
Green Beans with Sausages* (G.S.)   Kolacky*
Golden Bantam Corn, Baked*
Cream Puffs with Pistachio Ice Cream and Chocolate Sauce (p. 103)
or with Vanilla Ice Cream and Icebound Raspberry-Cranberry Sauce*

Princess Pea Soup
FOR SIX

4 tablespoons butter	¼ teaspoon mixed herbs
4 tablespoons flour	½ teaspoon parsley flakes
4 cups rich milk	1 cup chicken stock, jellied
1 cup frozen peas, cooked	1 small onion, cooked with stock
¼ teaspoon nutmeg	¾ cup light cream
½ teaspoon paprika	½ cup breast of chicken, cubed

Melt butter over low heat, rub in flour. Remove from heat. Add slowly a cup of milk, stirring carefully until it is smooth. Cook over low heat, stirring all the time until it thickens, about 3 minutes. Put it in the blender with half the cooked peas and the seasonings. Blend 2 minutes. Put in top of double boiler. Put the rest of the peas, the chicken stock into the blender, blend 2 minutes and add to the contents of the double boiler. Add the rest of the milk and cook over boiling water at least 20 minutes. At serving time add the cream and the chicken cubes. Serve very hot with Kolacky.

Kolacky (Slovak Nut Bread) (E.J.C.)

This was already in Mrs. Appleyard's freezer. She had been saving it for an emergency and was delighted that one had arisen. The Kolacky and directions for making it were a present from someone who had read one of Mrs. Appleyard's books and who thought she might like it. How right she was!

It may be made either with a raised dough or with a baking powder biscuit dough to which eggs are added. Given here are the directions for the raised-dough method.

8 cups flour, sifted 3 times and measured after sifting. Use the extra flour for rolling out dough.
salt to taste, about 1½ teaspoons
⅔ cup sugar

2 cups lukewarm milk
¾ pound butter, melted
3 yeast cakes dissolved in ½ cup lukewarm water
4 eggs

Filling:

1 cup pecans or walnuts, chopped and mixed with 1 cup sugar
a little water

Mix flour, salt, sugar, milk, butter, yeast and beaten eggs. Knead dough until it is smooth and elastic. Put it into a warm bowl, cover and let rise until double its bulk in a warm place. Turn onto a floured board, divide in 10 or 12 portions. Let rest a few minutes.

Make the filling. Chop the nuts fine, add the sugar and a little water, enough so it will stick together and spread easily.

Roll out each portion in oblong shape. Spread with filling, roll up like jelly roll. Put in large iron dripping pan. Cover.

Let rise till double in bulk. Brush top of each roll with a little butter or with beaten egg if you prefer. Bake at 400° for 10 minutes. Reduce heat to 350° and bake until golden brown, about 20 minutes longer.

Other kinds of filling such as would be used in filled cookies may be substituted for the nuts but Mrs. Appleyard recommends the original kind.

In serving the Kolacky that had been in the freezer, she thawed it out about half an hour, then sliced it about half an inch thick, spread it with soft butter, ran the slices briefly under the broiler and served them very hot.

Seafood Casserole

¾ pound frozen lobster meat
½ pound frozen or canned crabmeat
½ pound frozen shrimp
1 pound flounder fillets frozen
4 tablespoons butter
4 tablespoons flour
¼ teaspoon nutmeg
½ teaspoon paprika
½ teaspoon pepper; salt to taste
3 cups rich milk
1 cup cream

2 egg yolks
extra butter, 2 tablespoons
1 teaspoon minced onion
1 small green pepper, seeded
  and sliced thin
1 pimento, cut fine
8 mushroom caps, sliced vertically
2 tablespoons sherry
1 cup dry bread crumbs, rolled fine
4 tablespoons grated cheese

The shellfish should be thawed at room temperature for at least an hour. Steam the flounder fillets over boiling water for 10 minutes, flake them into fair-sized pieces. Set aside. Now make a cream sauce, melt butter over low heat, work in flour mixed with dry seasonings carefully; it must not brown. Remove pan from heat, blend in milk carefully a little at a time. Return to heat and cook slowly for 3 to 5 minutes. Add cream. Beat egg yolks with a fork, pour some of the sauce over them in

three lots, stirring well after each addition. Stir egg mixture
into the sauce. Mix well and set sauce aside where it will be
warm, not hot.

Now melt 2 tablespoons of butter and lightly cook the onion,
green pepper strips, pimento and sliced mushrooms in it. When
onion begins to turn straw-colored, add the seafood cut up, not
too fine. Cook 3 minutes. Add the sherry. Cook 2 minutes
more. Butter a 2-quart casserole. Put a layer of sauce in it, then
a layer of the seafood mixture. Repeat. Finish with some of
the sauce. Sprinkle the bread crumbs over it, dot with butter,
sprinkle with grated cheese.

Bake at 375° until crumbs are lightly browned. As the fish
is already cooked, 15 minutes will be long enough.

Green Beans with Sausages (G.S.)

This dish was the result of a fortunate accident. One of the
most talented cooks of Mrs. Appleyard's acquaintance once
baked enough sausages for 50 people. They were supposed to
surround platters of nicely broiled chicken breasts but somehow
the sausages stayed in the oven. Don't think for a moment that
they were wasted. Cutting them in halves rapidly, she thrust
them down into the big silver dishes of green beans and someone
said, "What a clever new idea! And delectable! I *must* find out
how she did it!"

For a family of eight, here's how:

2 packages French-cut green beans	½ pound link sausages, baked in a
1 tablespoon butter	350° oven for 40 minutes

Cook the beans in the smallest possible amount of hot water.
Watch them carefully and cook them until they are tender but

not mushy and the water has all cooked away. Add the butter. Put beans into a hot vegetable dish. Cut sausages, drained of fat on paper towels, in halves and thrust the cut half down into the beans, leaving tops half an inch above.

Golden Bantam Corn, Baked

1 package frozen Golden Bantam corn	½ stick butter
	½ teaspoon paprika — salt to taste
1 teaspoon sugar	¼ teaspoon pepper

Butter rather heavily a shallow iron enamel baking dish in which corn will be served. Mix seasonings with the corn, spread it out in the dish, dot all over with butter. Bake at 375° until golden brown around the edges — 20 to 30 minutes.

Cream Puffs

There is a blow-by-blow account of how to make cream puffs in *The Summer Kitchen* (p. 202). At the Icebound period she had some on hand, also some of Howard Johnson's Pistachio Ice Cream, also some of the Granite City Creamery's Real Ice Cream. She served a choice of Chocolate Sauce as made on (p. 103) or the Icebound Raspberry-Cranberry Sauce which she invented as the twilight waned.

Mrs. Appleyard's
Icebound Raspberry-Cranberry Sauce

½ package cranberries, cooked whole according to directions on the package	1 pint frozen raspberries
	1 glass currant jelly

Thaw the raspberries by setting the package in warm, not hot water. Cook the cranberries until berries are all popped. Remove from heat, add the currant jelly, stir till it is melted. Cool slightly. Add the partly thawed raspberries. Stir well. Keep in a cool place till needed.

By this time — the electricity had now been off for four hours — there was no difficulty in finding a cool place to set something. In fact the only really warm place was by the fire. They moved the table in front of it and lighted a variety of candles — pale green ones in brass candlesticks, twisted red ones in silver, a giant white and gold one that Mrs. Appleyard had for Christmas, others in glass or pewter or tin.

Perhaps it was the light of the fire and the candles and the last reflection from a pink and gold sunset coming in the window or Cynthia playing Bach on the piano before dinner or the girls all setting the table or the scent of woodsmoke — but something made that Icebound meal taste especially good to Mrs. Appleyard. When it was over, no one seemed anxious to melt icicles and wash the dishes.

"The most practical thing for you to do is to go to bed and get the bed warmed up — no electricity for your blanket tonight," Cicely said.

"That is certainly one place where candles don't make much of a substitute," Mrs. Appleyard agreed. "I'll be in bed and think what I'll write tomorrow."

So she did — for almost five minutes.

Why, she thought sleepily, sun's in my eyes, must be morning.

Then a weary tenor voice said in her ear, "On Feb'uary 15th we will bring you . . ." And she was back in the electrical world where it is so easy to purée peas and so difficult to pronounce the name of the second month in the year.

Appliances began to purr and hum and thump all over the house. Pills for indigestion and headaches and colds were seductively mentioned. Gunmen started to shoot, horses cantered, Schubert began where he left off on what Mrs. Appleyard decided must be his second *Unfinished Symphony*. Radiators hissed — ah, happy sound! The button on the control of her electric blanket glowed a cheerful bright gold.

Blessing the name of Thomas A. Edison, Mrs. Appleyard began to do a Double Crostic by a good bright light.

Now what, she asked herself happily, is "pertaining to the muscle sense"?

(Kinesthetic, in case you're interested.)

February

Jingle Bells

IT IS DIFFICULT, Mrs. Appleyard says, to arrange about snow.
It is often dumped on New York or Cairo, Illinois, where no one
wants it and in the meantime the supply in Vermont is inadequate. Lack of it is resented by weekend visitors from the city
who say gloomily, "There's better skiing on Broadway than
there is here." They consider, rather naturally, that it is the
duty of the natives, including of course Mrs. Appleyard, to get
at least two feet of fine powder piled up during the week, to
have the roads a good deal better plowed out than Fifth
Avenue, right down to the black-top in fact, and at the same

time to have the same roads with plenty of hard-packed snow on them so that they can go sleighing.

Mrs. Appleyard sympathizes with the wish to go sleighing. She wants her grandchildren to remember it half a century and more from now as she still does — a big sleigh packed with straw, with hot bricks in it, the creak of runners on crisp snow, the soft thud of horses' hoofs, fur coats and blankets and buffalo robes, trees dark against the moon, singing and laughing and — most important of all — sleigh bells.

It was not until February that enough snow was packed down on the roads so that she could telephone Hugh and say "If you come this weekend, I think there'll be sleighing. I'll ask Roger to be getting your house warmed up. Sam Flint has two big pungs ready and there are still four horses in town that are able to stand up and occasionally put one foot ahead of the other. Camilla and her friends in the 4-H Club are already making cookies so they can serve them here with hot chocolate afterwards."

"Fine," Hugh said, "and Erica says she wants the family at our house for supper beforehand. Just don't let the snow melt before we get there."

"I will preserve every flake," his mother said.

Mrs. Appleyard never did figure out just how many children were packed into the sleighs. She rode only from Hugh's house to her own, not a long distance but enough so that she had breathed all the 5-below-zero air she really needed and got plenty of straw in her fur boots and heard the silver sleigh bells under the silver moon. They were her own sleigh bells that usually hang in strategic places around her house. They sound — she noticed — quite differently on a cold night with the northern lights flickering in white and green and rosy streamers

across a green sky from the way they do when they call people
to supper on hot July evenings.

Supper tonight was served in two sections, the main course
at Hugh's before the sleigh ride, the dessert at Cicely's afterwards. The riders were stoked with the following menu:

Hamburg Strong-Enough* (E.R.K.)

Rice   Fresh Asparagus, Butter and Egg Sauce*

Mrs. Appleyard's Lemon Mint Chutney*

Garlic Bread*   Tossed Salad*

Later:

Hot Coffee Chocolate* with Whipped Cream

Coconut Cookies*   Flaming Angel Cake*

When Mrs. Appleyard asked Hugh's wife what she called
that tasty dish of meat balls in a hot zippy sauce, Erica replied
that Hugh had christened it. It was, she said, a sort of cousin of
Beef Stroganov only she hadn't used filet mignon so she asked
Hugh what she ought to call it.

He tasted the sauce and said "Call it Hamburg Strong-
Enough." So that was its family name. It was made that afternoon except for the final heating and the addition of the sour
cream.

Mrs. Appleyard promptly borrowed a not very co-operative
inkish pencil, a combination of pen and pencil with most of the
faults of both, and wrote down the formula.

Hamburg Strong-Enough
FOR TWELVE

4 pounds ground chuck	¼ teaspoon tarragon
4 tablespoons flour	½ teaspoon nutmeg
Wesson oil	¼ teaspoon curry powder
2 small onions, minced	1½ cups sour cream
1 pound button mushrooms	salt and pepper to taste
1½ cups beef stock	½ cup sherry
½ teaspoon thyme	½ cup vermouth

Make the meat into balls a little smaller than a ping-pong ball, pressing them firmly into shape. Put the flour into a bag and put the meat balls in and shake gently until they are well coated with flour. Put a little Wesson oil in an electric skillet over medium heat. Put in the meat balls, a few at a time and brown them all over. Pour off any surplus fat from time to time. Save it. (Such a substance is often just what you need.) Remove the meat balls as they are browned and in the same skillet sauté the onion and the sliced mushroom caps. Save the stems for soup. Now add the stock — it should be jellied — and about a cup of hot water. Stir it well and add the dry seasonings except the salt, the vermouth and the sherry. Add the meat balls. Simmer for 5 minutes. If the sauce seems too thin, thicken it with 2 tablespoons of flour, dissolved in cold water and rubbed through a fine strainer into the sauce. Turn off the heat. Cover the skillet and let the mixture stand for at least 2 hours. Just before serving time, bring it almost to the boiling point and let it simmer 2 or 3 minutes. Add a tablespoon of the sauce to the sour cream. Stir it in well. Add another and stir well, then stir the cream mixture into the sauce. Add the salt, vermouth and sherry. Taste it by dipping a crust of dry bread into it. Add more seasoning if you like. Don't let your assistants have too much dry bread or they will eat all the sauce before the dish ever gets to the table. After adding the cream, bring the mixture to the boiling point but do not let it boil. Serve it right in the skillet with a big bowl of freshly cooked rice beside it.

Garlic Bread
FOR TWELVE

If you have Italian or French neighbors they will tell you the name of the bakery where you can buy real crusty French or Italian bread, not the mushy crusted cottony stuff that masquerades under those honorable names.

2 loaves of crusty Italian   ½ pound whipped butter at room
    or French bread   temperature
            2 teaspoons garlic powder

Slice bread almost all the way through. Blend the butter and garlic powder. Spread the mixture between the slices of bread. This may be done ahead of time. Just before serving time put the loaves in a dripping pan and heat them 5 minutes in a 350° oven.

Mrs. Appleyard likes the primitive ferocity of real garlic put through the press and mixed with real butter, but she says a mixed group seemed to prefer this gentler version.

Tossed Salad
FOR TWELVE

The version on page 147 may be used. This is slightly different, chiefly because of the tomatoes. Do not use tomatoes at this season unless you can get real hothouse ones which have both color and flavor.

French Dressing

Erica mixed her dressing in a screw-type jar. She put into it:

⅓ cup olive oil	1 tablespoon chopped chives
3 tablespoons wine vinegar	⅓ cup Wesson oil
1 teaspoon sugar	1 teaspoon dry mustard
1 teaspoon salt	½ teaspoon pepper from the grinder
¼ teaspoon thyme	½ teaspoon paprika
1 bean garlic, crushed	¼ teaspoon orégano
1 tablespoon parsley, minced	

When this was well mixed she poured half of it into a big wooden salad bowl, crossed the spoon and fork and added the salad mixture.

1 head of iceberg torn into rather small pieces	half a carrot, shredded
	¼ pound Danish blue cheese
4 stalks of celery cut into ¼-inch cubes	1 cup cauliflower flowerets, raw
	2 green peppers, freed from seeds and pith, one sliced, the other cut in rings
5 large hothouse tomatoes, cut in eighths	

Mix all the vegetables together except the rings of green peppers. These are to decorate the top of the salad. Keep the bowl in a cold place for at least half an hour so the vegetables will be crisp. At serving time toss them gently but thoroughly in the dressing. Be sure not to crush the tomatoes. Add the cheese, crumbled not too fine. If salad seems too dry, shake up the jar of dressing and add a little more. The dressing should coat all the vegetables and not be in the bottom of the bowl. Just before serving lay on the pepper rings, pour over another table-spoon of dressing. For 12.

Asparagus, Country Style with Butter and Egg Sauce
FOR TWELVE

Some of the best asparagus of the year comes from California at this time; large stalks, tender, good flavor.

3 large bunches of asparagus	juice of one lemon
¼ pound butter	2 hardboiled eggs
salt and pepper to taste	

Cut off the ends of the asparagus stalks at the point where they break easily. Cut the stalks into inch pieces. Keep the tips in a separate dish. Cook the lower parts of the stalks in rapidly boiling water 15 minutes. Add the tips, cover and cook until tips and stalks are tender, about 5 minutes longer.

Have rounds of buttered toast ready on a big hot platter. Also have the sauce ready. It is made by heating the butter and lemon juice and then adding the hard-boiled eggs, cut up rather fine, and the seasonings. Drain off any water left in the asparagus. Cook it down to a tablespoonful and add it to the sauce. Heap the asparagus on the toast. Bring the sauce to a boil and spoon some over each heap of asparagus. This amount of asparagus will make 12 heaps — none extra.

Lemon Mint Chutney

In the life of everyone who has tomato plants in the garden the problem of what to do with the green ones arises. This was Mrs. Appleyard's solution for the summer of 1961.

6 large onions
8 pounds small green tomatoes
½ cup salt
7 lemons sliced thin and slices cut in eighths
1 pound sultana seedless raisins

2 cups cider vinegar
2 pounds brown sugar
3 pounds white sugar
1 cup mint leaves
4 cups cubes of green early apples
2 tablespoons ginger

2 cups green seedless grapes

Chop onions rather fine. Add the tomatoes, chop fine. Cover with salt and cold water. Let stand overnight. Next morning drain, wash thoroughly with cold water, then scald with boiling water. Put in a large kettle. Add the lemons and the raisins. Heat vinegar, dissolve sugar (brown and white) in it and pour it over the mixture. Cook 15 minutes. Next day reheat. Cook 10 minutes, stirring well. The third day pick your mint leaves (no stems). Your cupful should be solidly packed. Purée them in the blender with ¼ cup water. Add them, together with the cubes of apple (Golden Transparents in this case), the ginger and the green grapes. Bring mixture to the boil, cook 5 minutes. Put in jars and seal.

Until the last jar of this was used up, it never occurred to Mrs. Appleyard that she would ever wish she had some more green tomatoes. Well, the days are getting longer. Before she knows it she will be out in her garden, where passersby often confuse her with the scarecrow Roger Willard made for her. Even the indigo buntings, intelligent birds, can hardly tell them apart. Perhaps that is because the scarecrow is wearing some of Mrs. Appleyard's clothes so that both are suitably dressed for picking tomatoes.

As she thought happily of sunflowers in bloom with heavenly blue morning glories twining up their stems, of broccoli flowering like yellow butterflies because she forgot to pick it, of neglected zucchini the size of watermelons, of splendid stalks of grass ready and eager to be made into cake testers, Mrs. Appleyard suddenly heard something that brought her back to reality.

Yes, it was clear, it was crystal, it was silvery — as clear as zero air, as crystal as icicles, as silvery as moonlit snow — the sound of sleigh bells. She looked out the window. There they were, under the shimmer of the northern lights, coming down the hill, past the schoolhouse, past the white houses with their plumes of white woodsmoke, past the hidden brook, singing as they came.

> Jingle bells, jingle bells,
> Jingle all the way . . .

There was still singing after they came in and thumping of tunes that children already knew how to thump on the piano in 1897 and loud shrieks of delight when all the lights were put out and Erica brought in her flaming angel cake. There was even a moment of silence while it was being served and the scalding hot chocolate was being tasted.

Hot Coffee-Chocolate

There was plain hot chocolate or coffee or a mixture of both. Mrs. Appleyard likes coffee-chocolate. It should be rather a subtle blend, about half a teaspoon of instant coffee to a cup of chocolate is plenty and with whipped cream it is guaranteed to give the drinker a night with plenty of mental energy to think over the party.

Cicely had a good supply of miniature marshmallows on hand for putting into chocolate for those preferred them to cream. They disappeared rapidly and so did the coconut cookies made by the 4-H members.

Coconut Cookies (K.McK.)

1 cup softened butter	2 teaspoons baking powder
1 cup brown sugar	½ teaspoon salt
1 cup white sugar	2 cups quick oats
2 eggs, well beaten	2 cups Rice Krispies
2 cups sifted flour	1 cup coconut
1 teaspoon vanilla	

Cream butter and sugar together. Add the eggs, the flour sifted with the baking powder and salt and the oats, Rice Krispies and coconut. Add vanilla. Mix well, make into small balls (about 1 teaspoon in each), put on a cooky sheet, press out with a fork. Bake until delicately browned, at 350° for 15 to 20 minutes.

Flaming Angel Cake
FOR TWELVE

Mrs. Appleyard leaves the acquiring of the angel cake to your judgment. Make it from your great great grandmother's treasured rule using 13 egg whites, or bake the packaged kind or buy it from the supermarket.

1 large angel cake	2 packages frozen strawberries,
1 quart vanilla ice cream	slightly thawed
7 lumps of sugar	
2 tablespoons pure grain alcohol	

Split angel cake into 3 layers. Spread ice cream between the layers. Set the cake on a large paper plate covered with chef's foil. Fill the center with ice cream and set cake into the freezer

for at least half an hour. At serving time, pour the thawed strawberries over it, spreading them around the sides of the cake with
a spatula. Soak the sugar lumps briefly in the alcohol. Fish them
out with sugar tongs and place them on top of the cake. Light
them. Turn off all the lights. Carry the cake in blazing blue.

There were two this time so they gave a fine magical illumina-
tion as Bruce and Polly carried them in, smelled delicious and
tasted good too.

It is hoped that a suitable combination of ingredients can be
arranged for another sleighride next year.

Family Favorites

THIS sounds as if some of Mrs. Appleyard's family were her
favorites and though of course they are, all of them in fact, what
she is talking about was their favorite things to eat. During the
sleighing weekend she rashly said that she would have a family
dinner and that they all could choose something they specially
liked and she would cook it. This statement was greeted by a
chorus of "Oatmeal lace cookies" and the subject had to be
approached differently in order to supply a somewhat more
balanced menu.

What she finally did was to write slips saying Soup, Meat,
Vegetable and so forth, and let each guest draw one. This

system resulted in Nicholas's (almost two) choosing the meat. "Chicken," he said firmly, leaving the method to his grandmother.

When the results of the lottery were published — on the slate near the front door — the menu was as follows:

Appetizers
Sardines on toast   Stuffed Eggs*
Peanut Butter and Bacon (p. 126)

Onion Soup with Custard*
Chicken Simmered in Cream*
Baked Potatoes†   Green Peas*
Orange Sherbert with Bananas*   Oatmeal Lace Cookies (p. 110)

Stuffed Eggs

Choose large eggs. Hard-boil them and remove the shells. Cut them in quarters. Mash the yolks with a fork.

For four eggs allow:

2 tablespoons mayonnaise   2 tablespoons deviled ham

Blend yolks, mayonnaise and ham and fill the whites with the mixture. Mrs. Appleyard finds it easier to quarter eggs neatly if they are first cut in halves lengthwise.

Onion Soup with Custard
FOR FOUR

Make the custard early in the day:

1 egg	4 tablespoons cream
yolk of another egg	1 teaspoon salt
2 tablespoons consommé	¼ teaspoon pepper

Beat all ingredients together. Have a small buttered mold ready: the kind of tin that walnut meats come in makes a good one. Fill it two-thirds full of custard, put it on a rack in a pan, with hot water under the rack. Bake at 350° until it is set — about 10 minutes. Test with a silver knife. It is done when the knife blade comes out clean. Keep in a cool place until serving time.

For the Soup, allow for each person:

1 large onion	a few drops of Kitchen Bouquet
1 tablespoon butter	1 tablespoon red wine
6 ounces jellied beefstock	4 slices of French bread, toasted
6 ounces water	2 tablespoons grated cheese

Mrs. Appleyard keeps her own strong, well-seasoned jellied beefstock on hand but it is no secret from her that practically everyone else uses canned consommé. She doesn't really expect to make the world over this afternoon so go right ahead. Whichever you use, allow an equal amount of beefstock and water. Don't worry about its being too weak — it will cook out again.

Slice the onions and fry them gently in the butter. They should not brown, a delicate straw color is the right tint. Stir them well so that they will cook evenly. Now add the stock and water and the Kitchen Bouquet and let the soup simmer for an hour. At serving time add the wine. Toast the bread lightly on both sides. Into each hot soup plate put a slice of toast. Remove custard from the mold, slice it and lay a slice on each piece of toast. Ladle soup over the toast. Be sure the onions are evenly distributed. Sprinkle grated cheese over the custard and pass extra cheese in a bowl. You may use real Parmesan if you like but a piece of aged, dry Vermont cheddar grated is good too.

Chicken in Cream
FOR FOUR

Allow half a chicken breast, wing removed, for each person to be served. Use an electric skillet or a large frying pan over low heat.

1 small onion, cut fine	2 cups hot chicken stock, made
4 tablespoons butter	from the wings
4 tablespoons flour	½ cup thick cream
pinch of basil	4 chicken breasts
salt to taste	½ pound mushroom caps, sliced
½ teaspoon paprika	2 pimentos
¼ teaspoon nutmeg	2 tablespoons sherry
	watercress

Cook the onion in the butter until it is yellow and transparent. Remove and set aside. Mix flour and dry seasonings in a paper bag. (Choose one without holes . . . Yes, of course you know enough to do that . . . Excuse it, please. Powdering the floor is just something that happens to Mrs. Appleyard.) Put the chicken breasts in the bag and swing it around until they are well coated with the seasoned flour. Put the breasts into the skillet, skin side down, and cook over medium heat until they are golden brown. Turn and brown the other sides. Add hot stock slowly. Cover and simmer till tender over very low heat, about an hour and a quarter. Add the cream slowly during the last 5 minutes. Remove breasts to a hot platter. Add onions and mushrooms and the pimentos cut in strips to the sauce. Stir well, add the sherry. Simmer a minute. Pour sauce over the chicken. Wreathe the platter with fresh watercress.

Green Peas

There are especially good frozen green peas on the market now. S. S. Pierce has them but there are also other brands where the peas are picked when they are young and tender. When you find them, buy a good supply and put them in your freezer. They cost more than ordinary peas and are worth the difference.

This is the way Mrs. Appleyard cooks them. She says the directions on the package call for so much water that it has to be drained off, taking most of the flavor, vitamins and minerals with it. Thaw the peas, remove from the package for half an hour at room temperature. Put ¼ cup of water for each package of peas in a pan. When it boils, add the peas. Cover, cook 3 minutes. Add more boiling water if necessary. Add 1 tablespoon of butter. Cover, cook 2 minutes. Uncover. By this time the peas should be done and the water almost gone. Season according to taste. Serve in a very hot dish.

Orange Sherbet with Bananas

Before Mrs. Appleyard ever visited Appleyard Center she was told by her husband that Vermont bananas were better than other bananas. He had also made the same statement about butter, apples, cheese, sausage, turkeys, dried beef, and maple syrup. The air was different too in Vermont, he said. Hills were greener than other hills — or bluer if they were blue. Maple leaves were especially brilliant in the fall. Gravel on the roads was of a superfine texture.

Cool nights in summer, fresh-caught trout, Montpelier crackers, granite for tombstones and triple-etched rainbows were also favorably compared with other people's rainbows, granite and so forth. Mrs. Appleyard accepted it all as gospel. Before she ever crossed the Connecticut River, she had practically become a Vermonter. However, she had a slight mental reservation about the bananas.

Weren't bananas after all a tropical fruit? Would they really be improved by being taken north? Did they ripen especially well in igloos? Was it bananas, not grapes, that Eric the Red found growing so luxuriantly? Was Vineland really Lake Champlain?

Fortunately Mrs. Appleyard did not ask these questions aloud because Vermont bananas, as she soon found out, *are* better than other bananas. Long before the days of radio commercials Vermonters knew enough never to put bananas in the refrigerator and for an excellent reason: in most houses and shops there weren't any refrigerators. There were cellarways and — when a really cold place was needed — cellar cupboards, neatly screened from bats and mice. Ice was something you cut on the pond in winter and kept in sawdust in summer in case you wanted to make some ice cream.

The Appleyards — they were pioneers in such matters — had the first icebox in town. It was made by the local carpenter out of native ash, nicely matchboarded and lined with zinc. It held a hundred pounds of ice, an amount which can make rather a large lake in case anyone forgets to empty the pan underneath. This box was a little younger than Mr. Appleyard and it was his duty to keep it filled with ice and the pan emptied. Perhaps that was why he decided to go to Boston and take up desk work. Mrs. Appleyard keeps her paints in the icebox now.

In Vermont in 1912 bananas were bought in enormous green bunches and hung wrong-side up in the shady part of the store. Mrs. Appleyard was much surprised when she saw some growing and found out that bananas point up. They seem to ripen quite happily pointing down, however, and they can be picked off when they reach the right stage. There should be no green on them at all, not even on the tips, and they should be streaked and spotted with dark brown. Of course there is a school of thought that upholds those ripened under a mattress as being especially delicious but Mrs. Appleyard has not tried that method. All she knows is that when they are ripened slowly at an even temperature they develop the right flavor and texture.

The way she served them on the day of the family favorites was sliced horizontally around a big mound of orange sherbet. There were also slices of preserved kumquats and scoops of vanilla ice cream dusted over with grated tangerine peel.

Mrs. Appleyard had milk toast for supper that night. She has no idea what anyone else had.

Swing Your Partner

Mrs. Appleyard and her daughter were sitting quietly reading by the fire. At least Cicely was reading. Mrs. Appleyard shut her book. She had finished it and five minutes had elapsed without her starting another one. She was thinking.

Cicely did not realize her mother was indulging in this dangerous pastime until she heard her say: "Isn't it lucky Valentine's Day comes in vacation this year? And just when the floor needs waxing."

Cicely realized at once by her mother's trancelike tone that, though the groundhog had seen his shadow and whisked back into his hole, Mrs. Appleyard was not in a retiring mood.

"What are you planning?" Cicely asked apprehensively.

Mrs. Appleyard said she thought a simple little Valentine dance would be nice. Just enough dancers for two squares and Robin Viereck to fiddle and a few people to look on. Everyone must wear something at least a hundred years old — she said. And she'd take down the Japanese prints and hang up her own collection of old Valentines instead.

"We'll have candlelight and firelight and just a very simple supper —"

"Please don't keep saying how simple everything is," her child pleaded. "It's simple to sit and read after eating cold roast beef. Anything else I regard as extremely complicated. We'd have to go down to your house and get all those tall hats and tail coats."

"And the dancing wax and those good Viennese waltz records so Robin can rest occasionally and a few extra Paisley shawls," said her mother, "and —"

At this point Camilla began to do handsprings around the room, announcing: "I'm going to wear the red velvet jacket."

"And I'll wear the plaid silk dress with the hoopskirt," said Jane, taking a few practice spins.

"This party is evidently going to take place," said Cicely. "I'll wear that scarlet burnous — it's the only thing that fits me. I thought we were going to diet while we were writing this cookbook. What did you say you were going to have for supper?"

"Well, I thought I'd make some Tomato Tulip and some dips and real chicken à la King for the dancers to have first and then we'll have dessert later for everyone else who comes. We'll have lots of hot spiced punch for the children and champagne punch for the grownups and something deadly and delicious for dessert besides an ice-cream bar. Supper can be at your long table and I'll serve the dessert in my apartment. It will be perfectly simp — I mean it will be great fun."

Cicely agreed that anyway it would be fun.

All went as planned — with a few exceptions. Mrs. Appleyard thought she would polish the Franklin stove in her apartment before the party. This was a worthy idea but she found that all her stove polish, an heirloom inherited with the stove, was used up. It was a shock to find that no one in outer space seems to need stove polish now so shops don't carry it. The label on the can said the heirloom polish had been made in a town across the mountains so Mrs. Appleyard wrote to a friend there to see if he could get some, or the formula for making it.

He replied: "Yes, stove polish was made here until about twenty-five years ago. The formula was — luckily for Appleyard Center perhaps — a secret. One day a batch of polish exploded and blew the factory to bits while the owner was out for lunch. He has not been back. Perhaps that's why everyone in town has stoves enameled in pastel shades."

"I hope you won't try to make any," Cicely said nervously.

"Well, I thought I might just try a little honey and vinegar," Mrs. Appleyard replied. "Vermont folk medicine says it's fine for whatever is wrong with cows and people. I should think it might be worth trying."

"Does Vermont folk medicine say stoves have arthritis?" inquired her daughter.

Mrs. Appleyard regarded this question as frivolous. By controlled experiment she found that honey and vinegar, even when darkened with carbonized beets (easily produced by turning on the wrong burner of her electric stove) is not a polish. Finally she made a decoction of dark blue Esquire Boot Polish (advt.), some vinegar and some carbon of which she had plenty. Aside from the fact that people would say "what's cooking?" with a certain air of skepticism, this first batch was fine. There has never been a second because her kind friend has sent her a can of a professional brew. It seems to be nonexplosive. However, Appleyard Center folk medicine says it is no good as hand cream or for the alleviation of cracked ribs or housemaid's knee.

Having brightened up the stove and having removed a good deal of the polish from her hands, Mrs. Appleyard began serious consideration of her menu. After consultation with her grandchildren she began work on this one:

Flounder Balls*   Pink Dip*   Green Dip*
Tomato Mint Tulip*
Real Chicken à la King*   Green Beans and Beets with Almonds*
Candied Yams with Orange Marmalade Sauce*
Valentine Cheesecake with Glazed Raspberries*
Hot spiced Fruit Punch*   Champagne Punch*
Ice Cream with Crushed Strawberries
Baked Fudge Brownies (p. 117)

Flounder Balls
FOR SIXTEEN

Mrs. Appleyard began the day before by making the flounder balls. First she made a court-bouillon by cooking the bones, heads and trimmings of the flounders in water with 2 sliced carrots, 2 onions, chopped, 1 teaspoon of mixed herbs, and a bay leaf. This was to cook the flounder balls in. If you use frozen flounder, you will need only a 12-ounce package. Make the broth with an extra piece of flounder instead of the bones and heads. Add a little white wine to the bouillon just before you use it.

For the mixture:

2 pounds flounder, filleted	2 eggs
1 small onion, ground	2 Montpelier crackers (crumbs,
½ teaspoon sugar	rolled fine and sifted)
¼ teaspoon pepper	

While the court-bouillon is simmering, put the fish through the grinder unless you have the kind of blender that will do it for you. By all means use it if you have. Grind or blend the small onion with the fish. Add sugar, pepper and raw eggs, working them in thoroughly. Add the cracker crumbs. Do this with your hands and make the mixture into balls. Make them small, not over a teaspoon of the mixture because they will nearly double in size. The bouillon ought to be ready in about an hour. Add the white wine and strain the bouillon through a fine strainer into a saucepan big enough to hold your open-leaf steamer. Bring the bouillon to the boiling point, fill steamer with the flounder balls and lower it carefully into the boiling liquid. Cover tightly and cook 10 minutes.

Mrs. Appleyard cooked them in several batches without letting the bouillon dry out, an achievement of which she is quite proud, then laid them on a big platter and chilled them overnight. She served them impaled on scarlet toothpicks with the two dips.

Green Dip

½ cup mashed ripe avocado pear	bits of lemon rind
½ cup watercress, cut fine	1 tablespoon light cream
1 teaspoon onion cut fine	1 cup mayonnaise
2 tablespoons lemon juice	½ cup sour cream

Into the blender put the avocado, watercress, onion, lemon juice and rind. Blend 15 seconds. Add cream. Blend till smooth. Add this mixture to the mayonnaise. Add the sour cream. Chill.

Pink Dip

1 4-ounce tin of tomato paste	a few grains of cayenne
1 cup sour cream	2 tablespoons Worcestershire sauce
½ teaspoon garlic powder	4 ounces red caviar

Mix the tomato paste and the sour cream. Add the seasonings. Add the caviar. Chill.

Tomato Mint Tulip
SERVES SIXTEEN

2 lemons, sliced thin	3 drops peppermint extract
2 teaspoons garlic powder	ice cubes
1 teaspoon ginger	3 quarts tomato juice, chilled
sprigs of mint	1 quart pale dry ginger ale, chilled

Put the lemon slices into a large bowl. Crush them a little with a wooden pestle. Sprinkle in the garlic powder and the ginger. Add a few mint leaves and crush gently. Add the peppermint and the ice cubes and the tomato juice. Stir. Let it stand in a cool place 20 minutes. At serving time stir again. Add the ginger ale. Garnish with sprigs of fresh mint. Of course the easy way to get mint is to go out and pick it by your own pond when the hermit thrushes are calling in the woods and a deer is standing up to knock young apples off a tree on the hill and the click of croquet balls is heard from the lawn. However you can usually get it in winter by ordering it ahead of time.

Real Chicken à la King
FOR EIGHT

If you like the flour paste and ancient hen mixture that usually masquerades under an honorable name, do not read this receipt. If you persist in spite of this warning you will probably want to make it so start early on the day you are going to serve it.

2 3½-pound frying chickens
1 carrot
1 small onion
1 teaspoon mixed herbs
3 tablespoons butter
½ pound fresh mushrooms, caps
only, sliced vertically
1 green pepper, seeded, sliced
very thin
3 tablespoons flour
¼ teaspoon nutmeg

½ teaspoon paprika
salt and pepper to taste
2 cups light cream
1 cup heavy cream
½ cup jellied chicken stock
3 pimentos cut fine with sharp
scissors
2 egg yolks
juice of ½ lemon
½ cup dry white wine
1 tablespoon butter (extra)

triangles of toast or pastry

Have each chicken cut in 4 pieces. Cover with cold water. Add carrot, onion and herbs. Simmer slowly until meat falls from the bones. Remove meat from the bones. Return bones and skin to the broth and cook at least an hour longer. Strain and chill. When it has jellied, remove all fat from the top.

In the meantime cut up the chicken meat, not too fine. Do not use any very small pieces: save them for a casserole or pâté later. In a large frying pan, big enough to hold the whole mixture, or in an electric skillet, melt the butter and gently toss the sliced mushrooms and green pepper in it. Sprinkle on the flour, mixed with the dry seasonings. Cook one minute. Reduce heat to its lowest point. Stir in slowly first the light cream, then the heavy cream. Add stock. Cook over very low heat until the mixture begins to thicken — about 5 minutes. Add the sliced chicken. Cook a minute longer. Let stand at least one hour.

When serving time comes, reheat the mixture over low heat. Add the pimentos. In a pint bowl, beat the egg yolks lightly with a wire whisk. Add 1 tablespoon of the hot cream sauce to them. Keep beating. Add more sauce, beating all the time until you have about a cup. Add the lemon juice and the white wine. Stir them in well and stir the whole mixture into the chicken and cream mixture. Cook over very low heat until the mixture thickens. It will separate if you overheat it. Just before you serve it, slip in the extra tablespoon of butter. Have a hot platter ready. Serve the chicken on it. Garnish with triangles of toast or pastry. For the Valentine party Mrs. Appleyard baked pastry hearts. That is, they started as hearts but they puffed so enthusiastically that they were not anatomically recognizable. No one seemed to mind.

Green Beans and Beets
FOR EIGHT

2 packages frozen French-cut beans	1 tablespoon butter for beets
1 tablespoon butter for beans	½ cup blanched almonds
1 can S. S. Pierce's matchstick cut beets	2 tablespoons butter

Cook the beans till tender but not mushy in the smallest possible amount of water. Add 1 tablespoon of butter during the last few minutes of cooking. Heat the beets in their own juice with 1 tablespoon of butter. Watch them: they burn easily and suddenly. Toss the peeled, blanched almonds in 2 tablespoons of butter until they start to brown. On a hot circular dish, heap the beans, surround them with a ring of beets. Scatter the almonds over the beans. Serves 8.

Candied Yams, Orange Marmalade Sauce

The best yams available in Vermont come frozen in packages. Allow 2 packages for eight people. Follow directions on the package. They need only brief reheating.

Serve this sauce with them separately:

1 cup Seville orange marmalade   2 tablespoons lemon juice
2 tablespoons frozen orange juice,   1 teaspoon grated lemon rind
not diluted

Mix all together. Simmer, stirring carefully, until marmalade melts. Bring to the boil but do not boil.

Valentine Cheese Cake
FOR EIGHT

Follow the rule for glazed strawberry cheese cake (p. 87) but bake it in a shallow circular glass dish. Chill thoroughly. For the glaze use:

2 packages frozen raspberries,   1 glass currant jelly
defrosted   1 tablespoon instant tapioca

Strain juice from defrosted berries. Add currant jelly and cook until jelly is melted. Add tapioca and cook until it is clear — about half an hour. Cool until it begins to thicken. Top the cheese cake with the drained whole berries. Spoon glaze over the berries. Chill. Serves 8.

Hot Spiced Punch
FOR TWENTY

1 quart water   12 whole cloves
2 tablespoons tea   1 can frozen lemonade
2 cups sugar   2 6-ounce cans frozen orange juice
2-inch stick cinnamon   3 quarts cider

Bring a quart of water to the boil. When it boils hard, throw in the tea. Let it boil exactly one minute. Strain over sugar, spices and fruit juice. Let it stand at least 10 minutes. Longer will do no harm. Add the cider. Heat. Serve hot in pottery mugs.

Champagne Punch
FOR EIGHT

For each quart of champagne:

1 quart club soda	2 ounces curaçao
1 tablespoon sugar	1 tablespoon lemon juice
1 tablespoon orange bitters	1 can frozen orange juice
2 ounces brandy	4 ounces Bristol Cream sherry
	large block of ice

Chill champagne and soda for several hours. Mix all the other ingredients and chill thoroughly. At serving time put the block of ice in a punch bowl. Pour the mixture over it. Add the soda. Last of all add the champagne.

Diced pineapple and whole strawberries may be added if you like. Mrs. Appleyard prefers it plain.

The ages of the guests at the dance covered a wide span. James Harrison Ford IV was the youngest. He came in a basket, which was placed on Mrs. Appleyard's bed among the fur coats. He greeted his hostess with a courteous smile that showed where his teeth would be before long and went sound asleep. Mrs. Appleyard of course was the oldest person present. She is getting accustomed to being venerable, even thinks there are some advantages in it. For instance as she watched this dance with Camilla, in her great-grandmother's red velvet basque and, her partner, in an ancient sailor suit, she saw not just the dancers who were whirling over the shining floor in this kaleidoscope of color. Patterns that went back into the last century drifted before her eyes. She two-stepped by gaslight in a high-ceilinged room on Beacon Hill where a great square of Holland linen was spread over the Brussels carpet to make the dancing floor. She went to a cotillion in a big ball room copied from a room in Versailles, a cotillion with "favors" — spangled fans, enameled and gilt boxes, bunches of violets. She waltzed at a Monday German in Baltimore where one of her partners was as old, perhaps as she is now and who seemed of course to her, something that one would expect to find in an Egyptian tomb. There was Cicely's coming-out dance and Sally's. There were dances on the lawn in Appleyard Center and one in a mountain camp where she played the accordion until her arms ached.

Perhaps best of all she remembered a dance in her father's house on Woodbrook Green before she was married. Mr. Appleyard came to help her put up the decorations. They were loops and swags and wreaths of laurel with real fruit fastened to them. Just as he came into the front hall, she fell off a stepladder and landed at his feet.

He picked her up, saying as he did so: "Why is it girls always manage to fall so gracefully?"

Why, she thought, he must be in love with me! and her various bruises stopped hurting.

Not long after this they were waltzing at their wedding and a few weeks later he was teaching her to dance "Hull's Victory" in Appleyard Center.

Now, comfortably draped in a Paisley shawl, the one with the white center, she was happy to look on and rest her feet.

"It was a nice party," Cicely said after everyone had gone home and they were loading the dishwasher for the fourth time.

"Yes," said Mrs. Appleyard, "and I've just thought of something. It was my Apartment Warming — now I've had it, only no one knew it. You don't think I ought to have another, do you?"

"I think," said her daughter, "that enough is sufficient."

March

Soup's On

Mrs. Appleyard does not really spend much of her time making champagne punch and cheese cake. She is much more likely to be preparing a little homemade soup and a lettuce leaf or two. It is by eating such menus that she is able to wear the same wardrobe year after year. There is that blue and brown tweed suit for instance. It is so faded on the left sleeve, where the light strikes it in her car, that the two sleeves seem to be made out of entirely different pieces of material. At one time she thought of having the suit turned the other side out — after all it is one of her more recent ones, barely nine years old. Then Cicely brought her an interesting book on hooking rugs and it seemed as if the suit might be useful in that craft in case she should take it up. In the meantime she still wears the suit, which is the right width anyway though a little long in the skirt.

Fortunately for cooking she has some smocks and they never go out of style. Properly be-smocked you can imagine you have just stepped out of *Trilby* or that you are an ancient of some British village still chatting in Shakespearean style. Thus costumed, Mrs. Appleyard finds it natural to make soup rather than to open a can in which a few weary noodles float in a bath of monosodium glutumate, a substance Mrs. Appleyard would not offer to any visiting blue jay, no, not even to a starling. There was a time when consommé in a can used to be made as you would make it yourself with beef and veal bones and meat and vegetables and spices. Now it is constructed on the principle of the famous horse and rabbit stew which contained both — one horse and one rabbit. Probably modern consommé, in order to conform with the label on the can, does come briefly into contact with a shin of beef but such flavor as it has is supplied by MSG. The consommé costs more than it used to before this substance for raising blood pressure and promoting coronary thrombosis was discovered, but it does not cost four times as much, as it would have to if it were made of substances suitable for human consumption. MSG however is not really inexpensive. The flavor it gives is chiefly that of salt. If you must have it, get it out of a shaker.

Mrs. Appleyard could say more — pages in fact — on this topic but she refrains. When she says that, if a friend comes to supper she gives her soup and salad or soup and a dessert, she means that she made the soup herself. Here are a few menus for cold evenings when soup is welcome in the star role.

MENU 1

Fish Chowder* or Lord Baltimore Soup*
Souffléd Montpelier Crackers*
Tomato Aspic with Blue Cheese Dressing*

As the Lord Baltimore soup is a by-product of Fish Chowder,
Mrs. Appleyard will first reveal how she makes the chowder.

Fish Chowder (S.W.E.)

¼ pound beef suet or salt pork	¼ teaspoon black pepper
3 large onions, sliced thin	½ teaspoon mixed herbs
6 medium potatoes	salt to taste
4-pound haddock, head and all,	½ teaspoon paprika
cut for chowder	3 cups milk
Montpelier crackers	1 cup cream
butter for crackers	slices of lemon

Cut the suet or pork into very small dice. Try them out in a
large kettle until they are a delicate straw color. Remove them
with a skimmer and set aside. Add the sliced onions and cook
them gently in the fat, stirring often, until they are yellow and
transparent. Remove and set aside. Slice the potatoes very thin
and lay them in with the pieces of haddock. If you use frozen
haddock, cut the fillets in thirds. Cover fish and potatoes with
hot water and cook until potatoes begin to soften, about 20
minutes. By this time it should be possible to separate the skin
and bones from the fish and discard them. This is a nuisance,
Mrs. Appleyard admits. It's much easier to use frozen fillets.
The chowder does not taste quite so good, though, as when it is
made with the whole fish.

This first stage may be done any time during the day. Return the onion and diced suet to the kettle. The chowder is all the better if it stands and ripens. Just before serving time split and butter Montpelier crackers. Put them in a pan and set it into a 350° oven for 10 or 12 minutes. They should not get too brown. While they are heating, add the seasonings and the milk and cream to the chowder. Bring it to the boil but do not let it boil or your milk will curdle. It may just simmer a few minutes. Mrs. Appleyard likes to use the blue Canton tureen that her grandmother, who taught her how to make the chowder, used too. Any generous-sized bowl will do. Put in the chunks of fish, pour the rest of the chowder over them. Top the dish with some of the toasted crackers. Pass the sliced lemon and the rest of the crackers.

Lord Baltimore Soup (R.H.P. — G.S.)

The original version of this soup was made with that light-hearted disregard of the prices of food so characteristic of the nineteenth century. No housekeeper was so ill-bred as to mention the cost of things to eat. How could she tell you? — she didn't know. When she wanted a quart of oysters she ordered them from the fishman and he delivered them. At the end of the month her husband paid the bill. He also paid the cook the $4 a week she had earned by work every day, except every other Thursday and Sunday afternoons, from 6.30 A.M. to curfew, or thereabouts. When cooks began to demand $4.50 a week he grumbled a little but he never haggled over the price of a quart of Cape Cod oysters. He wanted the soup to taste the way it did when his mother's cook used to make it. This was the rule she followed.

Lord Baltimore Soup
19TH CENTURY VERSION (R.H.P.)

1 quart oysters	1 quart chicken stock
4 tablespoons butter	4 tablespoons flour
1 teaspoon Worcestershire sauce	1 teaspoon chopped parsley
1 cup heavy cream	a few grains of cayenne

"How many is a few grains?" Mrs. Appleyard once asked her grandmother, who replied unhesitatingly, "Nine."

Not being much of a counter of grains, Mrs. Appleyard usually leaves out the cayenne. If you like to put it in, that's the right number, she feels sure.

Pick over a quart of oysters, removing any pieces of shell. Parboil them 10 minutes in their own juice. Press them through cheesecloth. Add a quart of clear strong chicken stock. Make a roux of the butter and flour, blend in the oyster and stock mixture. Add seasonings and cook gently 5 minutes. Just before serving add a cup of heavy cream. Bring to the boil but do not let it boil.

A nice dish, Mrs. Appleyard thinks, in case royalty comes to visit you. She has just heard that in our great democratic country there is a society called the Illegitimate Descendants of Royalty in America. To become a member your papers have to be all in order just as if you were going to join the Mayflower Descendants or the Society of Colonial Wars. She would like it

clearly understood that when — if ever — she serves Lord Baltimore Soup (nineteenth century) none but legitimate royalty need apply. For the Queen Mother of England, a great favorite of hers, she will even include the cayenne, all nine grains.

Lord Baltimore Soup
20TH CENTURY - 1 (G.S.)

2 cups of leftover fish chowder	½ cup breast meat of fowl or
2 cups milk	chicken
2 cups of chicken stock, jellied	½ cup heavy cream

Put the fish chowder through your electric blender or chop fine and purée it by hand. If you use the blender, do it in two batches, adding a cup of the milk to each batch. Put the purée in the top of a large double boiler over hot, not boiling water. Add the chicken stock. Stock may be made from either fowl or chicken. Mrs. Appleyard uses a chicken breast cooked in water containing a slice of carrot, a sliced onion and half a teaspoon of mixed herbs. She chills the broth after it has cooked down to 2 cups and removes all fat from the top. While the soup is heating, cut the breast meat into neat cubes and add them to the soup. At serving time add the cream and bring the soup to the boil over direct heat. Put it into a hot tureen and serve it in well-heated plates. Serves four generously with second helpings.

Lord Baltimore Soup
20TH CENTURY - 2

When she has no chowder on hand as a basis, Mrs. Appleyard makes it this way.

½ cup breast meat of chicken, cubed
1 carrot
½ teaspoon mixed herbs
½ teaspoon paprika
¼ teaspoon pepper; salt to taste
3 medium onions, sliced
2 tablespoons butter
3 potatoes, sliced very thin
1 frozen haddock fillet (12 ounces)
2 cups chicken stock
2 teaspoons flour
2 cups milk
1 cup heavy cream
8 ounces oysters, frozen
sherry
slices of lemon

Cook the chicken breast with a carrot, herbs and seasonings. Cook the stock down to 2 cups. Strain, chill, skim off fat. Sauté onions in butter until they are pale yellow and transparent. Do not let them brown. Add the sliced potato and the haddock. Cover with boiling water and cook till the potatoes are done: 15–20 minutes. Put mixture through the blender in two batches. Put the purée into a large pan over low heat. Add the 2 cups of chicken stock and the cubes of breast meat. Dilute the flour with a little cold water and rub it through a fine sieve into the soup. Stir well. Scald the milk and cream in another pan. Be careful not to scorch them. Bring the chicken and fish mixture to the boil. Drop in the oysters and cook until the edges curl, about 3 minutes. Add the scalded milk and cream and bring soup to the boil but do not let it boil. Put some sherry and sliced lemon into hot plates. Soup's on — come and get it! Now!

This Lord Baltimore soup was so elegant that Mrs. Appleyard thought of serving Lady Baltimore cake with it, a ghoulish suggestion whch she discarded in favor of

Souffléd Montpelier Crackers

After making these for twenty or thirty years Mrs. Appleyard noticed that the top halves of the crackers puff more mountainously than the bottoms. Slow to catch on but prompt to act, she decided henceforward to use the bottoms for ordinary toasting or to use for casserole topping or in meat loaf. Occasionally, when a moment of efficiency attacks her, she rolls out the crumbs ahead of time and keeps them in a jar in the refrigerator.

These then are the ingredients she now uses:

water with ice cubes in it

top halves of Montpelier crackers   butter

The amount of butter used will depend on how many crackers you use. Be generous with it. Quarter of a pound should do 12 or more crackers. Have it at room temperature.

Into a large pottery bowl put cold water and ice cubes. As the ice cubes melt, split the crackers and drop the top halves into the water, split sides up. Light the oven: 450°. Watch crackers all the time. Have ready a cooky sheet covered with a clean damask napkin. At the end of 3 minutes — or sooner if they seemed to be softening too fast — remove crackers from water. Use a pancake turner with holes in it to do this. The crackers will be wider than when you put them in. Put them on the cooky sheet and set the sheet in the refrigerator for 5 minutes. Butter iron dripping pans and transfer crackers to the pans, working as quickly as possible. Dot them thickly with butter. Bake them until they are puffed, crisp and golden brown. This will take at least 35 minutes, longer if you have more than one panful. Check them at the end of half an hour. Add more butter if they look thirsty. Allow at least an hour for the whole process. If you try to hurry them, you may end with something resembling a moist blotter. What you want is something as dry and light as a dandelion ball. It is the sudden exposure of the soaked, chilled buttered cracker to intense heat that produces this effect. Customers must wait for them rather than the other way. If you put a second batch into the oven, to be ready when the salad is served, Mrs. Appleyard thinks you will not have much trouble in disposing of them.

Tomato Aspic

Make this the day before you plan to serve it.

4 envelopes (tablespoons) of plain gelatin	2 teaspoons sugar
	4 cloves
1 cup cold water	salt to taste
2 large onions, chopped fine	2 large cans of tomato
1 teaspoon grated lemon rind	juice (7 cups)
1½ teaspoons pepper	4 tablespoons lemon juice
1 tablespoon Worcestershire sauce	

Soften the gelatin in cold water. Simmer the onion, lemon rind and the seasonings with the tomato juice for half hour. Strain some of the juice over the soaked gelatin and stir well. Strain the rest of it into another kettle. Add the gelatin, lemon juice and Worcestershire sauce. Rinse a 2-quart ring mold with cold water. Pour in the tomato mixture. Set the mold into the refrigerator.

Ah, how steady the hands must be! How vital to see that a large enough space in the refrigerator is clear! How fatal if the corner of a rug is turned up!

Perhaps it is only Mrs. Appleyard who has to think of these things. Let us turn to the moment of unmolding, also a perilous time. You are — she suddenly recalls — supposed to stir the aspic twice before it sets. This however is a minor moment of danger. Even Mrs. Appleyard can usually manage the stirring without calamity; but the unmolding — that is really crucial.

Have ready a round chop plate, charger or silver tray. Put a little water on it, less than a teaspoonful, and spread it around evenly with a pastry brush. In case you do not center the mold exactly on the plate, the moisture will make it possible to tease the aspic into position without dislocating its personality. Now summon your courage, your judgment, your philosophy. Set the mold in warm (not hot) water for 5 or 6 seconds. Don't leave it too long. Loosen the aspic around the edges with a silver dinner knife.

Put your platter over the mold. Reverse the whole thing. Did you hear a gentle plop? Rather like the noise made by a ripe apple falling on sun-warmed grass? Good! Sink gracefully into a Chippendale chair, heave a sigh of relief, mop your brow. Mrs. Appleyard does so hope you won't have to mop the floor too. Perhaps you prefer to collapse into some other type of chair. Mrs. Appleyard's winter kitchen is also her living room so she has to use what is at hand.

When you are sufficiently rested, put the aspic back into the refrigerator. Before you serve it, make this filling to go in the center, if you used a ring mold, or to put in heaps around the edge if you used some other shape.

1 cucumber	lemon rind
1 small onion, thinly sliced	¼ cup French Dressing
green pepper	lettuce or watercress
2 tablespoons chives cut fine	½ cup sour cream
1 tablespoon fresh parsley, minced	½ cup Mayonnaise (p. 265)

Peel the cucumber. Engrave the edges by drawing the tines of a fork down the outside of it. Slice it thin. Add the onion slices. Slice the green pepper in very thin rings. Remove seeds and pith and add rings to cucumber mixture. Sprinkle with the chives, parsley and lemon rind. Add the French dressing and toss until the vegetables are well coated with it. When serving time comes, put sprays of watercress or leaves of Boston lettuce around the aspic. Put the cucumber mixture into the center of the ring. Mix the sour cream and the mayonnaise and mask the cucumber mixture with this dressing.

Pass Danish Blue or Roquefort cheese with the aspic. If the souffléd crackers have vanished, sesame crackers are good to put it on or homemade whole wheat bread or Melba toast. In fact Mrs. Appleyard likes it on pretty nearly everything. There is however no law that says you shouldn't use cream or cottage cheese if you prefer.

MENU 2

Beef chowder*   Popovers (p. 13)
Tossed Salad (p. 147)

A chowder is, of course, anything made in a kettle. Probably you knew that already. Mrs. Appleyard did not until she began to write a book about Champlain and noticed that one of the dangerous whirlpools he and his Indian guides had to portage around was called the Kettle — La Chaudière. For the first time chowder and chaudière struck together in her mind. Up to that moment she had always thought that chowder had to be made of fish. Laying down her pen and getting out her electric chaudière, she promptly invented

Beef Chowder Appleyard

¼ pound beef suet, diced	½ teaspoon mixed herbs
2 large onions, sliced thin	4 cups beef stock
3 carrots, sliced	1 tablespoon lemon juice
½ teaspoon cinnamon	1 teaspoon instant coffee
¼ teaspoon nutmeg	2 tablespoons sugar, caramelized

Dice the beet suet and try it out in the skillet over medium heat. Skim out the cracklings and set them aside. Spoon out 3 tablespoons of fat and set aside. Add the sliced onion and sauté until it is straw-colored. Add carrots and sauté 2 minutes. Add cinnamon, nutmeg and herbs. Add the beef stock, the onions, the instant coffee and the caramelized sugar. Rinse out the pan in which you caramelize it with a little stock so you will get all the brown color and flavor. Cook over low heat until carrots are done — about half an hour. Add the lemon juice.

In the meantime make some meat balls, using:

1 cup homemade bread crumbs	1 bean garlic or ¼ teaspoon garlic powder
½ cup milk	1 minced onion (small)
½ pound Vermont sausage	2 tablespoons butter
1½ pounds ground chuck	3 tablespoons flour
1 egg, lightly beaten	2 tablespoons minced parsley
3 tablespoons beef fat (from skillet)	

The sausage Mrs. Appleyard uses may be Colburn's in Montpelier or Harrington's in Richmond, Vermont. Both are made of excellent materials, finely ground and lightly seasoned. Jones Brothers and MacKenzie are also brands she likes.

Soak the bread crumbs in the milk 5 minutes and squeeze them dry. Mix sausage and ground beef thoroughly together. Add the egg and the bread crumbs. Put the garlic through the press and add it or sprinkle the garlic powder over the mixture. Sauté the minced onion in the butter until it is yellow and transparent and mix it in. Make the mixture into small balls, pressing them firmly. Put them into a paper bag with the flour. Shake the bag gently until the balls are well coated with flour. In the pan in which you sautéd the onion put the tried-out beef fat. Put in some of the meat balls and brown them on all sides over low heat. Repeat until all are done. Add more butter if necessary.

By this time the vegetables should be done. Add the meat balls, simmer 5 minutes. The chowder should now stand at least an hour barely simmering or until you are ready to serve it. At serving time if the gravy does not seem thick enough, add 2 tablespoons flour, diluted with cold water and strained through a fine sieve into the chowder. Let the mixture simmer a few minutes then bring it to the boil and serve it very hot with the diced cracklings and the parsley sprinkled over the top.

This is the basic rule for making it. Mrs. Appleyard varies it slightly according to materials on hand. If she has no stock on hand she substitutes tomato juice. Sometimes she adds mushroom caps sautéed in butter and broth made from mushroom stems to the kettle. A dozen small radishes may be sautéed with the carrots and added. They taste like very mild young turnips. If she has a few stalks of celery, she cuts them fine and adds when she starts the carrots.

Sometimes she adds

Dumplings

1 cup flour	2 teaspoons baking powder
½ teaspoon salt	2 tablespoons butter
	½ cup milk

Sift dry ingredients. Cut in butter with pastry blending fork, add milk. Pat out about ½ inch thick, cut with biscuit cutter. Butter top of steamer. Have water boiling hard in bottom part. Place biscuits in the top. Cover tightly. Steam until raised and light — 10–12 minutes. Put on top of the chowder.

If you *must* salt the chowder, do so just before you serve it. It only toughens the meat if it is added earlier. Another thing that Mrs. Appleyard found out while writing about Champlain was that the Huron Indians, the handsomest and healthiest people Champlain had ever seen, never ate salt. The Indians never had scurvy either until they ate the white men's salt meat and fish. Eating salt, Mrs. Appleyard concluded, is just a nervous habit. So, perhaps you may think, is having stock on hand. Skip this if the habit annoys you.

Stock

The ideal place to make stock is the top of an old-fashioned coal or wood stove. The invention of gas and electric ranges for a long time made the stock kettle a thing of the past. Even Mrs. Appleyard did not make stock. However, modern gas burners thermostatically controlled, deep-well electric cookers and electric skillets, electric burners with well-controlled low heat all make producing stock easy and practical.

Into the stockpot, whatever you use for one, should go bones from roasts, leftover vegetables, tomato juice, mushroom stems, celery tops, and any water left over from cooking vegetables. This is perhaps the most valuable thing in the stock since it contains vitamins and minerals, which otherwise would be lost. Mrs. Appleyard makes a practice of cooking vegetables in very little water and she usually comes out even — except of course when the telephone rings and she finds on her return some carbonized beans and an hour's work of saucepan scouring. With certain kinds of vegetables — asparagus and potatoes, for instance — even she has cooking water left over. That water goes into the stockpot instead of down the drain. Calcium, another substance valuable in your diet, gets into the stock from bones, which otherwise would be thrown away.

A stockpot also helps keep the refrigerator in order. Instead of serving small dabs of things, which you ultimately throw away because you are so tired of seeing them, put them in the stockpot. It is not necessary to keep stock cooking all the time. Make a kettleful two or three times a week, letting it simmer a few hours. Then strain it and cook it down until you have about a quart. It will take up much less room than all those saucers. You will be surprised by how often you use it.

MENU 3

Cream of Pea and Shrimp Soup*
Fruit Salad*

Cream of Pea and Shrimp Soup

Make cream of green pea soup. Use the rule for the Princess Soup (p. 178) but omit the breast meat of chicken. For four people make a quart of soup. Allow one 6-ounce package of flash-frozen cleaned shrimp to each quart of soup. Put the soup into the top of a double boiler over hot, not boiling water. Cook the shrimp, tightly covered, in a very small amount of water until tender — about 5 minutes. Add them and any liquid remaining to the soup. Bring to the boil but do not boil. Serve at once.

Fruit Salad with Cream Cheese Balls

Mrs. Appleyard uses the fruit that comes frozen in glass jars, drains it, saves the juice to drink. She adds a sliced ripe banana, 4 canned pears, halved, and some whole fresh strawberries to the fruit. She marinates it in the following:

Fruit Salad Dressing

1 tablespoon lemon juice	1 tablespoon honey
3 tablespoons Wesson oil	¼ teaspoon mustard
½ teaspoon paprika	½ teaspoon white pepper
salt to taste	1 teaspoon lemon extract

2 drops peppermint extract

While the salad is marinating make

Cream Cheese Balls

2 tablespoons powdered sugar	1 teaspoon thick cream
3-ounce package cream cheese	2 tablespoons candied ginger, cut fine

1 tablespoon chopped blanched almonds

Sprinkle a small cutting board with the powdered sugar. Mix cream cheese, cream and candied ginger. Sugar your fingers slightly and make the mixture into balls. Sprinkle chopped almonds on the sugared board and roll the balls in the mixture.

Line the salad bowl with watercress or Boston lettuce. Toss the fruit gently a few times in the dressing and heap it in the bowl. Put the cheese balls around the edge. Serve.

This is what Mr. Appleyard used to call feminine food. He was not unkind about it. He just wanted to make it clear that he would rather have a thick steak or tripe or hash or, in fact, pretty nearly anything else. Mrs. Appleyard feels it her duty to let it be known that when a man says: "How did you make this?" he is not necessarily paying you a compliment. He may just want to be sure that his wife never makes it.

More masculine is

MENU 4

Onion Soup in Casserole*
Deep-Dish Apple Pie (p. 102)
Vermont Cheese

Onion Soup in Casserole
FOR FOUR

4 large onions, sliced thin
4 tablespoons butter
1 quart stock
½ teaspoon Kitchen Bouquet

8 slices French bread, ½ inch thick
butter for toast
4 tablespoons red wine

8 tablespoons grated cheese

Slice the onions and fry them in the butter until they are straw-colored. Do not let them brown. Add the stock and 2 cups of water. This will cook out again, leaving the stock as strong as before. Add the Kitchen Bouquet and let the soup simmer for half an hour. Toast the bread on both sides. Spread lightly with butter. Put the soup into a large casserole, add the wine, put the slices of toast on top of the soup. Cover them thickly with the grated cheese. Set the casserole in the oven at 350° and cook until the cheese is well browned — about half an hour.

With sophisticated elegance Mrs. Appleyard serves Tuscarora Beaujolais with this meal. When she asked the wine expert at the Golden Dome Market if there were any difference between Tuscarora Beaujolais Claret and Burgundy, he replied: "Sure there's a difference. You make the Burgundy by pouring half a gallon of Beaujolais and half a gallon of Claret into a gallon jug . . . No, it won't spoil — it's pasteurized."

Mrs. Appleyard hopes no one in France will hear about this.

Quiet Please

Her friends in Boston find it hard to understand why Mrs. Appleyard has buried herself — that's what they call it — in the country. They realize that in the summer it is possible that someone might drop in but in the winter — ?!

"It must be so *quiet!*" they say.

Mrs. Appleyard's idea of a quiet place is the corner of Fifth Avenue and Forty-second Street. Some of her most peaceful moments have been spent outside the New York Public Library watching for a bus. There is also something relaxing about standing at the corner of Tremont Street and Temple Place in Boston. Things about it have changed since she was a girl but not so much as in most places. The spire of Park Street Church still thrusts itself into the sky as decoratively as it used to when it was the seventh tallest building in the world. The dome of the State House is still a golden bubble. The Masonic Temple where her grandmother went to school, where Bronson Alcott used to teach, is still on Temple Place. It is on top of Stearns's store. Mrs. Appleyard can remember when it was discovered, in the process of adding several stories to the store, that legally the Masonic Temple, part of the old building, must remain on the site forever. So, instead of being pulled down, it was pulled up. Watching the process was one of Mrs. Appleyard's favorite occupations. She liked to think that if it had happened when Alcott taught there that he might easily have been pulled up into the sky and never have noticed it.

The Common is a peaceful place. If Mrs. Appleyard's apartment were in Boston instead of in Appleyard Center, she could sit on a bench on the Common and no one would speak to her. An occasional squirrel might look at her skeptically. Pigeons would waddle around her feet but otherwise her reveries would be undisturbed. Yet the Common is not always completely impersonal. Nor is Fifth Avenue. Once, as she crossed the Common near the Frog Pond she smiled at a particularly attractive little Boston bambino. His Italian grandmother promptly snatched him up and made the sign of the evil eye at Mrs. Appleyard. Once at Forty-second Street J. P. Morgan, Jr., crossed Fifth Avenue to the library beside her. He removed his flat-topped pale gray hat and said "Good Morning" but not to her. On the whole social life in these centers of culture is limited.

Not so in Appleyard Center. Cicely's house is central and she has that nice big room. In it may be found at intervals the 4-H Club, the Bible Study group, the Development Council and other organizations too numerous to mention. Music lessons take place there and ballet dancing and parcheesi. Pictures cut into a thousand pieces are put together again. Mozart, Vivaldi, the sound of the typewriter and highbrow jazz echo through it, accompanied by descants from the canary's cage. He loves music whether by piano, dishwasher, washing machine or TV.

Kittens bat balls across the floor of the big room. Elkhounds drop in to call on their brother Eric and to play with the kittens. Each dog has his favorite kitten, which he carries around by the scruff of its neck. Nils, an especially amiable elkhound, drops in from time to time to get Cicely to pull the latest batch of porcupine quills out of his nose.

Then outside the house there is always something going on. Nils is tracking another porcupine. Eric is baying at the moon. A deer hears him and makes a great curve of bounding tracks across the snow. Blue jays frighten a flock of evening grosbeaks away from the sunflower seeds. Mrs. Appleyard frightens the blue jays, not on purpose, just by knocking over the inkbottle. She uses jet-black.

When snow falls deep, Sam Flint brings his ivory and scarlet jeep and plows out the garage, so Cicely can get out, and the drive, so that the oil truck and the gas truck can get in. In zero weather they are frequent and welcome visitors. The town plow and the sander often go up and down the hill. The drivers wave as they pass. The cars that make their cautious way to the store all belong to someone you know. They are not so numerous as the cars on Fifth Avenue but they have more personality.

Every now and then there is an out-of-state car. Above the roof, skis thrust their noses condescendingly into the air. Inside, summer residents clutch the steering wheels and peer out nervously upon the landscape as if — Mrs. Appleyard thinks — they are afraid the Vermont panther is going to pounce upon them for lunch.

A good many of these visitors stop at Cicely's to get news of the roads to their houses. Hearing statistics about the height of snow above the ground and the depth of frost below it, they often decide it would be simpler just to put their sleeping bags down on the floor of Cicely's living room and sleep there. Most of them eat at Cicely's house between visits to the top of Mount Mansfield.

Perhaps Mrs. Appleyard's favorite among these adventurers is one who carries an electric blanket with him. He and his bride just plug it in anywhere. Once, at Christmas time, they unplugged a community Christmas tree, plugged in the blanket, slept cozily till dawn, detached the blanket, plugged in the Christmas tree and drove on.

Usually Cicely's visitors are less efficient than these tourists. They seem to have thought chiefly about providing themselves and their hosts with good things to eat. Mrs. Appleyard is delighted to get involved in menus based on what they happened to bring from the city. Not being obliged to ski, she is able to experiment while they are away at work. It's lucky she has two kitchens available.

Skiers, she notices, are not interested in light nutritious snacks. Perhaps it is no endorsement of the following menus to say that they were eaten with enthusiasm. Probably TV dinners, about four apiece, would have done just as well. At least Mrs. Appleyard is able to report that the guests, after having washed the dishes, slept soundly. Soothed by the purr of the dishwasher, she slept all right too.

One of the guests brought a goose for roasting with him so this menu was constructed with the goose as the special feature.

MENU 1

Celery   Carrot sticks   Radishes
Goose Liver Pâté with Truffles*
Zippy Tomato Juice*   Sesame Seed Melba Toast
Roast Goose* with Chestnut Stuffing (p. 65)
Apple Sauce   Baked Potatoes with Sour Cream*
Cauliflower and Broccoli, Garlic Crumbs*
Peaches Cardinal with Orange Water Ice*
Red Wine   Pastry Pinwheels*   Coffee

Goose Liver Pâté with Truffles

There being only one goose liver and several sleeping bags full of guests, Mrs. Appleyard decided to combine goose and chicken liver.

2 tablespoons butter	½ teaspoon burnt onion powder
1 large goose liver	¼ cup bread crumbs,
1 package frozen chicken livers	dried and rolled very fine
¼ cup jellied chicken stock	2 tablespoons soft butter (extra)
½ teaspoon sugar	2 ounces truffles

Melt 2 tablespoons butter over meduim heat. Put in the livers — the goose liver cut in 6 pieces, the chicken livers, slightly thawed, in halves. Cover. Cook 3 minutes. Turn them over. Cover. Cook 2 minutes longer. Into the blender put the livers. Rinse the pan out with the chicken stock and add it. Add sugar, onion powder, bread crumbs and the soft butter. Blend until the mixture is smooth and of the consistency of thick cream. Part of the fun is dipping a piece of bread in it and sampling the mixture to see if it is smooth enough. Mrs. Appleyard's blender, an aged veteran, does it in about a minute. Stir some of the truffles, sliced thin, into the mixture. Do this with a small rubber scraper, which is also good for getting the pâté out of the blender. Pack the pâté into the dish in which you plan to serve it. Chill several hours.

Please, just as a special favor to Mrs. Appleyard, do not pronounce truffles to rhyme with ruffles or scuffles. She knows that American dictionaries, operating on the principle that if enough people do something wrong, it makes it right, have accepted this pronounciation but she has not. Tru as in true, please, when mentioning this fragrant delicacy.

Zippy Tomato Juice
FOR EIGHT

1 cucumber, peeled and diced	2 teaspoons sugar
4 tablespoons chopped green onions and tops	2 tablespoons Worcestershire sauce
thin peel of 2 lemons	3 drops tabasco
1 tablespoon prepared horseradish	salt and pepper to taste
5 cups Hunt's Tomato Juice	juice of 2 lemons
	lemon slices

Put the cucumber, onions and tops, lemon peel and horseradish through the blender into a cup of the tomato juice. Pour into a tall glass pitcher, add the seasonings, lemon juice and the rest of the tomato juice. Chill thoroughly. Add ice cubes and the sliced lemon. Serve.

Roast Goose

Mrs. Appleyard had never cooked a goose before. Someone else had always cooked the ones her family used to have at Christmas time. She approached the bird with respect and a certain amount of nervousness. She is glad to report that it yielded amiably to the slow method, being spied upon by a meat thermometer in Cicely's electric roaster.

She began by stuffing it with chestnut stuffing and then brushed it all over with Wesson oil and sprinkled it lightly with flour seasoned with pinches of sage, thyme and marjoram. She allowed 25 minutes to the pound at 300° and cooked it to 185° on the meat thermometer. It weighed a little over 12 pounds so she allowed 5 hours. It actually reached 185° in 4 hours and 20 minutes so she removed it from the roaster and set it in a warm place. It carved all the better for being taken out ahead of time.

Baked Potatoes with Sour Cream

Bake good-sized potatoes for 15 minutes in a preheated oven at 450°. Reduce heat to 350° and bake 35 minutes longer. Cut a slice from the side of each and remove contents to a heated bowl. To each potato allow ½ tablespoon of butter, 2 tablespoons soured cream, ¼ teaspoon paprika, salt and pepper to taste, and finely scissored fresh parsley.

Mash the potato with butter, seasonings and half the sour cream. Beat until light and pile into the potato shells. Use the rest of the cream to top each potato. Set the potatoes on a baking sheet and run them briefly under the broiler until the cream just starts to brown. Sprinkle with parsley and serve.

Cauliflower and Broccoli, Garlic Crumbs

1 large head of cauliflower	4 tablespoons butter
2 bunches fresh broccoli	½ teaspoon garlic powder
1 cup bread crumbs	salt and pepper to taste
yolks of 2 hard-boiled eggs	

Remove the stalk and leaves from a head of cauliflower, soak it in salted water 10 minutes. Use flowers of the broccoli, not the stems, and put flowers also in salted water. Drain and rinse well. Have water boiling hard in a large saucepan. Set your unfolding steamer into it. Place the cauliflower in the center of the steamer and surround it with the broccoli. Cover closely and cook until the vegetables are tender but not mushy — about 20 minutes.

Toss the crumbs in the butter until golden brown. Add the garlic powder and other seasonings. Mix well. Make the cooked egg yolks into rather coarse powder. Sprinkle the crumbs over the cauliflower and the broccoli and the powdered egg yolks over the broccoli. Mrs. Appleyard serves this combination on a rather shallow old yellow pottery dish that she thinks is rather becoming to it.

Peaches Cardinal with Orange Ice
FOR EIGHT

The day before she made this dessert, Mrs. Appleyard had rinsed out a melon mold with cold water, packed it with orange water ice and set it in the freezer.

2 packages frozen raspberries	2 packages frozen peaches
¾ cup sugar	1½ quarts orange water ice
½ cup blanched, shredded almonds	

Boil the raspberries with the sugar, strain them through a fine sieve to remove the seeds and boil the syrup until it is quite thick. Chill. Leave the peaches in the refrigerator for several hours so they will be partly thawed. At serving time unmold the orange ice in a large rather shallow bowl. Arrange the peaches around the ice. Springle almonds over the peaches. Pour raspberry sauce over ice and fruit and serve.

Pastry Pinwheels
ABOUT TWO DOZEN

These are sometimes called Pastry Leaves — taste good under either name.

Roll out pastry into an oblong 8 × 12 inches. It should be rather less than half an inch thick. Mrs. Appleyard uses her own pastry (p. 60) but she thinks the packaged kind ought to work all right. Dredge your molding board or pastry cloth well with sugar mixed with a pinch of cinnamon and a pinch of nutmeg. Allow at least ½ cup of sugar. Lay your sheet of rolled pastry on the sugared surface. Dredge it with another ½ cup of sugar and spice. Roll up the pastry like a jelly roll. Do it the long way so your roll will be 12 inches long. Dredge more sugar on any bare spots. Slice it as you would jelly roll only much thinner, about ⅜ of an inch. Lightly grease baking pans or heavy cooky sheets. Lay the pinwheels on them, not too close together. Bake at 450° for 5 minutes. Turn the pinwheels, using a pancake turner and a spatula. Reduce heat to 350°. Bake 10 minutes longer or until the sugar starts to turn to caramel. Do not overbake as they may burn suddenly. Keep them in a tightly covered tin box with wax paper between layers.

On another night of deep snow a guest arrived bringing a leg of lamb with him. This tactful gesture resulted in

MENU 2

Mushroom and Bacon Canapés*   Cheese and Chutney Appetizers†
Roast Lamb*
Mashed Potatoes   Spinach Ring with Peas*
Tossed Salad (p. 147)   Currant Jelly
Apricot Crossbar Pie*   Vanilla Ice Cream

Mushroom and Bacon Canapés

Mrs. Appleyard uses her own mushroom sauce (p. 169), made from mushrooms she picked in her own pasture for these. There is plenty of it in her freezer except in non-mushroom years.

In using it for the canapés, Mrs. Appleyard cooks the sauce down for an extra 3 or 4 minutes so that when it has cooled for about half an hour it will be a good consistency for spreading. In the meantime she cuts out small circles of thinly sliced bread and toasts them on one side. She cooks bacon until not quite crisp, drains it on a paper towel, cuts it into small squares. Then she spreads the untoasted side of the bread with the mushroom sauce, tops the sauce with squares of bacon. At serving time she runs a pan or baking sheet of the circles under the broiler just long enough to heat them thoroughly and crisp the bacon.

Roast Lamb

Let the lamb stand in a cool, not cold place for 24 hours before you roast it. A covered roaster with the vents open is a good thing to keep it in. For a 5-pound leg (trimmed) allow 30 minutes to the pound —2½ hours at 300°. Insert a meat thermometer. Be sure it does not touch the bone. Rub the lamb all over with Wesson oil and then with seasoned flour: 4 tablespoons of flour, ½ teaspoon mixed herbs, pepper from the grinder, ¼ teaspoon nutmeg, 1 teaspoon garlic powder.

Start it in a cold oven. Mrs. Appleyard likes to use an electric roaster for lamb. She and her family like it slightly pink so she considers it ready at 155°. Let it reach 160° or 165° if you like it well done. This will take perhaps half an hour longer. If it is not brown enough to please you, run the roast under the broiler for a few minutes.

On this hungry evening the family left only enough lamb to make soup for supper the next night. Perhaps this is the moment to tell how.

Lamb Soup

Leave the lamb right in the roaster. Cover it with hot water. Add 2 carrots, sliced, a large onion, also sliced, pinches of herbs — rosemary, basil, tarragon — a cup of thick tomato juice, ½ teaspoon of Worcestershire sauce, ½ teaspoon of instant coffee, a pinch of curry powder. Let the lamb simmer until the meat falls from the bones — about 3 hours. Remove and discard the bones. Pour the soup, meat, carrots and all, into a large bowl and set in a cold place.

At this point you may wash your roaster. Mrs. Appleyard calls it to your attention that you have roasted meat and made soup, and washed only one receptacle, also that it is practically washed already.

When you make the soup, skim all the fat from the broth. Sauté, in 2 tablespoons of the fat, 2 large onions sliced thin. Sprinkle in 2 tablespoons of flour seasoned with pinches of cinnamon, cloves, pepper and garlic powder. Blend it in well. Remove pan from the heat. Spoon in the cold broth, stirring well until you have a smooth mixture. Add the rest of the broth, the meat and the carrots. Taste it. Add more tomato juice and some lemon juice if you like. Serve with Montpelier crackers, split, buttered, sprinkled with sesame seeds and toasted until lightly browned. With a dessert this is a whole meal.

Spinach Ring with Peas
FOR EIGHT

2 bags washed spinach	1 teaspoon nutmeg
1 tablespoon chopped onion	¼ teaspoon pepper;
¼ cup water	salt to taste
1 cup milk	½ cup cream
3 tablespoons butter	4 eggs, not separated
3 tablespoons flour	1 package frozen peas

croutons from 2 slices homemade bread (lightly browned in 2 tablespoons of butter — do this while the spinach is baking)

Chop spinach and onion with the water until the spinach is limp. Keep chopping. It takes about 4 minutes. Now put ⅓ of the milk, water from the spinach and half the spinach into the blender and purée it. Add the rest of the spinach in two more lots. Now melt the butter, work in the flour and seasonings slowly. Remove from heat and stir in the rest of the milk. Be sure there are no lumps. Stir in the cream. Cook over low heat till it thickens. Remove from heat. Add the spinach purée. Mix well. Add eggs one at a time. Beat well after each addition. Put the mixture into a well-buttered 1½ quart ring mold. Have oven at 325° with a pan containing hot water on the lowest shelf. Set the ring on a shelf close above it. What you are baking is a little like a soufflé, rather more like a custard. Bake it until a knife blade comes out clean — about 35 minutes. Cook the peas during the last 6 or 7 minutes. Do not overbake the spinach or it will separate.

To get it neatly out of the mold, let it stand a minute. Run a spatula around the outside edge of the ring and a small dinner knife around the inner edge. Invert on a circular dish. Fill the center with the peas, cooked in as little water as possible and for the shortest possible time. After you have put the peas in the ring, cook the liquid remaining in the pan down to the last half teaspoonful. Add a tablespoon of butter and one of thick cream. Season to taste. Pour it over the peas. Scatter the croutons over the spinach.

Apricot Crossbar Pie

The apricots must be cooked at least 24 hours before you make this pie. They are really even better if they stand several days. This is how Mrs. Appleyard cooks them after experimenting with several different methods.

Conserved Apricots

2 cups water   2 packages dried apricots
1¼ cups sugar

Start water boiling. Put apricots into a folding steamer. Have the legs of the steamer long enough so that they hold apricots above the water. Cover tightly and steam till apricots are tender and have increased in bulk — 12 to 15 minutes. Be sure water does not cook away. You should have about 1¼ cups left in the pan. Pack the apricots into a quart jar. Press them down if necessary. Some of their flavor will be left in the water in the pan. Add the sugar to it and cook until the syrup just starts to color. Pour it over the packed apricots.

If you like apricots pallid, ragged, sour and watery, don't do them this way.

Now back to the pie. You will need:

2 eggs, well beaten	1 tablespoon Cointreau
2 tablespoons syrup from apricots	(optional)
2 tablespoons lemon juice	1 pint conserved apricots
grated lemon rind	½ cup blanched, shredded
1 tablespoon frozen orange	almonds
juice, not diluted	1 teaspoon butter, melted

Enough of Mrs. Appleyard's pastry for one pie (half the rule on p. 60). Line a 9-inch pie plate with the crust, fluting it neatly around the edge.

Mix the beaten eggs, syrup from the apricots, lemon juice and rind, orange juice and Cointreau together. Add the apricots. Put the mixture in the pie shell. Sprinkle over it the blanched and shredded almonds, brushed with the melted butter.

Light oven: 450°.

Now make the crossbars. Roll the pastry into a piece 9 inches long and cut it into strips. Moisten the places to which you fasten them slightly with a pastry brush dipped in cold water. Lay them across, the first strip north and south, the next one east and west and so on, until the pie is latticed. Do not put them too close together because they are going to expand. Chill the pie for a few minutes, then bake it at 450° for 15 minutes. Reduce heat to 350° and bake until pastry is well puffed and delicately browned — about 35 minutes longer. Turn it in the oven if it browns on one side more quickly than on the other.

Serve it warm with vanilla ice cream, thick Vermont cream in a pitcher or, for Mrs. Appleyard, some Vermont cheddar cheese.

MENU 3

The next pair of guests had prudently and generously equipped themselves for the rigors of a New England winter with an enormous ham, all cooked and sugary brown and bristling with cloves like an amiable porcupine. They told Mrs. Appleyard how they cooked it. They read the label, they said.

This already shows that they were promising cooks. The label tells you whether the ham has been precooked or not and this is something you had better know. This ham had been precooked and it weighed about 15 pounds. They estimated it would take 10 minutes per pound to bake it, and they used a meat thermometer and baked it at 300° until the internal temperature was 155°. First they scored it in diamonds and rubbed into it a mixture of brown sugar, a little mustard, a pinch of ginger, and finely rolled bread crumbs, and then stuck it with cloves. For a sauce with which to baste it they used ½ cup of ginger ale, ½ cup of dry white wine, one cup of light brown sugar, one teaspoon of mustard and one of ginger. They basted it every 20 minutes and when the ham was done they poured the sauce left in the pan over it.

It sliced beautifully. You could read *Paradise Regained* through a slice in case you had an early edition and were in the mood. The guests also endeared themselves by bringing half a bushel of oysters in the shell, beautifully packed in ice, the cold being reinforced by dry ice and Vermont weather. This menu was easy to plan:

Oysters on the Half-Shell
Oyster Bar Sauce*
Brown Bread and Cream Cheese Sandwiches*
Baked Ham (cold) with Minted Pears*
Cheese Croquettes*   Cole Slaw
Mocha Angel Cake*

Mrs. Appleyard had not seen so many oysters in one spot since she was last in an oyster bar on Broadway. She and Venetia Hopkins were going to the theater together. They had managed to get two tickets, one for *My Fair Lady* and the other for something depressing by Tennessee Williams. Mrs. Appleyard had already received a slight dose of melancholia from this in Boston and Venetia had already seen *My Fair Lady* so the only problem was where to eat. Luckily Venetia chose the Oyster Bar and fortunately Mrs. Appleyard told the barman she thought the cocktail sauce was the best she had ever eaten.

He recognized a kindred soul and said, "I have to make another batch before I go off duty. Wanta see me do it? Take notes if you like."

Mrs. Appleyard's notes were on the edges of a piece of paper which contained something she had found in the New York Public Library about John Paul Jones. She happened to be writing a book about him at the time. Using her own filing system (Pat. Applied For) she had filed it under two headings: J.P.J., watch, lost under interesting circumstances and Cocktail Sauce, Oyster Bar, Broadway. What is more she found it just now when she needed it.

Oyster Bar Sauce

Mrs. Appleyard's original manuscript calls for a gallon of Heinz Tomato Ketchup and a pint of horseradish among other things.

Using the set of Napier's Bones her grandson made her for Christmas she reduced the quantities to more homelike proportions.

1 cup Heinz Tomato Ketchup	1 cup Heinz Cocktail Sauce
1 cup Heinz Tomato Juice	1 tablespoon Lee & Perrin's
2 tablespoons prepared horseradish	Worcestershire Sauce
2 drops tabasco sauce	1 sliced onion, minced fine

thin peel and juice of ½ lemon

Mix everything together. Chill.

This turned out so well that her guests said they would get her a job on Broadway. She thinks however that she had better stick to off-Broadway (approximately 278 miles off) production. Drop in any time, bring your oysters and one of those twisty knives. She will supply the sauce.

Mrs. Appleyard usually makes her own brown bread but on this occasion no one wanted to wait three hours so it came out of a can. She says Friend's Brown Bread and Yellow-Eye Baked Beans are as much a part of New England as Plymouth Rock — more nourishing too.

Brown Bread Sandwiches

Slice brown bread about ⅜ inch thick. Have butter and cream cheese at room temperature. Into a 3-ounce cream cheese mash

1 tablespoon of thick cream. Spread rounds of bread thinly with the butter, more thickly with the cream cheese. Cut the circles in halves. Allow 3 halves for each person to be served.

Minted Pears

These were a garnish for the ham.

½ cup juice from can	1 tablespoon lemon juice
½ cup sugar	grated rind of 1 lemon
¼ teaspoon green coloring	5 drops peppermint extract
8 halves of canned pears	

Boil the pear juice and sugar till thick and syrupy. Add the green coloring, lemon juice and rind and the peppermint extract. Add the pears, 2 or 3 at a time. Turn them gently in the syrup until they are evenly colored. Remove with a slotted pancake turner and a perforated spoon. Hold the pear over the pan and let all the syrup drain back into the pan then place the pear on a cold plate and cook the others in the syrup till all are done. Use as a garnish for ham with watercress and half circles of sliced canned cranberry sauce.

Pears done this way may also be used as a dessert with lime or pineapple sherbet.

Cheese Croquettes

Mrs. Appleyard has never been down into the Grand Canyon on a mule, flown in a plane or fried anything in deep fat. All three ideas terrify her. Cicely, however, is made of sterner stuff and besides she has an electric fryer. Mrs. Appleyard marvels at her child's skill but she supposes it is natural to each generation to enjoy its own dangers. In her time she took being nearly drowned when a canoe upset or being missed by inches by a steamer in a thick fog with a certain amount of aplomb. For her grandmother a kettle of hot fat had no terrors. This was how she inspired her cook to make cheese croquettes, often frying the first ones herself, just as a form of sport. This rule served eight hungry ski maniacs generously.

6 tablespoons butter	1 teaspoon Worcestershire sauce
½ cup flour	few grains of cayenne
1⅓ cups milk	yolks of 6 eggs
salt and pepper to taste	1 cup dry cheese, grated
½ teaspoon paprika	1 cup mild cheese, cubed
1 teaspoon dry mustard	2 egg yolks (extra)
1 cup fine dry bread crumbs	

Make a thick white sauce of the butter, flour, milk and seasonings. When it is smooth, add the egg yolks, unbeaten. Add the dry cheese — Parmesan if you like but aged dry cheddar is all right — and stir well. Add the mild cheese. Do all this over rather low heat and take the pan off the fire as the cubes begin to melt. Cheese gets stringy and tough if overcooked.

Pour the mixture into a 9 × 13 pan. Spread it out. Cool. Mark in oblongs. Beat with a fork the extra 2 egg yolks and 2 tablespoons of water together. Roll each oblong of the cheese mixture into a cylinder. Dip them first into the dried crumbs, then into the egg mixture, then into crumbs again. Chill briefly. Fry in deep fat (Crisco) at 380°–390° till golden brown — about a minute. Do a few at a time. They should be crisp outside, a little like Welsh rabbit inside.

Mocha Angel Cake
FOR TWELVE

Making this was an adventure needing no special daring. Mrs. Appleyard gladly undertook the task. As the angel cake was handed to her in a neat carton the project seemed pretty well suited to her capabilities.

½ cup strong hot coffee	1 large angel cake, sliced
2 tablespoons Chocolate Sauce	in 4 layers
(p. 103)	1 cup thick cream
24 marshmallows	1 square bitter chocolate, shaved

Make the coffee with 1 tablespoon of instant coffee to half a cup of water. Make it in a pan big enough to hold the marshmallows and chocolate too. If you do not have chocolate sauce on hand, use 4 tablespoons of chocolate bits and melt them in the coffee. Add either sauce or bits to the coffee and then the marshmallows. Keep stirring until they melt. Cool until mixture begins to thicken. Spread it between the layers of cake, placing them on top of each other. Do this on the plate on which you plan to serve the cake. Cover it with four triangles of wax paper so that any spots will be on the paper instead of on the plate.

Mrs. Appleyard learned this example of culinary neatness by watching TV. If there were more cooking and fewer singers who cannot sing on it, she would probably never have any time to cook.

Chill the cake till serving time. Whip the cream and swirl it around on top. Sprinkle on the bitter-chocolate shavings. Pull out the paper triangles.

After the ham and the mocha cake and their donors had disappeared a strange era of peace descended upon Appleyard Center. Eric ran away, chasing an elk presumably. Nils, having had all his porcupine quills extracted, went off on a round of visits. One of the cats ate the canary. The TV stopped working, Cynthia stopped sandwiching Bach with Israeli folksongs and took up experiments in ESP, Mrs. Appleyard was presented with a new book of Double-Crostics, Jane taught Camilla how to set her new Italian haircut so it would be crooked in the right places. Cicely brought home six books from the library and censored them with a view to her mother's Victorian attitudes towards literature. She forbade Mrs. Appleyard to drive.

Since the roads were glare ice, and since Mrs. Appleyard had seen her former adversary zooming down the hill in a series of skids at 60 m.p.h. she agreed to stay indoors.

She sat in her suntrap. She wrote up her diary. She looked out at the hillside with its brocaded surface of blue and silver. She prepared delectable meals for the birds. The Escoffier of Appleyard Center, they called her. Or did she dream that? It's quite possible: she slept a good deal of the time.

One morning, we are a little embarrassed to report this, she woke up thinking, Peace — it's wonderful! But isn't anything going to *happen?*

Yes, it had been quiet enough even for Mrs. Appleyard.

Democratic Progress

I sometimes think," Mrs. Appleyard said to her daughter Cicely, "that it would be easier to get this book written if I went to prison. You know Cervantes was a prisoner for a while and he got a lot of writing done. And Bunyan — he wrote nine books in prison. One of them was a best seller."

"What kind of crime would you commit to get in?" Cicely inquired.

Mrs. Appleyard considered a few she had seen on TV lately and crossed them off.

"Something clean and neat," she said, "and that really wouldn't bother anyone much. I guess perhaps embezzling some money from a bank might be the best."

"You would have to be working in a bank," her child pointed out. "Does that seem likely?"

"My checkbook balances," Mrs. Appleyard asserted with natural pride.

"Oh, that's what you were groaning about before supper. I was afraid you were having sciatica. Besides didn't you tell me you have a list of forty-five different kinds of errors you've made at some time?"

"Yes," said her mother. "The list is very useful. I just glance it over and see if I forgot to write a stub or copied the

balance wrong or subtracted a deposit instead of adding it or
— well, there are ever so many kinds of mistakes, some I haven't
made yet, I daresay."

"You could learn to make the others if you worked in a bank,"
Cicely said encouragingly. "Besides you're practically a prisoner here at this season anyway."

Mrs. Appleyard admitted that this was true. The drive was a
sheet of glare ice. The mercury was at 20° below zero, and a
March gale was howling around the house.

"The trouble is the company is too good. It would be different in jail," she said.

"It's been very quiet lately," Cicely said. "I think your
trouble lies there."

She was right of course. Fortunately the quiet was temporary.

The next afternoon while Mrs. Appleyard was sifting flour for
a pound cake, just to calm her nerves, the telephone rang. Since
she has never outgrown the belief that something mystic and
magical lies behind each ring, she snatched up the receiver with
a floury hand.

"I'd like to speak to Cora Maxwell," said a man's voice.

Mrs. Appleyard knew how he had got her number instead of
the Maxwells. It's quite simple. You just dial the first three
figures of the exchange instead of the first two. She explained
this fact of life patiently and politely. The caller thanked her
and hung up. The telephone rang again. The young man —
his slight Southern accent sounded very attractive to Mrs.
Appleyard — still wanted the Maxwells.

No wonder, Mrs. Appleyard thought. Cora is a lovely girl.

She told the caller so and gave him a refresher course in how
to dial Cora's number.

"I think you're mighty nice," said the young man. "Why
don't you go out with me instead of Cora?"

"Because I think you're crazy," Mrs. Appleyard told him frankly and returned to her pastry.

It would have served him right if I had, she thought as she sifted the flour again, and I could have worn my black velvet and my new pretty nearly ermine cape.

Again the telephone, imperative, ingratiating.

"This must stop," Mrs. Appleyard said.

She floured the receiver once more and spoke in what her children call her dragon's voice, a combination of chill and fire, terrifying because so seldom used by the owner.

"My good young man," she began, but it was not her young man — good or otherwise.

This voice said:

"Mother, this is Anne?"

"Who?" Mrs. Appleyard asked.

"Your oldest daughter. The one whose house is where you are a prisoner — mother of Cynthia, Tommy, Jane and Camilla."

"I thought your name was Cicely," Mrs. Appleyard said. All conversation seemed peculiar this afternoon, so she added, "The voice is familiar but I don't remember the name."

Her daughter said patiently, "Don't you remember I was christened Cicely Anne so I would have a pretty name when I was a débutante. And Anne in case I grew up and turned out sensible. I've decided I'm going to be from now on."

"Did you call me to tell me that?" her mother inquired.

"No," Cicely said. "I am at the Hoyts and I called to tell you what we are planning. The Hoyts have some visitors, students from Brazil and two charming ladies from Portugal; one of them came from Brazil in the first place. We thought we'd have a progressive supper. It will be a chance for you to get out. Pamela Hoyt says to tell you it will be a Royal Progress and we want you to help us plan it."

"Fine," said her mother, "only if I have anything to do with it, we'll have a Democratic Progress. At a royal one they used to serve roasted peacocks with their tails on and enormous game pies and haunches of venison and whole salmon in jelly. I think we'll have to simplify it a little. Anyway, I'll have a pound cake — if the telephone doesn't ring again."

"We thought perhaps you and I would do the salads. Pamela will have the main course and we are going to ask Venetia to have the drinks and appetizers so we just have to find someone to have the dessert."

"I'll contribute my pound cake," said Mrs. Appleyard. "I mean it's only Half-a-Pound Cake but it might help."

"Pamela wants suggestions for the main course."

"All right. I will brood while I bake."

This process and several conferences resulted in the following menu.

Appetizers

Bacon Dip*   Marinated Haddock*   Sardine Dip*
Potato Chips   Melba Toast   Corn Crisps
Stuffed Celery

Main Course

Roast Capon*   Celery and oyster stuffing*
Green Beans with mushrooms (p. 67)   Mashed potatoes

Salad

Tossed Salad, French dressing*
Sea Food Salad*   Homemade Mayonnaise*
Curried Bread*   Deviled Biscuit*
Hot Coffee Chocolate (p. 193)

Dessert
Apricot Parfait*   Hot Mince Pie (p. 68)   Pound Cake*
Cheese   Coffee

"I think I'll ask the Maxwells to have the dessert," Cicely said.

"That's a fine idea," said Mrs. Appleyard. "Cora knows the nicest young man."

"Have you seen him?"

"No," said Mrs. Appleyard, "but I have private sources of information."

The night of the Progress was the night spring began. There was a full moon, the snowbanks were high along the roads so that no one slid off anywhere. Pussywillows were encased in ice. Plumes of smoke and steam rushed up from the Maxwells' sugar house and dimmed the moon. It had a rainbow of snow crystals around it. Maple sugar crystals perhaps, Mrs. Appleyard thought. How nice for astronauts!

On their way to Venetia's they passed Mrs. Appleyard's own house. It looked about as hospitable as an Egyptian pyramid would if it were made of ice and had two feet of snow on it. Mrs. Appleyard knows just how such a structure feels inside in winter and, as she shivered, she thought gratefully of her apartment. It had never needed an official warming. It had its own warmth, not just the sunshine of the southwest corner but companionship and happiness.

Voltaire, thought Mrs. Appleyard, said that happiness is a good that nature sells to us. But I never supposed it could be bought. After all, you can buy a prism but not a rainbow.

Then they came to Venetia's where Orion sparkled above the twisting branches of the big elm and Minet, the white cat, sat on the gatepost as if he were a snow angel among cats. Vermont hostesses can always tell when winter guests arrive because they hear them stamping snow off their boots on the porch. It is etiquette for the hostess to say, politely but insincerely, "Don't mind the snow. Come right in," and for the guest to reply, hopping on one foot: "No, no: I'll leave them here."

Perhaps the most remarkable thing about the Democratic Progress was that at the end of the evening sixteen people all had the same overshoes they started with.

There were big maple logs burning in Venetia's fireplace, their light shining on curtains of faded cherry-colored brocade and on walls the color of a chocolate ice-cream soda and picking out the gold on the backs of books. Here Mrs. Appleyard drank orange juice while other people drank whatever people do drink on such occasions and took note of the delicious things that people ate.

Bacon Dip

6 slices of bacon, cooked slowly till crisp, drained, cooled and crumbled
2 tablespoons lemon juice
1 tablespoon minced parsley

2 teaspoons onion, crushed through a garlic press
1½ cups thick soured cream
½ teaspoon grated lemon rind
1 tablespoon chopped chives

Mix all together in a pottery bowl. In summer the flavor may be varied by the addition of a little fresh tarragon or dill, very finely minced. Serve well chilled.

Marinated Haddock

1 12-ounce frozen fillet of
  haddock
1 tablespoon white wine vinegar
½ teaspoon each of dry mustard,
  sugar, paprika
1 tablespoon of mixed herbs
containing tarragon, basil,
marjoram, dill seed, parsley
and a pinch of garlic powder
2 tablespoons lemon juice
6 tablespoons olive oil
1 tablespoon piccalilli
1 small onion, put through garlic press

Cut the fillet in 4 pieces. Place them in a folding steamer in rapidly boiling water. Insert a meat thermometer in one of the pieces. Cover the pan and cook until temperature of the fish reaches 150°. This will take only 4 to 5 minutes. Longer cooking only toughens and dries the fish.

Place the pieces of fish in a shallow pan. Mix all the other ingredients in a small saucepan and heat them to the boiling point. Pour the mixture over the fish and let it stand in a cool place for at least 12 hours. When serving, drain the fish and cut it up into small cubes. Pass sesame crackers or melba toast with them.

Sardine Dip

12 ounces sardines
2 tablespoons olive butter
½ cup Mayonnaise (p. 265)
1 cup thick soured cream
1 tablespoon Oyster Bar Sauce
  (p. 248)
1 teaspoon lemon juice and a little grated rind

Mash the sardines and mix all the ingredients together. If it seems too thick for dipping, add a little more mayonnaise.

During this pleasant interval Mrs. Appleyard had an opportunity to use her seven words of Portuguese, learned from two of her grandchildren, Cariocans in their youth. Luckily the guests had many times seven words of English so communication was not difficult. When the fire had safely burned down, they set off for the Hoyts' house. The caravan now consisted of one Mercedes-Benz, one Saab, two Volkswagens, one Citroën and — just to show that there are American cars that can drive Vermont roads in winter — one Falcon. All arrived safely at the Hoyts' long, low, gray house where every window sent light across the snow.

Here the guests sat at small tables in several rooms. Magically, the roasted capons came out of the big oven cooked just right. There were two of them, weighing about 8 pounds apiece. They were set on a rack in an open roasting pan, brushed all over with softened butter, sprinkled with flour which was seasoned with mixed herbs and roasted at 300° until the meat thermometer read 185°. Pamela said she allowed 30 minutes to the pound, a little over four hours. She figured that one bird alone would have cooked in less time.

One of the great improvements of modern times, Mrs. Appleyard thinks, is the cooking of meat at a constant low temperature watched, not by you but by a meat thermometer. She supposes the result may be a little like the slow even cooking of the old brick ovens but use of the thermometer is really something new. However, cooks who depended on coal or wood stoves were often wonderfully skillful at estimating and controlling heat. Mrs. Appleyard can remember seeing a family cook put first the back of her hand, then the palm, then her cheek in the heat from the opened oven door and then hear her regulate the heat according to her diagnosis. She would clank the dampers, shake down the fire, add soft or hard wood, talking to the fire all the time in a sort of incantation of encouragement. The results were of memorable excellence.

Oyster Stuffing

For an 8-pound capon allow:

¼ cup juice from oysters	4 cups stale homemade bread
⅔ cup butter	cut into ¼-inch cubes
1 onion, minced	2 Montpelier crackers, rolled fine
1 cup oysters, cut in small pieces	pinch of thyme
1 cup celery, cut fine	pinch of nutmeg

In a saucepan big enough to hold the mixture, heat the oyster juice; add the butter, and as it melts, the onion, oysters and celery. Cook until butter froths up well. Remove from heat. Using a pastry-blending fork, stir in the bread and cracker crumbs, the seasonings and the beaten egg. Mix thoroughly and lightly. If you like a very moist dressing, add a little thick cream.

The Progress now overshod itself and moved on to Apple-yard Center. If this had been a Royal Progress — in Queen Elizabeth's time, for instance — there would have been beeves roasted whole for the common people. This is no longer true and for an interesting reason: there are, in the United States, plenty of beeves, which is after all merely the plural of beef. The trouble is there are no common people. So the Star-Spangled Banner, long may it wave o'er the land where everyone has two cars in the garage and half a Black Angus critter in the freeze locker. Even Mrs. Appleyard has two pounds of ground chuck.

At the moment she will give her attention to salad and salad dressings.

Seafood Salad
FOR EIGHT

2 12-ounce frozen haddock fillets   French Dressing (see below)
1½ pounds frozen lobster meat   Boston lettuce
2 pounds fresh crabmeat   watercress
2 pounds flash-frozen cooked   2 hard-boiled eggs
  shrimp   6 large stuffed olives
½ cup diced celery   mayonnaise

Cut frozen haddock fillets into quarters and cook them in a folding steamer until they flake easily. Time of cooking will depend on how much they have thawed: 4–6 minutes should be enough. Break into flakes and chill. Mix lobster and crabmeat, both cut up, not too fine; shrimp, left whole; celery and flaked haddock. Marinate in French dressing for several hours. When serving the salad, Mrs. Appleyard arranges it on a large platter. She mixes some of her own mayonnaise (see page 265) with the fish and makes it into individual mounds, each resting on lettuce, surrounded by watercress, masked with more mayonnaise and decorated with sliced hard-boiled eggs and olives.

Mr. Appleyard's French Dressing

Mrs. Appleyard has never eaten any that she prefers to Mr. Appleyard's. It was made with French red wine vinegar, with two beans of peeled garlic in the bottle, and the best olive oil. For a bowl of native lettuce, enough for four people, he used:

½ teaspoon salt   a few grains of cayenne
¼ teaspoon pepper from the grinder   1 tablespoon garlic red wine
1 teaspoon dry mustard   vinegar
½ teaspoon paprika   3 tablespoons olive oil

He put all the dry ingredients into a big wooden salad spoon and mixed them well together with the fork. (He did this over a soup plate.) When they were well mixed, he first poured the vinegar into the spoon, mixing it well in with the fork, and then added the olive oil a tablespoon at a time, always pouring it first into the salad spoon, then into the soup plate. He gave the dressing a final thorough mixing in the plate, then poured it over the bowl of salad greens and tossed them gently and carefully until every leaf was coated with the dressing.

For a marinade:

If you are making a marinade, it is easier to put the ingredients into a jar with a screw top and shake them well. Use double the amounts suggested for the Tossed Salad (p. 147) and keep it on hand to use when needed.

Now that Mrs. Appleyard has to get things ready without much help she sometimes uses the method described on page 149 in which the dressing is poured into the salad bowl, the spoon and fork laid on top of it, crossed, and the greens put in on top of the spoon and fork. If you can find a conscientious guest to toss it for you at the last minute this is an excellent method. In either case one of the most important points of a tossed salad is to be sure the lettuce is dry. Oil and water don't mix. If there's water on the leaves there won't be oil. You want the dressing on the leaves and not in the bottom of the bowl.

Mrs. Appleyard prefers pure olive oil in salad dressing. If you are going to use something else she suggests that, rather than corn or peanut oil — both of which have very definite flavors different from olive oil — you should try either Wesson (cotton-seed) oil or safflower oil. Both of these are more delicately flavored.

Here are a few winter salad combinations that she likes with French dressing.

Cooked shrimp, hothouse tomatoes, torn romaine and Boston lettuce, ripe olives.

Crabmeat, sliced avocado, celery, watercress. Make the dressing for this with lemon juice instead of vinegar.

Iceberg lettuce sliced in thin rounds, red onion rings, watercress.

Jerusalem artichokes, cooked, peeled and chilled, marinated in French dressing to which 2 beans of garlic crushed through the press have been added. Serve with a mixture of salad greens — romaine, endive, watercress — and toss well in the marinade.

Frozen tiny peas and French-cut green beans. Cook the vegetables *al dente*. Pour on French dressing while they are hot. Chill. Serve with watercress, red onion rings and garlic croutons.

Cauliflower flowerets, sliced avocado, hothouse tomatoes, Boston lettuce, French dressing to which 1 tablespoon of Roquefort cheese, crumbled, is added for each 4 tablespoons of dressing.

Avocado, sliced, with Bermuda onion rings, orange and grapefruit sections, watercress.

When no watercress or romaine or Boston lettuce are available, slice iceberg in rings and sharpen it up with one of these dressings:

Mix Mrs. Appleyard's Lemon Mint Chutney (p. 191) with French dressing — 1 tablespoon of chutney to 4 tablespoons dressing.

Add: 1 tablespoon Parmesan cheese to the dressing and sprinkle the lettuce rings with garlic croutons.

Or: 1 tablespoon olive butter, 1 tablespoon minced green pepper, 1 tablespoon onion, put through garlic press.

Or: 1 hardboiled egg, minced, thin rings of green pepper, anchovy fillets.

The dressing may also be varied by the addition of garlic

powder, mixed herbs for salad, finely scissored chives or parsley or aged Vermont cheddar cheese.

For "feminine" fruit salads omit garlic and onion and make the dressing with lime or lemon juice instead of vinegar.

Homemade Mayonnaise (M.W.)

Mayonnaise originated when the Duc de Richelieu was besieging the Fortress of St. Philip at Mahon on Minorca. The siege was going slowly. The Duc's chef was in despair. No milk, no cream, no butter — how was he going to make a sauce to sustain his master through the battle! But ah! — he said — even in this barbarous place we have eggs, we have olive oil. I will think of something . . . so he did.

Naturally the Duc led his men up a cliff never climbed before and took the fortress. Now try saying Mahonnaise fast three times and see how it sounds. Right! This is not exactly how the chef made it because he did not have a blender. If you have one and sixty seconds to spare you can have mayonnaise too.

1 whole egg unbeaten	1 teaspoon powdered sugar
1 tablespoon vinegar	¼ teaspoon pepper
salt to taste	1 teaspoon dry mustard
1 tablespoon salad oil — olive, Wesson, safflower	extra salad oil, at least 1 cup

Put everything in the blender except the cup of oil. Run the blender 10 seconds. Now in four batches add the rest of the oil, running the blender 10 seconds after each batch. After the last of the oil is added, run the blender an extra 10 seconds to be sure the oil has all been absorbed.

Your mayonnaise is now ready. You can of course also make it by hand with an eggbeater or with an electric mixer.

In case you are feeling restless, you can vary the mayonnaise in several ways.

For fruit salads make it with lemon juice instead of vinegar and add some thin lemon peel.

For Russian dressing add to 1 cup of mayonnaise, 1 minced green pepper, 1 tablespoon grated onion, 4 tablespoons chili sauce.

For iceberg lettuce cut lettuce in eighths or thin rounds and serve it with 1 cup mayonnaise, 1 tablespoon chopped stuffed olives, 1 bean of garlic, put through the press, 1 chopped hard-boiled egg, 1 tablespoon minced green pepper, 1 tablespoon finely cut parsley.

For Potato Salad: mix half sour cream and half mayonnaise, add celery and dill seeds.

Boiled Dressing

1 tablespoon sugar	2 eggs
½ teaspoon mustard	½ cup cider vinegar
½ teaspoon salt	2 tablespoons sweet butter
¼ teaspoon pepper	½ cup cream

Mix dry ingredients. Add eggs well beaten. Add vinegar and cook over hot water, beating all the time with a wire whisk until the mixture is thick and light. Add butter. Remove from heat. Chill. When ready to use it, whip the cream and add it (or add sour cream). Especially good for potato salad or cole slaw. The cooked dressing may be added hot to either and the mixture chilled. At serving time add sour cream.

Sour Cream Dressing

1 cup sour cream	1 teaspoon prepared horseradish
½ teaspoon curry powder	½ teaspoon sugar
2 tablespoons mayonnaise	

This is good on cucumbers, Jerusalem artichokes or avocados. For fruit try adding to ½ cup sour cream 1 tablespoon mayonnaise, 1 tablespoon crushed mint mixed with 1 tablespoon lemon juice, ½ teaspoon lime juice, and 1 teaspoon sugar.

As she makes these notes, Mrs. Appleyard begins to see a giant kaleidoscope of salads whirling around in front of her eyes. It makes her dizzy. Perhaps it does you too. She will cease and return to the Progress.

Curried Bread

Make this like garlic bread. Soften the butter. To ½ pound of butter allow 1 teaspoon curry powder, ½ teaspoon garlic powder. (Use half these amounts of seasoning if you do not like it pretty powerful.) Blend seasonings and butter. Cut a loaf of French or Italian bread in ½-inch slices almost all the way through. Spread slices with the softened seasoned butter. This may be done ahead of time. Just before you serve it put the bread in a pan into a 400° oven and heat until it starts to brown — about 10 minutes. Or you may cut slices all the way through, spread them with the mixture, lay them flat in a pan and bake them until they start to brown. Do not overbake in either case: the centers of the slices should be rather soft.

Deviled Biscuit

Make tiny baking powder biscuits. Use your favorite rule, or a packaged mix will do for these. Roll the dough rather thin. Brush half of it with melted butter. Lay the other half on top of it. Cut the dough into small squares. Bake until lightly browned at 450°, about 12 minutes.

Make this filling:

1 4-ounce tin Underwood's Deviled Ham	1 egg
	1 teaspoon onion, put through
1 cup grated mild cheese	garlic press
1 tablespoon mayonnaise	softened butter

Mix ham, cheese, mayonnaise, beaten egg and onion well together. While biscuits are still warm, split them and spread the insides of the top halves with the softened butter, then the lower halves with the filling. Put halves together again. At serving time put them into a 400° oven just long enough to heat through. Serve hot.

At Cicely's the long table was in front of a fire of birch logs. Her daughters joined some of the guests there. Others sat at a smaller table in Mrs. Appleyard's apartment. This table had Copenhagen onion-pattern cups, plates and napkins on it. The big one was set with blue willow ware. Both patterns had a characteristic much appreciated by the family dishwashers: they could be burned in the fireplace afterwards.

"So in your country you destroy the porcelain after a meal! This I have always wished to do. To go to college, I wash dishes," said one of the guests.

"You shall be the one to burn them," said Cicely.

The Maxwells, the next hosts, left while the sacrificial pyre was still burning. When it was safely out, the rest of the party, which now included Cicely's daughters, drove on towards the Maxwells'. The guests had now been in three houses — a brick one, a weathered gray one, a yellow one. All followed a basic Vermont pattern — a story and a half house with a long ell. Yet no two were really alike. Outside dormers and porches had changed the original roof lines. Inside you might find a wallpaper a hundred and forty years old with Spanish castles on it or silvery gray boards from the outside of an old sheep barn, or walls painted by the family with birds and flowers or — as in the Maxwells' big living room — panels from pines that were young when their ancestors came to Vermont from Massachusetts, walking beside an ox team. The house is white. That night even the roof was white, its thick meringue of snow sparkling in the moonlight. The pillar of white smoke still rose from the sugar house.

Inside, in the big kitchen, a coal fire burned in the old-fashioned iron stove, which somehow gives warmer heat than anything else. There was a delicious smell of maple syrup. In the pine-paneled room, apple wood scented the room and dropped pale pink coals among white ashes. Stereo jazz resounded. Alma's hooked rugs were rolled up in a corner. The floor was crowded with dancers from Brazil, Montpelier and other points south of Appleyard Center.

The Maxwells have only one child but luckily that one is Cora, who has enough charm for six, so there is always something going on in their house. Mrs. Appleyard enjoyed sitting and watching the dancing. After a while a young man brought her a small folding table and something delicious to put on it. He called her ma'am and treated her with so much gentle consideration that she began to feel fragile, exquisite and a hundred years old.

The Maxwell house is on the brow of a hill from which you can look down on the lights of Montpelier, stars dropped into a bowl of clouded marble, the pattern of trees and houses blurred against the snow. Mrs. Appleyard was glad to sit quietly and look down on the view and listen to half a dozen conversations at once and not talk herself. The young man who had brought her the apricot parfait (so good, she must get the rule from Alma) was entertaining a group that included two of her grand-daughters.

"And I said to this girl — well actually I reckon I ought to say lady — she had not been a girl for quite a while, I imagine, I said, 'You seem mighty nice. Why don't you go out with me instead of Cora?' and she said, 'Because I think you're crazy,' and hung up. And you know I'd have gone through with it. That is the kind I am. I'll always keep my word to a girl."

"How old do you think she was?" asked Jane in the tone of one awed by daring and chivalry.

"Well, it's hard to be sure — maybe twenty-four or five. But I'd have taken her out," he said gallantly, "even if she was thirty."

The girls gazed at him in admiration. Mrs. Appleyard did not dare to. She sat looking, she hoped, a little under one hundred in her black velvet and her almost-ermine cape and turned her smiles down upon star-spangled Montpelier.

She well remembered how, when she was eighteen, anyone over twenty-one seemed to her to be staring over a desert scattered with granite tombstones, mummies and a few ill-arranged skeletons.

I'll send him an autographed copy of my book with that picture of me that doesn't look a day over sixty-seven, she thought. That will teach him.

Of course she really did not expect to teach him anything. When he is a grandfather he will learn for himself how perplexing it is for a young man to have such old grandchildren.

At this moment he brought Mrs. Appleyard some of her own pound cake. She thanked him for his thoughtfulness. Did he start slightly? He certainly looked puzzled as he asked: "Have we met before, ma'am?"

"No," said Mrs. Appleyard, "but I hope we shall again."

She finished the pound cake (not bad really) collected her black lace mantilla, one of her best-known fur coats, her black velvet and fur boots and went out into the night.

"You look as if you'd been up to something, like a cat that's eaten a canary," Cicely said.

Her mother said: "Of course you are an expert in such matters but I would say offhand more like a benevolent owl who caught a kitten but decided to let it go. I have seldom," she added, "enjoyed an evening more."

Apricot Parfait
FOR SIX

1 large can apricots	2 egg whites, beaten stiff
½ tablespoon gelatin	2 tablespoons lemon juice
⅓ cup sugar	½ pint heavy cream, whipped

Drain the apricots. Soak the gelatin in 2 tablespoons of the syrup and cook the rest of it with the sugar till it threads. Pour it on the beaten egg whites. Stir the mixture all the time with a wire whisk. Stir in the gelatin. Cool. Put the lemon juice and apricots into the blender and blend until smooth. Add this mixture to the beaten whites. Chill thoroughly. Whip the cream and fold it into the apricot mixture. Put the parfait into a refrigerator tray or into a covered aluminum dish and set it into the freezer. Freeze 3 hours, stirring thoroughly to break up crystals three times during the first hour.

Unmold it on a circular dish. Surround it with vanilla ice cream and raspberries or with Conserved Apricots (p. 244).

Half-a-Pound Cake

Perhaps you are not in the mood this morning to use a dozen eggs and a pound of butter. That is what you'd have to do if you made a pound cake. Well, how about half-a-pound cake?

extra butter, melted	6 eggs, separated
½ pound (1 cup) butter at room temperature	1 tablespoon brandy
½ pound (1 cup) granulated sugar, sifted	½ pound (2 cups) cake flour, sifted 3 times with ¼ teaspoon nutmeg
¼ cup powdered sugar	

Light the oven: 300°.

Oil a Pyrex loaf pan and line it with wax paper, brushed lightly with the melted butter.

Cream the butter, beat in the sugar, using a pastry-blending fork. Beat the egg yolks and stir them well into the mixture. Stir in the brandy. Add the flour gradually, beating smooth after each addition. Beat the egg whites stiff, but not dry, and fold them into the mixture.

Bake until a testing straw comes out clean from the center of the cake — about one hour. Check it after half an hour's baking and reduce heat if cake seems to be browning too fast. Let it stand a few minutes after you take it out of the pan. Peel off the paper carefully. Turn it topside up. Cool. Sprinkle with powdered sugar.

There is a tradition in Mrs. Appleyard's family that pound cake will fall if anyone walks heavily past the stove during the first half hour of baking, or if the oven door is slammed shut. Apparently these offenses were never committed in her grandmother's kitchen, for the cake was always light, yet firm and it sliced beautifully. Mrs. Appleyard is not going to slam any doors to test this tradition scientifically. Let someone else try. She rather thinks that if you accept the superstition blindly, you will have a pretty nice loaf of pound cake at the end of an hour or an hour and a quarter. If you have self-control enough to keep it in a tightly covered tin box for three days, the texture will be especially good.

Maple Butternut Fudge

Cracking the butternuts is the really hard part of this job. You have to have a man in the family and he has to have a patient disposition. Mrs. Appleyard does not like to sound cynical but she will suggest that walnuts or pecans may be substituted for the butternuts.

Butter two plates lightly. Cover the plates with nuts. Using a candy thermometer cook 2 cups of maple syrup to 232°. Remove from the fire, stir until it just starts to thicken and pour it over the nuts, mark in squares before it hardens.

The batch the Maxwells served was especially good because it was made with butternuts and with syrup that had been sap, rising in century-old maples, only three days before.

You may add some thick cream during the last part of the cooking if you like. Mrs. Appleyard likes it better without.

For those who do not happen to have a sugar house handy, here is a palatable substitute.

Brown Sugar Pecan Fudge

1 cup pecans   4 cups golden brown sugar
1 cup thin cream   1 tablespoon butter
1 teaspoon vanilla

Butter plates and lay nuts on them, not chopped but as they come from a vacuum-packed can. Cook the cream and sugar to 238° (soft ball). Remove from fire. Add the butter. Beat hard until it is creamy and begins to thicken. Add vanilla. Pour over nuts. Mark in squares while it is still soft.

April

Ventilation Tour

Mrs. Appleyard said to her daughter — not entirely, we are afraid, without a slight air of complacency — that their book was practically finished.

"I've done March," she said, "and that's the last winter month. Now all I need to do is to put in the symbolism. You know — the way modern teachers of writing show their students how to do: a pinch of Freud here, a snip off a Jungian archetype there. Or perhaps I'd better put in philosophy, the way you do when you put sherry into Newburg Sauce, just at the end. Add philosophy, bring to the boil but do not boil. Or perhaps I'd better add symbolism and philosophy to taste and serve. For as many as will. What do you think?"

Cicely looked at her mother with indulgent pity.

"I think," she said, "that you have forgotten that in Vermont April is a winter month. So is most of May. You need not only philosophy but hearty sustaining food in both of them. After all, Vermonters have to build themselves up for the summer. Symbolism does not cure chilblains."

It was this remark, a truth as solid as a granite doorstep, that made Mrs. Appleyard decide to go south for the winter. She realized, of course, that she was lucky to have some winter left to go south in. A singularly grim cold spring prevailed as far south as Washington, where the cherry blossoms were late. In Philadelphia there were a few reluctant red buds on the maples but the country still looked bleak. In New York State the robins had come. There were hundreds of them beside the road with their wings so iced up in a sleet storm that they could not fly. Cold winds blew everywhere. In Boston it was the east wind right off a few icebergs.

"This," Mrs. Appleyard wrote to Cicely, "is my ventilation tour. My hat blew off in Washington and was picked up by a very pleasant-looking poodle. He looked it over carefully and decided he would wait for a more seasonable model, a fur one probably. Mine had violets on it. They are the only ones I have seen. However," she concluded, "nourishing and delightful menus have been thought up for me. I was brought up to think it a virtue to eat what was set before you. I'm afraid in my present circumstances it is not."

Here are some of the menus she encountered.

Menu 1

Clam and Chicken Soup*
Planked Porterhouse Steak with Broiled Stuffed Mushrooms
Mashed Potato   Asparagus — Butter and Egg Sauce (p. 191)
Tossed Salad (p. 147)
Sponge Cake*   Grapefruit*

Clam and Chicken Soup
FOR FOUR

2 cups strong chicken stock	salt and pepper to taste
1 tablespoon butter	2 tablespoons white wine
1 tablespoon flour	½ cup milk
8 ounces minced clams	½ cup heavy cream

Make the chicken stock by cooking a fowl with a carrot, a large onion, celery tops, a teaspoon of mixed herbs. Remove meat from the bones, use it as you wish — salad, creamed chicken, sandwiches. Return the bones to the broth and cook them at least an hour. Strain. Stock should jelly when chilled. Skim all fat from the top. In a frying pan melt the butter, blend in the flour, remove pan from heat and stir in a cup of the stock slowly. Cook until it starts to thicken, about 3 minutes. Put it into the blender with the clams and blend until you have a smooth purée, about half a minute. Put it into the top of a double boiler with the rest of the stock, then cook about 20 minutes over hot water. Add salt and pepper. When you are ready to serve it add the wine, the milk and the cream. Bring it to the boil but do not boil. Serve at once in hot soup plates.

Sponge Cake

grated rind of one lemon	1 cup flour, measured after
1 tablespoon lemon juice	sifting
¼ cup frozen orange juice,	1 cup sugar
not diluted	7 eggs separated
	sugar, extra, about ¼ cup

Grate lemon and mix it with the lemon juice and thawed orange juice. Sift flour 3 times and measure. Sift sugar twice and measure.

Light oven: 325°.

The cake may be baked in either a 9-inch tube pan or a 14 × 10 dripping pan, or in muffin tins. It will fill about 18. In any case the pan or pans must be lightly floured.

Beat the egg whites to soft peaks. Beat 4 tablespoons of sugar into them, one at a time. Beat egg yolks until thick and lemon-colored. Beat in the rest of the sugar alternately with the fruit juices and rind. Fold the whites gently into the yolks, alternating with the flour. Mrs. Appleyard used a wire whisk for this. It is important not to break up the air bubbles you have beaten in, as their expansion is what makes the cake rise. Put the batter into the pan or pans. If you use muffin tins oven should be at 350°.

Bake until well risen, about 10 minutes; then sift the extra sugar over the top. It is done when it springs back lightly when pressed with the finger. It will take almost an hour in the tube pan, 35–40 minutes in the dripping pan, 25–30 minutes in muffin tins according to their size.

Grapefruit

Mrs. Appleyard loves grapefruit. It is really her favorite dessert. It is farther around a grapefruit than you think but she does it pretty fast. The result however is not very much like those she encountered in Boston.

They were enormous Indian River Reds. Every single seed had vanished. They were perfectly cut, with all the divisions between the sections and the centers removed. Some epicure had mixed half honey and half Cointreau and dribbled a table-spoon of the mixture over each half. Try it, she says.

MENU 2

Shrimp, Crabmeat and Avocado Cocktail*
Roast Duckling*   Wild Rice and Mushrooms*
Currant-Orange sauce (p. 54)
Braised Celery*   Corn Dodgers†
Crème Brûlée†

Shrimp, Crabmeat and Avocado Cocktail

For each person to be served have half a ripe avocado brushed with lemon juice. Mix shrimp and fresh crabmeat, cut in rather small pieces, with mayonnaise, minced green pepper, finely minced onion and tomato cocktail sauce, 2 tablespoons of the sauce to half a cup of mayonnaise. Heap the mixture lightly into the avocado halves. Garnish with a little watercress.

Roast Duckling

People vary so much about how they like ducklings cooked that it is hard to please everyone. There is the idea of treating them like a wild duck, simply whisking them into a 450° oven and out again 18 minutes or you may go to the other extreme and cook them at 300° to 185° on the meat thermometer. In this case allow 25–30 minutes to the pound. It is not necessary to stuff ducks, either wild or tame — an apple quartered and with the seeds removed, a small whole onion and a few celery tops will help keep a duckling from drying out. A good deal of fat runs into the pan and that should be poured off twice at least during the roasting.

Wild Rice with Mushrooms

Directions for cooking wild rice better than Mrs. Appleyard can give you are on the package. Half a pound of mushroom caps, sliced and sautéd with a little finely minced onion, are often mixed with it. Crumbled crisp bacon is also sometimes added.

Brown rice may be treated in the same way and is an acceptable substitute to many people.

Braised Celery
FOR EIGHT

4 bunches, best parts only, of crisp celery
¼ pound butter
1 cup jellied chicken or beef stock, well seasoned with herbs and spices

½ cup coarse bread crumbs
grated cheese
minced chives
parsley

Cut the celery in pieces 4 inches long. Wash well. In a shallow enameled iron pan in which the celery can be served, melt the butter and toss the celery in it so that all sides are exposed to the heat. Cover and cook over very low heat 7 or 8 minutes. Add the stock and simmer over medium heat until celery is tender — about 20 minutes. If more convenient it may be baked in the oven at 375°. Just before serving time, brown the crumbs in the extra butter. Sprinkle them and the grated cheese over the celery. Run the pan under the broiler until the cheese melts. Sprinkle with chives and parsley.

It was a great pleasure to Mrs. Appleyard to get back into fish-eating country. Vermonters like to catch fish but except for trout they are not much interested in eating them. Along the eastern seaboard people take the matter more seriously. On a Friday night she was happy to encounter:

MENU 3

Celery   Eggs Stuffed with Crabmeat*   Radish Roses   Carrot Sticks
Shrimp Soup*   Planked Shad*
Baked Corn and Cheese*   Tossed Salad (p. 147)
Deep-Dish Apple Pie (p. 102)

Eggs Stuffed with Crabmeat
FOR FOUR

4 hard-boiled eggs
3 tablespoons mayonnaise
1 tablespoon finely minced green
pepper

¼ pound crabmeat
4 stuffed olives
parsley

Hard-boil 4 eggs. They will peel better if you have them at room temperature when you start them and cover them with water at 70°. You can acquire this by running some lukewarm water from the tap and letting it stand while the eggs are warming. Such is the magic of the law of thermodynamics — or something — that if the water is too cool it will get warm enough and if it is too warm it will get cool enough while time saunters on. Put the eggs in the water. Cover and bring rapidly to the boil. As soon as water boils, remove pan from heat and let eggs stand for 20 minutes. Then plunge them at once into running cold water. Crack shells under water and roll eggs in hands to loosen shells but do not peel them until they have cooled. Begin peeling them at the large end. This method produces eggs as smooth as Parian marble, not the kind that look as if they had been pecked by predacious blue jays. Perhaps you never shelled any like that. Congratulations from Mrs. Appleyard, who has only recently learned that it was not just a matter of luck.

Cut the eggs lengthwise. Mash the yolks with the mayonnaise and mix in the green peppers. Add more mayonnaise if necessary. The mixture should be easy to spread. Flake the crabmeat and fill the whites of the eggs with it. Top with the mashed yolk mixture, swirling it a little with a fork. Decorate with sliced stuffed olives. Serve with fresh parsley around them.

Shrimp Soup

3 tablespoons butter	1 tablespoon onion
3 tablespoons flour	6 tablespoons sauterne
1 teaspoon paprika	1 pimento, cut rather fine
½ teaspoon pepper from the grinder	2 cups heavy cream
	1 tablespoon butter (extra)
¼ teaspoon nutmeg	1 tablespoon finely scissored
¼ teaspoon garlic powder	parsley
2 cups milk	1 tablespoon chopped chives
1 pound flash-frozen shrimp	lemon slices

This was prepared in an electric skillet but could of course be done in a skillet over the fire and a double boiler.

Melt the butter over medium heat. Blend in the flour mixed with dry seasonings. Reduce heat to its lowest point and pour on the milk slowly, stirring all the time till the mixture is smooth. Leave it over very low heat while in the blender you purée the shrimp and onion with the sauterne. Add this mixture and the pimento to the skillet mixture. Cook covered over very low heat 20 minutes, stirring several times. At serving time add the cream. Bring to the boil but do not boil. At the last minute slip in the extra butter. Pour the soup into hot bowls, sprinkle with parsley and chives. Add lemon slices. This serves four generously. In cups it could serve six. A few whole cooked shrimp may be added to each bowl.

Planked Shad
FOR SIX

This was done not on a plank but on a large heatproof platter, but the effect was splendid. Mrs. Appleyard is delighted to be in a world where roe shad still exist, and also that geniuses have arisen who know how to bone a shad. Even under their skill, shad is not usually completely boneless — there always seem to be a few bones left. It is, however, very superior to the fishy pincushions of Mrs. Appleyard's youth.

4 large potatoes, mashed with hot milk and butter	shad roe
	¼ cup butter
2 or 3 large hothouse tomatoes	juice of 2 lemons
8 slices of bacon	½ teaspoon pepper from the grinder
matchstick carrots	
extra butter	1 teaspoon paprika
brown sugar	½ cup bread crumbs, browned in butter
tiny frozen peas	
6 boned serving pieces of shad	watercress

If you have a plank by all means use it, but you can get a very good planked effect by beginning with aluminum foil and using a fireproof glass, aluminum or fireproof enamel platter.

Begin by making plenty of good creamy mashed potato. Mrs. Appleyard prefers real potatoes but if you use the packaged kind, this is a handy place for it. Slice tomatoes into 6 slices. Cook the bacon till it is translucent but not crisp. Cook the carrots, glazing them with butter and a little brown sugar. Cook the peas till they are not quite done, in a very little water. Do not overcook the vegetables as they will get more cooking under the broiler.

Now lay the shad, skin side down, and the roe on a large piece of heavy aluminum foil. Turn the edges of the foil up carefully around it to make a box that will keep the juices in. Put the box on a cooky sheet. Melt the ¼ cup of butter with the lemon juice, add pepper and paprika and pour the mixture over the shad and roe. Broil 8–10 minutes. If you use gas and can turn flames down to pinpoints, have fish one inch from flame. Do not turn the shad but at the end of 5 minutes turn the roe and baste both shad and roe with the lemon and butter. Test fish for flakiness. Do not overcook it. Put the aluminum foil on your broiling platter. Spread out the edges. Make a wall of mashed potato around the outside edge, score the potato lightly with a fork, dot it with butter. Inside the potato make a ring of tomato slices, covered with the browned crumbs, partly cooked bacon, heaps of peas and carrots brushed with melted butter. Put the platter under the broiler and broil until the potatoes are brown — about 3 minutes.

A strong man, not only an excellent cook, but a painter of some of Mrs. Appleyard's favorite pictures, presided over this dish. He decorated it with watercress and carried into the dining room without slipping, tripping or spilling this artwork. Mrs. Appleyard wished she had a picture of it. Perhaps it's just as well she has none. She's already ravenous just writing about it.

It seems to Mrs. Appleyard that her host must be a man of rashness as well as courage to cook what is practically a soufflé at the same time he was dealing with the shad, but he did and it came out perfectly. She was allowed to toss the salad that went with it, a mixture of romaine, French endive, chicory, and Boston lettuce (which you can always buy in New York). She felt that great tribute was being paid to her reliability and conscientiousness and did her best to coat every leaf as neatly as if she had been using one of the painter's best sable hair brushes.

Baked Corn and Cheese Puff
FOR SIX

3 tablespoons butter	½ teaspoon paprika
½ teaspoon onion, minced	salt to taste
2 slices green pepper, minced	1 cup rich milk
1 pimento, cut fine	1½ cups cream style corn
2 tablespoons flour	½ cup grated mild cheese
¼ teaspoon pepper	3 eggs, separated

In a fireproof enamel dish put the butter over medium heat. Add the onion, green pepper and pimento and sauté till the onion is straw-colored. Sprinkle in the flour, mixed with the seasonings, and blend thoroughly. Remove pan from heat, pour in the milk and stir till smooth. Cook 3 minutes over low heat. Cool for a few minutes. Add the corn, grated cheese and egg yolks, beaten light, and mix well. Light oven: 350°. Beat the whites of the eggs to stiff peaks. Fold them gently into the corn-cheese mixture. Set the dish in the oven and bake until it has risen well and is nicely browned — about 35 minutes.

Mrs. Appleyard learned several things about cooking while she was on her ventilation tour. One of them was the use of aluminum foil in cooking fish. Here is an example of how to use it with halibut as the fish used. The same method may be applied to other kinds and of course the seasonings varied.

Halibut Steaks
FOR FOUR

4 tablespoons butter
½ pound mushroom caps, sliced
2 tablespoons finely cut celery
1 tablespoon onion, put through garlic press
1 pimento cut in strips

2 tablespoons lemon juice
grated rind of 1 lemon
½ teaspoon mixed herbs
4 small halibut steaks, 1 inch thick
2 hothouse tomatoes, sliced
1 tablespoon butter, extra

Light oven: 450°.

In the butter toss gently the mushrooms, celery and onion until onion is straw-colored. Add the pimento, lemon juice and rind and the mixed herbs.

Place each halibut steak on an oblong of aluminum foil and fold up edges to make a box. Put some of the mixture on each steak. Add tomato slices and dot with extra butter. Lay another piece of foil over the fish and fold the edges of the box up over it so that it is in a bag from which the juice will not escape. Put the bags on a rack in a dripping pan. Put a meat thermometer into one of the steaks. Cook to 145°: 10–12 minutes.

Have hot platter ready. Remove top pieces of foil. Lay the aluminum boxes right on the platter. Turn down the edges, overlapping them. Garnish the platter with lemon slices and heaps of asparagus, country style with Butter and Egg Sauce (p. 191).

With this dish were served:

Cheese and Chutney Crumpets
FOR FOUR

4 crumpets, split, buttered and lightly toasted	½ teaspoon paprika
2 tablespoons butter (extra)	1 teaspoon dry mustard
1 cup mild cheddar, grated	4 tablespoons Major Grey's chutney, chopped fine

1 tablespoon syrup from chutney

Melt the 2 tablespoons of butter, remove pan from the fire, mix in the grated cheese and stir till it just melts. Stir in seasonings and the chutney and syrup. Spread on the buttered crumpets. Mixture will spread, so keep it away from the edges. Put them on a baking sheet. Run them under the broiler till the cheese starts to bubble — about 2 minutes.

Mrs. Appleyard sometimes uses her own Lemon Mint Chutney (p. 191) in this way. Some people prefer it because it's milder. She rather likes the determined heat of Major Grey's herself.

Cheese has an affinity for fish, she thinks, and with another foil-cooked dish — frozen haddock fillets cut into serving portions and done in the same way as the halibut steaks — she served

Baked Cheese Balls

These are something that valiant characters might fry in deep fat but she does them by this peaceful method and finds them quite satisfactory.

½ cup grated Vermont cheese
½ cup grated Roquefort or
  blue cheese
1 egg, beaten
½ cup soft crumbs of Anadama
  white bread

1 teaspoon Worcestershire sauce
1 teaspoon mustard
1 cup dry crumbs, rolled very
  fine
½ teaspoon paprika
¼ teaspoon pepper

1 egg beaten light with 1 teaspoon of water

Mix both kinds of cheese with the beaten egg, soft bread crumbs, Worcestershire and mustard. Roll the mixture into balls about an inch in diameter. Then roll them in the fine crumbs, mixed with seasoning, next into the beaten egg and water mixture, then into the crumbs again.

Light oven: 450°.

While it is heating — about 5 minutes — chill the balls in the refrigerator. Put them on a lightly buttered iron frying pan. Do not let them touch each other. Bake until they are brown. Turn them, using a small pancake turner and a spatula, at the end of 5 minutes. The whole process, including turning, should take about 12 minutes. If you like them browner, run the pan under the broiler for a minute. Do not overcook them.

Luckily for Mrs. Appleyard it was still oyster season and she encountered them cooked in various ways, one of the most welcome of which was a de luxe version of scalloped oysters.

Oysters with Croutons

4 cups of cubes of homemade
  bread
extra butter
1 pint of fresh oysters
¼ pound butter
¼ teaspoon nutmeg

¼ teaspoon pepper from the
  grinder
¼ teaspoon garlic powder
½ teaspoon paprika
½ cup heavy cream
extra paprika

Slice homemade bread in ¼-inch slices. Trim off crusts, spread slices with soft butter. Cut into ¼-inch cubes. Pick over oysters, removing any bits of shell and of course saving any pearls you find to make earrings for your granddaughters. Drain oysters, mix the liquor with the ¼ pound of butter and heat the mixture. Sprinkle in the seasonings. Toss the bread cubes in the mixture. Do this a cup at a time, adding more butter if necessary. Light oven: 450°. Butter lightly a 9 × 12 Pyrex dish and cover the bottom with the bread cubes. Add half the oysters. Cover with more bread cubes. Add the rest of the oysters and the rest of the cubes. Pour the cream over all. Sprinkle with paprika. Put in the oven and bake until well browned — about 20 minutes.

More flattered than she can possibly say was Mrs. Appleyard when she went to dinner with one of her favorite composers and found that he had composed in her honor not a symphony, not a ballet, not a sonata, but something he called

Chicken Appleyard
FOR FOUR

For once — this is really an extraordinary compliment — she was so overcome that she forgot to ask for the rule but this is the way she has made it since and it is at least reminiscent of this happy occasion.

chicken breasts, wings removed
butter, about ¼ pound
2 cups chicken stock, made from
  wings and neck
4 tablespoons white wine

2 cups soft bread crumbs, not
  too fine, browned in butter
4 ounces liver pâté (French) or
  your own (p. 124)
watercress

Bread Sauce

Butter each chicken breast well. Put on a rack in a large skillet, put in chicken stock and wine, cover and simmer until tender — about one hour. Brush breasts again with butter. Slide pan under the broiler and brown the breasts. Sprinkle the breasts with browned crumbs. Top each breast with a small mound of pâté. Serve wreathed in watercress. Pass bread sauce with them.

If you have time to make gravy from the juices in the pan, you will find it good. Just take 2 teaspoons of flour, season it as you wish, dilute it with cold water, strain it into the pan, stir until it thickens and cook over medium heat for 3 minutes. Strain, add a little more white wine if you like, sprinkle it with minced fresh parsley.

An artistic triumph served with the chicken was a

Symphony in Green Vegetables

A large circular yellow dish had a mound of small tender green peas in the middle of it. Radiating out from the peas were thick stalks of asparagus. Between these were green beans and Brussels Sprouts and around the edge was a wreath of broccoli flowers. Lemon butter was passed with this.

The dessert for this meal was vanilla ice cream with a sauce made of

Marrons Glacés

What used to be practically a lifetime project, Mrs. Appleyard learned, is now a few minutes' work because chestnuts can now be bought shelled, cooked and cleaned of tough skin. You just open a can, drain and dry thoroughly 2 cups of chestnuts and fix this syrup:

2 cups sugar   1 cup water
1 teaspoon vanilla

Boil sugar and water without stirring until the syrup just starts to discolor. Watch it. The change can take place suddenly. You want thick syrup, not caramel. Remove from fire, put over warm (not hot) water. Put drained chestnuts into the syrup. Leave them exactly 5 minutes. Remove them with 2 silver forks to a warm steamer. The kind that opens out flat is good. Put it on a plate and leave the chestnuts on it overnight. Allow the syrup to cool to room temperature. Do not chill it. Next morning reheat it. Put the chestnuts in for another 5 minutes. Take them out again and put them back to drain again on the steamer, which has been washed in very hot water and thoroughly dried. If they are to be used that day or the next put them, when they have drained, into paper cases. (The easy way to get these is to save them from a candy box. In fact, to tell the truth, Mrs. Appleyard does not know how else you would get them. Stealing seems impractical and why should some rarely visited candy shop help set you up in business?)

If you are not going to use the marrons at once, put them, still handling them delicately with those silver forks, into a wide-necked jar or jars, bring the syrup to a boil and pour it over them. Add another teaspoon of vanilla. Cover tightly. Keep in the refrigerator till you need them. Mrs. Appleyard guarantees that they will not take up space long.

She remembers poignantly an occasion on which a dish, containing many different kinds of delicious candy including one — only one — marron glacé, was passed around a rather large table. The guests, that is the first eight, were all too polite to take the marron, but at last someone did take it. There was a general, an almost imperceptible sigh during which the lady next to the fortunate one said gently but sadly: "Ah! My favorite piece!"

It was every lady's favorite piece including Mrs. Appleyard's, alas. She believes however that she was probably the only one whose husband followed up his first meeting with her by sending her five pounds of marrons glacés. It occurred to her almost at once that this was no ordinary gesture. When he continued with the *Encyclopedia Britannica* (Eleventh Edition) she was sure she was right.

Luckily she was.

What Am I Offered?

REPORTS from Vermont were very cheering to everyone south of it. Snow, sleet, rain, mud, frost, glare ice and hail were reported with the gloomy pride Vermonters take in their weather. Mrs. Appleyard, admitting to Cicely that April was indeed a winter month, decided to stay in tropical Massachusetts for the Business Meeting and Auction of the Pinball and Scissors Club.

It is hard for Mrs. Appleyard to tell which she enjoys most

— the Business Meeting or the Auction. When the girls — they have been meeting for more than half a century — get together for a bout of parliamentary law, they sound like a murmuration of starlings in a high wind. Motions, sometimes three at once, are discussed and amended with bounce, brightness and benevolence. All except those who have a touch of laryngitis express their opinions but only to their next door neighbors, who agree or disagree with resonant enthusiasm. Every now and then the president remembers that remarks are supposed to be addressed to the chair and says so but of course no one hears her.

There is however a magic tranquilizer that always works. The hostess suddenly announces, "Lunch in five minutes, girls."

It is extraordinary how swiftly peace, order and agreement fall upon the assembly. From the eighteen organizations suggested as possible targets for their generosity, they quickly choose one to be endowed with the proceeds of the auction. Someone says, "Oh well, I'll be treasurer if you like," and the secretary casts one ballot for her amid applause before she has time to change her mind. They decide, as they have been doing ever since 1929, that the hostesses must keep the luncheons very simple. "Why don't we," someone asks, "just each bring a sandwich?"

"Splendid idea," everyone agrees and they all go into the dining room where under the family portraits, among Chippendale and Lowestoft, gilded glass and damask, they do full justice to the following menu.

Consommé with Rings of Green Pepper
Sesame Seed Sticks*
Lobster Newburg* with Pastry Diamonds   Cold Roast Turkey
Green Beans with Sausages (p. 181)   Parker House Rolls†
Ice Cream Bombes   Orange Ice with Vanilla Parfait

Chocolate Ice Cream with Marron Parfait
Scotch Shortbread*   Fruitcake (p. 116)   Madeleines†
Coffee   Hot Chocolate

Sesame Seed Sticks
FOR EIGHT

Use your favorite pastry mix for this if you do not feel like
making your own pastry (p. 60).

1 package of pastry mix   1 tablespoon butter
½ cup sesame seed

Roll out the pastry into an oblong about ¼ inch thick. Dot
with butter, fold, turn, and roll out again. Sprinkle with sesame
seed. Cut in 24 strips. Bake at 350° until delicately brown, 15–
20 minutes. Reduce heat to 325° after the first 5 minutes.

Lobster Newburg

Of course the Lobster Newburg at the Pinball and Scissors
Club was made of fresh lobster and the pastry diamonds were
light puffs of real pastry. Mrs. Appleyard heartily and enviously
endorses the freshest possible lobster. In her far-off childhood,
she spent her summers on an island off the coast of Maine. It
was a habit, in that country of pointed firs, of mountains thrusting out of the sea, of screaming eagles pouncing on ospreys and
stealing their fish, to keep, in the cove near the wharf, a lobster
car full of live lobsters. They used to be brought up to the
house, snapping and fighting, in a large basket. Their sudden
change from bronze-green to coral-scarlet was a daily miracle.

Monotony was avoided by serving them plain boiled with melted butter, as soup, stew or salad, broiled or as Lobster Newburg.

Mrs. Appleyard seldom sees as much as a lobster feeler any longer. She assumes that you probably don't have a lobster car in the front yard either and that, like her, you are grateful to gaze upon frozen lobster in a neat plastic-topped container, especially on winter evenings when it wouldn't be very convenient to row out to the lobster car in a northeaster. On the island the Newburg was made in a chafing dish. There was something charming about the chafing dish with its bright silver reflecting a flickering blue flame, only there was always the question whether you put in enough alcohol to finish the cooking. When you needed more, the bottle was often empty. The nearest shop was four miles across Frenchman's Bay, which was often blanketed in thick fog or else produced something called a short chop (pronounced shawt chawp) by the tide running against the wind.

Seen against this background an electric skillet looks reasonably attractive.

Lobster Newburg
FOR SIX

¼ cup butter	a few grains of cayenne
1½ pounds frozen lobster cut up, not too small	½ teaspoon paprika
	¼ teaspoon nutmeg
3 tablespoons good sherry (*not* "cooking" sherry)	1½ cups light cream
	3 egg yolks, lightly beaten

Melt the butter over low heat. Toss the lobster meat in it 2 minutes. Add sherry, mixed with the seasonings. Cook 2 minutes. Mix cream and beaten egg yolks in a small bowl. Add a tablespoon of juice from the pan and stir well. Add another tablespoon of juice. Stir again. Then pour cream and egg mixture over the lobster. Cook gently, without letting it boil, until the sauce is thick and smooth. Add the cognac. Stir. Serve at once with triangles of buttered toast.

This same method can be applied to shrimp, oysters, crab or scallops with excellent results.

Scotch Shortbread

½ pound butter   ½ cup sugar
3½ cups flour

All should be at room temperature.

Cream the butter until it stands in soft peaks. Use a pastry-blending fork. Work in the sugar, a little at a time. Work in a cup of the flour a tablespoon at a time. Use some of the remaining flour to flour a board. Put the mixture on it and knead in the rest of the flour. Light oven: 325°.

The more you knead it the "shorter" it will be, so add the flour in very small amounts. Turn the dough over and turn it around from time to time. When all the flour is used — get every bit on the board into it — press the dough into a 9 × 13 aluminum pan, not greased. Dough should be less than ½ inch thick. Mark dough in squares. This size pan will make 48 squares about 1¼ inches square, or 32 larger ones, but as the shortbread is very rich the small size may be what you prefer. Prick it all over with a fork. Bake 20 minutes. By that time the squares around the edge will be delicately brown. Remove them. Shove others against the edge of the pan. Bake 10 minutes longer. Remove those that show any brown and give the remaining ones an extra 10 minutes. They will be browner on the bottom than on top. It is important that they should not be browned too much. Their goodness lies in the rather sandy texture and the cooked but not scorched flavor of what advertisers coyly describe as "the more expensive spread."

Yes, it is more expensive than substitutes and for an excellent reason: it produces better flavor and texture than they do. Don't try to make shortbread with anything but the best butter.

Whose voice could it possibly be making this remark?

After lunch the girls were much relaxed, but the auction began before anyone went to sleep so they soon became mentally alert. The billiard room was the scene of the auction and the green table was covered with interesting lumpy packages. It seems miraculous, after all these years, that attics should still be producing treasures. Perhaps they are simply rotated from one attic to another and are brought down for some other auction. Ellen Pryor, who gave up her attic when she built her contemporary house, is still a generous contributor. She often buys things to present to the P. and S.C. auction. Not having become very familiar with these objects, she is apt to bid on them absent-mindedly and has been known to take them home again at a price rather higher than she originally paid.

She is that auctioneer's dream, a constant bidder. She even bids on hats. The part of the auction Mrs. Appleyard likes best is when the girls start trying on hats, all telling each other how becoming they are. Sometimes they model negligees too and hold up dresses on each other to get an idea of the probable cubic contents. In this way, last year, Mrs. Appleyard acquired her best black velvet dress, graduate of many Theater Guild openings with dinner beforehand. If it could only tell the menus at which it has presided! However, for $7.50 one could hardly expect the costume would have built-in clairvoyance.

The club is lucky in its auctioneer, Pauline French. She would, Mrs. Appleyard feels sure, make her fortune if she would take up auctioneering professionally. She is genial, skeptical, quizzical, relentless in getting the last penny. She has wit and friendliness and a repertoire of stories not learned from one of those auctioneering schools where men are taught to apply the mother-in-law joke to anything from a cracked plate to a photograph frame that won't stand up. ("Nice to keep your mother-in-law's picture in.")

Pauline's jokes are her own, told in her own way and in a voice which, Mrs. Appleyard thinks, must be the echo of an ancestral voice, as much a part of the family inheritance as the portraits by Copley and the silver by Paul Revere. Just as firm, sensible, cheerful and stronghearted must the Frenches have sounded as they hurried past the old elm on Boston Common dressed as Indians on their way to the Boston Tea Party.

No wonder everything in the billiard room changes hands. No wonder Erica Pryor goes home more heavily laden than she came and with three billiard balls (later returned by her chauffeur with suitable apologies) in her new Andalusian satchel. No wonder Mrs. Appleyard goes back to Vermont with a collection of real necessities such as a bronze bowl full of ivy, seven mystery stories (she needs some to lend), a cracked Lowestoft bowl (she's heard it can be made as good as new by boiling in milk and garlic), and a hat from Stella LaRose's intimidating little salon.

Stella will not sell hats to just anyone. Is it quite honorable for Mrs. Appleyard to have a Stella LaRose model? There is a terrifying story about a Boston woman on a train for New York. Realizing that of course there was no use in trying to look as if she belonged in New York, she decided to look as Bostonian as possible so she wore her LaRose hat, given to her by a cousin, Helen St. John, who had passed it on after only two years.

She was sitting quietly on the Merchant's Limited, reading

the *Saturday Review* and feeling liberal yet conservatively elegant, when Stella LaRose walked through towards the dining car. (The lady in the hat had a packet of sandwiches.)

Stella stopped in front of her and said, in a voice that would go through a wall of Roxbury puddingstone insulated with peacock feathers: "I see you are wearing one of my hats. Please tip it slightly forward over your right eye. It does not belong on the back of the head. Remember me to Mrs. St. John."

Would she be safe, Mrs. Appleyard wondered, if she wore her LaRose hat in public? She would hardly wear it in private, would she? In her apartment suntrap with only the chickadees at the feeder to enjoy it?

I might give it away, she thought. Why, of course! I'll take it to the auction next year. Now what am I offered?

May

The Right Mix

It was spring when Mrs. Appleyard left Boston. It was a wonderful hot day. There were as many tulips as people in the Public Garden. In the country flowering crabs, forsythia and daffodils had all rushed into bloom at once. Willows were raining green gold. Leaves smaller than a chipmunk's ear were quivering on white birches. She stopped to see some friends. When they saw her coming they rushed out and picked their own asparagus and made her stay to lunch. It was not difficult to persuade her. Probably it is gratifying to have a red carpet spread down for you but not, Mrs. Appleyard thinks, nearly so pleasant as being passed a platter of fresh asparagus with a delicious sauce of butter and thick cream.

She stayed to dinner. She stayed for the night. She saw a dogwood tree, loaded with greenish ivory flowers the day before, turn overnight to a shining white cloud. She saw the tight dark buds of lilacs change to waving plumes of fragrance with orioles flashing in and out of them. She saw elms cloud into green fountains and red knobs on the apple trees burst into pink and white stars. White candles started to open on the horse chestnuts. Evidently it was safe to pack up the Appleyard papers and go and tell Vermonters it was spring.

This was a project noble in purpose but a little hard to execute because, as she crossed the Connecticut River, it began to snow. It rather improved the looks of the hills, which were bare and bleak and gray close by and a sullen inky blue in the distance. The snow quickly capped them with white. This was no frivolous flurry, melting as it fell. It meant business. It frosted the chocolate of plowed fields and the dark green steeples of firs. It made red-winged blackbirds wish they had stayed south and cowslips wish they had not opened their shining gold flowers. Bloodroot was happy that its white petals were wrapped in cocoons of silver-green leaves. It made farmers glad that cows were still in the barn, and road commissioners groan. At Appleyard Center children were joyfully snowballing each other among the crocuses and a car that had skidded on the hill was being hauled out of the birch wood.

Cicely was so accustomed to the weather that she never even mentioned it. It was her mother who introduced the topic.

"Won't it even be spring for the christening?" she asked. "I was planning to open my house and have the party there. I might as well entertain on an ice floe."

Her child soothed her with an optimistic remark.

"Snow never lasts long in May and June," she said.

She was right. The next morning the fields were full of blue-eyed ponds. Cowslips were bright gold along darkly rushing brooks, spring peepers rang sleigh bell chimes. Ferns uncurled like the tops of cellos. Roger Willard opened the shutters of Mrs. Appleyard's house and let the sunshine in. She went into the front hall. She inhaled happily the smell of woodsmoke and potpourri, with faint overtones of pedigreed mice, descendants of those for whom the Appleyards have been keeping the house in good order since 1822. The house sheltered chimney swifts too. Mrs. Appleyard could hear their wings whirring. No doubt there were bats hanging upside down in the shed chamber. A weasel popped up in the woodshed, looked cynically at her and returned to his furnished apartment.

Human beings, Mrs. Appleyard reflected, are a great convenience to animals.

She began to make plans for the christening. It would be in the old church after the service on the Sunday nearest to Camilla's birthday, which was also her own birthday. They had meant to have Tim christened at this time last year, but he had the measles so it had been postponed. This year it could be his christening and Nick's too. Afterwards she would have a buffet lunch for everyone. The children could take their plates out on the grass — if it just didn't snow. She began to make lists.

Cicely picked one up off the pantry floor. "Silver polish, almonds, plastic plates, etc., Willow pattern, Mouse seed, Balloons, Flowers, Kaleidoscopes, Brandy snaps, Find stove polish, Telephone connected, Oatmeal cookies," she read.

"Is this the menu?" she asked.

"Just a rough sketch," her mother told her. "I haven't quite worked it out yet."

In its final form the menu was:

Chicken and Spaghetti with Sausages*   Veal Loaf, with Truffles*
Cold Sliced Ham   Shrimp Mold*
Tossed Salad (p. 147)   Homemade Whole-Wheat Bread*
Real Strawberry Ice Cream*   Oatmeal Cookies (p. 110)
Brandy Snaps*   Almond Cake*
White Grape Juice Punch*   Coffee

On the Friday before the party Mrs. Appleyard and Patience Barlow were already at work making almond cake and oatmeal cookies. It was a wonderful bright day, with bobolinks singing as they soared over the cowslips. Bluebirds were building a nest in Patience Barlow's mailbox. She told Frank Flint just to wrap the letters in the newspaper and throw it on the grass. Phoebes were announcing their name, a scarlet tanager was an instant of bright flame in a young maple and then burned away north. Forget-me-nots winked up at the sky.

It was, the experts decided, a perfect day to make oatmeal cookies. Patience worked on them and then on brandy snaps while Mrs. Appleyard made almond cake and polished silver. She went out occasionally to check up on the landscape. She was beside the pond helping Nicholas tickle the head of a very green frog with a piece of last year's witch grass when Cicely, Jane and Camilla arrived. Until she saw the Delft Posset Cup, the big bunch of roses and the carton of goldfish, she had forgotten it was her birthday.

"The goldfish," Cicely told her, "are for your pond. They will grow into carp and you can simmer them in red wine."

"I can't imagine doing anything so mean," Mrs. Appleyard said.

She slid the fish carefully into the pond. All promptly swam off except one which struggled in a tangle of forget-me-nots.

"Poor little thing — it doesn't seem to be able to swim!" Mrs.

Appleyard exclaimed bending over to help it, and falling into the pond with a rather loud splash.

"Luckily I can," she added as her descendants helped her out. She changed her swimming costume for something less moist. "From now on," she announced, "I'll attend to my cooking." Nothing else happened to interfere with the menu.

Chicken and Spaghetti with Sausages
FOR SIXTEEN

2 fowls weighing at least 5 pounds apiece
3 tablespoons butter
2 large onions, sliced thin and minced
3 green peppers, seeded, sliced thin, minced
1 pound mushrooms
3 tablespoons flour
2 teaspoons sugar
bit of bay leaf

¼ teaspoon each of cinnamon, clove, allspice, pepper
2 large cans of tomatoes
3 beans of garlic, put through the press
2 pounds small link sausages
1 pound spaghetti (2 packages)
4 pimentos, finely cut
1 cup dry Vermont cheddar cheese, grated
1 teaspoon paprika

2 tablespoons minced parsley

The day before you are going to serve this dish, cook the fowls. Simmer them in water in which you have put 2 sliced carrots, 2 sliced onions, celery tops and a teaspoon of mixed herbs. Cook until meat slips easily from the bones — 4–5 hours. Remove skin. Cut meat into serving pieces, wrap in wax paper and keep in the refrigerator till needed. Return the bones to the broth and cook until the broth is thick enough to jelly. Strain into a bowl. Add any small pieces of meat. Keep it in a cool place till needed. (Mrs. Appleyard wishes a warm one were as easy for her to find.)

The next day melt the butter in a large iron skillet. Sauté the onion, peppers and mushrooms — caps and the tender part of the stems — in it until onions are yellow. Skim the chicken fat from the broth. Add a tablespoon of it to the contents of the pan. Sprinkle in the flour mixed with the dry seasonings, except paprika. Blend it well with the fat over low heat. Add the tomatoes and garlic. Stir well, let the mixture simmer for an hour. Watch it. Add chicken stock occasionally. Stir mixture well from the bottom so it will not stick.

Half an hour before you plan to serve the spaghetti, start to cook it and the sausages. Put the chicken stock on to heat in a large kettle. Put the sausages into a frying pan. Pour warm water around them so that they are almost covered and let them simmer. The water should cook away in about 20 minutes. Turn them at the end of 10 minutes. Do not prick them. After the water has cooked away leave them in the pan until they brown. At the end of 5 minutes, drain off the fat and turn them. Cook 5 minutes more.

When the chicken stock boils hard — there should be 3 quarts — slip spaghetti into it slowly so that it curls up and the water never stops boiling. Coil it around in the water. Cook till it is tender but not mushy, about 7–8 minutes. Drain it and put it on a hot heatproof platter. Save the stock and reheat the cooked chicken in it for a few minutes. Skim it out and arrange the large pieces on top of the spaghetti. Add small ones to the tomato sauce. Add pimentos. Arrange sausages around the spaghetti and chicken. Pour the sauce over the whole thing. Set the platter in the oven for a few minutes. Sprinkle with grated cheese. Sprinkle the cheese with paprika and parsley. Serve.

Veal Loaf

½ pound calves' liver
1 tablespoon butter
½ pound baked ham, cubed
2 large onions
2 pounds of veal cutlet and
   1 pound of lean pork put twice
   through the grinder together
6 Montpelier crackers

salt to taste
pinch of nutmeg
1 teaspoon pepper
1 teaspoon poultry seasoning
2 truffles, sliced and quartered
2 eggs, well beaten
1 tablespoon flour
4 slices of bacon

extra butter

Your market man will grind the veal and the pork together for you. Cook the liver in the butter over low heat, covered, until it is tender — about 5 minutes. Chop it very fine. Dice the ham. Mrs. Appleyard used part of her baked ham for this but a slice of boiled ham cut ½ inch thick will do.

Chop onions very fine, chop liver into them, then the veal and pork until everything is well mixed. Roll crackers (Boston Commons will do if you can't get Montpelier crackers) into fine crumbs, add seasonings and mix them in. Next add the ham cubes and the sliced truffles. Their nutty fragrance is delicious with the veal and pork.

Butter a bread tin and put in the mixture. Press it well into the corners of the tin. Dredge the top with flour and a few very fine crumbs. Cover it with bacon cut into narrow strips. Set the pan on a rack in a covered roaster. Surround the pan with hot water. Bake at 350° for 2 hours.

When it is thoroughly chilled, it will slice beautifully.

Mrs. Appleyard sometimes serves it as a main dish with mushroom sauce. She had this plan the last time she made it, three loaves in Pyrex glass pans. She had intended them for the Pinball and Scissors Club. Unfortunately she dropped the roaster and contents, thus adding an extra ingredient, ground glass, to the mixture. She felt she was very lucky at such short notice to be able to get chicken breasts for twenty-four people. They were simmered in cream with mushrooms (p. 198) and were not unpalatable, but she advises baking veal loaf in tin pans.

Shrimp Mold

2 tablespoons plain gelatin soaked in ½ cup ginger ale	2 teaspoons onion, put through garlic press
2½ cups hot ginger ale	2 pounds flash-frozen cooked shrimp, thawed slowly
4 tablespoons lemon juice	
1 tablespoon lime juice	a little olive oil
1 cup celery, cut fine	watercress
1 green pepper, minced	tiny green peas
	Stuffed Eggs (p. 196)
mayonnaise	

Soak the gelatin in cold ginger ale. Dissolve it in hot ginger ale. Stir in lemon juice and lime, celery, pepper, onion and the shrimp. Brush a mold with olive oil. Add the mixture. Chill. Unmold on a platter. Surround with watercress, tiny green peas, cooked and chilled, and Stuffed Eggs.

When they are in season in her garden, Mrs. Appleyard surrounds the mold with cucumber and tomatoes, sliced, and sliced stuffed olives. Serve mayonnaise with it.

Homemade Whole-Wheat Bread (E. and H.B.)

Mrs. Appleyard is lucky enough to have a neighbor who grinds whole-wheat flour and he is lucky enough to have a wife who makes this bread.

Mix in a large bowl:

2 cups warm (not hot) water or milk
2 tablespoons (pkgs) dry baker's yeast
¼ cup honey, molasses or brown sugar

Stir in 3½ cups whole-wheat flour. Beat 300 strokes by hand (or about 8 minutes at low speed in the electric mixer). Work in another 3 to 3½ cups whole-wheat flour. Use your hands when necessary. Turn out on well-floured board and knead well. If it seems sticky, knead in more flour. When dough is smooth and elastic, return it to the bowl, cover, let stand in a warm place until double in bulk (about 2 hours). Punch down, turn out on a floured board, divide in half, shape in 2 loaves, place in oiled bread pans, cover, let double in bulk again (about 1 hour). Bake at 350° for 45 minutes. Turn out on wire rack to cool.

This flour is not "enriched." Enriching used to mean adding something extra to something rich already. It now means taking all the vitamins out of flour and putting some of them back in synthetic form. This is about as enriching as it would be if someone picked your pocket and then took pity on you and handed you back enough for carfare. Real home-ground whole-wheat flour has the wheat germ in it and will spoil if it is not kept under refrigeration. It is not enriched; it doesn't have to be.

Real Strawberry Ice Cream or Mousse

Mrs. Appleyard makes this in her electric freezer and it is like ice cream frozen by hand with ice and salt around it. It contains nothing but strawberries, cream and sugar. No isinglass, for instance. This is a substance used like gelatin. It comes out of a sturgeon. If you were growing your own caviar you could probably have isinglass too. It would not be any good to put in the windows of an old-fashioned cast-iron stove. They look like isinglass and are called isinglass but they are really mica. Neither should ice cream contain cornstarch or powdered eggs or artificial vanilla or any form of glue.

If you do not have an electric freezer you can make it quite satisfactorily in your deep-freeze or in the freezer section of your refrigerator. Put the mixture into a pan at least 3 inches deep. Stir it thoroughly to break up ice crystals three times during the first hour of freezing. Once during the second hour. Freezers vary so much in temperature that it's hard to be accurate about the length of time needed but three hours ought to be enough.

Of course if cream and fruit are not beaten continuously during freezing you are making mousse rather than ice cream. Its texture will not be quite so smooth but if you use only crushed and puréed fruit, sugar and whipped cream, the flavor will be delicious.

Strawberry Ice Cream

2 cups crushed strawberries   ½ cup sugar
1 pint heavy cream, not beaten

Put strawberries and sugar through the blender. Mix with the cream. Put into electric freezer. Freeze until dash will no longer move. Mrs. Appleyard makes this ahead of time, several batches of it, and stores it in her deep-freeze. A quart of ice cream is supposed to serve six. It is Mrs. Appleyard's duty to tell you that this will not do so unless your guests are on a diet. Make plenty.

Strawberry Mousse

2 cups crushed strawberries   ½ cup sugar
1 pint heavy cream, whipped

Put strawberries and sugar into the blender and blend until smooth. Chill. Whip cream until it stands in soft peaks. Fold it into the strawberry mixture until the mixture is a beautiful even color, like snow at sunset. Freeze according to the directions above.

Brandy Snaps

½ cup butter   ½ cup flour
½ cup sugar   ½ teaspoon mixed spices —
½ cup molasses   nutmeg, cinnamon, ginger
¼ cup coconut   2 tablespoons brandy

Melt butter over low heat. Stir in sugar, molasses and coconut. Heat to boiling point. Sift flour and spices. Add brandy to the molasses mixture. Stir in the flour and spice. Drop by half teaspoonfuls, well spaced to take care of spreading, on a lightly greased dripping pan. Bake at 325° for about 7 to 10 minutes. Have a second pan ready as the first one comes out. To get them off the pans is the problem. You need patience, a flexible spatula, a small pancake turner and a large spoon with a wooden handle. This spoon is so you can roll the snaps around the handle when you have removed them from the pan. Let them cool first. After a minute, test the edges with the spatula till you find the snaps are ready to leave the pan. Then you must work quickly, bending each one you detach around the spoon handle, or you may swiftly curve them over the edge of the mixing bowl. You may be skillful enough so you can roll them into cornucopias and serve them filled with whipped cream. (Mrs. Appleyard has never reached this adept level. She humbly admires those who have.) Don't try to make them on a sticky day with the barometer falling. Store them in a tin box with a tight cover, between layers of wax paper.

Almond Cake (S.H.L.)

1 pound butter	20 egg whites
½ pound almonds, blanched and skinned	4 cups flour, measured after sifting
2 cups sugar	1 teaspoon almond extract

Let butter warm to room temperature. Chop almonds. Cream butter, add sugar gradually, cream till light and fluffy. Add almonds, lightly floured. Beat whites to soft peaks. Add them alternately with the flour. Add the almond extract. Grease a large tube pan and line it with wax paper. The oven should be at 300°–325°. The cake requires long and uniform baking, about 2 hours. Test with straw, which should come out clean.

Boiled Frosting

2 cups sifted sugar	2 egg whites
1 cup cold water	1 teaspoon almond extract

Put sugar and water together in saucepan. Stir until sugar dissolves to keep crystals from forming, then boil without stirring. Use a candy thermometer. Cook till syrup will spin a thread that will turn up at the end — 238°. Remove syrup from the fire and let it cool a little while you are beating the egg whites stiff. Add the flavoring. Pour it over the egg whites in a thin stream, beating steadily. You need either an electric mixer or a co-operative friend for this process. Mrs. Appleyard much prefers the latter.

White Grape Juice Punch
FOR TWENTY

16 lemons	2 cans orange juice
2 cups sugar	(frozen)
1 gallon boiling water	2 gallons pale dry ginger ale ⎫ chilled
3 tablespoons tea	2 quarts white grape juice ⎭

Slice lemons thin. Add the sugar and crush it into the lemons with a wooden pestle till sugar disappears. Heat water. When it comes to full bubbling boil, throw in the tea and let it boil one minute, no more, no less. Strain at once over lemons and set mixture away to ripen overnight in a cool place. At serving time put ice cubes and the orange juice, not diluted, in a large punch bowl. Add the ginger ale and the white grape juice. Garnish with cubed pineapple, strawberries and mint.

White wine may be substituted for the white grape juice. Mrs. Appleyard sometimes makes two bowls, one for grownups with wine, the other for children with grape juice. She drinks from the children's bowl.

The day of the christening was soft blue and gold. The buds on the apple trees changed from red to pink. Lilacs began to open. Swallow-tail butterflies fluttered yellow and black among them and above the daffodil trumpets. Cicely brought a great bunch of narcissus and pink tulips and her mother arranged them with sprays of lilac in a big copper jug. It was cool enough to have fires in the Franklin stoves and warm enough to sit on the arched porch in the sunshine.

The old church shone in its new coat of paint. The weathervane, part arrow, part fish, flashed its new gold against the sky. Inside it was rather cooler, Mrs. Appleyard thought, than it had been on Christmas Eve but this morning she could look out on young pink and buff maple leaves, on Guernsey cattle eating emerald grass, on blue hills without a flake of snow on them. The peaceful hour of the service was over all too soon. During the last hymn, parents began to bring in the children who were to be christened. Some of them were small enough to join in the singing with soprano and tenor wails. Some, like Timothy, were dignified six-year-olds. Some, like Nicholas, were old enough to tramp emphatically on the wide pine boards in their shining new shoes. Few of them, however, thought Mrs. Appleyard, looked as benevolent as Nick, with as active a dimple, or as earnest as Timothy with such an impish gleam in his eyes. Of course she is completely unprejudiced.

When the old Adam had been cast out of everyone Mrs. Appleyard went home and sat peacefully in her music room while her daughters and daughters-in-law served the luncheon. She was so successful in pretending that she had never had anything to do with it that it really tasted pretty good. In fact the whole day was perfect. When she thought it over afterwards it was hard to choose the moment she had liked best. Was it when she expected to see Camilla's birthday cake with the thirteen candles she had arranged on it and then found that it had sprouted what looked more like seventy-six — so whose cake could it be? Was it helping Nick tickle a bullfrog? Was it hearing her children's and grandchildren's voices singing in the old church? Or feeling her house warm and full of life instead of cold and empty?

All these, of course, she thought of with happiness, but perhaps what she really liked best was Timothy's coming to her with three oatmeal cookies on a plate and offering them to her.

"You eat them," she suggested.

When he had politely co-operated he said: "Grandma, how do you make those cookies?"

"It's a little hard to tell without doing it," Mrs. Appleyard said, "but sometime I'll let you help me make some and then you'll know."

"Thank you," said Timothy. "I suppose," he added, "you have to begin by getting the right mix. And then cook them the right time."

Then he went off and began to turn cartwheels among the dandelions, leaving Mrs. Appleyard thinking about time.

She hopes that no one who reads this book will think she wants people to spend all their time in the kitchen. She wants you to have, literally, a good time. That means that you will use time as you like instead of its using you. In cooking, as in life, time is the most important element, especially if you are the kind of cook who is reading *The Wings of the Dove* while the bread is rising or doing a little painting on velvet while the pot roast is marinating.

A timer often saves this kind of cook from calamities. It is a mechanical device, but perhaps not quite so mechanical as it sounds as it ticks off the minutes. Perhaps you and Mrs. Appleyard are not precisely Einsteins of the kitchen. Yet, before you ever set that timer going, you thought of space-time. You know it takes longer to bake a 9 × 13 pan of brownies than an 8 × 8 pan but not twice as long. You have a sense of fire-time and of cold-time, of wet-and-dry time and of golden-brown time. You feed all those statistics into your mental computer before you ever set your timer for those oatmeal cookies.

Mrs. Appleyard admits that it isn't a giant computer. It would have to have ever so many more whizzing dials if you were going to do something useful like sending a giraffe to Venus.

Still it is helpful and so is your nose, which tells you how brown the johnnycake is, and your ears, which notice that the steak has just hissed three times so you'd better check the meat thermometer. Your ears will also tell you that the soufflé is still whispering so it isn't quite done. Your eyes detect that the cream puffs are done because the last iridescent bubbles have vanished. Your fingertips tell you when the sponge cake is ready. You use your sense of rhythm while you beat egg whites, your sense of weight when you lift a pan of fruitcake, your sense of taste when you decide to add a little more Bristol Cream sherry to the Lobster Newburg, your sense of beauty all the time.

Yes, Mrs. Appleyard says, you need the right mix. You need all the right kinds of time. And what is the result? Well, Aristotle knew. Mrs. Appleyard has her favorite books where she can reach them from her bed. Bostonians consider reading in bed rather dissipated. Mrs. Appleyard admits that she not only reads in bed; she also writes there. One of the books for which she often stretches out her hand is her grandmother's copy of *Miss Parloa's Cook Book* with her grandmother's handwriting on the extra pages in the back. Next to it is another favorite book called *Teach Yourself Greek*.

If someone else had taught her Greek about 1902, perhaps she would know more. However she has learned one or two sentences she likes. This one of Aristotle's is her favorite.

εὐδαιμονία ἐστὶν ἐνέργεια τῆς ψυχῆς κατ' ἀρετῆ ἐν τῷ τελείῳ βίῳ.

The word ἀρετη has no real counterpart in English. It can mean different things in different situations. For instance the ἀρετη of the soldier is courage, of a knife — sharpness, of a merchant — honesty, of a soufflé — lightness. It is a special excellence.

So Aristotle's sentence means to Mrs. Appleyard: "Happiness

is activity of the spirit used according to its special excellence in the complete life."

She hopes you will use your time according to your special excellence and that you will find the right mix — work and leisure, rain and sunshine, sugar and spice and, when you have to cook — friends to cook for.

Index